Empirical Knowledge

Empirical Knowledge

Readings from Contemporary Sources

edited by

RODERICK M. CHISHOLM
Brown University

and

ROBERT J. SWARTZ
The University of Massachusetts

Prentice-Hall, Inc., *Englewood Cliffs, New Jersey*

Library of Congress Cataloging in Publication Data

CHISHOLM, RODERICK M comp.
Empirical knowledge.

Includes bibliographical references.
CONTENTS: Nelson, L. The impossibility of the "Theory of knowledge."—Moore, G. E. Four forms of skepticism.—Lehrer, K. Skepticism & conceptual change. [etc.]
BD181.C49 1973 121 72-11723
ISBN 0-13-274894-0

Printed in the United States of America.

10 9 8 7 6 5 4 3 2 1

Prentice-Hall International, Inc., London
Prentice-Hall of Australia, Pty, Ltd., Sydney
Prentice-Hall of Canada, Ltd., Toronto
Prentice-Hall of India Private Limited, New Delhi
Prentice-Hall of Japan, Inc., Tokyo

Contents

Introduction

The various essays in this book, most of which were first published after World War II, and all but one of which belong to the present century, may be thought of as growing out of contemporary attempts to deal with the ancient problem of the criterion. The best statement of this problem may be the following, paraphrased from Montaigne's *Essays:*

> To know whether things really are as they seem to be, we have to have a *procedure* for distinguishing appearances that are true from appearances that are false. But to know whether our procedure is a good procedure, we have to know whether it really *succeeds* in distinguishing appearances that are true from appearances that are false. And we cannot know whether it really *does* succeed unless we *already* know which appearances are true and which ones false. And so we are caught in a circle.[1]

The philosophers who have attempted to deal with this problem may be subdivided into three groups.

[1] The passage we have paraphrased from Montaigne was translated by John Florio as follows: "To judge of the appearances that we receive of subjects, we had need have a judicatorie instrument: to verifie this instrument, we should have demonstration; and to approve demonstration, an instrument; thus we are ever turning round." *The Essays of Montaigne* (New York: The Modern Library), p. 544.

Some will ask the question "What is it that we know?" and then attempt to answer it on the basis of a prior decision with respect to the *criteria* of knowledge. ("We cannot find any genuine instance of knowledge," they will say, "unless we have a criterion enabling us to recognize it.") Others will ask the question "What are adequate criteria of knowledge?" and will then attempt to answer it on the basis of a prior decision concerning *what* it is that we know. ("We cannot formulate any adequate criteria of knowledge," they will say, "unless we can test our criteria by reference to genuine instances of knowledge.") Still other philosophers, more sceptical, say that we cannot answer the first of these two questions until we have an answer to the second and that we cannot answer the second until we have an answer to the first, and they conclude that we can never know whether or not there is anything that we know. Many philosophers will approach one area of knowledge (say, our knowledge of the external world) from the first of these points of view, another area of knowledge (say, logic and mathematics) from the second, and still another area of knowledge (say, our knowledge of our own states of consciousness or those of other people) from the third.

The results of adopting one or another of these methodological points of view are brought out clearly in the disputes about skepticism found in Part I of this volume. We have selected the papers and portions of books in the remainder of this volume so that running throughout, against the backdrop of the skeptical challenges discussed in Section I, the main theme one finds is in the form of a dialectic between two types of solutions to the problem of *actually finding* criteria for the different forms of empirical knowledge stemming from the use of the senses and memory. The two types of solutions here are those embodied in the classical idea that (1) such knowledge is, in an important sense, *indirect* knowledge, in some sense based on inference from bits of *direct* knowledge about our own states of consciousness; and in the more recent idea that (2) at least some knowledge we have about the past and about the world of objects and events around us is not *indirect* knowledge based on inference from, or justified by premisses about our own psychological states, but rather has at least some element of immediate and direct justification itself.

In the case of memory, for example, the latter can perhaps best be illustrated in this volume by Alexius Meinong's "Toward an Epistemological Assessment of Memory", first published in 1886. This work is concerned primarily with the credibility of memory. The problem that Meinong discusses has been put succinctly by C. I. Lewis in *An Analysis of Knowledge and Valuation* (La Salle, Illinois, The Open Court Publishing Company, 1946) :

> The assumption of certainty for memory in general would be contradicted by the fact that we remember remembering things and later finding them to be false. And memory in general being thus fallible, the claim of certainty for any particular memory, or class of them, becomes dubious. Such credence of any particular thing remembered, asks for some other and supporting ground beyond the immediate item which presents itself with the quality of recollection. And here we might well fall into despair; because we see in advance that in any attempt to provide for a memory such supporting grounds of its credibility, we are bound to encounter the same difficulty all over again, and in a more complex and aggravated form. Because we shall have to rest upon facts about like memories in the past and their subsequent confirmation—facts which can only be themselves disclosed by remembering. (p. 334)

Meinong's solution to the problem anticipates the following solution proposed by Lewis:

> The answer which, as we conceive, can be returned to the problem thus posed, has two parts. First; whatever is remembered, whether explicit recollection or merely in the form of our sense of the past, is *prima facie* credible because so remembered. And second; when the whole range of empirical beliefs is taken into account, all of them more or less dependent upon memorial knowledge, we find that those which are most credible can be assured by their mutual support, or as we shall put it, by their *congruence*. (*Ibid.*)

It is not difficult to see that an analogous problem arises in connection with "the evidence of the senses," our ostensible perception of material things external to our bodies, and that an analogous solution is available. Thus one may hold, as Russell does in the chapter entitled "Epistemological Premisses" reprinted here, that "beliefs caused by perception are to be accepted unless there are positive grounds for rejecting them." And one may say, paraphrasing Lewis's final sentence quoted above, and applying it to knowledge based on the use of the senses: when the whole range of empirical beliefs is taken into account, all of them more or less dependent upon perception, we find that those which are most credible can be assured by their mutual support or *congruence*.

The contrasting and more traditional view that one can find running throughout this volume is sometimes referred to as the doctrine of "the given". The knowledge a person has at any time, according to this doctrine, may be thought of as an "edifice" or "structure" which rests, in part at least, upon a foundation of absolute certainty. The "foundation" of this structure at any time is said to be the apprehension the person has at that time of (a) the ways in which things are appearing to him;

(b) certain of his own states of mind (how he feels, what he is thinking about, what he thinks he perceives, what he thinks he remembers) ; and (c) some of the *a priori* truths of logic and mathematics. "The given", as a technical term, has been applied primarily to (a)—to the ways in which things may appear to us at any time, or, as some philosophers put it, to the appearances we happen to sense at those times. This view is perhaps most clearly expressed in the writings of C. I. Lewis reprinted in this volume. Aspects of it are discussed critically in numerous works in the volume, including those of Malcolm, Reichenbach, Goodman, and Wilfrid Sellars. But this doctrine runs throughout all the different sections of this book and leads us to the more general question of the structure of human knowledge discussed in the last section.

The present book is not devoted solely to this contrast in contemporary epistemology. Among the other contemporary epistemological concerns discussed here are: how to define "S knows that p"; the meaning and relations between such epistemic concepts as "certain", "warranted", "evident", and "doubtful"; the explication of the concept of memory; and the nature of the knowledge that we have of our own psychological states. These problems, though, at least as treated in most of the works presented in this volume, grow out of one or another of the basic approaches to empirical knowledge we have outlined in this introduction.

RODERICK CHISHOLM
ROBERT J. SWARTZ

Brown University

Empirical Knowledge

I

CONTEMPORARY SKEPTICISM

Leonard Nelson

The Impossibility of the "Theory of Knowledge"

If we review the activity of this Congress so far, we become aware of two facts—facts of which other sources might have informed us but which it is good to find here corroborated. One of them is heartening, the other must sadden us. What is gratifying is that the mere existence of this Congress bears witness to a belief in the possibility of philosophy as science. That an international congress for philosophy is possible presupposes the conviction that there can be common philosophical endeavor; and such endeavor is possible only if we believe in philosophy as science. But this conviction is manifested even more clearly and strikingly in the unusually close connection, at this Congress, between philosophy and the exact sciences; and the union of science and philosophy in the personality of our honored president is a special symbolic expression of our faith that such union is possible.

An address, "Die Unmöglichkeit der Erkenntnistheorie," published in *Abhandlungen der Fries'schen Schule,* III (Göttingen, 1912), No. 4; also in *Die Reformation der Philosophie* (Leipzig, 1918), delivered on April 11, 1911, before the Fourth International Congress for Philosophy at Bologna.

Leonard Nelson, "The Impossibility of the Theory of Knowledge," in *Socratic Method and Critical Philosophy* (New Haven: Yale University Press, 1949, and New York: Dover Publications, Inc., 1965). Reprinted by permission.

As you know, there are many who ridicule a congress for philosophy, who feel that attendance at such a congress is beneath the true dignity of a philosopher. Such an opinion is necessary and natural to all those who regard philosophy as a matter of personal experience, as something that cannot be molded to precise, communicable forms—all those, in short, to whom philosophy is not a science. Those, however, who do not share this opinion must welcome the lively interest this Congress has aroused and the special emphasis its program lays on the relations of philosophy to the exact sciences, as refreshing testimony to the belief in philosophy as science.

But even though we who have convened here believe in the possibility of a scientific philosophy, we must ask ourselves whether we really possess such a philosophical science; and we must in all honesty confess—and this is the second, saddening fact of which this Congress makes us aware—that at present the state of philosophy is not that of a science. We have observed, and the discussions have borne it in upon us, that there is no unanimity among those present on even the most elementary philosophical questions. The more we are concerned with achieving the goal of philosophy as a science, the more important it must be to us not to gloss over this fact, that philosophy is not now a science, but rather to bring it out as clearly as possible. Thus we shall find occasion all the sooner to scrutinize the reasons *why* we have not yet succeeded in making a science of philosophy and to inquire in what way we may hope to put an end to this unseemly state of affairs.

This is the problem to the solution of which my address will attempt to make a contribution.

The nature of this task obliges me to deal primarily with the formulation of our problem and with questions of method. In so doing, I am undertaking nothing new: our age is strikingly rich in such methodological research. Indeed, it has been regarded as a failing, as a sort of morbid symptom, that current philosophy is preponderantly concerned with the question of its proper method. I cannot share that point of view. Whatever the case may be in other sciences, in philosophy it is not a sign of decline but a sign of convalescence, when attention is paid above all to the correct method. In other sciences the cognitive material that is to be reduced to scientific form is accessible to us through relatively simple procedures, and we do not require a special preliminary investigation to find out how we can make it our own; but in philosophy everything is based on just such a methodological preliminary study. For the sum total of the cognitions that are to form the content of philosophical science are not available to us without special effort, and everything turns on how we go about getting hold of them. Consequently, the trustworthiness of our results depends altogether on our choice of method.

Difficult though it may be to achieve unanimity regarding this method, it is futile to enter into a discussion of specific results until this has been achieved. Even though the many methodological efforts of recent times have not yet led to the desired goal, we may not on that account conclude that it would be better to abandon such methodological research in order finally to turn from the method to the real matter at hand. On the contrary, it is my opinion that if methodological work has not hitherto met with the hoped-for success, that is only because it has not attacked its task vigorously *enough*. If only this work is carried on with the necessary earnestness and energy, the correct way will soon be found to escape from philosophical anarchy to a harmonious and planned scientific endeavor.

It must strike a dispassionate observer of the development of philosophy in recent times as particularly remarkable that the contention and variety of philosophical opinions is greatest in just that discipline whose specific intention it has been to put an end to the fruitless quarrels of the earlier academic metaphysics, namely, in the studies on the "theory of knowledge" (*Erkenntnistheorie*).[1] These studies were originally undertaken with the sole purpose of making the philosophical problems, which without them appeared unsolvable, accessible to scientific treatment, either by establishing thus a scientific metaphysics or by ascertaining once and for all through a "theory of knowledge" the impossibility of such a scientific metaphysics. How is it to be explained that this apparently highly justified hope for a peaceful scientific form of philosophy has not only not been realized but on the contrary has immeasurably widened the dissension among the schools? I shall show that this curious phenomenon has a very simple cause, and that the problem of the "theory of knowledge" is similar to many allied problems in other sciences. We very often find that a problem we have disputed at great length, without getting a step nearer its solution, finally turns out to be one that simply permits of no solution or one whose solution (if we can call it that) is not the hoped-for positive finding but rather the proof of its unsolvability.

I shall, therefore, prove the impossibility of the "theory of knowledge," but in order not to conclude with a negative, unconstructive result, I shall enter into the question as to what positive consequences can perhaps be drawn from this fact—the question whether we are thus obliged to abandon the search for philosophy as science, whether, in other words, we must relapse into dogmatic metaphysics, or whether

[1] A comprehensive history of *Erkenntnistheorie* since Kant can be found in Nelson's "Über das sogenannte Erkenntnisproblem," *Abhandlungen der Fries'schen Schule,* II (Göttingen, 1908).

perhaps there is a third path, which really leads to our goal. I believe I can show you that this last is the case, and I hope that my address itself will provide you with an illustration that we can follow this path.

First of all, I shall say as much regarding the *method* I shall employ as is necessary to an understanding of my exposition.

When we concern ourselves with philosophy as science, it is natural for us to take the example of the exact sciences as a model, though we know, or at least we should know from Kant, that we cannot blindly transfer to philosophy a method that is appropriate to the mathematical sciences. Pre-Kantian metaphysics made precisely this mistake of trying to imitate in philosophy the usual dogmatic method of mathematics. Kant proved definitively the faultiness of this undertaking. But the relation of the two sciences, philosophy and mathematics, has changed in a curious way since Kant's time: during the last century modern mathematics has developed in what is called *axiomatics* a method that corresponds exactly to the one Kant demanded for philosophy. This is the *regressive* method, the importance of which does not lie in extending our knowledge, adding new truths to the fund of those already known, elaborating their consequences, but rather in examining the known truths with regard to their preassumptions. It serves as a means of investigating the conditions of the solvability of a problem before we attack the problem itself; it assures us whether or not the problem is solvable at all and what presuppositions are already implicit in the mere setting of the problem; it determines what presuppositions are necessary and sufficient for a definite solution of a problem.

I wish to apply this method to the problem of the "theory of knowledge," also called the problem of knowledge. This problem is that of the objective validity of our knowledge. It is the task of a "theory of knowledge" to test the truth or objective validity of our knowledge. I maintain that a solution of this problem is *impossible,* and I prove this as follows:

In order to solve this problem, we should have to have a criterion by the application of which we could decide whether or not a cognition is true; I shall call it briefly the "validity criterion." This criterion would itself either be or not be a cognition. If it be a cognition, it would fall within the area of what is problematic, the validity of which is first to be solved with the aid of our criterion. Accordingly, it cannot itself be a cognition. But if the criterion be not a cognition, it would nevertheless, in order to be applicable, have to be known, i.e., we should have to know that it is a criterion of the truth. But in order to gain this knowledge of the criterion, we should already have had to apply it. In both cases, therefore, we encounter a contradiction. A "validity criterion" is consequently impossible, and hence there can be no "theory of knowledge."

One need only take any example in order to make the content of this proof clearer. For instance, someone might assert that *agreement of thinking subjects with one another* is the criterion in question. To be able to apply this criterion, we should have to *know* that agreement of various subjects is a criterion of the truth of their knowledge. But in order to know this, we should have to apply this criterion itself to the assumption that agreement is the criterion in question. We should have to convince ourselves that all subjects agree on the assertion that agreement is a criterion of the truth of their assertions. But in order to realize from this the truth of this assumption, we should already have had to presuppose that it is correct, i.e., that agreement is a "validity criterion." Thus the possibility of achieving this knowledge would involve an inner contradiction.

Or someone might claim that *obviousness* is the criterion in question. In order for this criterion to be applicable, it would have to be known to us as such, i.e., we should have to *know* that the obvious cognitions are the true ones. But we could only know this if it were *obvious* that the obvious cognitions are true; however, in order to deduce the truth of this assumption from its obviousness, we should already have had to *presuppose* that obviousness is a criterion of truth. It is therefore impossible to achieve the knowledge in question.

Or let us take pragmatism. If the usefulness of a notion is to be the sought-after criterion of truth, we should have to *know,* in order to be able to apply this criterion, that usefulness is the criterion of truth. We should therefore have to know that it is *useful* to think that useful thinking is the true thinking, and thus we should have to presuppose that the usefulness of thinking is a criterion of its truth. So here, too, we meet the same contradiction; and it is the same in every other case.

Now, what is the *preassumption* that we make in setting the problem of a "theory of knowledge" and that involves the contradiction we have observed? It is important, first of all, to realize that such a preassumption is really implicit in the problem, and that the alleged absence of preassumptions, proudly proclaimed by the "theory of knowledge," is simply a chimera. If one asks whether one possesses objectively valid cognitions at all, one thereby presupposes that the objectivity of cognition is questionable at first, and that we can assure ourselves of this objectivity only indirectly, namely, through the process of the "theory of knowledge." What can be said about this preassumption, which is indispensable to the "theory of knowledge"?

Let us begin by drawing up a clearer picture of the meaning and content of this preassumption. It seems at first to be nothing more than an application of the logical principle of sufficient reason, according to which every assertion needs a *verification*. And indeed, the "theory of knowledge" stands or falls with the preassumption of the necessity of verifying every cognition; for the task of this discipline is none other than to verify our cognition. Although this very preassumption seems to aim at the elimination of all prejudgments, the contradiction it leads to, demonstrated above, makes us aware that some error must lie concealed here and that consequently the preassumption is itself a prejudgment.

This contradiction really lies in the following: If every cognition needs a verification, that is equivalent to saying that it presupposes another cognition as its ground, to which it must be traced back if it is to be asserted as truth. The contradiction lies in the proposition, here implied, of the *mediacy* of all knowledge. For if every cognition were possible only on the ground of another, we should have to execute an infinite regression in order to reach any true cognition, and hence no verification of cognitions would be possible.

We can phrase this result in another way. If one asserts the mediacy of all knowledge in the manner just outlined, one therewith asserts that every cognition is a *judgment*. The word "judgment" is here used in its usual sense to mean the assertion of a thought that is in itself problematic. Every judgment presupposes a notion that is not in itself assertoric but to which the assertion is only mediately added. However, this preassumption that every cognition is a judgment involves also another, namely, that the verification of a cognition can only be a *proof*. A proof is the tracing back of one judgment to another that contains the logical ground of the first. But if there is no other verification of judgments except proof, no verification of judgments is possible at all; for all proof consists only in the tracing back of the judgment to be proved to unproved and unprovable judgments. Therefore, either there is another means of verifying judgments besides proof, or no verification of them is possible at all.

The above-demonstrated preassumption in the "theory of knowledge"—and on this point I should like to lay particular stress—involves not only the logical contradiction we have discussed; it also contradicts psychological facts. It contains, as we have seen, the psychological conclusion that every cognition is a judgment; but this statement contradicts the facts of inner experience. To convince ourselves of the existence of cognitions that are not judgments, we need only consider any intuition at all, such as an ordinary sensory perception. For example, I have a sensory perception of the sheet of paper that lies here on the table before me. This perception is, first of all, a cognition, not merely a problematic notion. The existential assertion that is an element of this cognition is, however, not a judgment. To be sure, I can also render in a judgment the same circumstances that I here cognize through the perception; but when I judge that a piece of paper is lying before me on the table, that is an altogether different sort of cognition from the perception of this situation. I need concepts for the judgment, e.g., the concept "table," the concept "paper," etc. I connect these concepts in a certain manner and assert that objective reality pertains to this combination of concepts. Perception, on the other hand, has no need of any concepts nor of any problematic notion of its objects whatsoever; rather, it is itself an originally assertoric notion—is, in other words, an *immediate* cognition.

Thus we find that problematic notions are not that which is original, to which objectivity would have to be contributed from some other source, but that it is cognition itself that is original. It is correct that judgments are possible only on the basis of concepts, which are problematic notions; nevertheless, this does not apply to cognition as such. With this ascertainment the problem of the "theory of knowledge" disappears: the possibility of cognition is not a problem but a fact.

We must now scrutinize this *factual* character of cognition. Once one is clear in one's mind about it, one will see a problem not in the possibility of cognition but rather in the possibility of *error*. For if we originally have only cognitions, the question presents itself how error can arise at all. To solve this problem, we need only inquire into the relation of judgments to immediate knowledge. In and of itself a judgment is not yet a cognition; it is such only under the condition that it reiterates an immediate cognition. Judgments are acts of reflection, and to that extent arbitrary. The combination of concepts in judgments is arbitrary and hence depends on a factor that is foreign to cognition. The truth of *judgments,* namely, their correspondence with immediate knowledge, *is not an original fact;* it is rather a task that we arbitrarily set ourselves so far as our interest in truth motivates us; and in the choice of the means for the accomplishment of this task we can be mistaken.

Before I proceed to develop the consequences of my previous observations, I should like to illuminate the impossibility of the "theory of knowledge" from another angle. The impossibility of such theory can be proved also in the following manner. Since for this discipline knowledge is not a fact but a problem, the "theory of knowledge," in order to solve this problem, cannot assume any knowledge as given; rather, it must begin solely with problematic notions, that is, mere concepts. Now, only analytic judgments can be developed from mere concepts, and they never provide a new cognition, which can only consist in synthetic judgments. Thus our task amounts to deriving synthetic from merely analytic judgments.

That this task, however, is incapable of execution can be proved as follows. If we assume that it is possible to derive synthetic from merely analytic judgments, then there must appear somewhere in the series of syllogisms a syllogism both of whose premises are still analytic while the conclusion is already synthetic. But if both the premises of this syllogism, major as well as minor, are analytic, this means that, on the one hand, the major term of the syllogism is already contained in the middle term and, on the other hand, the middle term is already contained in the minor term. But with major term thus contained in middle, as well as middle in minor term, then the major term is also already contained in the minor term, i.e., the conclusion must also be analytic, contrary to our assumption. Thus it is impossible ever to derive a synthetic judgment from merely analytic judgments, and the task of the "theory of knowledge," to show how knowledge can arise from purely problematic notions, consequently cannot be accomplished.

I presuppose for this second proof of the impossibility of the "theory of knowledge" that one concedes my distinction between analytic and synthetic judgments. I shall therefore briefly consider the principal objection that is raised against this distinction. It has been held that this distinction is variable and unprecise, so that one and the same judgment can at different times and for different people be now analytic, now synthetic; consequently, a mutation of a judgment from the one type to the other is possible. This objection vanishes when we discriminate between judgments and their linguistic expression. What varies and is unprecise is only the co-ordination between the expression and the thought it stands for. The same words can, at different times and for different people, have different meanings, and for this reason, to be sure, one and the same sentence can stand here for an analytic, there for a synthetic, judgment. Whoever concludes from this that the division of judgments into analytic and synthetic is unprecise thereby confounds [fixed] concepts and [changing] word significations.

It is only through this same confusion that the dialectical illusion arises in attempts to solve the problem of the "theory of knowledge." All these endeavors tend toward a renewal of the old, logicizing metaphysics and accordingly can be no more than a repetition of the same old errors in new guise. The apparent success of attempts to create metaphysics from mere logic rests only on the ambiguity of words. This alone makes it possible, in "theories of knowledge," unconsciously to foist off an analytic judgment as a synthetic one by expressing them both in the same sentence.

I should like to adduce two examples of what I have just said, which at the same time will serve to clarify the importance of the basic thought I have presented and to distinguish it from other views with which it might perhaps be confused.

The answer to the question whether or not we possess valid knowledge—no matter what this answer may be—can only be sought in a synthetic judgment, since it is concerned with a fact. And yet it would appear as if we could prove our possession of knowledge purely logically by demonstrating a contradiction in the opposite assumption. This contradiction, with which absolute skepticism has time and again been reproached since Plato, is well known. It is said: Whoever asserts his inability to know anything is contradicting himself, for he claims to *know* what he is asserting, namely, his inability to know anything; and it follows from this contradiction that he knows something. This reasoning is not sound. It is, to be sure, contradictory if someone claims to know that he knows nothing; but it does not follow, by any means, from this contradiction that he knows something; it follows only that he does *not* know what he claims to know, namely, that he knows nothing. The contradiction lies not in the skeptical assumption that we know *nothing* but in the other assumption that we can *know* this. It is not judgment *A,* "I know nothing," but judgment *B,* "I know that I know nothing," that leads to a logical contradiction; hence it follows only that judgment *B* is false, not judgment *A.* The refutation of skepticism by such a theory rests only on the confusion of these two judgments.

This result, viz., insight into the impossibility of a positive validation of knowledge, might induce us to make the opposite attempt to decide the problem *negatively.* If no verification of the validity of our knowledge is possible, it seems to follow that we can know nothing about the validity of our knowledge, that we shall therefore have to regard it skeptically. But this skeptical conclusion from the impossibility of verifying knowledge is just as erroneous. It makes the tacit assumption that we can assert only that to be valid which can be verified; and this is precisely the same prejudice of the "theory of knowledge" on the basis of which we were, at the outset, led to the contradictory demand for a verification of knowledge.

I mention this last particularly because it might be objected that my proof of the impossibility of the "theory of knowledge" simply reiterates an old idea, often enunciated by the skeptics. It can be seen from what has been said that the skeptical arguments in question prove too little. *I do not assert the impossibility of the "theory of knowledge" in order to conclude that knowledge is impossible; rather, I assert that this skeptical conclusion, that knowledge is impossible, is itself merely a consequence of the prejudice held by the proponents of a "theory of knowledge."* The contradiction I have pointed out is characteristic not only of the positive solution of the problem of the "theory of knowledge" but indeed of every supposed solution, and hence also of the skeptical.

The opposite mistake from this skeptical reasoning is to be found in certain other arguments to which one might wish to call my attention in order to trace back my proof of the impossibility of a "theory of knowledge" to ideas that have long been known. I am thinking of the attacks on the "theory of knowledge" initiated by Hegel and Herbart and especially championed by Lotze and Busse; they all have in common the fact that they were launched in favor of dogmatism. Where the skeptical attacks prove too little, these prove too much in that they postulate the necessity of a dogmatic metaphysics—*a consequence that cannot be derived from the proofs I have offered.* Moreover, nothing can be decided by such vague arguments as, for example, the argument that one cannot swim before going into the water, or that cognition cannot cognize itself. In this way one could just as well prove the impossibility of philology with the assertion that one cannot use language with reference to language.

The alternatives of the "theory of knowledge" and dogmatism, i.e., of the necessity of verifying every cognition and the necessity of positing some judgments without any verification, are, to be sure, inevitable as long as one adheres to the already refuted presupposition that all cognitions are judgments. For on this presupposition one must necessarily extend the application of the principle of sufficient reason to *all cognitions whatsoever* and, on the other hand, confuse the obvious impossibility of verifying every cognition with the postulation of unverifiable *judgments.* If, however, one abandons the presupposition that every cognition is a judgment, the choice between a "theory of knowledge" and dogmatism disappears. The possibility then opens up of satisfying the postulate of the verification of all judgments without falling victim to the infinite regress of the "theory of knowledge."

The criterion of truth that we here use does not give rise to the contradiction that we have found in the concept of the "validity criterion." Indeed, the criterion of the truth of judgments cannot itself be a judgment, but it does not for that reason have to lie outside cognition; instead, it lies in immediate knowledge, which in its turn does not consist of judgments.

If philosophy wishes to be a science, it, like every science, will have to confine itself to this one task, the task of verifying judgments. It will only then assert its own scientific existence or, rather, will first be able to achieve it when, instead of setting itself above the competence of science and sitting in judgment on the rights and qualifications of the various sciences, it is satisfied to take over for treatment a particular field of knowledge alongside the other individual disciplines.

That this is possible and how we shall easily see if we call to mind the purpose the misinterpretation of which originally created the problem of the "theory of knowledge." If we disregard *proofs,* which only serve to trace judgments back to other judgments, and consider only the basic judgments, we find that these—unless they are analytic and have their ground in mere *concepts*—are verified by being traced back to *intuition* in accordance with the universal procedure in all special sciences. But, as Hume first pointed out, there are judgments where this means of verification fails, judgments that do not have their ground in intuition although they are not analytic: these are all the judgments through which we conceive a necessary connection between things. One such judgment is, for instance, the principle of causality. The verification of these judgments, which Kant called the "synthetic judgments evolved through mere concepts," is, indeed, the task to which metaphysicians have always, more or less gropingly, devoted their efforts but which Kant, through his generalization of the Humean problem, was the first to formulate scientifically. It is readily understandable that once the nature of these "metaphysical" judgments was clearly recognized, once the impossibility of tracing them back to the only recognized sources of knowledge—concept and intuition—was grasped, it was tempting (for lack of an immediate knowledge on which to ground them) to try to verify them through comparison with the object, i.e., through the "theory of knowledge."

Our rejection of this cast to the problem as an inadmissible misconstruction exposes Hume's original problem in its true significance. The possibility of verifying metaphysical judgments, and therewith the life or death of metaphysics as a science, depends on the solution of this problem. But it can easily be demonstrated that its solution can only be sought in *psychology*. We cannot develop the metaphysical judgments immediately from their source of knowledge in the way that geometry, for instance, can be developed from the intuition of space, for the nature and even the existence of this source of knowledge are precisely what are being questioned: this source is not readily at our disposal; rather, we must first *search* for it. The problem at hand, correctly understood, thus concerns the existence of a certain kind of cognition, namely, immediate metaphysical knowledge. This is first of all a *question of facts,* and consequently a question that can only be decided by way of *experience*. Secondly, the object whose factuality is in question is a *cognition;* and cognitions, whatever their object may be, are themselves only the object of *inner* experience. Therefore, the Hume-Kant problem can only be resolved through psychology, i.e., through the science of inner experience.

Now, what are the possible, that is, a priori conceivable, solutions of this problem?

Initially, the opinion is conceivable that the difficulty that gives rise to the problem only *seems* to exist, and that the so-called "metaphysical" judgments can actually, as the metaphysicians before Hume endeavored, be traced back to the then recognized sources of knowledge, i.e., mere reflection or intuition. Indeed, if we presuppose the completeness of the disjunction between reflection and intuition as sources of knowledge, any other way to verify the judgments in question is logically inconceivable.

If one chooses reflection as the source of knowledge of the metaphysical judgments, one arrives at metaphysical *logicism;* if intuition, metaphysical *mysticism.* If, however, one rejects both sources of knowledge for the metaphysical judgments, holding still to the exclusiveness of these two sources of knowledge, there remains only the conclusion that no source of knowledge exists as basis for the metaphysical judgments, that they are therefore altogether unverifiable, and hence are fraudulent assertions. This is the consequence of metaphysical *empiricism.*

These attempts at solution through metaphysical logicism, mysticism, and empiricism exhaust the logical possibilities available under the presupposition of the completeness of the disjunction between reflection and intuition as sources of knowledge. It has been generally assumed heretofore that therewith *all* the logically possible solutions of the problem have been exhausted. This would indeed be the case if the completeness of the disjunction between reflection and intuition as sources of knowledge were logically assured.

Now, it seems to be logically self-evident that a cognition that is not intuitive must arise from concepts and therefore from reflection, and vice versa, that a cognition we possess independently of reflection must pertain to intuition. This is true, to be sure, if we *define* intuition as nonreflective knowledge, but such a definition does not correspond to linguistic usage. According to general usage we understand "intuition" to mean a knowledge of which we are immediately conscious. But not every immediate cognition is necessarily a cognition of which we are immediately *conscious.* There is no contradiction in the assumption that a cognition that does not arise from reflection reaches our consciousness only through the mediation of reflection. Immediacy of cognition and immediacy of consciousness of the cognition are logically two different things. The illusion of the logical completeness of the disjunction between reflection and intuition as sources of knowledge arises only as a result of the confusion of these two concepts, in other words, as a result of the false conclusion of the immediacy of consciousness from the immediacy of cognition.

The demonstration of the logical incompleteness of this disjunction reveals to us a fourth possible solution of our problem. It consists in tracing back the metaphysical judgments to a cognition that belongs neither to reflection nor to intuition, that is, to a nonintuitive immediate cognition. I denote this solution, which follows from the criticism of the dogmatic disjunction of the sources of knowledge, as metaphysical *criticism.*

The disjunction, expanded by our indication of the possibility of a nonintuitive immediate cognition, is in its turn *logically* secured. Since thereby the completeness of the above-considered possibilities of solution is now guaranteed, we can turn to the further question of how we are to decide between these various attempts at solution, i.e., which of the various logically possible theories is psychologically correct. With this question we leave the realm of purely logical criticism and turn to the testimony of inner experience. And here we can avail ourselves of work done long ago.

Both the positive solutions possible under the dogmatic assumption of the completeness of the disjunction—metaphysical logicism and metaphysical mysticism—have already been refuted by Hume.

Logicism, such as formed the basis of scholastic metaphysics and which has been revived in the "theory of knowledge," breaks down on the psychological fact of the indirectness and emptiness of reflection. Reflection can analyze and elucidate cognitions elsewhere provided but cannot of itself creatively beget new cognitions, that is to say, it is a source only of analytic, but not of synthetic, judgments.

Metaphysical *mysticism,* such as forms the basis for neo-Platonic mysticism in its old and new forms, breaks down on the psychological fact of the original obscurity of metaphysical knowledge. There is no immediate obviousness in metaphysical truths; we cannot derive these cognitions from an "intellectual intuition"; they reach our consciousness only through thinking (reflection), through abstracting from the intuitively given content of empirical judgments.

If, then, we are not permitted to seek the source of the metaphysical judgments either in intuition or reflection, two ways are still open to us: either we can dispute altogether the existence of metaphysical knowledge; or we can abandon the assumption of the exclusiveness of reflection and intuition as sources of knowledge and assert the existence of nonintuitive immediate cognition.

Hume sought the basic fallacy of the theories he refuted in their assumption that we possess metaphysical cognition at all; in this way he was led to his negative attempt at solution and hence to metaphysical *empiricism.* His task then became not that of verifying the metaphysical judgments but that of explaining psychologically the illusion that calls forth these judgments, i.e., of explaining how the claim to knowledge asserted in these judgments is possible without presuppossing an actual source of knowledge, merely as a product of the blind mechanism of the association of ideas. The question now arises whether this task is capable of fulfillment.

Hume believed that he could find the basis for the judgments that were the object of his problem in the psychological principle of the expectancy of similar cases. But he was not unaware of the difficulty to be encountered in basing this principle on the laws of association. Association explains only that event *A* reminds me of a previous event *B* connected with it, but not that I expect the reoccurrence of *B*. The remembered thought, as such, is only problematic, whereas expectation comprises an assertion which—whether it be one of certainty or only of probability—cannot be explained by association alone. Hume tried to overcome this difficulty by presenting the difference between problematic and assertoric notions as merely one of degree, basing *this* difference on a difference in the intensity of the clarity of the notions. On this supposition our recollection would, indeed, after sufficiently frequent reproduction, be able to pass over into an expectation merely through the effectiveness of the association. But this Humean hypothesis, that the difference between problematic and assertoric notions is only one of degree, contradicts the facts of self-observation. This is generally admitted today; and so Hume's attempted solution collapses.

It is easy so to generalize this criticism of Hume's theory that through it any empirical attempt at solution, whatever its nature, is excluded. The problem lies in the actual existence of certain judgments through which we conceive a necessary connection of things. What is important here is not the assertion that the merely problematic thought of a necessary connection, which is to be found in these judgments, cannot be explained through association. To be sure, every *connection of ideas* must be explicable by the laws of association. What we must explain here, however, is not a connection of ideas but the *idea of connection*. This is in its content an entirely new conception vis-à-vis the ideas of that which, in this idea, is thought of as connected; accordingly, it can never arise from these other ideas through mere association but presupposes a source of knowledge of its own.

The critical analysis of metaphysical logicism and mysticism shows us that this source of knowledge can lie neither in reflection nor in intuition. If we now consider the above psychological analysis of empiricism together with the critical analysis of both these other theories, we have proof of the correctness of the fourth theory, the only one that still remains, viz., *criticism*. The mere exclusion of the first two theories permitted us only the conclusion that, *if* we possess metaphysical knowledge at all, the existence of nonintuitive immediate knowledge must be assumed. But we were not yet able to claim that this condition is valid;

rather, the possibility was still open to us of following Hume in the opposite direction and concluding, from the dogmatic disjunction of the sources of knowledge, that metaphysical knowledge is impossible. It is only after we have also refuted this empiristic consequence that we are able, in connection with the exclusion of metaphysical logicism and mysticism, to conclude the existence of nonintuitive immediate knowledge. We thus can, at the same time, supplement the proof of the logical incompleteness of the dogmatic disjunction with the proof of its psychological falsity.

At this juncture we perceive what we have gained from our previous logical analysis of the several possible solutions of the problem. In addition to the fact that this analysis at once precludes us from the contradictory attempt to find in the "theory of knowledge" a solution of the problem, it also prevented us from too hastily excluding from our range of choices what at first sight appeared to be a logically impossible course. The service that this analysis rendered us is all the more important since in our case the course that, by and large, has not even been considered heretofore is precisely the only one that really leads to a solution. Without this preparation through such a logical criticism one continually runs the danger of blinding oneself, through the deceptive illusion of the dogmatic disjunction, to the most obvious facts of self-observation. On the supposition of the completeness of this disjunction, as we have seen, the facts of the emptiness of reflection, the nonintuitive nature of metaphysical knowledge and the actual existence of metaphysical knowledge cannot be logically reconciled with one another because one of these facts always contradicts the consequences of the other two. And so—as, moreover, the history of philosophy bears in on us—without that critical analysis we are constantly driven hither and thither between these three equally necessary, but mutually contradictory, consequences. But the antinomy in which we thus become entangled is immediately resolved once we become aware of the prejudice that lies behind it, set aside all dogmatic suppositions, and look only the facts themselves in the eye.

We can accordingly epitomize the results of these critical observations as follows:

On the assumption of the exclusiveness of reflection and intuition as sources of knowledge, we have a choice only between metaphysical logicism, mysticism, and empiricism; that is to say, we have only the choice of contesting either the fact of the emptiness of reflection, or the fact of the nonintuitive nature of metaphysical knowledge, or the fact of the existence of metaphysical knowledge—or, finally, we may conclude from these three facts that nonintuitive immediate knowledge exists.

In conclusion, let us consider what we have gained in all this compared to the "theory of knowledge."

If we must admit the possibility of metaphysics, we still need a criterion by which to distinguish between legitimate and spurious metaphysical assertions. But here we are exposed to the difficulty that this criterion must itself be metaphysical in nature since we know it can lie neither in reflection nor in intuition.

The wish to escape this difficulty is the real reason why recourse had to be taken to the "theory of knowledge." For, since metaphysics can obviously no more contain in itself the basis of the validity of its judgments than can any other discipline, this basis had to be sought in another, higher discipline, which, however, in its turn could no more derive its content from mere reflection or intuition than metaphysics itself could. It is therefore not surprising that so far no one who has gone into this higher discipline has been able to disclose its origins.

But the embarrassment of which this enigmatic science is to relieve us is merely a consequence of the confusion of knowledge with judgment. If we discriminate between judgment and immediate knowledge, the fact that the ground of the validity of metaphysical judgments must itself be metaphysical in nature will not lead us to conclude that this ground itself must lie in metaphysical judgments, but we shall seek it in immediate cognition. In this immediate cognition, not in a higher discipline, lies the basis of metaphysical judgments.

To be sure, this immediate cognition is not intuition. And precisely here we see the really decisive reason why psychological critique is so fruitful for metaphysics. For even though we find the basis of metaphysical judgments in an immediate cognition, we do not become immediately conscious of this cognition in such a way as would enable us to compare it directly with the metaphysical judgments in order to verify them. Rather, in order to execute this verification, i.e., to trace back the metaphysical judgments to the immediate knowledge that forms their ground, we must first ingeniously bring this immediate knowledge to light and therefore make it the object of psychological investigation.

Hence we need a special science to verify metaphysical judgments. But this science is no "theory of knowledge": it does not itself contain the basis of metaphysical judgments but only serves to bring it to light. For this very reason, also, the empirical and psychological character of this science is entirely compatible with the rational and metaphysical nature of the propositions it is to verify. For the basis of the metaphysical propositions does not lie in the assertions of this psychological critique but in immediate metaphysical knowledge.

Perhaps we can best clarify this relation by drawing an analogy from critical mathematics. In geometric axiomatics is to be found the proposition of the unprovability of the parallel postulate. Here, then, we must distinguish between two propositions: proposition *A,* the parallel postulate, and proposition *B,* which states that proposition *A* cannot be proved. Now, proposition *B* can be proved. There is nothing paradoxical in this, because *A* is a proposition from the system of geometry, whereas *B* belongs only to critique. *B* does not contain the ground of *A* but simply has *A* as its object. The situation in the critique of the metaphysical propositions is altogether analogous. Let us take, for example, the principle of causality, which we shall call *C*. Then psychological critique proves proposition *D*: There exists a nonintuitive immediate cognition which contains the ground of *C*. *C* is a proposition from the system of metaphysics and as such is rational; *D* is a proposition from psychological critique and as such is empirical. *D* does not contain the ground of *C* but simply has *C* as its object.

Of course, this positive importance of psychology for the verification of metaphysics can only be asserted from the viewpoint of criticism. A logicistic or mystic metaphysics has no need of psychology. Nevertheless —and this should no longer be overlooked—psychology has a *negative* importance for every sort of metaphysics (and anti-metaphysics!), which manifests itself in the fact that every metaphysics—consciously or unconsciously—comprises a psychological preassumption regarding its source of knowledge, in view of which every metaphysics must submit to criticism through comparison with the psychological facts. In this general psychological criticism we are provided with a limiting principle, by the help of which, over and beyond logical criticism, we can at least exclude all those metaphysical doctrines, consistent in themselves, which stand from the very start in contradiction to psychological facts.

Herewith, also, the dispute is transferred to a field more accessible to scientific treatment, and in which it is possible to work on common problems according to a common method. Only after we have succeeded in making truly manifest the importance of the general logical and psychological criticism that we have been considering, can we hope to launch a program of cooperative and fruitful scientific endeavor in philosophy in the place of divisive and barren dogmatic quarrels.

G. E. Moore

Four Forms of Skepticism

My object in this lecture is to discuss four different philosophical views, each of which may, I think, be properly called a form of Skepticism. Each of these views consists in holding, with regard to one particular *sort* of thing, that no human being ever knows with complete certainty anything whatever of that sort; and they differ from one another only in respect of the sort of thing with regard to which each of them hold this.

I hope that nobody will be misled by my use of the word 'thing' in the above statement. I was not using it in the sense in which this pencil is one 'thing' and this piece of paper another. I was using it in the sense in which it is used, for instance, if one says: 'I know very little about American history, but there are two *things* I do know about it, namely that Washington was the first President of the United States, and that Lincoln was President at the time of the Civil War'. This use of 'thing' seems to me to be perfectly good and idiomatic English, and I intend to continue to use the word in this way; but obviously it is quite a different use of the word from that in which chairs or tables are 'things':

G. E. Moore, "Four Forms of Skepticism," in *Philosophical Papers* (London: George Allen & Unwin Ltd., 1959), pp. 196-226. Reprinted by permission of the publisher.

nobody would say '*that* Washington was the first President of the United States' is a 'thing' in the same sense in which this pencil is a thing.

At first sight it may seem as if, in this use, 'thing' is a mere synonym for 'fact', and as if, therefore, instead of speaking of four sorts of 'things', I might just as well have spoken of four sorts of *facts*. That Washington was the first President of the United States is a fact; and there is nothing strange in this use of the word 'fact'. But the use of 'thing' with which I am concerned is not only one in which it makes sense to say, e.g. 'That the sun is larger than the moon is a thing which I know for certain', but also one in which it makes sense to say 'That the sun is larger than the moon is a thing which *nobody knows for certain*'. Indeed, as we shall see, one of the four forms of skepticism with which I am concerned holds that the latter proposition is true; and though perhaps this is nonsense in the sense that it is obviously untrue, it is not nonsense in the peculiar sense in which, if we substituted the word 'fact' for the word 'thing' in this sentence, we should get a nonsensical statement. Consider the form of words 'That the sun is larger than the moon is a *fact* which nobody knows for certain'. Here the proposition 'That the sun is larger than the moon is a fact' is logically equivalent to the proposition 'The sun is larger than the moon'. But the proposition 'Nobody knows for certain that the sun is larger than the moon' is logically equivalent to the proposition 'It is possible that the sun is not larger than the moon'. Hence the combination of the two gives us 'The sun is larger than the moon, but it's possible that it's not' or 'That the sun is larger than the moon is a fact, but possibly it's not a fact'. And these are a peculiar kind of nonsense like 'I am at present sitting down, but possibly I'm not' or like 'I'm at present sitting down, but I don't believe I am'. But the person who says 'That the sun is larger than the moon is a *thing* which nobody knows for certain', though he may be talking nonsense, is certainly not talking *this sort* of nonsense. And hence it follows that this is a sentence in which 'thing' is not a mere synonym for 'fact'—a sentence in which the word 'fact' cannot be substituted for the word 'thing', without changing the meaning of the sentence.

Once it is realized that the word 'thing' in this usage is not a synonym for 'fact', it is natural to suggest that perhaps it is a synonym for 'proposition'. But this also, I think, will not do, for the following reason. 'I don't know that the sun is larger than the moon' certainly is logically equivalent to 'I don't know that the proposition that the sun is larger than the moon *is true*'; but it seems to me that it is not good English to use the expression 'I don't know the proposition that the sun is larger than the moon' to mean the same as the latter or to mean anything which is logically equivalent to the latter. This is a respect in which our use of the word 'know' differs from our use of the word 'believe'. Whenever a man believes a given proposition *p*, we can also rightly say that he believes that *p* is true; but from the fact that a boy knows the fifth proposition of Euclid, it by no means follows that he knows that that proposition is *true*. Hence for the expression 'That the sun is larger than the moon is a *thing* which I know' we cannot rightly substitute 'That the sun is larger than the moon is a *proposition* which I know'; since the former is logically equavalent to ' . . . is a proposition which I know *to be true*', while the latter is not. I may 'know' a given proposition in the sense of being perfectly familiar with it, and yet *not* know it to be true. We can, I think, say that the usage of 'thing' with which we are concerned is one in which the expression 'That the sun is larger than the moon is a *thing* which nobody knows for certain' is short for ' . . . is a proposition which nobody knows for certain *to be true'*; but we cannot always, in the case of this usage, simply substitute the word 'proposition' for the word 'thing', since it is not good English to use an expression of the form 'I know the proposition *p*' as short for the corresponding expression of the form 'I know that the proposition *p* is true'.

Assuming then, that my use of the word 'thing' is understood, we can say that I am so using the term 'skepticism' that anybody who *denies* that we ever know for certain 'things' of a certain sort can be said to be 'skeptical' about our *knowledge* of 'things' of that sort. And I think that this is *one* correct usage of the words 'skepticism' and 'skeptical'. But it is worth noting that, if it is so, then to say that a man is skeptical about certain sorts of things, or holds certain forms of skepticism, does not necessarily imply that he is *in doubt* about anything whatever. I think this is worth noting because people seem very commonly to assume that doubt is essential to any form of skepticism. But, if I am right in my use of the word, it is obvious that this is a mistake. For a man who *denies* that we ever know for certain things of a certain sort, obviously need not feel any doubt about that which he asserts—namely, that no human being ever does know for certain a thing of the sort in question; and in fact many who have made this sort of denial seem to have felt no doubt at all that they were right: they have been as dogmatic about it as any dogmatist. And also, curiously enough, a man who denies that we ever know for certain things of a certain sort, need not necessarily feel any doubt whatever about *particular* things of the sort in question. A man who, like Bertrand Russell, believes with the utmost confidence that he never knows for certain such a thing as that he is sitting down, may nevertheless feel perfectly sure, without a shadow of doubt, on thousands of occasions, that he is sitting down. And yet his view that we never do know for certain things of that sort can, I think, be obviously quite rightly called a form of skepticism—skepticism about our knowledge of things of that sort. In the case of all the four forms of skepticism with which I shall be concerned, it is, I think, the case that those who have held them have constantly felt no doubt at all about particular things of the very sort with regard to which they have held that nobody knows for certain things of that sort. Even if, on a particular occasion, such a man remembers his philosophical view that such things are never known for certain, and accordingly says quite sincerely e.g. 'I don't know for certain that I am at present sitting down', it by no means follows that he doubts in the least degree that he is sitting down. It is true that if he really believes that he doesn't know for certain that he is, he can also be truly said to believe that *it is doubtful* whether he is. But from the fact that he sincerely believes that it is doubtful whether he is, it certainly does not follow that he *doubts* whether he is. I think that the common opinion that doubt is essential to skepticism arises from the mistaken opinion that if a man sincerely believes that a thing is doubtful he must doubt it. In the case of sincere philosophical opinions this seems to me to be certainly not the case. Accordingly I think that all that is *necessary* for a man to be properly called a skeptic with regard to our knowledge of certain kinds of things is that he should sincerely hold the view that things of that kind are always doubtful; and that this is a thing which he may do both without having any doubt at all that such things always are doubtful and also without ever doubting any particular thing of the sort. There is, therefore, a sort of skepticism which is *compatible* with a complete absence of doubt on any subject whatever. But, of course, though it is compatible with a complete absence of doubt, it is also quite compatible with doubt. A man who sincerely holds that certain kinds of things are always doubtful *may* nevertheless doubt whether he is right in this opinion: he need not necessarily be dogmatic about it: and also he *may* sometimes be in actual doubt about particular things of the sort. All that I think is true is that he *need* not have any doubt of either of those kinds: from the fact that he does hold that all things of a certain kind are doubtful it does not logically follow that he has any doubts at all. At all events, whether or not I am right as to this, I wish it to be clearly understood that I am so using the term 'skepticism' that all that is necessary for a man to be a skeptic in this sense with regard to our knowledge of certain kinds of things is that he should hold the view (whether doubtfully or not) that no human being ever knows for certain a thing of the sort in question. It is only with skepticism in this sense that I shall be concerned.

All four of the skeptical views with which I shall be concerned have, I believe, been held in the past, and still are held, by a good many philosophers. But I am going to illustrate them exclusively by reference to two books of Russell's—his *Analysis of Matter*[1] and the book which in the English edition was called *An Outline of Philosophy,* and in the American edition *Philosophy*. When he wrote these books, Russell held, so far as I can make out, with regard to each of the four kinds of 'things' which I shall describe, that no human being has ever known for certain anything of that kind, and I shall give you quotations from these books to show why I think that this was his view. Now I can't help thinking that I myself have often known for certain things of all the four kinds, with regard to which Russell declares that no human being has ever known any such thing for certain; and when he says that no human being has ever known such things, I think he implies that I haven't, and that therefore I am wrong in thinking that I have. And the question I want to discuss is simply this: Was he right in thinking that I haven't, or am I right in thinking that I have? Of course, if I am right in thinking that *I* have, I think it is quite certain that other people, including Russell himself, often have too—that all of you, for instance, have very, very often known for certain things of each of these sorts with regard to which he asserts that no human being has ever known for certain anything whatever of that sort. But I don't want to discuss whether other people have, nor yet the very interesting question *why* it's certain that, if I have, other people have too. The question I want to raise is merely whether I am right in thinking that *I* have, or Russell is right in thinking that I never have.

I will now try to state what these four sorts of things are with regard to which Russell implies that I have never known for certain anything whatever of any of these sorts, whereas I can't help thinking that I have often known for certain things of all four sorts.

(1) The first sort is this. I have, according to him, never known with complete certainty anything whatever about *myself*. I do not, according to him, know now with certainty even that I am 'having a white percept',[2] and I never have known any such thing. This is a view which

[1] Bertrand Russell: *Analysis of Matter* and *An Outline of Philosophy;* Allen & Unwin, London, 1927.

[2] It should be noted that in the *Outline* Russell uses the word 'percept' in such a sense that by no means everything which would commonly be said to be 'perceived' is a 'percept'. I have, e.g., perceived each instance of the word 'the' which I have written on this paper; but no instance of the word 'the', though it is 'perceived', is a 'percept' in Russell's sense. It is a physical object, and no physical object is identical with what he means by a 'percept'. He uses the word 'percept' in the same sense in which others have used the word 'sense-datum', except that the word 'sense-datum' of course implies that sense-data are given, whereas his view seems to be that 'percepts' are not 'given', or at least that it's not certain that they are—two very different views, which he seems, in this case, not very clearly to distinguish from one another.

is implied by him in two different passages in the *Outline*. The first is where (on page 171), having raised the question whether Dr. Watson or Descartes is right as to 'the region of *minimum* doubtfulness', he goes on to say: 'What, from his own point of view, [Descartes] should profess to know is not "*I* think" but "there is thinking" . . . To translate this into "*I* think" is to assume a great deal that a previous exercise in skepticism ought to have taught him to call in question.' That is to say, Russell is saying: 'Your proposition "*I* am having a white visual percept" is not so certainly true as the proposition "There is a white visual percept"; it is not a proposition of *minimum* doubtfulness'. From which, of course, it will follow that 'I am having a white percept' is not a thing which I know with complete certainty. And the same is implied in a later passage (page 214) where he says that the difference between two such propositions as '*There's* a triangle!' and 'I see a triangle' is only 'as to surroundings *of which we are not certain*'. All that is *quite* certain, he says, is something common to both, namely, something which could be properly expressed by 'There is a visual triangle', where 'There is' means the same as '*Es gibt*' (page 216), not, as in the second expression, the same as '*Da ist*'. That is to say, '*I* am seeing a white percept' includes, according to him, besides something which is quite certain, something else which is not.

(2) The second class of things with regard to which he seems to imply that I have never known with certainty any such things is a class to which he refers as if it embraced all those things, and those things only, which I have at some time remembered. That is to say, he implies that, when I seem to remember, at a given time, e.g. that there was 'a white visual percept' a little while ago, I never know with complete certainty that there was. Thus, according to him I do not even know with certainty now that a sound like 'ago' existed a little while ago; still less, of course (because that involves the first point also), that *I* heard such a sound; and still less (because that involves a third point also) that I have been uttering words for some time past.

This view seems to me to be implied by him in the following passages.

Take first a passage in the *Analysis of Matter* (page 26). He there says: 'The inference from a recollection (which occurs now) to what is recollected (which occurred at a former time) appears to me to be essentially similar to the inferences in physics. The grounds for the trustworthiness of memory seem to be of the same kind as those for the trustworthiness of perception.'

Now he has repeatedly insisted that inferences in physics cannot give complete certainty; and I think, therefore, that when he wrote this he must have meant to accept the implication that I cannot be completely certain now even of such a thing as that there was a white visual percept a little while ago.

But a much stronger and clearer statement of this view is to be found in the *Outline*. The passage in which he gives this strong statement occurs in the place before mentioned (page 171), where he is considering whether Descartes or Dr. Watson is right as to the 'region of *minimum* doubtfulness'. He here (page 174) uses these words: 'In dreams we often remember things that never happened; at best therefore we *can be sure* of our present momentary experience, *not of anything that happened even half a minute ago.*[3] And before we can so fix our momentary experience as to make it the basis of a philosophy, it will be past, *and therefore uncertain*. When Descartes said "I think", he may have had certainty; but by the time he said "therefore I am", he was relying on memory, and *may have been deceived*.'

(3) The third kind of thing about which he implies that I can never know anything of that kind with certainty, is the sort of thing which I might express on a particular occasion by pointing at a particular person and saying 'That person is seeing something', 'That person is hearing something': or 'That person saw something just now' or 'That person heard something just now'; or, more definitely, 'That person is seeing now, or saw just now, a white visual percept'; or 'That person is hearing, or heard just now, the sound "that" '.

There can, I think, be no doubt whatever that Russell holds the view that I never do know for certain anything of this sort. I may refer first to a passage in the *Analysis,* in the chapter on what he calls 'The Causal Theory of Perception', where he is expressly dealing with the question: 'What grounds have we for inferring that our percepts and what we recollect do not constitute the entire universe?' (page 200). He here says: 'Someone says "There's Jones", and you look round and see Jones. It would seem odd to suppose that the words you heard were not caused by a perception analogous to what you had when you looked round. Or your friend says, "Listen", and after he has said it you hear distant thunder. Such experiences lead irresistibly to the conclusion that the percepts *you call other people*[4] are associated with percepts which you do not have, but which are like those you would have if you were in their place.' And it is obvious, I think, that the imaginary instances to which he refers in the first three sentences, are instances in which you might be either believing or knowing things of just the sort to which I have referred. In the first case, if, at the time when you saw Jones, you were seeing also the person who had just said 'There's Jones', you would

[3] My italics.

[4] My italics.

either be believing or knowing something which might be naturally expressed by pointing at the person who said it and saying 'That person saw just now a visual percept resembling this one'—where this one is the one you are now having in seeing Jones. And in the second case, if at the time when you heard the distant thunder you are also seeing your friend who has just said 'Listen'; you would similarly be *either* believing or knowing what would be expressed by pointing at your friend and saying 'That person heard just now a rumbling sound like this'. And if, in these cases, Russell would say, as we shall see he would, that you would not, under *any* circumstances, be knowing *for certain* that that person did see a visual percept like this or that this one did hear a rumbling sound like this, we may, I think, safely conclude that he would say that nothing of *any* of the kinds of which I have given instances is ever known for certain by any of us.

But in the case of Russell's last sentence, there is an important ambiguity to which I wish to call attention. He says that such experiences 'lead irresistibly' to a certain 'conclusion'; the conclusion, namely, 'that the percepts you call other people are associated with percepts which you do not have, but which are like what you would have if you were in their place'. And it is quite impossible to infer from this language whether what he means is that each such experience leads irresistibly to a conclusion different in each case and a conclusion which belongs to our class of things, namely the first to the conclusion 'That person saw just now a visual percept like this', the second to the conclusion 'That person heard just now a rumbling sound like the this', and so on. Or whether what he means is that a number of such experiences *taken together* lead irresistibly to the *general conclusion*: *Sometimes* other people have percepts which I don't have. Of course, neither of these things is what he actually says. In what he says he is implying, what seems to me certainly false, that it is *percepts of your own* which you call 'other people', i.e. that if I say now, pointing at Professor Stace, 'That person heard just now the sound "Stace" ', it is a *percept* of my own which I am calling 'that person'—that it is of a visual percept of mine that I am saying that *it had* an auditory percept of the kind 'Stace'. Surely this is absurd; and it is perhaps because Russell himself felt it to be absurd that he uses the queer expression 'other people are *associated with* percepts which you don't have', where what he seems to mean is merely 'other people *have* percepts which you don't have'. There is no absurdity in saying that a visual percept is *associated with* an auditory percept, nor in saying that another person *has* an auditory percept; but there is an absurdity in saying that a visual percept *has* an auditory percept; and these facts perhaps make it clear that it is certainly false that we ever 'call' a percept another person.

But this mistake which Russell makes, and his queer use of 'is associated with' to mean 'has', do not affect my present point. My present point is to call attention to the difference between the *general* conclusion 'Other people sometimes have percepts which I don't have but which are similar to percepts which I have had', and *particular* conclusions of the form 'This person had just now a percept which I did not have, but which was similar to that one which I did have'. I want to call attention to this difference, partly because the question whether we ever know for certain the *general* conclusion is, I think, easily confused with the question whether we ever know for certain any *particular* conclusion of the sort indicated; and I want to make it quite clear that in my view I often know for certain not merely the general conclusion, but particular conclusions of the sort 'This person had just now a percept of this sort'. And I call attention to it also partly because I gather from what immediatly follows in Russell, that his view is that the *general* conclusion is *more* certain than *any* particular conclusion of the form in question ever is; from which it would, of course, follow that in his view I never do know with complete certainty any particular thing of the kind we are now concerned with, since the degree of certainty with which I know such a thing is always, according to him, less than some degree of certainty with which I know the general conclusion.

But that Russell does hold that I never do know with complete certainty any particular thing of this sort is, I think, directly drawn from many things he says. He says, for instance, immediately after (page 205): 'We *may* be mistaken in any given instance'. And here, I think, clearly the force of 'may' is, what it often is, i.e. he is saying: In *no* particular instance do I *know for certain* that I am not mistaken. Moreover, he has just said that 'the argument is not demonstrative' in any of these cases; and it is clear that what he means by 'not demonstrative', is what he has expressed on page 200 by saying that 'it has not the type of cogency that we should demand in pure mathematics'; and he then says that what he means by saying that an argument has not this type of cogency is that its conclusion is *only* probable.

But here are three passages from the *Outline,* which seem to make it clear that this is his view.

That first is on pages 8–10, where he says:

'I ask a policeman the way, and he says: "Fourth to the right, third to the left". That is to say, I hear these sounds, and perhaps I see what I interpret as his lips moving. I assume that he has a mind more or less like my own, and has uttered these sounds with the same intention as I should have had if I had uttered them, namely to convey information. In ordinary life, all this is not, in any proper sense, an inference; it is a belief which arises in us on the appropriate occasion. But, if we are challenged, we have to substitute inference for spontaneous belief, and the more the inference is examined the more shaky it looks.' He concludes on page 10 with the words 'The inference to the policeman's mind certainly *may* be wrong'.

In these concluding words I think he certainly means by 'may' the same as before; i.e. he is saying that in no such case does anyone ever know for certain that the policeman was conscious.

The second passage in the *Outline* to which I wish to call attention is on page 157, where he says:

'For the present, I shall take it for granted that we may accept testimony, with due precautions. In other words, I shall assume that what we hear, when, as we believe, others are speaking to us, does in fact have "meaning" to the speaker and not only to us; with a corresponding assumption as regards writing. This assumption will be examined at a later stage. For the present, I will merely emphasize that it *is* an assumption, and that it may possibly be false, since people seem to speak to us in dreams, and yet, on waking, we become persuaded that we invented the dream. It is impossible to prove by a demonstrative argument, that we are not dreaming; the best we can hope is a proof that this is improbable.'

In this passage, it seems to me, Russell clearly means to say *both* that when in any particular case I either believe or think I know 'That person meant this', I *may* be wrong, i.e. that I never know for certain 'That person did mean this', *and also* that I never know for certain even the general proposition 'Sometimes other people have meant something'. And when he says I cannot *prove* this proposition to be more than probable, he means, I think, as usual, that, *since* I cannot prove it to be more than probable, it follows that I do not *know for certain* that it is true; since it is a kind of thing which, according to him, cannot be *known for certain* unless it can be proved by a demonstrative argument.

Finally I will quote a passage from the chapter on 'The Validity of Inference', to which I think he must have been referring when he said on page 157 'This assumption will be examined at a later stage', since I cannot find any other place in which he does seem to examine the assumption in question.

He here says (page 278):

'The belief in external objects is a learned reaction acquired in the first months of life, and it is the duty of the philosopher to treat it as an inference whose validity must be tested. A very little consideration shows that, logically, the inference cannot be demonstrative, but must be at best probable. It is not *logically impossible* that my life may be one long dream, in which I merely imagine all the objects that I believe to be external to me. If we are to reject this view, we must do so on the basis of an inductive or analogical argument, which cannot give *complete certainty*. We perceive other people behaving in a manner analogous to that in which we behave, and we assume that they have had similar stimuli. We may hear a whole crowd say "Oh" at the moment when we see a rocket burst, and it is natural to suppose that the crowd saw it too.' And he concludes with the words 'It remains possible . . . that there is no crowd watching the rocket; my percepts *may* be all that is happening in such cases'; where, I think, he clearly means that I never do know for certain in such a case 'There were other percepts, not mine, like those of mine', far less, therefore, such a thing as '*That* person had just now a percept like this of mine'.

I think, therefore, it is pretty clear that Russell did hold, when he wrote both books, not only that I never know for certain any things of the sort I have stated, but also that I never know for certain even the general proposition that some people have had percepts which I have not had, but like mine, or even that there have been percepts other than mine.

(4) The fourth class of things of which I think I have often known for certain particular specimens, whereas Russell seems to have thought that no human being had ever known for certain anything whatever of the kind, is as follows. It consists of such things as that this is a pencil; that this is a piece of paper, that this pencil is much longer than it's thick; that this piece of paper is longer than it's broad, and that its thickness is very much less than either its length or its breadth; that this pencil is now nearer to this piece of paper than it is to my left hand; and that now, again, it is moving towards this piece of paper, etc. etc. All these things that I have mentioned I think I knew with certainty at the time when I mentioned them; and though Russell does not talk very much *expressly* about things of this sort, there can, I think, be no doubt he did hold that no human being has ever known for certain anything whatever of the sort.

I will give references only from the *Outline,* where he comes nearest to expressly mentioning things of the sort in question. We have already seen that he raises the question whether Descartes or Dr. Watson is right as to 'the region of *minimum* doubtfulness'; and it is precisely in things of this sort (though Russell does not *expressly* say so) that Dr. Watson, according to him, finds the region of minimum doubtfulness. Russell gives as an example of the kind of thing which Dr. Watson takes to be particularly certain, what he calls 'the movements of rats in mazes', and says that a lover of paradox might sum up Watson's philosophy by saying that, whereas Descartes said 'I think, therefore I am', Dr. Watson says 'There are rats in mazes, therefore I don't think' (page 176). And here is a passage (page 140) in which he expressly deals, quite seriously, with

Watson's view about rats in mazes. 'Even', he says, 'when we assume the truth of physics, what we know most indubitably through perception is not the movements of matter, but certain events in ourselves which are connected, in a manner not quite invariable, with the movements of matter. To be specific, when Dr. Watson watches rats in mazes, what he knows, apart from difficult inferences, are certain events in himself. The behaviour of the rats can only be inferred by the help of physics, and is by no means to be accepted as something accurately knowable by direct observation.' What interests us here is that the kind of thing which Watson (according to Russell) takes himself to know with certainty when he watches rats in mazes is obviously (though Russell does not expressly say so) just the kind of thing I have illustrated: it is, e.g., 'This rat is now running down that passage' (which includes, of course, 'This is a rat' and 'That is a passage'), etc. etc. And we see Russell here says that such things are *never* what Watson is knowing most *indubitably; never* therefore things he is quite certain of, because there are other things of which he is more certain. And he says also that these things are things which can only be inferred *by difficult inferences*; the inferences meant being obviously of the kind we have seen he has already so often referred to, and which he says at best yield probability and not certainty. I think this leaves no doubt at all that he does hold that *nothing* of the kind I have mentioned is ever known by me *with certainty*.

But I will give one other example. On page 156, he tells us: 'When my boy was three years old, I showed him Jupiter and told him that Jupiter was larger than the earth. He insisted that I must be speaking of some other Jupiter, because, as he patiently explained, the one he was seeing was obviously quite small. After some efforts, I had to give it up and leave him unconvinced.' Now here what Russell said to his son must have been just one of the things with which I am now concerned: he must have pointed at the planet and said 'That is Jupiter', just as I now point at this pencil and say 'This is a pencil'. And while he is telling this story Russell speaks, you see, as if he himself entertained no doubt whatever that we sometimes do know for certain things of this sort as well as of all the other three *sorts* which we have found he really thinks no human being ever does know for certain. He speaks as if there were no doubt whatever that he *did* point out Jupiter to his son; that is to say as if at the moment when he said 'That is Jupiter', he knew for certain 'That is Jupiter'. He speaks, again, as if, when telling the story, he knew for certain that an incident of the kind he describes really did occur in the past, i.e. knew for certain something which he then remembered. He speaks, again, as if he knew for certain things about himself—that *he* did in the past see Jupiter, say the words 'That is Jupiter', etc. etc. And finally, as if, at the time of the incident in question, he knew for certain 'This boy is seeing Jupiter', 'This boy is having a very small percept', etc. etc. Yet we have seen that, as regards the two latter points at all events, he certainly holds that he *cannot* have known for certain any such thing. If, therefore, in telling the story he had been concerned to relate only what he thought he really knew, he would have had to have said: *It is highly probable* that, when my boy was three years old, I showed him Jupiter and told him that it was larger than the earth; but *perhaps* I didn't. It is highly probable that he insisted that I must be speaking of some other Jupiter; but *perhaps* he didn't. It is highly probable that after some efforts I had to give it up; but *perhaps* I never made such efforts. And we have now to see that he holds similarly that, if he ever did say in the past to his boy 'That is Jupiter', he did not know for certain that it was Jupiter. For he goes on to say, in the next sentence: 'In the case of the heavenly bodies, adults have got used to the idea that what is really there can only be *inferred* from what they see; but where rats in mazes are concerned, they still tend to think that they are seeing what is happening in the physical world. The difference, however, is only one of degree.' He holds, that is to say, that if he ever did say 'That is Jupiter', what he thereby expressed was only something which he had *inferred,* and *inferred* by the same kind of process by which Dr. Watson infers 'That is a rat, and that is a passage in a maze, and that rat is running down that passage'—a kind of information which we have seen he clearly holds can only give *probability,* not certainty. He holds, therefore, that he did not know for certain 'That is Jupiter', when (if ever) he said 'That is Jupiter'. And the same appears, I think, very clearly from what he says two pages later, viz:

'A lamp at the top of a tall building might produce the same visual stimulus as Jupiter, or at any rate one practically indistinguishable from that produced by Jupiter. A blow on the nose might make us "see stars". Theoretically, it should be possible to apply a stimulus to the optic nerve, which should give us a visual sensation. Thus when we think we see Jupiter, we may be mistaken. We are less likely to be mistaken if we say that the surface of the eye is being stimulated in a certain way, and still less likely to be mistaken if we say that the optic nerve is being stimulated in a certain way. We do not eliminate the risk of error completely unless we confine ourselves to saying that an event of a certain sort is happening in the brain: this statement may still be true if we see Jupiter in a dream' (page 138). Here, I think, he clearly means: *Always,* when we think we see Jupiter, we *may* be mistaken; and by this again: In no case do we know for certain that we are not mistaken; from whence it will follow: In no case does any human being know *for certain* 'That is Jupiter'. We have seen, then, that Russell implies that I have never at any time known for certain any things of any of the following four classes: viz. (1) anything whatever about *myself*, i.e. anything whatever which I could properly express by the use of the words 'I' or 'me'; (2) anything whatever which I remember; (3) any such thing as 'That person has or had a visual percept or an auditory percept of this kind'; nor even the truth of the *general* proposition: 'Some people have had percepts which I have not had but which were like what I have had'; and (4) any such thing as 'This is a pencil', 'This is a sheet of paper', 'This pencil is moving towards this sheet of paper', etc. etc.

Now I cannot help thinking that I have often known *with complete certainty* things of all these four sorts. And I want to raise the question: Is Russell right with regard to this, or am I? Obviously it is a logical possibility that he should be right with regard to some of these four classes of things, and I with regard to others. And it seems to me that, in respect of the arguments which he brings forward for his position, there is an important difference between those which he brings forward for saying that he is right as to the first two classes, and those which he brings forward for saying that he is right as to the last two. I propose, therefore, first to consider the first two classes separately.

To begin with the first. Russell says that I do not know with complete certainty now even that I am having a white percept; *only* that there *is* a white percept. And the only argument I can discover which he brings forward in favour of this position is the one already mentioned: 'the meaning of the word "I" evidently depends on memory and expectation' (page 215). If this premiss is to yield the desired result that I do not know for certain now that I am having a white percept, what it must mean is that in asserting that I have a white percept I am asserting something both with regard to the past and with regard to the future; and the argument must be: Since I don't know with certainty anything with regard to the past or with regard to the future it follows that a *part* of what I am asserting in asserting that I have a white percept is something that I don't know with certainty. Russell is therefore assuming two distinct things both with regard to the past and with regard to the future. With regard to the past he is assuming: (1) In asserting 'I have a white percept now' you are asserting something or other with regard to the past, and (2) You don't know for certain *that* (whatever it is) which you are asserting with regard to the past. And even if we grant, what I must confess seems to me by no means so evident as Russell thinks it is, that I *am* asserting something with regard to the past; I should maintain that there is no reason whatever why what I am asserting with regard to the past shouldn't be something which I do know with certainty. Russell's reasons for saying that it is not, must be those which he has for saying that I don't know for certain anything which I remember; so that so far as the past is concerned, the validity of his argument for saying that I don't know with certainty anything about myself entirely depends on the validity of his argument for saying that I don't know with certainty anything which I remember—to which I shall presently come. The only independent argument here offered is, therefore, that with regard to the future: and here again he is making two assumptions. He is assuming (1) that part of what I assert in asserting 'I am now having a white visual percept' is a proposition with regard to the future and (2) that *that* (whatever it is) which I am asserting with regard to the future is something which I do not know with certainty to be true. Now here, if it were true that in asserting 'I am now having a white visual percept', I were asserting anything whatever with regard to the future, I should be inclined to agree with him that that part of what I assert must be something that I do not know for certain: since it does seem to me very certain that I know little, if anything, with certainty with regard to the future. But Russell's first assumption that in asserting that I am seeing a white percept I *am* asserting anything whatever with regard to the future, seems to me a purely preposterous assumption, for which there is nothing whatever to be said. I now assert 'I am now having a white visual percept'. The moment at which I asserted that is already past, but it seems to me quite evident that the whole of what I then asserted is something which might quite well have been true, *whatever* happened subsequently to it, and even if nothing happened subsequently at all: even if that had been the last moment of the Universe. I cannot conceive any good reason for asserting the contrary.

The only argument, independent of the question whether I ever know with certainty what I remember, which Russell brings forward in favour of the view that I never know with certainty anything about myself, seems to me, therefore, to be extremely weak. But there is another argument, which he might have used, and which he hints at in the *Analysis of Mind,* though so far as I know he has not expressly mentioned it in either of these two books; and I want just to mention it, because it raises a question, about which there really seems to me some doubt, and which is of great importance in philosophy. You all know, probably, that there is a certain type of philosophers, who are fond of insisting that myself includes my body as well as my mind; that I am a sort of union of the two—a 'psycho-physical organism'. And if we were to take this view strictly, it would follow that *part* of what I am asserting whenever I assert anything about myself, is something about my body. It would follow, therefore, again that I cannot know for certain anything about myself, without knowing for certain something about my body; and hence that I cannot know for certain anything about myself, unless I can know for certain some things of my fourth class. For of course the propositions 'This is a body', 'This body has eyes', etc. etc., are just as much propositions of my fourth class, as the proposition 'That is a human body'. If this were so, then Russell's arguments to prove that I cannot know with certainty anything of my fourth class would, if they proved this, also prove that I cannot know with certainty anything of this first one—anything about myself. This, of course, does not seem to me to prove that I don't know with certainty anything about myself, since as I have said I think I do know with certainty things of my fourth class. But it seems to me important to point out that the two questions are possibly connected in this way: that, *if* the dogma that I am a psycho-physical organism were true, then I could not know for certain anything about myself, without knowing for certain things of my fourth class, and that hence any arguments which appear to show that I can't know for certain things of this class would be relevant to the question whether I can know for certain anything about myself. For my part I feel extremely doubtful of the proposition that when I assert 'I am now seeing a white visual percept', I am asserting anything at all about my body. Those who take this view seem to me to have overlooked one consequence of it, which constitutes a very strong argument against it. So far as I can see, if this view were true, then it would follow that the proposition 'This body is *my* body' was a tautology: and it seems to me that it is not a tautology. But nevertheless I don't feel perfectly confident that their view may not possibly be true.

However, so far as the arguments actually brought forward by Russell in the *Outline* are concerned, it seems to me he has no good reason whatever for the view that I do not know with certainty anything whatever about myself, *unless* he has good reasons for his second proposition that I do not know with certainty anything whatever that I remember.

Let us then now turn to consider this.

When I first described this second form of Skepticism (page 201), I said that the class of things which it denies that I have ever known for certain is one to which Russell refers as if it embraced all those things, and those things only, which I have at some time remembered; and I have since myself adopted his way of expressing this second skeptical view: I have spoken of it as if it really were the view that I have never known for certain anything whatever that I remembered. But I think that, in fact, this is a very incorrect way of expressing the view which Russell really holds and which constitutes this second form of Skepticism. For if, in the sentence 'We never know for certain anything that we remember', the word 'remember' were being used in accordance with ordinary English usage, the proposition expressed by this sentence would, I think, be a self-contradictory one. We ordinarily so use the word 'remember' that *part* of what is asserted by expressions of the form 'I remember that *p*' is 'I know for certain that *p*'; so that anybody who were to say, e.g., 'I remembered that I had promised to dine with you on Tuesday, but I didn't know for certain that I had' would be asserting the self-contradictory proposition 'I knew for certain that I had promised, but I didn't know for certain that I had'. Suppose you were to ask a friend who had failed to keep an engagement 'Didn't you remember that you had promised to come?', and he were to answer, 'Oh yes, I remembered all right that I had promised to come, but I don't know for certain that I had promised', what would you think of such an answer? I think you would be entitled to say: 'What on earth do you mean? What an absurd thing to say! If you did remember that you had promised, of course you knew for certain that you had; and if you didn't know for certain that you had, you can't possibly have *remembered* that you had, though you may possibly have *thought* you remembered it'. I think, therefore, that if the word 'remember' were being correctly used, the sentence 'We never know for certain what we remember' would express a self-contradictory proposition. But I have no doubt that the view which Russell intended to express was not a self-contradictory one. It follows, therefore, if I am right as to the correct use of 'remember', that he was not expressing his view correctly.

It is also worth notice that, although towards the beginning of the *Outline* (page 16) Russell says truly that the word 'memory' has a variety of meanings, he never, so far as I can discover, even tries to tell us to which of these various meanings his skeptical view is supposed by him to apply. I think, however, that there is one well-understood sense in which the word is used, which is the one in which he is using it in stating his skeptical view. It is a use which we can perhaps call 'personal memory', and which can be defined as that meaning in which nobody can be properly said to 'remember' that so-and-so was the case, unless he (or she) himself (or herself) either witnessed or experienced that it was the case. That this is a different sense of the word from others which are in common use can be seen from the fact that I can properly be said to 'remember' that 7×9 *is* 63, which differs from the usage in question in respect of the fact that we cannot properly say that 7×9 *was* 63, or, to use an expression used by Russell, that 7×9 *is* 63 is not something which 'happened' in the past; and we can also quite properly say we 'remember' that the Battle of Hastings happened in 1066, yet, though the Battle of Hastings was a thing which 'happened', no living person can have either witnessed or experienced that it happened at that time; in other words, this is not a 'personal' memory of any living person.

But where Russell gives as a reason for his skeptical view, as he does in my second quotation, that, in a dream we often 'remember' what never happened; he is, it seems to me, merely making a mistake. For though, in relating a dream, it is perfectly correct to say that I (or he or she) 'remembered' a thing which never happened, it is, it seems to me, a mere mistake to think that we are here using 'remember' in the sense defined above. In relating a dream, it seems to me, we use 'remember' in a special sense, namely as short for I (or he or she) *dreamt* that I (or he or she) remembered, which is not identical with any sense in which we ordinarily use the word; just as, in relating a dream, it is correct to use, e.g., 'I saw John' as short for 'I dreamt that I saw John'. And there is no difficulty in understanding why, in relating a dream, we should use 'remembered' in this special sense, since it is obvious that once we have made it quite plain that it is a dream which we are relating, it is unnecessary and would be tiresome to repeat with regard to every item in the dream the full phase 'I (or he or she) *dreamt* that so-and-so was the case'. In place of this, it is natural to say 'I (or he or she) remembered' or 'saw John', etc. etc. It follows, if I am right, that the use we make of the word 'remembered' in relating a dream, is one of that 'variety of meanings' in which Russell rightly declares that we use the word 'memory'. Yet this obvious possibility seems never to have occurred to him. He says that 'dreams would have supplied a sufficient argument' for his skeptical view (page 172). But if it is true, as I think it is, that the use of 'remember', in relating a dream, is different from any ordinary use, it is not true that dreams would have supplied a sufficient argument, for any ordinary use.

But even if, as I think, the reference to dreams as a proof of his skepticism is a mistake on Russell's part, because when we use 'remembered', in relating a dream, we are using 'remember' in a special sense, not identical with any ordinary sense, it is nevertheless true, that even when they are using 'remember' in the sense defined above, many people do (as Russell does not fail to point out) think they remember what, in fact, never happened. What is Russell's reason, based on this fact, for holding his skeptical view that it is always only probable, never quite certain, that what we think we remember to have happened did in fact happen?

He seems to come nearest to suggesting a reason in a passage in which he suggests that we can only know with certainty that so-and-so is true, if the 'so-and-so' in question belongs to some class of which it is true that no member of that class ever 'leads us into error'. This seems to be the principle to which he is appealing when he suggests that perhaps we can each be sure of 'our present momentary experience'; though he does not seem quite sure that we can be certain even of this, since he goes on to say only that 'there is no reason' to suppose that our present momentary experience ever leads us into error. But is it true that we can be certain of our present momentary experience and of nothing else? Russsell seems to suppose that his skeptical conclusion follows *directly* from this principle. But does it? If the principle is true at all, that it is true seems to require some further argument, which Russell does not supply. To me it seems certain that sometimes we do know with certainty things of classes which, like the class of what we think we remember, do sometimes lead us into error.

The truth seems to be that Russell has never noticed the fact that, sometimes at least, we use the word 'remember' in such a sense that if a thing did not actually happen we say that any person who thinks he remembers that it happened *only* thinks that he remembers its happening but does not in fact remember it. In other words we so use the word that it is *logically impossible* that what did not in fact occur should be remembered; since to say that it did not occur, but nevertheless is remembered, is to be guilty of a contradiction. This is certainly the case if we so use the word that in saying that a person remembers that so-and-so happened, we are not only saying something about that person's state of mind at the moment, but are also saying that the so-and-so in question did in fact happen in the past. Russell, on the contrary, expressly says that it is logically possible that 'acts of remembrance' should occur which are of things which never happened (*Outline,* page 7). This is certainly a mistake if, as I think, we often use the world 'remember' in such a sense that when we say that a person remembers that so-and-so was the case, part (but, of course, *only* a part) of what we are saying is something not concerned merely with what his state was at the moment, but also that the so-and-so which he thinks he remembers to have happened did actually occur in the past. If Russell was using 'remember' to include such cases, we must say that what he here calls 'acts of remembrance' are not 'acts of remembrance' at all, but only the sort of act which we perform when we *think* we remember that so-and-so was the case, but do not in fact remember that it was the case. He seems constantly to assume that whether a person 'remembers' what he thinks he remembers depends only on what his state was at the moment, never at all on whether what he thought he remembered actually occurred. And this assumption of his is, no doubt, partly responsible for his view that 'dreams would have supplied a sufficient argument' to prove his sceptical conclusion (*Outline,* page 172), a view which we have seen to be false, because, in relating a dream, it is correct to use 'I (or he or she) remembered' in the special sense 'I (or he or she) *dreamt that* I (or he or she) remembered'. So far as I can see, the only sense in which 'remember' can correctly be used (other than the special sense) whenever, as happens so often, the words 'remembers' or 'remembered' are followed by a clause beginning with 'that', is that sense in which, in saying that a person 'remembers' or 'remembered' so-and-so to have happened, we are not merely saying something about the person's state at the moment, but are also saying that what the person

(I or he or she) 'remembers' or 'remembered' did in fact happen at some time previous to that at which the memory occurred. When, on the other hand, the word 'remember' is followed by a noun, as often happens, it seems not incorrect to speak of remembering 'correctly' or 'incorrectly'; but such cases, so far as I can see, can always be analysed into cases where the word 'remember' is followed by one or more that-clauses, the memory being 'correct', if *all* the that-clauses say what is true, i.e. are remembered, and 'incorrect' if some of them say what is false, i.e. say what the person in question *only* thought he remembered, but did not in fact 'remember'.

If, therefore, we are to discuss whether Russell is right in the view which he expresses by saying that I have never known for certain anything whatever which I remembered, we must try to find out what view he is expressing in this self-contradictory way: we must try to find out in *what* unusual way he is using the word 'remember'; and I do not think that this is quite an easy thing to do. The natural way of trying to express it is to say that his view is: When we *think* that we remember so-and-so, we never do in fact know for certain the so-and-so in question, i.e. we never do in fact remember it. But obviously this is inaccurate, since the immense majority of the cases he really wants to consider are cases where we don't really *think* we remember, but simply either do remember or else do something else which is just what has got to be defined.

The best way I can find of stating what he means to say is this. He is saying that: In cases in which, *if* the question happened to occur to us whether we are remembering or not that so-and-so happened, we should feel very sure that we are remembering, we are never really knowing for certain that the thing in question did happen. I intend to speak of all such cases as cases where we *feel just as if we were remembering* a thing, using this expression in such a way that whenever (if ever) we *are* remembering the thing in question it is always true that we feel as if we were, though we sometimes feel as if we were when in fact we are not. Using this language, then, if I am right as to the proper use of 'remember', we can say Russell's view is that when we feel as if we were remembering, we *never* are in fact remembering.

Assuming that this, or something like it, is what he means, what arguments does he give for his view? In the *Analysis* he does not profess, so far as I can see, to bring forward any arguments at all in favour of the view there put forward, which, as we saw, implies this view; and in the *Outline* I can find only one argument, and that a very short one, which seems to be definitely put forward as an argument for this view. But, though short, it is, I think, very important to consider it carefully; because it is, if I'm not mistaken, of the same nature as one of the chief arguments put forward by Russell in favour of his view that I never know for certain things of the two last classes, which we are presently to consider.

The argument occurs in the passage I quoted before. And it is this: 'In dreams we often remember things that never happened. At best, *therefore,* we can be sure of our present momentary experience, not of anything that happened even half a minute ago.' That is all. What precisely is the nature of this argument, and is it a good one? Russell says to me: 'You don't now know for certain that you heard the sound "Russell" a little while ago, not even that there *was* such a sound, *because* in dreams we often remember things that never happened.' In what way could the alleged reason, if true, be a reason for the conclusion? This alleged reason is, of course, according to me, badly expressed; since if the word 'remember' were being properly used, it would be self-contradictory. If a thing didn't happen, it follows that I can't remember it. But what Russell means is quite clearly not self-contradictory. What he means is roughly: In dreams we often feel as if we were remembering things which in fact never happened. And that we do sometimes, not only in dreams, but also in waking life, feel as if we remembered things which in fact never happened, I fully grant. That this is true I don't feel at all inclined to question. What I do feel inclined to question is that this fact is in any way *incompatible* with the proposition that I do now know for certain that I heard a sound like 'Russell' a little while ago. Suppose I have had experiences which resembled this one in the respect that I felt as if I remembered hearing a certain sound a little while before, while yet it is not true that a little while before I did hear the sound in question. Does that prove that I don't know for certain *now* that I did hear the sound 'Russell' just now? It seems to me that the idea that it does is a mere fallacy, resting partly at least on a confusion between two different uses of the words 'possible' or 'may'.

What really does follow from the premiss is this: That it is possible for an experience of a sort, of which my present experience is an example, i.e. one which resembles my present experience in a certain respect, *not* to have been preceded within a certain period by the sound 'Russell'. Whereas the conclusion alleged to follow is: It is possible that *this* experience was not preceded within that period by the sound 'Russell'. Now in the first of these sentences the meaning of 'possible' is such that the whole sentence means merely: Some experiences of feeling as if one remembered a certain sound are not preceded by the sound in question. But in the conclusion: It is possible that this experience was not preceded by the word 'Russell'; or This experience *may* not have been preceded by the word 'Russell'; 'possible' and 'may' are being used in an entirely different sense. Here the whole expression merely means the same as: '*It is not known* for certain that this experience was preceded by that sound.' And how from 'Some experiences of this kind were not preceded' can we possibly be justified in inferring 'It is not known that this one was preceded'? The argument seems to me to be precisely on a par with the following: It is possible for a human being to be of the female sex; (but) I am a human thing; *therefore* it is possible that I am of the female sex. The two premisses here are perfectly true, and yet obviously it does not follow from them that I do not know that I am not of the female sex. I do (in my view) happen to know this, in spite of the fact that the two premisses are both true; but whether I know it or not the two premisses certainly don't prove that *I* don't. The conclusion *seems* to follow from the premisses because the premiss 'It is possible for a human being to be of the female sex' or 'Human beings may be of the female sex' is so easily falsely taken to be of the same form as 'Human beings are mortal', i.e. to mean 'In the case of *every* human being, it is possible that the human being in question is of the female sex', or '*Every* human being *may* be of the female sex'. If, and only if, it did mean this, then, from the combination of this with the minor premiss 'I am a human being' would the conclusion follow: It is possible that I am of the female sex; or *I may* be of the female sex. But in fact the premiss 'Human beings *may* be of the female sex' does not mean 'Every human being *may* be', but only 'Some human beings *are*'. 'May' is being used in a totally different sense, from any in which you could possibly assert of a particular human being 'This human being *may* be so-and-so'. And so soon as this is realized, it is surely quite plain that from this, together with the premiss 'I am a human being', there does not follow 'I may be of the female sex'. There may perhaps be something more than this simple fallacy in the argument that because experiences of this sort are sometimes not preceded by the sound of which they feel as if they were a memory, and this is an experience of this sort, therefore this experience *may* not have been preceded by that sound, i.e. that I do not know for certain that it *was* so preceded. But I cannot see that there is anything more in it.

The only argument, therefore, which Russell seems to bring forward to persuade me that I don't know for certain that I heard the word 'Russell' just now, does not seem to me one to which it is reasonable to attach any weight whatever. I cannot, therefore, find in him any good reason for doubting that I do know for certain things of both my first two classes: that I do know for certain things about myself; and that I also know for certain things about the past—in short that I *do* remember things.

But let us now turn to consider my third and fourth class of things. I take them together, because, so far as I can see, his arguments in both cases are the same. What arguments has he in favour of the view that I never know for certain such things as 'That person is seeing', 'That person is hearing' etc.?

Now here I think it is extremely difficult to discover what his reasons are: and in trying to distinguish them I shall very likely omit some or make mistakes. There is no passage, so far as I can discover, in which he tells us quite clearly 'These are the arguments in favour of this view', and, so far as I can see, he uses in different places arguments of very different orders, without being conscious of the difference between them. All I can do is to try to distinguish and consider separately each of the arguments which seem to me to differ in an important way.

I will begin by quoting three from the *Analysis* (page 205) which are the ones which lead up to his conclusion before quoted that 'we may be mistaken in any given instance'. The thing to be proved, I may remind you, is that when you hear your friend say 'There's Jones' and look round and see Jones, you can never be *quite* certain that your friend did just before have a visual percept like the one you're now having. And these are the supposed proofs: 'A conjurer might make a waxwork man with a gramophone inside, and arrange a series of little mishaps of which the gramophone would give the audience warning. In dreams, people give evidence of being alive which is similar in kind to that which they give when they are awake; yet the people we see in dreams are supposed to have no external existence. Descartes's malicious dream is a logical possibility.' 'For these reasons', says Russell, 'we may be mistaken in any given instance.'

Each of these three arguments seems to me to differ from the other two in important respects. I will take each separately, and try to explain what the differences are; beginning with the second, because that seems to me of exactly the same nature as the argument just considered in the case of memory.

Russell is trying to persuade me that I don't know for certain now that that person there is conscious; and his argument is: In dreams you have evidence of the same kind for the proposition 'That person is conscious'; yet in that case the proposition is *supposed* not to be true. Now it seems to me quite certain that in dreams the proposition in question often *is* not true; and that nevertheless I have then evidence for it of the same kind *in certain respects* as what I now have for saying that person is. I admit, further, that sometimes when I am awake I have evidence of the same kind *in certain respects* for 'That person is conscious' when yet the proposition is not true. I have actually, at Mme Tussaud's, mistaken a waxwork for a human being. I admit, therefore, the proposition: This percept of mine is of a kind such that percepts of that kind are in fact sometimes (to use Russell's phrase) *not* associated with a percept that belongs to someone else. But from the general proposition 'Percepts of this kind *may* fail to be associated with a percept that belongs to someone else', which means merely 'Some percepts of this kind are in fact not so associated', I entirely deny that there follows the conclusion '*This* percept *may* not be so associated', which means 'It's not known for certain that it is associated'. It seems to me a pure fallacy to argue that it does; and I have nothing more to say about *that* argument, if that is all that is meant. I don't see any reason to abandon my view that I do know for certain (to use Russell's language) that this percept which I have in looking at Professor Stace *is* associated with a percept that is not mine; I suspect that Russell may be at least partly influenced by the same fallacious argument when he tells me (as he does tell me, *Outline,* page 157) that I *may* now be dreaming. I think I know for certain that I am not dreaming now. And the mere proposition, which I admit, that percepts of the same kind *in certain respects* do sometimes occur in dreams, is, I am quite certain, no good reason for saying: this percept *may* be one which is occurring in a dream.

I pass next to the argument beginning 'A conjurer *might* make a waxwork'. The important difference between this argument and the last, is that Russell does not here say that a conjurer now *has* made a waxwork of the kind supposed and fulfilled the other supposed conditions; he is not therefore saying: Percepts like this in a certain respect *may* fail to be associated, meaning 'are sometimes actually not associated'; but merely 'Percepts like this *might* fail to be associated'. In that respect this argument is like one that he uses in the *Outline* on page 173, in dealing with our fourth class of cases, when he says: 'It would be theoretically possible to stimulate the optic nerve artificially in just the way in which light coming from the moon stimulates it; in this case, we should have the same experience as when we "see the moon" but should be deceived as to its external source.' He does not say that such a percept ever *has* been produced in this way; but only that it is theoretically possible that it *might* be. And obviously he might have used the same argument here. He might have said: 'It would be theoretically possible to stimulate the optic nerve artificially in such a way as to produce a percept like this one of yours, which would then *not* be associated with a percept belonging to another person.' But it is, I think, quite obviously just as fallacious to argue directly from 'Percepts like this *might* not be associated with a percept of another form' to '*This* percept *may* not be so associated' meaning 'It is not known that it is so associated': as from 'Percepts like this sometimes are not associated' to the same conclusion.

We pass next to the argument: 'Descartes's malicious demon is a logical possibility.' This is obviously quite different from both the two preceding. Russell does not say that any percepts are produced by Descartes's malicious demon; nor does he mean that it is practically or theoretically possible for Descartes's malicious demon to produce in me percepts like this, in the sense in which it is (perhaps) practically possible that a conjurer should, and theoretically possible that a physiologist should by stimulating the optic nerve. He only says it is a *logical possibility*. But what exactly does this mean? It is, I think, an argument which introduces quite new considerations, of which I have said nothing so far, and which lead us to the root of the difference between Russell and me. I take it that Russell is here asserting that it is *logically possible* that this particular percept of mine, which I think I know to be associated with a percept belonging to someone else, was in fact produced in me by a malicious demon when there was no such associated percept: and that, therefore, I cannot know for certain what I think I know. It is, of course, being assumed that, *if* it was produced by a malicious demon, then it follows that it is not associated with a percept belonging to someone else, in the way in which I think I know it is: that is how the phrase 'was produced by a malicious demon' is being used. The questions we have to consider are, then, simply these three: What is meant by saying that it is *logically possible* that this percept was produced by a malicious demon? Is it *true* that this is logically possible? And: If it is true, does it follow that I don't know for certain that it was *not* produced by a malicious demon?

Now there are three different things which might be meant by saying that this proposition is logically possible. The first is that it is not a self-contradictory proposition. This I readily grant. But from the mere fact that it is not self-contradictory, it certainly does not follow that I don't know for certain that it is false. This Russell grants. He holds that I do know for certain to be false, propositions about my percepts which are not self-contradictory. He holds, for instance, that I do know for certain that there is a white visual percept now; and yet the proposition that there isn't is certainly not self-contradictory.

He must, therefore, in his argument, be using 'logically possible' in some other sense. And one sense in which it might naturally be used is this: Not logically incompatible with anything that I know. If, however, he were using it in this sense, he would be simply begging the question. For the very thing I am claiming to know is that this percept was *not* produced by a malicious demon: and of course the proposition that it was produced by a malicious demon *is* incompatible with the proposition that it was *not*.

There remains one sense, which is, I think, the sense in which he is actually using it. Namely he is saying: The proposition 'This percept was produced by a malicious demon' is *not* logically incompatible with anything you know *immediately*. And if this is what he means, I own that

I think Russell is right. This is a matter about which I suppose many philosophers would disagree with us. There are people who suppose that I *do* know immediately, in certain cases, such things as: That person is conscious; at least, they use this language, though whether they mean exactly what I am here meaning by 'know immediately' may be doubted. I can, however, not help agreeing with Russell that I never do know *immediately* that that person is conscious, nor anything else that is *logically incompatible* with 'This percept was produced by a malicious demon'. Where, therefore, I differ from him is in supposing that I do know for certain things which I do not know immediately and which also do *not* follow logically from anything which I do know immediately.

This seems to me to be the fundamental question at issue in considering my classes (3) and (4) and what distinguishes them from cases (1) and (2). I think I do know *immediately* things about myself and such things as 'There was a sound like "Russell" a little while ago'—that is, I think that memory is *immediate* knowledge and that much of my knowledge about myself is immediate. But I cannot help agreeing with Russell that I never know immediately such a thing as 'That person is conscious' or 'This is a pencil', and that also the truth of such propositions never follows logically from anything which I do know immediately, and yet I think that I do know such things for certain. Has he any argument for his view that if their falsehood is *logically possible* (i.e. if I do not know *immediately* anything logically incompatible with their falsehood) then I do *not* know them for certain? This is a thing which he certainly constantly assumes; but I cannot find that he anywhere gives any distinct arguments for it.

So far as I can gather, his reasons for holding it are the two assumptions which he expresses when he says: 'If (I am to reject the view that my life is one long dream) I must do so on the basis of an analogical or inductive argument, which cannot give complete certainty' (*Outline*, page 218). That is to say he assumes: (1) My belief or knowledge that this is a pencil is, *if* I do not know it immediately, and if also the proposition does not follow logically from anything that I know immediately, in some sense 'based on' an anological or inductive argument; and (2) What is 'based on' an analogical or inductive argument is never certain knowledge, but only more or less probable belief. And with regard to these assumptions, it seems to me that the first must be true in some sense or other, though it seems to me terribly difficult to say exactly what the sense is. What I am inclined to dispute, therefore, is the second: I am inclined to think that what is 'based on' an analogical or inductive argument, in the sense in which my knowledge or belief that this is a pencil is so, may nevertheless be certain knowledge and *not* merely more or less probable belief.

What I want, however, finally to emphasize is this: Russell's view that I do not know for certain that this is a pencil or that you are conscious rests, if I am right, on no less than four distinct assumptions: (1) That I don't know these things immediately; (2) That they don't follow logically from any thing or things that I do know immediately; (3) That, *if* (1) and (2) are true, my belief in or knowledge of them must be 'based on an analogical or inductive argument'; and (4) That what is so based cannot be *certain knowledge*. And what I can't help asking myself is this: Is it, in fact, as certain that all these four assumptions are true, as that I *do* know that this is a pencil and that you are conscious? I cannot help answering: It seems to me *more* certain that I *do* know that this is a pencil and that you are conscious, than that any single one of these four assumptions is true, let alone all four. That is to say, though, as I have said, I agree with Russell that (1), (2) and (3) *are* true; yet of no one even of these three do I feel *as* certain as that I do know for certain that this is a pencil. Nay more: I do not thing it is *rational* to be as certain of any one of these four propositions, as of the proposition that I do know that this is a pencil. And how on earth is it to be decided which of the two things it is *rational* to be most certain of?

Keith Lehrer

Skepticism and Conceptual Change

People say they know. Almost no one doubts that he and others know for certain that at least some contingent statements are true. But I doubt it. Not only do I doubt that anyone knows for certain that any such statement is true, I also doubt that the lack of such knowledge is a serious epistemic loss. On the contrary, I believe that reasonable belief and action, reasonable theory and practice, do not depend on our knowing for certain that any contingent statement is true. I shall undertake to defend my skepticism and to explain why such knowledge is otiose. By so doing, I shall construct what James Ferrier called, an agnoiology, a theory of ignorance.[1]

Keith Lehrer, "Skepticism and Conceptual Change." The research for this paper was facilitated by National Science Foundation support of related research. Many of the ideas contained in the paper emerged from discussion of an earlier paper by the author, "Why Not Skepticism?," presented at the Pacific Coast Meeting of the American Philosophical Association in Los Angeles, March 28, 1971. Reprinted by permission of the author.

[1] James F. Ferrier, *Institutes of Metaphysics* (Edinburgh and London: William Blackwood & Sons, 1854).

I

There are immediate problems facing any would be skeptic. Language and the conventions of language are fraught with dangers. When a man asserts anything or argues for anything, it is natural to take him to be claiming to know. Skeptical speech must be understood differently. When I write something and argue, you must not take me as claiming to know anything but only as telling you what I believe with the hope that you will too. Even when I say that premisses logically imply a conclusion, you must not take me to be claiming to know. It is only a statement of what I believe. Of course, I have my reasons for believing what I do; you shall soon be told what they are.

Most of my argument for skepticism must be counterargument. The principal theses I shall advance have been advanced before and have been rejected as fallacious, unintelligible, inconsistent, and just plain false. Let me, therefore, lay down my premisses without comment and then turn to their defense. There are only two. First, if a man knows for certain that p is true, then there is no chance that he is wrong in thinking p to be true. Second, if a statement is contingent, then there is always some chance that one is wrong in thinking it to be true. Therefore, no one ever knows for certain that any contingent statement is true. If both premisses are conceded the conclusion is ineluctable. I now turn to a defense of the premisses.

The second premiss must be given some interpretation which makes the first premiss plausible. If by saying that there is some chance that a man was wrong in thinking something to be true, I meant no more than that it was logically possible that he was wrong; then, though the second premiss might be readily accepted, the first would become dubious. For it is doubtful that it need be logically impossible for a man to be wrong before he can know for certain that he is correct. Thus, we must find some stronger interpretation of the second premiss in order to sustain the first.

What, then, do I mean by saying that there is some chance that a man is wrong in thinking something to be true? Most simply put, I mean that there is some *probability* that he is wrong. Of course, introducing the notion of probability at this point is entirely unilluminating without some explanation of what is implied by that notion. What kind of probability is involved? Rather than giving a formal explication of the concept, I shall appeal to an intuitive conception of *objective* probability. Consider an ordinary penny and the statement that the probability is ½ that a fair toss of the coin will turn up heads. There are a number of possible interpretations of this statement. According to the subjective interpretation, it means the betting odds the agent would accept are one to one, according to the logical interpretation, it means one to one is a fair betting quotient, according to the frequency interpretation, it means that in an infinite sequence of tosses the limit of the relative frequency of heads in tosses would approach $1/2$ as a limit. But all of these interpretations suggest a more fundamental idea, to wit, that the coin has a certain physical property which explains why we expect the relative frequency to approach $1/2$, why we think $1/2$ is a fair betting quotient, and why we would accept such odds. This physical property is dispositional, like the property of being magnetized. It is manifested in the relative frequency with which the coin turns up heads when tossed, just as the magnetism of a nail is manifested in the movement of iron toward it.[2] This propensity has an explanation in the structure of the coin just as the magnetism has an explanation in the structure of the nail.

When I say that there is some chance that one is wrong, I mean that there is some probability that one is wrong in this last sense. The probability of being wrong is a property of the world which is manifested in cases of error concerning the truth value of contingent statements. It is this propensity to err that would lead me to reject any measure of probability as a fair betting quotient which assigned a probability of one or zero to any contingent statement. For I expect the relative frequency of error to be greater than zero no matter what kind of contingent statements one considered. However, it is no defense to argue that it is always logically possible that one is wrong. The logical possibility of error does not sustain the empirical claim that the world contains such a propensity.

I shall defend my claim with premisses concerning human conception. By considering the role of concepts in thought, we shall find reason to think that the world contains the kind of propensity in question, and, at the same time, explain that propensity. Kant is famous for his remark that intuitions without concepts are blind.[3] The idea is that experience by itself tells us nothing. The application of concepts to experience is required for any belief or knowledge about the world. Without concepts, cognition is impossible. To think that something is true, is to think that some concept applies. Hence, to think that any contingent statement is true, is to think that some concept applies. If all this seems obvious and commonplace, so much the better for my argument.

[2] The propensity interpretation is advocated by Karl R. Popper in "The Propensity Interpretation of Probability," *British Journal for the Philosophy of Science,* Vol. 10, 1959–60, pp. 25–42.

[3] Immanuel Kant, *Critique of Pure Reason,* A 51 = B 75.

Some philosophers have argued that the application of a concept entails the logical impossibility of misapplication. I believe this to be true, but it will not suffice. For, once again, I am arguing that there is a genuine propensity of the world manifested in our errors, and I cannot conclude that I am right by appeal to the logical possibility of error. The stronger conclusion may be obtained by consideration of the implications of conceptual change. No matter how well entrenched a concept may be in our beliefs about the world, it remains always and constantly subject to total rejection. To obtain our objectives, scientific or other, we may discard a concept as lacking a denotation. Any concept may be thrown onto the junkheap of discarded concepts along with demons, entelechies, and the like. Indeed, some philosophers have even suggested that mental concepts may one day meet that fate. It is difficult to understand how to describe such a situation without incoherence. For example, it will not do to say that we mistakenly *believe* mental concepts to apply. However, some alternative way may be found to say what it seems incoherent for us to say the way we now conceive of ourselves. Any concept, even mental ones, or the concept of existence, may be retired from conceptual service and be replaced by other concepts better suited to the job.

A few qualifications are important. First, any discarded concept can be refurbished. From ones own place in the history of thought, one thinks of progress as linear. This is natural, but sometimes mistaken. The concepts we reject may be better than the ones that supplant them. We may have to recycle what we have discarded. Second, the goals and objectives of empirical science, explanation and prediction most notably, are the ones that guide conceptual shifts today. This has not always been so, and there is no guarantee it will be so in the future. Today we think of conceptual change as being instigated by scientific revolutions, tomorrow some other kind of revolution may be the source of new conceptions.

Now we may draw our conclusions. The chance that we are wrong about the truth value of any contingent statement is the probability that we are wrong. The probability that we are wrong is a property, or feature, or propensity of the world that manifests itself in error. This propensity is explained in terms of human conception which continually shifts as a result of our attempt to apply concepts in order to facilitate our goals and objectives. Concepts are discarded to satisfy the goals of the day, and, as the day changes, so do our objectives. The continual flux in our acceptance and rejection of concepts explains why there is some chance that any concept does not apply to what we think it does. No concept is immune from the ravishment of conceptual change leaving it without any application whatever. Whatever contingent statement you think is true, there is some chance, some probability, that a concept applied in the statement lacks application. Hence, there is some chance you are wrong. However slender and not worth worrying about the chance or error may be, it is real. The reality of that chance is an objective feature of the world.

The foregoing is my argument in defense of the second premise, that, for any contingent statement, there is always some chance that one is wrong in thinking it to be true. This premiss describes a dispositional property of the world rather than a mere logical possibility. It says that, whatever contingent statement one thinks is true, the probability that one is wrong is greater than zero.

This probability interpretation of the chance of being wrong makes it difficult to extend the skeptical argument beyond contingency, because the usual calculus of probability contains an axiom affirming that all logical truths have a probability of one, and, even without this axiom, it may be demonstrated that some statements have a probability of one. Thus, one cannot argue that there is always some probability that one is wrong no matter what sort of statement one thinks is true without abandoning standard conceptions of probability. Whether some nonstandard conception of probability can be developed to give expression to the chance that we are wrong no matter what we think is a matter of speculation. Hence, I restrict my skepticism to contingent statements and standard conceptions of probability.

II

Having clarified the meaning of our second premiss, let us return to the first. If a man knows for certain that something is true, then there is no chance that he is wrong in thinking it to be true. It is difficult to muster direct support for this premiss. Many philosophers have said things that support it. Malcolm has contended that if a man knows for certain that something is true, then there is nothing he would count as evidence proving him to be incorrect.[4] Hintikka has concurred.[5] Locke held a similar opinion.[6] Other than appealing to the opinions of other philosophers, I can only appeal to you directly. Imagine that we agree that a man thinks some statement is true but also agree that there is some chance that he is wrong. Would it be correct for us to describe the man

[4] Norman Malcolm, "Knowledge and Belief," *Mind,* N. S., Vol. LXI, 1952, pp. 178–189, esp. pp. 179–180.

[5] Jaakko Hintikka, *Knowledge and Belief,* (Ithaca: Cornell University Press, 1962), p. 20.

[6] John Locke, *An Essay Concerning Human Understanding,* A. S. Pringle-Pattison ed. (London: Oxford University Press, 1924), p. 261.

as knowing for certain that the statement is true? Consider ones own case. If you admit that there is some chance that a statement is false, it would be incorrect for you to describe yourself as knowing for certain that the statement is true. If you ask me whether I know for certain that Oswald shot Kennedy, I would concede that there is *some* chance that Oswald did not shoot Kennedy, and hence, that I do not know for certain that he did. And you, I believe, would describe me in the same way for the same reason. It would be incorrect for you to describe me as knowing for certain that Oswald shot Kennedy, simply because there is some chance that I am wrong in thinking that he did.

The most important defense of the premiss in question is a proper understanding of it. When I say that if a man knows something for certain, then there is no chance that he is wrong, what I have said may remind one of a simple fallacy. The plausibility of the premiss depends on separating it from fallacious lines of thought. It follows from the statement that a man knows for certain that a statement is true, that the statement in question is true. Hence, it is logically impossible that a man should know for certain that something is true and be wrong, because his knowing for certain entails that he is right. It would be fallacious to argue from the logical impossibility of both knowing for certain and being wrong to the conclusion that if a man knows for certain, then there is no chance that he is wrong. I am not arguing in that way.

A second fallacious argument would be one based on conditional probability. When I have spoken of the probability of being wrong, I was speaking of the unconditional or antecedent probability, not conditional probability. Of course, a contingent statement may have a probability of one conditionally on the basis of some statement, for example, every contingent statement has a conditional probability of one on the basis of itself. When we speak of the probability or chance of being wrong, we may be speaking of the conditional probability of being wrong on the basis of what we know. If a man knows for certain that a statement is true, then the conditional probability of his being wrong on the basis of what he knows is zero, because the statement in question is included in what he knows. However, it is again fallacious to argue from this to the conclusion that if a man knows for certain, then there is no chance that he is wrong, where the chance of being wrong is an unconditional probability. I am not arguing in this way either.

It should now be somewhat clearer what I mean by the first premiss of my original argument. I mean that if a man knows for certain that a statement is true, then there is no chance that he is wrong in the sense that the objective unconditional probability of his being wrong is greater than zero. The objective unconditional probability is the dispositional property of the world that is explained, at least in part, by the nature of human conception. Moreover, it should also be clear why it is that ordinary men commonly, though incorrectly, believe that they know for certain that some contingent statements are true. They believe that there is no chance whatever that they are wrong in thinking some contingent statements are true and thus feel sure they know for certain that those statements are true. One reason they feel sure is that they have not reflected upon the ubiquity of conceptual application and conceptual change in all human thought. Once these matters are brought into focus, we may reasonably conclude that no man knows for certain that any contingent statement is true.

III

Having laid down my premisses and drawn my conclusions, I shall now consider what I consider to be the strongest counterarguments.

The first objection to my skeptical argument is a semantic one. It might be argued that there is an oddity in the speech of a man who denies that he knows for certain that he exists, that he has a hand on the end of his arm, and so forth. And this oddity may be taken as indicating that a skeptic such as myself either speaks without meaning or else must mean something different by the words he utters than is customary. But this conclusion is ill drawn. Anyone who denies what most men assert speaks oddly. There is more than one way to explain the systematic oddity of a man's speech. One way is to suppose that the man does not use certain words to mean what is ordinarily meant, that he means something different than what we ordinarily mean by some of his words. The other way is to suppose that such a person means what we ordinarily mean but has beliefs that are systematically different from the beliefs of other men. In my case, the simplest and correct explanation of why I say I do not know for certain when most men say they do, is that I have different beliefs concerning what people know than most men do. Most men believe that people know for certain that a variety of contingent statements are true. I do not believe that anyone ever knows for certain that such statements are true. That is why I say, oddly enough, that no one knows for certain that he exists or has a hand at the end of his arm. There is no simpler explanation for my speech, and therefore, the conclusion that I mean something out of the ordinary by the locution 'know for certain' is unnecessary and unreasonable.

A more serious objection is based on the assumption that there are contingent statements a man may incorrigibly believe to be true. This assumption has been disputed, and the concept of incorrigibility requires some explication. However, there is one familiar conception of incorrigibility that supports the assumption. Suppose that by saying a belief is incorrigible we mean that it is logically impossible that a man should believe such a statement to be true and yet be mistaken. It surely is very rare for a belief that a contingent statement is true to be incorrigible in this sense. Indeed, even beliefs about one's own immediate present experiences are not, for the most part, incorrigible. The reason is that one may believe something about what one is presently experiencing on the basis of inference, for example, from a premiss one accepts on medical authority affirming that whenever one is experiencing E, an itch say, one is also experiencing E*, a pain say. Consequently one may believe one is experiencing E* and be mistaken because a premiss of the inference leading to the belief is false. However, if I believe that I believe something, then I am believing a contingent statement, to wit, the statement that I believe something, and it is logically impossible that I should believe that statement and yet be mistaken. If I believe that statement, then it logically follows I believe something, which is the statement believed. So, I concede that there are at least some contingent statements a man may incorrigibly believe to be true.

However, if a man incorrigibly believes contingent statements to be true, it does not follow either that he knows for certain that the statement is true or that there is no chance that he is wrong in what he believes. A belief that a contingent statement S is true is incorrigible if and only if the conclusion that S is true follows logically from the premiss that S is believed to be true. However, the logical truth that a conclusion follows fom a premiss does not imply that the conclusion is known for certain or that there is no chance that the conclusion is false. First, it would need to be known for certain that the original conclusion did follow from the premiss, and, second, it would have to be known for certain that the premiss is true. Only then could the truth that the conclusion followed logically from the premiss imply that the conclusion was known for certain. The incorrigibility of a belief can only yield the conclusion the statement believed is known for certain *if* it is known for certain that the statement is believed. Put in the first person, the incorrigibility of my belief that S is true can yield the conclusion that I know for certain that S is true only if I know for certain that I believe S to be true. Thus, the incorrigibility of my belief that I believe something only warrants the conclusion that I know for certain that I believe something if we add the premiss that I know for certain that I believe that I believe something. This cannot be established by appeal to the incorrigibility of the belief without arguing in a circle. Hence, the appeal to the incorrigibility of beliefs fails to show that we know anything for certain. All it shows is that if we know for certain that we believe certain things, then there is something we know for certain. I concede that much because the concession is entirely harmless. For, as I suggested above, there is some chance, one that philosophers have worried about, that no one believes anything.

The third objection comes from philosophers of common sense who claim that we are warranted in saying that we know for certain that various statements expressing common sense beliefs are true.[7] The basic assumption is that at least some common sense beliefs are to be considered innocent until proven guilty. We may then argue that we know for certain that such beliefs are true until some proof to the contrary is presented on the other side.

The reply to this counterargument is that I have offered an argument on the other side, and the burden of proof now rests with my opponents. I agree that many of the beliefs of common sense are reasonable, though I do not think they are reasonable because they are beliefs of common sense. There is nothing sacrosanct about common sense. All that can be said for the beliefs of common sense is that they are what is believed, but the principle that whatever is, is reasonable, is no better principle of epistemology than of politics. Moreover, even if the beliefs of common sense are all reasonable, it hardly follows that there is no chance that they are wrong. So long as the belief of common sense is formulated in a contingent statement, there is some chance that the belief is wrong, and consequently, no one knows for certain that it is true.

The fourth objection is derived from those philosophers who argue that a statement is known to be true because of its explanatory virtues. Such a philosopher might argue that we know for certain that some contingent statement is true because it provides the best explanation of what we seek to explain or fits best into our total explanatory account.[8] My reply to this objection is based on the distinction between a correct and an incorrect explanation. An explanation, even the best explanation we have, may be incorrect because the explanatory statement is false. If the best explanation is incorrect for this reason, then we do not know for certain that the statement supplying the explanation is true. Thus, the argument proceeding from the premiss that a statement provides the best explanation to the conclusion that we know for certain that the statement is true is invalid. Moreover, even if the statement supplying the best explanation is true, it still does not follow that we know for certain that it is true. There is always some chance that even the best

[7] Cf. Thomas Reid, *The Works of Thomas Reid, D.D.* William Hamilton ed. (Edinburgh: Maclaugh and Steward, 1863), p. 234.

[8] Cf. Gilbert Harman, "Knowledge, Inference, and Explanation," *American Philosophical Quarterly,* Vol. 5, 1968, pp. 164–173.

explanation is incorrect, whether or not it in fact happens to be so, and consequently, for all we know, even the best explanation is incorrect. Therefore, we do not know for certain that a statement supplying the best explanation is true.

The fifth and last objection is closely related to the two preceding ones. Some philosophers have argued that if it is not only reasonable to believe something but also as reasonable to believe that statement as any other; then, if the statement is true, it is one we know for certain.[9] It might be added that there are some contingent statements that it is as reasonable to believe as any other. Thus, assuming some contingent statements of the kind in question are true, we know for certain they are true.

This objection is the most difficult to deal with in a satisfactory manner. The most tempting reply is that, no matter what statement one considers, we do not know for certain that it is true because there is some chance that we are wrong in thinking it to be true. However, this reply is not genuinely available because, as I conceded earlier, I cannot offer any satisfactory probablistic explication of the sense in which there is a chance of being wrong in thinking a statement is true which is a logical theorem. Nevertheless, from the premiss that a contingent statement is true and as reasonable for me to believe as any other statement, it does not follow that I know for certain that the statement is true. First, if, as I believe, there is no statement that we know for certain, then even those true statements that are as reasonable for us to believe as any other are not statements we know for certain to be true. Second, if even there are some noncontingent statements that we know for certain to be true, it does not follow that we know for certain each true contingent statement that it is as reasonable for us to believe as those noncontingent statements we know for certain. There is some chance that we are wrong in thinking any contingent statement to be true. Even if the contingent statement is one that is as reasonable for me to believe as any other statement, the chance that I am wrong about it precludes my knowing for certain that it is true.

Having defended my skepticism against the most plausible objections, I should note that my principle thesis applies to itself. I have argued that there is always some chance that we are wrong no matter what contingent statement we think is true. As I interpret this statement, it tells us something about an objective property of the world. It is therefore a contingent statement. I concede, therefore, that there is some chance that I am wrong in saying that it is true. If I am right, nobody

9 Cf. R. M. Chisholm, *Perceiving* (Ithaca: Cornell University Press, 1957), p. 19.

knows for certain that any contingent statement is true. I do not believe that anyone knows for certain that I am wrong.

IV

The conclusions reached so far are negative, or largely so. It is now time to consider the positive program that motivates what has gone before, and to explain why we need not mourn the passing of certainty as a great loss. Rational belief and rational action have been thought to depend upon a foundation of certain knowledge and to be impossible in the absence of such a foundation. But this is a mistake. We can offer a theory of reasonable belief and action that does not presuppose that we know for certain that any contingent statement is true. The broad outlines of such a theory may be sketched in a few words. Whether a belief or action is reasonable depends on two factors. One factor is what one values. The other factor is the probability of obtaining what one values. Once both values and probabilities are assigned, the reasonable belief or reasonable action may be calculated. The reasonable belief or action is the one that gives you a maximum of expected value. By construing rational belief and action in this way we can safely abandon the quest for certainty without giving up our claims to rationality.

First let us consider the matter of probability. It may seem that to assign probability we need to know for certain that some contingent statements are true. But this is incorrect. We may interpret probability in this context as subjective probabilities, as degrees of belief conforming to the calculus of probability, and as constituting our estimate of the objective probabilities discussed earlier. If you agree that there is always some chance of being wrong about any contingent statement, then, you will not estimate the probability of any such statement as being equal to one. So your subjective probability for any contingent statement will be less than one but greater than zero.[10] Such probabilities enable us to give an account of rationality without certainty.

A problem remains. It will often seem appropriate to consider the conditional probability of some outcome of belief or action relative to our evidence, and such evidence looks as though it must be both contingent and also be known for certain. The solution to this problem is to repudiate the idea that acceptance of statements as evidence means knowing them for certain or even assigning them a probability of one.

[10] For such an account of subjective probability, see *The Logic of Decision* (New York: McGraw Hill, 1965).

On the contrary, a statement is accepted as evidence because it competes favorably, that is, has a higher subjective probability, than other statements with which it competes for the status of evidence. I have argued that a statement may be regarded as competing for that status with any statement with which it could conceivably conflict, and therefore, with any statement except its logical consequences. What is accepted as evidence may change the subjective probabilities, but accepting a statement as evidence need not change the subjective probability of the statement at all. Hence, we need not assign evidence statements a probability of one, nor need we know for certain that such statements are true.[11]

With these considerations before us, the consequences of our theory may be drawn. Thomas Reid once suggested that a true skeptic would require the constant attention of his friends to keep him from stepping into dog kennels and walking in front of carriages. But the sort of skeptic we have been considering needs no such attention. Given the value he attaches to being unsoiled and uninjured and the high subjective probability he attaches to the statement that he will be soiled or injured if he steps in dog kennels or walks in front of carriages, it is only reasonable for him to avoid such actions. If he is reasonable in his actions, he need not suffer any indignity or harm not suffered by less skeptical companions.

Similar remarks apply concerning what one believes. Being a skeptic, I may for the most part believe what others do, excluding, of course, the belief of others that they know for certain that contingent statements are true. It may be reasonable for me to believe some contingent statement, not because I am willing to act as though the statement is true or know for certain that it is true, but because of what I value epistemically. Epistemic values differ from practical ones. For example, I may attach great epistemic value to believing those statements that explain what I seek to explain, though I attach no practical importance to explanation. If I value the understanding obtained from explanations, then it may be reasonable for me to believe contingent statements because of their explanatory utility. And, so, being a skeptic, it may be reasonable for me to believe what best explains what I find puzzling, though I do not assign a probability of one to what I believe or assume that I know for certain that it is true. In a skeptical world, rational belief and action is shaped against a panorama of shifting probabilities without need of a permanent foundation of certain knowledge.

11 I elaborate such a theory of evidence in "Induction and Conceptual Change," forthcoming in *Synthese.*

Willard V. Quine

Epistemology Naturalized

Epistemology is concerned with the foundations of science. Conceived thus broadly, epistemology includes the study of the foundations of mathematics as one of its departments. Specialists at the turn of the century thought that their efforts in this particular department were achieving notable success: mathematics seemed to reduce altogether to logic. In a more recent perspective this reduction is seen to be better describable as a reduction to logic and set theory. This correction is a disappointment epistemologically, since the firmness and obviousness that we associate with logic cannot be claimed for set theory. But still the success achieved in the foundations of mathematics remains exemplary by comparative standards, and we can illuminate the rest of epistemology somewhat by drawing parallels to this department.

Studies in the foundations of mathematics divide symmetrically into two sorts, conceptual and doctrinal. The conceptual studies are concerned with meaning, the doctrinal with truth. The conceptual studies are con-

Öffentlicher Vortrag im Rahmen des XIV. Internationalen Kongresses für Philosophie.

W. V. Quine, "Epistemology Naturalized," in *Proceedings of the XIVth International Congress of Philosophy* (Vienna: Herder & Co., Publishers, 1971), pp. 87–103. Reprinted by permission.

cerned with clarifying concepts by defining them, some in terms of others. The doctrinal studies are concerned with establishing laws by proving them, some on the basis of others. Ideally the obscurer concepts would be defined in terms of the clearer ones so as to maximize clarity, and the less obvious laws would be proved from the more obvious ones so as to maximize certainty. Ideally the definitions would generate all the concepts from clear and distinct ideas, and the proofs would generate all the theorems from self-evident truths.

The two ideals are linked. For, if you define all the concepts by use of some favored subset of them, you thereby show how to translate all theorems into these favored terms. The clearer these terms are, the likelier it is that the truths couched in them will be obviously true, or derivable from obvious truths. If in particular the concepts of mathematics were all reducible to the clear terms of logic, then all the truths of mathematics would go over into truths of logic; and surely the truths of logic are all obvious or at least potentially obvious, i.e., derivable from obvious truths by individually obvious steps.

This particular outcome is in fact denied us, however, since mathematics reduces only to set theory and not to logic proper. Such reduction still enhances clarity, but only because of the interrelations that emerge and not because the end terms of the analysis are clearer than others. As for the end truths, the axioms of set theory, these have less obviousness and certainty to recommend them than do most of the mathematical theorems that we would derive from them. Moreover, we know from Gödel's work that no consistent axiom system can cover mathematics even when we renounce self-evidence. Reduction in the foundations of mathematics remains mathematically and philosophically fascinating, but it does not do what the epistemologist would like of it: it does not reveal the ground of mathematical knowledge, it does not show how mathematical certainty is possible.

Still there remains a helpful thought, regarding epistemology generally, in that duality of structure which was especially conspicuous in the foundations of mathematics. I refer to the bifurcation into a theory of concepts, or meaning, and a theory of doctrine, or truth; for this applies to the epistemology of natural knowledge no less than to the foundations of mathematics. The parallel is as follows. Just as mathematics is to be reduced to logic, or logic and set theory, so natural knowledge is to be based somehow on sense experience. This means explaining the notion of body in sensory terms; here is the conceptual side. And it means justifying our knowledge of truths of nature in sensory terms; here is the doctrinal side of the bifurcation.

Hume pondered the epistemology of natural knowledge on both sides of the bifurcation, the conceptual and the doctrinal. His handling of the conceptual side of the problem, the explanation of body in sensory terms, was bold and simple: he identified bodies outright with the sense impressions. If common sense distinguishes between the material apple and our sense impressions of it on the ground that the apple is one and enduring while the impressions are many and fleeting, then, Hume held, so much the worse for common sense; the notion of its being the same apple on one occasion and another is a vulgar confusion.

Nearly a century after Hume's *Treatise,* the same view of bodies was espoused by the early American philosopher Alexander Bryan Johnson. "The word iron names an associated sight and feel", Johnson wrote.

What then of the doctrinal side, the justification of our knowledge of truths about nature? Here Hume despaired. By his identification of bodies with impressions he did succeed in construing some singular statements about bodies as indubitable truths, yes; as truths about impressions, directly known. But general statements, also singular statements about the future, gained no increment of certainty by being construed as about impressions; for Hume saw no rational basis for predicting what impressions might come.

On the doctrinal side, I do not see that we are farther along today than where Hume left us. The Humean predicament is the human predicament. But on the conceptual side there has been progress. There the crucial step forward was made already before Alexander Bryan Johnson's day, although Johnson did not emulate it. It was made by Bentham in his theory of fictions. Bentham's step was the recognition of contextual definition, or what he called paraphrasis. He recognized that to explain a term we do not need to specify an object for it to refer to, nor even specify a synonymous word or phrase; we need only show, by whatever means, how to translate all the whole sentences in which the term is to be used. Hume's and Johnson's desperate measure of identifying bodies with impressions ceased to be the only conceivable way of making sense of talk of bodies, even granted that impressions were the only reality. One could undertake to explain talk of bodies in terms of talk of impressions by translating one's whole sentences about bodies into whole sentences about impressions, without equating the bodies themselves to anything at all.

This idea of contextual definition, or recognition of the sentence as the primary vehicle of meaning, was indispensable to the ensuing developments in the foundations of mathematics. It was explicit in Frege, and it attained its full flower in Russell's doctrine of singular descriptions as incomplete symbols.

Contextual definition was one of two resorts that could be expected to have a liberating effect upon the conceptual side of the epistemology of natural knowledge. The other is resort to the resources of set theory as auxiliary concepts. The epistemologist who is willing to eke out his austere ontology of sense impressions with these set-theoretic auxiliaries is suddenly rich: he has not just his impressions to play with, but sets of them, and sets of sets, and so on up. Constructions in the foundations of mathematics have shown that such set-theoretic aids are a powerful addition; after all, the entire glossary of concepts of classical mathematics is constructible from them. Thus equipped, our epistemologist may not need either to identify bodies with impressions or to settle for contextual definition; he may hope to find in some subtle construction of sets upon sets of sense impressions a category of objects enjoying just the formal properties that he wants for bodies.

The two resorts are very unequal in epistemological status. Contextual definition is unassailable. Sentences that have been given meaning as wholes are undeniably meaningful, and the use they make of their component terms is therefore meaningful, regardless of whether any translations are offered for those terms in isolation. Surely Hume and A. B. Johnson would have used contextual definition with pleasure if they had thought of it. Recourse to sets, on the other hand, is a drastic ontological move, a retreat from the austere ontology of impressions. There are philosophers who would rather settle for bodies outright than accept all these sets, which amount, after all, to the whole abstract ontology of mathematics.

This issue has not always been clear, however, owing to deceptive hints of continuity between elementary logic and set theory. This is why mathematics was once believed to reduce to logic, that is, to an innocent and unquestionable logic, and to inherit these qualities. And this is probably why Russell was content to resort to sets as well as to contextual definition when in *Our Knowledge of the External World* and elsewhere he addressed himself to the epistemology of natural knowledge, on its conceptual side.

To account for the external world as a logical construct of sense data—such, in Russell's terms, was the program. It was Carnap, in his *Der logische Aufbau der Welt* of 1928, who came nearest to executing it.

This was the conceptual side of epistemology; what of the doctrinal? There the Humean predicament remained unaltered. Carnap's constructions, if carried successfully to completion, would have enabled us to translate all sentences about the world into terms of sense data, or observation, plus logic and set theory. But the mere fact that a sentence is *couched* in terms of observation, logic, and set theory does not mean that it can be *proved* from observation sentences by logic and set theory. The most modest of generalizations about observable traits will cover more cases than its utterer can have had occasion actually to observe. The hopelessness of grounding natural science upon immediate experience in a firmly logical way was acknowledged. The Cartesian quest for certainty had been the remote motivation of epistemology, both on its conceptual and its doctrinal side; but that quest was seen as a lost cause. To endow the truths of nature with the full authority of immediate experience was a forlorn a hope as hoping to endow the truths of mathematics with the potential obviousness of elementary logic.

What then could have motivated Carnap's heroic efforts on the conceptual side of epistemology, when hope of certainty on the doctrinal side was abandoned? There were two good reasons still. One was that such constructions could be expected to elicit and clarify the sensory evidence for science, even if the inferential steps between sensory evidence and scientific doctrine must fall short of certainty. The other reason was that such constructions would deepen our understanding of our discourse about the world, even apart from questions of evidence; it would make all cognitive discourse as clear as observation terms and logic and, I must regretfully add, set theory.

It was sad for epistemologists, Hume and others, to have to acquiesce in the impossibility of strictly deriving the science of the external world from sensory evidence. Two cardinal tenets of empiricism remained unassailable, however, and so remain to this day. One is that whatever evidence there *is* for science *is* sensory evidence. The other, to which I shall recur, is that all inculcation of meanings of words must rest ultimately on sensory evidence. Hence the continuing attractiveness of the idea of a *logischer Aufbau* in which the sensory content of discourse would stand forth explicitly.

If Carnap had successfully carried such a construction through, how could he have told whether it was the right one? The question would have had no point. He was seeking what he called a *rational reconstruction*. Any construction of physicalistic discourse in terms of sense experience, logic, and set theory would have been seen as satisfactory if it made the physicalistic discourse come out right. If there is one way there are many, but any would be a great achievement.

But why all this creative reconstruction, all this make-believe? The stimulation of his sensory receptors is all the evidence anybody has had to go on, ultimately, in arriving at his picture of the world. Why not just see how this construction really proceeds? Why not settle for psychology? Such a surrender of the epistemological burden to psychology is a move that was dissallowed in earlier times as circular reasoning. If the epistemologist's goal is validation of the grounds of empirical science, he defeats his purpose by using psychology or other empirical science in the validation. However, such scruples against circularity have little point once we have stopped dreaming of deducing science from observations. If we are out simply to understand the link between observation and science, we are well advised to use any available information, including that provided by the very science whose link with observation we are seeking to understand.

But there remains a different reason, unconnected with fears of circularity, for still favoring creative reconstruction. We should like to be able to *translate* science into logic and observation terms and set theory. This would be a great epistemological achievement, for it would show all the rest of the concepts of science to be theoretically superfluous. It would legitimize them—to whatever degree the concepts of set theory, logic, and observation are themselves legitimate—by showing that everything done with the one apparatus could in principle be done with the other. If psychology itself could deliver a truly translational reduction of this kind, we should welcome it; but certaintly it cannot, for certainly we did not grow up learning definitions of physicalistic language in terms of a prior language of set theory, logic, and observation. Here, then, would be good reason for persisting in a rational reconstruction: we want to establish the essential innocence of physical concepts, by showing them to be theoretically dispensable.

The fact is, though, that the construction which Carnap outlined in *Der logische Aufbau der Welt* does not give translational reduction either. It would not even if the outline were filled in. The crucial point comes where Carnap is explaining how to assign sense qualities to positions in physical space and time. These assignments are to be made in such a way as to fulfill, as well as possible, certain desiderata which he states, and with growth of experience the assignments are to be revised to suit. This plan, however illuminating, does not offer any key to *translating* the sentences of science into terms of observation, logic, and set theory.

We must despair of any such reduction. Carnap had despaired of it by 1936, when, in "Testability and Meaning," he introduced so-called *reduction forms* of a type weaker than definition. Definitions had shown always how to translate sentences into equivalent sentences. Contextual definition of a term showed how to translate sentences containing the term into equivalent sentences lacking the term. Reduction forms of Carnap's liberalized kind, on the other hand, do not in general give equivalences; they give implications. They explain a new term, if only partially, by specifying some sentences which are implied by sentences containing the term, and other sentences which imply sentences containing the term.

It is tempting to suppose that the countenancing of reduction forms in this liberal sense is just one further step of liberalization comparable to the earlier one, taken by Bentham, of countenancing contextual definition. The former and sterner kind of rational reconstruction might have been represented as a fictitious history in which we imagined our ancestors introducing the terms of physicalistic discourse on a phenomenalistic and set-theoretic basis by a succession of contextual definitions. The new and more liberal kind of rational reconstruction is a fictitious history in which we imagine our ancestors introducing those terms by a succession rather of reduction forms of the weaker sort.

This, however, is a wrong comparison. The fact is rather that the former and sterner kind of rational reconstruction, where definition reigned, embodied no fictitious history at all. It was nothing more nor less than a set of directions—or would have been, if successful—for accomplishing everything in terms of phenomena and set theory that we now accomplish in terms of bodies. It would have been a true reduction by translation, a legitimation by elimination. *Definire est eliminare.* Rational reconstruction by Carnap's later and looser reduction forms does none of this.

To relax the demand for definition, and settle for a kind of reduction that does not eliminate, is to renounce the last remaining advantage that we supposed rational reconstruction to have over straight psychology; namely, the advantage of translational reduction. If all we hope for is a reconstruction that links science to experience in explicit ways short of translation, then it would seem more sensible to settle for psychology. Better to discover how science is in fact developed and learned than to fabricate a fictitious structure to a similar effect.

The empiricist made one major concession when he despaired of deducing the truths of nature from sensory evidence. In despairing now even of translating those truths into terms of observation and logico-mathematical auxiliaries, he makes another major concession. For suppose we hold, with the old empiricist Peirce, that the very meaning of a statement consists in the difference its truth would make to possible experience. Might we not formulate, in a chapter-length sentence in observational language, all the difference that the truth of a given statement might make to experience, and might we not then take all this as the translation? Even if the difference that the truth of the statement would make to experience ramifies indefinitely, we might still hope to embrace it all in the logical implications of our chapter-length formulation, just as we can axiomatize an infinity of theorems. In giving up hope of such translation, then, the empiricist is conceding that the empirical meanings of typical statements about the external world are inaccessible and ineffable.

How is this inaccessibility to be explained? Simply on the ground that the experiential implications of a typical statement about bodies are too complex for finite axiomatization, however lengthy? No; I have a different explanation. It is that the typical statement about bodies has no fund of experiential implications it can call its own. A substantial mass of theory, taken together, will commonly have experiential implications; this is how we make verifiable predictions. We may not be able to explain why we arrive at theories which make successful predictions, but we do arrive at such theories. Sometimes also an experience implied by a theory fails to come off; and then, ideally, we declare the theory false. But the failure falsifies only a block of theory as a whole, a conjunction of many statements. The failure shows that one or more of those statements is false, but it does not show which. The predicted experiences, true and false, are not implied by any one of the component statements of the theory rather than another. The component statements simply do not have empirical meanings, by Peirce's standard; but a sufficiently inclusive portion of theory does. If we can aspire to a sort of *logischer Aufbau der Welt* at all, it must be to one in which the texts slated for translation into observational and logico-mathematical terms are mostly broad theories taken as wholes, rather than just terms or short sentences. The translation of a theory would be a ponderous axiomatization of all the experiential difference that the truth of the theory would make. It would be a queer translation, for it would translate the whole but none of the parts. We might better speak in such a case not of translation but simply of observational evidence for theories; and we may, following Peirce, still fairly call this the empirical meaning of the theories.

These considerations raise a philosophical question even about ordinary unphilosophical translation, such as from English into Arunta or Chinese. For, if the English sentences of a theory have their meaning only together as a body, then we can justify their translation into Arunta only together as a body. There will be no justification for pairing off the component English sentences with component Arunta sentences, except as these correlations make the translation of the theory as a whole come out right. Any translations of the English sentences into Arunta sentences will be as correct as any other, so long as the net empirical implications of the theory as a whole are preserved in translation. But it is to be expected that many different ways of translating the component sentences, essentially different individually, would deliver the same empirical implications for the theory as a whole; deviations in the translation of one component sentence could be compensated for in the translation of another component sentence. Insofar, there can be no ground for saying which of two glaringly unlike translations of individual sentences is right. Such is the doctrine which I have urged elsewhere under the title of the *indeterminacy of translation*.

For an uncritical mentalist, no such indeterminacy threatens. Every term and every sentence is a label attached to an idea, simple or complex, which is stored in the mind. When on the other hand we take a verification theory of meaning seriously, the indeterminacy would appear to be inescapable. The Vienna Circle espoused a verification theory of meaning but did not take it seriously enough. If we recognize with Peirce that the meaning of a sentence turns purely on what would count as evidence for its truth, and if we recognize with Duhem that theoretical sentences have their evidence not as single sentences but only as larger blocks of theory, then the indeterminacy of translation of theoretical sentences is the natural conclusion. And most sentences, apart from observation sentences, are theoretical. This conclusion, conversely, once it is embraced, seals the fate of any general notion of propositional meaning, or, for that matter, state of affairs.

Should the unwelcomeness of the conclusion persuade us to abandon the verification theory of meaning? Certainly not. The sort of meaning that is basic to translation, and to the learning of one's own language, is necessarily empirical meaning and nothing more. A child learns his first words and sentences by hearing and using them in the presence of appropriate stimuli. These must be external stimuli, for they must act both on the child and on the speaker from whom he is learning. It is only thus that the child can associate the sentence with the same stimulus that elicited the sentence from the teacher, and it is only thus that the teacher can know whether to reinforce or discourage the child's utterances. In these transactions a speaker's subjective imagery is beside the point. Language is socially inculcated and controlled; the inculcation and control turn strictly on the keying of sentences to shared stimulation. Internal factors may vary *ad libitum* without prejudice to communication as long as the keying of language to external stimuli is undisturbed. Surely one has no choice but to be an empiricist so far as one's theory of linguistic meaning is concerned.

What I have said of infant learning applies equally to the linguist's learning of a new language in the field. If the linguist does not lean on related languages for which there are previously accepted translation practices, then obviously he has no data but the concomitances of native utterance and observable stimulus situation. No wonder there is indeterminacy of translation—for of course only a small fraction of our utterances report concurrent external stimulation. Granted, the linguist will end up with unequivocal translations of everything; but only by making many arbitrary choices—arbitrary even though unconscious—along the way. Arbitrary? By this I mean that different choices chould still have made everything come out right that is susceptible in principle of any kind of check.

Let me link up, in a different order, some of the points I have made. The crucial consideration behind my argument for the indeterminacy of translation was that a statement about the world does not always or usually have a separable fund of empirical consequences that it can call its own. That consideration served also to account for the impossibility of an epistemological reduction of the sort where every sentence is equated to a sentence in observational and logico-mathematical terms. And the impossibility of that sort of epistemological reduction dissipated the last advantage that rational reconstruction seemed to have over psychology.

Philosophers have rightly despaired of translating everything into observational and logico-mathematical terms. They have despaired of this even when they have not recognized, as the reason for this irreducibility, that the statements largely do not have their private bundles of empirical consequences. And some philosophers have seen in this irreducibility the bankruptcy of epistemology. Carnap and the other logical positivists of the Vienna circle had already pressed the term 'metaphysics' into pejorative use, as connoting meaninglessness; and the term 'epistemology' was next. Wittgenstein and his followers, mainly at Oxford, found a residual philosophical vocation in therapy: in curing philosophers of the delusion that there were epistemological problems.

But I think that at this point it may be more useful to say rather that epistemology still goes on, though in a new setting and a clarified status. Epistemology, or something like it, simply falls into place as a chapter of psychology and hence of natural science. It studies a natural phenomenon, viz., a physical human subject. This human subject is accorded a certain experimentally controlled input—certain patterns of irradiation in assorted frequencies, for instance—and in the fullness of time the subject delivers as output a description of the three dimensional external world and its history. The relation between the meager input and the torrential output is a relation that we are prompted to study for somewhat the same reasons that always prompted epistemology; namely, in order to see how evidence relates to theory, and in what ways one's theory of nature transcends any available evidence.

Such a study could still include, even, something like the old rational reconstruction, to whatever degree such reconstruction is practicable; for imaginative constructions can afford hints of actual psychological processes, in much the way that mechanical simulations can. But a conspicuous difference between old epistemology and the epistemological enterprise in this new psychological setting is that we can now make free use of empirical psychology.

The old epistemology aspired to contain, in a sense, natural science; it would construct it somehow from sense data. Epistemology in its new setting, conversely, is contained in natural science, as a chapter of psychology. But the old containment remains valid too, in its way. We are studying how the human subject of our study posits bodies and projects his physics from his data, and we appreciate that our position in the world is just like his. Our very epistemological enterprise, therefore, and the psychology wherein it is a component chapter, and the whole of natural science wherein psychology is a component book—all this is our own construction or projection from stimulations like those we were meting out to our epistemological subject. There is thus reciprocal containment, though containment in different senses: epistemology in natural science and natural science in epistemology.

This interplay is reminiscent again of the old threat of circularity, but it is all right now that we have stopped dreaming of deducing science from sense data. We are after an understanding of science as an institution or process in the world, and we do not intend that understanding to be any better than the science which is its object. This attitude is indeed one that Neurath was already urging in Vienna Circle days, with his parable of the mariner who has to rebuild his boat while staying afloat in it.

One effect of seeing epistemology in a psychological setting is that it resolves a stubborn old enigma of epistemological priority. Our retinas are irradiated in two dimensions, yet we see things as three-dimensional without conscious inference. Which is to count as observation—the unconscious two-dimensional reception or the conscious three-dimensional apprehension? In the old epistemological context the conscious form had priority; for we were out to justify our knowledge of the external world by rational reconstruction, and that demands awareness. Awareness ceased to be demanded when we gave up trying to justify our knowledge of the external world by rational reconstruction. What to count as observation now can be settled in terms of the stimulation of sensory receptors, let consciousness fall where it may.

The Gestalt psychologists' challenge to sensory atomism, which seemed so relevant to epistemology forty years ago, is likewise deactivated. Regardless of whether sensory atoms or Gestalten are what favor the forefront of our consciousness, it is simply the stimulations of our sensory receptors that are best looked upon as the input to our cognitive mechanism. Old paradoxes about unconscious data and inference, old problems about chains of inference that would have to be completed too quickly—these no longer matter.

In the old anti-psychologistic days the question of epistemological priority was moot. What is epistemologically prior to what? Are Gestalten prior to sensory atoms because they are noticed, or should we favor sensory atoms on some more subtle ground? Now that we are permitted to appeal to physical stimulation, the problem dissolves; *A* is epistemologically prior to *B* if *A* is causally nearer than *B* to the sensory receptors. Or, what is in some ways better, just talk explicitly in terms of causal proximity to sensory receptors and drop the talk of epistemological priority.

Around 1932 there was debate in the Vienna Circle over what to count as observation sentences, or *Protokollsätze*. One position was that they had the form of reports of sense impressions. Another was that they were statements of an elementary sort about the external world, e.g., "A red cube is standing on the table." Another, Neurath's, was that they had the form of reports of relations between percipients and external things: "Otto now sees a red cube on the table." The worst of it was that there seemed to be no objective way of settling the matter; no way of making real sense of the question.

Let us now try to view the matter unreservedly in the context of the external world. Vaguely speaking, what we want of observation sentences is that they be the ones in closest causal proximity to the sensory receptors. But how is such proximity to be gauged? The idea may be rephrased this way: observation sentences are sentences which, as we learn language, are most strongly conditioned to concurrent sensory stimulation rather than to stored collateral information. Thus let us imagine a sentence queried for our verdict as to whether it is true or false; queried for our assent or dissent. Then the sentence is an observation sentence if our verdict depends only on the sensory stimulation present at the time.

But a verdict cannot depend on present stimulation to the exclusion of stored information. The very fact of our having learned the language evinces much storing of information, and of information without which we should be in no position to give verdicts on sentences however observational. Evidently then we must relax our definition of observation sentence to read thus: a sentence is an observational sentence if all verdicts on it depend on present sensory stimulation and on no stored information beyond what goes into understanding the sentence.

But this formulation raises another problem: how are we to distinguish between information that goes into understanding a sentence and information that goes beyond? This is the problem of distinguishing between analytic truth, which issues from the mere meanings of words, and synthetic truth, which depends on more than meanings. Now I have long maintained that this distinction is illusory. There is one step toward such a distinction, however, which does make sense: a sentence that is true by mere meanings of words should be expected, at least if it is simple, to be subscribed to by all fluent speakers in the community. Perhaps the controversial notion of analyticity can be dispensed with, in our definition of observation sentence, in favor of this straightforward attribute of community-wide acceptance.

This attribute is of course no explication of analyticity. The community would agree that there have been black dogs, yet none who talk of analyticity would call this analytic. My rejection of the analyticity notion just means drawing no line between what goes into the mere understanding of the sentences of a language and what else the community sees eye-to-eye on. I doubt that an objective distinction can be made between meaning and such collateral information as is community-wide.

Turning back then to our task of defining observation sentences, we get this: an observation sentence is one on which all speakers of the language give the same verdict when given the same concurrent stimulation. To put the point negatively, an observation sentence is one that is not sensitive to differences in past experience within the speech community.

This formulation accords perfectly with the traditional role of the observation sentence as the court of appeal of scientific theories. For by our definition the observation sentences are the sentences on which all members of the community will agree under uniform stimulation. And what is the criterion of membership in the same community? Simply general fluency of dialogue. This criterion admits of degrees, and indeed we may usefully take the community more narrowly for some studies than for others. What count as observation sentences for a community of specialists would not always so count for a larger community.

There is generally no subjectivity in the phrasing of observation sentences, as we are now conceiving them; they will usually be about bodies. After all, it is to discourse about bodies, and not about sense data, that we are first conditioned in our learning of language; for the inculcation of language is a social affair, and it is bodies that are out there for society to share. Since the distinguishing trait of an observation sentence is intersubjective agreement under agreeing stimulation, a corporeal subject matter is likelier than not.

The old tendency to associate observation sentences with a subjective sensory subject matter is rather an irony when we reflect that observation sentences are also meant to be the intersubjective tribunal of scientific hypotheses. The old tendency was due to the drive to base science on something firmer and prior in the subject's experience; but we dropped that project.

The dislodging of epistemology from its old status of first philosophy loosed a wave, we saw, of epistemological nihilism. This mood is reflected somewhat in the tendency of Polanyi, Kuhn, and the late Russell Hanson to belittle the role of evidence and to accentuate cultural relativism. Hanson ventured even to discredit the idea of observation, arguing that so-called observations vary from observer to observer with the amount of knowledge that the observers bring with them. The veteran physicist looks at some apparatus and sees an x-ray tube. The neophyte, looking at the same place, observes rather "a glass and metal instrument replete with wires, reflectors, screws, lamps, and pushbuttons". One man's observation is another man's closed book or flight of fancy. The notion of observation, as the impartial and objective source of evidence for science, is bankrupt. Now my answer to the x-ray example was already hinted a little while back: what counts as an observation sentence varies with the width of community considered. But we can also always get an absolute standard, nearly enough, by taking in all speakers of the language. It is ironical that philosophers, finding the old epistemology untenable as a whole, should react by repudiating a part which has only now moved into clear focus.

Clarification of the notion of observation sentence is a good thing, for the notion is fundamental in two connections. These two correspond to the duality that I remarked upon early in this lecture: the duality between concept and doctrine, between knowing what a sentence means and knowing whether it is true. The observation sentence is basic to both enterprises. Its relation to doctrine, to our knowledge of what is true, is very much the traditional one: observation sentences are the repository of evidence for scientific hypotheses. Its relation to meaning is fundamental too, since observation sentences are the ones we are in a position to learn to understand first, both as children and as field linguists. For observation sentences are precisely the ones that we can correlate with observable circumstances of the occasion of utterance or assent, independently of variations in the past histories of individual informants. They afford the only entry to a language.

The observation sentence is the cornerstone of semantics. For it is, as we just saw, fundamental to the learning of meaning. Also, it is where meaning is firmest. Sentences higher up in theories have no empirical consequences they can call their own; they confront the tribunal of sensory evidence only in more or less inclusive aggregates. The observation sentence, situated at the sensory periphery of the body scientific, is the minimal verifiable aggregate; it has an empirical content all its own and wears it on its sleeve.

The predicament of the indeterminary of translation has little bearing on observation sentences. The equating of an observation sentence of our language to an observation sentence of another language is mostly a matter of empirical generalization; it is a matter of identity between the range of stimulations that would prompt assent to the one sentence and the range of stimulations that would prompt assent to the other.[1]

It is no shock to the preconceptions of old Vienna to say that epistemology now becomes semantics. For epistemology remains centered as always on evidence, and meaning remains centered as always on verification; and evidence is verification. What is likelier to shock preconceptions is that meaning, once we get beyond observation sentences, ceases in

[1] Cf. *Word* and *Object*, pp. 31–46, 68.

general to have any clear applicability to single sentences; also that epistemology merges with psychology, as well as with linguistics.

This rubbing out of boundries could contribute to progress, it seems to me, in philosophically interesting inquiries of a scientific nature. One possible area is perceptual norms. Consider, to begin with, the linguistic phenomenon of phonemes. We form the habit, in hearing the myriad variations of spoken sounds, of treating each as an approximation to one or another of a limited number of norms—around thirty altogether, constituting so to speak a spoken alphabet. All speech in our language can be treated in practice as sequences of just those thirty elements, thus rectifying small deviations. Now outside the realm of language also there is probably only a rather limited alphabet of perceptual norms altogether, toward which we tend unconsciously to rectify all perceptions. These, if experimentally identified, could be taken as epistemological building blocks, the working elements of experience. They might prove in part to be culturally variable, as phonemes are, and in part universal.

Again there is the area that the psychologist Donald T. Campbell calls evolutionary epistemology. In this area there is work by Hüseyin Yilmaz, who shows how some structural traits of color perception could have been predicted from survival value. And a more emphatically epistemological topic that evolution helps to clarify is induction, now that we are allowing epistemology the resources of natural science. For induction is an extrapolation by resemblance, and resemblance is subjective. Our standards of resemblance are partly acquired; however, we had to have some innate standards of resemblance too, or we never could have begun to form habits and learn things. Natural selection, then, could explain why innate standards of resemblance have been according us and other animals better than random chances in anticipating the course of nature. For me this reflection already alleviates part of the discomfort that has been vaguely classified as the problem of induction.[2]

Acknowledgments: This paper is adapted in part from an unpublished Arnold Isenberg Memorial Lecture which I gave at Michigan State University on November 19, 1965, under the title "Stimulus and Meaning." I am indebted to Burton Dreben for helpful criticism of an earlier draft.

References

Campbell, D. T., "Methodological Suggestions from a Comparative Psychology of Knowledge Processes." *Inquiry,* 2 (1959), pp. 152–182.

[2] See my "Natural kinds."

Carnap, Rudolf, *Der logische Aufbau der Welt.* Berlin, 1928.

———"Über Protokollsätze," *Erkenntnis,* 3 (1932), pp. 215–228.

———"Testability and Meaning," *Philosophy of Science,* 3 (1936), pp. 419–471; 4 (1937), pp. 1–40.

Hanson, N. R., "Observation and Interpretation," Sidney Morgenbesser, ed., *Philosophy of Science Today* (New York: Basic Books, 1966), pp. 89–99.

Johnson, A. B., *A Treatise on Language.* D. Rynin, ed. Berkeley: University of California, 1947.

Kuhn, T. S., *The Structure of Scientific Revolutions.* Chicago: University, 1962.

Neurath, Hans, "Protokollsätze," *Erkenntnis,* 3 (1932), pp. 204–214.

Ogden, C. K., *Bentham's Theory of Fictions.* London, 1932.

Polanyi, Michael, *Personal Knowledge.* Chicago University, 1958.

Quine, W. V., *Word and Object.* Cambridge, Mass.: M. I. T., 1960.

———"Natural Kinds," in *Ontological Relativity and other Essays,* New York: Columbia University, 1969.

Russell, Bertrand, *Our Knowledge of the External World.* London, 1914.

Yilmaz, Hüseyin, "On Color Vision and a New Approach to General Perception." E. E. Bernard and M. R. Kare, eds., *Biological Prototypes and Synthetic Systems* (New York: Plenum Press, 1962), pp. 126–141.

———"Perceptual Invariance and the Psychophysical Law," *Perception and Psychophysics,* 2 (1967), pp. 533–538.

William W. Rozeboom

Why I Know So Much More Than You Do

What does it mean to say that person *X* "knows" that *p*? With a unanimity remarkable for philosophers, it is generally agreed that for this to be true, it must obtain that

(a) *p* is the case,
(b) *X* believes that *p*, and
(c) *X* is justified in believing *p*.

Whether conditions (*a*)–(*c*) jointly suffice for *X* to know that *p*, however, has recently been disputed by several writers.[1] I shall attempt to show

William W. Rozeboom, "Why I Know So Much More Than You Do," *American Philosophical Quarterly*, 4 (1967), 281–90. Reprinted by permission.

[1] See Gettier (8), Clark (7), Sosa (17), Saunders and Champawat (16), Lehrer (12), and Harman (9). The justified-true-belief view of knowledge has been well stated by Ayer (3, ch. 1), Chisholm (5, ch. 1), and Woozley (18, ch. 8, though Woozley rashly puts the justification condition as having *evidence* for what one knows), and recently defended in one respect or another by Arner (2), Saunders (15), and Harrison (10). While condition (*b*) has occasionally been disputed on the rather foolish ground that "believes" is sometimes understood to imply "does not feel sure of," the necessity of (*a*) and (*b*)

that these doubts are unfounded, and that the *justified true belief* analysis of knowledge (hereafter referred to as the "JTB thesis") is indeed adequate. But I shall then proceed to agitate related perplexities about the concept of "knowledge" and conclude with a possibly heretical suggestion about its continued usefulness for technical epistemology.

I

Estranged from his wife and beset by financial troubles, John Duosmith has become conspicuously despondent. Today, a man's body is found in Duosmith's hotel room with Duosmith's revolver in its hand, a bullet therefrom in its head, and a suicide note signed by Duosmith on the table. Mrs. Duosmith identifies the body as that of her husband, pointing out his characteristic birthmark, the private details of their recent quarrel cited in the note, and so on for many other items which make it overwhelmingly evident to Mrs. Duosmith that the corpse of John Duosmith lies before her, and hence that her husband is dead.

And John Duosmith is indeed dead. But what has happened is this: Last night, Duosmith received a secret visit from his identical twin brother Jim, a petty criminal whose existence John had concealed from his wife and who now begged John to hide him from certain colleagues seeking retribution for something Jim had done. Seeing a chance to make a new life for himself, John shot his brother and arranged the scene to appear as though he, John, had killed himself. But as John left the hotel, he was spotted by Jim's pursuers who, mistaking him for his twin, promptly executed their plans for Jim's demise. So John Duosmith is dead while his wife, for the best of reasons, also believes this to be so.

But does Mrs. Duosmith *know* that her husband is dead? Mr. Gettier and others[2] say "No," and my own linguistic intuition agrees with

---

for knowing that p is essentially noncontroversial. The status of (c), however, is more problematic. Armstrong (1, p. 120), Malcolm (13, p. 225ff.), [pp. 289ff., this volume Eds.] and Sosa (17) contend from an overly narrow equating of "justification" with "evidence" that justification is not always requisite to knowing. In contrast, Gettier (8), Clark (7), Lehrer (12), and Harman (9) accept the necessity of (c) for knowing p but deny its sufficiency given (a, b), while Saunders and Champawat (16) question the possibility of finding *any* set of conditions which are necessary and sufficient for all instances of "knowledge."

Though not strictly addressed to the analysis of "knowing," recent discussion by Chisholm (6), Brown (4), and Saunders (14) concerning self-justifying beliefs, and Hintikka's (11) widely acclaimed exploration of the modal logic of knowledge and belief are also background context for the present work.

[2] See n.1.

this judgment. The force of this and similar examples cited by Gettier *et seq.* is drawn from the principle that true beliefs grounded upon false premisses do not count as knowledge, no matter how reasonable those premisses may themselves be under the circumstances. That is,

> (A) If person X believes p—justifiably—only because he believes q, while he justifiably believes q on the basis of evidence e, then q as well as p must be the case if X's belief in p is to qualify as "knowledge."

Consequently, if p is true while q is false in such a case, as apparently illustrated by the Duosmith episode and Gettier's examples, it follows that a person may justifiably believe true proposition p and still not *know* that p. Now in fact, these examples do *not* show this, nor can the JTB thesis ever be threatened by principle (A). But before I point out why this is so, it is best to undermine confidence that linguistic intuition can be trusted to provide as sound interpretation of cases like these.

II

It is Sunday afternoon, and Mrs. Jones is on her way to borrow an egg from her neighbor, Mrs. Togethersmith. She fears that she may be too late, however, for she is aware that every Sunday afternoon for the past several years, the Togethersmith family—Mr. and Mrs. Togethersmith and their two children—has gone for a drive in the country. As she steps outside, Mrs. Jones sees the Togethersmith car departing with Mr. Togethersmith at the wheel, and thinks to herself, "Pity, there she goes." Mrs. Jones believes that Mrs. Togethersmith is driving away because, for excellent reasons, she believes that the entire Togethersmith family is in the departing car. But in fact, while Mrs. Togethersmith, her husband, and one of their children are indeed in the departing car, the other Togethersmith child is on this one occasion attending a friend's birthday party. Insomuch as it is not true that the entire Togethersmith family is driving away, is Mrs. Jones's justified true belief, that Mrs. Togethersmith is driving away, *knowledge*? Principle (A) appears to deny this, since Mrs. Jones arrived at her true belief about Mrs. Togethersmith by means of a justified but false belief about the whereabouts of the entire Togethersmith family. But the falsehood here seems so *irrelevant*. For "The entire Togethersmith family is driving away" is equivalent to the conjunction "Mrs. Togethersmith is driving away, Mr. Togethersmith is driving away, and all the Togethersmith children are driving away," the components of which are supported by Mrs. Jones's evidence just as well separately as conjoined—in fact, it is difficult to say whether Mrs. Jones's belief about

Mrs. Togethersmith derives from her belief about the Togethersmith family as a whole, or is a part-cause of it. In any event, linguistic intuition is disposed to deny that the absence of one Togethersmith child from the departing family car disqualifies Mrs. Jones's justified true belief about Mrs. Togethersmith's departure as an instance of knowledge.

But if so, what about Mr. Jones, who, wanting a 12-inch board, measures one with his new tape rule, obtains a 10-inch reading, and concludes "That's too small," when the tape rule is defective and this board is really 11 inches? (We assume that Jones has had much past experience with tape rules, all of which amply warrants his trust in the present reading.) Mr. Jones's justified belief, that this board is under 12 inches, is true even though it is derived from his false justified belief that this board is 10 inches. Since intuitively this case is no different in kind from Mrs. Duosmith's belief about her dead husband, we should deny that Jones *knows* this board is less than 12 inches. Yet "This board is 10 inches" is equivalent to the conjunction "This board is under 12 inches, this board is at least 10 inches, and this board is not between 10 and 12 inches," only the last component of which is false while its first component requires for its justification only a proper part of the evidence which supports Jones's belief in the whole conjunction. So by formal parallel, it might also seem that Mr. Jones's conclusion that the board is undersize should not be epistemically inferior to Mrs. Jones's belief in Mrs. Togethersmith's departure.

More intensive analysis of these two cases would show not so much that one or both violate principle (*A*) as that when a person's justified true belief *p* is accompanied by a justified false belief *q* it may well prove troublesome to decide whether or not his belief in *p* is related to his belief in *q* in such fashion that the falsity of the latter should disqualify the former as knowledge. That this is in general a failure of conception, not just an insufficiency of data concerning the believer's detailed reasoning, is shown by the following more sophisticated example.

Dr. Pillsmith, a competent practitioner of medicine, is well aware that

(1) Among persons who have not been vaccinated against Hypofluvia, 999,999 out of a million who show symptoms *S* are afflicted with this disease,

(2) Among vaccinated persons showing symptoms *S*, only one in ten is afflicted with Hypofluvia,

(3) Only one person in a million showing symptoms *S* has been vaccinated against Hypofluvia,

and that consequently,[3]

> (4) More than 999,998 persons in a million who show symptoms *S* are afflicted with Hypofluvia.

Attempting to diagnose the condition of his latest patient, Dr. Pillsmith observes that

> (5) Philip Blotely shows symptoms *S*,

and, lacking further information about Blotely's medical history, infers unhesitatingly from (1)–(5) both that

> (6) Philip Blotely has not been vaccinated against Hypofluvia

and that

> (7) Philip Blotely has Hypofluvia.

Now it so happens that Blotely was, in fact, vaccinated against Hypofluvia, but has contracted it just the same. So Pillsmith's diagnosis (7) is both justified and true—but is it knowledge? At first it might seem that the falsity of (6) thwarts this, for were Pillsmith to surmise the truth of Blotely's vaccination, his knowledge of (2) and (5) would prevent him from justifiedly accepting (7). Yet (6) is at the same time irrelevant to the diagnosis in that Pillsmith can get to (7) from (5) and (1)–(3) by way of (4) without ever considering whether or not Blotely has been vaccinated. And if Pillsmith does make his diagnosis in this way, must (6) still be true if Pillsmith's justified belief, that Blotely has Hypofluvia, is to count as knowledge? Surely not, since falsehood (6) takes no part in the inference. Yet we can also argue that justification of (7) by (5) and (1)–(3) via (4) implicity presupposes the truth of (6), for derivation of (4) from (1)–(3) argues in effect: Given any person with symptoms *S*, either he has or has not been vaccinated against Hypofluvia. If he hasn't, it is virtually certain that he has Hypofluvia; otherwise, Hypofluvia is counterindicated, but this is too unlikely a possibility to be considered seriously.

It seems to me that the intuition which was so sure in Sect. I that Mrs. Duosmith doesn't really know her husband is dead is quite at a loss to say whether or not Dr. Pillsmith knows that Blotely has Hypofluvia. There is quicksand underfoot here, and we must not too hastily presume

[3] Since for any three attributes *A*, *B*, and *C*, $\Pr(A/B) = \Pr(C/B) \times \Pr(A/BC) + \Pr(C/B) \times \Pr(A/BC) \geqslant [1 - \Pr(C/B)] \times \Pr(A/BC)$.

that Duosmith-type examples, which apparently refute the JTB analysis of knowledge by way of principle (*A*), are all that they seem to be.

III

It is now time to make explicit an important technical detail which is usually slighted in philosophical discussions of knowledge. This is that the judgmental attitudes in which a proposition can be held are not just belief and disbelief, or belief, disbelief, and uncertainty, but a whole spectrum of credibilities spanning many shades of uncertain belief and doubt. Consequently, assertion that knowing presupposes believing is specious unless it is made clear just how strong a belief is so required. Once this question of degree is raised, however, we can easily see from the absurdity of "He knows that *p* but isn't entirely sure of it." [4] or "I know that *p* but have some doubts about whether it is really so," that only maximal belief is acceptable for knowledge. Hence condition (*b*) of the JTB thesis must be explicated as "*X* feels completely sure of *p*" or "*X* believes *p* absolutely," while similarly, (c) must be read as "*X* is justified in believing *p* absolutely," "*X* has a right to have not the slightest doubt about *p*," or the like. (Also, since it may be argued that if *X* is justified in believing *p* in degree *d* then *X* is also justified to almost the same extent in believing *p* to a degree which is almost *d*, "*X* is justified in believing *p* absolutely" should be further explicated as "*X* has more justification for believing *p* absolutely than for feeling any doubt about *p*.")

When is absolute belief justified? While a convincing general answer is not easy to come by (see Sect. IV), a necessary condition for evidential justification is surely the following:

> (*B*) If person *X* feels completely sure of *p* on the basis of evidence *e*, then *X*'s belief in *p* is justified only if *e* necessitates *p*.

That is, *X* is not justified in feeling certain of *p* in virtue of his awareness of *e* unless *p is* certain, given *e*. This is entirely compatible with admitting that *X* may be justified in feeling *almost* certain of *p* on grounds

[4] At first thought, this might seem to make sense as a variant of "He really knows that *p* but can't bring himself to admit it." But *not admitting to belief in* is not at all the same as *having some doubts about*, and "He knows that *p* but won't admit it" implies not "He is not sure of *p* and won't admit that *p*," but either "He doesn't really have any doubt about *p* but can't bring himself to say so," or "He still isn't really convinced of *p* even though he has overwhelming evidence for it."

e if *p* is extremely likely, given *e*. It only denies that it is rational for *X* to close his mind completely to the possibility of not-*p* even though *e*, so long as this possibility does in fact exist. Moreover, while (*B*) does not specify what sense of necessity—logical, causal, or whatever—is required, it is in any case analytically true that

> (*C*) If *e* while not *q*, then it is not the case that *e* necessitates *q*.

Finally, I think it will be agreed that in general,

> (*D*) If person *X* feels completely sure of *p* only because he feels completely sure of *q*, but his belief in *q* is not justified, then neither is his belief in *p* justified.

(I would hold that (*D*) is always the case, but there is room for argument on this point when *q* is "basic" for X—see Sect. IV—and it is not essential here that (*D*) be completely universal.)

Let us now reconsider principle (*A*), which envisions a person's believeing *p* on the basis of his belief *q*, and *q* on the basis of evidence *e*. For this to pose any threat to the JTB analysis of knowledge, the degree of belief at issue must be *absolute* belief. But it follows from (*B*) and (*C*) that *X* can justifiedly believe *q*—absolutely—on the basis of evidence *e* only if *q* is the case; so stipulation of *q*'s truth in the final clause of (*A*) is in this case otiose. That is, if *X* feels completely sure of *p* only because he is convinced of *q*, and the latter only because he is aware of *e*, then to hypothesize that *q* is false is also, by (*B*) and (*C*), to presuppose that *X*'s absolute belief in *q* is unjustified, and hence by (*D*) that neither is he justified in feeling completely sure of *p*. Thus in our Duosmith example (and similarly for Gettier's cases), while Mrs. Duosmith had excellent reason to feel *virtually* certain that her husband was dead, the bare fact that, overwhelming evidence to the contrary notwithstanding, the body before her was not that of her husband shows that this evidence did not warrant her having no doubt whatsoever that her husband was dead. Likewise, for our more problematic examples in Sect. II, we can say without hesitation that Mrs. Jones, Mr. Jones, and Dr. Pillsmith did not *know* that Mrs. Togethersmith was departing, that this board was less than 12 inches, and that Blotely had Hypofluvia, respectively, because while the evidential bases for these conclusions made them extremely likely, a vestige of uncertainty still remained. In short, if the "belief" cited in principle (*A*) is allowed to include degrees of belief weaker than complete conviction, the truth of (*A*) resides in that the falsity of *q* is symptomatic that the degree of *p*-belief justified by *e* is less than absolute.

IV

But while the argument from principle (*A*) thus fails to impeach the JTB thesis, the claim that justification is always prerequisite to knowledge is far from unproblematic. Most conspicuously troublesome is that if *X*'s knowing *p* requires there to exist evidence *e* such that *X*'s belief in *p* is justified by *X*'s awareness (i.e., knowledge) of *e*, then *X*'s belief in *e* also requires such justification and we are off on a regress. In particular, the justification requirement might seem to exclude the possibility of perceptual knowledge and self-awareness where *X*'s belief in *p* is not inferred from other beliefs but is aroused directly by sensory stimulation or given introspectively. Moreover, as will be seen, the demand for justification undergoes a remarkable transformation when we turn from other-person to first-person knowledge, while the conditions of justification even for the inferred beliefs of others are not so straightforward as they might at first appear.

Actually, no puzzle of "justification" can even discredit the JTB thesis, for the simple reason that whatever is needed for *X* to know that *p*, if *X* does know *p* then he is certainly justified in believing *p*. (Witness, e.g., the absurdity of "*X* knows that *p*, but he has no right to believe it so strongly.") So we can maintain that *X* knows that *p* iff *p* is a justified true belief of *X*'s without concern for how murky the concept of justification may itself be. I submit, therefore, that the greatest philosophic challenge which issues from the JTB position is not to settle whether this view is entirely correct (though the import of my argument in Sect. III is that we have no good reason to doubt this), but to determine what it is about *X*'s knowing *p* that accredits *X*'s *p*-belief as "justified." The intent of this section is to rough out a tentative solution to this problem, which is more untidily complex than heretofore recognized, in full expectation that many more exchanges will be needed to round out the present survey in convincing detail.

Let a person's belief in *p* be described as "basic" if he does not believe *p* as a result of his believing something else. (For example, when *X* perceives that *p*, his belief in *p* is simply for him a *given* which becomes a basis for inference but is not derived from anything else he knows.) Then *X*'s *basic convictions* are beliefs of which *X* feels completely sure without having inferred them from evidence. Unless knowledge can be inferred from beliefs which do not themselves qualify as knowledge (a counterintuitive possibility which I shall not discuss), the regression argument shows that if *X* knows anything at all, he must also have basic knowledge, i.e. justified true basic convictions, and our first task in this section is to find some acceptable sense in which a basic conviction may be said to be justified. Two alternatives present themselves: either (1) basic convictions are self-justifying, or (2) some basic convictions have nonevidential justification.

In support of (1), it might be argued that the justification of *X*'s belief in *p* consists in *p*'s bearing a certain relation $\mathcal{J}$ to some set *B* of *X*'s true basic convictions. if b_i is such that each $b_i \in B$ is also related to *B* in manner $\mathcal{J}$, then all basic convictions in *B* are also by definition justified. For example, if "*X* is justified in believing *p*" were to be analyzed as "*p* is logically entailed by *X*'s true basic convictions," then *X*'s basic convictions are justified by the reflexivity of entailment. But this approach leaves much to be desired. For one, an intuitively acceptable $\mathcal{J}$-relation with the needed formal properties is not easy to come by. (It is simple to argue, e.g., that logical entailment does not in itself confer evidential justification.) Further, how is the set *B* to be circumscribed? Does veracity suffice for a basic conviction to belong to *B*—i.e., for it to be justified? If so, we should have to grant that a dogmatic thinker who habitually works himself into a state of absolutely closed judgment on controversial issues without considering any of the relevant evidence is justified in holding any such belief which by chance happens to be true. But if we hold that a basic conviction can be true without necessarily being justified, whatever else is needed for the latter constitutes a nonevidential source of justification and thus carries us into alternative (2).

There are many intriguing thought experiments by which our intuitions about nonevidential belief-warrants can be bared, starting with increasingly bizarre or futuristic ways (e.g., electrical stimulation of the retina) in which sensory input might elicit true perceptual beliefs; but here it will suffice to consider just one which cuts directly to the heart of the matter. Suppose that Tom Seersmith claims to be able to foretell the outcomes of horse races. Upon investigation, we learn that when Seersmith thinks about a forthcoming race, he is often overwhelmed, quite without any reason for it, with a feeling of complete certainty that a certain horse will be the winner. Before the last Kentucky Derby, Seersmith felt sure that it would be won by a horse named Fleetfoot, and as it turned out his prediction was correct. Did Seersmith *know* that Fleetfoot was going to win, and if so, in what sense was his belief justified?

Whatever the personal peculiarity which endows Seersmith with convictions about forthcoming horse races, if his prognostication record has shown only chance accuracy in the past, we would be loath to say that Seersmith either knew or was justified in believing that Fleetfoot would win the Derby even though his belief in this instance happened to be true. Even if Seersmith's previous race predictions have usually been correct, with a hit rate high enough to convince us that there is something extraordinary about this man, we would still deny that he was justified in feeling absolutely sure that Fleetfoot would win so long as his predictions are not infallible. But suppose we discover that Seersmith's horse race prognoses *are* infallible—i.e., we become convinced that whenever Seersmith feels sure that race r will be won by horse h, it is absolutely certain that h will win r. Then surely we would be forced to admit that Seersmith knew that Fleetfoot would win the Derby, even though how he knew would baffle us. (As I follow Seersmith through prediction after prediction and see that he is *never* wrong, I find myself saying, "I can't understand it, but somehow, he *knows*!") The justification—nonevidential—for Seersmith's belief is simply that since generalization

$$(\forall h)\ (\forall r)\ (\text{Tom Seersmith believes that horse } h \text{ will win race } r \supset h \text{ wins } r)$$

is a nomological principle of our world, Seersmith's basic conviction that Fleetfoot would win the Derby was true not by mere happenstance but of nomic necessity. For if Seersmith's horse race precognitions *cannot* be wrong, what better justification could there possibly be for his having them?

Now let's change the case slightly. Tom Seersmith's brother Dick also feels occasional convictions about the outcomes of forthcoming horse races, but unlike his brother, Dick's percentage of correct anticipations is substantially less than perfect. Careful research discloses, however, that Dick's accuracy depends critically upon the horse's name. Whenever Dick feels sure that horse h will win race r, he is never mistaken so long as h's name contains exactly two syllables, but when the predicted winner's name is shorter or longer than this, Dick's precognitive effectiveness is somehow impaired. Dick, too, felt sure that Fleetfoot would win the Derby—but did he *know* this? In principle, Dick's case is exactly like that of brother Tom, since by natural law his preconvictions about bisyllabically designated horse-race victors cannot err. Yet intuition is more hesitant here, for at times Dick also feels certain that h will win r when he should not, namely, when 'h' is not bisyllabic. And if Dick is unaware that the anticipated winner's name makes a difference for the reliability of his forecast, we might question whether he is entitled to feel such perfect confidence in his precognition even when, unknown to him, it is in fact nomologically infallible. Thus it might be denied that Dick *knew* of Fleetfoot's forthcoming victory if he did not recognize that this particular belief had stronger truth-credentials than his average forecast. But this line of argument is unsound. If Dick were aware of his general precognitive fallibility, it would indeed seem reasonable for him to have inferential meta-doubts about his belief in Fleetfoot's victory—if he had, in fact, had any. But to make a person's knowing p contingent upon his knowing that he knows p would precipitate an intolerable regress, nor should a person's true belief in p be disqualified as knowledge merely by his having additional erroneous convictions as well. (To hold that a person can know nothing if he ever believes falsely seems extreme to the point of absurdity, though as will be seen in Sect. V it contains an important grain of truth.) If Dick's conviction that Fleetfoot would win the Derby was truly basic for him, uninfluenced by any meta-beliefs concerning his general prognostic proficiency, then it was for him no less an instance of *knowing* than it was for brother Tom, and was justified on the very same grounds, namely, that insomuch as Dick felt certain Fleetfoot would win, it *was* certain that Fleetfoot would win.

And now one more twist. Suppose that Harry is still another Seer-smith whose case is like Dick's except that Harry's precognitions of form "horse h will win race r" are always (nomologically) correct when and only when r is run on a dry track. Insomuch as Fleetfoot won the Derby on a dry track, was Harry's conviction that Fleetfoot would win an instance of knowledge? Harry's belief, too, was infallible in that there exists a nomic principle in virtue of which, given that Harry felt sure that Fleetfoot would win and that the track was dry, it was certain that Fleetfoot would win. But Harry differs from Dick in that Dick's infallible precognitions are intrinsically identifiable as such—i.e., whether or not a forecast by Dick falls under the law which vouchsafes its accuracy is revealed by its syllabic composition—whereas the reliability of Harry's forecast cannot be determined without additional information which does not generally become available until race time. And since Harry thus cannot discriminate his infallible precognitions from those which are not (assuming that he does not also have advance knowledge of the track conditions), it might be argued that he had no right to feel so sure that Fleetfoot would win the Derby. But this doubt is only a refinement of the one we have already rejected in Dick's case. If it is not necessary for Harry to know that he knows p, or to know that he can trust his belief p absolutely, in order for him to know p or for his p-belief to be justified, then neither can we reasonably hold that his being *able* to acquire this meta-knowledge is requisite for the latter. (How could such an ability possibly be germane except by way of the knowledge which, with its help, Harry does acquire?) Consequently, so long as a person's basic believing of p belongs to a class whose members are nomologically infallible, its epistemological status should not depend upon whether or not this class is defined by properties inherent in the belief itself. (It is relevant to this point that knowing what *we* know about Harry, we could win a pretty penny at the races by noting Harry's prediction and waiting to see the track conditions before deciding whether to bet.)

The principle which appears to govern our Seersmith examples (though intuition speaks only with a subdued and halting voice here) is that a basic conviction counts as "knowledge," and is by the same token justified, if and only if it not merely *is* true, as could occur by chance, but is infallibly true by virtue of its being of a kind (perhaps defined in part by relational attributes) whose accuracy is guaranteed by natural law. This is at best an uneasy conclusion, however, for without further qualification it trembles on the brink of triviality: If V is the attribute of veridicality, then any belief of type V—i.e., any which happens to be true—is also infallibly true vis-à-vis type V and hence qualifies as knowledge unless "natural law" is defined to exclude generalizations which are logical truths. (That we would *like* to make some such exclusion is, I think, intuitively evident, but how to accomplish it effectively is another question.) Moreover, this criterion applies only to the basic convictions of other persons, for *my* beliefs, basic or otherwise, are justified by standards rather different from this.

Suppose that I set out to determine which of us, you or I, knows the more. I start by listing all propositions which you believe (or more precisely, all which I believe that you believe) and then prune this list by deleting everything on it which, in my judgment, is either false or is unwarranted for you. To display what *I* know, however, (or rather, what I believe that I know), I list all the propositions believed by me—*and stop*. For while I am perfectly willing to admit that there are facts of which I have no knowledge, I do not believe, nor can I bring myself to believe, any specific proposition of form "p, but I don't know that p." This is closely related to the oddity of "p, but I don't believe it," but has a significance the latter does not. I reject "p, but I don't believe it" because my believing this would entail my believing p and hence falsify the conjunction as a whole—i.e., it is impossible for me to believe a true proposition of this form. I could, however, truly believe "p, but I don't know it" were p to be the case while I believed but did not know that p.[5] Hence my refusal to admit, when I am convinced of p, that I may not know that p, has the force of maintaining that in *my* case, believing truly suffices for knowing. (And yet, when I reflect upon why I don't consider all *your* true beliefs to be knowledge, I am also willing to admit in general terms that some of mine may not be knowledge, either. This is an apparent inconsistency which will be resolved in Sect. V.)

[5] While Hintikka (11) has proposed essentially the same analysis of "p, but I don't believe it" as offered here, his modal system allows that a person *can* defensibly claim to believe "p, but I don't know it." However, Hintikka's intuitive apologia for this (11, p. 83) construes it to involve a degree of p-belief less than perfect conviction, and the fact that his system does not recognize the unacceptability of "I don't know that p even though I am absolutely sure of it" would seem to reveal a lacuna in its axioms.

This first-person/other-person difference in knowledge criteria is present even when, from your vantage point, my true belief is amply justified. Suppose that I believe mathematical theorem T because I have just discovered a convincing proof of it, and when I inform you that I know T, you ask me what grounds I have for thinking that I know this. The only reply which seems relevant is for me to recapitulate the steps by which I deduced T—except that when I do this, you quite properly point out that what I have given you is grounds for believing T whereas what you asked for is grounds for believing that I know T. My supplying of proof for T *demonstrates* to you that my belief in T is justified, but *asserts* nothing which implies this. On the other hand, if I try to give you an account of how it is that I know T, it will go something like: "Well, I know that L_1 and L_2 are logically true, so when I see that T is an immediate consequence of L_1 and L_2, this makes me aware that T is also the case." What I am telling you is that my awareness of certain facts, namely, that L_1 and L_2 are logically true and jointly entail T, is a *cause* of my knowing T. But from your perspective, my awareness of this evidence *provides* (noncausally, by fulfilling an existence requirement) the justification which is an analytic component of my knowing T. That is, in more general terms, when I have come to know p by a valid line of reasoning from unimpeachable premisses, the inferential procedure which to you is a *condition* on my knowing p is to me only the *occasion* for this. What justifies *my* believing p is simply p's being the case; for once I have convinced myself that p, I require nothing else to consider it right that I feel sure of p—what more could possibly be relevant? In fact, it is nomically impossible for me to accept "p, but I have no right to believe it so absolutely," for my believing the second component of this suffices to create some doubt in me about p. (This is why I am unable—nomically, not logically—to believe "p, but I don't know it.") So I reason about p not to transmute my base belief in p into golden knowledge, but to decide whether p is the case; whereupon, having convinced myself that it is, I rebuff all challenges to my conviction's epistemic credentials by the argument "p; therefore it is reasonable for me to believe that p."

What are my criteria for the justification of *your* beliefs? We have already explored the evaluation of your basic convictions, but it remains to see what is needed for your inferred beliefs to be reasonable. Ordinarily, the degree of p-belief which I consider evidence e to warrant in you is simply the confidence in p which I sense is aroused in me by conviction that e. However, closer analysis shows this not to be definitive. Let p and q be two propositions such that q logically entails p. If, somehow, I know that you know q, what will persuade me that you have evidential justification for believing p? For myself, merely being cognizant of q does not in itself convince me of p (I am, after all, often unsure of consequences of my beliefs when I have not discerned that they are such consequences), so for your q-awareness to warrant your p-belief, I would normally require you to know not only that q, but that q entails p as well. But is $q \;\&\; (q \vdash p)$, then *sufficient* evidence to justify your belief in p? If, either thoughtlessly or with good reason, I presume that our minds work alike, I will agree that it is; for belief in the former would cause me to believe the latter as well. But suppose I have learned that you just don't seem to grasp the significance of logical relationships; specifically, that you often accept propositions of form "α, and α entails β" while simultaneously doubting or even disbelieving β. Then I would no longer consider your belief in $q \;\&\; (q \vdash p)$ to be evidential justification for your believing p, for I could not regard the former as the *source* of the latter, nor would I have reason to regard your p-belief as knowledge insomuch as your veridicality in this instance may simply be the chance success of irrational thought. Conversely suppose I discover instead that your thinking is superrational in that for any two propositions α and β such that α entails β, and you believe α, your mere thinking of β when you believe α suffices for you to be convinced of β as well—i.e., you believe all logical consequences of your beliefs, so long as they come to mind at all, whether or not you are also aware of the entailment relations among these propositions. In this case, I must concede that your knowledge of q is fully adequate in itself to justify, and hence to dignify as knowledge, your belief in p. For if you accept all logical consequences of your convictions, rather than just a proper subclass of these constrained by your logistical perceptiveness, on what grounds can I hold your belief processes to be epistemically defective?

The preceding arguments show, first impressions to the contrary notwithstanding, that my other-person epistemology has exactly the same justificational standards for inferred beliefs as it does for basic ones. In both cases, the critical determinant is not whether the belief in question is "reasonable" in accord with some impersonal normative ideal, but whether it has arisen in circumstances which guarantee its accuracy. (This applies also to beliefs with derivational status intermediate between basic and inferred, thus bypassing the problems these would generate were the criteria of justification qualitatively different for the two extremes. For example, suppose that for a certain pair of attributes P and Q, whenever you perceive that $P(a)$ for an object a you find yourself also convinced that $Q(a)$. If I know that in our world P nomically implies Q, I must count your belief in $Q(a)$ as knowledge, justified by your awareness of $P(a)$, even if you are not consciously aware that $(\forall x)[P(x) \supset Q(x)]$.[6])

[6] I say "not consciously aware" rather than simply "unaware" to suggest the glide from inference episodes of the most paradigmatically rational sort down to believings which are patterned *as though* they were accompanied by additional supportive knowledge which the believer does not, in fact, have in any conceptualized form.

Harmony between first-person and other-person justification, however, is more elusive. At one level, these show a common pattern: Whenever I consider my/your conviction in *p* to be justified, I presume there to exist an argument of form "*S*; hence my/your belief in *p* is necessarily correct," where *S* is some state of reality.[7] But when it is my belief which is at issue, *S* is *p* itself; whereas I want the *S* which warrants your *p*-belief to do so nomically rather than logically. That I should adopt so flagrant an epistemological double standard is not a conclusion which I find esthetically pleasing, but if there is a deeper unity here I have yet to find it.

V

However lacking in clarity (and perhaps consistency) the epistemic concept of "justification" may be, it nonetheless appears that knowing *p* analytically requires not only that the knower feel completely certain of *p*, but also that there be some sense in which, considering the circumstances, it *is* completely certain that *p*. But since I reject the argument "*p*; therefore you are justified in feeling sure of *p*," and also doubt that our *de facto* world contains any nomic regularities perfect enough to vouchsafe any belief beyond all possibility of error, I do not think that you strictly know anything at all. Whereas in my own case, I have too much faith in my own fallibility to feel *absolutely* sure of anything, even if some of my perceptual beliefs fall short of this only negligibly. My admission (with high but not complete conviction) that probably not all of my beliefs are entirely correct, plus inability to meta-distinguish those which are true from those which are not, causally prevents me from ever entirely achieving an absolute extremity of belief, while my professional skills as scientist and philosopher enable me to find genuine even if minuscule chinks of uncertainty in any proposition I examine, even those which arise perceptually or feel analytically true. So technically speaking, I know nothing either.[8]

In short, my conception of "knowledge"—and presumably yours as well—is so impossibly idealized that no real-life belief episode ever satisfies it. Whenever you or I assert, as we often do, "I am aware that . . . ," "He knows that . . . ," etc., we are uttering falsehoods which would come closer to the truth if revised as "I approximate awareness that . . . ,"

[7] The scope of "necessary" here is of course $N(S \supset$ my-or-your *p*-belief is correct$)$, not $S \supset N$ (my-or-your *p*-belief is correct).

[8] Hence the title of this paper is something of a misnomer. Although my knowledge-criteria are enormously more liberal for me than for you, their extension is in both cases the null class.

"He almost knows that . . . ," or the like. The paradigm-case rejoinder, that what we mean by "know" is defined by these ordinary-life, applications, no more shows that this usage is literally correct than the everyday paradigmatic ascriptions of "spherical" to roundish objects of irregular curvature demonstrates that a thing's surface does not really have to be a constant distance from its center in order for it to be literally a sphere. On matters philosophical as well as scientific, ordinary language teems with simplistic presuppositions and coarse-grained, uncritical categories which do slovenly justice to reality; and intellectual maturity—represented most illustriously by technical science but by no means restricted thereto—consists first of all in learning to relinquish these cognitive crudities for a more sophisticated grasp of complexity and precise detail. It is all very well to recognize that the conceptual fluency of idealized approximations is often more convenient for everyday affairs than is the encumbrance of needless exactitude, but it is folly to construe the success of this practical usage as a sign that what is so asserted is precisely correct, or to begrudge its abandonment when, like outgrown clothing, its inaccuracies begin to chafe. In particular, there is no more reason for us to agonize philosophically over the esoterics of everyday knowledge-talk—e.g., why justified true beliefs at practical levels of assurance should sometimes be called knowledge and sometimes not—than for geometricians to puzzle over why some common-sense spheres have a larger cubed-surface-to-squared-volume ratio than do others.

To conclude, then, I propose that the subject of "knowledge" is no longer of serious philosophical concern for the simple reason that this concept is far too primitive for the needs of technical epistemology. No harm will be done, I suppose, by retaining a special name for true beliefs at the theoretical limit of absolute conviction and perfect infallibility so long as we appreciate that this ideal is never instantiated, but such sentimentality must not be allowed to impede development of conceptual resources for mastering the panorama of partial certainties which are more literally relevant to the real world. So far, however, the normative theory of practical belief has scarcely advanced beyond surmise that the structure of propositional credibilities is isomorphic to the probability calculus, and has not even begun to think technically about such vital subtleties as the ramifications of uncertainty in basic beliefs, reciprocal nondemonstrative supports among partially confirmed propositions, the credibility interplay between beliefs and meta-beliefs, and the like. With problems of "How strongly should X believe p?" lying dark and unfathomed before us, we stand to profit from continued epistemological preoccupation with the nature of "knowledge" to just about the same extent as would psychology from a return to study of the "soul."

References

1. Armstrong, D. M. *Perception and the Physical World.* London, Routledge & Kegan Paul, 1961.
2. Arner, D. "On Knowing." *The Philosophical Review,* vol. 68 (1959), pp. 84–92.
3. Ayer, A. J. *The Problem of Knowledge.* London, Macmillan, 1956.
4. Brown, R. "Self-Justifying Statements." *The Journal of Philosophy,* vol. 62 (1965), pp. 145–150.
5. Chisholm, R. M. *Perceiving: A Philosophical Study.* Ithaca, Cornell University Press, 1957.
6. Chisholm, R. "Theory of Knowledge." In: *Philosophy,* R. M. Chisholm, *et al.* Englewood Cliffs, Prentice-Hall, 1964.
7. Clark, M. "Knowledge and Grounds: a Comment on Mr. Gettier's Paper." *Analysis,* vol. 24 (1963), pp. 46–48.
8. Gettier, E. L. "Is Justified True Belief Knowledge?" *Analysis,* vol. 23 (1963), pp. 121–123.
9. Harman, G. H. "Lehrer on Knowledge." *The Journal of Philosophy,* vol. 63 (1966), pp. 241–246.
10. Harrison, J. "Does Knowing Imply Believing?" *The Philosophical Quarterly,* vol. 15 (1963), pp. 322–332.
11. Hintikka, J. *Knowledge and Belief.* Ithaca, Cornell University Press, 1962.
12. Lehrer, K. "Knowledge, Truth and Evidence." *Analysis,* vol. 25 (1965), pp. 168–175.
13. Malcolm, N. *Knowledge and Certainty.* Englewood Cliffs, Prentice-Hall, 1963.
14. Saunders, J. T. "Beliefs Which are Grounds for Themselves." *Philosophical Studies,* vol. 16 (1965), pp. 88–90.
15. ———"Does Knowledge Require Grounds?" *Philosophical Studies,* vol. 17 (1966), pp. 7–13.
16. ———and Champawat, N. "Mr. Clark's Definition of 'Knowledge'." *Analysis,* vol. 25 (1964) pp. 8–9.
17. Sosa, E. "The Analysis of 'Knowledge that p'," *Analysis,* vol. 25 (1964), pp. 1–8.
18. Woozley, A. D. *Theory of Knowledge.* London, Hutchinson, 1949.

II

THE EVIDENCE OF THE SENSES

H. H. Price

Belief and Evidence

THE EVIDENCE OF PERCEPTION, MEMORY AND SELF-CONSCIOUSNESS

We should all agree that a person can only believe reasonably when he has evidence for the propositions believed. Moreover, our evidence for a proposition *p* which we believe must be stronger than our evidence (if any) against that proposition, if our belief is to be reasonable. Nor is this all. Belief admits of degrees. And if we are to believe reasonably, the degree of our belief must be no greater than our evidence justifies. For instance, it would be unreasonable to believe a proposition with complete conviction if our evidence, though good as far as it goes, falls short of being conclusive, though it would still be reasonable to believe with a good deal of confidence.

But unfortunately the notion of 'evidence' is full of difficulties. For one thing, the meaning of the word in modern English is quite different from the one its etymology suggests. The Latin word 'evidentia' literally

H. H. Price, "Belief and Evidence," in *Belief* (London: George Allen & Unwin Ltd., and New York: Humanities Press, Inc., 1969), pp. 92–129. Reprinted by permission of the publishers.

means 'evidentness'. In the French word 'évidence' and the German 'evidenz' the etymological meaning is still retained. But in modern English it only survives in the term 'self-evident'. A self-evident proposition is one which is 'evident of itself'. You have only to consider the proposition itself and then it is evident to you that it is true. We notice however that here, in talking of 'self-evidence', we are concerned with the evidence *of* a proposition and not with the evidence *for* it. It does make sense to speak of the evidentness of a proposition, but it makes none at all to speak of the evidentness for it. And in modern English (apart from this one exceptional case), 'evidence' does always mean 'evidence for . . .'. The evidence for a proposition consists of those considerations which support that proposition or confer some degree of probability upon it, great or little. The evidence for a proposition may be strong or weak, whereas evidentness is a matter of all or nothing. Again, there may be evidence against a proposition, consisting of considerations which decrease the probability of that proposition; whereas the contrast between 'for' and 'against', or between favourable and unfavourable, does not apply to evidentness at all.

Presumably the word 'evidence' came to have this meaning in modern English, because we may acquire information which makes a proposition evident or obvious though it would not have been evident or obvious otherwise. The testimony of the witnesses makes it evident or obvious that the prisoner is guilty. But though this was presumably the first step in the divergence between the modern English sense of the word 'evidence' and its etymological sense of 'evidentness', there was more to come. 'Evidence' eventually came to mean not just considerations which make a proposition evident or obvious, but any considerations which make it in any degree probable.

Another point of terminology may be briefly mentioned. We speak of 'reasons' for believing something, and also of 'evidence' for believing it. What is the relation between the two? The answer is, I think, that the notion of 'reasons for' is wider. We may have reasons for doubting something, or for being surprised at it, or for suspending judgement about it. These three—doubting, being surprised, suspending judgement—are of course, fairly closely related to believing. But we may also have reasons for hoping or fearing, for being anxious, for liking someone or disliking him, or even for being angry with him. Again, we are expected to have reasons for the advice which we offer to someone, or the recommendations we make. Most important of all, we may have reasons for doing something, or for deciding to do it.

In this discussion, however, we are concerned only with reasons for believing. In some of the other cases just mentioned, when we speak of 'reasons for' such and such, it would be quite inappropriate to substitute the word 'evidence' instead. 'What evidence have you for being anxious about John's health?' would be a strange question. And 'what evidence have you for deciding to take the 4.15 train?' would hardly be intelligible. But in the special case of believing, the two questions 'what is your evidence for . . .' and 'what are your reasons for . . .' amount to pretty much the same thing. Perhaps 'reasons' here are primarily concerned with the mental attitude of believing (What reason have you for taking that particular attitude, rather than another, e.g. doubting or disbelieving?) whereas 'evidence' is primarily concerned with the proposition believed (what is the evidence for the proposition that this is the road to Aylesbury?). But when it is belief that we are talking about, there is at any rate a very close relation between the two questions. An answer to either would also serve as a satisfactory answer to the other.[1]

I think, then, that in this discussion we may safely confine ourselves to questions about evidence, though anyone who wishes to may translate what I am going to say into the terminology of 'reasons'.

THE EVIDENCE 'THERE IS' AND THE EVIDENCE X 'HAS'

Now it would often be said that the evidence for a proposition *p*, consists of some relevant fact or set of facts which 'support' that proposition, or increase its probability; and that the evidence against *p* consists of some relevant fact or set of facts which 'weaken' that proposition or decrease its probability.

But there are two objections to this formulation. If we are concerned to decide whether a particular person's belief is reasonable (or how reasonable it is, if reasonableness admits of degrees) what we must consider is not just what evidence there is for the proposition he believes, but the evidence which he has for that proposition. He may have evidence for it which others do not have, and equally he may fail to have evidence which others do have. Primitive people, we may suppose, believed pretty firmly that the sun is much smaller than the earth, and about the same size as the moon. Their belief was mistaken. But we must not conclude that it was therefore unreasonable. Neither telescopes nor trigonometry had been invented at that time. The evidence which we have about the size and position of the sun and the moon was not available. They only had the evidence of unaided sense-perception, and this

[1] Cf. also the parallel between 'What reasons are there for believing that *p*?', and 'What evidence is there for *p*?': and likewise between 'What reasons have you for believing that *p*?' and 'What evidence have you for *p*?'.

(as far as it goes) really does give some support to the proposition which they believed.

MUST THE EVIDENCE CONSIST OF KNOWN FACTS?

Secondly, there is a difficulty about the word 'fact' ('some relevant fact or set of facts which support the proposition believed'). It follows from what has just been said that if we are asking about the reasonableness of a particular person's belief, we must not just pay attention to the relevant facts which there are. Facts of which a man is completely ignorant, however relevant they may be, can have no bearing at all on the reasonableness of his belief. The only ones which do have a bearing on it are relevant facts which he himself is aware of.

And now we find that the word 'fact' gets us into difficulties. For when we say 'It is a fact that so-and-so', we are making a claim to knowledge. If I speak of the fact that to-day is Friday, I am claiming to know that to-day is Friday. Sometimes, no doubt, when I believe some proposition, my evidence really does consist of some relevant fact which I know. The primitive people I mentioned might fairly claim to know that the sun occupied a much smaller part of their visual field than the terrestial landscape did. But it is by no means obvious that when we believe reasonably our evidence must always consist of some relevant fact or facts which we know in any strict sense of the word 'know'. On the contrary, it seems (at first sight at any rate) that our evidence for a proposition which we believe consists quite often in other propositions which we believe—believe in a sense in which belief is contrasted with or inferior to knowledge. My evidence for believing that the Conservatives will win the next election consists of a lot of propositions which I have read in the newspapers during the last month or two. I believe these propositions more or less firmly: but can I claim to know in any strict sense of the word that all of them are true, or even that most of them are? It does look as if my belief about the next election was supported by nothing better than a set of other beliefs.

At any rate, there is a problem here, and we prevent ourselves from discussing it if we begin by laying down a rule that a belief cannot be reasonable, unless the evidence for it consists of relevant facts known to the believer. Instead of speaking of 'relevant facts' it is better to use some more colourless phrase like 'relevant considerations'; that leaves us free to enquire what kind of considerations they have to be. Might they just consist of other propositions which we already believe, but do not know to be true?

The suggestion that they might is strengthened when we consider the relations between belief and knowledge. As we have seen, we usually draw a distinction between belief and knowledge. It does not make sense to say 'John knows that it is raining, but it isn't': whereas it does make sense to say 'He believes that it is raining, but it isn't'—even though he believes this with complete and unshakable conviction. Here there is a very sharp distinction between belief and knowledge. Any belief, no matter how firmly held, can be mistaken: the proposition believed may still be false, and it still may be false, even when the belief is reasonable. But to speak of 'mistaken knowledge' would be self-contradictory.

We have also seen, however, that some philosophers have suggested that 'knowledge' itself can be defined in terms of 'belief'.[2] But even so, the distinction between knowledge and belief is not abolished. For we still have to distinguish between a belief which amounts to knowledge and a belief which does not; or, if you like, between knowledge on the one hand and 'mere' belief on the other. And thus the question asked just now can still be raised: does the evidence for a reasonable belief have to consist of propositions known to be true, or can it consist (wholly or partly) of propositions which are 'merely' believed?

The suggestion that it can is supported when we consider why we need to have 'mere' beliefs at all. Why not be content with such knowledge as we can get? The answer is that unfortunately we can get so little. If we are to live at all, we must constantly make practical decisions without knowing what the result of our action is going to be. Let us consider an academic person who has to give a lecture in a distant university this evening. When he gets into the train to go there, he certainly does not have conclusive evidence that the train will get him there in time to give his lecture. He has to be content with forming the most reasonable belief that he can on the evidence available. It is inductive evidence: most trains reach their destination not more than half an hour later than the timetable says they will. On the strength of this, he can reasonably believe with some confidence (but not with complete conviction) that he will arrive in time to address his audience. But if he had demanded conclusive evidence for this proposition before deciding which train to catch, he would never have got there at all.

Again, when he set out on his journey, he did not know that he would not be stricken by aphasia on the way, or otherwise incapacitated, whether physically or mentally, before he got there. Such things do happen, and he had no conclusive evidence that one of them was not going to happen to him. But on the evidence available to him about the state of his health, he could reasonably believe with considerable confidence

[2] Lecture 3, pp. 83–91. [H. H. Price, *Belief*. *Eds.*]

(but not with absolute conviction) that he was going to arrive there safe and sound.

One thing, then, which makes us believing beings is that we need beliefs for the guidance of our actions and our practical decisions. Belief is a second best, but it is much better than nothing. But we need it in another way too. Knowledge is something which we value for its own sake. (Everyone has some curiosity, and what is curiosity but a desire to know?) But here again, our trouble is that very often knowledge in any strict sense of the term is not available, especially, but not only, when the knowledge we should like to have concerns something rather remote in space or time. If we were to say 'we must have knowledge or nothing' then—very often—we should have to be content with nothing. We should have to remain in a state of suspended judgement, a state of complete 'agnosticism' about many of the questions which interest us (for example what were the motives of the Emperor Constantine when he adopted Christianity?). But though we have not got conclusive evidence which would enable us to know the answer, we may still have evidence which supports one answer rather than another. Thus we may have evidence which makes it probable, though not certain, that Constantine's motives were at least partly political ones, and improbable, though not certainly false, that they were purely religious. And here again reasonable belief is a second best; but still it is very much better than nothing, though knowledge would be better still if only we could have it.

BELIEF AND INFERENCE

Now let us consider what we do with our beliefs when once we have got them. The mathematical philosopher F. P. Ramsey suggested that when we come to believe a proposition, we 'add it to our stock of premisses'. I think he has put his finger on a very important function which our beliefs have. They enable us to draw inferences. Indeed, believing a proposition seems to consist at least partly in a tendency to draw inferences from the proposition believed. If someone claimed to believe that to-day is early closing day and yet set out on a shopping expedition this afternoon, we should doubt whether he did really believe what he claims to believe. For if he really does believe that it is early closing day, he must surely be capable of drawing the very simple inference 'The shops are shut this afternoon'.

As I have said already, we need beliefs for the guidance of our actions and our practical decisions. This is another way of saying that we draw practical inferences from the propositions we believe, or use them (when relevant) as premisses in our practical reasoning. But we draw theoretical inferences from them too. If one likes to put it so, we use them for the guidance of our thoughts as well as our actions. If I believe that the motives for Constantine's conversion were at least partly political, I shall think that this makes it likely that his motives for summoning the Council of Nicaea were partly political also. In other words, when we believe a proposition *p*, we do use that proposition as evidence to support other propositions. The inference we draw from the proposition *p* takes the form '*p*, so probably also *q*'. Indeed, this is one of the most important uses we have for our beliefs, once we have got them. When we come to believe a proposition *p* we consider its implications—what follows from it either certainly or probably. If we are reasonable, the propositions which follow from *p* with certainty are believed as firmly as *p* itself, though not of course more firmly.

Let us take the case of suspecting ('Suspecting' is the name traditionally given to the lowest degree of belief). If I suspect that to-day is early closing day, I am entitled to suspect that the shops will be shut this afternoon: indeed I am logically committed to suspecting this, since the second proposition is logically entailed by the first. But I am not entitled to be sure, or even almost sure, that the shops will be closed this afternoon.

If however the inference I make from the proposition believed is what we call a probable inference, '*p*, so probably also *q*', the degree of belief which I give to *q* must be lower than the degree of belief I give to *p*, if I am reasonable. For example, if I am absolutely sure that it is raining now, I am not entitled to be absolutely sure that it will still be raining in five minutes' time (unless I have some other evidence for believing so). But I am entitled to believe this second proposition with considerable confidence.

It will be seen that when we consider the consequences of some proposition which we believe, our belief attitude spreads itself as it were, or extends itself, from that proposition to its consequences. But in a reasonable believer it suffers some degree of diminution on the way, if they are only probable consequences, supported but not logically entailed by the proposition originally believed.

BELIEFS SUPPORTED BY OTHER BELIEFS

We may now return to the relation between belief and evidence. Our conclusion so far is this: on the face of it, it does not seem to be always true that when we believe reasonably our evidence consists of known facts (facts known to the believer). Quite often it seems to consist of other propositions which are themselves 'merely' believed.

But this involves us in an awkward problem. The problem is particularly awkward if we wish to define knowledge itself in terms of belief ('believing a true proposition on conclusive evidence and with full conviction'), and it must be admitted that this definition does fit some sorts of knowledge quite well. If the evidence for a proposition *p* is to be conclusive, surely it must consist of other propositions which are themselves known to be true? So according to this definition of knowledge, these other propositions too must be believed on conclusive evidence. And the evidence for them, in their turn, must consist of still other propositions which are believed on conclusive evidence. Here we seem to have committed ourselves to a regress which has no discernible end—a regress of 'evidence for our evidence for our evidence . . .'.

But the same sort of difficulty arises about beliefs which do not amount to knowledge. For instance, I do not even claim to know that John is away from home to-day; I only claim that it is reasonable for me to believe this with a considerable degree of confidence, the degree of belief which is traditionally called 'opinion'. What evidence do I have for this belief? Well, I am fairly sure (but not quite) that he told me so when I saw him last Tuesday. My opinion is supported by nothing better than another opinion.

To put it metaphorically: we seem to be in a bog or a quagmire with no firm ground anywhere. Or, if one prefers another metaphor, we build up an elaborate structure of beliefs supported by other beliefs, and the whole thing just hangs in the air like a cloud. Is it anything better than a more or less coherent fiction? Some philosophers might be willing to accept this situation. They would say that if a set of propositions is sufficiently coherent, that in itself makes them true. Yet it seems obvious that a highly coherent system of propositions might still be wholly fictitious. (I recently read Professor Tolkien's series of novels called 'The Lord of the Rings'. I was very much impressed by the coherence of this complicated story, and it occurred to me that if the Coherence Theory of Truth were correct the whole story would have to be true!)

Let me try to see whether we can solve the problem in another and more commonsensical way. We shall find, however, that we get into difficulties about two important sorts of evidence which we have for our beliefs, the evidence of memory and the evidence of testimony. In both cases the 'coherence' interpretation has very considerable plausibility.

What I shall try to show is that this regress of 'evidence for our evidence' does have a termination: so that in the long run (though not always immediately) the evidence we have for our beliefs does after all consist of known facts—that is, of facts known to the believer—if we are believing reasonably. But I shall only consider empirical beliefs, what Hume called beliefs concerning matters of fact, and shall not discuss *a priori* or logically necessary propositions. It is not clear to me whether the notion of believing (either reasonably or unreasonably) applies to *a priori* propositions at all, nor whether the notion of evidence applies to them, though the notion of proof certainly does. At any rate, when we speak of the evidence we have for believing something, the type of evidence we have in mind is always or nearly always empirical evidence. It may of course be maintained (and often has been) that some very simple mathematical and logical truths are self-evident. But as we have seen already, in the phrase 'self-evidence', 'evidence' means just evidentness. And in a discussion of belief the word 'evidence' has quite a different sense; it means evidence *for* . . . and that is something which is quite different from evidentness.

There seem to be four different ways in which the series of beliefs supported by other beliefs can be terminated. To put it differently, there are four different sorts of evidence which do not just consist in propositions which are themselves merely believed. They are: (1) the evidence of perception (2) the evidence of self-consciousness (3) the evidence of memory (4) the evidence of testimony. The fourth is the most puzzling, and moreover it is not wholly independent of the first and second. Testimony itself has to be perceived (e.g. heard or read) and it also has to be remembered if it is to be of any use to us. But we do normally think of it as a separate source of evidence for our beliefs, and it raises special difficulties of its own which do not arise about perception, self-consciousness or memory. So in the rest of this lecture I shall only consider the evidence of perception, of self-consciousness and of memory. The evidence of testimony needs a lecture to itself.[3]

THE EVIDENCE OF PERCEPTION

We all think that some questions can be conclusively settled by means of sense-perception; and not only that they can be conclusively settled in that way, but that they very frequently are.

It is true that the epistemology of perception is a complex and highly controversial subject. The analysis of such a simple-looking statement as 'I am now seeing a piece of paper' is very difficult, and many strange opinions have been held about it. The distinction between 'appears' and 'actually is' is puzzling too: for example, on a foggy evening the sun often appears oval, but it is not actually oval. How can something appear to have a quality which it does not actually have, and in what sense exactly can we be said to be 'experiencing' this quality when the

[3] See Lecture 5, below. [pp. 112–116, this volume. Eds.]

thing appears to us to have it? Or should we perhaps say that 'actually is' should itself be defined in terms of 'appears', and hold (as some philosophers have) that such a thing as this chair here is just a class or system of actual and possible appearances?

But in spite of these difficulties, we all do think that some questions can be conclusively settled by the evidence of sense-perception, for example the question 'Are there any matches in this box?' By looking inside, it is possible to know or be certain that there are some matches there, or that there are none. G. E. Moore was surely right in maintaining that we know many propositions of this sort to be true even though we do not know what the correct analysis of them is.

If so, it is perfectly proper to speak of observed facts, as we all do in practice, whatever philosophical theories we may hold. And this is one way (the most familiar way) in which the regress of beliefs supported by other beliefs comes to an end. This regress—the regress of evidence for our evidence, as I called it—is terminated sometimes by an observed fact, that is by a fact ascertained or discovered by means of sense-perception.

For example, suppose I have to go to Cambridge this afternoon, and I decide to take a bus to the railway station. My reason for this decision is that I believe I shall get very wet if I walk all the way. What is my evidence for believing this? It again is something which I believe but do not know. I believe that it will be raining at that time. And what is my evidence for that belief? This again might be something which I believe but do not know. I might have had the misfortune to be blind, or to be shut up all the morning in a room with no window; and then at half past twelve some kind person might have told me that it was raining steadily, and I might just have taken his word for it. But as it happens, I was not in this unfortunate situation. I was able to go out into the garden just before lunch and see for myself that it was raining steadily, to feel the raindrops on my hands and face, to look at quite a large area of the sky and see for myself that there was no break in the clouds there. This was enough to settle the question 'What is the weather like here and now?' It was an observed fact, a fact which I observed for myself at first hand, that at that place and time it was raining steadily and that there was no break in the clouds within my range of vision.

Some philosophers may maintain that this language I have used is too strong. They may tell me that even here I was still only believing, and had no right to use the word 'fact' (which implies a claim to knowledge). But perhaps this dispute is less important than it seems. Suppose we do say that I only believe that it is raining when I have the experience commonly described as 'actually seeing the rain and actually feeling the raindrops'. Nevertheless, we have to admit that my evidence for this believed proposition is as strong as the evidence for any empirical proposition could be, and we cannot well conceive what it would be like to have better evidence for the proposition 'It is raining'. To use an analogy suggested by Professor Ayer, so long as we agree that evidence of this kind gets 'top marks', it does not matter very much where we draw the line between knowledge and belief, or between the beliefs which amount to knowledge and the beliefs which do not. But in actual fact, we should all say that in the circumstances described a person does know that it is raining.

In our reaction against over-sceptical views of perception, we must not of course jump over to the opposite extreme and maintain that all propositions for which we have perceptual evidence are certainly true. There are illusions and hallucinations, and what we perceive is not always as it appears to be. There are perceptual mistakes, and there are several different kinds of them. But we have means of detecting them. Roughly speaking, we do it by finding that the expected consequences of our belief do not occur. For example, in a mirage there appears to be a pool of water some distance away. We go to the place, and instead of seeing the water more clearly and in greater detail (as we should expect to do if it were actually there) we see nothing but an expanse of sand or tarmac, and we cannot get the tactual experiences we expect to have when we put our hands in a liquid.

Again, quite apart from illusions and hallucinations, some perceptual experiences are better from the evidential point of view than others. A single glance is not always enough to settle the question which we wish to ask (for example, the question 'Is that a swan over there?') though it does provide us with some relevant evidence. Often we must move to another point of view. We must come closer, or look at the thing from another direction; or we must switch on the electric light, or put on spectacles. Sometimes we must touch as well as sight. In order to decide whether this is petrol or water, we may have to smell it or even taste it.

So, within the class of propositions for which we have perceptual evidence, we can still distinguish between (1) those which are known or certified and (2) those which are 'only' believed. In this sphere, as in others, there is plenty of room for mere belief which does not amount to knowledge, because our evidence is not conclusive, (although it is good evidence as far at it goes.) The important points for our present argument are these: (1) First, there are some propositions which are perceptually certified, conclusively established by perceptual evidence, and there are many others for which we have strong perceptual evidence although it is not conclusive. (2) Secondly, even when we have only relatively weak perceptual evidence, this is sufficient to bring the regress of 'evidence for our evidence' to an end. The series of beliefs supported by other beliefs is terminated when we get back to a belief supported by perceptual evidence. For this belief, though used to support other beliefs, is not itself supported by another belief. It is supported by something quite different, namely by an experience, for example an experience of seeing or touching or hearing.

THE EVIDENCE OF SELF-CONSCIOUSNESS

This phrase 'an experience' draws our attention to the second source of evidence I wish to consider—the second way in which the series of beliefs supported by other beliefs is brought to an end. This second sort of evidence is the evidence of self-consciousness. In the example I gave before about the rain, the experience of seeing and feeling the raindrops was my own. When someone has an experience of this sort, he need not of course attend to it. But if he does, he can know that he is having it. We can sometimes claim to have knowledge about ourselves, and here again the regress of beliefs supported by other beliefs is brought to an end. For example, I believe that I should make a hopelessly bad soldier or policeman or air-raid warden. What is my evidence? Well, I am a timid person. What is my evidence for believing this? My evidence is not just some other proposition which I believe. It is something I have noticed about myself. I have noticed on a great many occasions that I am easily frightened by persons, objects and situations which do not seem to frighten others at all. I feel fear in the presence of a large dog, or of a man who addresses me in a loud and angry tone of voice, or when I am driving a car on a main road on the day before Bank Holiday, or when I have to go to the dentist, or even sometimes when I have to deliver a lecture. My evidence for believing that I am a timid person is the evidence of self-consciousness, the frequent experiences of fear which I have noticed in myself on many different sorts of occasions.

In the present climate of philosophical opinion it is hardly necessary to point out that a person does need evidence for the statements he makes about himself, especially when they are statements about his own character. In these Behaviouristic days, we are in no danger of claiming that every human being (or every sane adult human being) has a vast store of infallible knowledge about his own mind. The danger nowadays is all the other way. We are more likely to assert that others know or can know far more about us than we know about ourselves, or even that each of us know almost nothing about himself or his own mind, and that most of the statements he makes about himself express 'mere' beliefs of a highly questionable sort. So if you want to know the truth about yourself you had better ask someone else, and preferably a person who does not like you very much.

No doubt this is a sphere in which we are peculiarly prone to error. That is why the precept γνῶθι σεαυτόν ('Know thyself') was needed. Self-knowledge is often a difficult achievement, and it is difficult in several different ways. One difficulty is that many mental states and happenings are so fugitive. They come and go so quickly and do not 'stay put' to be examined. Sometimes, however, the difficulty is just the opposite. A persistent state of mild melancholy or depression which 'colours' all our thoughts and feelings for the whole day, or even for weeks on end, or even throughout the whole of our waking life, is easily overlooked. One may fail to notice it, because there is nothing to contrast it with. More important still, self-knowledge and especially knowledge of one's own character (one's conative and emotional dispositions) is often painful. This is because we are moral beings. Self-knowledge is hardly separable from self-judgement, and only too often the self-judgement has to be of a disapproving kind. It is not very surprising that self-knowledge is something which we tend to dislike, and that when it comes to us we often do our best to forget about it.

All the same, there is such a thing as self-consciousness. The idea that the only good evidence a person can get for belief about himself is the evidence of testimony is too absurd to be taken seriously, however true it is that external observers may sometimes have more correct beliefs about us than we ourselves have. I can sometimes notice that I am feeling frightened or tired or surprised, that I still feel resentment about an unkind remark made to me yesterday. I do not have to look in a mirror and observe my bodily behaviour in order to ascertain these facts about myself. I can sometimes notice that I am hearing or seeing or thinking, that I am imagining this or wondering about that. I notice these things for myself at first hand and do not need the confirmation of others. Self-consciousness is one source of evidence, and an indispensable source of evidence, for the beliefs which each person has about himself, although the testimony of others who observe his bodily behaviour is also relevant. You may think that this is a platitudinous conclusion. So it is, but platitudes are just the things which Philosophers are liable to forget. What is called 'a firm grasp of the obvious' is less common among learned men than one might suppose.

THE EVIDENCE OF MEMORY

We may now turn to the third way in which the regress of beliefs supported by other beliefs may be brought to an end, namely by means of the evidence of memory. Since sceptical views about memory have been rather prevalent among philosophers, and some have doubted whether there can be memory-knowledge at all, I shall begin by considering the defects of memory.

There are two quite different ways in which a person's memory may be defective. Badness of memory is something like badness of character. There are sins of omission and there are sins of commission. I may fail to do the things I ought to do, or I may do the things I ought not to do; and very likely I have both these kinds of moral defect. There is a similar distinction between omission and commission where defects of memory are concerned. If you ask me where I was on this day of the month ten years ago, I cannot remember at all. Everyone has forgotten very many of his past experiences. And for some of our beliefs about the past—even though it was our own past—we have only the evidence of testimony, for example, what our parents or other relatives have told us about what we did in our childhood. Sometimes the testimony is in a way our own. I might be able to tell you what I was doing on this day of the month ten years ago if I could find my own diary for that year.

In such cases as these the defects of memory are defects of omission. It is important to mention then, but they do not raise any very difficult philosophical problem. The defects of memory which I compared to sins of commission are a different matter. For then it is not just a case of failing to remember but of mis-remembering, much as sins of commission are misdoings and not just failures to do something. And as reflection on our misdoings gives rise to pessimistic theories of human character, such as the doctrine that human nature is totally depraved, reflection on our mis-rememberings likewise gives rise to sceptical theories of memory. Memory is fallible. It sometimes turns out that what a man sincerely claims to remember did not in fact happen. Then how can we be sure that all our claims to remember are not equally mistaken? Whenever we claim to remember something, it is conceivable that we might be mis-remembering. In that case, how can we know anything about the past at all?

Now there is something wrong with this argument. It cannot even be stated unless we assume that some of our claims to remember are correct, that sometimes when we claim to remember we really are remembering and not mis-remembering. How do we know that memory claims are ever made at all? Because we remember making them ourselves and remember hearing others speak as if they were making them. And how do we know that some of these memory claims were incorrect? Because we are able, somehow, to find out what the facts about the past actually were. And in order to find out what they actually were, we ourselves must rely on memory at some point or other. For example, you claim to remember having lunch with Thomas in London last Thursday, but you must be mistaken. How do we know that you are mistaken? Because we all saw you having lunch in College in Oxford on that day. But we ourselves are relying on our own memories when we say this.

Let us now consider another way in which we might find out that our friend's memory claim is mistaken. Suppose he specifies the time. He claims to remember meeting Thomas in the restaurant in London at 1.5 p.m. Yet he was seen in Oxford at 1.6 p.m. on that day. Surely this is sufficient to show that his memory claim must be mistaken? It is, but only because we assume the validity of certain causal laws. It is not logically impossible that a person should travel from Oxford to London in one minute, but it is causally impossible, the laws of Nature being what they are. We must however ask ourselves what evidence there is for believing that the laws of Nature are of this particular sort. It is empirical evidence, the evidence of observations and experiments. And they are past observations and experiments. But if knowledge of the past is impossible (as the sceptic says it is) past observations and experiments cannot be evidence for anything. Nor will it do to say that we can rely on documentary evidence—books, articles in scientific journals, etc.

We do of course rely on documentary evidence, but here again it is reliance on what we have read, and not just on what we are at this present moment reading. And if it is not strictly correct to speak of the present as momentary, because it has a finite duration and is what is called 'a specious present', still the duration of the specious present is very brief indeed, only a very few seconds. There is another difficulty about documentary evidence which I will just mention. It would be absolutely useless to us, unless we were justified in assuming that ink-marks retain an approximately constant shape and approximately constant spatial relations to one another over long periods of time. But our evidence for this is again empirical (there is no *a priori* reason why they should not change their shapes every other minute or move about all over the page) and it again is the evidence of past experience.

I hope this is enough to show that we can have no ground for thinking that a particular memory claim is mistaken unless we assume that other memory claims are correct.

'SAVING THE APPEARANCES'

The pessimistic way of formulating our conclusion would be this. 'Do what we will, we have to depend on the evidence of memory in the end, however sceptical we try to be. So we must just make the best of it. There is no prospect of getting anything better.' If that is our view, we shall have to proceed in something like the manner recommended in the Coherence Theory of Truth. It will be a case of 'saving the appearances'.

We shall try to form a system of mutually supporting memory claims or memory propositions, in which as many of them as possible are retained and as few as possible rejected, though some, no doubt, will have to be rejected. In order to do this, we shall have to suppose that every memory claim has some degree of intrinsic weight or credibility. Unless we put in some proviso of this kind, our system of memory propositions, however coherent we make it, might be no more than a coherent fiction.

But once we have introduced this rather strange property of intrinsic weight or credibility, we can hardly fail to notice that it admits of degrees. Some memory claims have more of it than others. My claim to remember that I had several cups of tea at breakfast this morning has more 'credit-worthiness' than my claim to remember switching off the electric fire before I went to bed last Saturday night. Or again, I claim to remember (or, as we also say, I seem to remember) having seen this man before, when I was in California last winter; but the weight or credit-worthiness of this claim is small, and I could easily be persuaded that it is mistaken.

So if we do proceed in this way, and try to construct a coherent system which will include as many memory claims as possible, we cannot follow the democratic principle of Bentham, that each of them is to count for one and none of them for more than one. Our aim is to 'save the appearances'. But some of the appearances are more worthy of salvation than others, and we must save them first and be prepared to cast out the less worthy candidates, if there is a conflict between a more worthy one and a less.

But once we admit that this property of intrinsic credibility or credit-worthiness varies in degree, we may have to go farther. Might there not be cases where this property reaches a maximum? Might there not be some memory propositions which present themselves to us with a weight or credibility or credit-worthiness so great that no empirical proposition could possibly have more? On the face of it, there are such memory-propositions and we all of us are sure that there are.

For instance, could any possible adverse evidence induce me to reject the very clear recollection I now have that I have been sitting in a chair and writing for some time? Well, just conceivably it could. Unknown to me, a dose of lysergic acid might have been put into a cup of tea I had at breakfast, and for the past forty-five minutes I might have been in a state of hallucination. But even so, I very clearly recollect that I have for some time been having experiences which were as if I were sitting in a chair and writing, and I cannot conceive of any empirical evidence which would convince me of the contrary.

It seems likely that everyone has such memories pretty frequently, and can recognize them when he has them. Not all of them are memories of the very recent past, though these are the most obvious examples. They may be memories of something which happened many years ago, for example of some episode in a railway journey on one's first visit to the Continent. Such recollections of the distant past tend to be fragmentary and isolated. They usually come to us just as memories of 'long ago', and do not have a determinate date attached to them. To date them, we have to resort to causal inferences or to documentary evidence or oral testimony.

We should also notice that among these 'unshakable' recollections of our past experiences, recollections which no amount of adverse evidence would induce us to withdraw, there are some which have a *general* character. When put into words they take the form of statements which are in one way or another general statements: for example 'I have gone to bed many times', 'I have often been to London', 'I have sometimes played cricket and have very seldom enjoyed it'.

It follows, if I am right, that the task which confronts us in our study of memory is not just one of 'saving the appearances', that is, our apparent or ostensible recollections, with due regard to the fact that some of them are *ab initio* more worthy of salvation than others. For some of them, and not so very few of them either, are improperly described as 'apparent' or 'ostensible'. Mixed in among the appearances which have to be saved there are some realities. They are not just memory-claims but actual memories. Indeed, if this were not so, how could we talk of ostensible or apparent memories at all, or attach any meaning to the phrase 'claim to remember'? What is this which we claim to be doing, or are ostensibly or apparently doing but perhaps not really? It is remembering. There happens to be such a thing. It is logically possible that there might not have been. But if there had been no remembering, there would have been no persons either, and indeed no minds or minded creatures at all. Leibniz' *'mens momentantea seu carens recordatione'* would hardly deserve the name of *mens*.

So much for three sorts of evidence by which the series of beliefs supported by other beliefs is brought to an end: the evidence of perception, of self-consciousness and of memory. The problems we have considered in this chapter are at any rate familiar ones. They have been discussed by philosophers for many centuries. But that cannot be said about the fourth sort of evidence, to which we must now turn, the evidence of testimony. In practice, and in learned enquiries too, we do often rely upon it as a means of terminating the regress of beliefs supported by other beliefs. But to the best of my knowledge, epistemologists have had very little to say about it, and there are no 'standard views' which we might use as starting-points for our discussion. The next lecture, then, is bound to be difficult both for the lecturer and the audience.

THE EVIDENCE OF TESTIMONY

Epistemologists do not seem to have paid much attention to the evidence of testimony. But according to our ordinary way of thinking, testimony is one of our most important sources of knowledge. Everyone claims to know a very large number of geographical and historical truths, for which he has only the evidence of testimony. All of us here would claim to know that China is a very large and populous country, though none of us, perhaps, has been within three thousand miles of it. Every English schoolboy knows that Charles II was restored to the throne in 1660, and that Britain was once part of the Roman Empire, though these 'known facts' are facts about the remote past. The same applies to facts about the very recent past as well. If an important debate takes place in Parliament, millions of people claim to know about it next day, just by reading newspapers or listening to the wireless.

To take an even more striking example, each of us would claim to know how old he is, that is, how many years have elapsed since he was born. But he has only the evidence of testimony to assure him that he was born in such and such a year; and equally he has only the evidence of testimony to assure him that this present year is 1967. How do I know, or what grounds have I for believing, that to-day is January 23, 1967? If it is a case of 'being sure and having the right to be sure', I have acquired this right by reading what is written on a calendar, or at the top of the front page of the newspaper which was delivered at my home this morning. I am often uncertain what day of the week it is. Is it Wednesday or Thursday? But in my ordinary unphilosophical moments, I assume that this question can be conclusively settled by consulting the appropriate written sources, such as to-day's newspaper.

Indeed, each of us depends on testimony for almost all that he claims to know about anything which is beyond the range of his own first-hand observation and memory; and one of the most important functions of memory itself is the remembering of what we have learned from other people by means of speech and writing.

This reliance on testimony plays a fundamental part not only in our cognitive lives, but in our practical lives as well. In very many of our practical undertakings we depend in one way or another on the spoken or written information we receive from others. To catch a train, I must rely on the information I receive from the timetable. To catch a bus, I must rely on the written words which I see on the front of it, e.g. the word 'Paddington', which is an abbreviation for 'This object goes to Paddington'. I find my way about the country by relying on the written testimony of sign-posts and milestones, and if I use a map instead, I am relying on testimony too. It could even be said that we are relying on testimony whenever we use a ruler or a tape-measure to measure the length of something, e.g. the testimony of the manufacturer that this stretch on the ruler's edge is 8½ inches long.

But now let us imagine a detached and very reasonable observer of the human scene, brought up on Locke's principle that one must never believe any proposition more firmly than the evidence warrants.[4] Would he not think that our ordinary attitude to testimony is absurdly credulous? Of course, no one believes everything that he is told, nor everything that he reads; still less does he always believe it with complete conviction. But in nine cases out of ten we do give at least some credence to what we are told or what we read. There is of course the tenth case. The answer to some very important question, practical or theoretical, may depend on the correctness of so-and-so's testimony. Then we shall be more cautious. Or the event which he describes to us may be very improbable in the light of all the other relevant evidence which we have, for example, if he tells us that a Flying Saucer landed in the University Parks half an hour ago. Or perhaps it may be very much in the testifier's own interest that we should believe him; for if we do, we shall give him the money for which he asks. Or again, we may have found on many previous occasions that he himself or others like him (beggars for example) made statements which turned out later to be false. Even so, we are usually prepared to give some weight to the testimony which is offered to us, and it only happens very seldom that we just reject it 'out of hand'. Even habitual liars and romancers tell the truth sometimes. Improbable events do happen. Even when it is to the speaker's own interest that his statement should be true, it does sometimes turn out to be true all the same.

The principle which we follow in the great majority of cases seems to be something like this: What there is said to be (or to have been) there is (or was) more often than not. And that is why our disinterested Lockean observer might think us absurdly credulous. I do not think we extend this principle to the future ('What there is said to be going to be, there will be, more often that not'). We are not quite as credulous as that. We all know how unreliable even our own first-hand predictions can be. But even though we limit our principle to testimony about the present and the past, what justification can we have for accepting it? Must we not admit that our ordinary attitude to testimony is indeed unreasonably credulous?

But suppose we adopted the incredulous or non-credulous attitude which our disinterested Lockean observer would presumably recommend.

[4] Locke's 'ethics of belief' will be discussed in Lecture 6. [H. H. Price, *Belief*. Eds.]

Let us try to imagine a society in which no one would ever accept another person's testimony about anything, until he had completely satisfied himself about the *bona fides* of that person, his powers of accurate observation and capacity for recalling accurately what he had observed. Such a society would hardly be a society at all. It would be something like the State of Nature described by Hobbes, in which the life of every man is solitary, poor, nasty, brutish and short. What our Lockean observer calls credulity is a necessary condition for social cooperation. What he calls credulity is not only in the long-term interest of each of us. It has a moral aspect too. If some people make a virtue of accepting testimony so readily, they are not wholly mistaken. Am I treating my neighbour as an end in himself, in the way I wish him to treat me, if I very carefully examine his credentials before believing anything he says to me? Surely every person, just because he is a person, has at least a *prima facie* claim to be believed when he makes a statement? This claim is not of course indefeasible. But it might well be argued that we have a duty to trust him unless or until we find pretty convincing reasons for mistrust, and even to give him 'the benefit of the doubt' if we have some reasons for mistrusting him, though not conclusive ones.

A CONFLICT BETWEEN CHARITY AND THE 'ETHICS OF BELIEF'

It is true that there may be something like a conflict of duties here, or at any rate a conflict between two kinds of precepts, those of what is called 'The Ethics of Belief' and precepts of the moral kind, especially the precepts of charity. A charitable person might feel bound to give his neighbours 'the benefit of the doubt' long after Locke's reasonable man had decided that their statements were not worthy of even the lowest degree of belief. Other conflicts within the sphere of charity itself may also arise. For if I believe *A*'s story about *B*'s behaviour yesterday (on the ground that *A* is a person as I am, and must be treated so) I may find that I am being uncharitable to *B* by believing too easily what *A* tells me about him.[5]

Perhaps some religious moralists may think that these conflicts are illusory. Does charity really require that one should shut one's eyes to the facts or the empirically-supported probabilities? If it is an 'unconditional pro-attitude' towards other people, the knowledge or reasonable

[5] The Christian virtue of humility poses similar problems (concerning a person's beliefs about himself) and perhaps they are more difficult ones.

belief that your neighbour's statements are false will do nothing to weaken it—not even if you think that he is trying his best to deceive you or mislead you. 'He is rather a liar, of course, and I can't believe a word of it, but he is a good fellow all the same.' If you are a charitable person, you are supposed to have a pro-attitude towards him as he is, faults and all ('What he is' of course includes his capacities for becoming better). Surely it is at least logically possible to be at once charitable and clear sighted about the defects, intellectual or moral, of one's neighbours?

This combination of qualities is indeed logically possible, and is even occasionally achieved in some very admirable persons. It may well be true that the conflicts we have mentioned arise only for those who are trying to be charitable without yet being so, or are trying to be less uncharitable than they have hitherto been. But unfortunately this is the position in which many of us are most of the time; and then, for us, there can quite well be a conflict between the precepts of charity and the precepts of the Ethics of Belief.

As has been pointed out already, the study of belief is one of the regions where epistemology and moral philosophy overlap. But epistemological questions are our main concern at present.

'ACCEPT WHAT YOU ARE TOLD, UNLESS YOU SEE REASON TO DOUBT IT'

Whatever degree of charity we have, be it great or little, our ordinary practice is to accept what we are told unless or until we see reason to doubt it. We do seem to follow the principle 'What there is said to be (or have been) there is (or was) more often than not'. There are of course certain special occasions when the principle is temporarily switched off as it were, or put into cold storage for a while. When someone says 'I am now going to tell you a story' he is warning us that what he is about to say is not to be taken as testimony. The principle 'What there is said to have been there was, more often that not' is to be ignored for the time being. A similar switching-off occurs when we begin to read a book which we have borrowed from the section marked 'Novels' in the library. The sentences uttered by characters in a play are not to be taken as testimony either, though many of them have the form of statements about empirical matters of fact, for instance, 'The wind bites shrewdly, it is very cold'. We are not to take this as a weather-report. But the important point to notice about these occasions is that they are special and exceptional ones. Special conventions and devices have to be used to convey to us that for the time being the principle we ordinarily follow is not to be applied. And that principle *is* something like 'What there is said to be, or to have have been, there is, or was, more often than not'.

To follow this principle may be socially expedient or even socially indispensable. It may be charitable too. But considered in a cool hour, in the way our detached Lockean observer would consider it, it is a very curious principle indeed. It is not even easy to decide what kind of a principle it is. We are at first inclined to suppose that it is itself a proposition which we believe, something which is itself either true or false. In that case, we cannot dispense ourselves from the task of asking what grounds we have for claiming that it is true, or at any rate more probable than not. Certainly it is neither self-evident nor demonstrable. It looks like an inductive generalisation. If that is what it is, no one of us is entitled to believe it unless he himself, by his own personal observation, has been able to verify at least some of the testimony which he has received from others.

Such first-hand verification is in a way a wasteful procedure. No one would wish to verify all the statements he hears or reads, even if he could. The whole point of testimony is that it is a substitute for first-hand experience, or an extension of first-hand experience, whereby each of us can make use of the experiences which other persons have had. When a piece of testimony is verified by our own first-hand experience, we no longer need it. I want you to tell me what happened on the other side of the hill because I was not able to go there and see for myself. I want Tacitus to tell me what happened in the reign of the Emperor Claudius because I was not alive at the time. The testimony which I cannot verify for myself is the testimony which I need to have. I might as well not have had it, if I can find out for myself that what you tell me is true. On the other hand, unless I can find out for myself that at least some of the things I am told are true, the testimony I receive is equally useless to me, because I have no ground for believing that any of them are true.

The reasonable plan might seem to be that each person should test for himself a not very large part (one tenth perhaps?) of all testimony he receives, thereby rendering that part useless as testimony; and then he would be able to estimate what degree of confidence, great or little, he is entitled to have concerning the remaining nine-tenths. He would sacrifice a little of it in order to be able to use the rest to supplement and extend his own very limited first-hand experience. At least, this would seem to be the reasonable plan if the principle we are discussing ('What there is said to be (or to have been) there is (or was) more often than not') is indeed an inductive generalization.

Now certainly each of us is sometimes able to 'check' the testimony which he receives from others. In a strange town I have often had to ask a passer-by where the nearest post office is, or where the railway station is; and usually (though by no means always) I have found for myself that the information given to me was correct.

But when we consider the enormous number and variety of the beliefs which each of us holds on the evidence of testimony alone, it is obvious that the amount of first-hand confirmation he has is tiny indeed in comparison. It is nothing like large enough to justify the generalisation 'what there is said to be, or have been, there is, or was, more often than not'. In a very simple and primitive society, where no one can read or write or listen to the radio, the situation would be easier. Then, if someone tells me that there was a wolf sitting beside the village well at midnight, I can go to the well myself this morning and see what looks like the footmarks of a wolf in the mud beside it. But in a civilised and highly-educated community it is another matter. We have only to consider the vast mass of historical propositions which every educated person believes. I can personally remember a few of the events that happened in the reign of King Edward VII. But I certainly cannot remember anything that happened in the reign of King Edward the Confessor, to say nothing of the reign of Hadrian or Septimius Severus. Yet I do very firmly believe that both these Emperors visited Britain, and that Septimius Severus died at York. I hold this belief on nothing but the evidence of testimony. The best I have managed to do by way of 'checking' the testimony for myself is to read the Latin text of what I am told is a copy of the *Historia Augusta;* and this hardly amounts to first-hand verification.

Suppose however that we re-stated our principle in a much weaker form: 'What there is said to be (or to have been) there is (or was) in at least one case out of every five.' This seems a very modest principle, even a rather sceptical one. But if it is supposed to be an inductive generalisation, the evidence which any one person has for believing it would still be quite insufficient. In a civilized and literate society, the amount of testimony which each of us has been able to test and verify for himself is far too small to justify any inductive estimate of the 'overall' reliability of testimony in general: too small, that is, in relation to the enormous number and variety of all the beliefs he has, which are supported partly or wholly by testimony spoken or written, or conveyed in other ways (for example, by means of maps). Whatever estimate any one person tried to make of its reliability, whether favourable or unfavourable, he would not have nearly enough first-hand evidence to justify it. Indeed, the habit of accepting testimony is so deep-rooted in all of us that we fail to realize how very limited the range of each person's first-hand observation and memory is.

'FIRST-HAND' AND 'SECOND-HAND'

Before we consider whether there is some other way of interpreting our principle, it may be worth while to say something about the contrast between 'first-hand' and 'second-hand'. We contrast the first-hand knowledge which each of us acquires by means of his own observation, introspection and memory with the second-hand knowledge (or beliefs) which he acquires by means of testimony. Yet it is important to notice that there is, after all, something first-hand about the acceptance of testimony itself. Testimony has to be conveyed to us by means of perceptible events or entities—audible or visible words, or sometimes visible signs or gestures; or occasionally by tangible means, as when we converse with a deaf and blind person by 'tapping out' words on his hand. And the person who accepts the testimony must perceive these perceptible events or entities for himself. Unless he has this first hand experience, he cannot accept the testimony, nor even reject it.

It is true of course that I may believe what John said although I did not hear him say it. But then some third person, Bill for instance, must tell me that John said so-and-so; and I must still hear for myself what Bill tells me, or see it for myself if he tells me in writing. How ever many hands or mouths John's story has passed through before it reaches me, it will not reach me at all unless there is some first hand perceptual experience of mine at the end.

The acceptance of testimony is first hand in another way as well. Testimony has to be understood by the person who receives it, and he must understand it for himself. No one else can understand it for him. If it is offered to him in a foreign language which he does not know, or in a technical terminology which he cannot follow, he may ask someone else to translate it or interpret it for him. But he still has to understand for himself what the translator or interpreter tells him.

Sometimes this second condition is fulfilled, but the first—the perceptual one—is not. This happens quite frequently in dreams. In our dream we may have copious and complicated mental imagery, either visual or auditory; quite a complicated story may be presented to our minds, and often we understand it perfectly. We do not just dream that we understand it. Dreaming that one understands what one does not in fact understand can also happen. But I wish to consider the case where we really do understand the words which present themselves to us in our dream—and surely it is not at all an uncommon case. Very often these words are combined into sentences which preport to describe some empirical matter of fact. Sometimes it is as if we just heard them without even seeming to see anyone who utters them.

These sentences, however, do not count as testimony, not even if they turn out subsequently to be true, as they may if the dream is a telepathic or clairvoyant one. They do not count as testimony, because the words composing them are not physical sounds or physical marks which we perceived. The first hand experience we had, when they presented themselves to us, was not an experience of perceiving, but of imaging, though we were not aware of this at the time.

Much the same could be said of waking hallucinations. Suppose you are a motorist trying to find your way to a village in a remote part of Norfolk. You have a visual hallucination of a signpost with the words 'Great Snoring 2½ miles' written on it. What is written on signposts is a form of testimony. But they have to be real physical signposts with real physical letters written on them. Hallucinatory words on an hallucinatory signpost do not count as testimony, though here again it is conceivable that these hallucinatory words do decribe what is actually the case. Perhaps you do turn down the little lane which appears to be indicated by the signpost there appears to you to be, and perhaps you do arrive at Great Snoring after 2½ miles. Students of paranormal cognition might then suggest that the visual hallucination was a paranormal experience, the manifestation in consciousness of an unconscious 'extra-sensory perception' of the whereabouts of the village. But whatever we think of this explanation, we can hardly say that you accepted (and acted upon) a piece of testimony, as you would have been doing if the signpost had been a real one, perceived in the normal manner.

The conclusion we must draw is that the testimony received by a particular person can never be more reliable than the first hand experience by means of which he receives it. To be sure, when I am delirious the doctor may tell me that the spoken or written sentences which I claim to hear or to see are not to be taken as testimony, and that I am not to believe them or be at all worried or frightened by them. But then he himself is giving me testimony about the non-testimonious character of these hallucinatory words. Perhaps I believe what he tells me. But I am not entitled to believe it, unless I am first entitled to believe that the sounds he appears to be uttering really are what they appear to be—events in the public and physical world. If I suspect that the words I seem to hear him utter are hallucinatory too, I must also suspect that they are not to be relied on. It comes to this: before I am entitled to believe what someone is saying, I must make sure that it is really being said; and before I am entitled to believe what I read I must make sure that the written words really are there on the page or the signposts or the noticeboard.

Furthermore, one is only entitled to rely on testimony if one understands it correctly. When an English traveller in Italy sees the word 'calda' written on a water-tap he may think it means 'cold' and act accordingly, with unfortunate results. There is nothing wrong with his perceptual capacities. He is not having a visual hallucination or illusion, and he is not dreaming. The word 'calda' is really there on the tap just as it appears to be. But he misunderstands the testimony which is offered to him, and is therefore mistaken when he relies on it. Moreover, the understanding which is required may have to be something more than the mere 'dictionary-knowledge' which would have been quite sufficient in this example. One may need to be able to 'interpret' what is said or written. If the caller is told at the door that Mrs So-and-so is not at home, he may misinterpret what is said to him, and believe mistakenly that the lady is not in the house, though he understands the dictionary-meaning of the words perfectly well. The testimony which we accept can never be more reliable than our own capacity for understanding the words (or signs or gestures) by means of which it is conveyed to us.

If we prefer to put it so, our lack of understanding may prevent us from discovering what the testimony conveyed to us actually is, and what we believe will then be something different from what the speaker or writer was telling us. Viewed in this way, our lack of understanding has the same kind of results as an illusion or hallucination might have. If an Italian were to have an hallucination of the word 'fredda' when he looked at the water-tap, the results for him would be much the same as they were for our English traveller, who thought that 'calda' meant cold.

If we accept a proposition p on the evidence of testimony, this evidence can never be stronger than our evidence for believing (1) that certain words have in fact been spoken or written (2) that p is in fact the proposition which these words convey. And our evidence for these two beliefs has to be first-hand. Each of us must hear or see for himself, and no-one else can do it for him; and each of us must understand for himself if he understands at all. It is true that someone else may have to explain to me what a particular word or sentence means. But I still have to understand this explanation for myself.

No doubt these considerations are perfectly obvious. It is surely undeniable that there is something first hand about the acquisition of any belief whatever, whether it is based on testimony or not. But we tend to forget this, if we lay great emphasis on the concepts of public verifiability and public knowledge. We speak as though there were some formidable entity called 'the public' (or perhaps we call it 'Science' with a capital S). But there is no such entity, and if there were it could not know anything or verify anything. There are only human beings who co-operate with one another. One very important way in which they do it is by giving each other testimony. I tell other persons that I have verified a proposition *p*, and they tell me that they have verified it too. But each of us has to do his verifying for himself at first hand, however important it is for each of us to learn that others have done it.

What has now been pointed out is that there is also something first hand about this 'learning that others have done it', since each of us must hear or see for himself what others say or write, and each must understand for himself what they are telling him.

ANOTHER INTERPRETATION OF THE PRINCIPLE

We may now return to the principle 'What there is said to be (or to have been) there is (or was) more often than not'. Hitherto we have assumed that this principle is itself something which we believe; and if we interpret it in that way, we shall have to suppose that we believe it very firmly, perhaps even with complete conviction. At any rate, each one of us seems to be guided by it all the time. Of course, we do not believe that what there is said to be or to have been, there *always* is or was; still less do we believe this with complete conviction. The qualification 'more often than not' is an essential part of the principle itself. But even though this qualification is put in and borne in mind, it is difficult to see how such a belief could be reasonable. This is because the degree of our belief (if it is indeed belief) would still be far greater than our evidence justifies.

When we consider the vast amount of testimony which each of us accepts, especially if he is a civilized and educated person, we find that each of us is only able to verify a very small part of it by means of his own first-hand observation and memory. Perhaps there might be enough first-hand verification to justify him in suspecting or surmising that what there is said to be or have been there is, or was, more often than not. ('Suspecting' and 'surmising' are traditional names for the lowest possible degree of belief.) But any higher degree of belief than this would surely be too high, and could not be justified by the amount of first-hand confirmation each of us can get for the vast mass of statements, on all manner of subjects, which he hears or reads. Even if someone were to say 'I think, without being at all sure, that what there is said to be (or to have been) there is (or was) more often than not'—expressing a not very confident opinion—he would still be unreasonably credulous. Credulity may be socially expedient, even socially indispensable, and it may be charitable. But it is credulity still.

There is however another way of interpreting the principle we are discussing. Perhaps it is not itself a proposition which we believe, still less a proposition believed with complete conviction. Instead, it may be more like a maxim or a methodological rule. In that case, it is better formulated in the imperative than the indicative mood. We might put it this way: 'Believe what you are told by others unless or until you have reasons for doubting it.' Or we might say 'Conduct your thoughts and your actions as if what there is said to be (or to have been) there is (or was) more often than not'. If this is what our principle is, we no longer have to ask what evidence there is for believing it, because it is not itself something believed. It does of course concern believing, and could be described as a policy for forming beliefs. But a policy is not itself believable, since it is not itself either true or false. We could perhaps say that we believe 'in' it, in the sense in which some people believe in Classical Education and others believe in taking a cold bath every morning before breakfast. But believing in a policy or procedure is very different from believing that something is the case.

All the same, the adoption of a policy does have to be justified. We cannot ask what evidence there is for it (since it is not something which is either true or false). But we can ask what reasons there are for adopting it; or if it never was consciously adopted, we can ask what reasons there are for retaining it, once we have reflected on it and have noticed what sort of a policy it is. And there are in fact pretty cogent reasons for adopting, or retaining, this particular policy. They are economic reasons (in rather a broad sense of the term) because they are concerned with the intelligent use of scarce resources.

From one point of view, the scarcity from which each of us suffers is a scarcity of first-hand observations, or more generally of first-hand experiences. One of our misfortunes is that no human being is ubiquitous. If I am in Oxford at 10 a.m. this morning, I cannot directly observe what is going on in Newcastle at that time. Indeed, as I sit here looking out of the window, I cannot directly observe what is going on behind the thick screen of thornbushes ten yards away. Still less are we 'ubiquitous in time', if such a phrase is allowable. Each of us has some first-hand access to the past by means of his own memories. But the span of time which they cover is very limited. I certainly cannot remember the Norman Conquest, nor even what happened in the year 1890. Moreover, the past which each of us remembers is only his own past, what he himself perceived or felt or did on various past occasions, and what he then came to believe or came to know. He does not even remember the whole of his past, in the sense of being able to recall any part of it he pleases, though it is possible that in some subconscious or unconscious way he 'retains' a good deal more of it than he can now recall. And in the past which he is able to recall, he suffered from the same scarcity of first-hand observations as he does now. He cannot recollect even one occasion when he was able to see through a brick wall, or touch something from a distance of two hundred yards.

But 'scarce' is of course a relative term. After all, each one of us has had a good many first-hand experiences, and goes on having them all the time so long as he is alive and awake. If we call them 'scarce', we must have some good or end in mind, and we are pointing out that no one individual has enough of them to enable him to achieve it. What is this good or end? It is knowledge, which is something we desire for its own sake, and also as a means for achieving other goods which we desire.

To put it in another way, there are many questions which each of us desires to settle or to answer; and no one person has anything like enough first-hand evidence to enable him to settle more than a very few of them. Each of us would like to know what happened before he was born, and what is happening now on the other side of the wall. His own first-hand observations and his own first-hand memories will not enable him to answer these questions. If he cannot *know* the answers to them, he would still like to be able to hold the most reasonable beliefs that he can, on the best evidence he can get. And very often indeed the only evidence he can get is the evidence of testimony. He must either accept what others tell him, for what it may be worth; or else he must remain in a state of suspended judgement, unable to find any answer at all to many of the questions which he desires to answer.

The economic aspect of this situation comes out in another way when we notice that there is an *exchange* of testimony between different individuals. I have some information which you need but do not at present possess, and you have some which I need but do not at present possess. I tell you what I have observed and you have not; and you tell me what you have observed and I have not. This exchange is advantageous to both of us. Though both of us suffer from a deficiency of first-hand knowledge, I can do something to remedy your deficiency and you can do something to remedy mine. But in a way this is something better than an exchange. For I do not lose the information which I give you, as I should if I gave you my hat; and you do not lose the information which you give me in return, as you would if you gave me your umbrella. Both of us gain and neither of us loses.

As has been mentioned already, this exchange of testimony has a moral aspect too. The information you give me will be useless to me, or worse than useless, unless you give it honestly. And if I trust you to give it honestly, you too must be honest in giving your information to me. One way of formulating the policy we are discussing is 'Accept what you are told by others unless or until you have specific reasons for doubting it'; and this is closely related to the moral rule 'Trust your neighbour unless or until you have specific reasons for distrusting him'. Prudence and charity go hand in hand here. Or at least they go hand in hand some of the way, though a seeker after knowledge would probably stop giving his neighbour 'the benefit of the doubt' rather sooner than charity would recommend.

But at present it is the prudential or economic aspect of this exchange of testimony which mainly concerns us. The moral aspect of it is only relevant in so far as the policy we are considering will not in fact succeed, unless there is at least a modicum of honesty and mutual trust among those who practise it. In a community of incorrigible liars or incurable romancers, the exchange of testimony would not help very much to solve the problem which arises from the scarcity of each person's first-hand experiences. And the testimony of incurable theorisers, who cannot report an observed fact without putting their own interpretation on it, would not be much better. Our policy will work best in a community of honest and hard-headed empiricists who have a respect for facts and for one another. It must also be assumed, I think, that the majority of the persons from whom one receives testimony are sane or in their right minds, and are usually capable of distinguishing between hallucinations and normal perceptions. Finally, most testimony (though not all) is given 'after the event', perhaps a long time after. The recipient is then at the mercy of any defects there may be, whether of omission or commission,[6] in the memory of the testifier. So each of us has to assume that the memories of most other persons are not very defective in either of these ways.

We have been discussing a policy for forming beliefs. It is designed to remedy a certain sort of scarcity from which each individual person suffers, a scarcity of first-hand experiences. This policy may be formulated in two ways: (1) 'Accept what you are told, unless or until you have specific reasons for doubting it' (2) 'Conduct your thoughts and actions as if it were true that what there is said to be (or to have been), there is (or was) more often than not'.

Whichever formulation we prefer, we now see that a number of conditions must be fulfilled if this policy is to succeed. It is logically possible that none of them ever are fulfilled, and it is pretty certain that not all of them are always fulfilled in fact. There are incorrigible liars, romancers and theorisers. There are careless observations, defective memories, and hallucinations or dreams mistaken for normal perceptions.

It may well seem that if 'safety first' is one's motto, the wisest course would be not to accept testimony at all. The policy of accepting it, unless or until one has specific reasons for doubting it, is likely to yield a pretty

[6] Cf. Lecture 4, pp. 106–7 above. [pp. 95–111, this volume. Eds.]

mixed bag of beliefs, in which there will be many incorrect ones. It is likely that there will also be a good many others which will be inaccurate, correct in some respects but incorrect in others. You tell me that an airship is coming over. I believe you, and rush out into the garden to enjoy this unusual spectacle. There is indeed a lighter-than-air aircraft in the sky, but it is only a kite-ballon which has come adrift. Moreover there may in fact be specific reasons for doubting someone's testimony (for example, he has very poor eyesight, or he has a habit of telling others what they want to hear, whether it is true or not). But we may not know that he has these defects, nor have any evidence for believing that he has them. The policy we are considering does not say 'Accept what others say unless or until there are specific reasons for doubting it', and would be useless to us if it did. Instead, it says 'unless or until *you have* specific reasons for doubting' or 'unless you and them'. We may very well fail to find them, although they do exist.

But 'safety first' is not a good motto, however tempting it may be to some philosophers. The end we seek to achieve is to acquire as many correct beliefs as possible on as many subjects as possible. No one of us is likely to achieve this end if he resolves to reject the evidence of testimony, and contents himself with what he can know, or have reason to believe, on the evidence of his own first-hand experience alone. It cannot be denied that if someone follows the policy of accepting the testimony of others unless or until he has specific reason for doubting it, the results will not be all that he might wish. Some of the beliefs which he will thereby acquire will be totally incorrect, and others partly incorrect. In this sense, the policy is certainly a risky one. If we prefer the other formulation 'Conduct your thoughts and actions as if it were true that what there is said to be or to have been, there is or was, more often than not' we still have to admit that the policy is a risky one, and it would still be risky if we substituted 'in one case out of every three' for 'more often than not'.

But it is reasonable to take this risk, and unreasonable not to take it. If we refuse to take it, we have no prospect of getting answers, not even the most tentative ones, for many of the questions which interest us (for example 'What is the population of London?' 'Did London exist 300 years ago?' 'If it did, what was its population then?').

It must be admitted, of course, that many of these questions could not even be asked unless some testimony had already been accepted. The stay-at-home inhabitant of Little Puddlecombe has only the evidence of testimony for believing that there is such a place as London at all. And if he is a safety-first philosopher, whose policy it is to reject the evidence of testimony, or to ignore it on the ground that it is so unreliable, he does not even know, or has no ground for thinking, that there *is* the question 'what is the population of London?' and therefore cannot even wish to know the answer to it. Similarly, I could not even wish to know more about the character of the Emperor Severus Alexander unless I already believed that there was such a person; and for this belief I have only the evidence of written testimony. If I were to reject that evidence, I could not even ask what kind of a person he was.

So if anyone refused to follow the policy we are recommending, and preferred the contrary policy of rejecting all testimony unless and until he had conclusive reasons for accepting it, this would certainly save him a great deal of trouble. There would be very many questions about which he would not have to worry himself, because he would not be able to consider them at all. On the other hand, we might be inclined to think that he was rather less than human. He cannot value knowledge very highly, if he does not even attempt to get it when there is a risk that his attempt will fail. He rejects the policy we are recommending because he does not really care very much for the end which it is designed to achieve. He prefers to cultivate his own garden, and a very, very small garden it will be.

In our cognitive enterprises, as in some of our practical ones, 'nothing venture, nothing have' is a better motto than 'safety first'. But it is only better as a means. If you do not want to have, there is no reason why you should venture.

C. I. Lewis

The Bases of Empirical Knowledge

1. If the conclusions of the preceding discussion are to be accepted, then all knowledge has an eventual empirical significance in that all which is knowable or even significantly thinkable must have reference to meanings which are sense-representable. But this conception that even what is analytically true and knowable *a priori* is to be assured by reference to sense meanings, does not, of course, abrogate the distinction between what may be known independently of given data of sense and that which cannot be so known. Analytic statements assert some relation of meanings amongst themselves: non-analytic statements require relation of a meaning to what is found on particular occasions of experience. It is the latter class alone which may express empirical knowledge. They coincide with those the falsity of which is antecedently thinkable.

Empirical truth cannot be known except, finally, through presentations of sense. Most affirmations of empirical knowledge are to be justified, proximately, by others already accepted or believed: such justification involves a step or steps depending on logical truth. The

C. I. Lewis, "The Bases of Empirical Knowledge," in *An Analysis of Knowledge and Valuation* (La Salle, Illinois: Open Court Publishing Company, 1946), pp. 171–202. Reprinted by permission of the Open Court Publishing Company, La Salle, Illinois.

classification as empirical will still be correct, however, if amongst such statements required to support the one in question, either deductively or inductively, there are some which cannot be assured by logic or analysis of meaning but only by reference to the content of given experience. Our empirical knowledge rises as a structure of enormous complexity, most parts of which are stabilized in measure by their mutual support, but all of which rest, at bottom, on direct findings of sense. Unless there should be some statements, or rather something apprehensible and statable, whose truth is determined by given experience and is not determinable in any other way, there would be no non-analytic affirmation whose truth could be determined at all, and no such thing as empirical knowledge. But also there could be no empirical knowledge if there were not meanings capable of being entertained without dependence on particular occasions. No experience or set of experiences will determine truth of a statement or a belief unless, prior to such experience, we know what we mean; know what experiences will corroborate our affirmation or supposition and what experiences will discredit it. Apprehension of the criteria by which what we intend may be recognized, must be antecedent to any verification or disproof.

We shall find, however, that most empirical statements—all those ordinarily made, in fact—are such that no single experience could decisively prove them true; and it can be doubted that any experience would conclusively prove them false. We *do* entertain assertable meanings of a sort which *can* be decisively determined to hold or not to hold; but statements having that kind of significance are not usually expressed, both because there is seldom occasion to express them and because there is no language in which they can be easily expressed without ambiguity. It is items which belong somewhere in the upper stories of our structure of empirical beliefs which can be clearly put: it is those which are at or near the bottom, required to support the whole edifice, which there is difficulty to state without implying what does not genuinely belong to the import of them. Thus the analysis of an ordinary empirical judgment such as might indicate the foundations of it in given experience, encounters a difficulty which is primarily one of formulation. The reason for this is something which must be understood and appreciated at the start, if we are not to fall into some kind of misconception which would be fatal for the understanding of empirical knowledge in general.

2. Let us turn to the simplest kind of empirical cognition; knowledge by direct perception. And let us take two examples.

I am descending the steps of Emerson Hall, and using my eyes to guide my feet. This is a habitual and ordinarily automatic action. But for this occasion, and in order that it may clearly constitute an instance of perceptual cognition instead of unconsidered behavior, I put enough attention on the process to bring the major features of it to clear consciousness. There is a certain visual pattern presented to me, a feeling of pressure on the soles of my feet, and certain muscle-sensations and feelings of balance and motion. And these items mentioned are fused together with others in one moving whole of presentation, within which they can be genuinely elicited but in which they do not exist as separate. Much of this presented content, I should find it difficult to put in words. I should find it difficult because, for one reason, if I tried to express it precisely in objectively intelligible fashion, I should have to specify such items as particular muscles which are involved and the behavior of them, and other things of this kind; and I do not in fact know which muscles I am using and just how. But one does not have to study physiology in order to walk down stairs. I know by my feelings when I am walking erect—or I think I do. And you, by putting yourself in my place, know how I feel—or think you do. That is all that is necessary, because we are here speaking of direct experience. You will follow me through the example by using your imagination, and understand what I mean—or what *you* would mean by the same language—in terms of your own experience.

The experience I have as I approach the steps and look down is familiar: it is qualitatively specific, and undoubtedly supplies the clues on which I act. For example, if I had approached the steps with eyes shut, I should have been obliged to behave quite differently in order to avoid falling. Let us single out the visual part of the presentation for particular consideration. Ordinarily I have no occasion to express empirical content of this sort: it performs its office of guiding my behavior and thereupon lapses from consciousness. But if I attempt to express it, I might say: "I see what looks like a flight of granite steps, fifteen inches wide and seven inches deep, in front of me." The locution 'looks like' represents my attempt to signalize the fact that I do not mean to assert that the steps *are* granite, or have the dimensions mentioned, or even that in point of absolutely certain fact there are any steps at all. Language is largely pre-empted to the assertion of objective realities and events. If I wish, as I now do, to confine it to expression of a presented content, my best recourse is, very likely, to express what I take to be the objective facts this presentation signalizes and use locutions such as 'looks like', 'tastes like', 'feels like', or some other contextual cue, to mark the intention on this occasion to restrict what I say to the fact of presentation itself as contrasted with the objective state of affairs more usually signified by the rest of my statement.

This given presentation—what looks like a flight of granite steps before me—leads to a prediction: "If I step forward and down, I shall come safely to rest on the step below." Ordinarily this prediction is unexpressed and would not even be explicitly thought. When so formulated, it is altogether too pedantic and portentous to fit the simple forward-looking quality of my conscious attitude. But unless I were prepared to assent to it, in case my attention were drawn to the matter, I should not now proceed as I do. Here again, the language I use would ordinarily be meant to express an objective process involving my body and a physical environment. But for the present occasion, I am trying to express the direct and indubitable content of my experience only, and, particularly, to elicit exemplary items which mark this conscious procedure as cognitive. As I stand momentarily poised and looking before me, the presented visual pattern leads me to predict that acting in a certain manner—stepping forward and down—will be followed by a further empirical content, equally specific and recognizable but equally difficult to express without suggesting more than I now mean—the felt experience of coming to balance on the step below.

I adopt the mode of action envisaged; and the expected empirical sequent actually follows. My prediction is verified. The cognitive significance of the visual presentation which operated as cue, is found valid. This functioning of it was a genuine case of perceptual knowledge.

Let us take another different example; different not in any important character of the situation involved, but different in the manner in which we shall consider it.

I believe there is a piece of white paper now before me. The reason that I believe this is that I see it: a certain visual presentation is given. But my belief includes the expectation that so long as I continue to look in the same direction, this presentation, with its qualitative character essentially unchanged, will persist; that if I move my eyes right, it will be displaced to the left in the visual field; that if I close them, it will disappear; and so on. If any of these predictions should, upon trial, be disproved, I should abandon my present belief in a real piece of paper before me, in favor of belief in some extraordinary after-image or some puzzling reflection or some disconcerting hallucination.

I do look in the same direction for a time; then turn my eyes; and after that try closing them: all with the expected results. My belief is so far corroborated. And these corroborations give me even greater assurance in any further predictions based upon it. But theoretically and ideally it is not completely verified, because the belief in a real piece of white paper now before me has further implications not yet tested: that what I see could be folded without cracking, as a piece of celluloid could not; that it would tear easily, as architect's drawing-cloth would not; that this experience will not be followed by waking in quite different surroundings; and others too numerous to mention. If it is a real piece of paper before me now, then I shall expect to find it here tomorrow with the number I just put on the corner: its reality and real character I attribute in my belief imply innumerable possible verifications, or partial verifications, tomorrow and later on.

But looking back over what I have just written, I observe that I have succumbed to precisely those difficulties of formulation which have been mentioned. I have here spoken of predictable results of further tests I am not now making; of folding the paper and trying to tear it, and so on. Finding these predictions borne out would, in each case, be only a partial test, theoretically, of my belief in a real piece of paper. But it was my intention to mention predictions which, though only partial verification of the objective fact I believe in, could themselves be decisively tested. And there I have failed. That the paper, upon trial, would really be torn, will no more be evidenced with perfect certainty than is the presence of real paper before me now. It— provided it take place—will be a real objective event about which, theoretically, my momentary experience could deceive me. What I meant to speak of was certain expected experiences—of the *appearance and feeling* of paper being folded; of its *seeming* to be torn. These predictions of *experience,* would be decisively and indubitably borne out or disproved if I make trial of them. Both on this point, the reader will most likely have caught my intent and improved upon my statement as made.

3. Let us return to the point we were discussing. We had just noted that even if the mentioned tests of the empirical belief about the paper should have been made, the result would not be a theoretically complete verification of it because there would be further and similar implications of the belief which would still not have been tested. In the case of an important piece of paper like a deed or a will, or an important issue like the question whether "Midsummer Night's Dream" was written by Shakespere or by Bacon, such implications might be subject to test years or even centuries afterward. And a negative result might then rationally lead to doubt that a particular piece of paper lay on a certain desk at a certain time. My present example is no different except in importance: what I now believe has consequences which will be determinable indefinitely in the future.

Further, my belief must extend to any predictions such that I should accept the failure of them as disproof of the belief, however far in the future the time may be which they concern. And my belief must imply as probable, anything the failure of which I should accept as tending to discredit this belief.

Also it is the case that such future contingencies, implied by the belief, are not such that failure of them can be absolutely precluded in the light of prior empirical corroborations of what is believed. However improbable, it remains thinkable that such later tests could have a negative result. Though truth of the belief itself implies a positive result of such later tests, the evidence to date does not imply this as more than probable, even though the difference of this probability from theoretical certainty should be so slight that practically it would be foolish to hesitate over it. Indeed we could be too deprecatory about this difference: if we interrogate experience we shall find plenty of occasions when we have felt quite sure of an objective fact perceived but later circumstance has shocked us out of our assurance and obliged us to retract or modify our belief.

If now we ask ourselves how extensive such implied consequences of the belief are, it seems clear that in so simple a case as the white paper supposedly now before me, the number of them is inexhaustible. For one thing, they presumably will never come to an end in point of time: there will never be a time when the fact—or non-fact—of this piece of paper now lying on my desk will not make some trivial difference. If that were not the case, then it must be that at some future date it will become not only practically but theoretically impossible that there should be a scintilla of evidence either for or against this supposed present fact. It would not be possible for anyone even to think of something which, if it should then occur, would be such evidence. That even the least important of real events will thus make no conceivable difference after a certain time, is not plausible. If that should be so, then what belongs to the past, beyond a certain stretch, could be something worse than an unknowable thing in itself; it could be such that the very supposition of it could make no conceivable difference to anyone's rational behavior; and any alleged interest in its truth or falsity could be shown to be fictitious or pointless, or to be confined to having others assert or assent to a certain form of words. In that sense, this belief would then become meaningless, having no conceivable consequence of its truth or falsity which would be testable or bear upon any rational interest.

It will be well for the reader to come to his own clear decision on this question; whether it is or is not the case that the truth of an objective empirical belief has consequences which are inexhaustible and are such that there is no limited number of them whose determination theoretically and absolutely precludes a negative result of further tests and hence *deductively* implies all further and as yet untested consequences. It will be well to become thus clear because this point has decisive consequences for the nature of empirical knowledge. Also these consequences are disconcerting: those who are more interested in pretty theories than in facts will be sure to repudiate this conception, whether they acknowledge such repudiation or merely pass this point without making any uncomfortable admissions.

In fact, one objection to this conception is likely to occur to us promptly. It will strike us as dubious that we can believe, all in a minute, something whose consequences—which by implication we must also be believing—are not finitely enumerable. But that objection is not one which offers serious difficulty: what it reflects is principally a necessary comment on 'believing' and 'knowing'; and it cannot be more implausible than that we can know anything at all. This difficulty concerns the sense in which the 'consequences' of a belief—those statements whose proven falsity would discredit it—are 'included in' the belief. A little reflection will remind us that *every* proposition has innumerable consequences, deducible from it by laws of logic: or if that fact has escaped us, the logicians can easily make it clear, by providing us with formulas by which we can, from any given premise you please, deduce different conclusions without limit, so long as we can think of new terms to write in certain places in these formulas. The kind of deducible consequences of a proposition which such formulas would give are not entirely comparable to the kind we are here thinking of: the nature of the kind of consequences here in question will call for further examination; and other important questions are suggested, though we would best not pause upon them here. But on the point at issue, the comparison holds: it cannot be doubted that belief in *any* proposition commits us to innumerable consequences, disproof of any one of which would require rationally that the belief be retracted, whether we explicitly think of these consequences in believing what implies them or not. And surely, what is supposed to be or asserted to be empirical fact, cannot be supposed or asserted irrespective of what would, at some future time, be evidence concerning it, and irrespective of further possible tests the failure of which would discredit our supposition or assertion. The fact that such consequences of what we affirm are inexhaustibly numerous, cannot stand as a valid objection to this conception.

4. Let us now give attention to our two examples, and especially to the different manner in which the two have been considered. Both represent cases of knowledge by perception. And in both, while the sensory cues to this knowledge are provided by the given presentation, the cognitive significance is seen to lie not in the mere givenness of these sensory cues but in prediction based upon them. In both cases, it is such prediction the verification of which would mark the judgment made as true or as false.

In the first case, of using my eyes to guide me down the steps, the prediction made was a single one. Or if more than one was made, the others would presumably be like the one considered and this was taken as exemplary. This judgment is of the form, "If I act in manner *A*, the empirical eventuation will include *E*." We found difficulty in expressing, in language which would not say more than was intended, the content of the presentation which functioned as sensory cue. We encountered the same difficulty in expressing the mode of action, *A*, as we envisaged it in terms of our own felt experience and as we should recognize it, when performed, as the act we intended. And again this difficulty attended our attempt to express that expected presentational eventuality, *E*, the accrual of which was anticipated in our prediction.

As we considered this first example, the attempt was to portray it as a case in which a directly apprehensible presentation of a recognizable sort functioned as cue to a single prediction; the prediction that a certain directly recognizable act would lead to a particular and directly recognizable result. If we are to describe this cognitive situation truly, all three of these elements—the presentation, the envisaged action, and the expected consequence—must be described in language which will denote immediately presented or directly presentable contents of experience. We attempted to make clear this intent of the language used by locutions such as 'looks like', 'feels like'; thus restricting it to what would fall completely within the passage of experience in question and what this passage of experience could completely and directly determine as true. For example, if I should say, "There is a flight of granite steps before me," I should not merely report my experience but assert what it would require a great deal of further experience to corroborate fully. Indeed, it is questionable whether any amount of further experience could put this assertion theoretically beyond all possibility of a rational doubt. But when I say, "I see what *looks like* granite steps before me," I restrict myself to what is given; and what I intend by this language is something of which I can have no possible doubt. And the only possible doubt *you* could have of it—since it concerns a present experience of mine—is a doubt whether you grasp correctly what I intend to report, or a doubt whether I am telling the truth or a lie.

This use of language to formulate a directly presented or presentable content of experience, may be called its *expressive* use. This is in contrast to that more common intent of language, exemplified by, "I see (what in fact *is*) a flight of granite steps before me," which may be called its *objective* use. The distinctive character of expressive language, or the expressive use of language, is that such language signifies *appearances.* And in thus referring to appearances, or affirming what appears, such expressive language *neither asserts any objective reality of what appears nor denies any.* It is confined to description of the content of presentation itself.

In such expressive language, the cognitive judgment, "If I act in manner *A*, the empirical eventuality will include *E*," is one which can be verified by putting it to the test—supposing I can in fact put it to the test; can act in manner *A*. When the hypothesis of this hypothetical judgment is made true by my volition, the consequent is found true or found false by what follows; and this verification is decisive and complete, because nothing beyond the content of this passage of experience was implied in the judgment.

In the second example, as we considered it, what was judged was an *objective fact*: "A piece of white paper is now before me." This judgment will be false if the presentation is illusory; it will be false if what I see is not really paper; false if it is not really white but only looks white. This objective judgment also is one capable of corroboration. As in the other example, so here too, any test of the judgment would pretty surely involve some way of acting—*making* the test, as by continuing to look, or turning my eyes, or grasping to tear, etc.—and would be determined by finding or failing to find some expected result in experience. But in this example, if the result of any single test is as expected, it constitutes a partial verification of the judgment only; never one which is absolutely decisive and theoretically complete. This is so because, while the judgment, so far as it is significant, contains nothing which could not be tested, still it has a significance which outruns what any single test, or any limited set of tests, could exhaust. No matter how fully I may have investigated this objective fact, there will remain some theoretical possibility of mistake; there will be further consequences which must be thus and so if the judgment is true, and not all of these will have been determined. The possibility that such further tests, if made, might have a negative result, cannot be altogether precluded; and this possibility marks the judgment as, at the time in question, not fully verified and less than absolutely certain. To quibble about such possible doubts will not, in most cases, be common sense. But we are not trying to weigh the degree of theoretical dubiety which common-sense practicality should take account of, but to arrive at an accurate analysis of knowledge. This character of being further testable and less than theoretically certain characterizes every judgment of objective fact at all times; every judgment that such and such a real thing exists or has a certain objectively factual property, or that a certain objective event actually occurs, or that any objective state of affairs actually is the case.

A judgment of the type of the first example— prediction of a particular passage of experience, describable in expressive language—may be called *terminating*. It admits of decisive and complete verification or falsification. One of the type of the second example—judgment of objective fact which is always further verifiable and never completely verified—may be called *non-terminating*.

However, if the suggested account should be correct, then the judgment of objective fact implies nothing which is not theoretically verifiable. And since any, even partial, verification could be made only by something disclosed in *some* passage of experience, such an objective and non-terminating judgment must be translatable into judgments of the terminating kind. Only so could confirmation of it in experience come about. If particular experiences should not serve as its corroborations, then it cannot be confirmed at all; experience in general would be irrelevant to its truth or falsity; and it must be either analytic or meaningless. Its non-terminating character reflects the fact, not that the statement implies anything which is not expressible in some terminating judgment or other, but that no limited set of such terminating judgments could be sufficient to exhaust its empirical significance.

To be sure, the sense of 'verifiable' which is appropriate to the principle that a statement of supposed objective fact which should not be verifiable would be meaningless, is one which will call for further consideration. 'Verifiable', like most 'able' words, is a highly ambiguous term, connoting conditions which are implied but unexpressed. For example, the sense in which it is verifiable that there are lines on the other side of this paper, is somewhat different from the sense in which it is verifiable that there are mountains on the other side of the moon. But such various senses in which 'verifiable' may be taken, concern the sense in which the verifying experience is 'possible'; not the character of the experience which would constitute verification. And in general we may safely say that for *any* sense in which statement of objective fact is 'meaningful', there is a coordinate and indicated sense in which it is 'verifiable'.

It may also be the case that, for some judgments at least—those called 'practically certain'—a degree of verification may be attained such that no later confirmation can render what is presently judged more certain than it is at the moment. That turns on considerations which we are not yet ready to examine. But as will appear, these postponed considerations further corroborate, instead of casting doubt upon, the conclusion that no objective statement is theoretically and completely certain. For that conclusion—which is the present point—the grounds mentioned would seem to be sufficient.

5. The conception is, thus, that there are three classes of empirical statements. First, there are formulations of what is presently given in experience. Only infrequently are such statements of the given actually made: there is seldom need to formulate what is directly and indubitably presented. They are also difficult or—it might plausibly be said—impossible to state in ordinary language, which, as usually understood, carries implications of something more and further verifiable which *ipso facto* is not given. But this difficulty of formulating precisely and only a given content of experience, is a relatively inessential consideration for the analysis of knowledge. That which we should thus attempt to formulate plays the same role whether it is expressed, or could be precisely ex-

pressed, or not. Without such apprehensions of direct and indubitable content of experience, there could be no basis for any empirical judgment, and no verification of one.

To this there is no alternative. Even if one should wish to suppose that *all* empirical statements are affected by uncertainty; one could not—short of an absurd kind of skepticism—suppose them all to be doubtful in the same degree that they would be if there were no experience. And if there are some empirical statements not thus utterly doubtful, then there must be something which imparts to them this status of better-than-utterly-doubtful. And that something must be an apprehended fact, or facts, of experience. If facts of this order should not be clearly expressible in language, they would still be the absolutely essential bases of all empirical knowledge.

Those thinkers who approach all problems of analysis from the point of view of language, have raised numerous difficulties over this conception of the empirically given. We shall not pause to clear away all the irrelevant issues with which the point has thus been surrounded. That point is simply that there is such a thing as experience, the content of which we do not invent and cannot have as we will but merely find. And that this given is an element in perception but not the whole of perceptual cognition. Subtract, in what we say that we see, or hear, or otherwise learn from direct experience, *all that conceivably could be mistaken;* the remainder is the given content of the experience inducing this belief. If there were no such hard kernel in experience—e.g., what we *see* when we think we see a deer but there is no deer—then the word 'experience' would have nothing to refer to.

It is essential to remember that in the statement or formulation of what is given (if such formulation be attempted), one uses language to *convey* this content, but what is *asserted* is what the language is intended to convey, not the correctness of the language used. If, for example, one say, "I see a red round something," one assumes but does *not* assert, "The words 'red' and 'round' correctly apply to something now given." This last is not a given fact of present experience but a generalization from the past experience indicating the customary use of English words. But one does not have to know English in order to see red; and that the word 'red' applies to this presently given appearance, is not a fact given in that experience.

Knowledge itself might well get on without the formulation of the immediately given: what is thus directly presented does not require verbalization. But the *discussion* of knowledge hardly can, since it must be able somehow to refer to such basic factualities of experience. If there should be no understood linguistic mode of telling what is given, the analysis of knowledge would have to invent one, if only by arbitrary figure of speech. But our situation is hardly so bad as that: such formulations can be made, in a manner the intent of which, at least, is recognizable by what we have called the expressive use of language, in which its reference is restricted to appearances—to what is given, as such.

Apprehensions of the given which such expressive statements formulate, are not judgments; and they are not here classed as knowledge, because they are not subject to any possible error. Statement of such apprehension is, however, true or false: there could be no doubt about the presented content of experience as such at the time when it is given, but it would be possible to tell lies about it.[1]

Second, there are terminating judgments, and statements of them. These represent some prediction of further possible experience. They find their cue in what is given: but what they state is something taken to be verifiable by some test which involves a way of acting. Thus terminating judgments are, in general, of the form, "If *A* then *E*," or "*S* being given, if *A* then *E*," where *'A'* represents some mode of action taken to be possible, *'E'* some expected consequent in experience, and *'S'* the sensory cue. The hypothesis *'A'* must here express something which, if made true by adopted action, will be *indubitably* true, and not, like a condition of my musculature in relation to the environment, an objective state of affairs only partially verified and not completely certain at the time. And the consequent *'E'* represents an eventuality of *experience,* directly and certainly recognizable in case it accrues; not a resultant objective event, whose factuality could have, and would call for, further verification. Thus both antecedent and consequent of this judgment, "If *A* then *E*," require to be formulated in expressive language; though we shall not call it an expressive statement, reserving that phrase for formulations of the given. Also, unlike statements of the given, what such terminating judgments express is to be classed as knowledge: the prediction in question calls for verification, and is subject to possible error.

Third, there are non-terminating judgments which assert objective

[1] It would be possible to take statements of the given as involving judgment of correspondence between the character of the given itself and a fixed (expressive) meaning of words. But a judgment, "What is given is what '————' expresses" is not expression of the given but a relation between it and a certain form of words. There is such a 'judgment of formulation' in the case of *any* statable fact. Let *'P'* be an empirical statement which says nothing about language. "This fact is correctly stated by *'P'* " is then a different statement, stating a relation between the fact which *'P'* asserts and the verbal formulation *'P.'* Correlatively, it is always possible to make a mistake of formulation, even where there could be no possible error concerning what is formulated. (In Book I, where we were frequently concerned with matters of logic, we used small letters, *p, q,* etc., to represent statements, following the current logical usage. But from this point on, it will make for easier reading if we represent statements by capital letters, *P, Q,* etc.)

reality; some state of affairs as actual. These are so named because, while there is nothing in the import of such objective statements which is intrinsically unverifiable, and hence nothing included in them which is not expressible by some terminating judgment, nevertheless no limited set of particular predictions of empirical eventualities can completely exhaust the significance of such an objective statement. This is true of the simplest and most trivial, as much as of the most important. The statement that something is blue, for example, or is square—as contrasted with merely looking blue or appearing to be square—has, always, implications of further possible experience, beyond what should, at any particular time, have been found true. Theoretically complete and absolute verification of any objective judgment would be a never-ending task: any actual verification of them is no more than partial; and our assurance of them is always, theoretically, less than certain.

Non-terminating judgments represent an enormous class; they include, in fact, pretty much all the empirical statements we habitually make. They range in type from the simplest assertion of perceived fact—"There is a piece of white paper now before me"—to the most impressive of scientific generalizations—"The universe is expanding." In general, the more important an assertion of empirical objective fact, the more remote it is from its eventual grounds. The laws of science, for example, are arrived at by induction from inductions from inductions - - -. But objective judgments are all alike in being non-terminating, and in having no other eventual foundation that data of given experience.

6. The point of distinguishing expressive statements of given data of experience from predictive and verifiable statements of terminating judgments, and both of them from statements of objective fact, representing non-terminating judgments, is that without such distinctions it is almost impossible so to analyze empirical knowledge as to discover the grounds of it in experience, and the manner of its derivation from such grounds.

All empirical knowledge rests ultimately upon this kind of evidence and calls for the corroboration constituted by the facts of presentation. The cue to any statement of perceived actuality is in such presentation; and if there is to be any further confirmation of such statement, that can come about only through some further presentation. But unless the fact of presentation itself be distinguished from the objective fact it is cue to or corroborates, we shall never be able to understand or formulate the manner in which objective belief receives its warrant, or to explain how a belief which has some justification may nevertheless prove later to have been mistaken.

One says, for example, "I see a sheet of white paper," "I hear a bell," "I smell honeysuckle." Some datum of sense gives rise to the belief expressed. But what is believed does not coincide with the fact of sense: the belief expressed may be mistaken and the experience, as we say, 'illusory'; whereas the actual character of the given datum as such, is indubitable. If the belief expressed is corroborated by further investigation, there will be, again, data of sense. But these additional and corroborating data will not be the totality of the objective fact believed in and corroborated; and expression of the verifying event of experience will not coincide with expression of this objective fact.

Again; if the statement of objective fact, in whatever degree it may have become already assured, is further significant—if it implies what could be further and empirically determined but is not strictly deducible from past and present findings—then always it signifies something verifiable but as yet unverified, and is, in corresponding measure, itself subject to some theoretical uncertainty. We have concluded that all statements of objective fact do have this character. That conclusion being premised, it becomes essential to distinguish statements of the given and presently certain, as well as statements of terminating judgments which later experience may render certain, from such statements of objective fact. Otherwise it becomes impossible to assure objective truth as even probable. If what is to confirm the objective belief and thus show it probable, were itself an objective belief and hence no more than probable, then the objective belief to be confirmed would only probably be rendered probable. Thus unless we distinguish the objective truths belief in which experience may render probable, from those presentations and passages of experience which provide this warrant, any citation of evidence for a statement about objective reality, and any mentionable corroboration of it, will become involved in an indefinite regress of the merely probable —or else it will go round in a circle—and the probability will fail to be genuine. If anything is to be probable, then something must be certain. The data which eventually support a genuine probability, must themselves be certainties. We do have such absolute certainties, in the sense data initiating belief and in those passages of experience which later may confirm it. But neither such initial data nor such later verifying passages of experience can be phrased in the language of objective statement— because what can be so phrased is never more than probable. Our sense certainties can only be formulated by the expressive use of language, in which what is signified is a content of experience and what is asserted is the givenness of this content.

It is not, of course, intended to deny here that one objective statement can be confirmed by others; or to maintain that all corroborations of belief are by direct reference to immediate experience. Some objective beliefs are deductivly derivable from others; and many—or even most—

objective beliefs are inductively supported by other, and perhaps better substantiated, objective beliefs. It is only contended that in such cases where one objective belief is corroborated or supported by another, (1) such confirmation is only provisional or hypothetical, and (2) it must have reference *eventually* to confirmations by direct experience, which alone is capable of being decisive and providing any sure foundation. If one objective statement, '*Q*', is supported by another objective statement, '*P*', the assurance of the truth of '*Q*' is, so far, only as good as the evidence for '*P*'. Eventually such evidence must go back to something which is certain—or, as we have said, go round in a circle and so fail of any genuine basis whatever. Two propositions which have some *antecedent* probability may, under certain circumstances, become *more* credible because of their congruence with one another. But objective judgments *none* of which could acquire probability by direct confirmations in experience, would gain no support by leaning up against one another in the fashion of the 'coherence theory of truth'. No empirical statement can become credible without a reference to experience.

That we may have before us some presentation whose character as given we can be sure of, and that at the same time we know, through or by means of this presentation, some objective thing or event, is not here denied but affirmed. What is immediate and certain, however, is not the objective thing, even, or state of affairs which is known, but the content of experience which evidences it—as having some probability, which may be 'practical certainty'.[2] That the content of any such belief

[2] This statement has no implication of a dualistic or phenomenalistic interpretation of the relation of mind to reality in cognition. It is still possible, in terms of the conception here presented, to affirm that the content of presentation is an authentic part or aspect or perspective which is ingredient in the objective reality known. Such language is figurative, when measured against the ordinary meaning of 'part' or the ordinary meaning of 'ingredients' of objective things. But the view thus figuratively expressed may be consistently and literally correct provided one is prepared to accept the implications that an elliptical appearance may be genuine ingredient of a real round penny, the bent stick in the water an ingredient of the really straight stick, and one's nightmare an ingredient of mince pie for supper. The hiatus implied, in the view here presented, between immediate sense presentation and objective reality thus evidenced, is not the denial that the content of presentation may be 'numerically identical' with a part or aspect of the objective reality, but the denial that it is ever the whole of the objective reality believed in, or that it is ever unambiguously decisive of the statement of an objective property or existence of a specific objective thing or event. The kind of 'ingredients' which the sense-presented always are, can be 'ingredient' in such very different things and objective states of affairs! On the other hand, there is no implication here that the stuff of physical things is mind-stuff; or that both mind and matter are constituted out of neutral stuff. There is no implication at all on this metaphysical point.

is, at least theoretically, completely verifiable in experience, is also affirmed. But such *complete* verification of the belief, is at no time wholly given.

7. Perceptual knowledge has two aspects or phases; the giveness of something given, and the interpretation which, in the light of past experience, we put upon it. In the case of perceiving the white paper, what is given is a certain complex of sensa or qualia—what Santayana calls an 'essence'.[3] This is describable in expressive language by the use of adjectives of color, shape, size, and so on. If our apprehension ended with this, however, there would be no knowledge here; the presentation would *mean* nothing to us. A mind without past experience would have no knowledge by means of it: for such a mind the apprehension would be exhausted in mere receptivity of presentation, because no interpretation would be suggested or imposed.

If anyone choose to extend the word 'knowledge' to such immediate apprehensions of sense—and many do, in fact—there is no fault to be found with that usage. Such apprehensions of the given are characterized by certainty, even though what it is that we are thus certain of, is something difficult of clear and precise expression when separated from the interpretation put upon it. And without such sense-certainties, there could be no perceptual knowledge, nor any empirical knowledge at all. We have chosen not to use the word 'knowledge' in this way: and if it be given this broader meaning which would include apprehension of the immediate, it must then be remembered that one cannot, at the same time, require that knowledge in general shall possess a signification of something beyond the cognitive experience itself or that it should stand in contrast with some possible kind of error or mistake. Apprehension of the given, by itself, will meet neither of these requirements.

It is the interpretation put upon this presentation which constitutes belief in or assertion of some objective fact. This interpretation is imposed in the light of past experience. Because I have dealt with writing paper before, this presently given white oblong something leads me to believe there is a sheet of white paper before me. This interpretation is, in some measure, verified by the fact of the presentation itself: my belief has some degree of credibility merely because this presentation is given—a degree of credibility commensurate with the *im*probability of exactly such presentation as this if there were *not* a piece of white paper before me. For the rest, my belief is significant of other experience, taken to be in some sense possible, but not now given. This significance ascribed to the fact of the presentation and expressed by statement of the belief aroused, is equivalent to what *would be* accepted as complete verification

3 Though it would appear that Santayana calls some other things essences also.

of it. The *practical* possibility of such envisaged verification, or of any part of it, would not be here in point: it is the meaning which is here in question. When I entertain this interpretation of the given experience, this belief in objective fact, I must know what I thus mean in terms of experience I can envisage, if the meaning is genuine. Otherwise the truth of it would not be even theoretically determinable.

To construe this interpretation of the given experience—this belief in objective fact which it arouses—as verifiable and as something whose significance can be envisaged in terms of possible confirmations of it, is what dictates that the statement of this objective belief must be translatable into terms of passages of possible experience, each of which would constitute some partial verification of it; that is, it must be translatable into the predictive statements of terminating judgments. If we include the whole scope of the objective statement believed, endlessly many such predictions will be contained in its significance. This is correlative to the fact that, no matter to what extent the objective belief should have been, at any time, already verified, the truth of it will still make some difference to further possible experience; and correlative to the further fact that, at any moment, the truth of this objective assertion is something which I might now proceed to confirm in more than one way. That test of it which I choose to make, does not negate or extrude from the objective intent of the belief, what has reference to *other* possible confirmations which I choose *not* to put to the test. Thus it is not possible to make all possible confirmations of an objective belief or statement, and complete the verification of it. (Which is no more a contradiction than is the fact that one can never finish counting all the numbers that can be counted.)

The fact that both the meaning and the verification of empirical belief concern the predictions of further possible experience which the truth of it implies, makes the terminating judgments into which it is thus translatable centrally important for understanding the nature of empirical knowledge. We turn to that topic in the next chapter. The remainder of the present chapter will be occupied with certain further small matters which concern the conception of the meaning of objective empirical statements which the above account implies.

8. This conception that a statement of objective empirical fact is translatable into some set of predictive statements each of which formulates some possible confirmation in direct experience, the whole set of such statements being inexhaustible in number, will be sure to seem puzzling in certain ways and to suggest certain objections. Most of these questions which will arise are such as could not be answered satisfactorily here without anticipating much of what is to follow; and when the discussion of later chapters is before us, the answer to be given will be—we

hope—sufficiently clear. But it seems well to take preliminary notice of them here.

In the first place, the statement that the cognitive meaning of an objective statement is correlative with that of some set of predictive statements, each representing a theoretically possible confirmation, is not quite accurate. As has been indicated, the present sensory cue in given experience is already a partial verification and certainly has its place in the cognitive significance of the belief aroused. Amendment to include this should be understood. As has been pointed out, the givenness of present data may constitute a partial verification which renders the belief it arouses highly probable, since any datum of fact, *D*, justifies judgment that '*P*' is probable, in whatever degree *D* itself would be *im*probable if '*P*' should be false. My experience at this moment, for example, justifies my belief in a piece of white paper before me as probable in the degree in which it is improbable that I should have just this present given content of experience if there were *not* such a piece of paper here. And that, I may say, amounts to practical certainty. It is not strictly the present data of sense, all by themselves, which warrant this assurance: an infant seeing what I now see, would not believe what I believe or find my belief justifiable to him if he could understand it and assess it reasonably. It is my data of sense together with certain further beliefs, of which I feel assured, which are in point—that is a complication which must later engage us. But perhaps this notice of the significance of presently given experience in the verification of belief aroused, will be sufficient to remove one possible misunderstanding which might impede us.

Another possible point of difficulty concerns the interminable character of complete verification. It is difficult to deny that verification of objective fact is thus interminable, in view of the consideration that every objective fact has at all times some further empirical significance and later verifiability: the reader will, we hope, feel the weight of that consideration without additional discussion. But if the difficulty should be that where complete verification is interminable, we can never *come any nearer* to complete assurance of what we believe, and verification seems thus to fall into a situation affected by Zeno's paradoxes, then that difficulty can be removed. The interminability of verification—supposing that at *no* point it will become the situation that all further possible confirmations are *deducible* from the fact of those already made—does genuinely make it impossible to raise the probability of the objective belief to be verified to theoretical certainty. But it does not prevent new confirmations from increasing the antecedent probability. Unless skepticism is the only possible outcome of a just examination of empirical knowledge—and nothing here justifiably suggests that—it must be the case that every new confirmation of an objective belief (unless this new confirmation should be *deductively* and certainly predictable from past ones) must increase the antecedent probability of what is believed; and by the same token must increase the antecedent probability of each and every further possible but as yet untested confirmation of it.[4] Thus although the probability of empirical belief can never reach theoretical certainty, there is nothing in the present conception which denies the possibility of its being increased indefinitely, and nothing *a priori* incompatible with its being increased to any degree whatever, short of certainty.

Perhaps it is another sort of difficulty, however, which occurs to us; it strikes us as fantastic that the meaning of an objective statement should consist in an unlimited number of predictions of possible future confirmations (together with what is presently given). This kind of possible objection has a number of different aspects.

For one, it concerns the possible logical equivalance of a verbally simple objective statement such as "There is a piece of white paper now before me" with an unlimited set of predictions of its possible confirmations. The reader will already have observed that, however surprising it may be that a simple statement '*P*' should be equivalent to an unlimited set of other statements, there is no difficulty about that beyond the difficulty that such an unlimited set of statements cannot be conjointly stated. As has been noted, every statement, '*P*', has an unlimited number of implications, 'Q_1', 'Q_2', 'Q_3', ... And there will hardly be objection to the supposition that there is nothing in the meaning of a statement beyond what is contained in some implication of it.

The reader will already have observed a connection between what was said about sense meaning in Book I and the present analysis of empirical objective statements. And perhaps he is puzzled to determine whether that earlier account and the one here given are compatible. We there defined sense meaning as the criterion in terms of sense by which the application of expressions is determined. And we indicated, by a forward reference, the necessity of further consideration of the question whether the application of a meaning would be determinable with theoretical certainty. But we did not observe the reason for such possible doubt. As we now see, the sense meaning of assertion that a thing is square or white or hard, must be in terms of the terminating judgments

[4] The principle governing such increase of antecedent probability by additional confirmations, is the general principle of 'inverse probability', already alluded to: after confirming events V_1, V_2 . . V_n, a new confirmation, $V_n + _1$, increases the probability of '*P*' in measure as event $V_n + _1$, was antecedently improbable if V_1, V_2, . . V_n be the case but '*P*' be false.

implied in attribution of these properties. It is only such terminating judgments which express the meaning of objective attributions directly in terms of sense. And by the same token, a sense meaning must have a kind of complexity not previously noted. The criterion of objective squareness, for example, cannot be expressed as a criterion of sense determination by specification of a single test which could be carried out with completely decisive results. Because no actual test would be thus theoretically decisive. Rather, a sense meaning is a criterion of possible *confirmations,* and would be exhibited *in extenso* by the totality of terminating judgments implied or included in objective attribution of the property or character to be tested.

However, this fact that a sense meaning represents a criterion of confirmations and not of any decisive verification which is possible, does not prejudice the possibility of comparing sense meanings amongst themselves with a result which is decisive. (It was this which was in point in Book I.) It is still possible in these terms to compare, for example, square and rectangle, or square and round, with results which will be certain; because while we cannot perhaps determine beyond peradventure that a thing is absolutely square or is rectangular, we can nevertheless determine *a priori* that *if* it is square it is rectangular. We can determine this through comparison of these sense meanings as criteria of confirmation: through observing that whatever confirms squareness must *ipso facto* confirm rectangularity in like degree; and that what disconfirms rectangularity must in like measure disconfirm squareness. Similarly we may observe from inspection of the criteria of possible confirmations, that whatever confirms the applicability of 'square' will disconfirm the applicability of 'round'; and hence determine *a priori* that nothing can be both square and round.

There are further complicating considerations which must later be remarked. But already we may observe that the set of possible confirmations, verification of which would together constitute verification of an objective statement, also exhibit discursively the sense meaning which this objective empirical statement has. Perhaps that is as clear a way as any of indicating what the phrase 'sense meaning' would signify, as applied to a statement of objective empirical fact: the sense meaning of such a statement coincides with what it would mean, in terms of experience, to determine fully that it is true. This will very likely be met by the objection that in such terms the meaning of any objective statement could not be specified: exhaustive recital of all that the truth of it would imply in terms of possible experience cannot finitely be accomplished. But is not that exactly the fact? I cannot tell you precisely and completely and in all detail what it signifies that there is a piece of white paper on this desk. Yet if I did not know what that means, in just those terms, I could not find out whether it is the case—could not verify it. I can tell you this 'well enough' for all practical purposes; can indicate a few critical tests whose positive result would suffice for practical certainty. But if one substitute this limited 'practical' significance for the full force and import of the objective belief, even the practical mind will soon point out the inadequacy of such a 'practical' delimitation of an objective empirical meaning. It would be quite plausible to say that all the remote and exquisite consequences which would 'theoretically' be involved are never really included in what one means to affirm in making ordinary empirical judgments. So be it. Our ordinary meanings are more or less rough and ready, and correspondingly limited in their actually implied and testable consequences. Thus—it may be—they are finitely statable in terms of sense verification. But where, then, do such 'practical' meanings leave off? They leave off in their significance precisely at that point at which we can say, "Beyond this, nothing that experience can present to us could make any difference to the truth of what we *mean.*" When that can truly be said, such limitation of meaning is genuinely to be accepted. But clearly one sets such a limit to empirical meanings at some risk: statements for which this would be possible are 'rough and ready', 'inexact', 'slipshod', as measured against what may at any moment and in some connection be demanded of statement of objective empirical fact. Clearly we should do ill to take *all* objective statements as of such limited meaning: an adequate account of empirical knowledge must at least leave room for meaning beyond any particular such limitation that could be set. If acceptance of meanings as in sense terms not exhaustively statable, is uncomfortable, it would seems to be a discomfort we shall do best to put up with. The alternative likewise is uncomfortable and, as a generalization, would seem to have the further defect of being false.

However, if it appears to constitute a difficulty that, as here conceived, what an objective statement means in terms of experience is not finitely statable, then let us not forget that "There is a piece of white paper here on my desk" precisely is the required verbally simple way of stating all these interminable consequences of it in terms of sense. This statement, in relation to explication of its sense meaning, in terms of all the terminating judgments it implies, is like a universal proposition in relation to all the particulars of fact it subsumes; like, for example, the statement "All men have noses" in relation to "Socrates had a nose, and Plato had a nose, and this man has a nose, and that man has a nose—and I can't tell you how many other men have lived or are alive or will live, but each of them severally has a nose." (Or like "All the natural numbers can be counted" in relation to "1 can be counted; 2 can be counted; 3 can be counted; . . .") When I say "All men have noses," I *mean* something about each and every particular man; and I know that now, and know what I mean about each. That I can't tell it to you, naming each, should not be thought a difficulty: I tell it to you in saying "All men have noses." And when I tell you (or myself) "There is a piece of white paper here on my desk," I tell more detailed consequences, testable in possible confirming experience, than I could recite exhaustively, or explicitly remind myself of, one after another; particularly because most, or perhaps all, of them depend on *conditions* of verification which it is a trouble to think of. But I now mean all of them by my statement; and if conditions should arise making test of any one of them the practically indicated test of what I say, then I could explicitly remind myself of it—if genuinely it is contained in what I now mean to assert. The answer to the difficulty would appear to be that it is not a difficulty but a fact. That seems to be the kind of empirical meanings which we entertain, and we seem to have the kind of minds capable of entertaining them.

If there is a moral to be drawn, perhaps it is that we would best not confuse the analysis of meaning with formal logical analysis. The implication, by a statement of objective fact, of the terminating judgments which represent its particular possible confirmations, is not a formal implication (in the old fashioned sense of 'formal'), which can be derived by rules of logic. Rather it is like the implication of "Today is Friday" by "Yesterday was Thursday," or the implications which one might discover through consulting a dictionary—implications which can only be determined by *knowing a meaning* and which, without that, cannot be discovered by any application merely of logical rules.

9. Another kind of objection which we might encounter, and which would relate to the same question whether the statement of objective fact is non-terminating in its testable consequences, is one which could be raised by reference to the operational conception of meaning. That conception may appear to explicate meaning in terms of verification, but of a verification which can be decisive and complete. On examination, however, this difference from the present view will turn out to be unreal, or else of doubtful validity. If the operationist, for example, defines "A has hardness m" by "If a certain pointed instrument falls on A from height h, it will make a dent of depth n," this does not indicate that the test consequences in experience which would establish the objective fact tested are a single one, or even finitely recitable.

In the first place, though hardness m is here defined by a 'standard test', it is *not* defined by anything which a single *trial* will establish with theoretical finality. This test itself, as stated, is in terms of other objective facts—that the test instrument is in proper working order and the depth to which it penetrates the material tested is really so and so. Such defining test operations are carefully regulated so as to be determinable as easily and as surely as possible in a single trial. But no physicist will maintain that any observer's single test observation of the test conditions and test result is theoretically beyond all question as determination of the objective fact tested. The 'standard test' must also, in order to define satisfactorily what is in question, be an operation which is repeatable. And if repetition gives a different result, then the earlier determination will be subject to revision. It is not theoretically certain as a result determined by one trial. Thus if an operational definition be expressed, not in terms of test results as objective fact, but of test results *observed,* any such result of a single test is not decisive verification but merely a confirmation —though perhaps sufficient, in many cases, for 'practical certainty'.

In the second place, even if the objective property be 'defined' by test operations of a certain kind, this property will have *other implications,* and hence other *confirmations* than those mentioned in its operational definition. For example, the test of hardness mentioned would have implication of the behavior of the material tested under many other conditions than the test conditions. And if that were not the case, this definitive test of it would be a relatively useless one to perform. The operationist merely picks out a kind of test the result of which is relatively simple to determine with a high degree of assurance and *is widely indicative of other testable consequences* which as a scientist, he demands of what has the property tested. The operationist merely selects, with some degree of arbitrariness, a certain *objective* test result, and says that *that alone* is what he will mean by, for example, 'hardness *m*'. But as a matter of fact he doesn't mean that *only* by predication of the objective property tested. He is merely cutting the Gordian knot of a difficult problem of meaning by a little harmless dogmatism.

Thus when the operational conception of meaning is examined with care, it may be seen to have no different consequences, which can be made to stand up, from the view we present.

10. A different kind of objection which has been raised against views like the one here put forward, is that interpretation of objective statements as meaning what would verify them does violence to our knowledge of the past. By depicting the meaning of "Caesar died" as consisting in what would verify it to us in future possible experience, this conception may be charged with translating what is past into something which is exclusively future. The force of this objection is something which will be felt as obvious. But just what this obvious point is, it is a matter of some difficulty to elicit. In fact, the one who raises it lays himself open to equally 'obvious' objections. Does he wish to maintain that what is really essential in past fact is independent of all

possible verification? If so, what is his, or anybody's, interest in knowing it? Is it merely sentimental attachment to an indeterminable property of a thing in itself?

The real point of the objection is the patent one, nevertheless. It is felt to be an unacceptable paradox that what "Caesar died" means, should be interpreted in terms of what you and I might find by initiating a historical investigation, because when we say "Caesar died" we are pointing back to an irrecoverable past event. The past just can't be identified with the present or future, or with anything that anybody can any longer experience. But one who advances such an interpretation of empirical meaning as is here put forward will not—if he knows what he is about—have any such intention. The trouble is that the objector—quite naturally, perhaps—understands us to be affirming that the past event of Caesar's death really is something belonging, in piecemeal fashion, to future time, as certain events of verification. But we intend no such patent absurdity: we are speaking of meaning in the sense of intension, for which two empirical statements have the same meaning if each is deducible from the other. For example, if anyone asks us, "What does it mean that it was Monday yesterday?", we might reply, "It means that it will be Wednesday tomorrow." That would not be a good explanation of meaning because it would be unlikely to clarify anything not already understood: those who fail to understand the statement "Yesterday was Monday" are not any more likely to grasp what is meant by "Tomorrow will be Wednesday." Nevertheless it would meet the requirement that the statement offered as explanatory genuinely has the same intensional meaning as the one to be explained. And one who thus said that "It was Monday yesterday" and "It will be Wednesday tomorrow" have the same meaning—have the same logical consequences and are each deducible from the other—would not be asserting that yesterday is tomorrow or Monday is the same day as Wednesday or that the event of yesterday's falling on a Monday is the same event as tomorrow's falling on a Wednesday.

There is really more to this kind of objection than meets the eye; and further examination of it will reveal that several different issues are involved at one and the same time. Some of these only are well illustrated by the example offered above. But first let us confine attention to those for which it will be sufficient.

It is conceivable that there might be objection to presuming that "Yesterday was Monday" and "Tomorrow will be Wednesday" are genuinely equivalent in meaning. But if so, then the points which could be in question have already been discussed in Book I. Either of them is deducible from the other. For a deduction by formal rules of logic, definitions of 'Monday' and 'Wednesday', 'yesterday' and 'tomorrow' would be requisite; but these definitions will be granted, and also they would be explicative statements which, as analytic, are implicitly given when any premise like "Yesterday was Monday" is assumed.

Since each of these statements is thus deducible from the other and they have the same intensional meaning, they have also the same meaning in every mode of meaning except that of analytic meaning. With respect to analytic meaning, however, they are different. The one of them speaks of yesterday as subject and asserts that it is a member of the class of Mondays; the other speaks of tomorrow and asserts that it is a member of the class of Wednesdays; and the constituents 'yesterday' and 'Monday' in the one of them find no equivalent in the other. It is this sense of analytic meaning that they refer to different things or events: the one of them refers to yesterday and the other to tomorrow, but taken as whole statements each of them asserts, by implication, the truth of the other also.

Since they have the same logical consequences and the same intension, they must also signify the *same state of affairs.* And it is here, perhaps, that what strikes the objector as unacceptable begins to appear. He will, perhaps, demur that yesterday being Monday is *not* the same fact or event as tomorrow being Wednesday. But we have already granted everything which that objection could be intended to assert without falling into errors which are demonstrable. Yesterday isn't tomorrow and a Monday isn't a Wednesday; and we have identified the sense in which "Yesterday was Monday" speaks of something to which "Tomorrow will be Wednesday" does not refer. But either of these two statements does refer to what the other refers to in the sense of implying whatever the other implies. Each of them thus signifies the *same state of affairs*: what either of them requires to be the case in order to be true is exactly and completely the same as what the other requires to be the case; anything which decisively verified the one would decisively verify the other, and whatever confirms the one must in equal measure confirm the other also. But we have also pointed out that the state of affairs signified by a statement is not an event in the sense of a space-time slab or chunk of reality. In so identifying the state of affairs asserted by a statement with an event, in the sense of such a space-time slab, one would commit what Whitehead has called the fallacy of simple location.

In terms of these conceptions, it would seem that we can express the only point which any objector could consistently have in mind in saying, for example, that yesterday being Monday is not the same event as tomorrow being Wednesday, and that one who translated the past event of yesterday being Monday into terms of the future event of tomorrow being Wedneseday would be doing violence to something or other. The space-time slab or chunk of reality correctly denoted by 'yesterday' and by 'Monday' is not the same chunk of reality denoted by 'tomorrow' and 'Wednesday'. But the objector will have to grant that any verification or confirmation of tomorrow being Wednesday is an equal verification or confirmation of yesterday being Monday; and that whoever knows beyond peradventure that tomorrow will be Wednesday can fail to know that yesterday was Monday only by failing to observe something which what he believes commits him to and implies. If he still feels that there is some further kind of fact not here noted with respect to which this kind of analysis is defective, it would appear in order to ask that he elicit the remaining issue and characterize the alleged defect more sharply than seems as yet to have been done.

It is an important consideration with respect to empirical knowledge that *no* theoretically sufficient verification of any past fact can ever be hoped for. In that respect our example above—or our discussion of it—fails to bring out a point which is pertinent. Not only is the past event of Caesar's death a different chunk of reality from any space-time slab belonging to the future, but nothing that any human knower can ever determine in future with theoretical certainty will be quite equivalent to the fact that Caesar died at a certain past time. In saying that "Caesar died (at such and such a time)" means what would verify it, we also recognize that possession of such theoretically sufficient knowledge is as impossible as it is to turn time backward and find ourselves presented in experience with the occurrence of Caesar's death. The 'equation' of past fact with possible verification, or 'translation' of the one into terms of the other expresses a limit or ideal of empirical knowledge which never can be fully realized.

11. It is much the same issues which are involved in another kind of criticism often made of the view of empirical knowledge here advanced; the charge, namely, that it is subjectivistic or phenomenalistic.[5] And it is to be feared that those who hold a pragmatic or 'verification' conception of meaning have never adequately explained why this particular criticism leaves them unmoved—though they would not admit to an idealistic metaphysics. To those who raise this objection, the present view appears to belong to the same family with Berkeleian empiricism, which might be thought of as asserting that the fact or event of there being a tree out there before me means that I have a certain content of perception now in my mind. Any account of knowledge which seems to say that what a certain believed-in state of affairs *means* is such and such *in terms of experience,* strikes these objectors as being subjectivistic. It

[5] This objection has been urged by R. W. Sellars, *The Philosophy of Physical Realism,* pp. 145 *ff.* See also, J. B. Pratt, "Logical Positivism and Professor Lewis," *Journal of Philosophy,* vol. XXXI, p. 701.

would be thus subjectivistic if the sense of meaning in question were that of identifying the content of experience which evidences what is believed with the existence and character of the external reality of which it is accepted as being evidence. And the objection fails of its point precisely because *no* such sense of meaning as that is here intended.

Berkeley was an idealist because he *did* intend what may be suggested by saying, " 'There is a tree out there' refers to the same event or chunk of reality as does the statement 'I have a percept of a tree'." If he had intended to assert only that the existence of the tree was inferable from the occurrence of the percept; and the occurrence of the percept under certain conditions from the fact of the tree; and hence that there was an equivalence of intension between the two kinds of statement; then he would not have committed himself—so far—to either idealism or realism. That would have remained another question, over and above his empiricistic account of knowledge. To be sure, Berkeley fails to do justice to the further point which we have observed—that no single experience of sense can be adequate to insure beyond possible doubt an objective existence believed in on the basis of it. The possibility of illusion and of mistakes of perception is, by itself, sufficient to preclude the genuine equivalence of intensional meaning between two statements "I have such and such a given content of perception" and "The objective facts of reality are so and so." But passing this point, it should be observed that two statements may have such equivalence of intension though the terms in which they are expressed my have quite different reference. The equivalence asserted is simply that of consequences implied. And if it were true—as it is not—that "I have such and such a percept" is a sufficient premise for exactly the same inferences as "So and so objectively exists," there would still be no implication whatever, contained in that fact, that what 'percept of a tree' denotes is the same thing which is denoted by 'tree'—any more than the logical equivalence of "Yesterday was Monday" with "Tomorrow will be Wednesday" implies identity of the existent or event named by 'yesterday' with that named by 'tomorrow'. Such equivalence of intension, and hence coincidence of what may verify or confirm one statement with what will verify or confirm another, argues no identity whatever between items mentioned in the one and in the other affirmation, These may be as various and incomparable in other respects as the quite different kinds of events in which we may nevertheless find evidence of the same fact or from which we may draw the same conclusion.

There are serious difficulties which the kind of analysis of empirical knowledge here advanced will have to meet, if it can. But the objections mentioned above are not of them, because such objections spring from erroneous assumption that logical equivalence of statements argues existential identity of things referred to in them, and that what evidences an objective reality or verifies it must somehow be included in a metaphysical nature of it. As we shall see in the next chapter, the conceptions here put forward do not fail to have a bearing on the metaphysical question of realism versus idealism. But these critics have mislocated the issues which are most pertinent.

Norman Malcolm

The Verification Argument

1

A number of arguments have been used by various philosophers to prove that the truth of no empirical statement is absolutely certain. In this paper I wish to examine *one* of these arguments. The argument has, to the best of my knowledge, been stated more forcefully by C. I. Lewis than by any other writer. I will quote from him in order to obtain a strong presentation of the argument.

While engaged in discussing the statement "A piece of white paper is now before me," Lewis says the following:

> This judgment will be false if the presentation is illusory; it will be false if what I see is not really paper; false if it is not really white but only looks white. This objective judgment also is one capable of corroboration. As in the other example [the other example, to which Lewis refers, is the statement "There is a flight of granite steps before me"], so here too, any test of the judgment would pretty surely involve some way of acting—*making* the test, as by continuing to look, or turning my eyes, or grasping to tear, etc.—and would be determined by finding or failing

Norman Malcolm, "The Verification Argument," in *Philosophical Analysis,* ed. Max Black (Englewood Cliffs, N.J.: Prentice-Hall, Inc., 1950). Reprinted by permission.

to find some expected result in experience. But in this example, if the result of any single test is as expected, it constitutes a partial verification of the judgment only; never one which is absolutely decisive and theoretically complete. This is so because, while the judgment, so far as it is significant, contains nothing which could not be tested, still it has a significance which outruns what any single test, or any limited set of tests, could exhaust. No matter how fully I may have investigated this objective fact, there will remain some theoretical possibility of mistake; there will be further consequences which must be thus and so if the judgment is true, and not all of these will have been determined. The possibility that such further tests, if made, might have a negative result, cannot be altogether precluded; and this possibility marks the judgment as, at the time in question, not fully verified and less than absolutely certain. To quibble about such possible doubts will not, in most cases, be common-sense. But we are not trying to weigh the degree of theoretical dubiety which common-sense practicality should take account of, but to arrive at an accurate analysis of knowledge. This character of being further testable and less than theoretically certain characterizes every judgment of objective fact at all times; every judgment that such and such a real thing exists or has a certain objectively factual property, or that a certain objective event actually occurs, or that any objective state of affairs actually is the case.[1]

The same argument is stated more dramatically by Lewis in *Mind and the World Order*. He says:

Obviously in the statement "This penny is round" I assert implicitly *everything the failure of which would falsify the statement.* The implicit prediction of *all* experience which is essential to its *truth* must be contained in the original judgment. Otherwise, such experience would be irrelevant. All that further experience the failure of which would lead to the repudiation of the apprehension as illusory or mistaken is predicted in the judgment made. Now suppose we ask: How long will it be possible to verify in some manner the fact that this penny is round? What totality of experience would verify it completely beyond the possibility of necessary reconsideration? . . . it seems to be the fact that *no* verification would be absolutely complete; that all verification is partial and a matter of degree. . . . Is it not the case that the simplest statement of objective particular fact implicitly asserts something about possible experience throughout all future time; that theoretically every objective fact is capable of some verification at any later date, and that no totality of such experience is absolutely and completely sufficient to put our knowledge of such particulars beyond all possibility of turning out to be in error?[2]

1 C. I. Lewis, *An Analysis of Knowledge and Valuation* (La Salle, Ill.: Open Court Publishing Co., 1946), p. 180. [p. 135, this volume. Eds.]

2 *Mind and the World Order* (New York: Charles Scribner's Sons, 1929), pp. 279–281.

For the purpose of refuting it, Lewis considers the supposition that at a certain time, designated as t_1, the verification of such a statement as "This penny is round" could be complete. He continues the argument:

> Now suppose further that at some date, t_2, we put ourselves in position to meet the consequences of this fact, which was accepted as completely established at t_1. And suppose that these consequences fail to appear, or are not what the nature of the accepted fact requires? In that case, will there still be no doubt about the accepted fact? Or will what was supposedly established at t_1 be subject to doubt at t_2? And in the latter case can we suppose it was absolutely verified at time t_1? Since no single experience can be absolutely guaranteed to be veridical, no limited collection or succession of experiences can absolutely guarantee an empirical fact as certain beyond the possibility of reconsideration.[3]

Many other philosophers have made use of this argument.

Carnap, for example, uses it in his paper "Testability and Meaning."[4] He says:

> Take for instance the following sentence "There is a white sheet of paper on this table." In order to ascertain whether this thing is paper, we may make a set of simple observations and then, if there still remains some doubt, we may make some physical and chemical experiments. Here . . . we try to examine sentences which we infer from the sentence in question. These inferred sentences are predictions about future observations. The number of such predictions which we can derive from the sentence given is infinite; and therefore the sentence can never be completely verified. To be sure, in many cases we reach a practically sufficient certainty after a small number of positive instances, and then we stop experimenting. But there is always the theoretical possibility of continuing the series of test-observations. Therefore here . . . *no complete verification is possible* but only a process of gradually increasing *confirmation*.[5]

He continues: "For such a simple sentence as e.g. 'There is a white thing on this table' the degree of confirmation, after a few observations have been made, will be so high that we practically cannot help accepting the

[3] *Ibid.*, pp. 281–282.

[4] Rudolph Carnap, "Testability and Meaning," *Philosophy of Science*, III, IV (1936, 1937). This argument is also used by Carnap in *Philosophy and Logical Syntax* (London: Routledge & Kegan Paul, Ltd., 1935), pp. 11-13 and in *Logical Syntax of Language* (New York: Harcourt, Brace & World, Inc., 1937), p. 246; by A. J. Ayer, in *Foundations of Empirical Knowledge* (New York: The Macmillan Company, 1940), pp. 42–45; by K. Popper, in *Logik der Forschung* (Vienna: J. Springer, 1935), pp. 60–62.

[5] *Philosophy of Science*, III (1936), 425.

sentence. But even in this case there remains still the theoretical possibility of denying the sentence." [6]

Before proceeding to an analysis of this argument, which I will call "the Verification Argument," I wish to say something about the nature of the conclusion which it is thought to prove. Previously I said that it is thought to prove that no empirical statements are absolutely certain. But this remark is not sufficiently clear because of a haziness in the meaning of the expression "empirical statements." Certainly no philosopher who has used the Verification Argument has intended that the argument should apply to necessary or a priori truths. But there is a class of statements with regard to which philosophers have had difficulty in deciding whether to classify statements of that class as empirical statements; and among those philosophers who have used the Verification Argument there would be disagreement and hesitation about saying whether the argument applies to statements of that class. Statements of the class in question have been called "incorrigible propositions" or "basic propositions" or "expressive statements" or "sense statements." The sentence "It *seems* to me that I hear a scratching sound at the window," when used in such a way as not to imply that there is a scratching sound at the window, would express a statement of this class. The sentence "It *looks* to me as if there are two candles on the table," when used in such a way as not to imply that there are two candles on the table, would express another statement of this class. I will call statements of this class "incorrigible statements," and henceforth I will use the expression "empirical statement" in such a way that the class of empirical statements will be understood to exclude incorrigible statements as well as necessary truths and necessary falsehoods. It is in this sense of "empirical statement" that the conclusion of the Verification Argument will be understood to be the proposition that every empirical statement is "less than absolutely certain."

The class of empirical statements is, of course, enormous. The following are examples of such statements: "There is an ink bottle on that table," "I see a goat in the garden," "We were in Lugano last winter," "I closed the door a moment ago," "There is no milk in the ice box," "Gottlob Frege was not a Spaniard," "Michelangelo designed the dome of St. Peter's," "Water does not flow uphill," "Chickens are hatched from eggs," "This man's neck is broken," "My wife is angry." The Verification Argument is thought to prove that whenever any person has ever asserted that the truth of any one of these statements is absolutely certain his assertion was false or mistaken, and also to prove that if anyone

[6] *Ibid.*, p. 426.

should, in the future, make such an assertion his assertion will be false or mistaken.

It is to be noted that the phrase "It is absolutely certain" is only one of several phrases which are used synonymously in certain contexts. Some of the other synonymous phrases are "It has been completely verified," "It has been established beyond a doubt," "I have made absolutely certain," "I have conclusively established," "I know for certain," "It has been proved beyond any possibility of doubt," "It is perfectly certain." The Verification Argument is thought to prove something with regard to each and every one of these phrases. It is thought to prove that whenever anyone applies one of these phrases to any empirical statement the assertion which he thereby makes is false or mistaken or incorrect or unjustified. It is thought to prove, for example, that if any art historian has ever made the assertion that it is conclusively established that the dome of St. Peter's was designed by Michelangelo, his assertion was false or mistaken or incorrect or unjustified; and if any art historian should, at any time in the future, make this assertion, his assertion will be false or mistaken or incorrect or unjustified. It is thought to prove that if a physician who has just examined a man struck down by a bus should ever assert "I have made absolutely certain that his neck is broken," what he asserts is wrong or improper or unjustified, *no matter how careful his examination has been.*

It is common knowledge that assertions of this sort are *often* mistaken and that it frequently happens that someone asserts that he has made absolutely certain that so-and-so is true, when either so-and-so is not true or else, even if so-and-so is true, he has not made so thorough an investigation as to justify his assertion that he has made absolutely certain that so-and-so is true. The Verification Argument is thought to prove, not simply that many assertions of this sort are mistaken or unjustified, but that *all* such assertions are, *in all cases,* mistaken or unjustified. In short, it is thought to prove that it is not even *possible* that anyone should, in *any* circumstances, make such an assertion without the assertion being false or unjustified or improper or mistaken or incorrect.

In order to state the Verification Argument as clearly as possible I will make use of an example. Let us suppose that a dispute has arisen between a friend and myself as to whether William James used the phrase "the stream of thought" as the title of a chapter in his book *The Principles of Phychology,*[7] my friend contending that James did not use that phrase, but did use the phrase "the stream of consciousness" as the title

[7] Two volumes, 1890.

of a chapter. Whereupon I take from a bookshelf Volume I of James's book, turn the pages until I come to page 224, where I see the title "The Stream of Thought" occuring just under the heading "Chapter IX." Then I say, "You are wrong. Here is a chapter entitled "The Stream of Thought." He says, "Have you made absolutely certain?" I reply, "Yes, I have. Here, look for yourself."

I believe that this example provides a natural usage of the expression "I have made absolutely certain." It is, furthermore, a good example for my purposes because I do wish to maintain that on June 17, 1948, I did make absolutely certain that the phrase "the stream of thought" was, on that day, on page 224 of my copy of Volume I of James's *The Principles of Psychology.* The statement "The phrase 'the stream of thought' was, on June 17, 1948, on page 224 of my copy of Volume I of James's *The Principles of Psychology"* I will call *"S."* The Verification Argument is thought to prove that I did *not* make absolutely certain that *S* is true. Let us see whether it does prove this.

The first step in the argument consists in saying that *S* has "consequences" or "expected results in experience," or that from *S* one can infer statements which are "predictions about future observations." It seems to me that it is not difficult to see an important thing that is meant by these expressions. If, for example, someone said "Just now a cat went into the closet," and I believed the statement, I should *expect* that if I were to search about in the closet I should see or hear or touch a cat. If I did not believe his statement he might naturally say "I assure you that if you look in the closet you will see a cat." And if I did look and did see a cat it would be natural to regard this as *confirming* his first statement "Just now a cat went into the closet." Another way of expressing this matter would be to say that if it is true that a cat went into the closest just now, then it *follows* or is a *consequence* that if I were to search about in the closet I should see or hear or touch a cat. This is a natural use of "follow" and of "consequence." And it is easy to understand what is meant by saying that the conditional statement "If I were to search about in the closet I should see or hear or touch a cat" states a "prediction about future observations." Henceforth I will use the word "consequence" to express these relationships. I will say that it is a "consequence" of the statement "Just now a cat went into the closet" that if I were to search in the closet I should see or hear or touch a cat; and I will say that the conditional statement "If I were to search in the closet I should see or hear or touch a cat" expresses a "consequence" of the former statement. In this use of "consequence" it is a consequence of the statement *S* that if now, on June 18, 1948, I were to look at page 224 of my copy of Volume I of James's *Principles* I should see the phrase "the stream of thought." I should certainly expect to see that phrase if

I were to look at that page now, and I should be greatly astonished if I did not see it.

It may be said that what I have called a "consequence" of *S* is not a consequence of *S* alone, but of *S* conjoined with some other statements. If I thought that since yesterday someone had erased from page 224 of James's book the phrase "the stream of thought," then I should not expect that if I were to look on that page I should see that phrase. Also I should not expect to see it if I knew that my vision was abnormal or that the room was so dark that I could not make out printed words. The statement "If I were to look on that page now I should see that phrase" expresses a consequence, not of *S* alone, but of the conjunctive statement "The phrase was on that page yesterday, and there is no reason to think that the printing on that page has been altered or has changed since then, and my vision is normal, and the light is good." I cannot see any objection to saying this. I believe that it is a natural way of speaking to say that if *S* is true then it is a consequence that if I were to look at page 224 now I should see that phrase; and I will continue to speak in that way. But it will be understood that this consequence of *S* is not a consequence of *S* alone, but of *S* conjoined with the other statements mentioned.

A difficut question now arises, namely, what *kind* of statements are the conditional statements that express consequences of *S*? Consider the statement "If I were to look now at page 224 of my copy of James's book I should see the phrase 'the stream of thought.' " I will call this statement *"c."* *c* is of the form "If *A* then *E*." Now a view has been put forward by Lewis that implies that this consequence of *S* should really be expressed in these words: "If it were the case that it should *seem* to me that I was looking at page 224 of James's book then it would be the case that I should *seem* to see the phrase 'the stream of thought.' " I will call this statement *"k."* Lewis holds that in a conditional statement which expresses a consequence of an empirical statement, both *A* and *E* (that is, both antecedent and consequent) must be regarded as what I call "incorrigible statements" and what he calls "expressive statements." [8] Lewis calls the statements which express consequences of an empirical statement "predictions"; and so does Carnap. Lewis talks about his believing such a statement as "There is a piece of paper before me." He

[8] "The hypothesis *'A'* must here express something which, if made true by adopted action, will be *indubitably* true. . . . And the consequent *'E'* represents an eventuality of *experience,* directly and certainly recognizable in case it accrues, not a resultant objective event, whose factuality could have, and would call for, further verification. Thus both antecedent and consequent of this judgment 'If *A* then *E*,' require to be formulated in expressive language . . ." (*An Analysis of Knowledge and Valuation,* p. 184). [p. 138, this volume. Eds.]

says that this belief involves numerous predictions, e.g., that if he were to fold it, it would not crack; that if he were to try to tear it, it would tear easily.[9] A moment later, however, he says that he has not expressed himself accurately. He says:

> But it was my intention to mention predictions which, though only partial verification of the objective fact I believe in, could themselves be decisively tested. And there I have failed. That the paper, upon trial, would really be torn, will no more be evidenced with perfect certainty than is the presence of real paper before me now. It—provided it takes place—will be a real objective event about which, theoretically, my momentary experience could deceive me. What I meant to speak of was certain expected experiences—of the *appearance and feeling* of paper being folded; of its *seeming* to be torn.[10]

He is saying that the statement "If I were to try to tear this, it would tear easily" is not a "prediction" and does not express a "consequence," in his use of "prediction" and "consequence," of his belief that there is paper before him. This passage and the one which I quoted from page 184 show that he would regard the statement "If it *seemed* to me that I was trying to tear this, then it would *seem* to me that it was tearing easily" as the sort of statement that is a "prediction" and expresses a "consequence" of his belief and if it were true would partially confirm or verify his belief. Thus it is clear that Lewis's use of "consequence," as this word occurs in his presentation of the Verification Argument, is such that he would say that k is a "consequence" of S, and c is not. There is, of course, an enormous difference between k and c. The difference could be expressed in this way: If I were to look now at page 224 of James's book and were to see there the phrase "the stream of thought," that would *entail* that page 224 of James's book does exist and that the phrase "the stream of thought" is on that page. But if now it were to *seem* to me that I was looking at page 224 of James's book and if it were to *seem* to me that I was seeing there the phrase "the stream of thought," that would *not* entail that page 224 of James's book exists or that that phrase is on any page of any book.

No other philosopher who has used the Verification Argument has, to the best of my knowledge, expressed himself on this point. Carnap, for example, says that when we are trying to verify an empirical statement what we do is to infer from it statements that are "predictions about future observations."[11] But he does not say whether these "pre-

[9] *Ibid.*, p. 175. [p. 130, this volume. Eds.]
[10] *Ibid.* [p. 131, this volume. Eds.]
[11] *Philosophy of Science,* III (1936), 425.

dictions" are statements like *c* or statements like *k*. Since he does not even allude to the distinction it would be natural to assume that by "predictions" he means statements like *c*. Whether this is so or not I will henceforth mean by "statements which express consequences of *S*" statements like *c* and not like *k*. I have two reasons for this decision. One is that statements like *k* are awkward and unnatural. The other and more important reason is that I am not sure that there is any natural usage of "confirm" or "verify" according to which the discovery that *k* is true would confirm or verify that *S* is true. Suppose that I were in doubt as to whether *S* is true. If I were to look now at page 224 of James's book and see there the phrase "the stream of thought," that would indeed confirm that the phrase was on that page yesterday. But if it were merely the case that it *seemed* to me now that I was looking at page 224 of James's book and that it *seemed* to me that I was seeing there that phrase, in a sense of the preceding words that is compatible with its being the case that I am dreaming now or having an hallucination and am not seeing any page or any printing at all, then how would this confirm that the printed words "the stream of thought" were on page 224 of James's book yesterday? It is not clear to me that it would in the least confirm *S*, in any natural sense of "confirm." This is, however, a difficult point and I do not wish to argue it here. I believe that no important part of my treatment of the Verification Argument is affected by the decision to interpret the statements that express consequences of *S* as statements like *c* and not like *k*, and it is open to anyone reading this paper to interpret them in the other way.

There is, however, a fact about the relationship between *S* and the statements that express consequences of *S* which should be clearly understood. This is the fact that *S* does *entail* any statement that expresses a consequence of *S*, in whichever of these two ways one interprets these statements. For example, *S* does not entail *c*, i.e., the statement "*S* but not *c*" is not self-contradictory. It is not self-contradictory to say "The phrase 'the stream of thought' was on page 224 of James's book yesterday but it is not the case that if I were to look on that page now I should see it there." Nor is *c* entailed by the conjunctive statement "The phrase 'the stream of thought' was on page 224 of James's book yesterday, and there is no reason to think that the printing on that page has changed or been altered since then, and my vision is normal, and the light is good." Even though there is no reason to think that the phrase "the stream of thought" has disappeared from that page since yesterday it *may* have disappeared, and if it has then if I look at that page now I shall not see it there. It should be even clearer that *S* does not entail *k*. The whole statement "The phrase 'the stream of thought' was on page

224 of James's book yesterday but it is not true that if it were the case that it should *seem* to me that I was looking at that page it would be the case that I should *seem* to see that phrase" is not self-contradictory. Nor is *k* entailed by the previously mentioned conjunctive statement of which *S* is one conjunct. When Carnap says that in order to verify an empirical statement we "infer" or "derive" from it statements that are "predictions about future observations," [12] the words "infer" and "derive" must be understood in a sense in which to say that one infers or derives *q* from *p* is *not* to say that *p* entails *q*. When Lewis speaks of the "implied consequences" [13] of a belief it is to be understood that to say that a belief "implies" certain consequences is not to say that it entails the statements that express those consequences. Whenever the word "consequence" occurs in my discussion of the Verification Argument it is to be understood that an empirical statement does not entail any statement that expresses a consequence of it. This being understood, I see no reason for not accepting the first step in the Verification Argument. When it is said that *S*, or any similar statement, has "consequences" or "expected results in experience," or that from *S* one can infer "predictions about future observations," it seems to me that this has a fairly clear meaning and is also true.

The second step in the argument consists in saying that the number of "consequences" or "expected results in experience" or "predictions about future observations" that can be inferred from *S* is "infinite" or "unlimited." This step in the argument offers some difficulty, but the following considerations may help to explain it. I said before that it is a consequence of *S* that if I were to look now at page 224 of this book I should see the phrase "the stream of thought." But it is also a consequence that if I were to look a second from now I should see that phrase, and if I were to look two seconds from now I should see it, and three seconds from now, and so on for an *indefinite* number of seconds. What it means to say that this number of seconds is "indefinite" is that *no* number of seconds from now can be specified such that, after that number of seconds had elapsed, I should no longer expect that if I were to look at that page I should see that phrase. At some future time that page may be destroyed. But for as long a period of time as it continues to exist and is not injured or tampered with, and provided that during that period my vision remains good, I should expect that if at *any* moment during that period I were to take a good look at that page in a good light I should see that phrase, *however long* that period of time shall be.

[12] *Ibid.*
[13] *An Analysis of Knowledge and Valuation*, p. 176. [p. 132, this volume. Eds.]

There is a second consideration: I do not expect merely that if *I* were to look at that page now *I* should see that phrase, but also I expect that if my wife were to look at that page now she would see that phrase, and that if the man who lives on the floor below were to look at that page he would see that phrase, and that, in short, if anyone of an *indefinitely* large number of persons of good vision were to take a good look now at that page he would see that phrase. What is meant by saying that the number of persons in question is "indefinitely" large is that *no* number of persons, however large, can be specified such that I should not expect that if any person of this number were to look at that page he would see that phrase. There is a third consideration that is a combination of the preceding two and may be stated as follows: I should expect that if anyone of an indefinitely large number of persons of good vision were to take a good look at that page either now or at any second of an indefinite number of seconds from now, he would see that phrase, provided that the page had not been injured or tampered with and that he looked at it in good light. I think that the statement that the number of "consequences" or "predictions" or "expected results in experience" that can be inferred from *S* is "infinite" or "unlimited" or "indefinitely large" means what I have expressed in these three considerations; and if that is so I am prepared to accept the second step in the Verification Argument.

The third step in the argument consists in saying that any of these "consequences" or "expected results in experience" may not turn out as expected and that any of these "predictions about future observations" may prove to be false. What this implies with regard to *S*, for example, is that if I were to look now at page 224 of James's book I might not see the phrase "the stream of thought," or that if I were to look a second from now I might not see it, or if my wife were to look now she might not see it, and so on. This proposition in the Verification Argument seems to me to require very careful examination, and I shall return to it later.

The fourth step in the Verification Argument consists in saying that if some of these "consequences" or "expected results in experience" or "predictions about future observations" that can be inferred from *S* should not turn out as expected or should prove to be false, then doubt would be thrown on the truth of *S*. Lewis expresses this when he says: "And suppose that these consequences fail to appear, or are not what the nature of the accepted fact requires? In that case, will there still be no doubt about the accepted fact?" [14] This fourth proposition in the argu-

[14] *Mind and the World Order,* p. 282.

ment seems to me to express an important truth but one that is difficult to state. If I were to take a good look now at page 224 of James's book and were *not* to see the phrase "the stream of thought," I should not simply conclude that I was mistaken when I asserted previously that it is there, and so dismiss the matter. The truth is that I should at first be too dumbfounded to draw any conclusion! When I had recovered from my astonishment what I should conclude or whether I should conclude anything would depend entirely on the circumstances. Suppose that if I were to look now on that page I should see, or seem to see, the phrase "the stream of *consciousness*" occurring as the title, under the heading "Chapter IX," instead of the phrase "the stream of thought." As I said I should at the first moment be enormously astonished and not know what to say. But suppose that I looked again and again and that I still saw, or seemed to see, the phrase "the stream of consciousness"; that everything else in the room and the things seen through the windows appeared to look the same and to be placed as I remembered them to be the moment before I looked at the page; that I did not feel ill, dizzy, or queer but perfectly normal; that I had assured myself that the book *was* my copy of Volume I of James's *Principles* and that the page *was* page 224; and that there was no reason to believe that the printing on that page had been altered since the last time I had looked at it. If all of these things were to occur, then I must confess that I should begin to feel a doubt as to whether the phrase "the stream of thought" ever was on page 224 of James's book. What is more important is that this would be a *reasonable* doubt. When Lewis asks the rhetorical question, "Will there still be no doubt about the accepted fact?" [15] he means to imply, of course, that there would be a doubt. But, furthermore, he must mean to imply that the doubt that would exist in those circumstances would be a *reasonable* doubt, i.e., that there would be *good* grounds for doubting. For if the doubt were not a reasonable one then the fact that it existed would be no evidence that that which had been accepted as a fact was not a fact. Now when I say that if certain things were to happen I should doubt whether the phrase in question ever did appear on the page in question and that this would be a reasonable doubt, I am accepting the fourth step of the Verification Argument. I am accepting the statement that if certain consequences of *S* should "fail to appear" then I should have good grounds for believing that I was mistaken when I asserted previously that I had made absolutely certain that *S* is true. I should have good grounds for believing that the phrase "the stream of thought" was not there on page 224 of James's book, but also for believ-

[15] *Ibid.*

ing that that phrase *never* had been on that page. I do not see any mistake in this fourth step in the Verification Argument.

There is a fifth step in the argument that is also difficult to state. It is implied, I believe, in these remarks by Lewis:

> Now suppose . . . that at some date, t_2, we put ourselves in position to meet the consequences of this fact, which was accepted as completely established at t_1. And suppose that these consequences fail to appear, or are not what the nature of the accepted fact requires? In that case, will there still be no doubt about the accepted fact? Or will what was *supposedly* established at t_1 be subject to doubt at t_2? And in the latter case can we suppose it was absolutely verified at time t_1? [16]

The last two sentences in this quotation express the proposition which I have called "the fifth step" in the argument. This proposition may be stated as follows: If at any time there are good grounds for believing that a given statement p is false then at no previous time was it known with certainty that p is true. This proposition is implied by the rhetorical question, "And in the latter case can we suppose it was absolutely verified at time t_1?" The "latter case" referred to is the time t_2 at which there is supposed to exist a reasonable doubt as to whether something that was accepted at t_1 as a fact is really a fact. What the rhetorical question implies is that if there is a reasonable doubt at t_2 as to whether something is a fact then it cannot have been the case that at t_1 it was absolutely verified that that something is a fact. This proposition will, perhaps, be clearer if expressed in the following way: The proposition "There are now good grounds for doubting that p is true" *entails* the proposition "At no previous time was it known with absolute certainty that p is true."

Should we accept this proposition which is the fifth step in the Verification Argument? Let us substitute for p the statement "Hume was the author of *An Abstract of A Treatise of Human Nature*." Is there any contradiction in supposing that some person, say a publisher, had made absolutely certain in 1740 that Hume was the author of *An Abstract of a Treatise of Human Nature,* but that in 1840 some other person, say a historian, had good grounds for believing that Adam Smith, and not Hume, was the author of it? Is there any contradiction in supposing that some person at one time should possess a body of evidence that conclusively established that so-and-so was the case, but that at a later time another person should possess none of that evidence but should possess *other* evidence on the basis of which it was reasonable to doubt that so-

[16] *Ibid.*

and-so was the case? I cannot see any contradiction in this supposition. Consider this actual example: Some competent Greek scholars are unable to decide whether Plato was the author of the *Lesser Hippias*. They can cite grounds for saying that he was and grounds for saying that he was not. The view that he was the author is subject to a reasonable doubt. But Plato may have been the author. If he was the author then Plato himself, or a contemporary, may have known with certainty that he was the author.[17] Now are the two statements, (*a*) "Someone at some time in the past knew with absolute certainty that Plato was the author of the *Lesser Hippias*," and (*b*) "Someone now has good grounds for doubting that Plato was the author of the *Lesser Hippias*," incompatible with one another? They are not at all. The proposition that is the conjunction of (*a*) and (*b*) is not self-contradictory. Nothing is easier to imagine than that it should be the case *both* that Aristotle knew with absolute certainty that Plato was the author of that dialogue *and* that 2400 years later a professor of Greek, not having the evidence which Aristotle had and noticing in the dialogue certain features of style uncharacteristic of Plato, should have a reasonable doubt that Plato was the author. There is no contradiction whatever in this supposition, although it may be false. If this supposition is not self-contradictory, then (*b*) does not entail that (*a*) is false. Therefore, the fifth step in the Verification Argument is an error.

Why should anyone fall into the error of thinking that the proposition "There are now good grounds for believing that *p* is false" entails the proposition "At no previous time was it known with absolute certainty that *p* is true"? I believe that there is something which may explain why this error should be made. What I have in mind is the following: If some person were to make the assertion "Aristotle knew with absolute certainty that Plato was the author of the *Lesser Hippias* but I doubt, and with good reason, that Plato was the author," then his assertion would contain an odd absurdity. The most ordinary use of the phrase "knew with absolute certainty" is such that "*x* knew with absolute certainty that *p* is true" entails "*p* is true." Therefore, the above assertion *entails* the assertion "Plato was the author of the *Lesser Hippias* but I doubt that he was." But if anyone were to assert "Plato was the author of the *Lesser Hippias*" he would *imply*, by his assertion, that he *believed* that Plato was the author of the *Lesser Hippias*. By his assertion "Plato was the author of the *Lesser Hippias* but I doubt that he was" he would

[17] This statement might be thought to beg the question. It *does* conflict with the conclusion of the Verification Argument. It does *not* beg the question with regard to any premise in the argument. It could do so only if some premise in the argument contained the assertion that no one can know with certainty that any empirical statement is true. But if this were contained in a premise then the Verification Argument itself would beg the question.

assert that he doubted something, but also *imply* that he did *not* doubt that something but believed it.[18] The same absurdity would be contained in the assertion "It is raining but I doubt it." If a philosopher had sensed the peculiar absurdity of this sort of assertion he might be led to conclude that since it would be absurd for anyone to *assert* "At a previous time someone knew with absolute certainty that p is true but I doubt, and with good reason, that p is true," that therefore the proposition "At a previous time someone knew with absolute certainty that p is true and now someone doubts, and with good reason, that p is true" is self-contradictory.

It would be a mistake, however, to draw this conclusion. Although it would be absurd for anyone to assert "It is raining but I doubt, and with good reason, that it is raining," it does not follow that this proposition is self-contradictory. That it is not self-contradictory is shown from the fact that the proposition "It is raining but *he* doubts, and with good reason, that it is raining" is clearly not self-contradictory. Since the latter proposition is not self-contradictory, how can the former one be so? Indeed, I can easily imagine that it should happen *both* that it was raining *and* that, at the same time, I had a reasonable doubt as to whether it was raining. This supposition is certainly not self-contradictory. Thus the proposition "It is raining but I doubt, and with good reason, that it is raining" is not self-contradictory, although it would be an absurdity if I were to *assert* it. If this proposition *were* self-contradictory then "I doubt, and with good reason, that it is raining" *would* entail "It is not raining." But once we see clearly that this proposition is not self-contradictory then, I think, all temptation to believe that this entailment does hold is removed.

It would also be absurd for anyone to assert "Aristotle knew with absolute certainty that Plato was the author of the *Lesser Hippias* but I doubt, and on good grounds, that he was." But it does not follow that the proposition "Aristotle knew with absolute certainty that Plato was the author of the *Lesser Hippias,* but someone now doubts, and on good grounds, that Plato was the author" is self-contradictory. It would be a great mistake to think that the statement "Someone now doubts, and on good grounds, that Plato was the author of the *Lesser Hippias*" entails the statement "It is false that Aristotle knew with absolute certainty that Plato was the author of the *Lesser Hippias.*" Lewis makes this mistake, I believe, when the assumes that if something was accepted as a fact at time t_1 but that at time t_2 there arose a reasonable doubt as to whether

18 Moore has called attention to the peculiarity of this sort of statement. Cp. G. E. Moore, "Russell's 'Theory of Descriptions,'" *The Philosophy of Bertrand Russell,* P. A. Schilpp, ed. (Evanston: Northwestern, 1944), p. 204.

this something was a fact, then it follows that it was not absolutely verified at t_1 that this something was a fact. With regard to *S*, which is the statement, "The phrase 'the stream of thought' was on June 17, 1948, on page 224 of my copy of Volume I of James's *The Principles of Psychology*," this fifth step in the Verification Argument claims the following: *If* today, June 18, 1948, those things which I have imagined as happening *should* happen, so that I should have good reason to believe that *S* is false, then it would follow logically that I did not make absolutely certain yesterday that *S* is true.

I have tried to show that that claim is false. It is true that it would be an absurdity for me, or anyone, to assert "I made absolutely certain on June 17 that *S* is true but today, June 18, I doubt, and with good reason, that *S* is true." This assertion would have the same peculiar absurdity as the assertion "*S* is true but I doubt that *S* is true." But it does not follow in the least that the proposition "On June 17 I made absolutly certain that *S* is true and on June 18 I doubted, and with good reason, that *S* is true" is self-contradictory. It does not follow at all that the proposition "On June 18 I doubted, and with good reason, that *S* is true" entails the proposition "It is false that on June 17 I made absolutely certain that *S* is true." It might be objected that if I had made absolutely certain on June 17 that *S* is true, then on June 18 I should remember this fact and, therefore, should not be able to doubt that *S* is true. But it is logically possible that I should not remember on June 18 that on June 17 I had made certain that *S* is true. There is no logical contradiction whatever in the supposition that on June 18 I should have a reasonable doubt that *S* is true, although on June 17 I had made absolutely certain that *S* is true. Thus it seems to me that there is no reason to accept the fifth step in the Verification Argument and that, in fact, it is a definite error.

Can the Verification Argument be restated in such a way as to avoid this error? It seems to me that this can be done by the following two measures. The first measure consists in *strengthening* the fourth step in the argument. The fourth step is the proposition that if certain things were to happen then I should have good grounds for doubting that *S* is true. This step could be strengthened by substituting the proposition that if a sufficient number of things were to happen I should have *absolutely conclusive* grounds for thinking that *S* is false. It seems to me that if the fourth step were strengthened in this way it would still be a true proposition. When discussing the fourth step I imagined certain things as happening such that if they *were* to happen I should have grounds for doubting that *S* is true. But let us imagine that certain additional things should occur. Let us imagine that, being astonished and perplexed at seeing the phrase "the stream of consciousness" on page 224 of James's book, I should ask my wife to look at that page and that she too should see the phrase "the stream of consciousness." Let us suppose that I should examine the manuscript of this paper in order to verify that there was in it the statement that I had made absolutely certain that the phrase "the stream of thought" was on page 224, but that I should find instead that in the manuscript was the statement that I had made absolutely certain that the phrase "the stream of consciousness" was on page 224. Let us imagine that I should then examine other copies of Volume I of *The Principles of Psychology* and see that in each of them the title of Chapter IX was *"The Stream of Consciousness"*; that I should find a number of articles written by psychologists and philosophers which quoted from page 224 of James's book and that each of them quoted the phrase "the stream of consciousness" and that not one quoted the phrase "the stream of thought"; that my wife should declare sincerely that she had read page 224 of my copy of James's book on June 17, 1948, and that she recalled that the phrase "the stream of consciousness" was on that page and not the other phrase; that everyone of several persons who had recently read Chapter IX in other copies should declare sincerely that to his best recollection James had used the phrase "the stream of consciousness" in that chapter and had not used the other phrase. *If* all of these things were to happen then there would be *more* than good grounds for doubting that *S* is true; there would be, I should say, absolutely conclusive grounds for saying that *S* is false. In other words, it would be absolutely certain that the phrase "the stream of thought" was not on page 224 of my copy of James's book on June 17, 1948; and it would be absolutely certain that my seemingly vivid recollection of seeing it there was a queer delusion. The fourth step of the Verification Argument could, therefore, be reformulated as saying that *if* a sufficient number of things were to occur then there would be absolutely conclusive grounds for saying that *S* is false.

The second measure involved in revising the Verification Argument would be to change the fifth step by substituting for the false proposition "If at any time there should be a reasonable doubt that *S* is true then at no previous time did anyone make absolutely certain that *S* is true," the true proposition "If at any time there should be absolutely conclusive grounds that *S* is false then at no previous time did anyone make absolutely certain that *S* is true." The latter proposition is clearly true. It is a plain tautology. In ordinary discourse the expressions "I made absolutely certain that *p* is true" and "There are absolutely conclusive grounds that *p* is false" are used in logical opposition to one another. It would be a contradiction to say "There are absolutely conclusive grounds that *p* is false but I made absolutely certain that *p* is true." The statement "I made absolutely certain that *p* is true" entails "*p* is true"; and the statement "There are absolutely conclusive grounds that *p* is false" entails "*p* is false." Thus the statement "There are absolutely conclusive grounds that p is false but I made absolutely certain that p is true" entails the contradiction "p is false and p is true." Therefore the proposition "If at any time there should be absolutely conclusive grounds that S is false then at no previous time did anyone make absolutely certain that S is true" is a tautology.

If the Verification Argument were revised by strengthening the fourth step and changing the fifth step, in the way that I have suggested, then the argument *would* prove (provided that there were no other error in the argument, which, I think, there is) that on June 17, 1948, I did not make absolutely certain that S is true. But if the argument were revised in this way then it could not be used to prove the *general* proposition that *no* empirical statement can be conclusively established as true, for an obvious reason. In its revised form the argument would contain as a premise the proposition "If at any time there are absolutely conclusive grounds that S is false then at no previous time did anyone make absolutely certain that S is true." Even if the argument could be used as a valid proof that I was mistaken when I asserted that I had made absolutely certain that S is true it could not be used as a valid proof that no empirical statement can be conclusively established as true, *because* one premise of the argument relies on the supposition that a particular statement, the statement "S is false," can be conclusively established as true. The situation with regard to the Verification Argument is, therefore, as follows: When stated in its original form, as presented by Lewis, the fifth step in the argument is a logical error. When the argument is revised so as to avoid this error, then it cannot be used to validly prove the proposition that no empirical statement can be conclusively established as true, which is the conclusion that it was intended to prove.

2

I wish to point out another error in the Verification Argument, an error that I believe to be of very considerable philosophical importance. The whole argument may be stated as follows:

I. S has consequences.
II. The number of consequences of S is infinite.
III. The consequences of S *may* fail to occur.
IV. *If* some of the consequences of S *were* to fail to occur, then there would be a reasonable doubt that S is true.
V. If at any time there should be a reasonable doubt that S is true then at no previous time did anyone make absolutely certain that S is true.

Conclusion: No one did make absolutely certain that S is true.

I will call this the "original" Verification Argument. Before I try to show the second error in the argument I wish to make some remarks. In the first place, I have stated the argument as if it applied only to the statement *S*. But it is intended, of course, to be a perfectly general argument. There could be substituted for *S* any other empirical statement. If the argument as stated is sound, then by substituting any other empirical statement for *S* we could obtain a parallel, sound argument. In this sense the Verification Argument, if it were sound, would prove, with respect to any empirical statement whatever, that no one did make absolutely certain that that statement is true. Indeed, it would prove that no one *can* make absolutely certain that that statement is true, because the argument applies at any *time* whatever. In the second place, I have tried to show that premise V is false. I suggested that this false step could be eliminated by the adoption of these two measures: First, to substitute for IV the proposition, which I will call "IV*a*," "If a sufficient number of the consequences of *S* were to fail to occur, then it would be absolutely conclusive that *S* is false"; second, to substitute for V the proposition, which I will call "V*a*," "If at any time it should be absolutely conclusive that *S* is false then at no previous time did anyone make absolutely certain that *S* is true." Is seems to me that both IV*a* and V*a* are true. If these substitutions are made then the whole argument may be restated as follows:

I. *S* has consequences.
II. The consequences of *S* are infinite in number.
III. The consequences of *S* may fail to occur.
IV*a*. If a sufficient number of the consequences of *S* were to fail to occur then it would be absolutely conclusive that *S* is false.
V*a*. If any time it should be absolutely conclusive that *S* is false then at no previous time did anyone make absolutely certain that *S* is true.

Conclusion: No one did make absolutely certain that *S* is true.

This second statement of the argument I will call the "revised" Verification Argument. The revised argument is different from the original argument in two respects. First, premise V of the original argument is false but the corresponding premise of the revised argument is true. Second, premise IV*a* of the revised argument contains the assumption that an empirical statement "*S* is false" can be conclusively established as true. If we substituted for *S* in the revised argument any other empirical statement *p* then IV*a* would contain the assumption that it can be conclusively established that the contradictory of *p* is true. No premise of the original argument, however, contains the assumption that any empirical statement can be conclusively established as true. This difference between the two arguments might be expressed in this way: If all of its premises were true the original argument would prove, with regard to any empirical statement that was substitued for *S,* that that statement cannot be conclusively established; and no premise of the argument assumes that any empirical statement can be conclusively established; therefore it could properly be said that if all of its premises were true the original argument would prove the general proposition that *no* empirical statement can be conclusively established. If all of its premises were true the revised argument would also prove, with regard to any empirical statement that was substituted for *S,* that that statement cannot be conclusively established; but since one premise assumes that an empirical statement can be conclusively established, it would be wrong to say that the revised argument, if its premises were all true, would prove the general proposition that *no* empirical statement can be conclusively established. No matter what statement was substituted for *S,* premise IV*a* would assume that the contradictory of that statement can be conclusively established. The revised argument has this peculiar logical character, that if all of its premises were true it would prove, with regard to *any* empirical statement, that that statement cannot be completely verified, but it would not prove that *no* empirical statement can be completely verified.[19]

[19] [I was mistaken in this assessment of the revised argument. Peter Geach pointed out to me that a proponent of the Verification Argument does not have to assume *categorically* that an empirical statement can be conclusively established. He might assume it *hypothetically* in order to prove that any given empirical statement (for example, *S*) is not conclusively established. Let us substitute for IV*a* the following proposition (call it "IV*b*"): "*If* any empirical statement can be conclusively established as true or false, then if a sufficient number of the consequences of *S* were to fail to occur, it would be absolutely conclusive that *S* is false." With this alteration, the revised argument would still be deductively valid. And it would not be the case that any premise of the argument assumes categorically that some empirical statement can be conclusively established. Nothing in the *form* of the argument, therefore, prevents a proponent of it from concluding that *no* empirical statement can be conclusively established.

My criticism of premise III is not affected by this amendment.

In an interesting study of my essay, Harry G. Frankfurt suggests another way of amending the "original" argument ("Philosophical Certainty," *The Philosophical Review,* LXXI, No. 3, July 1962, 303–327). He proposes to retain IV without change and to substitute for V the following proposition (called "V*b*"): "If at any time t_2 there should be a reasonable doubt that *S* is true, then at no previous time t_1 did anyone make absolutely certain that *S* is true, *provided that the evidence possessed at* t_2 *includes all the evidence possessed at* t_1" (*ibid.,* p. 306). As far as I can see, Frankfurt is right in saying that his reformulation of V "is an accurate expression of what is intended by proponents of the Verification Argument" (*ibid.,* p. 305), and he is also right in saying that his revised argument is deductively valid (*ibid.,* p. 307). Furthermore,

The revised argument, however, does *seem* to prove, with regard to my statement *S*, that no one can make absolutely certain that *S* is true. If it does prove this then it follows that I was mistaken when I asserted that on June 17, 1948 I made absolutely certain that *S* is true. I have previously accepted premises I, II, IV*a* and V*a*. This leaves premise III. I believe that III contains a serious mistake. I expressed III in this way: "The consequences of *S* *may* fail to occur." Lewis makes use of III in the following passage:

> No matter how fully I may have investigated this objective fact, there will remain some theoretical possibility of mistake; there will be further consequences which must be thus and so if the judgment is true, and not all of these will have been determined. The possibility that such further tests, if made, might have a negative result, cannot be altogether precluded; and this possibility marks the judgment as, at the time in question, not fully verified and less than absolutely certain.[20]

When Lewis says, "The possibility that such further tests, if made, might have a negative result, cannot be altogether precluded," he is asserting the proposition which I have called "III." Carnap, in discussing the statement "There is a white thing on this table," says that "the degree of confirmation, after a few observations have been made, will be so high that we practically cannot help accepting the sentence." When he adds, "But even in this case there remains still the theoretical possibility of denying the sentence"[21] he is, I believe, making use of III. It is unlikely that he is merely saying that it is possible that someone should deny the statement to be true, because the fact that someone had denied the statement to be true would in no way tend to show that the statement cannot be completely verified. It is likely that what he is asserting is that there "remains still the theoretical possibility" that some of the statements, which are "predictions about future observations" and which can be inferred from the statement in question, should turn out to be false. If this is a correct interpretation of his remarks then he is asserting III.

In order that we shall be clear about the meaning of III let us remind ourselves of what are some of the "consequences" or "expected results in experience" or "predictions about future observations" that

---

his version of the argument does not even appear to possess the "peculiar logical character" that I attributed (mistakenly) to the "revised" argument.]

New footnotes, which have been added to the original text of the previously published essays, are enclosed in brackets.

[20] *An Analysis of Knowledge and Valuation,* p. 180. [p. 135, this volume. Eds.]

[21] "Testability and Meaning," *Philosophy of Science,* III (1936), 426.

can be inferred from *S*. If *S* is true then one consequence is that if I were to look now at page 224 of James's book I should see the phrase "the stream of thought." Another consequence is that if I were to look again two seconds later I should again see it; another is that if my wife were to look a second later at that page she would see that phrase; and so on. What proposition III says is that it is *possible* that some or all of these things should fail to occur, that it is *possible,* for example, that if I were to look at page 224 now I should *not* see that phrase. Although it may appear obvious to some philosophers what is meant by saying that such a thing is "possible," it does not appear at all obvious to me, and I wish to scrutinize proposition III.

In order for the Verification Argument to be a valid deductive argument (i.e., an argument in which the premises entail the conclusion) III must be understood in such a way that it implies the following proposition, which I will call "III*a*": "It is not certain that the consequences of *S* will occur." Why must III be understood in this way? For this reason, that someone might agree that it is *possible* that some or all the consequences of *S* should fail to occur but at the same time maintain that it is *certain* that they will occur. I might agree, for example, that it is *possible,* in some sense of "possible" that if I were to look at page 224 of James's book now I should not see the phrase "the stream of thought," but maintain, nevertheless, that it is certain that if I were to look at that page now I should see that phrase. The assertion of proposition III*a* is, therefore, a required step in the argument. If III is understood in such a way that it implies III*a* then the revised argument is a valid deductive argument. This will be seen if we substitute III*a* for III and write down the whole argument, which I will call the "finished" Verification Argument:

I. *S* has consequences.
II. The consequences of *S* are infinite in number.
III*a*. It is not certain that the consequences of *S* will occur.
IV*a*. If a sufficient number of the consequences of *S* should fail to occur then it would be absolutely conclusive that *S* is false.
V*a*. If at any time it should be absolutely conclusive that *S* is false then at no previous time did anyone make absolutely certain that *S* is true.

Conclusion: No one did make absolutely certain that *S* is true.

It seems to me that the conclusion does follow logically from the premises. To put the argument more briefly: If it is the case that were certain things to happen then it would be conclusively established that *S* is false, and if it is not certain that those things will not happen, then it follows that no one has made certain that *S* is true. I have accepted premises I, II, IV*a*, and V*a*. I have admitted that the conjunction composed of these premises and of III*a* entails the conclusion. Therefore, if I were to accept III*a* I should be agreeing that the finished argument is sound and that its conclusion is proved. I should have to admit that I was mistaken when I asserted that I had made absolutely certain that *S* is true. I do not see, however, any good reason for accepting III*a*. I believe that it has seemed obvious to the proponents of the Verification Argument both that III is true and that III implies III*a*. I wish to show that this is a mistake. I wish to show that III may be understood in several senses, that in some of these senses III is true and that in some it is false, and that only in the senses in which III is false does III imply III*a*.

I expressed proposition III in the words "The consequences of *S* *may* fail to occur." I could have expressed III in several other ways. I could have expressed it by saying "It is *possible* that the consequences of *S* will not occur," or by saying "The consequences of *S* *might* not occur" or by saying "*Perhaps* the consequences of *S* will not occur," or by saying "It *may be* that the consequences of *S* will not occur," or by saying "The consequences of *S* *could* fail to occur." The words "may," "possible," "might," "perhaps," "may be," "could," "can" are related to one another in such a way that for any statement that uses one of these words there may be substituted an equivalent statement that uses another of them. But whichever one of this class of statements we employ to express III, its meaning will be open to several different interpretations.

Let us consider some of the different things which might be meant by the proposition "It is possible that the consequences of *S* will not occur." One thing which might be meant is that the statement "The consequences of *S* will not occur" is not self-contradictory. Frequently in philosophical discourse and sometimes in ordinary discourse when it is said "It is possible that so-and-so will happen" or "So-and-so may happen," what is meant is that the statement "So-and-so will happen" is not self-contradictory. If, for example, I were to say that it is possible that beginning tomorrow the temperatures of physical objects will vary with their colors, or that it is possible that in one minute the desk on which I am writing will vanish from sight, one thing which I should mean is that the statements "Beginning tomorrow the temperatures of physical objects will vary with their colors" and "In one minute this desk will vanish from sight" are not self-contradictory. When III is interpreted in this way what it says is that it is not the case that the contradictory of any statement which expresses a consequence of *S* is self-contradictory. It says, for example, that the statement "If I were to look now at page 224 of James's book I should *not* see the phrase 'the stream of thought' " is not self-contradictory. This interpretation of III I will call "III_1."

Another thing which might be meant by III is that no statement that states the *grounds* for holding that any consequence of *S* will occur *entails* that it will occur. Let me make this clearer by an example. If someone were to ask me why I am sure that if I were to look now at page 224 of James's book I should see the phrase "the stream of thought," I might reply "I saw it there yesterday and there is no reason to believe that the page has changed or been altered since then and my vision is normal and the light is good." But what I offer as reasons or grounds for saying that if I were to look at that page now I should see that phrase, does not *entail* that if I were to look at that page now I should see that phrase. In the sense of "possible" which is used in III_1, it is possible that the following statement is true: "I saw the phrase on that page yesterday and there is no reason to believe that the printing on that page has changed or been altered since then and my vision is normal and the light is good, *but* if I were to look on that page now I should *not* see that phrase." This statement is not self-contradictory. I have called the following statement,*"c":* "If I were to look now at page 224 of James's book I should see the phrase 'the stream of thought.'" *c* expresses one of the consequences of *S*. Let us call the statement that I have just used to state the reasons for holding *c* to be true, *"R."* The proposition "*R* but not *c*" is not self-contradictory. In other words, *R* does not entail *c*. It is possible, in the sense of "possible" that is used in III_1, that *c* is false even though *R* is true. It is possible, in this sense, that the phrase "the stream of thought" has vanished from page 224 even though there is no reason to think that it has; and if it had vanished I should not see it there. It is not self-contradictory to suppose that it has vanished although there is no reason to think that it has. It seems to me, that with regard to any statement *p* that expresses a consequence of *S*, it is the case that it is not entailed by any statement *q* that states the grounds for saying that *p* is true. This is one natural interpretation of the meaning of III. I will call it "III_2" It must not be supposed that III_1 and III_2 are equivalent. With regard to *c*, for example, III_1 says that the phrase "not *c*" or "*c* is false" is not self-contradictory. What III_2 says, with regard to *c*, is that the statement "*R* but not *c*" is not self-contradictory. III_1 says that the negative of *c* is not, by itself, self-contradictory. III_2 says that the conjunction of *R* and the negative of *c* is not self-contradictory, or, in other words, that *R* does not entail *c*. III_1 and III_2 are entirely different propositions and both of them seem to me to be clearly true. The conjunction of III_1 and III_2 is, I believe, what would ordinarily be meant by the statement "It is *logically* possible that the consequences of *S* will not occur."

I wish now to point out other uses of "possible" and the correlative words that are of a quite a different *kind* than the two so far mentioned. When it is said in ordinary life that "It is possible that so-and-so will happen," what is very frequently meant is that *there is some reason to believe* that so-and-so will happen. Suppose that my wife were to say, "It's possible that Mr. Jones will come to see us this evening." If I were to ask "Why do you think so?" she might naturally reply "He said to me this morning that he would come if he did not have to work." In this example the reply consists in stating a piece of *evidence* in favor of saying that he will come. Suppose that a friend, who looks to be in perfect health, should say "I may be extremely ill tomorrow." To may question "Why do you say that?" he might reply "Because I ate scallops for lunch and they have always made me very ill." Here again the reply offers a *reason,* some *grounds* for saying that he will be ill. This usage of "possible," "may," "might," and their correlatives is enormously frequent in ordinary discourse, and it is strikingly different from the usages noted in III_1 and III_2. When my friend replied to my question "Why do you say that you may be ill tomorrow?" his reply did not consist in pointing out the logical truth that the statement "I shall be ill tomorrow" is not self-contradictory; nor did it consist in pointing out the logical truth that no statement which expressed grounds for saying that he will not be ill tomorrow would entail that he will not be ill tomorrow. It did consist in giving some reason, or evidence, or grounds, for believing that he will be ill tomorrow. My question "Why do you think so?" or "Why do you say that?" would be naturally understood as a request for the reason for believing that he will be ill tomorrow. It would be quite absurd for him to reply to my question by saying, "Because the statement 'I shall be ill tomorrow' is not self-contradictory" or by saying, "Because it does follow logically from the fact that my health is excellent and that I feel perfectly well that I shall *not* be ill tomorrow." If he were to reply in this way it would be regarded as a joke. If a Greek scholar were to remark "It's possible that Plato was not the author of *The Republic*" we should ask "Why do you say so?" and it would be only a joke if he were to reply "The statement 'Plato was not the author of *The Republic*' is not self-contradictory," or to reply "The evidence we have for saying that Plato was the author does not *entail* that he was the author." We should naturally interpret his first remark to mean "There is evidence that Plato was not the author of *The Republic*"; and our question "Why do you say so?" would be naturally understood as a request for him to say what the evidence was. His reply gave no evidence. He failed to show that it is *possible* that Plato was not the author of *The Republic,* in the sense of "possible" which was appropriate to the context.

A radical difference between the use of "possible" that I am now describing and its uses in III_1 and III_2 consists in the fact that the kind of "possibility" now being described admits of *degree,* whereas those other kinds do not. The ordinary expressions "There is some possibility,"

"It is barely possible," "There is a slight possibility," "There is a considerable possibility," "There is a greater possibility that so-and-so than that such and such," "It is very possible," "There is a strong possibility," all belong to the use of "possible" now being described and not to its uses in III_1 and III_2. If the man who says "It is possible that I shall be ill tomorrow" supports his statement by saying that he had just eaten scallops and scallops had always made him ill, then he could have correctly expressed his statement by the words "It is *very* possible that I shall be ill tomorrow" or "There is a *strong* possibility that I shall be ill tomorrow." But if he supports his statement by saying that "I shall be ill tomorrow" is not self-contradictory, or by saying that the fact that he is in excellent health does not entail that he will not be ill tomorrow, then he could *not* have correctly expressed his statement by the words "It is *very* possible that I shall be ill tomorrow" or "There is a *considerable* possibility that I shall be ill tomorrow." The expressions "There is some possibility," "There is a considerable possibility," "There is a greater possibility that so-and-so than that such and such" mean roughly the same as the expressions "There is some evidence," "There is a fair amount of evidence," "There is more evidence that so-and-so than that such and such." The expressions of both types are expressions of *degree*. If the man who says "It is possible that Plato was not the author of *The Republic*" means that the statement "Plato was not the author of *The Republic*" is not self-contradictory, then he is not using "possible" in a sense that admits of degree. There can be more or less evidence for a statement, the reasons for believing it can be more or less strong, but a statement cannot be more or less self-contradictory. The statement "There is a slight possibility that the Smiths are in Paris this week but a greater possibility that they are in Rome" illustrates a use of "possibility" which is totally different from *logical* possibility. The statement obviously does not mean that "The Smiths are in Rome" is *less* self-contradictory than "The Smiths are in Paris." It does not make sense to say that one statement is "less" self-contradictory than another. And it obviously does not mean that the evidence as to the whereabouts of the Smiths entails "The Smiths are in Rome" *more* than it entails "The Smiths are in Paris." It does not make sense to say "*p* entails *q* more than it entails *r*." The statement obviously means that there is some reason to think that the Smiths are in Paris but greater reason to think that they are in Rome.

I hope that I have made it sufficiently clear that there is a common use of the word "possible" and of the correlative words, according to which the statement "It is possible that so-and-so" means "There is some reason to believe that so-and-so." When proposition III is interpreted in this sense it is equivalent to the proposition "There is some reason to believe that the consequences of *S* will not occur." I will call this interpretation of III, "III_3."

There are other common uses of "possible" closely analogous to its use in III_3. Suppose that the members of a committee are to meet together. All of the committee, save one, turn up at the appointed time and place. Someone asks "Does *K.* (the missing member) know that there is a meeting?" Inquiry reveals that no one recalls having notified *K.* of the meeting. It is also pointed out that, although an announcement of the meeting appeared in the local newspaper, *K.* frequently does not read the newspaper. A member of the committee sums up the situation by saying, "Then it is possible *K.* does not know about the meeting." This latter statement means that *there is no reason* to think that *K.* does know about the meeting; and this seems to me to be a very common usage of the word "possible" and its correlatives. The proposition "It is possible that the consequences of *S* will not occur," which is proposition III, if interpreted in the sense just described, would mean "There is no reason to think that the consequences of *S* will occur." This interpretation of III, I will call "III_4."

Suppose that the question arises as to whether *M.* was in a certain theater at the time when a murder was committed there. It is known that he left a bar only fifteen minutes before and that it would be extremely difficult for any man to go from the bar to the theater in fifteen minutes. The situation might be summed up by saying "It is unlikely that *M.* was at the theater at the time of the murder but it is *possible* that he was." This statement means that there is good reason to believe that *M.* was not at the theater but that the reason is not absolutely conclusive. It is a very common use of "possible" to say that although there are strong grounds for believing that so-and-so is the case, it is still *possible* that so-and-so is not the case, where this is equivalent to saying that although the grounds for saying that so-and-so is true are strong, they are not absolutely conclusive. If III were interpreted in this way it would mean "The grounds for saying that the consequences of *S* will occur are not absolutely conclusive." This interpretation of III, I will call "III_5."

I have wished to show that sentences of the sort "It is possible that so-and-so," "It may be that so-and-so," "Perhaps so-and-so," have several different uses. The very same sentence has, in different contexts, quite different meanings. I do not know that there are not still other uses of those sentences; but if there are I cannot think of them. The third premise of the Verification Argument is expressed by a sentence of this sort. When it is said "It is possible that the consequences of *S* will not occur," the question arises, therefore, in which of these different ways is this sentence being used? When Lewis says "The possibility that such further tests, if made, might have a negative result, cannot be altogether precluded" his statement is equivalent to "It is possible that further 'tests,' if made, will have negative results." How are we to understand the use of "possible" in this important premise of the argument? In what sense of "It is possible that so-and-so" is it possible that if I were to look now at page 224 of James's book I should not see the phrase "the stream of thought"? A proponent of the Verification Argument cannot reply that it is possible in the *ordinary* meaning of "It is possible." There is not such a thing as *the* ordinary meaning of that phrase. A sentence of the sort "It is possible that so-and-so" does not have just *one* meaning that is the same in all contexts. The only course open to us is to examine each of the several different interpretations of the third premise in order to see whether there is any interpretation of it which will make the "revised" Verification Argument a sound argument.

III is the proposition "It is possible that the consequences of the statement *S* will not occur." III*a* is the proposition "It is not known that the consequences of *S* will occur." I pointed out previously that in order for the revised argument to be a valid deductive argument III must be understood in such a way that it implies III*a*. In order for the revised argument to be a *sound* argument it must also be the case that III is true. (I am using the phrase "a sound argument" in such a way that a deductive argument is a sound argument if and only if it is both the case that it is a valid deductive argument and that all of its premises are true.) Is there an interpretation of III in accordance with which III implies III*a* *and* III is true? The following are the different interpretations of III which arose from the description of the several meanings of sentences of the sort "It is possible that so-and-so":

- III_1. The statement "The consequences of *S* will not occur" is not self-contradictory.
- III_2. No statement *p* which expresses a consequence of *S* is entailed by any statement *q* which states the grounds for holding that *p* is true.
- III_3. There is some reason to believe that the consequences of *S* will not occur.
- III_4. There is no reason to think that the consequences of *S* will occur.
- III_5. The grounds for holding that the consequences of *S* will occur are not absolutely conclusive.

With regard to these propositions I think that the following is the case: III_1 and III_2 are true. But neither of them implies III*a*. III_3, III_4, and III_5 each implies III*a*. But each of them is false. I wish to defend these statements, and I will do so by discussing each of these interpretations of III.

(III_1) It is clearly not self-contradictory to say either that all or that some of the consequences of *S* will not occur. It is possible, in one sense of "It is possible," that they will not occur. But it does not follow in the least that it is not absolutely certain that they will occur. Here is a source of philosophical confusion. With regard to any contingent statement, it is the case that "*p* is false" is not self-contradictory. A natural way to express this logical truth about *p* is to say "It is possible that *p* is false." This provides the temptation to say "Since it is possible that *p* is false, therefore it is not certain that *p* is true." But this is a confusion. From the sense of "It is possible that *p* is false" in which this means that "*p* is false" is not self-contradictory, it does not follow either that there is some reason to believe that *p* is false, or that there is no reason to believe that *p* is true, or that the reason for holding that *p* is true is not conclusive. The fact that it is possible that *p* is false, in this sense, *has nothing to do with the question of whether p is false.* In this sense of "It is possible that *p* is false" it is not self-contradictory to say "It is certain that *p* is true although it is possible that *p* is false." In the senses of "It is possible that *p* is false" that are expressed by III_4 and III_5, it *is* self-contradictory to say "It is certain that *p* is true although it is possible that *p* is false." In the sense of "It is possible that *p* is false" that is expressed by III_3, it is not self-contradictory to say "It is certain that *p* is true although it is possible that *p* is false," for the reason that I gave in discussing proposition V. But in the sense of III_3 to say "It is possible that *p* is false" *is* to say something that counts *against* saying "It is certain that *p* is true."

It is easy to be misled by these different uses of "It is possible" and to conclude that from the fact that it is possible that *p* is false, when this means that "*p* is false" is not self-contradictory, that therefore it is not certain that *p* is true. But in the use of "It is possible" that is expressed by III_1, "It is possible that *p* is false" only tells us what *kind* of statement *p* is. It only tells us that *p* is a contingent statement and not a necessary truth or a necessary falsehood. It tells us *nothing* about the state of the evidence with respect to *p*. In the uses of "It is possible" that are expressed by III_3, III_4, and III_5, the statement "It is possible that *p* is false" does tell us something about the state of the evidence. It tells us that there is some evidence for believing that *p* is false, or that there is no evidence for believing that *p* is true, or that the evidence for *p,* although strong, is not conclusive. In these latter uses the statement "It is possible that *p* is false" says something *against* its being certain that *p* is true. The statement " '*p* is false' is not self-contradictory" says nothing whatever against its being certain that *p* is true. That statement is *neutral* with regard to the question of whether *p* is true or of whether it is certain that p is true. To say that " 'p is false' is not self-contradictory" entails "It is not certain that p is true" amounts to saying that "p is a contingent statement" entails "It is not certain that p is true." But to say the latter would be to say something false. It is not self-contradictory to say "There are many contingent statements which I know with certainty to be true." c is the statement "If I were to look now at page 224 of James's book I should see the phrase 'the stream of thought.' " c is a contingent statement, which entails that "c is false" is not self-contradictory. It is correct to express this logical fact about c by saying "It is *possible* that if I were to look now at page 224 I should *not* see the phrase 'the stream of thought.' " But although this statement expresses a truth it is not a truth which is even *relevant* to the question of whether it is certain that if I were to look now at that page I should see that phrase.

(III_2) Previously I said that the grounds for saying that c is true are expressed by the statement "I saw the phrase when I looked there yesterday, there is no reason to believe that the printing on that page has changed or been altered since then, my vision is normal, and the light is good." I said that this statement R does not entail c. A natural way of expressing this fact about the logical relationship of R to c is to *say* "Even though R is true it is *possible* that c is false." This expresses the fact that the inference from R to c is not a deductive or demonstrative inference. But it provides another great source of philosophical confusion. There is a temptation to conclude from the fact that it is possible, in this sense, that c is false even though R is true that, therefore, it is not *certain* that c is true. It does not, however, follow from the fact that R does not entail c either that it is not certain that c is true or that R does not state the grounds on the basis of which it is certain that c is true. The temptation arises from the fact that there are several uses of "It is possible that p is false" and that frequently these words mean that there is some reason to believe that p is false, or that there is no reason to believe that p is true, or that it is not absolutely conclusive that p is true. When one says "Although R is true c may be false" and expresses by this the fact that "R and not c" is not self-contradictory, it is easy to be misled by the variety of uses of "possible" and "may be" into supposing that one has said something that counts against its being certain that c is true. But the statement that R does not entail c, i.e., that "R and not c" is not self-contradictory, says nothing that counts either for or against its being certain that c is true. Whether it is certain that c is true depends upon the state of the evidence with regard to c. The statement "R does not entail c" says no more about the state of the evidence with regard to c than does the statement " 'c is false' is not self-contradictory." Both statements are irrelevant to that matter. The statement "The fact that *R* is true makes it absolutely certain that *c* is true" is in no way contradicted by the statement "*R* does not entail *c*." The two statements are perfectly compatible with one another. One statement describes the evidence concerning *c*. The other describes a logical relationship between *R* and *c* of which one could be aware even though one knew nothing whatever about the state of the evidence concerning *c*.[22] The fact that *R* does not entail *c* provides no ground for doubting that *c* is true. It is a mistake to suppose that because it is possible that *c* is false even though *R* is true, in the sense of III_2, that therefore "It is possible that *c* is false," where these latter words imply that it is not quite certain that *c* is true. What I have said about *c* applies equally to every other statement which expresses a consequence of *S*.

22 [Frankfurt ("Philosophical Certainty," *The Philosophical Review*, LXXI, 309) disagrees with me here. He says that the statement that *R* does not entail *c* "is obviously about the evidence for *c*." But as Frankfurt acknowledges, it is irrelevant to the question of *how much* evidence there is for *c*, and in this sense it has nothing to do with the state of the evidence for *c*. In what sense *is* it about the evidence for *c*? In supposing that it "obviously" is, Frankfurt would appear to be thinking that if *R* does not *entail c*, then it is not certain that *c* is true. He goes on to indicate, however, that he is not sure about this point and that I may be right in my view of the matter (*ibid.*, p. 310). But he says that I have offered "surprisingly little" support for my view (*ibid.*, p. 309). The only support I know how to give is examples—that is, cases in which we should *say* that something is "perfectly certain" or "conclusive," and yet in which it is clear to us that the evidence does not entail the thing in question. In the essay I do this. I go on to mention, for example, the fact that if the printed words "the stream of thought" were on page 224 of James's book yesterday, "then it is perfectly certain that they have been there as long as the book has existed" (see p. 38). This *is* perfectly certain: and it is also perfectly obvious that there is no entailment. Countless other examples lie at hand. (It is perfectly certain that Harry G. Frankfurt is the author of an article entitled "Philosophical Certainty," but my evidence that he wrote it does not *entail* that he wrote it.) The aim of the examples is to bring out the fact that our use of the locutions "certain," "perfectly certain," "conclusive," "absolutely conclusive," and so on, as applied to empirical propositions in everyday life, is not tied up with the question of whether the evidence for the propositions *entails* the propositions. This latter question is generally *irrelevant*. (It is not always irrelevant because sometimes an empirical proposition is based on a calculation, e.g., "I spent a total of $12.42 at the grocer's.") Why is it so difficult to see this? Why are we so strongly inclined to think that III_2 entails III*a*? Partly because of the ambiguity of III. Partly (I am now inclined to think) because the verb "entails" incorporates *one* use of the verb "follows," and in ordinary speech we have another more frequent use of it, in which to say such a thing as "It does not follow from the evidence you offer that *p*" just *means* that the evidence is not good enough, is not conclusive, does not make it certain that *p*. In our philosophical thinking about empirical certainty, it is easy for us to confuse these different uses of "follows." (The topics of certainty and entailment are discussed, in a special connection, in my review of Wittgenstein's *Investigations*, pp. 113–117.)]

(III_3) III_1 and III_2 provide no basis whatever for accepting III*a*. The same thing cannot be said of III_3. If there is some reason for believing that any consequence of *S* will not occur, this counts in favor of holding that it is not certain that it will occur. But is III_3 true? Is there some reason or ground or evidence for thinking that any consequence of *S* will not occur; for thinking, for example, that if I were to look now at page 224 of James's book I should *not* see there the phrase "the stream of thought"? There is none whatever. Let us consider what *would* be a reason for thinking that any consequence of *S* will not occur. If some person of normal vision had carefully looked for that phrase on that page a few minutes ago and had not found it there, then that would be a reason, and a powerful one, for thinking that if I were to look now I should not see it there. Or if my copy of James's book possessed the peculiar characteristic that sometimes the printing on the pages underwent spontaneous changes, that printed words were suddenly replaced by different printed words without external cause, then that would be a reason for doubting that if I were to look now at that page I should see that phrase. But there is no reason to think that any person has looked for that phrase and has not found it there, or to think that my copy of James's book does possess that peculiar characteristic.

It might be objected that although there is no reason to think that these things are true nevertheless they *may* be true. In which of the several senses of "may be" is it that these things *may* be true? If it is in the senses of III_1 and III_2 then it does not follow that it is not certain that they are false. It cannot be said that they may be true in the sense that there is some reason to think that they are true, for we are supposing it to be admitted that there is no reason. May they be true in the sense that there is no reason to think that they are false, or in the sense that the grounds for saying they are false are not conclusive? But there *is* reason to think that they are false. There is reason to think that no one has tried and failed to find that phrase on that page. The reason is that I did make certain that the phrase was there yesterday, and if those printed words were there yesterday then it is perfectly certain that they have been there as long as the book has existed. This is not only a reason but is what would ordinarily be regarded as a conclusive reason for saying that no one of normal vision who has carefully looked for that phrase on that page in good light has failed to see it there. The reason is obvious for saying that my copy of James's book does not have the characteristic that its print undergoes spontaneous changes. I have read millions of printed words on many thousands of printed pages. I have not encountered a single instance of a printed word vanishing from a page or being replaced by another printed word, suddenly and without external cause. Nor have I heard of any other person who had such an encounter. There is overwhelming evidence that printed words do not behave in that way. It is just as conclusive as the evidence that houses do not turn into flowers—that is to say, absolutely conclusive evidence.

It cannot be maintained that there is any particular evidence for thinking that the consequences of *S* will not occur. It might be held, however, that there is a *general* reason for doubting whether they will occur. The reason is that the consequences of *some* statements *do* fail to occur. It might be argued that, since sometimes people are disappointed in expecting the consequences of a certain statement to occur, therefore I may be disappointed in expecting the consequences of *S* to occur. This would be similar to arguing that since people are sometimes mistaken when they declare a statement to be true therefore I may be mistaken when I declare *S* to be true, or that since people sometimes suffer from hallucinations therefore I may have been suffering from an hallucination when I thought that I was making certain that *S* is true.

There is undoubtedly a temptation to argue this way. The following remarks by Russell are but one example of it. "Lunatics hear voices which other people do not hear; instead of crediting them with abnormally acute hearing, we lock them up. But if we sometimes hear sentences which have not proceeded from a body, why should this not always be the case? Perhaps our imagination has conjured up all the things that we think others have said to us." [23] Here Russell is arguing that since sometimes people imagine voices, therefore in every case when one "hears a voice" one may have imagined the voice. I cannot undertake to examine in this paper all of the sources of the temptation to argue in this way. They lie in some serious difficulties surrounding the philosophical question, "How do I know that I am not dreaming or having an hallucination?" To investigate them would lead us away from the Verification Argument.

I do want to point out that this sort of arguing is, on the face of it, entirely invalid. To argue that since people sometimes make mistakes therefore I may be mistaken when I say that *S* is true is like arguing that Francis Bacon may not have been an Englishman because some men are not Englishmen, or that Bismarck may not have been a statesman because some men are not statesmen or that I may be blind because some men are blind. This is a travesty of correct reasoning. There are *some* circumstances in which reasoning of that sort is acceptable. If the door to the adjoining office is closed and we are wondering what the man in there is doing and someone says that surely he is sitting at his desk, one of us might reply "He may not be sitting at his desk because sometimes he sits

[23] Bertrand Russell, *An Outline of Philosophy* (W. W. Norton & Company, Inc., 1927), p. 9.

on the floor." In these circumstances the fact that sometimes he sits on the floor *does* count against saying that it is surely the case that he is sitting at his desk. But if we were to open the door and see him sitting at his desk then it would be absurd for anyone to say "He may not be sitting at his desk because sometimes he sits on the floor." This sort of reasoning is acceptable in those circumstances where one has not yet investigated the question at issue, where one is not in a position to know the answer, where one can only make conjectures. If there is an unexamined chair in the closet and someone assumes that it is wooden, we might reply "It may be metal because some chairs are metal." But once we have looked at it, felt it, and scratched some splinters from it then it would be only amusing to say "It may be metal because some chairs are metal." Here is a type of reasoning that is appropriate in some circumstances but not in all circumstances. There might be circumstances in which it would be reasonable to say "I may be having an hallucination because people do have hallucinations" or to say "I may have imagined that I heard a voice because sometimes I do imagine that I hear voices"; but it is an error to suppose that this is a reasonable thing to say in *all* circumstances.

These remarks apply to what we were considering as a general reason for doubting that the consequences of *S* will occur. The suggestion was that the consequences of *S* may fail to occur because the consequences of some statements do fail to occur, that since sometimes people make false statements and are disappointed when they expect their consequences to occur, that therefore when I asserted *S* I may have made a false statement and may be disappointed in expecting its consequences to occur. There are circumstances in which it is highly reasonable to temper the confidence with which I assert something, by reminding myself that sometimes other people and myself make erroneous assertions. But it is a mistake to suppose this to be reasonable in *all* circumstances, to suppose, for example, that it is reasonable to conclude that, since sometimes I am mistaken, therefore when I say that I am more than ten years old I may be mistaken and that it is not quite certain that I am more than ten. Thus the suggestion that there is a general reason for believing that the statements that express consequences of *S* are false, and that the reason is that *some* statements that people expect to be true turn out to be false, is completely in error and presents nothing more than a caricature of good reasoning. It would be a caricature of good reasoning if a member of a society of Greek scholars were to declare to the society that there is reason to believe that Plato was not the author of *The Republic* and when asked for the reason were to reply that people often believe propositions which are false.

I conclude that III_3 is false. It asserts that the consequences of *S* may fail to occur in the sense that there is some reason for thinking that they will not occur. But there is no reason at all, neither any particular reason nor any general reason, for thinking that any of the consequences of *S* will not occur.

(III_4) Proposition III_4, which expresses another common usage of "It is possible," says that there is *no* reason to believe that the consequences of *S will* occur. III_4 is false because there is a very good reason for saying that the consequences of *S* will occur. The reason is that *S* is true. What better reason could there be? Two objections might be made to this. First, it might be said that no empirical statement, *p*, is evidence for another empirical statement, *q*, unless *p* entails *q*: *S* does not entail any statement that expresses a consequence of *S* (e.g., *S* does not entail *c*); therefore the fact that *S* is true is no evidence that any statement is true that expresses a consequence of *S*. This objection, however, cannot be made use of by a proponent of the Verification Argument. The fourth premise in that argument says that if some of the consequences of *S* were not to occur then there would be some reason to think that *S* is false. But the contradictory of a statement which expresses a consequence of *S* does not entail that *S* is false (e.g., "*c* is false" does not entail "*S* is false"). Therefore, one step in the Verification Argument assumes what is clearly correct, that a statement, *p*, can be evidence for a statement, *q*, even though *p* does not entail *q*. The second objection that might be made is that if *S* is true then there is good reason to think that the consequences of *S* will occur, but that it is not absolutely certain that *S* is true. If a person made this objection it would be necessary to ask him what his reason is for saying that it is not absolutely certain that *S* is true. Is his reason that he has looked at that page of James's book and failed to find that phrase there? In other words is he saying that there are particular grounds for thinking that it is not certain that *S* is true? But there are no such grounds. Is his reason the general philosophical proposition that no empirical statement is absolutely certain? But that is the very proposition that the Verification Argument is meant to prove and so that proposition cannot be used as a step in the argument. There is no way in which it can be consistently upheld, within the context of the Verification Argument, that there is no reason to believe that the consequences of *S* will occur. III_4 cannot be accepted as an interpretation of proposition III in the argument, because not only is III_4 false but also its use as a premise would lead either to an inconsistency or to a circular argument.

(III_5) It is unlikely that any philosopher who has used the Verification Argument would wish to maintain either that there is some reason to believe that the consequences of *S* will not occur or that there is no reason to believe that they will occur. But undoubtedly he would wish to maintain that the grounds for saying that they will occur are not absolutely conclusive. The statements that express consequences of *S* are empirical statements and the Verification Argument is intended to prove that the grounds for no empirical statement are absolutely conclusive. If the conclusion of the argument is true then III_5 is true, and it would be inconsistent to accept the conclusion and not to accept III_5. But we are now regarding III_5 as a *premise* in the argument intended to prove that conclusion. Within the context of the Verification Argument the proposition that is the conclusion of it cannot be offered in support of premise III_5, because the argument would then be circular. What is to be offered in support of III_5?

The Verification Argument is subject to a serious logical difficulty. It cannot be a valid deductive argument unless it contains the premise that it is not certain that the consequences of *S* will occur. The fact that this premise is required is obscured by the ambiguity of proposition III, which is the proposition "It is possible that the consequences of *S* will not occur." The meaning of III is open to several interpretations. Only if III is interpreted in such a way that it implies III*a* is the argument valid. III_5 is one natural interpretation of III, and III_5 implies III*a*. In fact, III_5 and III*a* are logically equivalent propositions. III_5 entails III*a* and III*a* entails III_5. But III*a* (or III_5) is a proposition which requires *proof*. Proposition III*a* is extremely similar to the proposition which is the general conclusion of the Verification Argument. The conclusion says something about every member of the entire class of empirical statements—it says that the truth of not one of those statements is completely certain. Proposition III*a* says the same thing about every member of a certain subclass of empirical statements, namely, the class of conditional statements which express consequences of *S*. *S* was but one example of an empirical statement, picked at random, and could be replaced by any other empirical statement. Whatever statement may be substituted for *S*, proposition III*a* would say that it is not certain that the conditional statements that express consequences of *that* statement are true. In effect, therefore, proposition III*a* says that the truth of not one of an enormous class of statements—namely, all conditional statements which express consequences of any empirical statement—is completely certain. This sweeping and paradoxical claim requires to be justified as much as does the general conclusion of the Verification Argument. Every one of us in ordinary life frequently makes assertions of the following sort: "It is absolutely certain that if you look through these binoculars you will see a canoe on the lake," "We know for certain that if you pour that acid into this solution you will see a red precipitate form," "It is perfectly certain that if you were to touch that wire you would receive a shock." That is to say, every one of us frequently asserts of some conditional, empirical statement that its truth is entirely certain and beyond question. Shall it be said that the conditional, empirical statements which express consequences of *S*, or of any statement substituted for *S*, are not certainly true because *no* conditional, empirical statement is certainly true? What is the justification for the latter proposition? What is the justification for saying that every time anyone has made an assertion of the preceding sort his assertion has been false or mistaken or unjustified?

Here is a gap in the Verification Argument and the Verification Argument itself cannot be used to fill that gap. What is to fill it? Some other philosophical argument? Hume produced an argument that, if it were sound, would prove that it is not certain that any of the conditional statements that express consequences of *S* are true. But Hume's argument could not be used by a proponent of the Verification Argument to prove premise III*a*. Hume's argument was intended to prove that no inferences about matters of fact are "founded on reasoning." [24] He meant that there can be no reason to accept any inference about matters of fact —that there can be no reasonable inferences about matters of fact. But premise IV of the original Verification Argument asserts that if some of the consequences of *S* were not to occur then there would be reason to think that *S* is false. That premise implies that there can be reasonable inferences about matters of fact. Thus Hume's argument is incompatible with the Verification Argument. Perhaps there is some other philosophical argument that could be offered in support of III*a*; but until it has been presented we cannot determine whether it is sound or whether it is compatible with the Verification Argument.

The Verification Argument does not stand on its own feet. Proposition III*a*, a required premise, makes a claim which is of the *same nature* as the general conclusion of the argument and only slightly less grandiose. The philosophers who have used the argument have tended to tacitly assume III*a*. They have not clearly seen that III*a* needs to be set down as a premise and to be *supported*. The explanation for this, I believe, is that these philosophers have been confused by the variety of uses of the phrases "It is possible," "It may be," and their equivalents. When they have said that "It is possible that further tests will have a negative result" or that "The predictions about future observations may prove to be false," they have thought that they were saying something that is so obviously true that it does not require support *and* that shows that it is not certain that those further "tests" will have a "positive result" or that those "predictions" will prove to be true. The fact is, however, that

24 David Hume, *An Enquiry Concerning Human Understanding,* Part II, sec. 4.

although there are natural interpretations of III according to which III is obviously true, none of those interpretations show that III*a* is true; and although there are natural interpretations of III which, if true, would show that III*a* is true, there is no reason to think that III is true in any of those interpretations. The result of this confusion is that III*a*, although a required premise, is an unsupported premise.

There is one passage in his exposition of the Verification Argument in which it is clear that Lewis is asserting a proposition corresponding to III_5 and, therefore, to III*a*. He is discussing his "belief" that there is a piece of paper before him. He says:

> And my belief must imply as probable, anything the failure of which I should accept as tending to discredit this belief. Also it is the case that such future contingencies implied by the belief are not such that failure of them can be absolutely precluded in the light of prior empirical corroborations of what is believed. However improbable, it remains thinkable that such later tests could have a negative result. Though truth of the belief itself implies a positive result of such later tests, the evidence to date does not imply this as more than probable, even though the difference of this probability from theoretical certainty should be so slight that practically it would be foolish to hesitate over it. Indeed we could be too deprecatory about this difference: if we interrogate experience we shall find plenty of occasions when we have felt quite sure of an objective fact perceived but later circumstance has shocked us out of our assurance and obliged us to retract or modify our belief.[25]

When he says "The evidence to date does not imply this as more than probable" ("this" refers to "a positive result of such later tests") it is clear that Lewis is asserting that the evidence for any statement that expresses a consequence of his belief is not absolutely conclusive. (If the evidence for a statement is not absolutely conclusive then it follows that it is not certain that the statement is true, i.e., III_5 entails III*a*.) What is his reason for saying that there is no absolutely conclusive evidence that later "tests" will not have a "negative result"? I think that part of his reason lies in the statement "However improbable, it remains *thinkable* that such later tests could have a negative result." It is clear that he is using "thinkable" as equivalent to "conceivable." The phrase "It is conceivable" is used in ordinary language in exactly the same way as are the phrases "It is possible" and "It may be." The expression "It is conceivable that so-and-so" is open to the same variety of interpretations as is the expression "It is possible that so-and-so." How shall we understand the statement "However improbable, it remains conceivable that later

25 *An Analysis of Knowledge and Valuation,* p. 176. [pp. 131–32, this volume. Eds.]

tests will have a negative result"? If it means that it is not self-contradictory to suppose that later "tests" will have a "negative result," or that the evidence for saying that later "tests" will have a "positive result" does not *entail* that they will, then this statement is true; but it provides no ground for denying that the evidence is absolutely conclusive that later "tests" will have a "positive result." If the statement means that there is *some evidence* that later "tests" will have a "negative result," then the statement is false. With regard to *c*, it is not true that there is some evidence that if I were to look at page 224 of James's book I should *not* see the phrase "the stream of thought." The statement does not mean that there is *no* evidence that later "tests" will have a "positive result"; for Lewis clearly holds that it may be probable or even highly probable that later "tests" will have a "positive result." The only thing left for the statement to mean, so far as I can see, is that the evidence, although strong, is not absolutely conclusive that later "tests" will have a "positive result." But if the statement "However improbable, it remains conceivable that later tests will have a negative result" has this meaning, then it provides no justification at all for the statement that "the evidence to date does not imply as more than probable that later tests will have a positive result." The two statements are then *identical* in meaning and the former statement can provide no justification for the assertion of the latter statement. Both statements are equally in need of support.

I believe that there is something else in the paragraph just quoted from Lewis that he may have regarded as supporting his claim that "the evidence to date does not imply this as more than probable, even though the difference of this probability from theoretical certainty should be so slight that practically it would be foolish to hesitate about it." He continues: "Indeed we could be too deprecatory about this difference: if we interrogate experience we shall find plenty of occasions when we have felt quite sure of an objective fact perceived but later circumstance has shocked us out of our assurance and obliged us to retract or modify our belief." In terms of my statement *S*, I understand Lewis to be saying the following: It is no more than probable that the consequences of *S* will occur; but it may be so highly probable that there is no "practical difference" between this high probability and "theoretical certainty." It may be so highly probable that it would be foolish to hesitate over this difference and to feel any doubt that the consequences of *S* will occur. But then, he warns, perhaps we are deprecating this difference too much. ("Indeed we could be too deprecatory about this difference.") I understand him to be saying that we should remember that it is not certain that the consequences of *S* will occur and that perhaps we should hesitate a little, i.e., feel a slight doubt that they will occur. Why? *Because* there have been numerous occasions when we felt sure of something and then discovered later that we were mistaken. If I understand Lewis correctly, he is using the latter fact both to reinforce his claim that it is not conclusive that the consequence of *S* will occur and as a ground for suggesting that perhaps it would be reasonable to feel a slight doubt that they will occur. But if he is doing this then he is making a mistake that I mentioned in my discussion of proposition III_3. That mistake consists in thinking that there is a *general* reason for doubting any particular statement that we believe to be true, the reason being that it has frequently happened that what we believed to be true turned out to be false. I am not entirely confident that Lewis is arguing in that way; but if he is then enough was said in our discussion of III_3 to show that this alleged general reason for doubt is no good reason at all for doubting that the consequences of S will occur and that to argue in this way is to commit a travesty of correct thinking.

The passage that I have just quoted contains the clearest assertion of proposition III_5 that I can find in Lewis' writing or in the writing of any other proponent of the Verification Argument. In this passage no good grounds are offered in defense of III_5 and the assertion of it seems to obtain its plausibility from the ambiguity of the expression "It is conceivable" ("thinkable"), which has the same ambiguity as the expression "It is possible." Almost anyone who reflects on these matters will, indeed, feel an inclination to say that III_5 is true. What is the source of this strong inclination? I believe that it lies exactly in that ambiguity. Consider *c*, which is the statement "If I were to look now at page 224 of James's book I should see there the phrase 'the stream of thought,' " and which expresses a consequence of *S*. One feels compelled to say that it is possible that *c* is false. And this is correct. It *is* possible that *c* is false *in the sense* that "*c* is false" is not self-contradictory, and *in the sense* that the grounds for affirming *c* do not entail *c*. Now feeling assured that the statement "It is possible that *c* is false" is undeniably true, one wants to conclude "Therefore it is not *certain* that *c* is true." And from the latter statement one correctly concludes "Therefore the grounds for affirming *c* are not conclusive." Reasoning in this way leads one to accept III_5. But this reasoning is fallacious. The error lies in the step from "It is possible that *c* is false" to "Therefore it is not certain that *c* is true." In the senses of "It is possible" in which it is undeniably true that it is possible that *c* is false, the fact that it is possible is irrelevant to the question of whether or not it is certain that *c* is true. The fact that, in those senses, it is possible that *c* is false is entirely compatible with the fact that the grounds for affirming *c* are perfectly conclusive and that it is perfectly certain that *c* is true. The grounds I should give for affirming *c* are that I saw the phrase "the stream of thought" when I looked at page 224 of James's book yesterday and that there is no reason to believe that the printing on the page has changed or been altered since then, and that my vision is normal, and that the light is good. These grounds would be accepted as absolutely conclusive by everyone in ordinary life. In what way do they fail to be conclusive?

It will be said "It is possible that you had an hallucination yesterday and did not see the page of a book at all." As I said before, there are connected with this statement problems of great importance which cannot be studied in this paper. I will limit myself to these remarks: The meaning of the statement is not that there is *some reason* to think that *I* had an hallucination yesterday. The philosopher who makes this statement does not intend to claim that by virtue of a particular knowledge of me and of my circumstances yesterday he has evidence that I suffered from an hallucination. This statement is intended to make the general claim that *every time anyone* has believed that he did perceive a certain thing it is possible that he did not perceive that thing at all and that he had an hallucination instead. Furthermore this statement does not claim merely that whenever anyone has believed that he perceived a certain thing it is possible that he was having an *hallucination*. It is intended to claim that it is *also* possible that he was *dreaming* or that he had an *optical illusion*, or, in short, that he suffered from *an error of some sort*. The philosophical statement "Whenever anyone has made a perceptual judgment it is possible that he was suffering from hallucination" is a disguised way of claiming "Whenever anyone has made a perceptual judgment it is possible that his judgment was in error," or of claiming "It is possible that every perceptual statement is false."

Now is it possible that every perceptual statement is false in any sense of "It is possible" from which it follows that it is not *certain* that any perceptual statement is true? Let us review the uses of "It is possible" that we have described. Any perceptual statement may be false in the sense that the contradictory of any perceptual statement is not self-contradictory; but it does not follow that it is not certain that any perceptual statement is true (III_1). It is true, I believe, that the evidence that one could offer in behalf of any perceptual statement does not *entail* that the statement is true; but, again, it does not follow that it is not certain that any perceptual statement is true (III_2). It cannot be maintained that with respect to each perceptual statement there is some particular evidence that that statement is false; e.g., there is no evidence at all that my statement that I saw a page of a book yesterday is false (III_3). To argue that since some perceptual statements are false therefore it is not certain that any particular perceptual statement is true is unsound reasoning (III_3). It would be absurd to contend that there is no reason to accept any perceptual statement (III_4).

Nothing remains to be meant by the statement "It is possible that every perceptual statement is false" except the claim that the grounds for accepting any perceptual statement are never conclusive (III_5). As I said, I believe that the grounds which one could offer in behalf of any perceptual statement do not *entail* that the statement is true. It does not follow in the least, however, that the grounds are not perfectly conclusive. I can produce enormously good grounds for accepting my perceptual statement that I saw the phrase "the stream of thought" on page 224 of James's book yesterday. The best way to show that those grounds are not conclusive would be to offer *some evidence* for saying that I did not see that phrase yesterday. But no philosopher is prepared to do this. Therefore, the philosophical claim that those grounds are not conclusive does not rest on *evidence*. On what does it rest? On a confusion, I believe. One is inclined to argue "It is not conclusive that that perceptual statement is true because it is possible that it is false." But examination of this statement shows that the words "It is possible that it is false" do not mean that there is *evidence* that it is false. They mean that it is *logically* possible that it is false. But the fact that it is logically possible that it is false does not tend to show in any way that it is not conclusive that it is true.

The inclination to contend that it is possible that every perception is hallucinatory rests, in part at least, upon the same confusion which lies at the root of the Verification Argument, a confusion over the usage of the expression "It is possible." One can construct an argument intended to prove that it is not certain that I did not have an hallucination yesterday, which closely resembles, in an important respect, the Verification Argument. This argument may be stated as follows:

If certain things were to happen there would be good reason to believe that I had an hallucination yesterday.

It is possible that those things will happen.

Therefore, it is not certain that I did not have an hallucination yesterday.

The second premise of this argument corresponds to premise III of the Verification Argument. In order that the conclusion should follow, this second premise must be understood in such a way that it implies the proposition "It is not certain that those things will not happen." I contend that there is no natural interpretation of this premise in which it is both the case that the premise is true and that it implies that proposition.

I have tried to show that there is no sense of the expression "It is possible," and the correlative expressions, in which the statement "It is possible that the consequences of *S* will not occur" *both* is true *and* implies the statement "It is not certain that the consequences of *S* will occur." To show this is to expose the most important error in the Verification Argument. The Verification Argument is a very tempting argument. From the propositions that *S* has an infinite number of consequences and that it is *possible* that these consequences will not occur and that if a sufficient number of them did not occur it would be conclusive that *S* is false and that if it were conclusive that *S* is false then no one previously made certain that *S* is true, it *seems* to follow that I did not make certain yesterday that *S* is true. The proposition that it is *possible* that these consequences will not occur is the premise of central importance. When one first meets the argument one feels that this premise cannot be questioned. It seems so obviously true that there is scarcely need to state it. This apparently invulnerable premise conceals a serious fallacy. This premise must be understood in such a way that it implies that it is not certain that the consequences of *S* will occur. Anyone who undertakes to examine carefully the several ordinary usages of "It is possible" should see that in the usages expressed by III_1 and III_2 this premise does not imply in the least that it is not certain that the consequences of *S* will occur. He should see that in the usages expressed by III_3 and III_4 this premise is clearly false. He should see that in the usage expressed by III_5 this premise stands in need of support and that the proponents of the Verification Argument have offered nothing valid in support of it and that if it were to be supported by philosophical argument it could not, without circularity, be supported by the Verification Argument itself. The persuasiveness of the Verification Argument arises from the failure to distinguish several usages of "It is possible" that occur in different contexts in ordinary discourse. The result of this failure is that in the philosophical context of the argument one tries to make that phrase straddle several different ordinary usages all at once. In the usages expressed by III_1 and III_2 the proposition "It is possible that the consequences of *S* will not occur" is an obvious logical truth. In the usages expressed by III_3, III_4, and III_5 this proposition expresses a *doubt*, implies an *uncertainty*. Through neglecting to distinguish these two sets of usages one is led to think *both* that the proposition "It is possible that the consequences of *S* will not occur" is an obvious truth *and* that it implies that it is not certain that the consequences of *S* will occur.

The proponents of the Verification Argument have emphasized their proposition that the consequences of an empirical statement are *infinite* in number. They have exerted themselves mainly in arguing for that premise of their argument, while they have said hardly anything at all about proposition III*a*. If, however, III*a* is true then it does not matter, in a sense, whether II is true or not. If *S* has only *one* consequence and if that consequence is such that if it failed to occur *S* would be refuted and if it is not certain that the consequence will occur, then it follows both that it is not certain that *S* is true and that I did not make certain yesterday that *S* is true. It will be replied, of course, that if *S* had only one consequence then we could put that one consequence to the test. If *c*, for example, expressed the only consequence of *S* then we could find out whether *c* is true by my performing the action of looking now at page 224 of James's book. If we knew that *c* is true and if *c* expressed the only consequence of *S*, then we should know with certainty that *S* is true. But *S* has not just one or several consequences, but an infinite number. We cannot put an infinite number of consequences to the test. Therefore we cannot know with certainty that *S* is true.

This argument makes an important assumption. The assumption is that I cannot know that any consequences *will* occur. I can know that it *is* occurring and, perhaps, that it *has* occurred, but not that it *will* occur. It assumes that I cannot know that *c* is true *until* I perform the action of looking at page 224 of James's book. *This assumption is identical with proposition* III*a*. Why should we accept this assumption? The philosophers who use the Verification Argument have given us no reason at all. This assumption goes against our ordinary ways of thinking and speaking. I should say, for example, that it is certain that if I were to look now at page 224 of my copy of James's book I should see there the phrase "the stream of thought." My grounds for saying this are that I saw the phrase there yesterday, that there is no reason to think that the printing on that page has changed or been altered since then, that my vision is normal, and that the light is good. These are not merely "very good" grounds; they would ordinarily be regarded as absolutely conclusive. What grounds do those philosophers have for saying that it is not certain that if I were to look now at that page I should see that phrase? None at all! There is nothing whatever which prevents me from knowing now that *c* is true. *I do not have to perform the act of looking now in order to know that if I did perform it now I should see that phrase.* I should also say that it is certain that if my wife were to look at that page now she would see that phrase and that it is certain that if my neighbor were to look now he would see it and so on for an indefinite number of persons. If I can know now that *c* is true I can also know now that *any* number of other statements, which express consequences of *S*, are true. That this number of statements is infinite or unlimited or indefinitely large does not prevent me from knowing that they are all true. I cannot perform an infinite number of actions of looking; but it does not follow in the least that I cannot know what the results would be *if* any of an infinite number of possible actions of looking were performed. With regard to any one of an infinite number of statements which express consequences of *S*, I can give grounds for saying that it is certain that that statement is true and the grounds are what would ordinarily be regarded as perfectly conclusive. The philosophers who use the Verification Argument have put their emphasis in the wrong place. The critical step in the argument is not the proposition that an empirical statement has an infinite number of consequences; it is the unjustified assumption that it cannot be certain that those consequences will occur.

3

Our attention has been concentrated on the fallacies contained in propositions III and V of the original argument. There are, however, other errors involved in the thinking that surrounds the argument. One of these errors consists in a misunderstanding of the ordinary usage of expressions such as "verify," "establish," "make certain," "find out." The proponents of the argument say that if I want to find out whether a certain proposition is true I make a few "tests" or "observations." These few tests may be enough "for practical purposes" but, they say, I can go on making tests forever. "But there is always the theoretical possibility of continuing the series of test-observations. Therefore here also *no complete verification is possible* but only a process of gradually increasing *confirmation*." [26]

Let us take an example. Suppose that I think that *Paradise Lost* begins with the words "Of Man's first disobedience," but that I am not sure and wish to verify it. I take from the shelf a book entitled *Milton's Poetical Works*. I turn to the first page of verse and under the heading *Paradise Lost, Book I,* I see that the first four words of the first line of verse are "Of Man's first disobedience." It would ordinarily be said that I had verified it. The proponents of the Verification Argument would say that I had not "completely" verified it. They would say that I had not even "completely" verified the fact that the first four words of verse on *the page before me* are the words "Of Man's first disobedience." What shall I do to *further* verify this latter fact? Shall I look again? Suppose that I do and that I see the same thing. Shall I ask someone else to look? Suppose that he looks and that he sees the same thing. According to this philosophical theory it is still not "completely" verified. How shall I further verify it? Would it be "further verification" if I were to look *again* and *again* at this page and have more and more other people look again and again? Not at all! We should not describe it so! Having looked once carefully, if I then continued to look at the page we should not say that I was "further verifying" or "trying to further verify" that the first four words of verse on that page are "Of Man's first disobedience." Carnap declares that although it might be foolish or impractical to continue

[26] Carnap, "Testability and Meaning," *Philosophy of Science,* III (1936), 425.

"the series of test-observations" still one could do so "theoretically." He implies that *no matter what the circumstances* we should describe certain actions as "further verifying" or "further confirming" this fact. That is a mistake. Suppose that I continued to look steadily at the page and someone wondered why I was behaving in that way. If someone else were to say "He is trying to further verify that those are the first four words," this would be an absurd and humorous remark. And this description would be equally absurd if my actions consisted in showing the book to one person after another. In those circumstances there is nothing which we should *call* "further verification." To suppose that the "process of verification" can continue "without end" is simply to ignore the ordinary usage of the word "verify." It is false that "there is always the theoretical possibility of continuing the series of test-observations." It *is* possible that I should continue *to look at the page*. It is *not* possible that I should continue the verification of that fact because, in those circumstances, we should not describe *anything* as "further verification" of it. The verification *comes to an end.*

Carnap would say that the statement "The first four words of verse on this page are 'Of Man's first disobedience' " is not "completely" verified because "there remains still the theoretical possibility of denying the sentence." [27] What does he mean by "there remains still the theoretical possibility of denying the sentence"? Does he mean that it is logically possible that someone should *deny* that statement? This is true, but irrelevant to the question of whether it has been established that the statement is true. Does he mean that the contradictory of the above statement is not self-contradictory? This is also true and also irrelevant. Does he mean that there is *some reason* for thinking that the statement is false, or that there is *no reason* for thinking it true? But there is the best of reasons for saying it is true, namely, that I looked carefully at the page a moment ago and saw that those were the first four words; and there is no reason whatever for saying that it is false. Does he mean that the fact that I looked at the page and saw that those were the first four words of verse does not "completely" establish that the statement is true? In what way does it fail to establish it "completely"? Shall we repeat that it does not "completely" establish it because "there remains still the theoretical possibility of denying the statement"? But this is circular reasoning. Carnap's statement "There remains still the theoretical possibility of denying the sentence" embodies the same confusion that surrounds premise III of the Verification Argument, the confusion produced by the failure to distinguish the several different usages of the expression "It is possible."

[27] *Ibid.*, p. 426.

Some philosophers have thought that, when it is said in ordinary discourse that it is absolutely certain that so-and-so, what this means is that it is *practically* certain that so-and-so. This is clearly a mistake. The ordinary usage of "practically certain" is quite different from the ordinary usage of "absolutely certain." It is "practically certain" normally means "It is almost certain." To say that it is practically certain that so-and-so implies that it is *not* absolutely certain. "It is practically certain that *p* is true" implies that it is reasonable to have a slight doubt that *p* is true and implies that the evidence that *p* is true is not absolutely conclusive. "It is absolutely certain that *p* is true" implies, on the contrary, that the evidence that *p* is true is absolutely conclusive and implies that in the light of the evidence it would be unreasonable to have the slightest doubt that *p* is true.

Lewis and Carnap do not, of course, make the mistake of identifying absolute certainty with practical certainty. They make a different mistake. They identify absolute certainty with "theoretical certainty." Lewis, for example, uses the expressions "absolutely certain" and "theoretically certain" interchangeably.[28] Both he and Carnap say that the truth of an empirical statement can be practically certain but not "theoretically certain." How are they using the expression "theoretical certainty"? What state of affairs, if it could be realized, would they call "theoretical certainty"? In what circumstances, supposing that such circumstances could exist, would it be "theoretically certain" that a given statement is true? The answer is clear from the context of their arguments. It would be "theoretically certain" that a given statement is true only if an *infinite* number of "tests" or "acts of verification" had been performed. It is, of course, a *contradiction* to say that an infinite number of "tests" or acts of any sort have been performed by anyone. It is not that it is merely impossible in practice for anyone to perform an infinite number of acts. It is impossible *in theory*. Therefore these philosophers *misuse* the expression "theoretically certain." What they call "theoretical certainty" cannot be attained even *in theory*. But this misusage of an expression is in itself of slight importance. What is very important is that they identify what they mean by "theoretically certain" with what is ordinarily meant by "absolutely certain." If this identification were correct then the ordinary meaning of "absolutely certain" would be contradictory. The proposition that it is absolutely certain that a given statement is true would *entail* the proposition that someone had performed an infinite number of acts. Therefore, it would be a *contradiction* to say, for example, "It is absolutely certain that Socrates had a wife." Statements of this sort are often false, or they are often unjustified on the strength of the evidence at

[28] Cp. *An Analysis of Knowledge and Valuation,* p. 180. [p. 135, this volume. Eds.]

hand. But to say that such statements are one and all *self-contradictory* is perfectly absurd. A philosophical theory that has such a consequence is plainly false.[29]

[29] [Frankfurt very properly raises the question as to what certainty, and the highest degree of certainty, *is*. He complains that I have not "ever attempted seriously and precisely to say what certainty is and what its general criteria are" ("Philosophical Certainty," *The Philosophical Review*, LXXI, 317). I do not do this in the present essay, but I do attempt it in "Knowledge and Belief." I try to describe what I call "the strong sense of 'know,'" and I make the conjecture that it is what various philosophers have had in mind when they have spoken of "strict," "perfect," or "metaphysical" certainty (see p. 70). I return to the subject in "Direct Perception" (see p. 90). Frankfurt himself tries to characterize the notion of certainty by drawing a connection between a person's regarding a statement as certain and his being "willing to take the risks associated with the statement if there is nothing to be gained by refusing to do so" (*The Philosophical Review, op. cit.*, p. 319). He goes on to say that "a statement *is* certain only if it would be reasonable for anyone possessing the evidence available for it to regard the statement as certain" (*ibid.*). Finally, he characterizes the *highest* degree of certainty, which he calls "philosophical certainty," as follows: "A statement enjoys the highest degree of certainty only if it is supported by evidence which justifies a willingness to risk the greatest possible penalty on the truth of the statement. For a person to regard a statement as being certain in the highest degree, he must be willing to risk *anything* on its truth" (*ibid.*, p. 323).

There appears to be *some* sort of connection between certainty and risk taking. "How much will you bet?" is often a good question to ask when someone has claimed that something is certain. But it is doubtful that Frankfurt has stated any *necessary conditions* of certainty. For one thing, it is a dubious assumption that whenever it is certain that a statement is true it is "supported by evidence." (If this were so, philosophical certainty would not apply to "protocol statements," as Frankfurt thinks: *ibid.*, p. 323.) For another thing, the notion that there should be *any* statement at all (whether empirical, protocol, or a priori) with respect to which it would be *reasonable* for a person to risk *"anything"* (disgrace, torture, eternal hell-fire?) on its being true, does not seem intelligible to me. Finally, Frankfurt appears to assume that whenever a person is entitled to assert that something is certain, there is a *risk* ("the risks associated with the statement") of his being *mistaken*. This must mean that the person *could be mistaken*. But it is precisely the *impossibility of being mistaken* that is fundamental to the concept of certainty. And we are most inclined to speak of "perfect," "metaphysical," or "philosophical" certainty, or of certainty in "the highest degree," in those cases where there is a *conceptual absurdity* in the suggestion that one could be mistaken. Furthermore, there are *different kinds* of that sort of conceptual absurdity. Some of these kinds are discussed in "Knowledge and Belief," "Direct Perception," and in Part IV of "Memory and the Past." For a report of some remarks of Wittgenstein about certainty "in the highest degree," see my *Ludwig Wittgenstein: A Memoir* (New York: Oxford University Press, 1958), pp. 87–92.]

Roderick Firth

The Anatomy of Certainty

It is no exaggeration to say that almost all the traditional problems of epistemology can be construed so that they depend for their solution on decisions about the relationship between knowledge and certainty. Some philosophers have maintained, for example, that certainty is the criterion that makes statements about sense experience epistemically prior to statements about physical objects. Thus, from their point of view, to deny all epistemic priority in favor of a pure coherence theory of knowledge is to take an alternative position with respect to the relationship between knowledge and certainty. Some philosophers have maintained that certainty is a criterion of some kinds of self-knowledge, and have argued on this basis against attempts to analyze statements about oneself by reference to other people or to physical objects. From their point of view, to defend certain forms of materialism, or to hold that statements about oneself are logically parasitical on statements about other people, is to take an alternative position with respect to the relationship between knowledge and certainty. Some philosophers have thought that certainty is a criterion that enables us to distinguish necessary from contingent

Roderick Firth, "The Anatomy of Certainty," *The Philosophical Review,* 76 (1967), 3–27. Reprinted by permission.

truths, so that from their point of view to reject this distinction is to take an alternative position with respect to the relationship between knowledge and certainty.

The term "certain" has played a leading role in discussion of these and other epistemological issues, and it is clear that if this term is ambiguous, or if its meaning in epistemological contexts is inadequately understood, the resulting confusion can have serious consequences for epistemology in general. Yet very few philosophers have attempted to explore the concept of certainty in a systematic way. Even C. I. Lewis, who made this concept a cornerstone of his theory of empirical knowledge, had very little to say about the precise *sense* in which he thought that "expressive judgments" are certain and "objective judgments" are not.[1]

During the past two decades the most notable exception to the rule has been Norman Malcolm, whose influential essays on knowledge and certainty have recently been republished in a single volume.[2] Malcolm's explorations of the concept of certainty are guided by an admirable kind of philosophical sympathy that cannot fail, I believe, to make a deep impression on anyone who rereads these essays one after another. Malcolm is always reluctant to conclude that a philosopher whom he has some reason to admire has made an important mistake—however strong the superficial evidence may be—until he feels that he understands *how* the mistake was made. When confronted by a puzzling statement in the writings of C. I. Lewis, for example, or G. E. Moore, Malcolm's characteristic reaction is to ask himself again and again: "What *could* he have meant?" and "What else *could* he have been trying to say?" In searching for an answer he is led to formulate interesting positions that might otherwise have escaped our notice. It is this reluctance to embrace the easy refutation that makes Malcolm, in the best sense of the term, a philosopher's philosopher, and makes his essays an unrivaled source of ideas about alternative ways of interpreting the term "certain" as it occurs in epistemological contexts.

Malcolm has not, however, provided us with anything resembling a complete map of the concept of certainty, and without such a map we cannot be sure that we have not overlooked still other possibilities of philosophical interest. I shall try to show in the following pages, moreover, that even those uses of "certain" that Malcolm and others have

1 I have discussed this matter in some detail in an essay to be published in *The Philosophy of C. I. Lewis*, ed. by P. A. Schilpp.

2 *Knowledge and Certainty* (Englewood Cliffs, 1963). The ten essays include two (on memory) published here for the first time. My frequent page references to this book will be inserted in the text without footnotes.

already defined will be seen in clearer perspective if we can plot their relationships to one another in some systematic way. There are, of course, many different principles on which a map of the concept of certainty could be based, and to the extent that we increase the number of coordinates we can achieve finer and finer discrimination at the cost of greater and greater awkwardness in use. The particular map that I shall outline represents a practical compromise. It is based on just three coordinates, is intended only as a map of the concept of *empirical* certainty, and seems to me to be particularly useful when reading Malcolm's essays and attempting to solve epistemological problems of the kinds he discusses. And I should perhaps add, to forestall a possible confusion, that the map takes no account of those purely *psychological* uses of "certain" in which the word is roughly synonymous with "confident" or "completely convinced."

Most philosophers who have maintained that some empirical statements are absolutely certain have used the word "certain" in such a way that a statement can never be certain "intrinsically" but only relative to a particular person or group of people at a particular time. To understand what they have meant by the word "certain," therefore, we must explore the various meanings that might reasonably be attached to a "relativized" assertion of the form: "The statement *S* (e.g., the statement 'This is a hand,' 'This afterimage is pink,' or 'I am in pain') is certain for person *A* at time *t*." Because of the egocentric ambiguity of words like "this" and "I," however, and hence of statements like "This is a hand" and "I am in pain," there are many important cases in which our formula cannot uniquely identify statement *S* except by reference to a speaker and the time at which he speaks. I believe that the simplest way to meet this difficulty is to use the word "statement" in the familiar sense that allows statements to be dated by reference to the time they are made. We can then alter our formula to read: Statement *S*, made by *B* at *t*, is certain for *A* at *t'*. But of course the cases that have seemed most important to philosophers are all cases in which *A* and *B* are the same person and *t* is identical with *t'*; and so for the sake of simplicity we may concentrate our attention from the outset on assertions of the form:

(1) Statement *S*, made by *A* at *t*, is certain for *A* at *t*.

The assertion that a statement *S* is certain has been understood by most philosophers to entail that *S* is warranted (credible); and the idiom "certain for *A* at *t*," as I have used it in (1), is intended to relativize assertions about certainty in the same way that I shall later relativize assertions about warrant by using the corresponding idiom "warranted for *A* at *t*." In both cases the reference to a *person* is essential. The relativity represented by the expression "for *A* at *t*" is not merely the "logical" relativity that allows us to say, without reference to any person at all, that *S* is certain (or warranted) in relation to one statement *T*, but not certain (or warranted) in relation to another statement *T′*.[3] Knowing such purely logical facts about the relation of *S* to another statement *T* might enable us in some cases to draw the hypothetical conclusion that if *T* is certain (or warranted) for a person at *t*, then *S* is also certain (or warranted) for that person at *t*. But (1) is intended to assert *categorically* that *S* is certain for some person at *t*. Furthermore, it implies nothing at all about the relation of *S* to any other statement, but something about the relation of *S* to a particular person, *A*. And since *S* bears this relations to *A* because of *A*'s characteristics, (1) implies, we can say, that *A* happens at *t* to have those "certainty-conferring" (or "warrant-conferring") characteristics (whatever they may be) in virtue of which it is true that *S* is certain for him at *t*. We may, of course, go on to ask the general question: what *are* the characteristics of a person in virtue of which a statement is or is not certain (or warranted) for him? And to this question there can in principle be as many answers as there are forms of the coherence theory of knowledge and distinguishable alternatives to it. Some philosophers would maintain, for example, that whether or not *S* is certain (or warranted) for *A* at *t* depends entirely on the nature of the *other* statements that *A* believes to be true. Other philosophers would assign a special warrant-conferring role to *A*'s "immediate experience" at *t*. And there are interesting ways of combining these two positions.[4] But no issues of this kind are prejudiced by our neutral use of the expressions "certain for *A* at *t*" and "warranted for *A* at *t*."

It should perhaps also be noted at this point that to use the expression "statement *S*, made by *A* at *t*" as the grammatical subject of (1) is not to assume that certainty can be construed only as a property of statements, or of statements that someone actually *makes*. Many philosophers have used the word "certain" in a way that allows us also to attribute certainty to judgments and beliefs, including judgments and beliefs that are *unexpressed*. And some of the most important uses of "certain" are broad enough so that a statement may be certain although it is *neither* made *nor* believed. Assertions of form (1), of course, cannot fully represent the scope of any of these broad uses of "certain." But alternative formulas are less convenient, and for present purposes it is enough that

[3] For a discussion of this "logical" relativity of certainty and warrant, see Carl G. Hempel, "Deductive-Nomological vs. Statistical Explanation," *Minnesota Studies in the Philosophy of Science* (1962), pp. 133 ff.

[4] I have discussed some of these possibilities in "Coherence, Certainty, and Epistemic Priority," *The Journal of Philosophy*, LXI (1964), 545–557.

every epistemological use of "certain," including each of the broad uses, will require a different interpretation of (1). In principle we can eventually map all the important epistemological uses of "certain" simply by asking ourselves how various philosophers have interpreted, or might have interpreted, assertions of form (1).

Limiting ourselves, then, to assertions of form (1), it seems to me that all the important epistemological uses of "certain" fall into one or more of three classes. There are

(*a*) truth-evaluating uses,
(*b*) warrant-evaluating uses, and
(*c*) testability-evaluating uses.

Since these three classes are not mutually exclusive, they can be taken to represent three co-ordinates of a map that enables us to determine the approximate position of any particular use of the word "certain." (I say "approximate" because, as we shall see, there is a variety of possible uses of "certain" within each area located by the three co-ordinates.) To distinguish classes (*a*), (*b*), and (*c*) from one another it is helpful to consider a few relatively simple examples taken from recent philosophical literature.

(*a*) *Truth-evaluating uses.* When contrasting the certainty of "expressive" judgments about "the given" with the uncertainty of "objective" judgments, Lewis sometimes says that the judgments we make about our own present sense experience "cannot be mistaken." "One cannot be mistaken," he asserts, "about the content of an immediate awareness."[5] It is hard to decide just what Lewis means here by the words "cannot be mistaken," for elsewhere he speaks of the "difficulties which the psychologist encounters in dealing with reports of introspection" and grants that "these *may be sources of error* in any report of the given."[6] Ordinarily, however, to say that some person *A* makes a judgment that cannot be mistaken would surely entail that *A*'s judgment is *true,* so it would not be unreasonable to conclude that for Lewis, at least in some contexts, our basic formula

(1) *S,* made by *A* at *t,* is certain for *A* at *t*

entails

[5] *Mind and the World Order* (New York, 1929), p. 131. Cf. *ibid.,* p. 125, and *An Analysis of Knowledge and Valuation* (La Salle, Ill., 1964), p. 188. [p. 142, this volume. Eds.]
[6] *Mind and the World Order,* p. 62. Italics mine.

(2) *A* cannot be mistaken at *t* in believing *S*, made by *A* at *t*,

and that (2) in turn (assuming that the truth or falsity of *S* cannot depend on anybody's believing it) entails

(3) *S*, made by *A* at *t*, is true.

This is sufficient to make Lewis' use of "certain" what I have called a *truth-evaluating* use; and we may say, in general, that any use of "certain" is truth-evaluating if it allows us to deduce (3) from (1). It is important to observe that (3) is deducible from (1) if we accept the two maxims, "Certainty entails knowledge" and "Knowledge entails truth." If we grant, to put the point more precisely, that (1) logically entails

(4) *S*, made by *A* at *t*, is known to be true by *A* at *t*

and if we use "know" (as we usually do) in such a way that "*S* is known to be true" entails "*S* is true," then we are necessarily committed to a truth-evaluating use of "certain."

(*b*) *Warrant-evaluating uses.* In his *Human Knowledge,* Bertrand Russell says that a proposition is certain in the "epistemological" sense "when it has the highest degree of credibility, either intrinsically or as a result of argument." [7] "Perhaps," he adds, "no proposition is certain in this sense; i.e., however certain it may be in relation to a given person's knowledge, further knowledge might increase its credibility." I shall say that Russell's use of "certain" in this context is warrant-evaluating because it meets two requirements. In the first place (*i*) it allows us to deduce from (1) that *S*, made by *A* at *t*, has a certain specified degree of warrant (credibility, justification) for *A* at *t*. But it does not allow us to deduce merely that *S* is warranted for *A* at *t*, or that *S* is more warranted than *not-S* for *A* at *t*. For (*ii*) the degree of warrant is identified by reference to a logically independent standard—a standard that is not defined either by reference to the warrant that *S* has for *A* at *t* or by reference to the warrant that *not-S* has for *A* at *t*. It is true that Russell has not defined his standard with any precision. He has not told us, even in principle, exactly how to identify a statement that has "the highest degree of credibility." (I shall say something later about how that might be done.) But whatever his standard may be, the fact that he is able to wonder whether *any* statement has maximum credibility for *any* actual person is probably enough to show that it has the logical independence necessary to meet requirement (*ii*). Thus Russell's use of "certain" seems

[7] (New York, 1948), p. 396.

to be warrant-evaluating. And it should be noted that it seems *not* to be truth-evaluating. To say that a statement is warranted, or even that it is highly warranted, does not of course logically entail that it is true; and in the absence, therefore, of any textual evidence to the contrary, there is no reason to suppose that Russell would consider it self-contradictory to say that a false statement might even possess the very *highest* degree of warrant or credibility. To say this is not, of course, to say that someone can *believe rationally* both that a statement is false and that it has for him the very highest degree of warrant. Nor is it to say that a person can *be* rational if he believes that a statement is false when it *in fact* has for him the highest possible degree of warrant.

These remarks naturally raise a question about the relationship between certainty and knowledge when "certain" is used in a warrant-evaluating way. We have already observed that any use of "certain" is *truth*-evaluating if it makes (1) entail

(4) *S,* made by *A* at *t,* is known to be true by *A* at *t.*

We can now see that if requirement (*ii*) were not included in our definition of "warrant-evaluating," any use of "certain" that makes (1) entail (4) would also be *warrant*-evaluating; for surely (4) tells us *something* about the degree to which *S* is warranted for *A* at *t,* even if only that *S* is more warranted than *not-S*. Because of requirement (*ii*), however—the requirement that the degree of warrant be identified by reference to what I have called a "logically independent standard"—we cannot decide whether (4) is sufficient in itself to make (1) warrant-evaluating until we are told just how strictly we are to interpret the verb "know" as it occurs in (4). If a philosopher wishes to use "know" in a very strict way, there is obviously *no* warrant-evaluating implication of "certain" that he cannot construe as an implication of "know." He could say, paraphrasing Russell, that a proposition is known only if "it has the highest degree of credibility"; and in that case, of course, the fact that (1) entails (4) would insure that "certain" is being used in a warrant-evaluating way. Since this is not so for weaker (and, I think, more normal) uses of "know" that admit a distinction between knowing and knowing with certainty, each case must be decided on its own merits.

It will facilitate later discussion if we consider at this point a few of the most obvious ways in which warrant-evaluating uses of "certain" might differ from one another. I think we may assume that the most interesting warrant-evaluating uses of "certain" are those that allow a statement to qualify as certain only if it has a degree of warrant that is, in some definable respect, *maximum;* but there are many ways of construing expressions like "maximum warrant" and "highest degree of credibility," and to each of these there corresponds a different possible use of "certain." These various possibilities reflect the fact, previously discussed, that the expression "for *A* at *t*" relativizes warrant in the same way that it relativizes certainty. The maximum warrant entailed by warrant-evaluating uses of "certain" is to be construed neither as an "intrinsic" property of statements nor merely as a "logical" property that one statement may have in relation to another. It is, like lesser degrees of warrant, a property that statements possess in relation to what I have called the "warrant-conferring" characteristics of a particular person at a particular time. And since the logically independent *standard* that determines whether *S* has maximum warrant for *A* at *t* must be relativized in the same way, it is possible to define many different warrant-evaluating uses of "certain" simply by ringing changes on the personal and temporal variables.

What I have called a "logically independent standard" for determining whether *S*, made by *A* at *t*, has maximum warrant for *A* at *t*, cannot be defined by reference to the warrant that *S*, made by *A* at *t*, has for *A* at *t*. But in principle it *can* be defined by reference to the warrant that *S*, made by *A* at *t*, has for *A* at times other than *t*, or the warrant that *S*, made by *A* at times other than *t*, has for *A* at those other times, or the warrant that other statements have for *A* at *t*, or the warrant that *S* has for other people (actual or possible) at times when they assert *S*, and so on for various permutations and combinations. In general, the highest standards for determining whether *S* has maximum warrant for *A* at *t* will be those that are defined without reference to either *A* or *t*. We could interpret "maximum warrant for *A* at *t*" so strictly, for example, that *S* cannot have maximum warrant for *A* at *t* unless *S* has at least as much warrant for *A* at *t* as *S* *ever* has for *anyone* who asserts *S*. This sets what might be called a "universal human standard" for maximum warrant, a high standard definable without reference to either *A* or *t*. But it is possible to go still further and say that for *S* to have maximum warrant for *A* at *t* it must not be possible to *imagine* circumstances in which *S* would have more warrant for someone who asserts *S* than *S* has for *A* at *t*. This sets a very high standard indeed—perhaps the one that Russell has in mind when he says that no proposition is certain for a given person if "further knowledge might increase its credibility." Yet it is possible to formulate still higher standards by referring to statements other than *S* and classifying these statements by *subject matter* in various ways. A philosopher might maintain that if the statement "This is a knife" is to have maximum warrant for *A* at *t* it is not enough that it be as warranted as *it* can be under any imaginable circumstances: it must also be as warranted as *any* statement about a physical object can be under any imaginable circumstances. (This would raise the interesting question whether any statement about a knife or other *inanimate* physical object can ever be as warranted for *A* as the statement "This is a hand" might sometimes be—for example, if *A* were talking about his own hand while looking at it and moving his fingers.) Other reference classes determine still other standards, and if we finally remove all restrictions on subject matter we can say that for *S* to have maximum warrant for *A* at *t* it must not be possible to imagine circumstances in which *any* statement would have more warrant for *anyone* than *S* has for *A* at *t*. This is the highest possible standard of maximum warrant, and one that seems to have played a role in the arguments of Descartes and others to show that no statement about the "external world" is ever certain.

On the other hand there are also various ways in which the standard that determines whether *S* has maximum warrant for *A* at *t* can be defined by reference to *A* and nobody else. These have the effect, so to speak, of restricting the statements with which *S* must compete for the status of maximum warrant. We might say, for example, that *S* has maximum warrant for *A* at *t* if and only if there is no other statement *known to be true by A at t* to which *A*'s warrant-conferring characteristics at *t* give more warrant than they give to *S*. Or we could raise the standard by reformulating this so that *S* must compete with all of *A*'s *past, present, and future* knowledge. Or we could raise the standard in a different way simply by eliminating the words "known to be true by *A* at *t*"; [8] for these words would normally be taken to restrict the competition to statements actually *believed* by *A*, or at least to statements that *A* would immediately infer to be true if his attention were directed to them. These are of course only a few of the possibilities, but enough to suggest that some of the traditional debates about certainty may have been generated and sustained by the ambiguity of the term "maximum warrant" and its synonyms

(*c*) *Testability-evaluating uses.* From the assertion that *S* has maximum warrant for *A* at *t*, we may be able to deduce something about the extent to which *S*, made by *A* at *t*, can be *tested* (confirmed or disconfirmed) under actual or hypothetical conditions. Even a fairly weak definition of "maximum warrant" would allow us to deduce, for example, since *S* has *maximum* warrant for *A* at *t*, that future experience cannot confirm *S* to the extent of making *S more* warranted for *A* than it already is at *t*. But there are, on the other hand, some propositions about the testability of *S*, made by *A* at *t*, that *cannot* be deduced from the

[8] This particular alternative is illustrated by Chisholm's definition of certainty in his *Perceiving* (Ithaca, 1957), p. 19: "'*S* [a person] is certain that *h* [a hypothesis] is true' means: (*i*) *S* knows that *h* is true and (*ii*) there is no hypothesis *i* such that *i* is more worthy of S's belief than *h*."

assertion that *S* has a specified degree of warrant for *A* at *t*; and I shall say that any use of "certain" is *testability-evaluating* if it allows us to deduce *these* propositions from assertions of form (1). In his essay entitled "The Verification Argument," for example, Malcolm points out that in some contexts Lewis seems to accept the following statement:

> (5) If at any time there should be reasonable doubt that *S* is true then at no time did anyone make absolutely certain that *S* is true [p. 21].[9] [p. 173, this volume. Eds.]

If we assume that Lewis intends (5) to follow from the meaning of "certain," then we may conclude that in some contexts Lewis' use of "certain" is testability-evaluating. From the bare assertion that *S* has maximum warrant for *A* at *t* we cannot deduce

> (6) *At no time after t* can *A* reasonably doubt that *S* is true.

And since (6) nevertheless tells us something about the extent to which *S* can be disconfirmed (namely, that *S* cannot be disconfirmed at any time after *t* to the point at which *A* can reasonably doubt *S* at that time) any use of "certain" that makes (1) entail (6) is a testability-evaluating use. It should be observed, furthermore, that such a use of "certain" might be neither truth-evaluating nor warrant-evaluating. To know whether it falls into either of these two classes we should have to know what *else,* if anything, is supposed to be entailed by (1). For it is clear that from (6) alone we cannot deduce that *S* is true. Nor can we deduce from (6) anything at all about the degree of warrant that *S* has for *A* at *t*. Perhaps I should add, parenthetically, that in other contexts Lewis seems to me to use "certain" in other ways. This particular testability-evaluating use of the word clearly fails to make the epistemic distinction that is basic to his theory of knowledge, for *any* empirical statement, even one of the kind Lewis calls "expressive," can reasonably be doubted by any one of us at some future time under some imaginable future circumstances.

With this map of the concept of certainty to guide us, I think it is possible to see more clearly just what is proved, and what is not proved, by various types of argument for and against the thesis that some of our knowledge is certain. To show this I shall discuss three arguments selected from Malcolm's *Knowledge and Certainty,* beginning with one

[9] Nelson Goodman has made a similar statement: "I cannot be said to be certain about what occurs at a given moment, even at that moment, if I may justifiably change my mind about it at a later moment." In "Sense and Certainty," *Philosophical Review,* LXI (1952), 161.

in the essay "Knowledge and Belief" that is intended to persuade us that in some circumstances the statement "This is an ink-bottle" is absolutely certain. There is no doubt about the importance of this argument, since it constitutes an influential challenge to the traditional doctrine that no statement about the "external world" can be certain. And at this juncture in our discussion it has the additional merit of drawing attention to at least two testibility-evaluating uses of "certain" that are more important than the one we have just considered.

Malcolm grants that it is logically possible that the ink bottle on his desk should suddenly vanish from his sight, and that when he reaches for it his hand should seem to pass through it without any feeling of contact; and he grants that if these thing should happen he might, at that *future* time, come to believe that there has not been an ink bottle on his desk. But this is not to deny, he argues, that in the strong sense of "know" (implying strict certainty) he *now* knows that there is an ink bottle before him; for the fact remains, he says, that "no imaginable future occurrence would be considered by me *now* as proving that there is not an ink-bottle here" (p. 68). The same point can be made with respect to some mathematical statements. "I should not admit," Malcolm says, "that any argument or any future development in mathematics could show that it is false that $2 + 2 = 4$" (p. 63). And on this basis he concludes: "If it is not a certainty that $5 \times 5 = 25$ and that this is an ink-bottle, then I do not understand what it [certainty] is" (pp. 69–70).

As I interpret this argument (I hope correctly), the emphasis that Malcolm puts on the word "now" is intended to remind us, so to speak, of the *position* he is in at the time (t) when he asserts "This is an ink-bottle." He is in the position of a man who has just dipped his pen into ink, who is transferring ink from pen to paper with one hand, whose other hand is touching an object that looks like an ink bottle, and so forth. (If this seems to beg some questions we can say that he is at least in the position of a man who *seems to himself* to be doing, or to have done, these things.) Malcolm's argument is intended to imply that a man in his position (which I have not of course attempted to describe fully) cannot rationally deny the statement "This is an ink-bottle" no matter what he *imagines as occurring* in the future. It is important to observe, however, that the words which I have italicized, although used by Malcolm himself (p. 68), are probably not strong enough to express his full intent. I think he would argue that in his position at t he could not rationally deny the statement "This is an ink-bottle" *even if he were given some good reason* at t—for example, the prediction of a reliable soothsayer—to believe that the object before him is about to vanish from sight, will soon seem to elude his grasp, and so forth. Strictly speaking, of course, to suppose that a reliable soothsayer is present at t is to suppose that Malcolm's position has *changed* so that he is *not* in what we originally called "his position at *t*"; but it does not seem hard to draw the distinctions that we need to clear up this point and put the argument into general terms. Let us say, reverting to the language of formula (1), that a possible change in *A*'s position at *t* has "epistemic import" for *S* in relation to *A* at *t* if and only if it would either increase or decrease the warrant that *S* has for *A* at *t*. And let us say that this epistemic import is "predictive" if it exists only in virtue of the fact that the change also has epistemic import for some statement about events occurring *after t*. Using this terminology Malcolm might be prepared to maintain that given his position at *t* there are no imaginable changes in it (such as hearing the prediction of a soothsayer) that would make it rational for him to deny at *t* the statement "This is an ink-bottle" *provided that* all the epistemic import of such changes for *S* in relation to *A* at *t* is predictive. And it seems to me that Malcolm might be quite right in asserting this, for under the circumstances it might be more rational to explain away the expected future events—perhaps as hallucinations or even miracles—than to deny at *t* the statement "That is an ink-bottle." If we assume that it *is* in fact rational to "protect" the statement in this way at *t* against all predictions of future events, including the most trustworthy ones we can imagine, the statement is, we might say, "ideally irrefutable" for Malcolm at *t*. (This is not to say, we must remember, that the statement is irrefutable for Malcolm at some time after *t* when the ink has dried on the paper and memory begins to fade.) But what conclusion can we draw from all this about the *certainty* of the statement at *t*?

On the basis of the distinctions already drawn, it is not difficult to define a testability-evaluating use of "certain" that would allow us to maintain that ideal irrefutability is relevant to certainty. Since to say that *S* is irrefutable is to imply that *not-S* cannot become warranted, we can maintain that *S* is ideally irrefutable for *A* at *t* if and only if

> (7) There is no imaginable event such that if *A* were justified at *t* in believing that it will occur after *t*, *not-S* would therefore become warranted for *A* at *t*.

And then we can say, if we want to follow Malcolm in making certainty entail knowledge, that statements of our basic form (1) are equivalent to the conjunction of (7) and

> (4) *S*, made by *A* at *t*, is known to be true by *A* at *t*.

This use of "certain" is truth-evaluating because of the implications of "know." It is testability-evaluating because (7) tells us something about the extent to which *S* could be disconfirmed under certain conditions (in this case hypothetical conditions). And whether or not it is warrant-evaluating depends entirely on the way we interpret "known" as it occurs in (4); for it is clear that from (7) alone we cannot deduce anything at all about the degree of warrant that *S* has for *A* at *t*—unless, perhaps, merely that *S* is not less warranted than *not-S*.

As soon as we spell out and classify this particular use of "certain," however, it becomes clear that it is a *weak* use of the term—weak, that is to say, in relation to other uses that are easy to define. A philosopher who is "skeptical" to the extent of maintaining that the statement "This is an ink-bottle" is never certain might nevertheless grant that the statement is sometimes ideally irrefutable—that is, that it sometimes meets the requirement defined by (7). But to be certain, he might say, it must not only be safe from *refutation* but safe from even the slightest degree of *disconfirmation*. He might maintain that *S* is in this sense "ideally disconfirmation-proof" for *A* at *t* if and only if

> (8) There is no imaginable event such that if *A* were justified at *t* in believing that it will occur after *t*, S would therefore become less warranted for *A* at *t*.

And it does indeed seem clear that the statement "This is an ink-bottle" fails to meet this strong requirement even under the conditions Malcolm has described. For suppose that a soothsayer whom Malcolm had good reason to trust were to tell him at *t* that the object before him would soon seem to vanish from sight, that he would then seem to see and hear his own doctor telling him that he had been behaving as though he were having hallucinations, and so forth. It might be rational to protect the statement "This is an ink-bottle" by concluding that these experiences, if they should occur, would be hallucinations. And from a practical point of view such a prediction might have only negligible epistemic import for the statement. But surely it would decrease to some *slight* degree, however "negligible," the warrant that the statement has for Malcolm at *t*. Perhaps Malcolm would deny this, for in the essay entitled "Direct Perception" he says of a similar case that he might be unable to conceive of a future happening, "that would show, *or tend to show* that he was having a hallucination" (p. 93; italics mine). This statement may reflect an ultimate difference in epistemic judgment, one that is not subject to argument, and for that reason I should perhaps limit myself to saying that to *me* the difference between (7) and (8) seems to be crucial. Malcolm's distinctions are illuminating, I feel, and his conclusion probably correct, when he argues that in his position no additional information would "prove" that there is no ink bottle, or "show" that the statement is false. But if a "skeptical" philosopher is asked what *more* anyone can look for than the certainty that this gives him, he is free to reply that he is looking for certainty of a kind that meets requirement (8). Perhaps statements like "$5 \times 5 = 25$" and "I am in pain" are sometimes certain in this strong sense. (To discuss this would carry us far beyond the limits of the present essay.) But it seems clear to me that empirical statements about the "external world" are not.

By reference to our map, furthermore, we can see that we have so far considered only one of the respects in which Malcolm's conception of certainty might seem *weak* to a philosopher who denies that a statement like "This is an ink-bottle" can ever be certain. Requirements (7) and (8), as we have remarked, are testability-evaluating and not warrant-evaluating. They stipulate that to be certain *S* must not be refutable (7) or disconfirmable (8) under certain specified hypothetical conditions. But from the fact that a statement is irrefutable, or proof against any degree of disconfirmation, we cannot deduce that it is highly warranted; and for this reason requirements (7) and (8) will not satisfy a philosopher who maintains, with Russell, that to be certain a statement must have the "highest degree" of warrant. Malcolm does not neglect the issues raised by warrant-evaluating uses of "certain," however, for in a later essay ("Direct Perception") he argues that statements about physical objects are sometimes as warranted as they could possibly be. He maintains that if we are looking for a dinner plate under the bed, the suggestion that what we see is a shadow, and not a plate, would be quite understandable. But if the plate is in plain sight, he says, "neither of us has any conception of what would be better proof that it is a plate" (p. 92). Malcolm makes this particular statement while arguing that in one sense of the words it is sometimes true that a report about a physical object "cannot be in error." These words, as we have noted, are truth-evaluating. But the statement I have quoted seems to be warrant-evaluating. It seems to imply that we have no conception of conditions under which the report that this is a plate would be *more warranted.* At this point, therefore, I shall consider it simply as a warrant-evaluating statement, and save until later the questions I want to raise about the expression "cannot be in error."

It is probably already clear, on the basis of our brief survey of possible warrant-evaluating uses of "certain," that there is more than one standard of maximum warrant which might make Malcolm's statement true. It might be true, for example, with respect to a standard defined by reference to plates only. Perhaps no report about a *plate* is ever more warranted than the one Malcolm makes, though the statement "This is a hand" is sometimes more warranted for someone speaking about his own hand. Perhaps no statement about a *physical object* is ever more warranted, although the statement "I am in pain" sometimes is. And so on.

Stricter and stricter standards can be formulated, and it seems clear that there is one of these, at least, that is never met by the statement "This is a plate"—the standard, namely, that I have previously attributed to Descartes. For even if we grant for the sake of the argument that no empirical statement of any kind is, has been, or will be more warranted for anyone than "This is a plate" is for Malcolm in the circumstances he has described, we can surely *imagine* a world in which some statements—indeed this very statement—would be more warranted. For in the actual world, as Descartes reminds us, we have good reason to believe that people sometimes experience hallucinations and sudden lapses of memory, and that we are all subject without warning to the disorders that produce these effects. (Descartes's argument is based on the fact that such disorders *do* occur, not that they *might* occur.) Yet we can surely imagine a world in which people are immune from such disorders, just as we are now immune from certain diseases of dogs and cats; and if people in that imaginary world had good reason to think that they were immune, it does not seem reasonable to deny that the statement "This is a plate" might sometimes be at least *slightly* more warranted for them than it ever is for us.

Again it must be granted that this conclusion may represent an ultimate and undebatable epistemic judgment. But what should we say if the situation were reversed? If we learned that there had recently been a sharp *increase* in the frequency of hallucinations and lapses of memory —as a result, perhaps, of the testing of a new military weapon—this fact would surely *reduce* the warrant of a statement like "This is a plate" at least to some slight degree. It appears, indeed, when we develop this analogy, that we can consistently reject Descartes's argument only by taking a very implausible position with respect to the disorders that affect perceptual judgment: we should have to maintain that the degree of warrant that the statement "This is a plate" has for a particular person can *never* be affected by anything that person knows about his susceptibility to such disorders. Thus it seems clear that the "skeptic" is right if he maintains that no statement that *we* make about the physical world is ever certain in the strictest warrant-evaluating use of "certain." In one sense of the words it is probably true, as Malcolm suggests (pp. 90, 94), that we are sometimes in *"the best possible"* circumstances for examining a particular physical object; and in such cases, to use Malcolm's words, we cannot be in doubt "in that sense of 'being in doubt' that implies that he who is in doubt has some conception of what is lacking and what to look for" (p. 90). But if we mean by "the best possible" not the best possible in *this* world—the best we can "look for"—but the best *imaginable,* and if the best imaginable circumstances are those in which our statements have a maximum warrant in the strictest sense of "maximum," then we are *never* in the best possible circumstances for making a statement about a physical object. (It is an interesting question whether the same can be said of a statement like "I am in pain"; but again this would carry us beyond the limits of the present essay.)

In discussing Malcolm's arguments I have so far tried to show that there are at least two possible uses of "certain," one of them testability-evaluating and one of them warrant-evaluating, in which statements about the "external world" are never certain. Since I have said almost nothing about *truth*-evaluating uses of "certain," however, I shall conclude by raising some questions about the truth-evaluating expression "cannot be mistaken." In his essay, "Direct Perception," Malcolm attempts to define a strict use of this expression in which it is true to say that some statements about an afterimage—those that describe its shape or color—cannot be mistaken, but false to say that there is some statement about a physical object that cannot be mistaken. This argument has an important bearing on the traditional doctrine that the epistemic status of "immediate experience" is very different from that of physical objects. And I think that once again our map of the concept of certainty helps us to see more clearly just what is proved by the argument and what is not.

It is useful to reconstruct Malcolm's argument (pp. 77–86) by dividing it into two steps, the first of which can be formulated without raising any question at all about the expression "cannot be mistaken." The "first step" is an attempt to establish something like the following, which I shall call the "Incorrigibility Thesis":

> (9) If any person *B*, in any imaginable situation at any time *t′*, were warranted in believing (*i*) that at an earlier time *t* some specified person *A* (who may be *B* himself) sincerely made the statement "My present afterimage is red," and also (*ii*) that *A* did not immediately revoke or otherwise discredit it, then *B* would not be warranted at *t′* in believing that at *t A* had an afterimage that was not red.

(We might say for short that in this particular respect *B* must *trust A*, must refrain from "correcting" him, and that to this extent *A*'s statement is "incorrigible.") The terminology I have used here is different from Malcolm's and calls for two comments.

It should be noted, first, that to say that *A* "made the statement" is not to say merely that *A* "uttered the words." *A* might utter the words "My present afterimage is red" in all sincerity, but if his tongue slipped, or if he does not know how these words are commonly used, others might easily be misled. To satisfy the antecedent clause of the Incorrigibility Thesis, therefore, *B* must be justified in believing that these "errors of use and expression," as Malcolm calls them (p. 86) were absent at *t* and that *A* really took his own afterimage to be red. It should be noted, second, that the consequent of the Incorrigibility Thesis, as formulated in (9), does not read simply "then *B* cannot be warranted at *t′* in believing that *A's statement at t was false.*" The reason for this lies in the fact that *A*'s statement can be taken to imply or presuppose that the thing described as red is an afterimage and not, for example, an image of some other kind (for example, hallucinatory)—a reflection, a speck of ink on *A*'s glasses, or a patch of paint on the wall. With respect to *this* implication or presupposition, the Incorrigibility Thesis does not assert that *B* must necessarily trust *A*'s statement, for on this score it is possible for *A* to be mistaken in essentially the same ways in which one can be mistaken about physical objects. As it stands, in other words, the Incorrigibility Thesis requires that *B* trust *A*'s statement only to the extent of refusing to believe both that *A* had an afterimage at *t* and that it was not red. It does not assert that *A*'s *statement* is incorrigible.

Since it does not assert that *A*'s statement is incorrigible, we cannot convert the Incorrigibility Thesis directly into a definition of "certain" in the context of our basic formula (1). This difficulty can be met, however, by substituting a somewhat different case for the one described in (9). I shall change the case by supposing that *B* is warranted at *t′* in believing that at *t A* said "It looks exactly as if I am seeing a red afterimage," and I shall suppose, furthermore, that this statement is understood by both *A* and *B* in such a way that it is true if and only if *A* sees a red afterimage *or* sees something that looks to him exactly like a red afterimage. This allows us to generalize the Incorrigibility Thesis as follows, taking *S* to be some statement of the form "It looks exactly as if I am seeing a red afterimage":

> (10) If *S′* is the statement that at some past time *t* a specified person *A* asserted *S* and did not immediately revoke or otherwise discredit it, then there is no imaginable situation in which some person *B* would be warranted both in believing *S′* and denying *S*.

Since everything that I shall say about (10) has its analogue in the more complex terminology of (9), I shall not pause for further discussion of the idiom "It looks exactly as if I am seeing a red afterimage."

I think that the Incorrigibility Thesis can be made more plausible by adding several qualifications. In the first plase (10) fails as it stands to take account of the fact that *A* may believe and assert *S* with varying degrees of *conviction,* most conspicuously in the case of a statement presupposing fine discrimination (for example; "It looks exactly as if I am seeing a red afterimage slightly darker in the center than around the edges"). If *S* is warranted for *B* only because *S′* is warranted, and then *B* finds new evidence indicating that if *A* asserted *S* he did so with less than complete conviction, it seems to me that the warrant that *S* has for *B* might decrease to a point at which *B* is still justified in believing *S′* (the statement that *A* did in fact assert *S*) but no longer justified in believing that *not-S* is false. This defect in (10) can be remedied by speaking directly of *A*'s convictions rather than his assertions. This change also allows us to omit the clause stipulating that *A* must not have immediately "revoked or otherwise discredited" *S*; for any act of *A* that discredits *S* can be construed simply as evidence that *A* was not convinced that *S* is true. (10) also fails, however, to take account of an evidential conflict that might conceivably arise in the special case in which *A* and *B* are the same person. For if *S* is the statement "It looks exactly as if I am seeing a red afterimage," *A* might now be warranted in believing that he asserted *S* with complete conviction several minutes ago; but in attempting to "recover" the image in memory *A* might seem to remember it as orange. The rational resolution of this conflict would no doubt depend on the *degree* to which *A* is warranted in believing that he asserted *S* with complete conviction, and also on the time that has elapsed and the kinds of events that have transpired since he asserted *S*.

By taking all these considerations into account in one way or another, we can convert the Incorrigibility Thesis into a variety of interesting definitions of certainty quite different from any that we have so far considered. We might say, for example, that our basic formula

(1) *S*, made by *A* at *t*, is certain for *A* at *t*

can be defined as follows:

> (11) If at any time *t′*, considerably later than *t*, *A* or anyone else should be highly warranted in believing that at *t* *A* was completely convinced of the truth of *S*, that person would not be warranted under any imaginable conditions in believing at *t′* that *S*, made by *A* at *t*, is false.

It is obvious enough that no statement about the "external world" is ever certain in the sense defined by (11); but whether (11) allows statements like "I am in pain" and "It looks exactly as if I am seeing a red afterimage" to be certain is once again a question that I cannot try to answer here. For the present I want only to locate (11) on our map of the concept of certainty, and to ask, in particular, whether (11) defines a use of "certain" that is truth-evaluating. It is clear that this use of "certain" is testability-evaluating since (*i*) it is not possible to deduce (11) from the statement that *S* has maximum warrant for *A* at *t*, and (*ii*) we are informed by (11) that *S* is not disconfirmable under certain specified conditions. It is also clear that this use of "certain" is *not* warrant-evaluating: it entails nothing at all about the degree of warrant that *S* has for *A* at *t*. Furthermore, it surely seems—at first thought, anyhow—that this use of "certain" is *not* truth-evaluating; and we must therefore look with special care at the move Malcolm makes (which I shall call the "second step" of his argument) from the testability-evaluating thesis that some statements about an afterimage are *incorrigible* to the truth-evaluating thesis that they *cannot be mistaken*.

It is important to observe at this point that Malcolm expresses his conclusion in two quite different ways. On the one hand he maintains that apart from errors in use and expression (errors already discounted by the definition of incorrigibility) the supposition that someone might be mistaken about the color of his own afterimage is "entirely without meaning" (p. 85). Taken by itself this might perhaps be read merely as a rough and colloquial restatement of the Incorrigibility Thesis, for it might be possible to express the fact that a statement *S* is incorrigible by saying that it would be foolish, absurd, senseless, nonsensical, or (less happily) "entirely without meaning" to suppose (that is, to suppose *seriously*) that *S* is false. But I think that Malcolm probably means to say more than this, for he immediately summarizes his position in a more forceful way. He asserts that the significant difference between descriptions of afterimages and descriptions of physical realities consists in the fact that the former "cannot embody errors of perception" (p. 86). This seems to show that Malcolm's conclusion is not that it would be foolish to take the possibility of such errors *seriously*, but that in some important sense of the words there just *is no possibility* of such errors. (This interpretation is confirmed by a new footnote appended by Malcolm to "The Verification Argument." He says there: "But it is precisely the *impossibility of being mistaken* that is fundamental to the concept of certainty," and then adds that in his "Direct Perception" he has discussed the "conceptual absurdity" that may sometimes lie in the suggestion that one could be mistaken [p. 57].) [p. 202, this volume. Eds.]. In any case this would be an interesting and important conclusion, and one that I think other philosophers may have reached by the route that Malcolm seems to follow.

So far, however, I have not been able to find any good reason for thinking that if a statement is incorrigible it cannot be mistaken. The relationship between incorrigibility and absence of error is not one of direct logical entailment, for there is surely no paradox in supposing that a statement might be both incorrigible and false, and no paradox in supposing that anyone who believed such a statement would be *incorrigibly mistaken*. It would indeed be self-contradictory to say that we can *identify* statements that are both incorrigible and false, or to say that we can sometimes *know* that a particular belief is incorrigibly mistaken. To say such things would imply that we are able to correct an incorrigible statement. But we cannot infer from this that it would be, in Malcolm's words, "entirely without meaning" or a "conceptual absurdity" to suppose that somewhere among the incorrigible statements (we know not where) are some that are false. It would of course be possible to make the statement "Some incorrigible statements are false" self-contradictory by redefining the term "incorrigible" in some unnatural way that would make it truth-evaluating. We might perhaps interpret the assertion that *S* is incorrigible to entail that *S* is known to be true and hence that *S is* true. But such a use of "incorrigible" would be very different from the use defined by the Incorrigibility Thesis and irrelevant, therefore, to the present question. The Incorrigibility Thesis asserts only that under certain specified conditions we can never be *warranted in believing* that afterimage statements of a certain kind are false; and obviously this by itself does not entail that such statements cannot *be* false.

It seems clear, therefore, that to move from the premise that *S* is incorrigible to the conclusion that *S* cannot be false, we shall need an additional premise. The fact that Malcolm uses expressions like "senseless," "entirely without meaning," and "conceptual absurdity" suggests that this premise might be a principle that follows from some form of the so-called "verification theory of meaning." (This is also suggested by the concluding pages of Malcolm's essay "Wittgenstein's *Philosophical Investigations*." For having argued with respect to a sensation of pain that "nothing counts as mistaking its identity"—a point about *verifiability*—he concludes: "When I identify my sensation . . . my identification, one might say, *defines* its identity" [p. 129].) But it is hard to find a suitable principle of that kind which has even the slightest tinge of plausibility. It cannot be a simple principle to the effect that a sentence is meaningless unless it can *sometimes* be used to make a verifiable statement, for the Incorrigibility Thesis asserts only that the denial of an afterimage statement *S* is unwarrantable (and hence unverifiable) *under specified contingent conditions*. It does not assert that *not-S* can *never* be warranted *for anyone*. It implies, on the contrary, that *not-S* *would* be warranted for *B* at *t′* if *B* had good reason to think that *A* had actually *asserted not-S*.[10] Thus the Incorrigibility Thesis defines a thor-

[10] The status of *not-S* is consequently quite different from the one Malcolm assigns in his "Meaning and the Past" to the hypothesis that the earth sprang into being five minutes ago (pp. 199–202). For this hypothesis, he maintains, is conceptually absurd because *nobody* could *ever* believe it rationally.

oughly relativized concept of incorrigibility that would have to be matched by an equally relativized verification principle of meaning. And unless truth and error are also to be relativized, such a principle could scarcely yield the conclusion that *S* "cannot embody errors of perception."

It should not be overlooked, finally, that there is *some* very familiar sense of the words in which we believe that it *is* possible for someone to be mistaken in describing his own present afterimage. There are circumstances in which it would be quite natural for someone to say "I am fairly confident that my afterimage is slightly darker in the center than around the edges, but I may be mistaken." There is room for debate about the function here performed by the words "but I may be mistaken"; but whatever else they do, they surely express the speaker's *doubt* about *something*. And unless we suppose that in such a case the doubt must *always* be doubt about the meaning of words (a supposition quite incredible when the words are as commonplace as "darker" and "center") we must conclude that it is not entirely without meaning to say, in *some* familiar sense of the words, that we might be mistaken about the color of our own afterimage. The significance of this fact should not be exaggerated, but I think it does place the burden of clarification on those who use the words in some other sense. It adds to our reasons for caution whenever we are tempted to say that a particular warrant-evaluating or testability-evaluating use of "certain" can also be classified as truth-evaluating.

Roderick M. Chisholm

On the Nature of Empirical Evidence

The present paper[1] is divided into five parts. The first is a sketch of what I take to be the basic concepts and principles of epistemic logic; the second is an attempt to characterise in terms of these epistemic concepts those propositions that may be said to be basic to a man's knowledge at any given time; the third is concerned with the notion of evidential support or justification; the fourth is concerned with the problem of defining knowledge; and the fifth is an attempt to formulate criteria of application for some of the concepts of the theory of evidence. Much of what I have to say is by way of correction and emendation of what was said in my book *Theory of Knowledge* (Englewood Cliffs, N. J., 1966). I choose this occasion to make these corrections and emendations, since the topic is basic to the question of "Experience and Theory" and since

A revision of a paper that first appeared in *Experience and Theory,* edited by Lawrence Foster and J. W. Swanson (Amherst: The University of Massachusetts Press, 1970). Parts of the original paper are reprinted by permission. The present version of the paper was prepared under NSF Grant GS-2953. Reprinted by permission of the University of Massachusetts Press from *Experience and Theory,* copyrighted 1970.

[1] I am indebted to Herbert Heidelberger, Ernest Sosa, Robert Swartz, Edmund Gettier, Robert Keim, and Mark Pastin for criticisms of earlier versions of this paper.

I wish to deal with problems that have been pointed out by Professor Gettier and Professor Heidelberger of the University of Massachusetts.[2]

I

We may think of the theory of evidence as a branch of the theory of preference, or, more accurately, of the theory of *right* preference, or preferability. Let us take *epistemic preferability* as our undefined epistemic concept. Thus we begin with the locution, "*p* is epistemically preferable to *q* for *S* at *t*," where the expressions occupying the place of "*p*" and "*q*" are terms referring to states of affairs (or propositions) and where "*S*" and "*t*," respectively, refer to a particular person and to a particular time.

There are two ways of throwing light upon what is intended by an undefined expression. The first is to paraphrase it into ordinary language. And the second is to make explicit the basic assumptions it is used to formulate.

So far as the first is concerned, we might paraphrase the locution "*p* is epistemically preferable to *q* for S at t" in somewhat the following way: "If S were a purely intellectual being, a being capable only of believing and of withholding belief, and if at *t* he had just the duty of trying his best to bring it about that, for every proposition *h,* he then believe *h* if and only if *h* is true, then it would be more fitting to the situation in which he finds himself at *t,* for him to bring about *p* at *t* than for him to bring about *q* at *t.*"

So far as the second method of explication is concerned, we may set forth the following seven principles as axioms of epistemic preferability.

1) Epistemic preferability, like other types of preferability, is such that, for any states of affairs *p* and *q,* if *p* is preferable to *q* for *S* at *t,* then it is not the case that *q* is preferable to *p* for *S* at *t.* (2) Again like other types of preferability, epistemic preferability is such that, for any states of affairs, *p, q,* and *r,* if it is not the case that *p* is preferable to *q,* and if it is not the case that *q* is preferable to *r,* then it is not the case that *p* is preferable to *r.* (3) For any propositions *h* and *i,* believing *h* is epistemically preferable to believing *i* for *S* at *t,* if and only if, believing *not-i* is epistemically preferable to believing *not-h* for *S* at *t.*[3] (4) For

[2] See Edmund L. Gettier, "Is Justified True Belief Knowledge?" *Analysis,* XXIII (1963), pp. 121–123, and Herbert Heidelberger, "Chisholm's Epistemic Principles." *Nous,* III (1969), pp. 73–82.

[3] I have called the terms of the relation of epistemic preferability "propositions or states of affairs" and I have used the letters as "*p,*" "*q,*" and "*r*" as variables designating such terms. I have called the objects of such attitudes as believing "propositions" and

any proposition *h*, if withholding *h* (that is, neither believing *h* nor believing *not-h*) is *not* epistemically preferable to believing *h*, then believing *h* is epistemically preferable to believing *not-h*. "If agnosticism is not epistemically preferable to theism, then theism is epistemically preferable to atheism." (5) For any propositions *h* and *i*, withholding *h* is the same in epistemic value as withholding *i* for *S* at *t*, if and only if, either believing *h* is the same in epistemic value as believing *i* for *S* at *t* or believing *not-h* is the same in epistemic value as believing *i* for *S* at *t*. (To say that one state of affairs is "the same in epistemic value" as another is to say that neither one is epistemically preferable to the other.) (6) For any propositions *h* and *i*, if believing *i* is epistemically preferable to believing *h* for *S* at *t* and also epistemically preferable to believing *not-h* for *S* at *t*, then withholding *h* is epistemically preferable to withholding *i* for *S* at *t*. And finally (7) withholding a proposition is the same thing as withholding its negation.[4]

In order to explicate the basic concepts of the theory of epistemic preferability, let us consider what is involved in asking, for any given proposition and any given subject and any given time, which is epistemically preferable: believing the proposition, disbelieving the proposition (that is, believing the negation of the proposition), or withholding the proposition (neither believing nor disbelieving the proposition). We may consider six different states of affairs which, together with their negations, give us twelve possibilities.

a) The proposition may be such that believing it is epistemically preferable to withholding it (for the particular subject at the particular time). In this case, we may say that the proposition (for that subject at that time) is one that is *evident*. The propositions falling within the

---

have used the letters as *"h," "i,"* and *"j"* to designate such objects. I believe, however, that the entities which are called in th on case "propositions or states of affairs" and in the other "propositions" are one and the same, but this belief is not essential to any of the points of the present paper. Some further defense of it may be found in my paper, "Language, Logic, and States of Affairs," in Sidney Hook ed., *Language and Philosophy* (New York, 1969), pp. 241–248, and in "Events and Propositions," *Nous,* IV (1970).

4 These axioms are used in "A System of Epistemic Logic" by Roderick M. Chisholm and Robert Keim, *Ratio,* Vol. XV (1973). The last three were proposed by Mr. Keim. Versions of the others may be found in: *Theory of Knowledge,* p. 22n; Roderick M. Chisholm, "The Principles of Epistemic Appraisal," in *Current Philosophical Issues: Essays in Honor of Curt John Ducasse,* ed. F. C. Dommeyer (Springfield, Illinois, 1966), pp. 87–104, and "On a Principle of Epistemic Preferability," *Philosophy and Phenomenological Research,* XXX (1969); and Roderick M. Chisholm and Ernest Sosa, "On the Logic of 'Intrinsically Better,'" *American Philosophical Quarterly,* III (1966), pp. 244–249.

negation of this category are those which are such that believing them is *not* epistemically preferable to withholding them. Let us say that such propositions are epistemically *gratuitous.*[5]

b) The proposition may be such that believing it is epistemically preferable to disbelieving it (believing its negation). Let us say that a proposition of this sort is one that has *some presumption in its favor.* The phrase "more probable than not" is sometimes used to express this concept. Our principles imply that whatever is evident also has some presumption in its favor, but they do not imply the converse. Propositions falling within the negation of this second category—propositions which are such that believing them is not epistemically preferable to disbelieving them—will be such as to have no presumption in their favor.

c) The proposition may be such that withholding it is epistemically preferable to believing it. Let us say that a proposition of this sort is one that is *unreasonable* or *unacceptable.* Hence any proposition not such that withholding it is epistemically preferable to believing it may be said to be *reasonable* or to be *beyond reasonable doubt.* Our principles imply that any reasonable proposition is a proposition that has some presumption in its favor, but they do not imply the converse. They also imply that any proposition that is evident is one that is beyond reasonable doubt, but again they do not imply the converse. Hence we have the beginnings of an epistemic hierarchy. (The hierarchy may be illustrated as follows. If the state is justified in bringing you to trial, then the proposition that you did the deed alleged must be one which, for the appropriate officials, has some presumption in its favor. If the jury is justified in finding you guilty, then the proposition should be one which, for it, is beyond reasonable doubt. And its decision should be based upon propositions which, for it, have been made evident during the course of the trial.)

d) The proposition may be such that withholding it is epistemically preferable to disbelieving it. Hence any proposition falling within this category is one having an unacceptable negation. And any proposition falling within the negation of this category—any proposition such that withholding it is not epistemically preferable to disbelieving it—is one that has a reasonable negation.

e) The proposition may be such that disbelieving it is epistemically preferable to believing it. In this case, the negation of the proposition is such that there is some presumption in its favor. And any proposition

[5] In *Theory of Knowledge* and the works cited in the previous footnote, the terms "beyond reasonable doubt" and "acceptable," respectively, were defined as we are here defining "evident" and "beyond reasonable doubt." The term "evident" was defined in *Theory of Knowledge* as we are here defining "certain."

falling within the negation of this category will be one such that there is no presumption in favor of its negation.

f) Finally, the proposition may be such that disbelieving it is epistemically preferable to withholding it. In this case, the negation of the proposition will be evident and the proposition itself, therefore, will be unacceptable. A proposition falling within the negation of this category will be one that has a gratuitous negation.

If we use "*Bh*" for "believing *h*," "*B*~*h*" for "believing *not-h*" (or "disbelieving *h*"), "*Wh*" for "withholding *h*," and "——*P* . . ." for "——is epistemically preferable to . . . for *S* at *t*," then the following formulae will illustrate the categories just discussed:

a) $(Bh)P(Wh)$	d) $(Wh)P(B{\sim}h)$
b) $(Bh)P(B{\sim}h)$	e) $(B{\sim}h)P(Bh)$
c) $(Wh)P(Bh)$	f) $(B{\sim}h)P(Wh)$.

We may use the letters, "*a*," "*b*," "*c*," "*d*," "*e*," and "*f*," respectively, as further abbreviations for these six formulae, and "~*a*," "~*b*," "~*c*," "~*d*," "~*e*," and "~*f*," respectively, as abbreviations for their negations.

Some of the consequences of our first and fourth axioms may now be abbreviated as follows:

a implies: *b*, ~*c*, *d*, ~*e*, *f*
b implies: *d*, ~*e*, ~*f*
c implies: ~*a*
d implies: ~*f*
e implies: ~*a*, ~*b*, *c*
f implies: ~*a*, ~*b*, *c*, ~*d*, *e*
~*b* implies: ~*a*, *c*
~*c* implies: *b*, *d*, ~*e*, ~*f*
~*d* implies: ~*a*, ~*b*, *c*, *e*
~*e* implies: *d*, ~*f*.

These formulae thus exhibit some of the relations holding among the various epistemic concepts defined above. For example, since ~*c* implies *d* (that is, since any proposition which is such that withholding it is not epistemically preferable to believing it is also one which is such that withholding it is preferable to disbelieving it), we may say that if a proposition is reasonable it has an unacceptable negation. Hence any proposition is such that either it or its negation is unacceptable.

Making use of some of the terms just defined, we may introduce still other epistemic categories. Thus we may say that a proposition is *counterbalanced* if there is no presumption in its favor and also no presumption in favor of its negation. In other words, a proposition is counterbalanced, for *S* at *t*, if believing it is not epistemically preferable to disbelieving it for *S* at *t* and if disbelieving it is not epistemically preferable to believing it for *S* at *t*. In still other words, *h* is counterbalanced if believing *h* and believing *not-h* are the same in epistemic value. We may say that a proposition *ought to be withheld* provided that both it and its negation are unacceptable. Our principles imply the Pyrrhonistic thesis according to which any proposition that is counterbalanced is also one that ought to be withheld.

The term "indifferent" is sometimes taken in the present sense of the term "counterbalanced"; in the book, *Theory of Knowledge,* I defined it in this way. But "indifferent" is sometimes taken, in analogy with one of its uses in ethics and deontic logic, to suggest that, if a proposition is thus indifferent to a man, then the doxastic attitude (believing, disbelieving, or withholding) that he may take toward the proposition is one that "does not matter." If we are right in saying that every proposition is such that either it or its negation is unacceptable, then, although there are many propositions that might be said to be "indifferent" in the first sense, there are no propositions that may be said to be "indifferent" in the second. Hence we shall avoid the term in the present discussion.

We have not mentioned the term "certain," or "absolutely certain," in its epistemic sense, but it should be obvious how to define it within the present conceptual scheme. A proposition could be said to be *certain,* or *absolutely certain,* for a given subject at a given time, provided that it is then evident for him and that there is no other proposition which is such that believing that other proposition is then epistemically preferable for him to believing it. Presumably the propositions which are thus certain coincide with the class of *basic propositions* to be discussed below.

Among the consequences of our seven axioms cited above are the following. For our subject *S,* at any given time *t,* every proposition *h* falls into one and only one of seven categories: (1) *h* is evident; (2) *h* is beyond reasonable doubt but not evident; (3) *h* has some presumption in its favor but is not beyond reasonable doubt; (4) *h* is counterbalanced; (5) not-*h* has some presumption in its favor but it is not beyond reasonable doubt; (6) not-*h* is beyond reasonable doubt but is not evident; and (7) not-*h* is evident. The axioms also imply that withholding a proposition that is counterbalanced is epistemically preferable to withholding a proposition that is not counterbalanced.

We now list for future references some of the definitions we have proposed for the fundamental concepts of the theory of evidence. We assume that a temporal reference is constant throughout, but for simplicity we keep it implicit.

(D1) *h* is *evident* for *S* = Df Believing *h* is epistemically preferable to withholding *h* for *S*.

(D2) There is *some presumption in favor* of *h* for *S* = Df Believing *h* is epistemically preferable to believing not-*h* for S.

(D3) *h* is *unacceptable* for *S* = Df Withholding *h* is epistemically preferable to believing *h* for S.

(D4) *h* is *beyond reasonable doubt* for *S* = Df It is not true that withholding *h* is epistemically preferable to believing *h* for *S*.

(D5) *h* is *counterbalanced* for *S* = Df Believing *h* is not epistemically preferable to believing not-h for *S*, and believing not-*h* is not epistemically preferable to believing *h* for *S*.

(D6) *h* is *certain* for *S* = Df *h* is evident for *S*, and there is no *i* such that believing *i* is epistemically preferable to believing *h* for *S*.

II

We now consider briefly a somewhat different type of epistemic concept. Certain propositions may be said to be *directly evident*, or as we will say, *basic*, for a man at any given time. Of the propositions that are thus directly evident, or basic, some may be said to be empirical and other *a priori*. Leibniz referred to these two types of directly evident proposition as "the first truths of fact" and "the first truths of reason," respectively.[6]

We will say that directly evident propositions of the first sort are propositions which are "self-presenting" for the person to whom they are evident, and that directly evident propositions of the second sort are "*a priori*." In defining them, we will make use of the concepts of *necessity* and *truth*, as well as that of the *evident*, defined above.

The term "self-presenting" was used by Meinong and suggested by Brentano.[7] We will construe a self-presenting proposition as being a proposition which is such that, whenever it is true, it is evident. Because of the "whenever," we make the temporal reference explicit in th following definition:

(D7) *h* is *self-presenting* for *S* at *t* = Df (i) *h* is true at *t* and (ii) necessarily if *h* is true at *t* then h is evident for S at *t*.

[6] G. W. Leibniz, *New Essays Concerning Human Understanding*, Book IV, Chapter 9. Compare Franz Brentano, *The True and the Evident* (London: Routledge and Kegan Paul, 1966), English edition edited by Roderick M. Chisholm, esp. pp. 123–132.

[7] Compare A. Meinong, *Über emotionale Präsentation* (Vienna: Kais. Akadamie der Wissenschaften, 1917), p. 3ff., and Franz Brentano, *Psychologie vom empirischen Standpunkt* (Hamburg: Felix Meiner, 1955), Vol. I, pp. 176–180.

(For those who cannot accept the presupposition that a proposition may be true at one time and not true at another the expression "is true" may be replaced by "occurs or obtains" and "*h*" construed as referring to an event or state of affairs.)

Among the propositions which are thus self-presenting for a man at a given time are propositions about his state of mind at that time—his thinking certain thoughts, entertaining certain beliefs, his sensing in certain ways. For it is impossible for a man to think such thoughts, have such beliefs, or sense in such ways unless it is then *evident* to him that he is thinking those thoughts, entertaining those beliefs, or sensing in those ways. We will return to this concept in Section V below.

What now of the *a priori*? It is traditional to say that an *a priori* proposition is a proposition that is "independent of experience" and such that "if you understand it then you can see that it is true." To get at what is intended by these descriptions, let us first say what it is for a proposition to be *axiomatic* for a person at a given time:

(D8) *h* is *axiomatic* for *S* = Df (i) *S* accepts *h*, (ii) necessarily *h* is true, and (iii) necessarily if *S* accepts *h* then he is evident for *S*.

The second clause tells us the sense in which an axiomatic proposition is "independent of experience," the third tells us the sense in which an axiomatic proposition is such that "if you understand it then you see that it is true," and the first and third together tell us that the man for whom the proposition is axiomatic does thus "see that it is true." We next define the somewhat broader concept of the *a priori:*

(D9) *h* is *a priori* for *S* = Df There is an *e* such that (i) *e* is axiomatic for *S* and (ii) the proposition that *e* entails *h* is also axiomatic for *S*.

Now we may define a basic proposition as one which is either self-presenting or *a priori:*

(D10) *h* is *basic* for *S* = Df Either *h* is self-presenting for *S* or *h* is *a priori* for *S*.

Instead of "*h* is basic for *S*," we may also say "*h* is *directly evident* for *S*."

III

The epistemic concepts defined up to now pertain to the epistemic status a single proposition may have for a given subject at a given time. There is also a family of epistemic concepts pertaining to the relations that may hold between two propositions when one of the propositions may be said to confer some epistemic status upon another. Thus one proposition may be said to *confer evidence* upon another, or to make the other evident. Or it may confer a lower epistemic status—that of being beyond reasonable doubt, or that of having some presumption in its favor. In the latter case, where one proposition confers upon another the status of having some presumption in its favor, the one proposition may be said to *confirm* the other proposition. We will call these various relations "justifying relations" for they exemplify different ways in which one proposition may be said to *justify* another.[8]

Our major concern in this section will be to say what it is for one proposition to *make evident* another proposition for a given subject at a given time. It is one of the tasks of epistemology to show ways in which a man's basic propositions at any time may make evident to him other propositions at that time. We will express the relation we wish to define in the locution "*e* makes *h* evident for S." Let us first consider some of the things we wish to be able to say about this relation.

Presumably we will want to say that, if *e* makes *h* evident for *S*, then *e* as well as *h* is evident for S. But there will be many propositions *e* and *h* which are evident for S (e.g. "There is a sheep" and "There is a stone") which will not be such that either one of them makes evident the other for S. We will want to be able to say that an evident proposition may make evident some of the propositions it entails. But an evident proposition need not make evident every proposition it entails. Hence for an evident proposition *e* to make evident a proposition *h* for S, it will not be sufficient that *e* entail *h*.

Nor will it be necessary. Any adequate theory of evidence must provide for the fact that a proposition *e* may make evident a proposition *h* for a subject S even though e does not entail *h*. We reject the sceptical view according to which there is no reason to believe that the premises of an inductive argument ever confer evidence upon the conclusion. If this sceptical view were true, then we would know next to nothing about the world around us. We would not know, for example, such propositions as are expressed by "There are 9 planets," "Jones owns a Ford," and "The sun will rise tomorrow." [9]

[8] One proposition may also confer negative epistemic status upon another; it may render the other nonevident, for example, or unacceptable. What may be said about the positive cases may also be said *mutatis mutandis* about the negative cases.

[9] ". . . in common discourse we readily affirm, that many arguments from causation exceed probability, and may be received as a superior kind of evidence. One would appear ridiculous who would say, that it is only probable that the sun will rise tomorrow, or that all men must die; though it is plain we have no further assurance of these facts than what experience affords us." David Hume, *A Treatise of Human Nature,* ed. L. A. Selby-Bigge (Oxford, 1888), Book I, Part III, Section XI, p. 124.

We will distinguish, therefore, between *deductive* (or *demonstrative*) justification and *inductive* (or *nondemonstrative*) justification. Given a definition of "*e* makes *h* evident for *S*," we will be able to say that *e* deductively (or demonstratively) makes *h* evident for S, provided only that *e* makes *h* evident for *S* and also entails *h;* and we will be able to say that e inductively (or nondemonstratively) makes *h* evident for *S*, provided only that *e* makes *h* evident for *S* and does not entail *h*. What, then, will be our strategy for defining "*e* makes *h* evident for *S*"?

First we will say what it is for one of a man's basic propositions to *tend to confer evidence* for him upon some other proposition. Then we will be able to define an *absolute* sense of the relation "*e* confers evidence upon *h*," where this is construed as a relation that holds necessarily between the two propositions, *e* and *h*, no matter what epistemic status they may happen to have for any subject at any time. A proposition *e* will be said to confer evidence, in this absolute sense, upon a proposition *h* if the following is necessary true: for any subject *S*, whatever tends to confer evidence upon *e* for *S* entails something that also tends to confer evidence upon *h* for *S*. Then, given this absolute sense of the relation of conferring evidence, we may define the *applied,* or *relativised,* locution, "*e* makes *h* evident for *S*." We will say that a proposition *e* makes evident a proposition *h* for a given subject *S* provided only the following two conditions hold: (i) *e* is evident for *S* and (ii) for every proposition *i*, if *i* is evident for *S*, then the conjunction, *e* and *i*, confers evidence, in the absolute sense, upon *h*. In other words, if *e* makes *h* evident for S, then *e* is evident for *S*, and the conjunction of *e* with any other proposition that is evident for *S* confers evidence, in the absolute sense, upon *h*.

Why the latter condition? Why not say, more simply, that if *e* makes *h* evident for *S*, then (i) *e* is evident for *S* and (ii) e confers evidence in the absolute sense upon *h*? The reason lies with the fact that in rejecting scepticism, as we have said, we must allow for the possibility of inductive, or nondemonstrative, justification. We want to be able to say that a proposition *e* may make evident a proposition *h* for *S* even though *e* does not entail *h*. But if we thus allow inductive, or nondemonstrative, justification, we must provide for what may be called the fact of *defeasibility*—and the simpler definition does not provide for this fact.

The fact of defeasibility is this: it is possible for there to be a conjunction of mutually consistent propositions *i* which is such that (1) *i* is evident for S, (2) a proper part *e* of *i* confers evidence in the absolute sense upon a proposition *h*, and yet (3) *i* itself does not confer evidence in the absolute sense upon *h*. When this occurs *i* may be said to *defeat* or *override* the justification that would be provided by *e*. The possibility of such defeat may be illustrated as follows. Consider that conjunctive proposition *e* which makes evident for me the proposition *h*, that there are exactly 9 planets. Doubtless it is possible to find among the things that are known by some learned astronomer a set of propositions *e′* which are such that the conjunction, *e* and *e′*, is a consistent proposition *i* which does *not* confer evidence, in the absolute sense, upon the proposition *h*, that there are exactly 9 planets. (These propositions, of course, must be carefully selected if, as we may suppose, the astronomer himself knows that there are exactly 9 planets. They are propositions which, if I were suddenly to come to know them, would give *me* pause in my confidence in the proposition that there are exactly 9 planets. But the astronomer has still additional information which I don't have and which justifies him in *his* confidence in that same proposition.) The result, then, of conjoining these propositions *e′* with my present evidence *e* for the proposition that there are exactly 9 planets would be such as to defeat or override the evidence that *e* thus provides. If now I were taught just these propositions *e′* but retained those propositions *e*, which as a matter of fact now do make evident for me the proposition that there are exactly 9 planets, then the fact of defeasibility would be exemplified: there would be a set of propositions *i* which are evident to me and which are such that a certain subset of *i*, but not *i* itself, confers evidence in the absolute sense upon the proposition *h*, that there are exactly 9 planets.

And this is why it is not enough to say that, if *e* makes *h* evident for *S*, then (i) *e* is evident for S and (ii) *e* confers evidence in the absolute sense upon *h*. For the two conditions are satisfied in the case where the evidence that *e* would provide for *h* is defeated or overridden by a larger body of evidence *i*. So, to rule out this possibility, we say that, if *e* makes *h* evident for *S*, then (i) *e* is evident for *S* and (ii) for every proposition *i*, if *i* is evident for *S*, then the conjunction, *e* and *i*, confers evidence, in the absolute sense, upon *h*. The second condition assures us that the evidence *e* provides has not been defeated or overridden by any other proposition that is evident to S.

And so, in D14 below, we define the applied or relativised concept "*e* makes *h* evident for *S*" in terms of the absolute or nonrelativised concept "*e* confers evidence upon *h*." In D13, we define the absolute or nonrelativised "e confers evidence upon *h*" in terms of "*e* tends to confer evidence upon *h*" where "*e*" is understood to refer to a basic proposition. In D12, therefore, we define the requisite sense of "*e* tends to confer evidence upon *h*."

In formulating D12, we wish to say what it is for one of a man's basic propositions to *tend to confer evidence* for him upon some other proposition. Speaking roughly, we may say that our definition of "*e* tends to confer evidence upon *h* for *S*" would be similar in essential respects to one which defined it by saying: "(i) *e* is basic for *S* and (ii) if *e* were the *only* proposition that is basic for *S*, then *h* would be evident for S." But in place of the counterfactual we will have a more precise statement.

Suppose, to oversimplify somewhat, the proposition *S* would express by "I seem to see a sheep" tends to confer evidence for him upon the proposition he would express by "I see a sheep." Then, still speaking roughly, we could say that if "I seem to see a sheep" were the only proposition that was then basic for *S*, then "I see a sheep" would be evident for *S*. Our statement would imply that "I seem to see a sheep" *is* evident for *S*, but it would leave open the possibility that "I see a sheep" is evident for *S*. (The latter *would* be evident if the former were the *only* proposition that were basic for S, but it is hardly conceivable that "I seem to see a sheep" could be the only proposition that is basic for a man.) Why do we thus leave open the possibility that "I seem to see a sheep" is evident and "I see a sheep" is not? The answer is that there are certain other propositions—e.g., "I seem to remember having had visual hallucinations all day"—which are such that, if they were *also* basic for *S*, at the same time that "I seem to see a sheep" is basic for *S*, then "I see a sheep" would *not* be evident for *S*. In such a case the epistemic work done by the "I-seem-to-see" proposition would be defeated or overridden by the "I-seem-to-remember" proposition.

Our problem, then, in formulating a definition of "tends to confer evidence upon," is to make precise a set of conditions which will accomplish what was intended by the counterfactual, "if *e* were the only proposition that were basic for *S* then *h* would be evident for *S*." One difficulty with the counterfactual is that, for any proposition *e*, it may be very difficult to contemplate the possibility that *e* is the *only* proposition that is basic for *S*. Even if, so to speak, *S*'s immediate experience does not go beyond *e*, won't *some* at least of the propositions that *e* entails also be basic for *S*—in which case it will be false that *e* is the only proposition that is basic for *S*? *This* difficulty may be met by reformulating the antecedent of our counterfactual and saying, "if everything basic for S were entailed by *e* then *h* would be basic for *S*." But how are we to interpret this conditional?

It will not be enough to think of the conditional as a material conditional and thus equivalent to "either it is false that everything basic for *S* is entailed by *e* or *h* is evident for *S*." For the material conditional would be true if it *were* false that everything basic for *S* is entailed by *e*. And in such a case our definition of "tends to confer evidence upon" would require us to say that, if *e* is evident for *S*, then *e* tends to confer evidence upon *every* proposition for *S*.

Shall we construe the conditional, then, as a statement of necessity? Then we would be defining "e tends to confer evidence upon *h* for *S*" by saying: "(i) *e* is basic for *S* and (2) *necessarily,* if everything basic for S is entailed by *e,* then *h* is evident for *S*." But what if there is a basic proposition *e* which is such that it is *impossible* that everything basic for *S* is entailed by *e*? Our definition would require us to say, of any such *e,* that it tends to confer evidence upon *every* proposition for *S*. To meet this difficulty, therefore, we add a third clause to our definiens, saying "(iii) it is possible that everything basic for S is entailed by *e*."

We are now in a position to put our definitions more precisely:

(D11) *e tends to confer evidence* upon *h* for *S* = Df (i) *e* is basic for *S,* (ii) necessarily, if *e* is basic for *S,* and if everything basic for *S* is entailed by *e,* then *h* is evident for *S,* and (iii) it is possible that everything basic for *S* is entailed by *e*.

We now define the absolute sense of "confers evidence upon":

(D12) *e confers evidence upon h* = Df Necessarily, for every *i* and every *S,* if *i* tends to confer evidence upon *e* for *S,* then *i* entails something that tends to confer evidence upon *h* for *S*.

And, finally, we define the applied, or relativised, sense of "makes evident":

(D13) *e makes h evident* for *S* = Df (i) *e* is evident for S and (ii) for every *i,* if *i* is evident for S, then the conjunction, *e* and *i,* confers evidence upon *h*.

Definitions of other justifying relations would be analogous. Thus if we consider *confirmation* as a matter, not of conferring evidence upon a proposition, but of conferring upon it the status of having some presumption in its favor, we would have:

(D14) *e* tends to confirm *h* for *S* = Df (i) *e* is basic for *S,* (ii) necessarily, if *e* is basic for *S,* and if everything basic for *S* is entailed by *e,* then *h* has some presumption in its favor for *S,* and (iii) it is possible that everything basic for *S* is entailed by *e*.

(D15) *e* confirms *h* = Df Necessarily, for every *i* and every *S,* if *i* tends to confer evidence upon *e* for *S,* then *i* entails something that tends to confirm *h* for *S*.

(D16) *e* confirms *h* for S = Df (i) *e* is evident for *S* and (ii) for every *i,* if *i* is evident for S, then the conjunction, *e* and *i,* confirms *h*.

Definitions of the corresponding senses of "confers reasonability upon" would be analogous.[10]

Let us now turn to the concept of knowledge.

IV

The traditional definition of knowledge may be put as follows:

> *S* knows at *t* that *h* is true = *Df h* is true, *S* believes at *t* that *h* is true, and *h* is evident for *S* at *t*.

In countenancing the possibility that a proposition *e* may inductively confer evidence upon a proposition *h,* we also countenance the possibility that *e* is true and *h* is false and therefore that there are some propositions that are both evident and false. But Professor Gettier has shown that, if there are propositions that are both evident and false, then the traditional definition of knowledge is inadequate. It is necessary, therefore, to revise the traditional definition. I wish now to suggest that we can revise the traditional definition in terms of the vocabulary that we have introduced here.

What Gettier has shown is that the traditional definition is inadequate to the following situation. (i) There is a set of propositions *e* such that *e* inductively confers evidence for *S* upon a certain false proposition *f;* (ii) *S* accepts the false but evident *f;* (iii) *f* confers evidence for *S* upon a true proposition *h;* and (iv) *S* accepts *h.* The traditional definition, in application to this situation, would require us to say that *S* knows that *h* is true. But it is clear that, in such a situation, *S* may not know that *h* is true.

Gettier cites the following example. (i) There is a set of propositions *e* such that *e* inductively confers evidence for Smith upon the false proposition *f* that Jones owns a Ford. We may suppose that *e* contains such propositions as these: "Jones has at all times in the past within Smith's

[10] Our account of confirmation may be compared with the following informal explication by Carnap of a closely related concept: "To say that the hypothesis *h* has the probability *p* (say 3/5) with respect to the evidence *e,* means that for anyone to whom this evidence but no other relevant knowledge is available, it would be reasonable to believe in *h* to the degree *p* or, more exactly, it would be unreasonable for him to bet on *h* at odds higher than $p : (1 - p)$." Rudolph Carnap, "Statistical and Inductive Probability," in Edward Madden, ed., *The Structure of Scientific Thought* (Boston, 1960), pp. 269–279; the quotation appears on page 270. Compare Carnap's *Logical Foundations of Probability* (Chicago, 1950), p. 164. In the latter passage Carnap refers to a subject who "knows *e,* say, on the basis of direct observations, and nothing else."

memory owned a car, and always a Ford" and "Jones has just offered Smith a ride while driving a Ford."[11] (ii) Smith accepts the false but evident *f* ("Jones owns a Ford"). (iii) We may assume that *f* deductively confers evidence upon the disjunctive proposition *h* that either Jones owns a Ford or Brown is in Barcelona. And we will suppose that, as luck would have it and entirely unsuspected by Smith, Brown *is* in Barcelona. Therefore *h* ("Either Jones owns a Ford or Brown is in Barcelona") is true. And (iv) Smith, who sees that *f,* which he believes to be true, entails *h,* also believes that *h* is true. Hence the proposition "Either Jones owns a Ford or Brown is in Barcelona" is a proposition which is such that: it is true, Smith believes that it is true, and it is evident for Smith. But our description of the situation does not warrant our saying that Smith knows it to be true.

What has gone wrong? Is it that the evidence *e* that Smith has for *h* also confers evidence upon a false proposition? This isn't quite the difficulty. For we may assume that *e* itself is a proposition that S knows to be true; but *e* confers evidence upon a false proposition; therefore whatever confers evidence upon *e* also confers evidence upon a false proposition; and so a proposition can be known even though what confers evidence upon it confers evidence upon a false proposition. The problem might seem to be, rather, that *e* confers evidence upon a false proposition *f* and that *h* does *not* confer evidence upon that false proposition *f*. To repair the traditional definition of knowledge, we must add a qualification roughly to the effect that, if *S* knows *h* to be true, then the evidence he has for *h* will not confer evidence upon any false proposition *f* unless *h* itself confers evidence upon *f*. But just how shall we formulate the qualification? Of the possibilities that first come to mind, some exclude too much and others exclude too little.

Shall we say, for example: "If a man knows a proposition *h* to be true, then *nothing* that confers evidence upon *h* for him confers evidence upon a false proposition *f* unless *h* also confers evidence upon *f*"? This would exclude too much. Consider some proposition *k* that the Smith of

[11] Some authors, I believe, have been misled in two respects by Gettier's example: (a) He has used "justify" where I have used "confer evidence upon." But "justify" may also be taken to mean the same as the weaker "confer reasonability upon" or even "confirms." The example given would not be counter to the traditional definition of knowledge, if *e* could be said, only in one of these weaker senses, to justify *h;* it is essential that *e* confer evidence upon *h*. (b) The two propositions which Gettier cites as members of *e* ("Jones has at all times in the past within Smith's memory owned a car and always a Ford" and "Jones has just offered Smith a ride while driving a Ford") are not themselves sufficient to confer evidence for Smith upon the false proposition *f* ("Jones owns a Ford"). At the most, they justify *f* only in the weaker sense of making *f* reasonable. In discussing the example, however, we will imagine that *e* contains still other propositions and that it does confer evidence upon *f* for Smith.

Gettier's example does know to be true and suppose that Smith accepts the conjunction of *k* and *f*, where *f* is the false but evident "Jones owns a Ford." Since the conjunction, *k* and *f*, confers evidence upon *k* for Smith and also upon the false proposition *f*, the proposed qualification would require us to say that Smith does not know that *k* is true.

Should we say: "If a man knows a proposition *h* to be true, then *something* that confers evidence upon *h* for him is such as not to confer evidence upon a false proposition *f* unless *h* confers evidence upon *f*"? This would exclude too little. Suppose that the *h* of Gettier's example ("Jones owns a Ford or Brown is in Barcelona") does not confer evidence upon any false proposition for Smith. Then there will be something which deductively confers evidence upon *h* for Smith and which confers evidence upon no false proposition; this something could be *h* itself as well as the conjunction of *h* with various other evident propositions that do not construe evidence upon false propositions. Hence the proposed qualification would require us to say that the Smith of Gettier's example does know *h* to be true.

Should we say: "If a man knows a proposition *h* to be true, then something that *inductively* confers evidence upon *h* for him is such as to confer evidence upon no false proposition *f* unless *h* itself confers evidence upon *f*"? This too, would exclude too little. Consider the disjunction, *e or h,* where *e* is the set of propositions that inductively confers evidence upon *h* for Smith. Like *e* itself, the disjunction, *e or h,* inductively confers evidence upon *h* for Smith. And if it is such as to confer evidence upon no false proposition, then, once again, the proposed qualification would require us to say that Smith knows *h* is true.

Should we say: "If a man knows a proposition *h* to be true, then something that inductively confers evidence upon *h* for him is such that (i) *h* does not confer evidence upon *it* for him and (ii) it confers evidence upon no false proposition *f* for him unless *h* confers evidence upon *f* for him"? This, too, excludes too little. Suppose Smith accepts the disjunction, " *e* or (*h* and *p*)," where *p* is any other proposition. If this disjunction confers evidence upon no false proposition, we will still be committed to saying that Smith knows that *h* is true.[12]

Have we construed "*e* confers evidence upon *h*" too broadly? We began by considering a single "*h*-evidencer"—a single set of propositions *e* which conferred evidence upon *h* for *S*. But we have seen that even our simple example involves many additional *h*-evidencers. In addition to *e* there are: *h* itself; the disjunction "*h* or *e*"; the disjunction "(*h* and *p*) or *e*," where *p* is any proposition; the disjunction "(*e* and *p*) or *h*"; the

[12] I am indebted to Professor Gettier for the points made in this paragraph and the one that precedes it.

conjunction "*e* and *k*," where *k* is any other evident proposition; thus also the conjunction "*e* and *f*," where *f* is a false but evident proposition; and such disjunctions as "(*e* and *f*) or *h*" and "(*h* and *p*) or (*e* and *k*)." [13]

Though we thus seem able to construct *h*-evidencers *ad indefinitum*, some of them would seem to be parasitical upon others. If we had a way of marking off the parasitical *h*-evidencers from the nonparasitical ones, then we could formulate the desired qualification in terms merely of *S*'s nonparasitical *h*-evidencers. A nonparasitical *h*-evidencer would be one which, so to speak, did not derive any of its epistemic force from any of S's other *h*-evidencers. What, then, would be an instance of such a nonparasitical *h*-evidencer?

The answer is obvious: S's nonparasitical h-evidencers are to be found among those *basic propositions* which make *h* evident for *S*. And so we might say:

(D17) *h* is *defective* for *S* = *pf* *h* is not basic for *S*, and no proposition which is basic for *S* makes *h* evident for *S* unless it makes evident a falsehood which some proposition which is evident for *S* does not make evident.

Then the desired definition of knowledge would be this:

(D17) *S knows* that *h* is true = Df (i) *S* accepts *h*, (ii) *h* is true, and (iii) *h* is equivalent to a conjunction of propositions each of which is evident and nondefective for *S*.

V

What now of the applicability of our various epistemic terms—"evident," "beyond reasonable doubt," "confirmed," and so on? In considering this question we turn from epistemic logic to epistemology. To answer it, we may attempt to formulate certain epistemic rules or principles—rules or principles describing the conditions under which a proposition may be said to be evident, or to be beyond reasonable doubt, or to be confirmed, and similarly for our other epistemic terms. In attempting to formulate these rules, we should procede as we do in logic when we formulate

[13] Still other *h*-evidencers for S may be constructed by disjoining any of the *h*-evidencers above with certain propositions *e*' which confer evidence in the absolute sense upon *h*. Suppose, for example, *e*' is "Jones has just bought a car from the local Ford dealer; the Registry of Motor Vehicles and other reliable and trustworthy authorities affirm that Jones owns a Ford; etc." Then, whether or not *e*' is true, and whether or not not it is evident for *S*, the epistemic state of *S* may be such that such disjunctions as "*e* or *e*'" and "*h* or *e*'" also make *h* evident for him.

rules of inference, or as we do in ethics when we formulate rules telling one the conditions under which a state of affairs may be said to be good, bad, or neutral, or an action may be said to be obligatory, or wrong, or permitted. The procedure is thus essentially Socratic. We begin with certain instances which the rules should countenance and with certain other instances which they should not countenance. And we assume that by reflecting upon these instances and asking ourselves, Socratically, "Just why should our rules countenance cases of the first sort and not countenance cases of the second sort?", we will arrive at certain general criteria.

It is sometimes said that such ethical theories as hedonism are theories telling us what sorts of characteristics are "good-making characteristics" or "better-making characteristics." One could say, analogously, that the attempt to formulate epistemic criteria of the sort described is an attempt to say what sorts of characteristics are "evidence-making characteristics," or "reasonability-making characteristics," or even "epistemically-better-making characteristics."

In the book, *Theory of Knowledge,* I proposed "a sketch of a theory of empirical evidence" and formulated nine such principles. The set of principles was conceded to be incomplete and I noted that "corrections of detail may well be required." As a result of Professor Heidelberger's criticisms, in his article "Chisholm's Epistemic Principles," I now see that the latter observation was true and that the principles I had formulated should be modified in a number of respects.

In what follows, I shall describe briefly certain types of principles or rules which, I believe, are essential to any adequate theory of evidence. The reader who is interested in further details is referred to the original sketch and to Professor Heidelberger's paper. I shall describe eight different types of rule or principle.

1) The first type of principle was summarized in *Theory of Knowledge* as follows: "If there is a 'self-presenting state' such that *S* is in that state, then it is evident to *S* that he is in that state" (p. 44). The formula should be thought of as holding for any subject and any time. It should also be thought of a being an abbreviation for a large set of principles that are more specific—more specific with reference to the "self-presenting state" that is involved. Meinong's technical term "self-presenting state" was used to refer to certain thoughts, attitudes, and experiences which were assumed to be such that it is evident to a man that he is thinking such a thought, taking such an attitude, or having such an experience if and only if he *is* thinking such a thought, taking such an attitude, or having such an experience.

Examples of the more specific principles of this first type would be: "Necessarily, for any *S* and any *t*, if *S* believes at *t* that Socrates is mortal, then it is evident to *S* at *t* that he then believes that Socrates is mortal"; "Necessarily, for any *S* and any *t*, if *S* thinks at *t* that he perceives something that is red, then it is evident to *S* at *t* that he then thinks he perceives something that is red." Other principles of this sort would refer to such intentional phenomena as hoping, fearing, wishing, wondering; for example, "Necessarily, for any *S* and any *t*, if *S* wonders at *t* whether the peace will continue, then it is evident to *S* at *t* that he then wonders whether the peace will continue." Still others would refer to certain ways of sensing or being appeared to. Thus there is a possible use of "is appeared to redly" which is such that, if we give the expression that use, then we may say: "Necessarily, for any *S* and any *t*, if *S* is appeared to redly at *t*, then it is evident to *S* then he is then appeared to redly."

2) To introduce the second set of principles, I shall begin with the earlier, inadequate formulation that appears in *Theory of Knowledge:* "If *S* believes that he perceives something to have a certain property *F*, then the proposition that he does perceive something to be *F*, as well as the proposition that there is something that is *F*, is one that is *reasonable* for *S*" (p. 43). The expression "*S* believes that he perceives something to have a certain property *F*" was used in a rather special sense to refer to what is sometimes called a "spontaneous act of perception." The expression "takes," or "perceptually takes," is sometimes used in a similar way. Thus if a man can be said to *take* something to be a dog, in this sense of "take," his act will be entirely spontaneous and not reached as the result of reflection, deliveration, or inference.[14] And if the man is rational and honest, then, in answer to the question, "What is your justification for thinking you know there is a dog here?", he will say that he *perceives* something to be a dog—that he sees, or hears, or smells, or feels there to be a dog. A man can thus take there to be a dog, in the present sense of the term "take," when in fact no dog is there to be taken.

Why not have the simpler rule: "If a man *perceives* there to be a dog then the proposition that a dog is there is one that is reasonable for him"? What this simpler rule states is, of course, true. But to apply it one would need a criterion for deciding when in fact one *does* perceive a dog.

[14] *In Perceiving: A Philosophical Study* (Ithaca, New York, 1957), I have discussed "perceptual taking" in more detail; see pp. 75–77. "Taking" is preferable to "believing that one perceives," in the present context, for the latter expression, unlike the former, suggests a higher-order propositional attitude (believing) which has *another* propositional attitude (perceiving) as its object. If a man takes there to be a dog, in our present sense of "take," the object of his attitude is, not another propositional attitude, but simply the being of a dog. "Taking," in this sense, might be said to be related to "perceiving" in the way in which "believing" is related to "knowing." Perceiving (or "veridical perceiving") and unveridical perceiving are both species of the common genus that is here called "taking," or "thinking-that-one-perceives."

Our more complex rule, on the other hand, was intended to provide such a criterion; for the *taking* to which it refers is one of the "self-presenting states" with which the first set of rules is concerned.

The second rule, then, was designed to tell us of certain conditions under which we would say that, for a given subject, a proposition is beyond reasonable doubt. But the rule is much too permissive. For it countenances as being beyond reasonable doubt certain propositions which are hardly worthy of this epistemic status. The point was clearly made by Heidelberger:

> As applied to a particular case, principle (B) tells us that if a man believes that he perceives a certain object to be yellow then the proposition that he does perceive that object to be yellow and the proposition that that object is yellow are reasonable for him. But let us suppose that the following facts are known by that man: there is a yellow light shining on the object, he remembers having perceived a moment ago that the object was white, and at that time there was no colored light shining on the object. Suppose that, in spite of this evidence, he believes that he perceives that the object is yellow. It would not be correct to say that for our man the proposition that the object is yellow is a reasonable one. Merely from the fact that a man believes that he perceives something to have a certain property *F*, it does not follow, accordingly, that the proposition that that something is *F* is a reasonable one for him; for, as in our example, he may have other evidence which, when combined with the evidence that he believes that he perceives something to have *F*, may make the proposition that something is *F* highly unreasonable. (Op. cit., p. 75)

Our rule was intended to give the senses their due, so to speak, but it gave them far more than they deserve. Clearly some kind of restraint is necessary.

In what sense, then, can we say that taking, or thinking-that-one-perceives, confers reasonability upon the proposition that one does in fact perceive? We could say this: if the only things that were evident to a man were the proposition that he does, say, take something to be yellow, along with various propositions this proposition entails, then, for such a man, the proposition that he does in fact perceive something to be yellow could be said to be beyond reasonable doubt. But this fact does not constitute a principle we could apply to any particular case, since there is no one whose evidence is thus restricted. In order to have a principle we can apply, I suggest we say this: the proposition that one perceives something to be yellow is made reasonable provided *(i)* the man takes, or thinks-he-perceives, something to be yellow and *(ii)*, of the things that are evident to him, none is such that the conjunction of it and the proposition that he *takes* something to be yellow will *fail* to confirm the proposition that he perceives something to be yellow.

Consider again the man to whom Heidelberger refers. He takes something to be yellow—he thinks he perceives something to be yellow. But he also happens to know that the following set of propositions *i* is true: "there is a yellow light shining on the object, he remembers having perceived a moment ago that the object was white, and at that time there was no colored light shining on the object." Although for the man who knows nothing else, taking, or thinking-that-he-perceives, confers reasonability upon the proposition that he does in fact perceive, the present man, as Heidelberger observes, is not one for whom the proposition that he is perceiving something yellow is thus beyond reasonable doubt. And, I would say, the reason that it is not beyond reasonable doubt lies in this fact: the man's independent information *i* is such that the conjunction of *i* and the proposition that he takes something to be yellow does not confirm the proposition that he does in fact perceive anything to be yellow. Thinking-that-one-perceives something to be yellow not only confirms but also makes reasonable the proposition that one does perceive that something is yellow; but thinking-that-one-perceives something to be yellow in conjunction with the proposition *i* referred to above does *not* confirm the proposition that one does perceive something to be yellow.

I suggest, then, that the members of our second set of epistemic principles might be put in the following form:

> Necessarily, for any *S* and any *t*, if (i) *S* at *t* believes himself to perceive something to be *F*, and if (ii) there is no proposition *i* such that *i* is evident to *S* and such that the conjunction of *i* and the proposition that *S* believes himself to perceive something to be *F* does not confirm the proposition that he does then perceive something to be *F*, then the proposition that he does then perceive something to be *F*, as well as the proposition that somthing is, or was, *F*, is one that is beyond reasonable doubt for *S* at *t*.

The letter "*F*" may be replaced by any predicate which is such that the result of replacing "*F*" by that predicate in "*S* takes something to be *F*," or "*S* thinks-he-perceives something to be *F*," where "takes" and "thinks-he-perceives" have the special use we have attempted to characterize here, is meaningful.

3) A third set of principles may be obtained from the second in the following way: (a) the predicates that can replace "*F*" in our formulation are restricted to those connoting sensible characteristics; and (b) the expression "is beyond reasonable doubt" in the final clause is replaced by "is evident."

Examples of sensible characteristics are: such visual characteristics as being blue, being green, being black; such auditory characteristics as sounding or making a noise; such somesthetic characteristics as being rough, being smooth; those characteristics that were traditionally called "the common sensibles"; and the relations that are connoted by such expressions as "is louder than," "is similar in color to," and "is more fragrant than."[15]

The third set of principles would tell us, then, that taking something to have a certain sensible characteristic confers, not only reasonability, but also evidence, upon the proposition that one does in fact perceive something to have that characteristic. Is this too permissive? I have argued elsewhere that, if we are not to be sceptics with respect to our perception of the external world, we must say that the spontaneous act of *taking* confers evidence and reasonability.[16] Otherwise, I believe, we will not be able to say of any synthetic proposition about a physical thing that that proposition is evident to anyone.[17]

4) To be able to apply the members of our second and third sets of principles, we must also be able to apply principles of still another sort. For the members of the second and third sets of principles each contain a *proviso*. They tell us that taking something to be F confers reasonability or evidence upon the proposition that one perceives something to be F

[15] See *Theory of Knowledge,* pp. 46–47, for a fuller list.

[16] See *Perceiving: A Philosophical Study,* chap. 6 ("Some Marks of Evidence"), and "'Appear,' 'Take,' and 'Evident,'" *Journal of Philosophy,* LIII (1956), pp. 722–731, reprinted in Robert Swartz, ed., *Perceiving, Sensing, and Knowing* (Garden City, New York, 1965).

[17] Heidelberger proposes what he calls the "traditional empirical" alternative to our third set of principles. This may be suggested by: "the proposition that an object looks rectangular to a man makes evident the proposition that the object is rectangular" (p. 82). I think this principle, too, is sound—provided that "looks rectangular" is taken in that phenomenal or noncomparative sense which is such that, if it has that sense in the sentence "All rectangular things look rectangular under conditions that are optimum for viewing shape," then the sentence is both true and synthetic. But the proposed principle has other possible interpretations under which it would not be satisfactory. Thus it would be inapplicable if "looks rectangular" were taken to mean the same as "looks the way rectangular objects look under conditions such as those that now obtain" or "looks the way I remember rectangular objects to have looked when I have perceived them in the past." And the proposed principle would be less plausible than any of my third set of principles if "looks rectangular" were taken to mean the same as "looks the way I think-I-remember rectangular objects having looked to me when I have thought-I-have-perceived them in the past" (for surely the object of thinking-that-one-remembers-having-thought-that-one-perceived is not *more* worthy of credence than that of thinking-that-one-perceives). And although the proposed principle, when taken in its first sense above, may be an alternative to my third set of principles pertaining to sensible characteristics, it does not provide an alternative to the *second* set of principles pertaining to other types of perceptual taking.

provided that the following condition holds: there is no evident proposition *i* such that the conjunction of *i* and the proposition that one takes something to be *F* *fails* to confirm the proposition that one perceives something to be *F*. Hence our fourth set of principles should tell us what types of proposition *i* are such that the conjunction of *i* and the proposition that one takes something to be *F* *fails* to confirm the proposition that one perceives something to be *F*. How are we to specify such propositions *i*? I shall attempt only a general characterization.

Such propositions *i* would be propositions casting doubt upon the particular testimony of the senses. They could do this in two ways—either "internally" by constituting conflicting testimony, or "externally" by suggesting the possibility of some perceptual malfunction.

The "internal" case presents no problem. Consider a man who thinks-he-sees something to be the only object in his hand and to be round and who, at the same time, things-he-feels something to be the only object in his hand and to be rectangular. We may say that each of these takings casts doubt upon the intentional object of the other. The two takings in conjunction are such as to fail to confirm the proposition that there is just one object in his hand and that object is round, and they also fail to confirm the proposition that there is just one object in his hand and that object is rectangular.

What of the "external" case—those evident propositions *i* which suggest the possibility of perceptual malfunction? If it *were* evident to our subject that his senses were not functioning properly, then, of course, there would be an *i* of the sort described. But we have not yet specified any conditions under which such a proposition *i* might be evident to him. Can we describe such a proposition *i* without assuming that our subject has any evidence beyond that so far countenanced by our principles? Heidelberger's criticisms suggest that he might put the problem in the following way: Can we describe such propositions *i* without abandoning the "program of establishing as evident propositions about physical things entirely on the basis of subjective propositions" (p. 76), where "subjective propositions" are those propositions about "self-presenting states" referred to in our first set of principles?

Here we must distinguish at least two different questions. The first question would be: "Suppose we wish to describe conditions under which the proposition that a man is perceiving some object to be *F* is one that is evident or beyond reasonable doubt for him. Can we do this without assuming that some *other* proposition about a physical object is evident to the man?" The answer to *this* question would seem clearly to be affirmative. For our principles say merely that as long as propositions of a certain sort are *not* evident to the man, then, if he takes something to be *F*, it is evident or reasonable to him that something is *F*.

The second question would be: "Consider the situation of a man taking something to be *F* and his *not* being such that it is evident or reasonable to him that he is then perceiving something to be *F*. Can we describe this situation without assuming that some other proposition about a physical thing is evident or reasonable for him?" Here, too, I think the answer is affirmative. Consider a set of believings, takings, and seemings-to-remember of the following sort: the various propositions which are the intentional objects of the members of the set (the propositions that one believes, takes, or seems to remember to be true) are such that, in conjunction, they are consistent and logically *confirm* the proposition that one is *not* perceiving anything to be *F*. Consider this situation: a man takes something to be yellow; he seems to remember having had a sensory disorder causing him to mistake the colors of things; and he believes that the circumstances that now obtain are of the sort that have always misled him in the past. I suggest that the propositions which are the intentional objects of this seeming-to-remember and this believing are such that they logically confirm the proposition that he is not now perceiving anything to be yellow. And these propositions need not themselves be evident in order for the present testimony of the senses to be discredited. They need only be the objects of believing and of seeming-to-remember; and, by our first set of principles, if they are such objects, then it will be evident to the man that he does thus believe or seem-to-remember.

An adequate formulation of our fourth set of principles, then, would tell us what propositions would *confirm* the proposition that one is *not* perceiving anything to be *F*. And our principles will say that such propositions are of this sort: the proposition *i* asserting that one believes, takes, or seems-to-remember them to be true will be such that the conjunction of *i* and the proposition that one takes something to be *F fails to confirm* the proposition that one perceives something to be *F*.

We should remind ourselves that our principles are intended only to formulate *sufficient* conditions for the applicability of our epistemic terms. They are not intended to formulate *necessary* conditions. Thus, from the fact that a man takes something to be yellow under conditions where there is no *i* of the sort we have described, we may infer that it is evident to him that he is perceiving something to be yellow. But, from the fact that he takes something to be yellow under conditions where there is such an *i,* we may *not* infer that it is *not* evident to him that he is perceiving something to be yellow.

5) Our fifth set of principles, pertaining to "thinking-that-one-remembers," or "seeming-to-remember," will be analogous to our second set, pertaining to "thinking-that-one-perceives." But where our second set tells us that thinking-that-one-perceives confers *reasonability* upon

the proposition that one does perceive, this fifth set will tell us that thinking-that-one-remembers confers some presumption in favor of the proposition that one does remember. I suggest that the members of this fifth set might be put in the following form:

> Necessarily, for any *S* and any *t*, if (i) *S* at *t* believes himself to remember having at a certain time perceived something to be *F*, and if (ii) there is no proposition *i* such that *i* is evident to *S* and such that the conjunction of *i* and the proposition that *S* believes himself to remember having at that time perceived something to be *F* does not confirm the proposition that he does then remember having perceived something to be *F*, then the proposition that he does then remember having perceiced somthing at that time to be *F*, as well as the proposition that he did perceive something at that time to be *F* and the proposition that something at that time was, or had been, *F*, is one that has some presumption in its favor for *S* at *t*.

6) Our sixth set of principles will be analogous to the third. Where the third describes conditions under which thinking-that-one-perceives confers evidence, the sixth will describe conditions under which thinking-that-one-remembers confers reasonability. The sixth may be obtained from the fifth as follows: (a) the predicates that replace "*F*" in our formulation are restricted to those connoting sensible characteristics; and (b) the expression "has some presumption in its favor" in the final clause of our formulation is replaced by "is beyond reasonable doubt." In short, thinking that one remembers having perceived something to have had a certain sensible characteristic not only confirms, but also confers reasonability upon the proposition that one does in fact remember having perceived something to have had that characteristic.

7) The seventh set of principles would be analogous to the fourth. The fourth set of principles, it will be recalled, tells of certain conditions under which taking something to be *F* fails to confer evidence or reasonability upon the proposition that one perceives something to be *F*. The seventh set, analogously, would specify conditions under which thinking-that-one-remembers having perceived something to be *F* fails to confirm or confer reasonability upon the proposition that one does remember having perceived something to be *F*. *If* it is possible to formulate an adequate set of principles of the fourth type, then, I think, it is also possible to formulate an adequate set of principles of this seventh type.

8) Our eighth set of principles would make use of the notion of *concurrence,* where this notion is defined as follows: any set of propositions that are mutually consistent and such that no one of them entails any other of them is concurrent provided only that each member of the set is confirmed by the conjunction of all the other members of the set. In *Theory of Knowledge,* I proposed the following, somewhat over-

simplified example of a set of concurrent propositions: (h) "There is a cat on the roof today"; (i) "There was a cat on the roof yesterday"; (j) "There was a cat on the roof the day before yesterday"; (k) "There was a cat on the roof the day before the day before yesterday"; and (l) "There is a cat on the roof almost every day." [18]

One example, then, of an epistemic principle making use of this concept of concurrence would be the following, which tells us, in effect, that every perceptual proposition belonging to a concurrent set of reasonable propositions is evident:

> Necessarily, for any *S* and any *t*, if (i) *S* at *t* believes himself to perceive something to be *F*, if (ii) there is no proposition *i* such that *i* is evident to *S* and such that the conjunction of *i* and the proposition that *S* believes himself to perceive something to be *F* does not confirm the proposition that he does then perceive something to be *F*, and if (iii) the proposition that he does then perceive something to be *F* is a member of a set of concurrent propositions each of which is beyond reasonable doubt for *S* at *t*, then the proposition that he does then perceive something to be *F*, as well as the proposition that something is, or was *F*, is one that is evident for *S* at *t*.

Any adequate theory of empirical evidence would include canons of inductive logic and doubtless many other epistemic principles as well. But, I am certain, it would also include principles of the sort I have tried to describe.

[18] The notion of concurrence is similar to what H. H. Price has called "coherence" and to what C. I. Lewis has called "congruence"; see Price's *Perception* (New York, 1933), p. 183, and Lewis' *An Analysis of Knowledge and Valuation* (La Salle, Ill., 1946), p. 338. Compare also Bertrand Russell, *An Inquiry into Meaning and Truth* (New York, 1940), pp. 201–202, and Roderick Firth, "Coherence, Certainty, and Epistemic Priority," *Journal of Philosophy*, LXI (1964), pp. 545–557.

III

MEMORY

Alexius Meinong

Toward an Epistemological Assessment of Memory

People who reflect on psychological matters have always been intrigued by the ability to call past events into the present through memory. We all know that not even the ordinary person can avoid forming an opinion about the efficiency of his memory, and that the development of a good memory is one of the few things that even superficial common-sense pedagogy regards as an educational goal which is easy to comprehend but just as easy to overestimate. Thus, it is only natural that, since the days of Plato and Aristotle, psychological researchers have dealt with a set of problems which seemed to combine relatively great accessibility with an easy transformability into the needs of everyday life, thus affording, above all, the prospect of practical application which is so valuable for any type of theoretical work. Realizing, in addition, that present-day psychological researchers, who rightly strive for greater and greater exactness, are very well aware of the phenomenon of memory,[1] no one will

Translated by Linda L. McAlister and Margarete Schättle. Reprinted with permission. This work first appeared in the *Vierteljahrsschrift für wissenschaftliche Philosophie,* Band X (1886), pp. 7–33. It is reprinted in Band II of the *Gesamt Ausgabe* of Alexius Meinong, edited by Rudolf Kindinger and Rudolf Haller (Graz: Akademische Druck- u. Verlagsanstalt, 1971), pp. 185–213.

[1] The recently published investigations by H. Ebbinghaus, *"Über das Gedächtnis"* (Leipzig: 1885) are evidence thereof.

be tempted to say that the area in question has been neglected by psychology.

On the other hand, it seems fairly obvious that the study of memory is not one of the main concerns of the rather young science of epistemology. There are some epistemologists who do occasionally mention memory as a source of knowledge along with the senses; but so far hardly anyone has assumed that the phenomenon of memory could be of basic interest for epistemological investigation. Yet a very simple deliberation seems to bear out the suspicion that the preference for the large and ultimate questions so typical of earlier metaphysics, which preference has been carried over into modern epistemological theory, has had less than favorable effects on the study of the elementary data of knowledge. Whatever the truth of the matter might be, one thing seems certain—no one has as yet planted the flag of epistemology in an area to which it has more than a valid claim. To take possession of this area in the name of epistemology shall be the aim of the following sketch. If the claim is good and if the ground is worth the effort, then my own strength, as well as that of others, should be devoted to securing the possession and to cultivating the newly won ground.

A first fleeting glance might easily give the impression that what are commonly considered activities of memory can have no claim at all to the name "knowledge," and cannot, therefore, be the subject of epistemological investigations, since association and reproduction belong exclusively to the process of presentation, which, no matter how important it might be for the creation of knowledge, can never be regarded as knowledge itself. A second glance, however, is enough to show how little justice we do the facts under discussion if we try to force them into the framework of presentation, in which, strictly speaking, the difference between true and false, justified and unjustified, does not exist. The traditional meaning of the German word "Erinnerung" shows with sufficient clarity that the demands made upon the memory are not restricted to recalling various contents of presentation back into consciousness. But we are not concerned here with the characteristic activity so often attributed to remembering, but rather, if one can say so, with the much more obvious fact that he who remembers must remember *something,* and this "something" can by no means be interpreted as referring only to a certain content of presentation. The contrast set forth here can be further clarified by means of an example. The painter can imagine a picture before he sets out to put it on canvas; the musician can think of a piece of music before he writes it down. Each of them, in so doing, has a presentation of something, but this "something" exists only in their respective thoughts, it is nothing but the content thereof. If a person remembers a shape or a musical theme, he is certainly thinking of a content, but what distinguishes these cases is that something is added to the presentation and this is neither the simple fact that the contents originated in the earlier experiences of the person remembering, or the knowledge of such origins gained from psychological investigation—for both might also be present in the artist who creates out of "pure fantasy." What is added is the clear and, here, very essential conviction of the person remembering, that the image in his memory relates to a real experience, i.e., that he is thinking of something that actually happened, and not of something that, whatever the causes, he arbitrarily or accidentally thought up or invented. It would certainly never occur to anybody to say that he remembers this or that, if he lacks such a conviction. This judgement, which is made with a distinct claim to credibility, and which usually stands up to doubts voiced later on, must be subject to epistemological investigation just as is any other case of actual or purported knowledge. Whether or not such an investigation will reveal certain peculiar or marked aspects which call for a more thorough investigation is something that cannot be presupposed, but is bound to be revealed if one looks at the epistemological characteristics of the phenomena under discussion. Since we attempt to do this below, it is perhaps not superfluous to point out that judgements which are made, so to speak, on the basis or authority of memory, which from now on we will call memory judgements for short, are in no way always expressed in the following form: "I remember this or that," or even better, "I remember that this and that has taken place." Because I remember, or rather, while I am remembering, I can easily make a judgment about that which I am remembering, without, at the same time, making a special judgement about the remembering itself. Thousands of experiences seem to bear this out: If I remember the experiences of last summer after I have returned home, I can be making judgements about a very great variety of things. I may be thinking of a pine forest, and in the middle of it a cozy working place under a simple wooden roof, or many stimulating conversations with dear friends, or the deep green waters of a little mountain lake, or two little churches on the mountain slope, or of a thousand other things, yet it seems there is no necessity to think about remembering *per se*. Cases like the one we discussed above, where the remembering itself forms the content of the judgement, must be regarded as more complicated and, in this respect, as secondary constructs, for here the simple act of memory is supplemented by reflection on itself. Since, however, our further observations will be relevant to both forms of memory judgements, it is not necessary to continue the investigation of the above-mentioned difference.

Nor do we have to discuss the question what it really means to say that memory must refer to, or, so to speak, correspond to, things that actually happened. This is nothing but a new form of the old, and recently so much discussed, question of the reality of the external world, of immanence and transcendence, or whatever more or less misleading names you want to use. As far as can be predicted at present, memory judgements do not offer a genuine contribution to the solution of this controversy. We remember reality in exactly the same way or at least in the same sense as we are able, in general, to judge reality in order to know about reality. It seems that even in the area of memory judgements an understanding between opposing views could easily be achieved. Almost everybody would be willing to admit that I cannot remember something that I have not experienced; similarly, most people would also agree that I really cannot experience what takes place outside of me, but only what goes on within me. Thus we have admitted that we can actually and directly remember only the data of the mental life, i.e., thoughts and feelings, judgements and desires; everything beyond these data that may form part of the memory can do so only on the basis of such data, provided that one succeeds in establishing a bridge between them and the world outside the mind. We may regard all memory judgements as directly related to mental data, but naturally only to those belonging to the past, and in so doing we need not fear that we are prejudicing epistemological or metaphysical controversies without prior investigation.

With this last formulation we have arrived at the point where epistemological interest is specifically directed to memory judgements, although at first only to the simple question of their legitimacy, if we may use that expression. On what right, on what authority does a person base his use of memory to make a judgement about his mental past? In asking such a question the epistemologist need not, by any means, consider himself the supreme judge of truth and falsity; [2] one often asks in order to prove something, but much more frequently and naturally in order to learn. The epistemologist may well leave the question of proof to the logician, for the epistemologist is satisfied if he succeeds in understanding the nature of human knowledge and can follow it on its various paths. With this in mind, we now ask the question of "quid juris" in memory judgements: It shall not be our aim to doubt their trustworthiness, but, taking that for granted, we shall attempt to determine whether this trustworthiness is based on something which these judgements have in common with others that epistemologists have already investigated, or whether it is based on something which, due to its special nature, requires special consideration.

2 Compare the exhaustive exposition in my *Über philosophische Wissenschaft und ihre Propädeutik* (Vienna: 1885), p. 6. [This work is to be reprinted in Band V of the *Gesamt Ausgabe,* edited by Roderick M. Chisholm.]

It is superfluous to point out expressly that the above-mentioned requirement of legitimacy does in no way imply that everything that we can justifiably call knowledge must be proven or provable. Aristotle, too, pointed out that every proof must rest directly upon premisses which are unproved and cannot be proven. We could add here that the relationship between premisses and conclusion itself constitutes the content of a cognition,[3] which guarantees that it is possible and necessary to give up the search for proofts at a certain point. Even the layman is familiar with many judgements which carry the guarantee of truth in themselves because they contain, in addition to the firmness of conviction, which might also be present in erroneous judgements, that peculiar, perhaps irreducible element that we have traditionally attempted to describe with phrases such as, "directly evident," or "self-evident," and others; but this is merely to give them a name, something which is unavoidable with irreducible data such as these.

We are even less likely to fall into error if we insist that every judgement which claims to be knowledge must either be directly evident or contain sufficient basis for its proof within itself. Nor can memory judgements avoid these alternatives; and it is the next task of epistemological investigation to answer the basically rather elementary, but up to now seldom asked question, whether the trustworthiness of memory comes from direct insight or must be based upon proof.

It is natural to discuss the possibility of direct evidence first. It is well known that in the theoretical treatment of ultimate data, very special difficulties arise; we could say that this is due to the fact that, should insecurity or difference of opinion arise in connection with such data, the traditional remedy of proof cannot be employed, but the indirect procedure may not always be applicable either. This is why, if someone insists that something is evident or not evident to him, it may be very difficult to convince him otherwise, even if what he claims is obviously wrong. Indeed, by pointing to the necessity of recognizing ultimate truths, epistemology would have provided the forces of arbitrariness and prejudice with very effective weapons, had it not, on the other hand, provided the means for combatting such dangers. A survey of the various forms in which direct evidence actually occurs—a classification based upon empirical investigations—is not the least of these means. Taking into consideration the great improbability of the assumption that a judgement whose evidence is questionable would have nothing in common with judgements of unquestionable evidence, other than this very evidence, we seem to be justified in rejecting the doubtful evidence of a judgement if this judgement cannot be subsumed under one of the cate-

3 Compare my "Zur Relationstheorie," pp. 106ff. [Reprinted in Band II of the *Gesamt Ausgabe,* pp. 1–183.]

gories established by this classification. Yet the present case differs insofar as we are not concerned with the question of evidence in relation to an individual judgement, but in relation to a whole group of judgements, i.e., memory judgements. Nevertheless, it might be of value even here to attempt to subsume them under previously established categories of evidence.

The best way to survey the cases of direct evidence seems to be the old distinction, first expressly formulated by Hume, between judgements of "fact," and judgements of "relations of ideas," [4] or as we can say for the sake of brevity, existential and relational judgements. This distinction, although it may not be completely immune to objections posed by a more penetrating epistemological analysis, nonetheless serves many practical needs. With regard to the evident in particular we notice immediately that it plays a part in both of the above-mentioned kinds of judgements, and occurs in each of them in a very characteristic form. What our inner perception tells us about the conditions of our consciousness is directly evident, carries in itself the guarantee of infallible certainty; on the other hand, difference or similarity, or again incompatibility between certain presentational contents seem to be just as compelling. Judgements of inner perception claim that mental realities present to the perceiver exist; judgements of difference or similarity, on the one hand, and of incompatibility, on the other hand, concern relations or presentational contents, and their validity is completely independent of whether or not the judged contents correspond to something in reality.[5] Leaving aside memory for the time being, one can also claim that apart from judgements of inner perception there are no directly evident existential judgements, and, apart from the area of relations of comparison and compatibility there are no other directly evident relational judgements.[6] That means that we can formulate the question which concerns us at present more precisely as follows: Are memory judgements existential or relational judgements? And when we have clarified that, we can ask: Do they belong to one of the special areas in which we ordinarily find the directly evident?

To many people the thought that memory judgements could be relational would not even seem to be worth mentioning. This thought, however, is not as far-removed from the host of ordinary reflections as one is inclined to believe at first. For the person who remembers, it is very natural to claim and to emphasize the correspondence of his memory image with what has actually happened: isn't it possible that this very

[4] Cp. "Zur Relationstheorie," p. 174.

[5] Cp. "Zur Relationstheorie," p. 163.

[6] Concerning the latter point, cp. "Zur Relationstheorie," *loc. cit.*

relation of correspondence constitutes the content of memory judgements as such? Obviously the answer to this question will point first to the fact that the claim to a correspondence is as inessential to memory judgements (or only connected with them in the majority of cases) as the above-mentioned reflection on the remembering process. But more important and even more obvious is the fact that when we actually have the correspondence judgement in question, it can by no means be equated with the memory judgement; as a matter of fact, the latter is the indispensible precondition of the former. For on what else could the correspondence judgement be based? Certainly not on a comparison between the presentational image we have at the moment and the "reality" to which this refers; this reality is, in any case, already past, and whatever aspects of it may have remained, and in whatever way, they have meaning only as a memory image.[7] If I trust this memory, then, on the basis of this trust, the correspondence with the past that cannot be brought back may seem wholly plausible to me. That, however, does not change a memory judgement into a relational judgement, certainly not into a directly evident one, since that is only possible if both terms of the relation are given, and not if one of these terms must, as a precondition, belong to the past.

Thus we find ourselves forced into the area of existential judgements, and, indeed, it is not difficult to subsume the memory judgements here, since they refer by their very nature to realities, even though these realities are past. But what about evidence, however, in the existential area, is it attributed only to judgements of inner perception? Should memory judgements, which, as mentioned above, also refer only to the mental, themselves be regarded as cases of inner perception? People who still think of memory in the old Platonic sense of an aviary or some other kind of storehouse in which the presentation itself is stored, to be called up when the need arises, should not regard such a view as particularly strange: if the state of consciousness which I can remember at first only directly, is actually retained in me, and now crosses the "threshhold," isn't it true then, that *now* I actually experience inwardly what happened *then,* in the past? This peculiarity, however, does not have to be imposed upon the theory in question; it can be maintained that what I inwardly perceive now is actually identical with something that existed some time ago, without drawing from this the conclusion that the knowledge of this identity is a matter of inner perception in itself. Furthermore, it is interesting to note how the observations automatically return to the paths which we abandoned as impassable before, for the memory judgement seems to come out as an identity judgement, which is itself

[7] Cp. also Windelband, "Uber die Gewissheit der Erkenntnis" (Leipzig, 1873), p. 87.

a kind of relational judgement. In conclusion, we have to say, however, that memory judgements are homogeneous neither with relational judgements nor those existential judgements which otherwise are the only ones that can justifiably claim to be directly evident. Should we, therefore, assume that they constitute a separate category of the evident? Such an assumption would not be excluded *a priori;* more detailed consideration will reveal, however, that there is a difference between memory judgements and the directly evident cognitions, which makes it particularly difficult if not impossible to posit direct insight for the memory. As mentioned briefly above, there is no question about the fact that evidence and certainty are not the same thing. It is possible for a person to be absolutely convinced of something that he has accepted from his youth as an irrefutable truth, and yet realize later that this conviction is completely without basis or justification; even the greatest errors were firmly believed in, yet nobody will be inclined to suppose that a wrong judgement, too, could be made with insight. The greatest certainty can be accompanied by a lack of evidence; but would it also be possible to have evidence where we do not yet have a firm conviction? Almost everyone would deny such a possibility; it seem obvious that direct evidence, wherever it occurs, has the characteristic of imposing an absolutely firm conviction. If this is so, we are only one step away from the realization that we have been on the wrong track from the very beginning, if we hoped to apply the element of direct evidence to memory judgements. Or do these judgements actually contain that certainty which we just regarded as being connected with the presence of direct evidence? Are the data of memory really as certain as the fact that red is not blue, that two times two is four—or even that we are at this moment having such and such a thought or feeling, etc.? It is possible that a completely naive person might entertain that thought; but many people will find it rather difficult to regard such naiveté as anything but thoughtlessness, and the person who has learned to reflect to a certain extent on his experiences will definitely regard the fallibility of his memory as one of the most trivial truths. Nothing is more common than to mistrust ones memory, at least within certain limits, even though one continues to be guided by it; thus one does not discard what the memory offers, but neither does one build on it with that degree of confidence that excludes all possibility of error. If such confidence occurs wherever the directly evident exists, the latter cannot be connected with mistakes that are made by people who rely too strongly on the memory; thus we have, on the basis of these considerations, the proof that direct evidence is definitely not a characteristic of memory judgements *per se.*

At this point the relationship between the confidence in our memory and the confidence in our experiential knowledge seems to come clearly to the fore. If a person spends enough time in one place, and has fairly acute powers of observation, he can easily get to the point where he is just as good at predicting the weather as frogs and barometers; but unless someone is absolutely convinced of his talents, he will not rely on his prophesies to such an extent that he excludes the possibility of their not coming true. This holds true, *cum grano salis* obviously, of everything that experience teaches us,[8] from the simplest rules of thumb to the laws of gravitation and inertia. If, as we pointed out above, the same holds true of memory, what would be more natural than to answer the question under investigation in the way most obvious to the empiricist: that our confidence in, as well as our distrust of, memory is simply the result of our accumulated experiences? In order to judge the value of such a view, it is of primary importance to see clearly the nature of the instances which we have to employ in an inductive proof. It seems that we can use only those cases in which the data of our memory are subject to empirical verification; the way in which such verification takes place is demonstrated by numerous graphic examples from everyday life, because every time a person loses confidence in the testimony of his memory concerning a certain matter, he seeks confirmation. If someone committed an image of a landscape to memory, and later on has some doubts as to its various details, he simply has to return to the original place in order to be able to subject the accuracy of this memory to a completely adequate test; if a person travels in a group and if he distrusts his memory in respect to a certain incident, all he has to do is ask his companions and accept their concurring testimony as confirmation. Obviously any of these cases might be further complicated; the appearance of a landscape may change to a certain extent, but traces of what was there before remain. In such cases the tree-trunk verifies the memory image of the tree, the charred remains that of the house, etc. But also with regard to witnesses, one does not have to, and one cannot always, resort to direct participants; occasionally it suffices to call on those who had earlier heard a report about the things to be testified to, or who were involved in the consequences thereof. If we attempt to reduce what everyone does wholly or partly by instinct in individual cases to principles, we soon see that all cases of verification fall into two groups. (1) Cases in which the verification does not go beyond the person remembering: here proof is established by means of direct sensory perception. If we assume that the reality we believe we remember has not changed from the time of the perception until the time it is tested, the correspondence of the memory image with a renewed perception will constitute the verification. If the object of memory is subject to change in

[8] Cp. "Uber philosophische Wissenschaft und ihre Propädeutik," pp. 43ff.

accordance with known regularities, the renewed perception constitutes a verification even in those cases where the above-mentioned changes in relation to the memory image have taken place.

(2) Cases in which other individuals, in addition to the person remembering, assist in the verification. In these cases the memory image to be tested is compared with the memory images of others (which obviously can only be done in a limited way, through the medium of linguistic expression). Another case in which confirmation means correspondence is when different memory images relate to the same reality and the same time, or to the same reality at different times, given the consistency of the object in question; analogously to the first group, memory images of different contents can serve as verification, if the variations are in line with the regularities according to which the different realities represented in the memory images change.

We can hardly assume that memory could be verified in any other way; we may, therefore, rely on the principal determinations just set forth above when we attempt to establish whether processes suitable for confirming individual activities of the memory could not also serve as the basis for the trustworthiness which we generally accord to memory judgements.

In fact there seems, at first, to be no objection to such a statement; it is perfectly natural that every single instance which helps to prove the trustworthiness of the memory should serve the same function for memory judgements, and it is moving only a few more steps in the same direction if we finally base the entire belief in the trustworthiness of memory on empiricism. But anyone who argues in that way must obviously be able to assume that the individual cases which are subject to induction are treated on their own merits, i.e., not under the presupposition of inductive conclusions to be derived therefrom. This is an assumption whose admissability is normally so obvious that is is superfluous to draw special attention to it, unless the instances we use are chosen from the outset with a certain intention which continues to preserve its meaning or, rather, only becomes meaningful if that which we want to prove from individual cases is already presumed to be valid. And that is exactly the case here. The practical man is not at all concerned with proving the trustworthiness of memory in general; he already believes in it. What he really wants to know is whether his memory, apart from the question of its general trustworthiness, has been deceived in this or that particular case. Take, for example, the tourist who is studying the weather at the place where he is staying, and who might become interested in the question of whether the westerly wind, which he usually expects to bring bad weather, might not possibly bring good weather here. It just might happen that the valley in which he is carrying out his observations is situated in such a way that the genuine, bad westerly wind has no access to it; but there is a side valley which opens up toward the west which allows the north or northeasterly wind to penetrate into the main valley where it blows from west to east.[9] If our observer is aware of this, it might easily happen that on the general presupposition that the wind bringing rain usually comes from the west, he arrives, in this particular case, at the conclusion that, under these special circumstances, the westerly wind will bring no rain. If a person tests a case of memory by one of the above methods, and comes across an error, should we reject *a priori* the thought that his case is analogous to that of the weather example, insofar as he derives the untrustworthiness of the special instance from the general trustworthiness of the memory? If that were so, could we in any way escape the objection of circularity if we go in the other direction and try to prove the trustworthiness of memory on the basis of favorable instances of verification? One can easily see that we are not dealing with mere possibilities. Let us concentrate once more on the characteristics of the simplest cases in the first of the two groups mentioned above: the later sense perception, as we said above, can only serve as a proof if the thing to which it refers has remained unchanged in relation to the memory image. Certainly it is easy to assume that a house or a mountain does not change its place or undergo other essential alterations within a year's time; no matter how insignificant such a presupposition appears, however, the epistemologist cannot avoid the question of where we get such commonplace knowledge. Obviously the answer sounds just as commonplace: we get it directly or indirectly through experience. On the basis of past consistency, either directly, or through reference to regularities which in themselves use such a consistency [10] as a basis for proof, we draw conclusions as to the future, the present, and also the past. But how can we utilize past consistency for present knowledge? Certainly only on the presupposition that we have the ability to remember the past, that is to say, on the presupposition that we regard ourselves, in general, as entitled to trust the memory. This trust in no way impairs the importance of verification so long as the interest is directed only toward the individual case; but what happens if this individual case should serve to establish the justification for that trust? The more complex cases of the first group differ only very

9 The example is not a fictional one.

10 Or, from time to time, regularly occuring changes; for the sake of simplicity we will leave this eventuality unexamined for the moment because it will be taken up explicitly below. [p. 264, this volume. Eds.]

insignificantly from the simple ones just discussed: here the knowledge of a change based on regularities replaces the knowledge of consistency. Whatever type of regular succession we may encounter, it is even more obvious here than in the case of consistency, that experience must be employed, and that memory and the trust therein, being integral parts of that experience, play their inevitable roles.

What about the second group? Here, the subject matter, beginning again with the relatively simple case, is completely transparent. The memory of A is verified by the memory of B; what significance could be attributed to the whole process, if the memory of B had not been accorded a certain degree of trustworthiness? At first we could hope to fall back on a consideration of probability, which could be formulated as follows: if A and B reproduce the same image, it is much more improbable that both deviate from the original impression in exactly the same way, than that they both retain an unaltered impression. But supporting sameness by considerations of probability is a rather dangerous undertaking to begin with, since sameness, if understood in the strictest sense, is usually opposed, *a priori,* to all probability. In our case, however, it suffices to point out that A and B not only have to reproduce the same impression in those cases where the original impression of both has not changed, but also in those cases where it has changed for both in the same way; what would speak against the *a priori* acceptance of a regularity according to which, in those cases where we (mistakenly) talk about reproduction, we actually have a production regulated in a certain way? We can see how reflection loses its grip if it seriously attempts to anticipate nothing which would in any way imply trust in the memory; thus, also, the second group is characterized by anticipation, and if we replace the simple instances by the more complicated ones in this group, we change the situation only insofar as we add to the overt anticipation of the things to be proved, the more covert one, which has already been explained in our discussion of the first group.

So far we have concentrated only on individual verifications which must inevitably be the basis of an attempt to legitimize memory through induction. If we now think, for a moment, of the instances as being set out in the proper way, and if we look at the presumptive process of induction itself, we will encounter the inconvenience just mentioned, in a different form. Again we have to survey and to evaluate experiences which could be collected only in the past; in this case the experiences are the individual cases of verification themselves. But then again might it not be the case that the memory is necessary to hold them together in thought? And would there remain any basis for induction if we could not trust our memory to report the instances to us correctly? Thus it becomes clear that should someone succeed in avoiding the error of *petitio principii* in performing the individual verifications, he would try in vain to avoid it when summarizing the individual cases; in reality, there is no way out, in either direction.

Although of secondary importance, it should also be pointed out that the appeal to the inductive process gives rise to another kind of concern with respect to our problem. We are again faced with the previously rejected correspondence theory, formulated in such a way that every single memory judgement would have to derive its justification from the right generally attributed to memory, a rather roundabout statement which clearly contains an element of artificiality. This considerable complication is even further intensified by the fact that the proof always has to be supported by additional relevant external things. Thus, what must appear to the ordinary man as a relatively primary fact—the correspondence between the mental phenomenon and the memory image thereof—could be achieved only by means of a number of intermediate factors. Among these factors we should at least mention in passing the presupposition of causal influences on the part of external things, and the consistency of the relevant subject (the latter at the same time being a possibility for *petitio principii*). All in all, this is more than enough for us to discard as completely impossible our attempt to base memory on induction.

If we look back on the ground we have covered so far, we need only a few words to characterize it; it seems that we have employed practically everything that other forms of knowledge seem to offer for the theory of knowledge for the epistemological interpretation of memory judgements, and all attempts have been complete failures. Memory judgements participate neither in the direct evidence of relational nor of existential judgements. It seems, indeed, that direct evidence cannot be attributed to them, for they lack the absolute certainty such evidence requires. Yet the trust in them is not based on experience either, because any attempt to support this trust by empirical means leads inevitably to circularity, or rather to a whole complex of *circuli viciosi*. Should we then conclude, in view of this complete failure, that our belief in the memory is actually unjustified? No ordinary person would like to think so; if someone would attempt this, however, the above discussion on induction should immediately convince him that a renunciation of memory would be equivalent to a renunciation of all experiential knowledge, and it could easily be demonstrated that in this case very little would remain even of *a priori* knowledge. What can we do to overcome a seemingly hopeless situation?

It has often been said that it is easier to destroy than to build, that it is easier to negate than to affirm. But even the easy tasks need to be done, and very often this is a precondition that must be fulfilled before one goes on to undertake the more difficult tasks. Thus, if all that has been said so far serves no other purpose, at least it expresses the conviction that the epistemological discussion of memory, although of utmost importance, has yet to be undertaken. This mention of tasks yet to be done hardly justifies the reprimand often directed at people who demand from others what they themselves are unable to do. I have no intention of leaving entirely up to others the risk involved in venturing positive statements concerning the matters under discussion. Thus, I would like to add a few more comments about the direction, as I see it at this moment, that the epistemological assessment of the phenomena of memory should take.

We had the opportunity to establish that memory judgements are seriously lacking in the certainty which is so characteristic of the statements of inner perception or of the mathematical axioms. While here we encounter absolute knowledge, memory judgements represent conjectures (*Vermutungen*). If the talk about more or less firm convictions in the ordinary terminology is more than a rather far-fetched metaphor, the difference under discussion can be described in terms of psychology as a difference in the intensity of the act of judgement, in the same way as we feel justified in talking of different degrees of intensity with regard to feelings and acts of will. It is a well-known fact that in the area of conjecture we encounter a great variety of degrees of confidence; sufficient evidence to that effect can also be found with regard to memory judgements if we compare the memory of the immediate past with the events that happened a day or a year ago, etc.

Even though there seems to be no doubt that epistemologists will have to make up for their neglect of conjectures, the somewhat new question arises whether, after having left the ground of absolute certainty, every conjecture has the same value, or whether there, too, we find a difference which could be analogous to the difference between truth and falsity. The answer to the latter question will almost unanimously be affirmative, while the answer to the first one will be negative. In practice, we find ample testimony to the difference under discussion; some conjectures which are regarded as justified are treated completely differently from those which seem to be rather arbitrary. We can, therefore, proceed immediately to the next question as to the nature of the epistemological criterion for justified conjectures.

The analogy between this question and the question of the criteria of truth already well established for knowledge characterized by certainty is obvious; but if in the latter area the commonplace answer,

"Correspondence with reality," is still regarded by some as not completely objectionable, the same answer loses, even at a fleeting glance, all appearance of validity if applied to conjectures. It is a fact that conjectures are tested as to their justification, and for practical reasons must usually be tested long before the reality occurs, which would provide the proof for the conjecture, according to the viewpoint discussed. Even more important is the fact that there are conjectures which "come true" yet are unjustified, while there are others whose justification is in no way diminished by the fact that they do not come true. If someone has misgivings about a business matter which he has to begin on Friday the 13th, and then if something actually does go wrong, no reasonable person would regard the superstitious conjecture as justified; on the other hand, if the fire department, as a result of a false alarm, draws up in front of a house which is in absolutely no danger at all, no reasonable person would say that the fire department acted on the basis of an unjustified conjecture. Thus, conjectures, much more than knowledge, point toward characteristics immanent in the types of judgement concerned. If in the area of certainty, direct and indirect evidence (the latter term designating evidence resulting from proofs) are well established criteria, is there any reason why the analogy between the uncertain and the certain, so effective until now, should fail at this point?

At the beginning of this investigation,[11] we were faced with the alternative that memory judgements, provided they belong to the area of knowledge at all, must either be directly evident or provable; a closer investigation seemed to exclude both eventualities, and yet it is unthinkable to say that the memory does not constitute a source of knowledge. Perhaps the alternative is basically correct, and all it lacks is a determination which was overlooked because we did not take into consideration the difference between certainty and conjecture. We have actually investigated two things so far: first, direct evidence as it appears in connection with absolute certainty, which we had to deny to memory judgements because they lack such certainty; second, indirect evidence which concerned only conjecture and not certainty. Even if we have not reached a positive result, does not a purely formal concern for external completeness point to a third eventuality which has not yet been considered? If the reason for our failure to recognize the indirect evidence of memory judgements lies in the fact that every attempt at proof must resort to memory data, and, therefore, makes inevitable the anticipation of the things to be proved, doesn't that clearly indicate that memory judgements do not have to be verified by proofs, but are directly evi-

[11] [Above, p. 257, this volume. Eds.]

dent, the only difference being that this time the evidence does not relate to certainty, but simply to conjectures?

Indeed, I see no other possibility for escaping the difficulties into which we have fallen as a result of our investigation, than to attribute direct conjectural evidence to memory judgements. Although the acceptance of such an assumption may seem inappropriate and *a priori* inadmissible, the fact that the assumption easily solves the difficulty mentioned may certainly be regarded as an important element of proof. This is, by no means, one of those hypotheses which those people, who consider Newton's proud words neither fulfilled nor fulfillable, avoid "making up" at all costs. The meaning of the term "evidence for conjecture" can be easily discovered by anyone, simply by observing what he does with his memory. There is no reason to suppose that a person listens to the voice of his memory in order to obtain a general ground for proof. Every individual judgement carries its whole guarantee in itself; at least no ordinary person would look elsewhere for it. Yet the memory judgement is by no means a blind and thoughtless opinion which is then thoughtlessly retained; on the contrary, it is accompanied by a certain consciousness of correctness which the ordinary person tends to overestimate rather than underestimate. If we are aware, to this extent, of the relation to the behavior of the person who makes a judgement of a geometrical axiom, fully conscious of its direct evidence, we cannot help but recognize the peculiarity of the memory judgement, especially in those cases where an attempted verification thereof fails or seems to fail. If a person, out of naive self-confidence, increases the intensity of his memory judgement to certainty, then the failure of verification will obviously reveal his error; but is he now going to renounce his memory judgement in the same way as he would have to cease to trust a mathematical axiom at any time if this axiom had, on an experimental basis, been included in a calculation and led to a wrong result? By no means; his exaggerated confidence is somewhat reduced but not destroyed, and no one has succeeded in exorcizing it. Here we have a case of the characteristic element of conjectures, as indicated above—that the justification of the conjecture and its nonfulfillment are by no means incompatible; nothing but *conjectural evidence* can exist if reality, so to speak, denies its approval.

But would it not be, in every case, methodologically rather questionable to assert that memory judgements have a quality which would put them in a completely isolated position relative to other judgements? Assuming this to be the case, one could reply that the class of memory judgements is large enough to be governed by its own special laws. It would be wrong, however, to equate the sphere of direct conjectural evidence to that of memory judgments. It is well-known how vast the area of human conjecture is and that almost all practical interests are governed by conjectures; [12] yet, is there a possibility of going from completely certain premises to uncertain consequences by employing a completely conclusive process of inference. If not, we have the further analogy between knowledge and conjecture, that in both cases every appearance of direct evidence is a sure sign of the simultaneous existence of indirect evidence. It certainly cannot be denied that, from this point of view, the probability theory in particular, whose relation to the matter under discussion is clear, might have to be modified slightly; yet, on the other hand, everybody knows how far epistemological and logical interpretation have fallen behind mathematical practice; it could also be taken for granted that mathematics can set up fractions and work with them, but could never turn them into probability fractions.

Will it be possible to arrange the, at first sight rather large, diversity of directly evident conjectures into a relatively small number of groups? To begin with, there would be no reason why theoretical work should have less chance here than in the area of certainty. Such an attempt would not, by the way, relieve us of all preparatory work; we have to note, above all, that the so-called Law of the Uniformity of Nature has often been employed as a final principle [13] even after Hume explained that the violation of this law would not involve a contradiction, i.e., would not violate the evidence of certainty. The fact that the theoretician should try to create as few special classes of evidence as possible applies to conjectures in the same way as to knowledge; but even then it is clear that memory judgments are by no means the sole carriers of direct conjectural evidence.

The advantages memory judgements have over other evident conjectures are, firstly, that they form a clearly deliniated and immediately recognizable class of directly evident conjectures, which could, in a special way, be compared to the evident judgments based upon inner perception; secondly, they are freer from presupposition, and thus lend themselves better to demonstrating the indispensibility of conjectural evidence. In this sense they are the natural starting point for research work which interests instinctively directed toward perfection have not permitted up until now, but which nevertheless, must finally be started.

[12] Locke has said, "He that will not eat till he has demonstration that it will nourish him; he that will not stir till he infallibly knows the business he goes about will succeed, will have little to do but sit still and perish." (*Essay,* Bk. IV, Ch. XIV, Sect. 1). [N. B. this is the correct citation; Meinong's reference was incorrect. LM]

[13] For example by Alexander Bain (*Logic,* II, p. 8) in connection with John Stuart Mill —cp. also Lotze (*Logik,* pp. 527f).

Perhaps the investigations just begun can throw some light on the border regions of an area that has, until now, remained so much in the dark, but yet is the true home of the human spirit, which, so imperfect in itself, always strives for perfection.

Richard Brandt

The Epistemological Status of Memory Beliefs

Many philosophers have been concerned with the central epistemological question of the logical reconstruction of science; in other words, with the question of what sort of systematic noncircular justification can be given by a person for his whole system of beliefs. Inevitably such philosophers have been forced to consider the more specific problem of which, if any, of one's recollections are properly to be accepted as veridical.

There are simple but decisive reasons why the general problem of epistemology leads to consideration of the acceptability of memory beliefs. For one thing, there is no evidence at all except memory for many events in the past, such as unrecorded personal enjoyments or disappointments. And in fact a good many predictions of future events—e.g., of the trustworthiness of our friends—are based largely on our recollections of past occurrences. But more important, anyone who seriously regarded memory as untrustworthy and misleading could give no reasons for accepting any statement of empirical science; for it is easy to show that if we discount memory beliefs we have no reason to suppose that certain observations were made, or that certain experimental arrangements were of a particular kind.

Richard Brandt, "The Epistemological Status of Memory Beliefs," *The Philosophical Review,* 64 (1955), 78–95. Reprinted by permission.

The precise nature of the problem is apt to be obscured by the ambiguities of words like "remember" and "recall." Let us therefore make some decisions about how such terms will be used in this paper. In the first place, let us use "remember" only in that sense in which we speak of remembering past experiences (in a broad sense) of our own. Thus we shall not use this term in a sense in which it is correct to say that we remember how to ride a bicycle or that we remember the multiplication table or the fact that England was invaded in A.D. 1066. We thus limit ourselves to what Professor Furlong has called "retrospective" memory. I am assuming that remembering in this sense includes a judgement, doubtless usually along with a memory image, about the past experience. And I am assuming that this kind of judgment—which differs from judgments about our past experiences which we make on another's authority or on the evidence of photographs—can be distinguished from other judgments about past experiences which are not rememberings, however difficult this may be in border-line cases. Second, we shall distinguish between the achievement and phenomenological senses of "remember." We sometimes use "remember" in the achievement sense, for instance, when we say, "You don't really remember that; you only think you do." The term is used correctly in this sense only if what a person remembers (in the phenomenological sense) actually happened.[1] But we use "remember" in its phenomenological sense when we say, "Your evidence clearly shows that I didn't do so-and-so; but I'd have sworn I did, and I *remember* it very distinctly." (We might say that we are remembering in the phenomenological sense when we *seem* to remember in the achievement sense.) I shall distinguish between these two senses by using "ostensibly remembers" to refer to remembering in the phenomenological sense, and "genuinely remembers" ("genuine recall," etc.) to refer to remembering in the achievement sense. Third, we shall see that we need a dispositional term to correspond with ostensible recall (since we can remember ostensibly only one thing at a time). For this purpose I shall use the term "memory belief." This distinction parallels one sometimes drawn between judgment and belief. (Note how we may say of a child, who is asleep, that he believes in Santa Claus.) Sometimes we use "remembers" in the sense of just memory belief, for instance when we say of an old man, "He remembers the Civil War." I shall say that a person has a *memory belief* that p (where p is a statement about a past experience) as a way of saying that, if he tried, he *would* remember that p, in

[1] Probably when we speak of "really remembering" in this sense we demand more than simply that what is (phenomenologically) remembered is true. Probably we demand that there be a simple causal chain leading from the original experience to the present recollection. For our purposes, however, this question can be ignored.

the occurrent and ostensible sense. (It may be that we ordinarly say we *believe* something only if we are not certain; but I am proposing to use the term here so as not to carry implications about the correctness of the belief, or about the degree of conviction on the part of the person who has the belief.) What we shall be concerned with is the reliability of our ostensible occurrent recollections and memory beliefs.

The epistemological problem about the trustworthiness of memory in this sense is not a problem about the *nature* of occurrent ostensible recollections or of memory beliefs. There are also problems about this which may be classified as epistemological or phenomenological. For instance, there is the question whether an ostensible occurrent recollection is always the occurrence of an image along with a "yes-feeling" or a judgment "Something like that occurred." But the problem, our problem, about the *justification* for relying on memory is entirely different. This problem *begins* with the assumption that we have memory beliefs, dispositions to remember past events ostensibly (the phenomenological account being left unspecified)—indeed, a vast storehouse of them—and the problem is to show how to decide which, if any, of them are properly to be accepted as accurate reports of a real past experience.[2]

There will be some philosophers who can see no problem of *justifying* ostensible recollections or memory beliefs; for they will say that when we remember an occurrence, we clearly *know* that it happened. The past event, it may be said, is present to our mind for inspection just as is our present phenomenal field. And it may be added that there is no contradiction in holding that *past* events are presently inspectable, viz., stand in a certain relation to a knower. But this theory cannot be

[2] Skepticism might carry us back a further stage. It might be asked how, since we can remember only one thing at a time, we are to justify, at any given time, the claim that we do have a *storehouse* of memory beliefs. Are we not relying on memory to know that we do? And if we are trusting memory so far at the start, is not our justification of memory beliefs thereby rendered circular?

In answer to this we may remark, first, that if we are in doubt about the existence of many memory beliefs about a certain topic—or about their content—, we can always resolve the doubt by producing as many of them as we wish, one after the other. If even this is objected to ("How do you know you just had a different recollection about the topic on which you are now having a recollection?"), at least we can say, as Wesley Salmon recently suggested, that there is *a* problem of determining the minimum possible assumption about memory necessary for the reconstruction of science—that we can construe our problem as one of ascertaining how small an "epistemological present" we can get on with.

At any rate I am deliberately setting myself here a limited task: to determine whether, *if* we can properly assume that we have a store of memory beliefs of a particular character, we can then justify accepting certain ones of them as a genuine record of the past. For some relevant discussion, see C. I. Lewis, *An Analysis of Knowledge and Valuation* (LaSalle, Illinois, 1946), pp. 329ff.

taken seriously. It is true that our knowledge that some recollections have been mistaken does not imply that no recollection are direct inspections of the past.[3] But it is disconcerting doctrine to be told that sometimes ostensible recollection is inspection of the past and therefore knowledge (apart from carelessness or mistakes in verbal formulation), although some other cases of ostensible recollection, not noticeably different in character, are known to be erroneous. If the past was *not* present for inspection in the case of the erroneous recollections, have we not some ground for doubting that it was present in other cases of ostensible recollection, not distinguishable in character from the former? It would be more plausible to claim that *something* is always given for inspection in the case of ostensible recall; but in view of errors, some argument at least seems needed to establish that this something is a past event. In any case we cannot identify the past experience with the present memory image, for, assuming that memory in general is reliable, we know that the experience was different in many respects from the present image, e.g., in vivid detail and flickeringness.[4] Moreover, notice that if we are looking at the garden gate, we can tell how many vertical bars it has; but we are unlikely to be able to tell this from memory. Why not, if the original is presented? In view of these considerations, it is difficult to see how it can reasonably be claimed that in recollection the event being judged about is somehow present and accessible for inspection in a way very similar to that in which the present phenomenal field is accessible for inspection. And if so, it is not obvious what can be meant by saying that there is noninferential *knowledge* in memory. Indeed, as Ayer pointed out,[5] when we ask what is the precise meaning of the talk about the past being directly presented, it appears that no more is being said than simply that sometimes recollections are genuine recall.

I believe, then, that those writers are correct who, like E. J. Fur-

[3] It has been thought that we must assume that some recollections are genuine in order to demonstrate that some are mistaken. This is a mistake. For either (a) all recollections are, and have been, correct, or (b) some are or have been incorrect. But (a) is false. For we can remember cases when we first recalled that *p*, and then later (perhaps because of being reminded of more details, so that the whole situation became more vivid) recalled ostensibly that not-*p*. Then, either the earlier memory that *p* or else the later one that not-*p* was mistaken; or else our recollection that there ever was a change of memory opinion of this sort is mistaken. It does not make any difference which possibility we pick; any way (a) is false. Hence (b) must be true. This reasoning, of course, does not tell us *which* recollection was or is faulty.

[4] H. H. Price has reviewed such differences in "Memory Knowledge," *Supplementary Volume 15, The Aristotelian Society*, cf. esp. p. 26. See also E. J. Furlong, *A Study in Memory,* ch. iii.

[5] A. J. Ayer, "Statements about the Past," *Proceedings of the Aristotelian Society,* 1951–1952, p. vii.

long, Bertrand Russell, and C. I. Lewis,[6] think that the epistemologist who wishes to use memory as a source of evidence in his reconstruction of science must provide a justification for so doing. In this paper I shall argue for two propositions central to the theory of such a justification. (1) I shall argue that use of a rule providing for the acceptance of memory beliefs can be justified in a sense to be made clear later. (2) I shall argue that such a justification can be non-circular, although in important senses it does not establish the acceptability of memory beliefs prior to or independently of establishing the acceptability of beliefs about physical things and laws (which in some sense are evidenced by memory). I shall begin with a discussion of the second of these points, although I shall not be able to complete it, or even, I fear, to make the issue wholly clear, until the close of my discussion of the first point.

1. *Must Memory Beliefs Be Justified First?* We may assume that circular arguments are unacceptable in epistemology. Hence, any justification of the reliability of memory is unacceptable if it must use *as premises* assertions that recollections are genuine—or any other assertions which themselves cannot be justified except upon the assumption that memory is trustworthy.

We cannot reasonably deny, however, that *some* recollections are properly tested by considering evidence which could not be accepted as good evidence unless some recollections were known to be genuine. For instance, I think I wrote a certain letter to Mr. X, but I am not sure. Then I find a letter in his handwriting acknowledging receipt of my letter. We properly take this as decisively establishing our original recollection. This procedure may seem to be circular, for, unless I can rely upon memory, how shall I be sure that what I have before me is a letter from Mr. X (since perhaps that isn't like his handwriting after all), or even a piece of paper (since my belief that it is can only be justified by recollections that appearances like this have on previous occasions turned out to be appearances of a piece of paper)? But, clearly, there is only an apparent circularity here. It is perfectly reasonable to support *some* memory beliefs by reference to propositions themselves epistemologically dependent on memory beliefs, if it so happens that somehow these propositions can be established prior to and independently of the question at issue—if, in this case, we can justify our belief that this is a piece of paper before me independently of justifying the belief that I did indeed write to Mr. X, as I seem to remember I did.

[6] The reader who is familiar with Lewis' discussion will notice that my conclusions and reasoning differ rather substantially from his. But I believe that his discussion is the most helpful and important that has been written. The present paper developed from a study of the difficulties in his view; and some of my arguments are adaptations of his.

It is evident, however, that the epistemologist could not, without circularity, establish *all* memory beliefs in the way in which this particular belief about writing Mr. X can be established as valid. For, somewhere along the line, he would inevitably be using as premises some assertions which could not be established independently of the justification of relying on some of the ostensible recollections he is attempting to establish as valid. (It may be, of course, that in some sense *inquiry* can proceed usefully without troubling to justify the whole system of beliefs at all; but this is merely to say that the problem of epistemology is different from some other problems.)

But does it follow from these considerations that the status of memory beliefs in general is a *prior* question in epistemology, to be completely settled before one can properly go on to consider the justification of laws or thing-statements? [7] It is quite tempting to answer this question, "Yes." And some things which Lewis, for example, has said suggest that he is inclined to answer it in this way. For knowledge, he suggests, is a kind of pyramid, and we must attend to the foundations before we can appropriately busy ourselves with the upper stories. Any belief about a physical object, he says, "presumes the validity" of statements about prior experience and generalizations from these. He goes on to say, "Before I can accredit the present belief on the basis of given sense data and a generalization about past like occasions, *I must first accredit the presently given recollections or sense of past fact,* which are the only available witnesses to actual past experience." [8]

I believe, however, that one can consistently deny that the justification of memory is a prior question in epistemology, and at the same time agree that the justification of memory must not be circular and

[7] Some philosophers seem to imply that unless and until we have shown that memory is reliable to some degree, we are not justified in having beliefs about our present experience—or at least in accepting the verbal statements expressing beliefs about present experience. (The same would hold for a statement that we ostensibly remember an event of a certain sort.) I cannot agree with this conclusion; and I think that anyone who does is committed to conceding the impossibility of epistemology in the traditional sense. I am preparing a paper on basic propositions, in which this view of the implications of the above conclusion is defended, and in which I argue that no such concession need be made.

In the present paper I am assuming that statements expressive of (descriptive of) present experience and of ostensible recollections can be justified at least as probable independently of a justification for regarding ostensible recollections as genuine.

[8] *Op. cit.,* pp. 335–356, my italics; see also pp. 261–263, 327–334. On the other hand, it may be that Lewis wants to argue only that epistemology requires that all ostensible recollections be recognized as enjoying some antecedent probability of being genuine. Notice that one might admit this, but deny that any *high* probability could be attributed to any of them except by appeal to the consequences of rejection for one's total system of beliefs.

must not *employ as a premise* any proposition the justification for believing which requires prior knowledge that memory beliefs in general, or some specific memory beliefs, are very likely true. The only question is how this can be done—how a justification can avoid circularity while at the same time making appeal, in a sense, to the whole system of one's beliefs, so that the warrant of memory beliefs is not achieved prior to that of laws, thing-statements, and so on. In the next section I shall propose a justification of this sort, and at the end I trust it will be evident that at least it is not circular.

Before turning to this, however, let me point out one misconception to be avoided.

In recent years a good many philosophers have come to the conclusion that one cannot justify believing a proposition simply by showing the logical connections of that proposition with other propositional candidates for belief, viz., by an appeal to system. And the objection they have raised against the Coherence Theory is that it is an attempt to do just that. Our system of beliefs, they have argued, cannot be justified unless there are some beliefs that are justifiable independently of an appeal to system, that is, independently of the logical relations of the propositions believed to other propositions. And these independently credible beliefs may properly be regarded as the epistemological premises of knowledge. Among such beliefs which can serve as the premises of knowledge, these philosophers have held, are beliefs about the present content of experience, including the belief that I am now ostensibly recalling a past event.

Now the error to be avoided is this. A person might think, on the basis of this showing that some beliefs must somehow be independently credible if any are to be justified, that no further argument is needed to demonstrate that the required set of independently credible premises must include some statements about past experience—the propositions about past events which are the content judged in an ostensible recollection, or the propositions which are the content of memory beliefs. But this is not so. All the general argument shows is that *some* synthetic statements must be independenly credible, not that some particular type of synthetic statements must be. The difficulties of the Coherence Theory do not by themselves show that statements about the past (the content of memory beliefs) cannot somehow, all of them, be given a systemic justification. It may perfectly well be that propositions about the content of present experience, and to the effect that certain other propositions are the content of present memory belief or ostensible recollection, are all that is needed as a base for an epistemological justification of science. This is what I shall contend.

2. *The Justification of Memory Beliefs.* The epistemologist interested in justifying memory beliefs will do well to consider the import of

the following two facts. (1) Our memory beliefs include beliefs in an immensely rich and complex set of propositions. All of us can trace back the events of the preceding few days or weeks in major outline, and we can fill in many details if need be. Given proper stimulus, we could doubtless recall thousands of incidents in the past few years. And incidentally, we recall having had reason to reject very few of such memory beliefs. (2) We all have a great many beliefs—*not* memory beliefs—either about general laws, or theories, or physical facts, or events in the past which we did not ourselves witness, etc. And we are aware of the identity of those recollections which are our evidence for those beliefs, if we have evidence. If we are scientists, we can remember the experiments we performed, or recall the oral or written testimony of others about their experiments. At a subscientific level we believe that aspirin reduces fever—and recall incidents when administration of aspirin was followed by this effect in our children. Or we believe that physical things do not change their properties (e.g., that our books retain the same printed marks on the same pages, day after day), and we can recall many events consistent with these beliefs and none conflicting with them. (Sometimes we can recall that there were events of a certain sort, without being able to recall the particular occasion, time, or circumstance.)[9]

With these points in mind, let us proceed to formulate our problem. I am assuming as a fact which the epistemologist can take for granted, that each of us (more strictly, I am assuming that each epistemologist can take for granted that he) has a storehouse of memory beliefs, and a vast number of beliefs which are not memory beliefs, and that we can make correct statements about their detailed character when we need to. Now what I wish to find is how many and which types of the propositions forming the content of memory beliefs can reasonably be accepted as part of one's scientific base—as propositions to be acted upon or used as premises wherever they are relevant. Since these propositions are all about past experiences, what I am aiming at is to justify accepting a very large number of propositions about past experiences into one's scientific base. Unfortunately, perhaps, I am not aiming to say in advance—for the obvious reason that I do not think it possible to justify any such thing—exactly *which* propositions are to be included in the base. The inductive logician may possibly be disturbed by this, if he is accustomed to thinking of the instantial base for inductive generalization as consist-

9 I believe there are good reasons why epistemologists should construe the content of memory beliefs in phenomenal language. Thus a statement like "I gave Dick an aspirin at six o'clock" is not in the form in which the content of a memory belief should ideally be put. But, for the sake of simplicity, I am allowing myself to speak as if this were not the case. For a helpful discussion of what is remembered see Furlong, *op. cit.*, ch. vi.

ing of unquestionable singular statements like "Crow no. 1 is black"; but at present probably most inductive logicians are reconciled to the idea of working with a base of instantial propositions which can be regarded as only provisionally acceptable.

Now let us ask ourselves which propositions, among those which are the content of our total memory beliefs at the present, we seriously think it justifiable to accept, and what degree of confidence we ought to feel in them. I believe we could agree on the following points. (1) We all think that the vast majority of our recollections should be accepted as true, and can properly be used as instantial evidence for a system of laws, theories, etc. (2) We think that some of our past recollections have been in error (unless we are endowed with an unusually accurate memory), and we are therefore inclined to think that some of our present memory beliefs are also erroneous. We have been led to this conclusion about occasional error in past recollections partly by the fact that memory itself sometimes discovers a previous recollection to have been wrong (or seems to; see footnote 3), and partly by the recollection that some of our past memory beliefs have been shown to be incompatible with the scheme of things evidenced by the vast majority of our recollections. (For instance, we think our memory belief that on a certain date we were at a certain place has sometimes been overthrown by conclusive evidence —from other observers, diaries, newspaper accounts, etc.—that we were somewhere else.) Thus we are prepared to allow that some of our present memory beliefs are mistaken, if it can be shown that it would be very inconvenient for our whole system of beliefs to regard them as veridical. (3) Finally, I believe we all hold that the credibility of our recollections is enhanced by the support they receive from our system of beliefs, and reduced by conflict with this system, to a degree corresponding with the extensiveness of the support or conflict. (For instance, my recollection of having turned out the light last night is made more credible by the facts that it is now out and that there is no other physically possible way in which it could have got turned off, if I had not done so. Or again, my recollection that I did a certain thing yesterday is rendered more credible by the consideration that I remember many occasions on which similarly recent and vivid recollections were subsequently strongly supported by further evidence, and none on which such a recollection had to be rejected as erroneous.)

Let us now try to formulate a rule which corresponds with these convictions about justifiable attitudes toward our memory beliefs; and then let us see if we can justify using this rule. The best formulation I can give will be loose and tentative. But I suggest the following:

Rule: (a) Accept as a basis for action and for accepting other beliefs all your clear recollections except those (but not more than a few) of which the system (laws, theories, etc.) of beliefs supported by the vast majority of your recollections requires rejection or makes rejection convenient. (b) Believe (disbelieve) any particular recollection *more* firmly and confidently corresponding to the degree of support by (seriousness of conflict with) the system which can be erected on the base consisting of the vast majority of your recollections.[10]

The rule is vague in a number of respects, for instance, in the phrases "degree of support" and "seriousness of conflict with." Nor does the rule make clear exactly how much conflict with a system of laws and theories is required before one is advised to remove a particular recollection from the instantial base. But I believe that in most cases there will be no serious question how to apply the rule, when we work out the details. Rather obviously, if a couple of recollections are inconsistent with the proposition that I have a mother, it would be ridiculous for me to retain them. And again, if the only thing against a pair of recollections is that they do not jibe with some moderately well supported theory in social psychology, at least there is not a clear case for rejecting them. (Remember that the status of a memory belief may change from one time to another, since in general the memory data will be more numerous, and one's system of theories more complex, at a later time. I might be inclined to place little credence in a faint recollection that I hated my father when I was six years old; after reading psychoanalytic literature I might—conceivably—be properly inclined to put more stock in it.)

The rule is stated as an imperative. But since it is an imperative enjoining belief, it differs little in effect from corresponding assertions,

[10] Notice that this rule advises accepting recollections when there is no positive support from the system, and does not advise rejection except where the conflict is considerable.

It might be thought that this rule advises rejecting memory beliefs about an experiment the outcome of which conflicts with an established theory. But this is not the case. For our recollections strongly support the view that we are most unlikely to be in error about a recent occurrence in which we take a strong interest. Moreover, we should doubtless in any case wish to repeat the experiment or observation several times, making notes of our observations at the time. Thus in practice we shall confront an established theory with quite a strong system of connected memory beliefs. (In any case, it will hardly ever be a question of choosing between a theory and recollections; there is almost always a possibility that the experimental arrangements were not satisfactory, that one's calculations contain an error, or even that one's original perceptions were illusory.) Of course there are occasions on which it *is* proper to question memory, when memory beliefs conflict with theory. If I were an anthoropologist studying the kinship terminology of a tribe and were (very unwisely!) writing my report of an informant's statement *after* an interview, and came to a statement of his which was in conflict with a well-supported theory and perhaps also with the statements of other informants, I should certainly think it proper to go back and inquire a second time.

e.g., "All of your memory beliefs . . . except . . . are veridical." Nevertheless, I believe it preferable to use the imperative form as I have done, since there are fewer misleading suggstions associated with it, about the kind of justification that must be given for it. For instance, we do not naturally demand an inductive justification for an imperative, but we do instinctively think of this when we are considering justification for asserting a universal statement. We must be careful not to assume in advance that some particular kind of justification must be given for our policy concerning memory beliefs.[11]

What reasons can be given which justify acting in accordance with this rule? We cannot, of course, expect an inductive argument showing that following the rule will lead to true beliefs; this would inevitably be circular. Nor, on the other hand, is it enough to show merely that in fact scientists act in accordance with the rule (or cannot seriously doubt the truth of corresponding statements), although I believe this is in fact the case. For perhaps scientists follow in their practice some rules which have no justification. And of course there cannot be given any deductive proof of the rule. But what we can do in justification is this: We can show that for one who is looking for a system of predictive theories which will explain (and hence, be supported by) a nonarbitrary set of instantial propositions about experience, there is no alternative. Whether this is a sufficient justification for intelligent human beings, the reader must judge.

We cannot possibly consider the detailed reasons for heeding all parts of the rule. Let us therefore confine ourselves to the basic idea: the proposal that almost all but not necessarily all memory beliefs are to be accepted, the decision about the elimination of some to be based upon the difficulties raised for the system by acceptance or rejection. Why should we pay attention to memory beliefs at all, say, more than to the creations of fantasy? Or, why should we not hang on to *all* consistent

[11] One naturally wonders whether it would not be simpler to reformulate the rule as an indicative making use of the notion of probability. Such a course would, however, lead to difficulties at least on some explications of "probable," such as Reichenbach's. (For instance, if one started out by saying that all recollections have a low degree of probability, but greater than 0, in his sense, it is not easy to see how this statement could be supported without circularity.)

Lewis has proposed an important alternative theory along this line. He first gives arguments supporting the assertion that every recollection enjoys a degree of antecedent probability—more than it would have enjoyed had it not been recollected. He further thinks that consideration of the logical connections of these propositions remembered will justify ascribing to some of them a consequent probability very close to 1, and to others a consequent probability close to 0. I believe, however, that there are difficulties when we come to working out the details of this theory, difficulties which I discuss in a paper scheduled to appear in *Philosophical Studies*.

memory beliefs, at all costs? Let us consider some reasons that bear on these points.

(1) The first reason is one of necessity—for one who is looking for a predictive system of general propositions based upon a nonarbitrary set of statements about experience. Why should a person not believe all that he remembers, no matter what? The answer is that—except of course for contradictions—there is no reason why he should not, providing he is interested only in reminiscing about his ostensible past. But if he wants to predict, if he wants an explanatory theory of a comprehensive sort, then he must concede occasional error of memory. We can show him (see footnote 3) that some ones of his recollections, now or former, must have been erroneous; and we can also show him that known comprehensive explanatory and predictive systems are inconsistent with saving all of his memory beliefs. (If he happens to have an extremely accurate memory, he may not have to give up any, at least at present.) But suppose he is of a skeptical turn of mind, and does not want to use the content of memory beliefs at all. Well, then we can show him that the coherence of systems alone will not enable him to make a rational choice among the unlimited number of possible systems he could consider—even if we add the requirement that the system selected entail or be compatible with the presently given facts of experience. Nor will coherence with facts he is able to *imagine* help him; for he can imagine facts coherent with many different systems. So, if he wants to select from among possible systems by reference to some datum, at least ostensibly a clue to past events, there is nothing for him to do but give the palm to the only candidate. At least we do not know in advance that memory beliefs are erroneous. And, furtheremore, if one is to use memory-beliefs as an evidential base, there appears to be no nonarbitrary decision about which ones we are to adopt, other than that we take the clear ones, and of these as many as possible—as many as are compatible with our aim of setting up a general predictive system. A person seeking an explanatory predictive system, then, cannot refuse to accept the bulk of his memory beliefs, or to deny that some of them—unless he happens to be extremely fortunate in point of memory—are unacceptable. The rule offers him the only nonarbitrary compromise: rejecting only those recollections which are awkward for the system he erects on the vast majority as a base.[12]

It may be pointed out that the above argument overlooks a certain fact: that we can use, as a means of deciding between competing scientific systems, not only the presently given facts of experience, but also the

[12] This reason is similar to one Lewis has offered, at least if I understand him correctly (*op. cit.*, pp. 358, 362). It is also similar to William Kneale's and others' defense of induction as a policy.

fact that we have the *memory beliefs* we do have. And, it may be said, one can use memory beliefs as a means for deciding between competing theories, even if we are still in doubt whether we should regard the propositions which are the content of these beliefs as mostly true. And perhaps, if so, we do not after all need anything more in the way of facts, in order to choose among competing systems. This objection I am prepared to grant. Indeed I shall work out its implications in the course of a second argument for our rule, for it can be shown that a person who decides to use just the fact of his memory beliefs as a device for choosing among possible systems of belief will inevitably be led to accept our rule! But for those who for some reason do not find it plausible to regard just the fact of memory beliefs themselves as evidence capable of deciding between scientific theories (and in favor of our rule, as we shall see), this first argument will have considerable force.

(2) But the detailed content of our memory beliefs is itself good reason for accepting our rule. Let us see how this is so.

Any satisfactory theory of nature obviously has to be based on, and to explain, the unquestionable facts: the facts of present experience, and the fact of our memory beliefs—an intricate, ever expanding complex fact. Of course, a theory which explained and was based on these facts need not necessarily assert that any or all of one's memory beliefs correspond to the actual facts of one's past experience. But, as it happens, when we begin looking about for a theory which will do what is wanted, we find that there is only one type of theory which comes near to success: a theory which postulates an historical sequence of events and human beings with a capacity to recall (not exactly as things were, but in a somewhat simplified form, as described by psychologists), and which hence explains memory beliefs as the precipitate of a process of interaction between human brain-minds and the world. In other words, the only acceptable theory is one which asserts that a large proportion of our memory beliefs are veridical. No alternative to such a theory has been proposed; nor can one imagine what one would be like. So at least we can say this about our rule. The only serious type of theory for explaining the unquestionable data conforms closely to it. If we seriously rejected it, we should in consistency have to reject the only theory we know that can explain the facts that any theory has got to explain.

Consider the consequences if we rejected the rule, and urged that all or almost all our recollections are nonveridical. In this case we should have a very serious puzzle on our hands. For in fact we have (again unquestionably) beliefs in a system of interlocking laws and theories which we remember to have been put to repeated experimental test; and we recall the outcome of these tests to have been almost uniformly successful. Now the puzzle is this. If our recollections are almost uniformly erroneous, how is it that our laws and theories, erected on the assumption of past events attested in the end by memory, have so frequently predicted experimental events which, at least according to present memory beliefs, actually occurred as predicted? Why should our memory beliefs have this kind of consistency if they have no reliable connection with nature? If memory beliefs are not admitted to be genuine in the measure our rule proposes, then at least this coherence among them demands an explanation from any theory which competes with actual science (which, in large part, accepts memory). Will it be proposed that some demon has cooked up our memory beliefs to deceive us? This and similar suggestions are fantasies, which cannot be worked out in their details, and are wholly without evidential foundation. And clearly we can say a person is unreasonable if he rejects our rule without any detailed proposal explaining why our memory beliefs are as they are.[13]

Whether these reasons are good reasons for adopting the rule we may leave to the reader. But at least they are not circular reasons. They do not assume the genuineness of any recollections, or the truth of any thing-statement, law, or theory. All they assume is that no alternative to the common-sense scientific view of the world is known which explains memory beliefs equally well or better. The reader may decide whether this assumption is correct, for his own knowledge.

Let us now revert to the question how far, on the above proposal, the status of memory beliefs is or must be decided before the status of laws, theories, etc., is decided.

It is clear that according to our rule the final appraisal of a particular one among the total set of memory beliefs held at a certain time can be made only in connection with the development and confirmation—by appeal to the system of memory beliefs—of a whole system of beliefs. (We need not say that the *total* system of one's beliefs is involved, if different areas of these beliefs are only loosely connected.) For instance, if I want to know whether I really did return a book to the library, as I remember having done, although the desk assistants made no record of the fact and I find a suspiciously similar book on my shelf, I have to decide, according to the rule, on the basis of my system of beliefs. Will books fly through the air back to my room, unassisted? Are

13 This line of reasoning was first suggested to me by Lewis' argument (*op. cit.*, pp. 356–362), which he calls "a trial of Cartesian doubt." I cannot, however, accept what I believe to be the particular turn he gives it. But I think he suggests the acceptable formulation when he says, "The attempt to carry through a circumstantial supposition that would actually conform to what we have attempted to suggest, must inevitably end in nonsense" (p. 360)—although even here I cannot agree that the doubter's proposal must necessarily be meaningless.

the desk assistants apt to make no record of the fact, if I do return a book? These possibilities must be considered. What excludes the recollection that I did return the book is the fact that none of these possibilities can be fitted into a theory which jibes with any large proportion of my recollections. It is because we know positively what sorts of theories can and cannot be developed consistently with the large body of memorial evidence, that according to the rule we must reject this particular recollection. (We must include also the reputation of our own memory, based on the appraisal of similar recollections.) It appears, then, that the adjudication of the status of particular memory beliefs can be properly carried out, according to our rule, only as part of a process in which theories correspondingly get established. There is no necessity or possibility, according to the rule, of a justified appraisal of a particular recollection prior to having an at least partially confirmed system of beliefs about the world.

It may be said, however, that according to the rule at least the general strategy of saving memory beliefs is secured, in advance of any consideration of the details of science. In fact, it may be pointed out, the criterion for accepting an empirical theory is in part that it must succeed in saving the vast proportion of memory beliefs.

It is important to see, however, that there are certain qualifications to be added to this dictum. (1) There are other equally basic points in general strategy: that the system of beliefs against which individual memory beliefs are to be tested contain general statements enabling predictions, that it be free from *ad hoc* hypotheses—and so on for the other properties any acceptable theory must have. (2) The reasons for adopting the rule derive much of their weight from the fact that a detailed theory can be worked out, which explains memory beliefs in accordance with the rule. We know that such a theory can be worked out only because we are familiar with the general system of common-sense and science. In so far, the justification of the strategy of saving memory beliefs depends upon knowledge of at least the outlines of the accepted system of science.[14]

[14] The foregoing paper was written during a leave of absense supported by a grant from the Fund for the Advancement of Education. In an earlier form, it was read by Monroe Beardsley, Roderick Firth, John Goheen, Patrick Suppes, and Richard Taylor. I am grateful to these individuals for their helpful critical comments.

Norman Malcolm

A Definition of Factual Memory

Enough has been said in the previous two lectures to show that factual memory (remembering that *p*) holds an important position in the family of concepts of memory. Some forms of memory can be defined in terms of factual memory plus the purely logical notion of existential quantification. Other forms are related to factual memory as *species* to *genus*.[1] Still other forms, not related to factual memory in either of these two ways, *imply* it.[2] I have not been able to discover any form of memory which does not have at least this latter relation to factual memory. I will not undertake to provide an account of the exact position that factual memory occupies among the concepts of memory, but it has sufficient importance to make it worthwhile to attempt to *define* it.

In my second lecture I produced definitions of perceptual and per-

Norman Malcolm, "A Definition of Factual Memory," in *Knowledge and Certainty:* Essays and Lectures (Englewood Cliffs, N.J.: Prentice-Hall, Inc.), pp. 222–40 Reprinted by permission of Prentice-Hall, Inc., Englewood Cliffs, N.J.

[1] For example, if a man "remembered to" water his horse it follows that he remembered that he should water his horse and also that he watered it. Remembering *to* do something appears to consist of remembering that one should do it plus doing it.

[2] Both personal and perceptual memory imply factual memory.

sonal memory. As we noted they are not definitions of *memory,* but only of the adverbs "personally" and "perceptually," as these modify the verb "remember." That they are not definitions of *memory* is shown by the fact that the verb "remember" occurs in the *definiens* of each of those definitions. The definition of factual memory which I shall propose will really be a definition of *memory*—not of memory in general, but of one use of the verb "remembers." In this definition that verb will not occur in the *definiens.*

The definition is very simple. It is the following: A person, B, remembers that *p* if and only if B knows that *p* because he knew that *p.* It will be convenient to say that this definition is composed of three elements: the present knowledge that *p,* the previous knowledge that *p,* and the relationship between the present and the previous knowledge expressed by saying that B knows that *p because* he previously knew that *p.* Each element is a logically necessary condition and the conjunction of them a logically sufficient condition of factual memory.

I wish to discuss each of these three elements in turn. But before I do so I want to anticipate one objection to the definition. Let us suppose that a man saw a bird of striking appearance in his bird feeder last week, but did not know what bird it was. While looking through a book about birds he comes upon a picture of a cardinal and now knows it was a cardinal he saw. He might naturally say "I remember that I saw a cardinal in the feeder last week." But it is false that *previously* he knew that he saw a cardinal. It might be concluded that the element of *previous* knowledge is shown not to be a necessary condition of factual memory.

I deal with this kind of case by distinguishing between what I call "elliptical" and "nonelliptical" uses of the expression "remembers that *p.*" I believe that the man in our example would agree to substitute for his sentence "I remember that I saw a cardinal" the *conjunctive* sentence "I remember that I saw this bird (or: a bird of this kind) *and* now I know it was a cardinal." The sentence he originally uttered was an ellipsis, in the grammarian's sense, the meaning of which is given by the conjunctive sentence. In this conjunction the first conjunct expresses factual memory, the second conjunct expresses the new information. Another way of putting the distinction is to say that the original sentence did not express "pure" factual memory. In the conjunctive sentence substituted for it, the first conjunct expresses pure factual memory, the second conjunct expresses something other than memory. The whole conjunction expresses "impure" memory.

There could be many different kinds of impure factual memory. For example, suppose that someone had often noticed, as a boy, that the house in which he lived faced the setting sun. Years later, when conversing with someone, he suddenly realizes, for the first time, that this implied that his house faced the west, and he says "I remember that our house faced the west." This sentence of his expresses impure factual memory, which is a compound of pure factual memory and present inference or realization. The definition I am presenting is intended solely to be a definition of *pure* factual memory, with no admixture of inference or present realization.

I turn now to a consideration of the three elements in the definition. The first two elements are present and previous knowledge, and so whatever is true of knowledge will apply equally to both. In the history of the philosophy of memory there has been a considerable amount of puzzlement and confusion about the relation of memory to knowledge. First, if memory involves knowledge what *kind* of knowledge is it? Second, if a person remembers that *p* just *how certain* is it that *p*? Third, when a person remembers that *p* does he have *grounds* for saying that *p*? These are some of the questions that puzzle us, and I hope that this discussion will help to answer them.

Obviously one necessary condition for the knowledge that *p* is that *p* should be *true*. If *p* is false then B does not know, and did not know, that *p*; and also B does not remember that *p*.

A second necessary condition for someone's knowing that *p* may be expressed, roughly, as the condition that he should be *sure* that *p*. Being unsure whether *p* is true counts both against knowing that *p* and against remembering that *p*. If a man previously knew that *p* and now not only is not sure but does not even believe that *p*, we are sometimes ready to say "He really remembers it": but what we mean would also be expressed by saying "He *will* remember it" or "His forgetting it is only *temporary*." We should have to admit that at present he does not remember it.

Of course there are many differences of degree in the confidence with which one believes or is sure of something. A person can be *inclined* to believe something and at the same time be quite unsure about it. Sometimes we should say he knows the thing in question and sometimes that he does not, depending on what contrasts we were making. Suppose some pupils were being tested on their knowledge of Roman history. They are supposed to tell who killed Caesar. Suppose that one of them, A, is inclined to think it was Brutus, but has little confidence in this answer. Should we say A *knows* that Brutus killed Caesar? If we were comparing him with B, who believes that Cassius was the assassin, we should say that A knows the answer but B does not. If we were comparing A with C, who is *certain* that Brutus slew Caesar, we should say that C knows the answer but A does not "really *know*" it, or does not know it "very well." The same considerations apply to the question of whether

A *remembers* that Brutus killed Caesar. Thus we can say, in summary, that if someone has *no* inclination to believe that *p*, this counts absolutely against either his knowing or remembering that *p*. If he has some inclination to believe that *p* but is unsure about it, whether we say he does or does not know, or remember, that *p* depends on the comparisons we are making. In short, if one is unsure about something this *can serve*, in some circumstances, to justify the claim that one does not know, and does not remember, the something.

The considerations about truth and certainty, so far adduced, apply equally to knowledge and memory. A third consideration is that of *grounds* for being sure that *p*.[3] It has often been supposed that, in addition to being right and being sure, a further thing necessary for knowledge is the possession of grounds, or adequate grounds, or conclusive grounds. I am not convinced that this third feature is a requirement for knowledge, although I admit that not just any true belief is knowledge. My discussion of this difficult point will necessarily be skimpy.

In the first place, I call attention to the knowledge that human beings normally have of their own voluntary actions, both of what they are doing and what they are going to do. Suppose a man was for a while undecided as to whether he would quit his job, but now *knows* he will quit it. Should we expect him to have *grounds* for being sure he will quit it? It is hard to see what this could mean.[4] Could one say that his grounds for being sure he will quit is his *decision* to quit? But in the case, which is common enough, where a person is trying to make up his mind whether or not he will quit his job, not through the consideration of evidence that he will or will not quit it, but of reasons for and against quitting it—in this case, what *is* his deciding to quit other than the transition from his being unsure about it to his being sure that he will quit? In this example, his deciding what he will do is the same thing as his becoming sure what he will do, and is not his grounds for being sure. Nothing can be put forward as his grounds for being sure he will quit: yet it is correct to say "He knows now that he will quit his job."

In the second place, sometimes people know in advance about things they do *in*voluntarily. A nervous amateur actor, about to make his first appearance on the stage, might say with conviction, "I know I shall forget my lines." Sure enough, he does forget them. This use of "know" is entirely natural. Did he have grounds? He could have been relying on some statistics—but that would not be the normal case. We

[3] It is worth noting that we do not speak of a person's grounds for *knowing* something, but of his grounds for believing it, being sure of it, asserting it, denying it, saying it, or doubting it. On the other hand, we ask *how* he knew it.

[4] Of course we might expect him to have grounds or reasons *for* quitting his job—a different matter.

are willing to say that he knew he would forget his lines, yet we do not expect him to have had evidence or grounds.[5]

In the third place, I can imagine a man who has unusual knowledge of the whereabouts of various persons, of what they are engaged in, what will happen to them, and so on. The man I am imagining (let us call him "the seer") is sure about these things and apparently is always right, but he does not have *grounds* for being sure. He has no special sources of information, he does not make use of tips or hints, and he does not guess. But he can tell someone the whereabouts of the son who left home five years ago and has not since been heard from. As his powers became known, people would come to him to inquire about their relatives and friends. I am supposing that in a large number of cases his answers have proven true and in no cases have they proven false. It is unquestionable that people would regard the seer as a source of *information*. "He informed me of the whereabouts of my son" would be a natural thing to say about him: and also "He knew the whereabouts of my son." The seer, as said, does not have grounds for being sure of the things he is sure of. He might even admit that he does not know *how* he knows the things in question. Sometimes when a question is put to him he has to wait a bit until the answer comes to him, like an inspiration; and sometimes he knows the answer immediately. But never is it a matter of grounds, evidence, or reasoning.

It is sometimes held that a person cannot properly be said to know something unless he is *in a position* to know it. But one might say that what is extraordinary about the seer is that he knows things which he is *not in a position to know*. A. J. Ayer says that "the necessary and sufficient conditions for knowing that something is the case are first that what one is said to know be true, secondly that one be sure of it, and thirdly that one should have the right to be sure." [6] I question the third condition. I believe Ayer would agree with me that the seer *knows* the things he reports, for Ayer says that if someone "were repeatedly successful in a given domain" although "without appearing to have any adequate basis for it," then "we should grant him the right to be sure, simply on the basis of his success." [7] But I think it is odd to say that the seer has a right to be sure of what he is sure of. The rest of us would have a right to be sure of something because the seer told us so, and because (to the best of our knowledge) he is invariably right. *We* have

[5] A friend of mine died after an illness of several weeks. Those who were with him reported to me that *he knew* he would die on the night he did die. Am I supposed to think that either they were wrong, or else that he had grounds for his conviction? "He felt his life ebbing away." What does this mean, except that he knew he was dying?

[6] *The Problem of Knowledge* (London: Macmillan & Co., Ltd., 1956), p. 34.

[7] *Ibid.*, p. 32.

grounds for being sure. But the seer does not have our grounds, or any other grounds. As said, he is not, in the ordinary meaning of the phrase, *in a position to know* what he tells us. I cannot understand, therefore, the expression "has a right to be sure" when it is applied to the seer, unless it merely means "*knows* what he is sure of," in which case it cannot express an element in the *analysis* of knowledge.

I have argued, from several different kinds of cases, that having grounds for being certain of something is not a necessary condition of knowing it. I imagine there are still other kinds of cases. I suspect that a stronger candidate than grounds or evidence, for being a necessary condition of knowledge, is the negative requirement that to know something one should not be certain of it because of a *mistake,* e.g., because of mishearing what someone said or because of fallacious reasoning.

The connection of this discussion of grounds with the definition of factual memory is that if having grounds is not a necessary condition of knowing something there is then no reason to suppose it is a necessary condition of remembering something.

When people do have grounds for being sure of something the grounds can differ in strength. If an American living in England converts his dollar holdings into pounds because he is sure that the American government is going to devalue the dollar, his grounds for being sure could be of many sorts. Let us suppose there are three people, A, B, and C, each of whom converts from dollars to pounds because he is sure the dollar will be devalued. A's grounds for being sure of this are that several of his friends, who are "generally well-informed about developments in international finance," are convinced it will happen. B's grounds are that a friend of his was told in confidence by an American Treasury official that it was "bound to happen." C's grounds are that the Secretary of the Treasury himself, in his last news conference, said he "did not see how this step could be avoided." All three are right; the dollar is devalued.

A person commenting on the matter afterwards could correctly say that all three *knew* the devaluation would occur (in contrast, for example, with D, whom the devaluation took by surprise). The person commenting on the matter would allow that B's grounds for being sure of it were stronger than A's, and that C's grounds were stronger still. Indeed, he would think that C's grounds were "just about as strong (or conclusive) as one could have in a matter of that sort." As he might put it, A's grounds were pretty good, B's grounds were even better, and C's grounds were as good as one could have. Another way to express the difference would be to say that on A's grounds it was "reasonably certain" it would happen; on B's grounds it was still more certain; and on C's grounds it was as certain as could be. Finally, another way to express it would be to say that although A knew it would happen his knowledge of it *was less certain* than B's, and B's knowledge was more certain than A's although not as certain as C's, and C's knowledge of it was as certain as knowledge can be in such matters. The interesting point here, if I am right, is that in ordinary discourse we conceive of *knowledge* as being *more or less certain.* We *grade* knowledge in terms of certainty. This grading of knowledge is solely in terms of the strength of the grounds. Grading *knowledge* as more or less certain is *equivalent* to grading *grounds* as more or less conclusive. If this is right, the assumption we are often tempted to make in philosophy, that if someone really knows that *p* then he must have grounds which make it perfectly certain or perfectly conclusive that *p,* is shown to be false. Knowledge is not all wool and a yard wide.

Our definition of factual memory requires the elements of present and previous knowledge. Let us raise again the questions that we put before: First, what *kind* of knowledge is involved in memory? Second, when someone remembers that *p* does he have *grounds* for being sure that *p*? Third, when someone remembers that *p,* just *how certain* is it that *p*?

Let us consider the first question, keeping in mind that memory involves both previous and present knowledge. The element of *previous* knowledge involved in memory can be any kind of knowledge at all. It might be the knowledge that a person has of his own voluntary or involuntary actions; it might be knowledge based on a newspaper report, or on a mathematical demonstration, or on an inference from what someone said; it might be the kind of knowledge that the seer has. Of what kind is the *present* knowledge involved in memory? Of exactly the *same* kind that the previous knowledge was. I think that here it may be misleading to speak of *two* elements of knowledge in memory, previous and present knowledge. There are not two pieces of knowledge but one piece. Memory is the *retention* of knowledge. One knew something and still knows it. The present knowledge in memory is the *same* as the previous knowledge.

Let us go to the second question: When someone remembers that *p* does he have grounds for being sure that *p*? The answer is that he has the same grounds, if any, that he previously had.[8] If B remembers that his friend, Robinson, was ill last year, then B previously knew of the illness. His previous knowledge may have been based on perception (He saw Robinson when the latter was ill); or on testimony (Jones told him about Robinson's illness); or on inference (B inferred that Robinson was

[8] This is true insofar as his present knowledge that *p* is solely *memory.* I am not dealing with the case in which it is partly memory and partly present evidence.

ill from his absence from work). B's *present* knowledge that Robinson was ill, if it is solely memory, has the *same* grounds. If the ground of his previous knowledge was testimony then the ground of his present knowledge is that same previous testimony. And so on. If what made him sure, previously, that Robinson was ill was that Jones told him so, his present ground for being sure is that Jones told him so previously. If a man's previous knowledge that *p* had *no* grounds, then in remembering that *p* his present knowledge has *no* grounds.

There is an interesting problem that arises here. If a man previously had grounds for being sure that *p,* and now remembers that *p,* but does not remember what his grounds were, does he *have* grounds for being sure that *p*? I will not go into this point, but I am inclined to say that he *has* the *same* grounds he previously had. In some cases if a man cannot give any grounds for believing something it follows that he has no grounds. But I think this does not hold for the special case of his *forgetting* what his grounds were. I should say it does not follow that he *has* no grounds for being certain that *p,* any *more* than it follows that he *had* no grounds. But by hypothesis he had grounds.

Our third question was: When someone remembers that *p,* how *certain* is it that *p*? The answer I give is that his present knowledge that *p* has the *same* degree of certainty that his previous knowledge that *p* had. Of course, if he has forgotten what his grounds were, *he* may be less certain then he was—but that is a different matter.

One thing which is obvious is that no matter how well a person remembers something, his present knowledge cannot be *superior* to his previous knowledge. His present knowledge that *p,* if it is solely memory, cannot be *more* certain than was his previous knowledge that *p.* This fact provides one clear sense for the claim that memory is not a *source* of knowledge.

When I remember that *p,* does my *remembering* it have grounds? If we are not merely asking again whether my certainty that *p* has grounds, then this seems a nonsensical question. If by "my remembering it" is meant the *relation* between my present any my previous knowledge that *p,* then my remembering it cannot be said to have or to lack grounds. This is reflected in the definition of factual memory—knowing that *p* because one previously knew that *p.* It would be unintelligible as well as ungrammatical to ask whether one had grounds for *that.*

Let us try to summarize briefly the place of knowledge in factual memory. If a person remembers that *p* then he knows that *p* and he knew it before. Knowing implies being sure, save for the qualification noted. There can be and are cases in which people know things without having *grounds* for being sure. If the previous knowledge was without grounds then the present knowledge is without grounds (if the present knowledge is solely memory). When a man had grounds for his previous knowledge that *p,* his previous knowledge was more or less certain, depending on the strength of his grounds; and his present knowledge (if it is solely memory) has this same degree of certainty regardless of whether he *remembers* his grounds.

I turn now to the third element in the definition of factual memory. What does it mean to say that someone knows that *p because* he previously knew that *p*? Could it mean that the past knowledge *caused* the present knowledge? W. von Leyden says that "it is part of the meaning of memory that, when it is correct, it is causally dependent upon a previous perception."[9] He is saying, for example, that someone's memory of having seen the *Queen Mary* in drydock is causally dependent on his having seen the *Queen Mary* in drydock. One might object to the idea that the supposed effect is *causally* dependent on the supposed cause, for the reason that the "effect" is *logically* dependent on the "cause." It is logically impossible that one should remember having seen *x* unless one saw it.

But we are concerned now with factual memory and whether it is a possibility that the present *knowledge* that *p* is causally dependent on the previous *knowledge* that *p*. Here it is not true that there is logical implication, in either direction, between supposed effect and supposed cause. Furthermore, one might think that we must be justified in speaking of a "causal dependence" here, simply because it is at natural use of language to say that someone knows that *p* "because" he knew it before, or to say that his present knowledge is "due to" his previous knowledge.

Granting this to be so, it does not tell us what this "causal dependence" *means.* There is an important sense of "cause" in which a singular causal statement of the form "*x* caused *y*" implies a general proposition of the form "In like circumstances, whenever *x* then *y*." But *this* meaning of "cause" cannot be involved in factual memory, since in saying that someone remembers that *p,* we are certainly not committing ourselves to the truth of the general proposition that "In like circumstances, whenever a person has previously known that *p* then he knows that *p*," even if we could give any clear meaning to it.

To come back to von Leyden, he holds that recollecting something implies that there is "a memory process or causal chain stretching continuously from the occurrence of *x* and the original experience of *x* up to the present recollection of *x*."[10] Another way he puts it is to say that there is a "continuous connexion" between a remembered fact and a

[9] *Remembering* (London: Gerald Duckworth & Co., Ltd., 1961), p. 31.
[10] *Ibid.*, p. 42.

present memory of it.[11] Sometimes he calls it an *unbroken* connection.[12] But this requirement, he holds, creates a problem about knowing whether *anyone* remembers *anything!* For, "the process of retention," say von Leyden, is "unobservable." [13] The "causal chain" implied by memory is "elusive." [14] It is difficult if not impossible, he says, to prove that an unbroken connection or persisting process intervened between a past experience and one's present recollection of it.[15] The conclusion drawn by him is that "no memory statement is, strictly speaking, verifiable." [16] I think he means by this remark that it is *never* verifiable that someone remembers something!

I should have thought a more reasonable conclusion would be that the concept of memory carries *no* implication of a continuous process of retention or of an unbroken causal connection. The imagery suggested by what von Leyden says is fairly definite. Remembering consists in a certain *process* which begins at the time a person witnesses or learns something. What the process is *in its own nature* is not known. But it is there, going on, and the person's occasional recollection of what he witnessed or learned is a *manifestation* of this underlying process.

This picture gives rise to two sorts of skeptical reflection. First, perhaps the underlying process is not *always* in operation during the intervals between the manifestations of it, and consequently we are sometimes mistaken in thinking that we remember certain things even though we give the right answers. Second, perhaps the required process is *never* there, and occurrences of so-called "recollection" are *never* manifestations of a process of remembering, and we are *always* deceived in thinking we remember something. It merely *looks as if* people remember!

Rather than to dwell on the absurdity of this conclusion, I want to try to explain the third element in the definition of factual memory. What does it mean to say that A knows that *p* *because* he previously knew that *p*? It does not mean that there is a "continuous" or "unbroken" connection between the previous and the present knowledge, even if this were an intelligible notion. I am afraid my explanation of the meaning of the "because" will be disappointing. I believe its meaning is essentially *negative*. This will be brought out by reflecting on one sort of consideration which would *disprove* the claim that A remembers that *p*. Suppose we know that A had known at a previous time that Rob-

11 *Ibid.*, p. 45.
12 E.g., *ibid.*, p. 40.
13 *Ibid.*, p. 55.
14 *Ibid.*, p. 46.
15 *Ibid.*, p. 53.
16 *Ibid.*, p. 43.

inson walked across Cayuga Lake when it was frozen. Suppose we also know that A knows it now. Could it turn out that A's present knowledge is not memory? Yes. If A were to tell us that he would not have had his present knowledge of the incident had not someone informed him of it *just now*, or had he not read about it in his diary a moment ago, or had he not inferred it from some remarks he overheard just now, then we should know that A's present knowledge that Robinson walked across the lake is not memory.

In this example, A had *forgotten* that *p*. But his having previously forgotten it is not a sufficient condition of his not remembering it. He might have forgotten it and then later remembered it, just as it often happens that one is for a time unable to remember a name and then finally does remember it. What keeps it from being true that A remembered the incident is not that he had previously forgotten it, but that he had just now *learned about it over again*. To say that A knows that *p* because he previously knew that *p* implies that A has *not* just now learned over again that *p*. This brings out, in part, the negative sense of the "because."

Another expression we can use here is "source," i.e., the *source* of A's present knowledge that *p* is his previous knowledge of it. This word carries a certain physical imagery. A river has a source and stretches continuously from its source to its mouth. The imagery of this word might play some part in producing von Leyden's inclination to postulate a "continuous connexion." But when the word "source" is used in the analysis of memory it must, like "because," be understood in a negative sense. To say "His previous knowledge is the source of his present knowledge" implies that he has not just now learned over again that *p*.

The meaning of "just now" is, however, pretty indefinite. If I was told something two hours ago would that be "just now"? Or would "just now" have to be ten minutes or ten seconds ago? I believe this is an artificial problem. I think that when we say "A remembers that *p*," we refer, more or less vaguely, to a more or less definite previous time when A knew that *p*. We are asserting that A remembers that *p from that time*. This will imply that A has not learned over again that *p* since that time. If this is correct we can get rid of the phrase "just now" in stating our analysis of factual memory. The statement "He remembers that *p*" will imply: "He knows that *p, and* at a previous time, *t*, he knew that *p, and* he has not learned over again that *p* since *t*." It would be up to the person who made the original statement to specify the time, *t*, to which he refers.

There is another objection to this analysis of factual memory. Let us imagine the following case: A man, B, learned that *p*. B then suffered an injury to a certain part of his brain, as a result of which he no longer knew that *p*. Later an operation was performed on his brain which had the effect that again he knew that *p*. At this later time it would be true that B knows that *p* and also that he knew that *p* at a previous time, *t*, and that he had not learned over again that *p* since *t*. (The operation on his brain, or the effect of it, cannot be called "*learning* over again" that *p*.) Our proposed definition of factual memory is satisfied: yet should we really wish to say that B remembers that *p*?

Whether we should say this or not may depend on what we suppose to be the efficacy of the brain surgery.[17] If we supposed that what was done to B's brain would cause him to know that *p*, *regardless of what his previous knowledge had been*[18] (i.e., he would know that *p* even if he had not ever previously known that *p*) then we should be disinclined to say that the operation had "restored his memory," and also disinclined to say, "Now he remembers that *p*." If, on the other hand, this operation could cause a person to know that *p* *only if* he had previously known that *p*, then we should be inclined to say those doings.

It appears, therefore, that in this described case we should call B's present knowledge that *p* *memory*, only if we supposed that he would not now know that *p* had he not previously known that *p*. This fits in with the general feature of knowing something on the basis of memory, namely, that the present knowledge must be dependent on previous knowledge. As suggested before, when we claim that someone remembers a certain thing, we refer (more or less tacitly) to a previous time, t_1, when he knew the thing, and we are claiming that he remembers it *from* that time. Our claim implies that he has not learned the thing over again since t_1.[19] More generally, our claim implies that nothing whatever has occurred at some later time, t_2, such that his knowledge "dates" from t_2 instead of from t_1. This general requirement eliminates the possibility that, for example, a brain operation at t_2 should have been a sufficient condition of B's present knowledge.

The most concise and accurate formulation of this requirement which I have been able to think of is this: A person, B, remembers that *p* from *t*, only if it is the case that had B not known that *p* at *t*, he would not now know that *p*. The negative counterfactual conditional statement "If B had not known at *t* that *p*, he would not now know that *p*" does not express a *law*. It is similar in meaning to such a statement as the

[17] In my discussion of this point, I am indebted to John Rawls and David Sachs.

[18] I do not assume that this is, or ever will be, a factual possibility. I am not entirely sure that it even makes sense. But it is not clear to me that it does not, and so my analysis of factual memory should take account of it.

[19] It is worth remarking that if I have forgotten something temporarily, and then suddenly remember it, it cannot be said that I have *learned* the thing over again. This is because my present knowledge of it is "due" to my previous knowledge of it.

following: "If you had not given me a cigar I should not have one now." This would simply mean that, in fact, no other opportunity of my obtaining a cigar presented itself. Similarly, our negative counterfactual conditional about B's knowledge means that, as a matter of fact, if he had not obtained this knowledge at *t* he would not have it now. This is a kind of thing we often know to be true, just as we often know it to be true that this man would not have a cigar now if someone had not given him the one he has. Nothing is implied, in either case, about the existence of a causal chain or of a continuous process.

I have been trying to explain the meaning of the third element in our definition of factual memory, namely, the meaning of saying that someone now knows that *p because* he previously knew it. Our definition of factual memory can now be stated in full as follows: A person, B, remembers that *p* from a time, *t,* if and only if B knows that *p, and* B knew that *p* at *t, and* if B had not known at *t* that *p* he would not now know that *p*.

One point should be mentioned here. Something may *remind* one of some fact. You remember the latter *because* of something you saw or heard or thought. This meaning of "because" is different from the meaning it has in the definition of factual memory. Without going further into the matter, I will say that these two meanings of "because" are quite compatible. It can be true both that a man should now remember that *p* (which implies that he now knows that *p because* he previously knew it) and also that something made him remember that *p* (i.e., he remembered it *because* of something he perceived or thought). I think that this second "because" has a genuine *causal* meaning.

It must be admitted that one feels some mystification about my negative interpretation of the words "because" or "source" in our definition of factual memory. It seems mysterious that a man should know that *p,* having previously known it, unless there is something that comes *between* his previous and present knowledge and *ties them together.* It is probably this feeling that chiefly contributes to von Leyden's view of memory. We feel that there is a *gap* between the previous and the present knowledge, but at the same time we do not know how to fill in the gap. Should we say that what fills it is some persisting state of the brain or neural process? Whether or not it makes sense to postulate a specific brain-state or neural process persisting between the previous and the present knowledge that *p,* such a postulation is obviously not required by an analysis of the *concept* of remembering. Our everyday verifications of whether some person does or does not remember that *p* are not bound up with any questions about what is and has been going on in his brain. Our use of the language of memory carries no implications about inner physiology. Nor can we fill the gap with a continuous process of thinking about what is remembered. People could not think, continuously and simultaneously, of all the things they remember. If we resorted to *unconscious* thoughts in order to bridge the gap, we should then be in a difficulty about the *criterion* we should use for the existence of those unconscious thoughts. If we had no criterion our "solution" would, in a sense, be unintelligible. If we used the existence of the gap itself as our criterion for the existence of the unconscious thoughts that bridge the gap, then our solution would solve nothing.

This feeling of the mysteriousness of memory, unless we assume a persisting state or process between the previous and the present knowledge, provides one *metaphysical* aspect of the topic of memory. I believe this feeling explains why it is so commonly taken for granted, by philosophers, psychologists, and physiologists, that there is a "*process* of retention." It would be a valuable piece of philosophical work to explain why we have this feeling—what comparisons, what analogies, give rise to it. My own guess would be that our strong desire for a mechanism (either physical or mental) of memory arises from an abhorrence of the notion of action at a distance-in-time.

Leaving aside the question of why we have it, the idea of there being a gap between the previous and the present knowledge in memory is certainly a confusion. There is a gap only if there is something *missing*. But what is missing? We have no idea.

What *could* fill the gap? I have mentioned three candidates: a persisting physiological state or process; continuous thinking about what is remembered; continuous unconscious thinking about what is remembered. We see that for different reasons none of these candidates can be included in the truth conditions for statements of the form "A remembers that *p*." I believe we do not have the conception of anything else that might fill the gap. In a sense, therefore, we do not know what it means to speak of a *gap* here.

All of us (myself too) tend to have a piece of imagery, namely, of a *physical* gap. I can express that imagery with gestures. With a wave of the hand I can say, "Over *there* is the previous knowledge that *p*, and over *here* is the present knowledge that *p*: but what *connects* the two?" Yet if someone were to take seriously my pointing gestures and my expressions "Over there" and "Over here," I should be embarrassed. I have the imagery, together with the feeling that it illustrates something significant; but at the same time I cannot take it seriously. This is a frequent predicament in philosophy.

Two additional objections to our definition of factual memory must be considered. The first one is the following: Bodily sensations are among the objects of memory. A person can remember that he had an earache and that the pain was excruciating. But it is senseless, it may be said, to speak of someone's *knowing* that he is in pain.[20] Our definition cannot be satisfied, therefore, since it requires that a person who remembers that he had an earache should have previously known that he had one. The time at which he had this previous knowledge would have to be the very time at which he had the earache. For if it were at a later time, his knowledge at this later time would itself be memory and, by our definition, would require a previous knowledge. And so on. Our definition really requires that a person who remembers that he had a certain sensation (solely on the basis of having had it) must have shown that he was having it at the time he was having it. But since this latter is nonsense, it would follow that one could not remember a sensation. We can and do remember sensations, and so the definition is wrong.

My reply to this objection is to point out that *a* sense can be given to saying that a person knows that he has a sensation at the time he has it. He knows it in the sense that *he can tell you* that he has it. This is a significant thing to say, because a dog or a human baby *cannot* tell you that he has a painful ear, although it could be determined that he has one. In this sense, there are various sensations that lower animals and human infants have without knowing it, whereas human adults both have them and know it. As a human being learns language he acquires the capacity to know that he has those sensations. Therefore he can subsequently remember that he had them. Our definition of factual memory in terms of knowledge does not presuppose that knowledge is always the *same kind* of thing. Any legitimate sense of "know" yields a legitimate sense of "remember."[21]

The second and final objection to our definition, which I am going to consider, is the following: A person can remember that he had a dream and what it was. But a person cannot know that he is dreaming while he is dreaming. Remembering that one had a dream cannot be analyzed, therefore, into knowing that one had a dream because one previously knew it.

I believe this argument is sound. In my monograph on dreams I argue that the sentence "I am asleep" cannot be used to express a judg-

[20] It can't be said of me at all (except perhaps as a joke) that I *know* I am in pain" (Ludwig Wittgenstein, *Philosophical Investigations*, tr. G. E. M. Anscombe [New York: The Macmillan Company, 1953], sec. 246. See p. 110).

[21] I do not believe there is any sense in which a dog or infant can be said to know that it has some sensation. I accept the consequence that a dog cannot be said to remember that he had a painful ear, and also the more interesting consequence that a human being cannot be said to remember that he had one, if he had it at a time before he knew enough language to be able to tell anyone that he had it. This point is connected with what Wittgenstein says about William James's Ballard (*Investigations*, sec. 342).

ment about one's own condition, i.e., one cannot judge that oneself is asleep.[22] If this is correct then there cannot be such a thing as knowing that oneself is asleep, and from this it follows that one cannot know that one is dreaming. One can know that one *dreamt* but not that one *is* dreaming.

Is this knowledge that one dreamt *memory,* and if so, does our definition of factual memory fit it? There is no doubt that often the knowledge that one had a dream is memory, e.g., when one knows that one had a dream last week or last month. But if a person awakened suddenly from sleep and immediately declared that he had a dream, should we call this *remembering* that he had a dream? I am not sure: but if so then this use of "He remembers that *p*" does not fall under our analysis of factual memory. We cannot hold that here "He remembers that he dreamt" is equivalent to "He knows that he dreamt because he knew that he dreamt," since we should not know how to determine a previous time at which he knew that he dreamt. It would not be satisfactory to hold that "At some previous time he knew that he dreamt" means the same as "If he had been awakened at some previous time he would have said that he dreamt," since, in our example, the latter might be false.

The conclusion I draw is, not that our definition of factual memory is wrong, but that this special sense of remembering that one dreamt differs sharply from the central use of the factual memory locution.[23] Our definition gives a correct account of the central use, but perhaps not of absolutely every use of this locution.

[22] Norman Malcolm, *Dreaming,* second impression (New York: Humanitics Press and London: Routledge & Kegan Paul, Ltd., 1962). See especially Chapters 3 and 9.

[23] See *Dreaming,* pp. 56–59, for a discussion of the notion of remembering dreams.

C. B. Martin and Max Deutscher

Remembering

I. INTRODUCTORY DISTINCTIONS

We intend to define what it is to remember. Our account covers direct memory of events, remembering information, and remembering how to do things. There are differences between these three sorts of memory. Someone may remember how to swim and yet not remember those occasions on which he learned to swim. A man in the twentieth century may say truly that he remembers that Julius Caesar invaded Britain. What is impossible is that he remembers Caesar invading Britain. There are differences between "He remembers going swimming," "He remembers that he went swimming," and "He remembers how to swim."

Remembering How

To say that someone remembers how to swim is at least to say that he has learned how. He may have taught himself or learned from an-

C. B. Martin and Max Deutscher, "Remembering," *The Philosophical Review*, 75 (1966), 161–96. Reprinted by permission.

other. It is also to say that, as a result of his learning to swim, he still has the skill needed to swim. He need not be able to swim; he may be paralyzed and unable to employ his skill. An account of the causal connection involved would not be the same as the one which we will give for remembering, but we shall not discuss this here. Some people insist that if a person can, for instance, give a fair account of how to swim, then he may be said to remember how to swim, though he has no skill at all at swimming. Perhaps it is better to speak here of remembering how a stroke goes, than of remembering how to do it. The difference between remembering and remembering *how* to do something cannot show itself better than in the case where some swimming *is* an example of remembering and not, as is usual, an example of remembering *how*.

Suppose that someone has never dog-paddled. He is not good at visualization and has never learned any words which would describe swimming. His method of representing the one time at which he saw a man dog-paddle is his actually doing the dog-paddle stroke. We can imagine him trying to remember the curious action that the man went through in the water. He cannot describe it, and cannot form any picture of it. He cannot bring it back. He gets into the water, experimenting a little until suddenly he gets it right and exclaims, "Aha, that's it!" To anyone who complains that the man would have no test for whether the stroke was remembered, unless he could visualize or describe the process, we point out that exactly the same difficulty attaches to answering the question "What test does a person have for his visual imagery or description being correct?"

Two Types of Remembering That

A person can remember that something happened even though it was before he was born, or was within his lifetime though not within his experience. In the same sense a person may be said to remember *that* he spent the first year of his life in a certain town, even though in this case what he remembers is within his experience. There is, however, a distinction between two radically different types of remembering that *p*. In the first type one sufficient reason why a man may be said *only* to remember that *X* happened is that he did not experience *X* happening. Another sufficient reason would be that his representation of the event is not (in a way which we shall describe in Sections VI and VII) due to his experience of it. In such a case, he will have previously worked it out or heard about it quite independently of his own original perception of it. When speaking of this first type of case, we shall say that someone remembers that_1 something.

In the second type of case, the reason a man might be said only to remember that something happened is merely that there is a lack of detail in his *direct* memory. Thus the second type is quite unlike remembering $that_1$, where his source of information is not his own past experience of what he recounts. Here we shall speak of his remembering $that_2$ something. If someone is asked whether he remembers what he did last Friday at lunchtime, he may be able to say that he went down the street. Yet he may feel scarcely in a position to say that he remembers actually going down the street. What he needs in order to be able to say that he does remember going down the street is at least more detailed remembering $that_2$ certain things happened when he went down the street. As we shall go on to argue, this addition of detail must be due to the original perception. However, no amount of detailed remembering that various things happened on the walk is relevant to the question whether he remembers the walk unless his remembering that they occurred is of the second type. A precisely analogous point could be made in connection with the construction "remembering what happened," or "remembering what something was like," and we shall use the numbers 1 and 2 as subscripts in the same way. This second use of remembering that (or *what*) allows us to describe cases of remembering where we can bring back very little detail, although it is not restricted only to such cases. A considerable amount of remembering $that_2$ is *involved in* remembering an incident.

To say that someone remembers some fact such as Caesar's invasion of Britain is to say more than that he represents it correctly (we shall discuss "representing" later). It is to say also that it or a representation of it has come within his experience or that he has worked it out. It is to say still more than this, too, since someone's learning a fact at some past time may have nothing to do with his now representing it. He may have no retention of his school lessons, and have just worked it out from various things he has read recently. Although in remembering a fact he learned at school a man does not *ipso facto* remember the learning of it, his present account must be given because of this previous learning. It is interesting that he might not have accepted what he was taught, experienced, or worked out on the past occasion, but later may remember that it was the case. For instance, he may have been in a mood which made him irrationally reject what he was taught. Later, with no new information, he may simply remember it.

We claim that a person can be said to remember something happening or, in general, remember something directly, only if he has observed or experienced it. This is not to be confused with the false doctrine that we always remember *only* what happened to ourselves.[1] Of course

[1] Cf. A. Flew, "Locke and Personal Identity," *Philosophy,* XXVI (1951), 56.

someone can remember his brother being married although it didn't happen to him. Still, unless he saw it, heard it, or otherwise perceived it happening, it is false to say he remembers his brother being married.

If someone remembers $that_1$ *p*, then some source of information, other than his own perception that *p*, is part of the cause of his now recounting what he learned. If someone was told something false, then naturally he cannot be said to remember that it was the case. This is in no way a failure of memory on his part (see Section III for an analogous and fuller discussion of this type of problem); he legitimately can be said to remember what he was told, whether it is true or false.

Normally one does not trouble to make a distinction between remembering what one was told a day ago and what one was told a year ago, when the very same fact is involved. Yet there is a basis for such a distinction, if we wished to draw one, and, furthermore, there could be a reason to insist on making this distinction—namely, where consideration is given to the *responsibility* of the acceptance. For example, a year ago someone was told something by a reliable authority and also, a week ago, accepted the same fact from someone he had no reason to trust. In that case, the question whether he remembered what he was told a year ago rather than, or as well as, what he was told a week ago, would affect the answer to the question "Does he now accept irresponsibly what he was told a week ago?" If the distinction were drawn as just suggested, then if a person is to remember what he was told *at a certain time,* his being told at that time must stand in the causal relation (which we shall specify in Sections V, VI, and VII) to his representation of what he was told. A point must be made about what is demanded of the representation involved in remembering what one was told. It is not necessary either to represent one's being told, nor the fact which one was told, because it might not *be* a fact. Remembering $that_2$ is remembering directly, and so our discussion of the causal connection in Sections V, VI, and VII will automatically cover this concept also.

Reliving the Past and the Role of Imagery

Although it is a mistake to insist that a person must have mental images of what he remembers, imagery is of importance for a number of reasons. For one thing, some people to whom imagery is very vivid and impressive *insist* that they do not "really" remember something unless they can see it again in the mind's eye, or hear it again with the mind's ear. Furthermore, many things we remember might have been extremely difficult to describe in the first place. For instance, if someone cannot form a mental image of the sound of a *cor anglais,* or the look of affected concern on a person's face, or the taste of an avocado pear, then he may well be completely at a loss to recall such things in any other way.

Thus, it is easy to think that the notion of reliving the past, as something more than just remembering it, is coextensive with getting vivid imagery of it, supposing that the other conditions for memory are fulfilled. This, however, is not accurate. Two people engaged in animated discussion of something they were both involved in may be said to be reliving the incident, although they are not having mental images of the incident. Something of their past involvement with the events they remember comes out in their present feelings and in the way they describe the incident. Yet, although reliving something is not merely remembering it, reliving *need* not involve the sort of return of the past emotions and feelings which we have just described. It would seem at least that either imagery or the return of the old emotions about the incident must occur, each by itself being enough to allow us to speak of reliving as something more than merely remembering.

It may be said that two old soldiers are reliving the past when they are discussing and joking about some terrible events which they lived through. These old men may be having neither mental imagery of the events, nor may the original horror be, as it were, felt again. In such a case, we are more inclined to say that they would be merely reminiscing.

One last minor distinction should be made before we begin the main discussion. In our analysis we claim that to remember is at least to do something. Yet one can say of a person asleep, "His memory is quite remarkable. He remembers the details of every car he has ever owned." The difference between such a sense and the one we discuss is not the difference between two sorts of memory. It merely reflects the difference between remembering and the ability to remember. Since understanding of such a general ability is immediately dependent upon understanding of actual occurrences of remembering, we concentrate our attention on an analysis of the latter. Our discussion will deal primarily with cases of remembering. From time to time, however, we will point out how some of our remarks apply to cases of remembering *that* certain things happened.

II. THE PROPOSED ANALYSIS

If someone remembers something, whether it be "public," such as a car accident, or "private," such as an itch, then the following criteria must be fulfilled:

1. Within certain limits of accuracy he represents that past thing.
2. If the thing was "public," then he observed what he now represents.[2] If the thing was "private," then it was his.
3. His past experience of the thing was operative in producing a state or successive states in him finally operative in producing his representation.

These three statements express the condition which we consider to be separately necessary and jointly sufficient, if an event is to be an instance of remembering. The main body of the paper will be taken up with elucidation and argument for the necessity and sufficiency of these conditions. It will be found that two more clauses must be added to criterion 3, and these will be introduced and explained as the need for them arises. Obviously an explanation of the first criterion is needed, and in due course we also discuss "limits of accuracy," "representation," "prompting," and "operative."

III. BELIEF AND REMEMBERING

There is some reason to say that the list of conditions is not sufficient. Locke in his *Essay Concerning Human Understanding* (Bk. II, ch. x, sec. 2) and Russell in *The Analysis of Mind* (ch. ix) claim that if a person remembers something, then he must believe that it happened. Also Furlong in his recent book, *A Study in Memory* (pp. 73, 75, 93) and Harrod in an article, "Memory" (*Mind,* LI [1942], 53) require that a person believe that an event occurred before he can be said to remember it. These philosophers hold the position as something obvious, not as something to be stated and argued for. Hume, too, seems to require belief as a criterion. Russell and Harrod rely on belief as one of the necessities of a logical distinction between imagination and memory. B. Benjamin ("Remembering," *Mind,* LXV [1956], 321, 322) is one of the few who has challenged the view that one must believe if one remembers. More recently, J. T. Saunders ("Does All Memory Imply Factual Memory," *Analysis Supplement,* [1965], 109) in criticism of Professor Norman Malcolm has claimed that memory is possible without belief.

If philosophers are in the egocentric predicament and an introspective mood when they try to define memory, then they will feel that they must find the difference between real and delusory remembering within their own experience. In that case they are very likly to assume that it is not possible for someone to remember something unless he be-

[2] See Sec. IV, 2nd par.

lieves it happened. With Hume, they may wonder which of their apparent memory images are real representations of the past, but they will not pick on an image as a memory unless at least they *believe* that it is a "copy" or representation of a past event. This fact does not show that the philosophers we criticize are wrong, but it is an adequate explanation of their assumption.

It may seem obvious that a person does not remember something unless he believes that it occurred. The "obvious" leads to trouble, however. For one thing, surely people say, "I don't know whether I am remembering this or imagining it," suggesting that they could be remembering something, though they neither believe nor disbelieve that it happened. It may seem even more obvious that, even if belief is not necessary in remembering, absence of disbelief certainly is. But consider the following case.

Suppose that someone asks a painter to paint an imaginary scene. The painter agrees to do this and, taking himself to be painting some purely imaginary scene, paints a detailed picture of a farmyard, including a certain colored and shaped house, various people with detailed features, particular items of clothing, and so on. His parents then recognize the picture as a very accurate representation of a scene which the painter saw just once in his childhood. The figures and colors are as the painter saw them only once on the farm which he now depicts. We may add more and more evidence to force the conclusion that the painter did his work by no mere accident. Although the painter sincerely believes that his work is purely imaginary, and represents no real scene, the amazed observers have all the evidence needed to establish that in fact he is remembering a scene from childhood. What other explanation could there be for his painting being so like what he has seen?

Let us approach the matter from another direction. It is quite common in ordinary life to describe some past event, and then to be uncertain whether the description was from memory, or was founded on something one was told after the event. If it were impossible to remember while believing one is not remembering, one would be saved the embarrassment of thinking that one is originating a tune or an argument when one is not. Now, we can prove that if one may remember *X*, but not believe that one is remembering *X*, then it is possible that one should remember *X* and not believe that *X* happened.

Suppose that:

1. *A* remembers *X*, and *A* holds no belief that he remembers *X*.

We can easily suppose that, in addition, *A* is prepared to believe that the past event occurred only if either he believes that he remembers it, or believes that he has been told that it occurred, or has worked it out from something he has been told. (For brevity, let us say that in both the last two alternatives he believes that he has been "told.")

That is to say:

2. *A* holds the belief that *X* occurred only if either he believes that he remembers *X*, or believes that he was told that *X* occurred.

Now, *A* tells some story about his past, and in fact this story is true, although he does not know it. He wonders whether he is remembering the story but, thinking it most implausible, he rejects this possibility. On the same ground, he rejects the idea that he has been told such a story.

This we may set down as:

3. *A* neither believes that he remembers *X*, nor believes that he has been told that *X* occurred.

From 3 and 2 we deduce that *A* does not hold the belief that *X* occurred. In conjunction with 1 this allows us to deduce that *A* does not believe that *X* occurred, but that he does remember that it did. Given that the three premises may express contingent truths, and are mutually consistent, we cannot deny that it can be true that *A* remembers something, but does not believe that it happened. It is impossible to deny that each premise may express a contingent truth. The set as it stands is formally consistent, and makes no assumption about the analysis of remembering. It can be proved inconsistent only by someone who simply presupposes that 1 entails that *A* believes that *X* occurred.

We suggested that introspection as a means of discovering the nature of remembering was likely to make the idea appear inescapable that to remember is at least to believe. On the other hand, if we adopt an uncritical linguistic approach to the matter, we are equally likely to be misled, since to say "I remember *X* but believe that *X* did not happen" is bound to be incoherent. We must be wary about such first-person present-tense expressions of belief as "I have boots on, but I believe that I do not." This is equally incoherent, but the incoherence does not prove that, if I have boots on, I cannot believe that I do not have them on.

The incoherence of any utterance of the sentence in question is an important matter which merits considerable discussion, but in the context of this paper the following remarks must suffice.[3] It is generally ac-

[3] For further remarks on this topic, see Max Deutscher, "A Note on Saying and Disbelieving," *Analysis* (1965), 53–57.

cepted that "*A* remembers an event *X*" entails "The event *X* occurred." Hence the incoherence of the remark "I remember *X*, but *X* never took place" needs no special explanation; it is the incoherence of sheer contradiction. Therefore when a person asserts that he remembers *X*, what he says can be true only if *X* did occur. From this we can proceed to explain why "I remember *X*, but I *believe* that *X* did not occur" is incoherent. When a man says that he has a belief, there are two avenues for argument with him—that is, that he does not have the belief which he says he has or, alternatively, that he is mistaken in holding the belief which he holds. In holding a belief a person must be either correct or mistaken. The incoherence of "I remember going for a walk, but I do not believe that I went for a walk" is quite straightforward. Only if *X* did happen can a person be right when he asserts "I remember *X*." Only if *X* did not occur, however, can he be correct in his belief that *X* did not occur. Therefore it is impossible for a person to be right both in his claim to remember *X* and in his belief that *X* did not occur. Whatever the facts are he must be wrong. Since what the person *says* could be true, though he must be mistaken, this is not the same as a contradiction, although it is very like one. Thus we can explain why "I remember going for a walk, but I believe that I did not go for a walk" is incoherent without assuming that to remember is at least to believe.

Since we do not include belief in our analysis of memory, we avoid puzzles of the sort which Miss Anscombe produces in her article, "The Reality of the Past" (in *Philosophical Analysis,* edited by Max Black). She puts forward the case of someone who at a certain time sees a wax dummy which he takes to be a man. Later on he says without lying that he remembers seeing a man at that time. What he says must be false. Yet, as she says, it is not his memory which is at fault. Von Leyden in a recent book, *Remembering* (New York, 1961), describes a similar case (p. 60) in an effort to deal with this very puzzling matter and is led to think that one can remember no physical thing, but only one's own experiences. Now, since we do not require that a person should believe that *X* happened when he remembers *X*, we do not require that he believe correctly. We argue that the man in Miss Anscombe's case may remember seeing the wax dummy, although he believes that he saw a man.

All the same, a problem arises for us from such a case. Is our first criterion correct? Does the person represent correctly what he remembers? It might be thought not. We have agreed that when the person says that he saw a man, his memory is not at fault, though he actually saw a wax dummy and not a man. But though his memory is not at fault, he cannot be said to remember seeing a man for the simple reason that there was not a man at that time to be remembered. Our criterion requires only that he represent correctly what he *does* remember. What could the person be said to remember here? It would depend on details of the case which are not mentioned by either Miss Anscombe or Von Leyden. Depending on how the person did see it, it might be said that he remembered seeing how the wax dummy looked—namely, like a man—supposing that what he later recounted was that he *saw* a man. Furthermore, it could be said that he remembers the shape of the nose of what he saw, the set of the eyes, the stance, and so on.

Yet is there not still a difficulty for criterion 1? What he may say is "I remember the shape of the man's nose. It was crooked and rather short." He is not correctly representing what he saw, since what he saw was a wax dummy's nose and so, according to the first criterion, he is not remembering. This, however, would be a misunderstanding. What the man does remember is the shape of the nose of what was in fact a wax dummy. Just as we can say that, so we can also say that he does correctly represent the shape of the nose of what was in fact a wax dummy. That he can correctly represent the shape of the nose is in no way vitiated by the fact that he is wrong about the stuff the nose was made of, or the nature of the nose's owner.

IV. CONCLUDING INTRODUCTORY REMARKS

Someone might think that our treatment of Miss Anscombe's case permits us to speak of a person remembering more than he has ever seen. (This would conflict with our second criterion.) It might be argued: "If *A* sees *B* who is covered in a sheet, and later remembers the incident, then, although he might not believe it, *what he remembers* is *B* covered in a white sheet. All that *A* saw, however, was a white sheet." But this is just an equivocation on the "what" in "what he remembers" and in "what he saw." Just as we may say that what he remembers, although he does not believe it, is a man covered in a white sheet, so we may say that what he saw, although he does not believe it, was a man covered in a white sheet. Or we may wish to speak "strictly" in both cases, and say that all he saw and all that he remembers is a white sheet. So long as one does not work with a double standard, there is no trouble for the criterion.

We can offer no argument for the sufficiency of our list of criteria other than the failure, after examination of cases, to find the need for a longer list. We move on to argue for the necessity of the conditions which we have named. Criterion 1 states: *Within certain limits of accuracy he represents that past thing.* Failure to fulfill this criterion is the most typical failure to remember. Somebody may have observed an event, but unless he is recounting it to himself, telling others or in some other way representing it, then, roughly speaking, he is not remembering that event. Even if it is true, as some psychoanalysts claim, that under suitable conditions we are able to remember anything which we have experienced, nobody actually remembers anything until he comes to the point of representing in some way what he has observed or experienced. We *intend* the vagueness of the phrase "represents the past." Already in connection with memory without belief, we have described an example in which painting was a case of remembering. At the beginning of the article we suggested that even to swim might be a form of representation.

What we have said about the types of representation is insufficient, and this is a claim rather than an admission, since we want to bring to notice that no philosophical writing on memory has so much as recognized the problem. On anyone's account of memory, it is not enough that someone should have observed or experienced something in the past. He must do something in the present. "What sort of thing must he do in the present, in order to be said to remember?" is a difficult and very general question. It is similar to the question "What sort of thing must a person do in order to be right or wrong about something?" and requires a full treatment by itself.

V. THE CAUSAL CRITERION

In his article, "The Empiricist Theory of Memory" (*Mind,* LXIII [1954], 474) Holland maintains that the following conditions are adequate to determine that someone is remembering something.

(*a*) What he is recounting did in fact happen, exist, and so forth.
(*b*) He is not being currently informed about what happened, existed, and so forth.
(*c*) He observed what he now recounts.

It must be obvious that (*b*) is not a necessary condition for remembering, since someone might be remembering as well as being informed about the events which he remembers.

It must be equally clear that Holland has given an inadequate analysis. One has only to reflect on the case of a man who can tell you what happened to him when he was three months old but can do so only because his mother told him. As well as Holland's, Ryle's account of memory (*The Concept of Mind* [New York, 1949], pp. 272–279) does not leave enough room for real doubt about whether someone is remembering an event rather than remembering what he has been told about it, or making it up, or imagining. We have already argued that it is not necessary that a person believe what he remembers or believe that he remembers. Even if such conditions were necessary they would not, in conjunction with the first two criteria, be sufficient for remembering.

In the argument which follows for the necessity of the third criterion, we begin with clause (a) of it. Later we shall show why clauses (b) and (c) must be added.

> Clause (a). *To remember an event, a person must not only represent and have experienced it, but also his experience of it must have been operative in producing a state or successive states in him finally operative in producing his representation.*

For brevity we consider only the memory of "public" events, but the same considerations would apply to the memory of "private" episodes and the memory of processes, physical objects, relations, dreams, and recollections themselves. First support for the principle arises from a consideration of the following case.

A man whom we shall call Kent is in a car accident and sees particular details of it, because of his special position. Later on, Kent is involved in another accident in which he gets a severe blow on the head as a result of which he forgets a certain section of his own history, including the first accident. He can no longer fulfill the first criterion for memory of the first accident. Some time after this second accident, a popular and rather irresponsible hypnotist gives a show. He hypnotizes a large number of people, and suggests to them that they will believe that they had been in a car accident at a certain time and place. The hypnotist has never heard a thing about Kent nor the details of Kent's accident, and it is by sheer coincidence that the time, place, and details which he provides are just as they were in Kent's first accident. Kent is one of the group which is hypnotized. The suggestion works and so, after the act is over, Kent satisfies criterion 1 again. He believes firmly that he has been in an accident. The accident as he believes it to be is just like the first one in which he was really involved. All along he had satisfied criterion 2, of course. Thus, while it is clear that he satisfies the first two criteria, it is very doubtful that he remembers.

If Kent's loss of memory had been due to psychological causes, then it would have been easy to suppose that in the case as described hypnosis had actually brought his memory back. Kent does not repeat anything else about the period of his life which had been blotted out, however; he just repeats what the others in the group repeat. Kent is certainly "describing correctly" the first accident, as they all are, but his recounting of the first accident is not due, even in part, to his observing it. Like the others, he says what he does only because of the hypnotist's suggestion. It is for this reason that he cannot be said to be remembering the accident, despite the fact that he correctly recounts what he saw. Therefore the first two criteria are inadequate. If a person's account of what he saw is not due even in part to his seeing it, it cannot be said that he remembers what he saw. If a person *remembers* what he saw, his recounting it must be due in part to seeing it. Anyone who rejects this causal interpretation must himself explain its force. At the end of this article we shall argue against Malcolm's attempt to do so.

Ryle, in *The Concept of Mind* (p. 278), and Benjamin (*op. cit.*, pp. 323, 324), have expressly denied that any causal criterion is part of the definition of memory. Writers such as Harrod (*op. cit.*), Furlong (*op. cit.*), and Holland (*op. cit.*) have ignored it. Let us make it quite clear that we do not claim that any causal connection is a logical connection. All we claim is that there is a causal connection between *A*'s past observation of *X* and his present representation of it, and a logical connection between "*A*'s past observation of *X* is causally related to his present representation of it" and "*A* remembers *X*."

Malcolm (*Knowledge and Certainty,* [Englewood Cliffs, 1963], p. 237, par. 2) [pp. 298–299, this volume. Eds.] feels that someone who gave a causal account of memory would have to say that a statement of the actual causal mechanism involved would be entailed by "*A* remembers *X*." He says that "our use of the language of memory carries no implication about our inner physiology." We can agree with him, for what we claim in our causal account is that our use of "language of memory" carries implications only that there is *some* continuous causal process or other. Nor, to use Benamin's phrase, do we require that the actual causal connection which does exist is "known by the vast majority of people." Benjamin suggests that it is curious that people should be sure that some process has gone on without knowing just what process it is. It seems to us not in the least curious to claim this. It is just what many people do when they say that dialing a number makes the phone ring at the other end. They think that there is some process linking their action with the effect, but they have little or no idea what it is.

We offer the following subsidiary arguments for the general version of the causal criterion. Consider the example of the painter which we gave earlier. The onlookers were compelled to the conclusion that the painter was remembering something he saw in childhood. It would have been unreasonable for them to think that he would have done what he did if it had not been for some particular past observation. Criteria 1 and 2 were fulfilled, but this did not by itself establish that it was a case of memory. What finally established it as such was this: the only reasonable explanation of the fact that the painter put details, colors, people, and so on into his picture, just as he saw them only once in his childhood, is that he was remembering that scene from his childhood. (We talk of the "only reasonable explanation" in the case described, of course. We do not suggest that in no case would there be an alternative explanation.) If to remember an event, however, were merely to represent it and to have observed it, then it would be absurd to pretend to *explain* the fact that someone gave a description which fitted something he had seen, by asserting that he must be remembering it.

To clinch this line of argument, we bring forward one of many similar cases from real life. A person has an apparent recollection of something from early childhood, and wonders whether he really remembers it. His parents may tell him that what he describes did happen, and that he witnessed it, but the discussion of whether he remembers it still goes on. They wonder whether his witnessing of the event has any connection with his now giving the story or whether his discription can be completely explained by what he heard later. Whether he has been told about it in the meanwhile, how young he was at the time, and whether he has seen things very similar at many other times are all relevant to deciding whether he actually remembers the event. These facts are the same as those which are used to decide whether or not he would have given the story if he had *not* witnessed the event in his childhood. To decide that he would not have done so is to decide that his past witnessing is causally necessary for his present account. (We shall see that a cause need not be a necessary condition. Naturally, in such cases it is difficult to verify that someone does remember what he recounts.)

Yet another supplementary argument can be developed from the following considerations. Benjamin (*op. cit.*, p. 324) claims that there are no strict rules to decide whether a certain amount of correct description of a witnessed event is enough. Harrod (*op. cit.*, pp. 54, 56) says that there are no strict rules to decide between imagination, dreams, and so forth, and genuine memory. Neither of them saw quite how loose the rules are, if there are no criteria for memory other than those recognized in their analyses.

The person who recounts an event from early childhood may be perfectly accurate in giving details of the event. Yet, as we have seen, he may well not be remembering it, but only remembering that certain things happened to him then. Suppose that someone sees a scene with just one very unusual feature. Later on he is asked to describe what he saw at that time. All he gets right is that one unusual feature. Here we have good reason to say that he remembers the one feature, even when all the rest of his description is mistaken. The feature in the scene was unusual, so it was not likely that he would have put it in if he had not seen it. It is useful to see that a similar point also holds with respect to the first type of *remembering that.* If someone had been asked to remember a telephone number (to adapt a case from Benjamin's article) and had been correct about only one digit of the number, there would be no reason to think that he remembered even that one digit. Suppose, though, that he is able to say that the last number is 7, and that is all he can say. We might then be prepared to allow that he does remember what he says, since it is comparatively unlikely that he should have been correct by chance.

It seems that our "rules" for how much a person must get right in order to be said to remember are completely confused, unless we use more criteria than are used by those philosophers we are criticizing. Even clause (a) of the causal criterion makes a considerable degree of order out of this chaos. For instance, Harrod's difficulties about distinguishing imagination and dreams from genuine memory are resolved. Sometimes what we take to be imagination may be memory, but usually it is not. In those cases where we take ourselves to imagine something, and our "imagining" it is caused (in the way which we shall explain) by some previous experience or observation of it, then we are remembering whether or not we take ourselves to be. Unless Malcolm in his book *Dreaming* is right, dreams also may sometimes be memories. What we show is that one cannot expect to be able always to distinguish between these things for oneself.

VI. NECESSARY AND OPERATIVE CONDITIONS

When philosophers speak of a necessary condition, they usually mean a generally necessary condition. Thus when they say that C is necessary for E, they are talking of types of events, not of events. To say that C is generally necessary for E is to say that there is no way of bringing about an event of type E, without an event of type C. For the most part, however, people speak of particular events as necessary for other particular events. It is not generally necessary for the production of flame that someone strike a match. Nevertheless, on a particular occasion, someone's striking a match can be necessary for the lighting of his cigarette at that time if there was then no other way of lighting the cigarette.

The above distinction may be made even if a particular event C is necessary for E, only when some description C' would hold of C, and some description E' would hold of E, such that "If E' then C'" is a universal law. So, when we consider necessary causal conditions in examining occurrences of remembering, we are interested in the idea of occurrent conditions which are causally necessary for others. When we discuss the question whether, in remembering, the past experience must be causally necessary for the subsequent representation of it, we shall not be interested in the question whether the past experience is of a *type* which is *generally necessary* for a type of events of which the subsequent representation is an instance.

It might be thought that since we defend the causal criterion we are committed to saying that the past experience is causally *necessary* for the subsequent representation, since the past experience is clearly never *sufficient* for it. There are, however, causal conditions which are neither necessary nor sufficient.

For example, if a person is about to recount something and someone butts in and tells him about it anyway, then his having observed it himself is not necessary for his recounting it at that time. Yet that does not mean that he does not remember the past event, when he goes on to tell someone about it after being interrupted. Only if he had not recounted what he does, had he not experienced what he did, would his past experience be causally necessary for his present account. Had he not experienced what he did, he still would have recounted the same story, since he would have accepted his trustworthy friend's story. It seems scarcely believable, though, that he should not be remembering the event after his friend has butted in, and be remembering only what his friend told him.

There is another type of case in which someone could be said to remember something, though his having observed it is not causally *necessary* for his now recounting it. Suppose that he happened to glance around and notice a monkey turning a somersault. Someone else was watching then and would have told him that the monkey had turned a somersault, had the person not seen it doing so. Supposing that all the man can say later is that the monkey turned a somersault (second type of remembering that), it would then be false to say that his having seen it for himself was a causally *necessary* condition of his being able to say later that the monkey had turned a somersault. (Of course, his having experienced what he recounts is always a *logically* necessary condition of his later remembering it.)

In both of the types of cases described it is improbable that the person should have recounted what he did at exactly the same time, had he not seen for himself what he later recounted. It may be thought that at some level of accuracy a time discrepancy would be discoverable. Whether true or not, however, this is scarcely relevant. Within those same limits of accuracy which we use to decide at what moment particular events of the type under discussion have occurred, we may be able to say that the person would have recounted what he did at the same time, but from other causes.

In order to speak of a causal condition which may be necessary or sufficient but need be neither, we introduce the term "operative." A condition may be operative in producing another, even though the result would have been obtained at the same time by another method, had the operative condition not been present.

In order to discuss fully the need for this term, we would have to consider cases in which it seems that there may be two conditions, fulfilling exactly the same causal role, present simultaneously. Certainly neither could be described as necessary. Yet it can be very embarrassing to have to say that both, *or* either, are operative. A discussion of this tantalizing issue must be ruled out of court here.

Even the inclusion of clause (a)—*to remember an event, a person must not only represent and have experienced it, but also his experience of it must have been operative in producing a state or successive states in him finally operative in producing his representation*—in the list of criteria for remembering allows the admission of unwanted cases. It will be found that clause (b), which we shall introduce, excludes these.

To tell another story about the accident-prone Kent, let us say that he has told his friend Gray what he saw of an accident in which he was involved. Kent has a second accident in which he gets a blow on the head which destroys all memory of a period in his past, including the time at which the first accident occurred. When Gray finds that Kent can no longer remember the first accident, he tells him those details which Kent had told Gray in the period between the first and second accidents. After a little while Kent forgets that anyone has told him about the first accident, but still remembers what he was told by Gray. It is clear that he does not remember the accident itself. Think how Gray would feel about Kent's claims to remember the first accident again. He would know that Kent had been quite unable to say anything about it after the second accident, and that when he, Gray, had told him the story, there had been no signs of recognition on Kent's part. Kent had quite a period of his past blotted out, and he can tell nothing about that period except what Gray told him. So we have no reason to say that Gray's retelling Kent about the first accident actually revived Kent's memory. Kent witnessed the first accident, can now recount what he saw of it, but does not remember it. But if criteria 1 and 2 and clause (a) were sufficient, we should have to say that he did remember the first accident. In the case as just described, the causal chain between Kent's witnessing of the first accident and his correct retelling of it at the later date (after Gray had told him) is this: Kent's observation of the first accident resulted in his telling Gray the account of the accident as he witnessed it. Gray's hearing of Kent's story resulted in Gray's telling Kent about the first accident as Kent witnessed it. Kent's hearing Gray tell him about the accident resulted in Kent's retelling, at a later date, the account of the first accident.

This is to say that in the case as described, Kent's observation of the first accident was operative in producing his subsequent account of the event. Despite this, Kent does not remember, and therefore some additional clause must be introduced. The condition that the past observation be an operative condition for the present retelling is correct so far as it goes, but it is too weak. Strengthening the criterion so that the past observation must be a causally sufficient condition for the present retelling would be far too strong. Innumerable other factors and events are always necessary for representation of a past observation to occur. If all there was to say about causal conditions was that they were either simply operative or sufficient, either in general or in particular circumstances, this difficulty would be insuperable.

The most simple rule which would dismiss the troublesome case just described, and which fits the facts in our world, is that the causal chain between the past observation and present representation of it should continue without interruption within the body of the person concerned. In the troublesome case the causal chain goes from Kent to Gray and back to Kent again. This criterion rules out conceivable cases of memory, however. We do not want to say that we can conceive only of humans remembering. Surely it is imaginable that we might find creatures who could represent the past as efficiently as we do, in the various ways we do, but who differ from us in the following respects. They carry a metal box around with them and, if they are separated from it, then they can remember nothing, no matter how recent. They are not born with the boxes. The boxes are made in a factory, and given them at birth, after which the creatures gradually develop the ability to remember. They do not ask the box questions about the past, but when they are connected with the box they remember as we do. This case shows that the suggested criterion is not strictly necessary.

We can also show that the proposed additional criterion does not rule out other spurious cases of memory, and in that sense is not strong enough. Suppose that a student could not remember$_2$ what he read in a chemistry book for an examination, and inscribed what he read into his palm with a hot needle. In the examination he writes down the correct formulae by feeling the marks on his palm. Here the causal chain does not extend beyond the body of the person and yet he does not remember$_2$ what he read in the chemistry book, but only what he inscribed on his palm. (We owe the idea for this case to Professor J. L. Mackie.) The alterations we do propose to the causal criterion deal correctly with these cases.

Although the rule we just tried, and the next we shall try, are both straw men, it is important to see that they do not work, and to understand why. Let us try out the addition to the causal criterion:

> "A subsequent *strict or complete prompting* concerning the thing remembered is not causally necessary for his representation of the thing at the later date."

"Complete prompting" is a technical term, and is explained in the following way.

A prompting is *complete* if the person cannot correctly give back any more in his representation of what happened in his past than was supplied by the prompting.

Let us speak of someone being *prompted* whenever he observes what he has seen before, or observes a representation of it, whether or not a person intentionally or unintentionally prompts him. A person is prompted if he just happens to read an account of something he once did, or if he happens to read a fictional story which by chance matches something in his own past, or if he sees some event very like another which he previously saw, or sees an object in much the same state as he saw it previously.

There is one important difference between being prompted verbally and being prompted by an observation of something resembling what one has observed before. If someone sees something which he has seen before, then even if he can give *no* detail of what he saw before which he did not gain from being prompted, his prompted representation *contains* the idea that he did see something like this before. No matter how much detail is supplied by observation of a replica of what has been previously observed, there is always, in such cases, the *additional* "detail" of recognition. Only if he is being prompted verbally can he, in a *very* strict sense, be "fully" prompted. When he is thus verbally prompted, so that he is even told that he has experienced before what he is being informed about, we shall say that he is *strictly prompted.*

It is important to realize that he need not, when verbally prompted, represent what he does as having happened in the past. If he is not told that it was in the past, and does not say so when he recounts what he has been prompted to say, then he has been fully but not strictly prompted. But if he is told that it happened some time in the past, and he can add nothing to that, then he has been strictly prompted.

The connection between strict prompting and linguistic prompting is this: only linguistic prompting can be strict prompting, but it can be complete without being strict. The proposed rule copes with the second accident case, since Kent could tell the story of the first accident only after Gray had told him *everything* about it again, and Kent could tell nothing of the accident which he was not told by Gray. The rule also allows that the people with the boxes do remember. Furthermore, it accords with the common-sense thought that someone who remembers something does not have to see it again, or something like it, or hear a full description of it, in order to tell about it.

VII. A DISTINCTION BETWEEN OPERATIVE IN THE CIRCUMSTANCES, AND OPERATIVE FOR THE CIRCUMSTANCES

Despite the apparent success of this modification described above, it is far too stringent as a general rule. What we need is a criterion which makes sense of the possibility that after a person is fully or even strictly prompted, he may or may not be remembering. If we can find such a criterion, then it will in fact allow us to say that a person who must be strictly prompted may or may not be remembering when he recounts what he has been prompted about. The cases which we shall describe to show this will, in fact, lead us to the correct rule. Very often a person must be prompted before he can remember, and this fact seems to be ruled out by the suggested extra criterion, although many cases of prompting would be accommodated since it is required only that *complete or strict* prompting should not be causally necessary. Nevertheless, the rule will not do for the following kind of reasons. Suppose that a person tries to remember what type of pancake he had at a place where fifty different sorts of pancakes are served, and cannot. After he is told, or it is suggested, that he had a banana pancake, he says, "Ah, yes, now I remember." But he can give no detail at all. He could be deceiving us and he could be deceiving himself, but such possibilities serve to emphasize that he might be correct, and deceiving nobody. He might be remembering that$_2$ he had a banana pancake, and not merely remembering that$_1$ he had a banana pancake, although he has been strictly prompted. Take another case. Someone cannot remember what he did the previous afternoon. He is told quite a long story about driving through certain towns, eating such-and-such foods at a picnic, and so on. Then he says, "Now it all comes back." He then recounts the whole story. Suppose that he had already been told the story in such a full way that there was nothing which he could reasonably add. It is more convincing if he can add important details, but the mere fact that he can repeat such a long story would normally show that he does genuinely remember many of the things he did on that afternoon. It would be highly unlikely that he could have retold such a story detail for detail, if he had not actually been on the picnic himself. (Of course, if he is a person with highly accurate short-term retention, then his ability to give the story word for word will not allay our suspicions that he remembers nothing but the story we have just given him.)

Even when a person has had to be strictly prompted it may be very unlikely that he would have followed this prompting with his own duplicate account if it had not been for his observation of whatever is in question. In such a case we normally have strong evidence to suppose that he remembers the event and not the prompting. Even in such a simple case as the one where someone "remembers" only $that_2$ he had banana pancakes after he has had to be told that he had banana pancakes, we could find evidence for or against genuine remembering. If someone is given a list of fifteen pancakes including the one he is trying to remember, and picks the right one, we accept this as evidence for memory rather than for chance.

There *will* be cases of *strict* prompting where we will have no idea whether or not that prompting would have been followed by the correct account without observation of what the account is about. In such cases we will not be able to decide whether the person is remembering, but this is no objection to our theory, but the very reverse. One of the faults of analyses of memory which have recently been given is that they leave insufficient room for the real doubts which can arise concerning whether or not someone is remembering something. It is a common fact that there *can* be doubt whether a person who gives a true account of his own past is remembering. For instance, as pointed out earlier, we may fail to have enough evidence to decide whether someone who gives a true account of an incident from his childhood is remembering it or is merely repeating what he has been told by his parents.

We are now using clause (b) of criterion 3, which is:

> In those cases where prompting is operative for the representation, his past experience of the thing represented is operative in producing the state (or the successive set of states) in him which is finally operative in producing the representation, *in* the circumstances in which he is prompted.

The past experience must not be operative only *for* the man's being prompted.

This may appear forbidding. What we must make clear is the difference between:

> *E* (experience) being operative *for* the circumstance *P* (prompting) which helps to bring about *R* (representation)

and

> *E* (experience) being operative *in* the circumstance *P* (prompting) which helps to bring about *R* (representation).

If *A* is operative for *B* and *B* is operative for *C*, then we shall say that *A* is operative *for* the circumstance *B* which is operative for *C*. If *A* is operative for *B* and *B* is operative for *C*, however, and as well as this *A* is operative for a factor *B′* other than *B* which acts with *B* to bring about *C*, then we shall say that *A* is operative for *C in* (as well as *for*) the circumstance *B*, which is operative for *C*. Clearly, *A* may be both operative for the circumstances *B* which help to bring about *C*, and operative in those circumstances.

Clause (b) deals with the troublesome version of the accident case in the following way. Kent was involved in the original accident and as a result told Gray about it. Because he had been told about it, Gray related the story back to Kent, after Kent had lost his memory in the second accident. Thus, Kent's original observation of the accident was a factor in bringing about his final account of it. His observation of the accident, however, is not operative in producing (through a successive set of states) his account of the accident *in* the circumstance of his being prompted. For that reason we do not say that he remembers the accident. We might put the matter another way. We could say that his past observation was not operative in bringing about his representation of the accident, *upon* prompting. Again, we might put it thus: his past experience is not operative in bringing about his representation of the accident, *given that* he is prompted.

VIII. THE IDEA OF A MEMORY TRACE

Even when someone represents something from his own past and his past experience is part of the cause of his representing it *in* the circumstance of being prompted, still he may not be remembering anything. Suppose that someone sees something and as a result becomes suggestible to all sorts of "promptings" whether true or false, concerning what he has done and observed. For brevity we shall say that this past experience has produced in him a "suggestible" state. He is strictly prompted about something he really did see, and due to the suggestible state produced in him by that past observation he accepts the prompting. According to all the criteria which we have so far set down, he is remembering what he has seen. Yet surely in the case just described it does not follow that he is remembering anything beyond the story with which he was prompted.

Once this point is accepted, it might be thought obvious that it follows from the description of the case that he is *not* remembering anything beyond the story with which he was prompted. It might be thought that if someone has some memory of something, then he must be able to select correct from incorrect promptings. If there exists in him a suggestible state, then he accepts a true or false prompting equally readily. Presented with both he may not be able to choose, and he will be as liable to accept the false one as he is to accept the true one. If he is in this condition then, although he may be correctly representing something because he has seen it, it does not follow that he is remembering it. We shall see, however, that it does not follow that he is *not* remembering it.

This latest difficulty has been raised by means of a case in which the person's representation involves his holding a belief about the past. In fact, a precisely analogous problem arises in those cases in which his representing something does not involve belief, as in the case of the painter in Section III. It is logically possible that someone should see something and as a result gain the power of highly accurate short-term retention. Then he might relate a story with which he had been prompted, due to this power produced in him by his own past observation of the matter which he relates. Thus he would satisfy all the criteria which we have enunciated so far. Yet it does not follow that he remembers anything beyond the story with which he has been prompted. Evidence for the supposition that he was remembering only the story and not the past event would be supplied if it were found that the truth of the promptings put to him about his own past had nothing to do with whether he related these stories upon being prompted with them. We must be careful to say that it does not follow in such a case that he is remembering; we must not say that it follows that he is *not* remembering. (The solution which we will give to the problem raised by the "suggestible" state will also solve this problem.)

It is easy to see why it would be a mistake to say that a person *could* not be remembering, if the past experience recounted had produced a suggestible state in him. Sometimes he might remember the matter perfectly well if left alone. His past experience might have left him with a fair memory of what he experienced, but also it might have produced in him a suggestible state due to which he accepts any credible prompting. Thus it is possible that when he needs full prompting, it may revive his memory, even though, due to the suggestible state in him, he would have accepted a false prompting with equal readiness.

This may appear to make our problem insoluble. If we do not rule out his being in a suggestible state when we define remembering, we seem bound to admit inadmissible cases. Yet if we *do* rule that he must not be in a suggestible state, we rule out admissible cases.

The following rule might be thought to do the trick:

> If the prompting elicits his representation from a "memory state" (rather than a "suggestible state") then, if a false prompting at that time would have elicited a false representation of the event, the state to which this false prompting would be due must be something other than that state which led him to give a true representation upon being correctly prompted.

A difficulty arises with this common-sense method of coping with the difficulty, however. Call the memory state, taken together with the suggestible state, state M'. We can then say that M' is the basis of someone's representing his past upon being prompted about it, although the basis of his giving a false representation upon being falsely prompted would have been the very same state M'. Thus the proposed rule fails in its purpose, since the person may be remembering when his representation of the past, upon being prompted, is due to M'. According to the proposed rule he would *not* be remembering it. It is pointless to attempt to defend the rule thus:

> "Don't be silly! If the memory part of the M' state is responsible for his representation of the past, and the suggestible state is not operative for his representation, then he remembers, otherwise not."

The defense is pointless, since the rule simply fails to give an effective statement of the difference between the memory part of M' and the suggestible part of M'.

It is natural to attempt a counterfactual account of the memory state, thus:

> The memory state for X is that state in the person, produced by his past experience of X, which leads him to accept or select a true prompting, and which is such that if no other state existed which would lead him to accept true or false promptings about X, then he would accept or select only true promptings about X.

This rule does at least avoid the difficulty raised in terms of the state M'. M' is not the memory state, since it is not true that if no other state relevant to the acceptance of prompting existed in him, he would select true from false promptings. This is because M' is a combination of the memory and the suggestible states. The rule suffers, however, from a far more radical defect than the previous one, which was merely inadequate. Who is to say what the man would do if no other state relevant to his accepting promptings, true or false, existed in him? It is not improbable that he would be a zombie.

The problem can be solved by recourse to the idea of a memory trace. This idea is an indispensable part of our idea of memory. Once we accept the causal model for memory we must also accept the existence of some sort of trace, or structural analogue of what was experienced. Even if someone could overcome the many difficulties of various kinds surrounding the idea of action at a distance, it could not be true to say that someone was remembering an event if his past experience of that event caused him, over a temporal gap, to recount it. There is an inevitable recourse to metaphors about the storage of our past experience involved in our idioms and thought about memory. Furthermore, if our past experience could act directly on us now, there would no longer be any reason to suppose that we could remember only what we had experienced ourselves. So long as we hold some sort of "storage" or "trace" account of memory, it follows that we can remember only what we have experienced, for it is in our experience of events that they "enter" the storehouse. If we did not hold such an account, why should we not suppose that events which occurred years before we were born could cause us to recount their occurrence?

Some philosophers are inclined to think that to hold the notion of a causal connection to be part of the idea of memory is to hold the notion of actual causal connection to be part of the idea of memory. (See the section to follow on Professor Norman Malcolm.) Similarly, no doubt, they would think that our latest move commits us still more deeply to the idea that the common notion of memory contains the ideas which are found only in specialized areas of knowledge such as neurophysiology. But this is not so. People can understand the general requirements for a memory trace though they have little or no idea of the specific nature of such a trace. They may rely on as simple an explanation as that of a print of a coin in wax, or they may, like Wittgenstein, use examples such as the structural analogy between music and the groove in a gramophone record. For any increase in pitch of the music, there is an increase in the number of wriggles per unit length in the groove. For any increase in loudness of the music, there is an increase in deflection of the groove, and so on. Only a "perfect" structural analogue would have a system of differences which mirrored, one to one, the differences in the original. Perhaps there is no sense to the idea of mirroring all the features of a thing, for there may be no sense in the notion of all the features of anything. But it is enough for our purposes that we can make sense of the idea of an analogue which contains at least as many features as there are details which a given person can relate about something he has experienced.

We can now deal directly with the problem of distinguishing between the suggestible and the memory state. It must be clear on the one hand that someone *may* not be remembering, if a past experience of an event has put him into a suggestible state in which he is prone to accept promptings whether true or false, for this suggestible state may not be a structural analogue of what was observed of the past event. At the same time, our past experience of the event may have produced a memory trace in us as well as a suggestible state. (This has the consequence that if we are put into both states and we need to be fully prompted, it is impossible to verify that we are remembering upon being prompted, without appealing to the sort of detailed physiological knowledge which is at the moment possessed by no one. It also might seem possible that the memory trace should itself be a suggestible state. This suggestion is full of difficulties, however, and we do not intend to pursue it.) Thus clause (c) of criterion 3 completes our analysis of remembering:

> The state or set of states produced by the past experience must constitute a structural analogue of the thing remembered, to the extent to which he can accurately represent the thing.

IX. MALCOLM ON REMEMBERING

Since the substance of this article was written, Professor Norman Malcolm has published a valuable contribution to the subject of memory in three chapters of his book, *Knowledge and Certainty* (Englewood Cliffs, 1963). Our account differs from his in various ways.

Malcolm claims that a person *B* remembers that *p* if and only if *B* knows that *p*, because he knew that *p*. This definition has three elements: the present knowledge that *p*, the previous knowledge that *p*, and the relationship between the present and previous knowledge expressed by saying that *B* knows that *p* *because* he previously knew that *p*. The elements are separately necessary and jointly sufficient conditions of factual memory. We shall consider these three conditions in turn.

Previous Knowledge

Suppose that someone sees something, but thinks that he is suffering a hallucination. The person sees something, but since he does not accept that he is seeing it, he fails to gain the knowledge that it is there in front of him. Some time later he learns that there had been nothing at all the matter with him at the time, and that he had really seen what he thought he had hallucinated. He is able to give a detailed and faithful account of what he saw. It is incorrect to insist that he cannot be remembering what he saw simply because at the time he had not believed his eyes. The question whether he remembers having distrusted his senses is quite distinct from the question whether he remembers seeing what he did. Naturally this case is different from the one described by Malcolm as a possible difficulty for his analysis (p. 223) [p. 287, this volume. Eds.]. In the case we suggest, the person is given no new information about what he saw. When he discovers that he had not been hallucinated previously, surely he will say, "Well, of course, in that case, I remember *seeing*. . . ." This cannot be considered as one of Malcolm's "elliptical" uses of "remembers."

Malcolm thinks that someone can know that he has a particular sensation only if he has a language in which to express this fact. It would take us too far afield to discuss this, but in conjunction with his requirement of previous knowledge for remembering, it leads Malcolm, in the following passage, to accept as an "interesting consequence" what we consider to be a *reductio ad absurdum.*

> I do not believe that there is any sense in which a dog or infant can be said to know that it has some sensation. I accept the consequence that a dog cannot be said to remember that he had a painful ear, and also the more interesting consequence that a human being cannot be said to remember that he had one, if he had it at a time before he knew enough language to be able to tell anyone that he had it. This point is connected with what Wittgenstein says about William James's Ballard (*Philospohical Investigations,* sec. 342) [p. 300n, this volume. Eds.].

We wonder what Malcolm would say about an adult deaf-mute.

Present Knowledge

We have argued that present belief is not a necessary condition for remembering (Section III). It is clear that those arguments apply also to Malcolm's claim that present knowledge is a necessary condition.

The "Because" Relationship

Malcolm presents arguments against a causal interpretation of the "because" in "He now knows that *p* 'because' he previously knew that *p*." If these arguments are correct, then any causal analysis of remembering is mistaken.

Malcolm professes not to understand what would be meant by causal dependence in connection with remembering. He says:

> What *could* fill the gap? I have mentioned three candidates: a persisting physiological state or process; continuous thinking about what is remembered; continuous unconscious thinking about what is remembered. We see that for different reasons none of these candidates can be included in

> the truth conditions for statements of the form "A remembers that p." I believe we do not have the conception of anything else that might fill the gap. In a sense, therefore, we do not know what it means to speak of a *gap* here [p. 238] [p. 299, this volume. Eds.].

It seems that Malcolm has put forward the following invalid argument. "*P*" does not entail "*Q*." "*P*" does not entail "*R*." "*P*" does not entail "*S*." Therefore "*P*" does not entail "*Q* or *R* or *S*."

Whether or not Malcolm is right and his three alternatives are in fact the only conceivable ones, he has given no valid argument to show that "*B* remembers that *p*" does not entail the existence of some continuous causal process.

Our own view is that the relations between "Some causal process exists" and "This particular process exists" is not the same as the relation between a disjunction of statements that particular processes exist and any one of those statements. He feels that it is a mere piece of imagery to require that *some* (unknown) continuous causal connection should exist. He says, "This feeling of the mysteriousness of memory, unless we assume a persisting state or process between the previous and the present knowledge, provides one *metaphysical* aspect of the topic of memory" (pp. 237–238) [pp. 299, this volume. Eds.]. This is very strange. The ordinary idea of a slot machine logically involves the idea of a device in which some mechanism or other is set in operation by the coin, which in some way delivers the appropriate goods. Is this idea a "mere piece of imagery"? Although most ordinary people do not know how a slot machine works, they would not be prepared to call something a slot machine if it were opened up and found to have no works. To parody Malcolm: "This feeling of the mysteriousness of a coin-in-the-slot machine, unless we assume a persisting state or process between the insertion of a coin and the appearance of cigarettes, provides, one *metaphysical* aspect of the topic of coin-in-the-slot machines."

There is evidence that Malcolm thinks that a singular causal statement, "*X* causes *Y*" must entail a statement of the form "In like circumstances, whenever *X*, then *Y*" (pp. 232, 236 [pp. 294, this volume. Eds.]; cf. Section VI of this article). This makes him think that a causal account of memory is impossible. (As a matter of fact, he himself accepts as "genuinely causal" [p. 237] [p. 298, this volume. Eds.] a case in which it is no easier to formulate a law than in the cases which he dismisses. This slip of his suggests that the notion of *cause* which he actually uses is more liberal than the one he states.) He nowhere argues that there *is* no law relating past knowledge and present knowledge, in "like" circumstances, in cases of remembering. (Given the unspecified phrase "in like circumstances," it is surely in no way obvious that there is no law relating his knowing a thing of a certain sort at one time with his knowing that thing at a later, *in like circumstances.*) Nor does he canvass any fresh arguments to resolve the well-known dispute whether causal statements can *ever* be analyzed in terms of regularities. Malcolm's account, "*B* now knows that *p, because* he knew that *p*," is:

> "A person *B* remembers that *p* from a time, *t,* if and only if *B* knows that *p,* and *B* knew that *p* at *t,* and if *B* had not known at *t* that *p* he would not know that *p*."

This account is at once too strong and too weak. It is too strong for reasons given in Section VI (pp. 178–179). A person who remembers something might have another independent source of information. This point has recently been made by Stanley Munsat ("A Note on Factual Memory," *Philosophical Studies,* XVI [1965], 33). The account is too weak for reasons similar to those given in Section VI (pp. 180–181). For consider a case in which a person knows that *p* at time *t,* writes it in his diary, forgets it completely, and relearns that *p* from what he wrote in his diary. If he had no other source of information, then he would not now know that *p,* if he had not known that *p* at time *t.* Yet it does not follow that he remembers that *p* from time *t.* Often he will only remember that *p* from the time at which he subsequently reads his diary.

X. *CONCLUSION*

In conclusion we must guard against a certain misconstruction of our analysis of memory. It is this:

> "Take any case in which *A* observes an event *E, P* is a prompting, and *R* is *A*'s representation of *E; P* is part of the cause of *R.* In such a case, when *A* gives *R* he is not only remembering *E* but, according to the causal analysis of remembering given, he must be said to be remembering *P* as well as *E* since any representation of *E* is *ipso facto* a representation of any representation of *E.* Thus in remembering an event a person willy-nilly remembers any prompting which is part of the cause of his now giving the representation of his observation of the past event. But this is absurd and so the analysis is in some way incorrect."

Such an objection is based on a misunderstanding. Consider the case of a bird watcher who saw a yellow-tufted titmouse. He had never seen one before and so he described it in his diary. Suppose that years later his reading of his diary is part of the cause of a subsequent description he gives of what he originally saw. Such a supposition does not in the least imply that his reading of the diary is part of the cause of his representation of reading the diary, for the simple reason that he does *not* represent his reading the diary. There is a difference between his remembering the occasion of first seeing a yellow-tufted titmouse and his remembering reading what he put in his diary. Someone may remember with great clarity the occasion of seeing the bird, and yet not remember reading what he put in his diary. Or he may remember with great precision reading what he put in his diary, and yet not remember seeing the bird.

Summary

As well as the usual distinctions made between remembering how to do something, remembering that something occurred, and remembering an occurrence or object, there is a distinction to be drawn between two different uses of "remembers that." Despite these various distinctions, the uses of "remembers" resemble each other in their requirements of past perception, of correctness about what was perceived or learned, and of a causal connection between past perception and a subsequent representation of what was perceived or gained by perception. The exception is that in remembering how to do something, the requirement in the present may be that what was learned is done again, rather than represented. A careful examination of all that is required of the causal connection brings to the surface the complex and partly theoretical nature of our commonplace notion of remembering.

The analysis of remembering which we have given may be used to answer some skeptical questions about memory, and it has importance for other problems about knowledge, but an investigation of these implications is altogether another enterprise.

IV

OUR KNOWLEDGE OF OUR PSYCHOLOGICAL STATES

Alfred J. Ayer

Basic Propositions

Philosophers who concern themselves with the theory of knowledge are apt to be haunted by an ideal of certainty. Seeking a refuge from Descartes' malicious demon, they look for a proposition, or class of propositions, of whose truth they can be absolutely sure. They think that once they have found this basis they can go on to justify at least some of their beliefs, but that without it there can be no defense against scepticism. Unless something is certain, we are told nothing can be even probable.

The discussion of this problem is not usually confined to the case of empirical propositions. For what is required is certainty about matters of fact, in Hume's sense of the term; and while it is generally agreed that *a priori* propositions can be certain, it is also held that they do not afford us knowledge about matters of fact. But even the claim that *a priori* propositions are certain is not without its difficulties. For surely it is possible to doubt them. People do make mistakes in mathematics and in logic; they miscalculate, they draw invalid inferences, they construct abstract systems which turn out to be self-contradictory. And I suppose that someone who had discovered that he was addicted to such

A. J. Ayer, "Basic Propositions," in *Philosophical Analysis,* ed. Max Black (Englewood Cliffs, N.J.: Prentice-Hall, Inc., 1950). Reprinted by permission.

errors might come to doubt the validity of any *a priori* statement that he made. Admittedly, his only ground for supposing that a particular answer was wrong would be that it failed to tally with some other answer which he took to be right; nevertheless the assumption that he was justified in so taking it would be one that he could still go on to question. Recognizing that some answers must be right, he would remain eternally in doubt as to which they were. 'Perhaps', he would say to himself, 'the procedures that I am trying to carry out are not the correct procedures; or, even if they are correct, perhaps I am not applying them properly in this particular case.'

But all that this shows, it may be said, is that we must distinguish the propositions of mathematics and logic as such from empirical propositions about the behaviour of persons who do mathematics or logic. That someone is carrying out the right procedure, or that someone is carrying out a certain procedure rightly, is an empirical proposition which can indeed be doubted. But the result at which he arrives, the *a priori* proposition of logic or mathematics itself, is either certainly true or certainly false; it is certainly true, if it is true at all. But what is meant here by saying of such a proposition that it is certain? Simply that it is *a priori*. To say that the proposition is certainly true, or that it is necessary, or that it is true *a priori,* is, in this case, just to say the same thing in three different ways. But what then is the point of saying that *a priori* propositions are certain if it is to say no more than that *a priori* propositions are *a priori*? The answer is that people wish to pass from '*p* is certainly true', in this sense, to '*p* can be known for certain to be true'. They make the tacit assumption that the truth of an *a priori* proposition can be 'clearly and distinctly perceived'. But if their ground for saying that such a proposition can be known for certain is simply that it is certain in the sense of being *a priori,* then their use of the word 'certain' gains them nothing. They are still saying no more than that an *a priori* proposition is an *a priori* proposition. And if by saying that such propositions can be known for certain they mean that they sometimes are known for certain, then their conclusion does not follow from their premiss. For in any case in which such knowledge is claimed, there is room for the empirical doubt; perhaps this is not the correct procedure, or perhaps it has not been applied correctly in this instance. Thus, while there is a sense in which *a priori* propositions are unassailable, to explain which would be to explain what was meant by calling them *a priori,* there is also a sense in which they are not. They are not unassailable, inasmuch as it can always be asked of any 'clear and distinct perception', in Descartes' sense of the term, whether it really is clear and distinct. Of course, such a question easily becomes futile. If I doubt whether I have done a sum correctly, what can I do except look up the rules as set out in the textbooks, check my result with those of other people, go over the sum again? And then it remains possible that I have misread the textbooks, that other people are deceiving me, that if I went over the sum yet again I should get a different answer. Now clearly this process can go on for ever, and just for that reason there is no point to it. If nothing is going to satisfy me, then nothing is going to satisfy me. And if nothing counts as satisfying me, then it is necessarily true that I cannot be satisfied. And if it is necessarily true, it is nothing to worry about. The worrying may, in fact, continue, but at this point the state of doubt has become neurotic. It is never settled because it is not allowed to be.

For the most part, however, philosophers are not troubled in this way about *a priori* propositions. They are content to say that these propositions are certain, and they do not regard it as an objection to this way of speaking that people often reason incorrectly or that they get their calculations wrong. On the other hand, they are very often troubled about empirical propositions, just because they are not *a priori*. For, following the same line as before, they argue that since these propositions are not necessary, they are not certain; and that since they are not certain they cannot be known for certain to be true. But, reasoning in this way, they find themselves exposed to the taunts of the G. E. Moore school. 'Of course empirical propositions are not certain in the way that *a priori* propositions are. Of course they can be denied without self-contradiction. If this were not so, they would not be empirical propositions. But it does not follow from this that they cannot properly be said to be certain in any sense at all. It does not follow that they cannot be known for certain to be true. 'Do you mean to tell me', says Professor Moore, 'that you do not know that you are awake and that you are reading this? Do you mean to tell me that I do not know that I have a pen in my hand? How improper it would be, what a misuse of English, to say that it was not certain that I had a sheet of paper in front of me, but only highly probable. How absurd it would be to say: "Perhaps this is not a pen. I believe that it is but I do not know it".'

Now clearly Professor Moore and his friends are right. It is good English to use the words 'know' and 'certain' in the way that they encourage us to use them. If someone wants to know what day of the week it is and, when I tell him it is Monday, asks me whether this is certain, then an answer like 'Yes, quite certain; I have just seen it in the newspaper, and anyhow I remember that yesterday was a Sunday' is a correct answer. To answer, 'Well, I seem to remember that yesterday was a Sunday, and I believe that this is to-day's newspaper, and I seem to see "Monday" written on it; but I may be wrong about the newspaper, and anyhow both memory and perception are fallible. Therefore I cannot be certain that it is Monday but I think it very probable'— to give an answer of this sort would be tiresome, and not only tiresome but misleading. It would be misleading because, in the ordinary way, we say that something is not certain, but at best highly probable, only in cases where we have some special reason for doubting, some reason which applies particularly to the case in question. Thus, in the example that I have just given, I might be justified in saying that I did not know that it was Monday if my memory were frequently at fault in matters of this kind, or I had glanced at the newspaper only carelessly, or the newspaper could not be relied on to print the right date. But if my reason for saying that it is not certain is merely the general reason that all empirical beliefs are fallible, then it is not consonant with ordinary usage to say that it is only probable. It is correct to say that it is certain. It is correct for me to say that I know.

All the same, this does not take us very far. It is all very well for Moore to prove the existence of external objects by holding up his hands and saying that he knows that they exist;[1] the philosopher who sees this as a problem is unlikely to be satisfied. He will want to say that Moore does not really know that these physical objects exist, that he cannot know it. At the very least he will want to raise the question, 'How does he know it?' Now it may be argued that this is not a sensible question. But one is not going to stop people from asking it merely by giving them an English lesson, any more than one is going to make people feel comfortable about induction merely by arguing that it is correct for a schoolmaster to say that he knows the truth of Archimedes' law, that he would be misleading his pupils if he said that he did not know it to be true but only thought it probable. Even if this is so, it is beside the point.

But in that case what is the point? Why are people not satisfied with Moore's sort of answer? Presumably the reason is that they feel that it does not meet the question which they are trying to ask. After all, it is to be supposed that the philosopher who says that Moore does not really know, that he cannot really know, what he says he knows is as well acquainted with the English language as Moore. He is not making a philological blunder, nor is he casting doubts upon Moore's honesty. If he says that Moore does not know for certain the truth of such a proposition as 'this is a human hand', it is because he thinks that nobody can know for certain that such a proposition is true, that it is not the sort of proposition that can be so known. But this means that he has decided to use the word 'know' in an unconventional way. He is making it inapplicable to a set of propositions to which it does apply in ordinary usage. And this, we may assume, is not a mere piece of eccentricity on

1 *Proof of an External World* (British Academy Annual Philosophical Lecture, 1939).

his part. He has some reason for his procedure. Let us consider what it might be.

I can think of two reasons for taking such a course, both of which are good reasons in the sense that they call attention to valid points of logic. In the first place, it may be suspected that someone who claims to know, without giving any proof, that such and such is the case, is relying on an act of intuition; and then the rejection of the claim proceeds from the denial that any act of intuition can constitute knowledge. The logical point is that from the fact that someone is convinced that a proposition is true it never follows that it is true. That *A* believes *p* may be a good reason for accepting *p*, if *A* is a reliable person; but it is in no case a conclusive reason. It is never self-contradictory to say both that *A* believes *p* and that *p* is false. It is indeed self-contradictory to say that *A* knows *p* and that *p* is false, but the explanation of this is just that part of what is meant by saying that *A* knows that *p*, as opposed to merely believing it, is that *p* is true. If *p* turns out not to be true, then it follows that it was not known, though it does not follow that it was not believed. Now one way of bringing out this distinction is to say that knowledge guarantees the truth, or reality, of its object, whereas belief does not; and this can be allowed to pass so long as it is nothing more than a picturesque way of expressing the linguistic fact that it is self-contradictory to speak of knowing something which is not the case, but not self-contradictory to speak of believing what is not the case. But what such formulations are all too often taken to imply is that the property of guaranteeing the truth or reality of its object belongs to knowledge as a special kind of mental activity; from which it is concluded that the truth, or reality, of the supposed 'object of knowledge' can be inferred simply from the occurrence of the act of knowing, considered in itself. And this is a serious mistake. For knowledge, in the sense which is here alone in question, is always knowledge that something or other is so. In order that it should be knowledge, it is necessary that the symbols which express what is known should state something true; and whether this is so depends upon the existence or non-existence of the situation to which the symbols refer. It is not to be decided merely by examining the 'state of apprehension' of the knower. My own view is that it is extremely misleading to speak of 'acts of knowing' at all. But even if we allow that something is described by this expression, it can never follow from the occurrence of such an act, considered in itself, that anything is known.

Thus, if Moore's ground for saying 'I know that this is a human hand' were merely that he apprehended that it was so, it would not be conclusive; and it may be because some people have thought he was maintaining that it was conclusive that they have wished to reject his claim. But, in fact, one's reason for making an assertion like 'This is a human hand' is never just that one is convinced of it. It is rather that one is having certain visual or tactual experiences. And this brings us to the second of my reasons why people may be dissatisfied with the 'What I know, I know' technique. It is that in the case of propositions like 'This is a chair', 'This is a human hand', 'There is more than one picture in the room'—all of which I should say that I now knew—it is not absurd for someone to ask me 'How do you know?' And the answers he will get are 'Because I can see it', 'Because I can touch it', 'Because I have counted them', 'Because I remember seeing it', and so on. In short, a proposition like 'I know this is a chair' cannot be true unless some propositions of the form 'I am seeing . . .', 'I am touching . . .', 'I remember . . .' are true. On the other hand, a proposition of this type can be true in cases where the corresponding proposition at the 'I-know-this-is-a-chair' level is false. Next, let us give the name 'sense-datum statement' to a description of what is seen, touched, or otherwise perceived in a sense of words like 'see' and 'touch' which does not carry the implication that what is so perceived is a physical object. Then, no statement like 'This is a chair' can be true unless some sense-datum statement is true; but once again the converse does not hold. And this, I think, explains why some philosophers have wished to deny that any proposition which asserts the presence of a physical object can be known for certain to be true. The point that they are thereby making is that such a proposition does not follow from any one sense-datum statement; it is based upon the fact that somebody is having some sensory experience, but the description of the experience in question does not logically entail it.

This gives us the clue also to what is meant by those who say that propositions about physical objects can never be certain. They are not denying that there is a good and familiar sense of the word 'certain' in which it can apply to such propositions, nor that it is good usage to say that one knows them to be true. What they are maintaining is simply that they do not follow from any finite set of sense-datum statements. The suggestion is that however strong the evidence in their favour may be it is never altogether sufficient; it is always consistent with their being false. Now this, indeed, may be disputed.[2] It might be argued that we should in fact take a finite quantity of sensory evidence to be sufficient; and that if subsequent evidence proved unfavourable we should account for it in some other way than by saying that what we took to be a physical

2 Cp. C. Lewy, 'On the Relation of Some Empirical Propositions to Their Evidence', *Mind,* vol. liii (1944), 289, and 'Entailment and Empirical Propositions', *Mind,* vol. lv (1946), 74; also A. H. Basson, 'The Existence of Material Objects', *Mind,* vol. lv (1946), 308, and my own paper, 'Phenomenalism', pp. 135–137.

object never really was one; we might prefer to distrust our present experience, or to save the appearances by introducing some new physical hypothesis. The difficulty is that there is no established rule to meet such cases. A procedure has to be laid down; and this, I think, is what is being done by those who deny that any proposition about a physical object can be certain. They are expressing a resolve to treat all such propositions as hypotheses, which are liable to revision in the light of further experience.

Now we may or may not agree with this proposal. But even if we reject it in favour of allowing the existence of a physical object to be conclusively established by a finite number of sensory experiences, we shall still have to recognize that no description of any one such experience entails the descriptions of the others. So that, if the test which a proposition has to satisfy in order to be certain is that it should follow from the description of a particular experience, we shall still reach the conclusion that all propositions about physical objects are uncertain. But all that this then comes to is that a proposition about a physical object is something more than a description of some particular experience. To say that it is therefore uncertain is to imply that of all empirical statements only those that refer exclusively to some immediate, present, experience are to be regarded as certain. Now this, again, is not an account of ordinary usage. It is a philosophers' recommendation. The question which concerns us is why anyone should wish to make it.

The answer is that 'certainty' is reserved for statements of this kind because it is thought that they alone can not be challenged. If I make a statement of the form 'I perceive . . .' or 'I know . . .' or 'I remember . . .', the truth of my statement can be questioned. It may turn out that I was having an hallucination, or that what I claimed to know was false, or that my memory was betraying me. But suppose that I am more cautious. Suppose that I merely say 'It looks to me . . .', 'I have a feeling that . . .', 'I seem to remember. . . .' How can these statements be challenged? In what way could one set about refuting them? Of course, someone who says 'I feel a headache' or 'There is a red patch in the centre of my visual field' may be lying. But surely, it is argued, he must know whether he is lying or not. He can deceive others about what he sees or feels. But if his statement refers only to the content of his present experience, how can he possibly be mistaken? How can he even be in doubt as to whether it is true?

Let us look into this. Is it impossible that someone should wonder whether he was in pain? Certainly it would be a queer sort of doubt. Suppose that someone were to tell me 'You think you are in pain but you really aren't'. What should I understand him to be saying? Perhaps that nothing was wrong with me physically, that it was all my imagination, or, in other words, that the cause of my pain was psychological; and this might very well be true. But it would not follow that I was not feeling pain. To suggest to me that I do not feel it may be a way of making the pain stop; but that is a different matter. It does not alter the fact that when I feel the pain, I feel the pain. This is, indeed, an analytic truth.

But this, it may be objected, is not the point at issue. The question is 'What am I feeling?' Might I not think that it was pain when it was really something else? Might I not think that such and such a coloured patch was magenta when it was really scarlet? Might I not think that such and such a note was E sharp when it was really E natural? Surely one can misdescribe one's experience. And if one can misdescribe it, can one ever be certain that one is describing it correctly? Admittedly, I see what I see, feel what I feel, experience what I experience. That is a tautology. But, so it may be argued, it does not follow that I know what I am seeing, or that I know what I am feeling. For my knowing what I am seeing entails that some set of symbols, which I use to describe what I am seeing, does describe it correctly; and this may not be so.

But what is 'misdescribing' in this case? What is the test by which it is determined that the coloured patch which I have called 'magenta' is really scarlet? Is it a physical test? In that case I can very well be making a mistake, and a factual mistake. Is it what other people would say? Here again I can easily make a factual mistake. But suppose I intend merely to name what I am seeing. Can I be mistaken then? Plainly the answer is that I can not, if I am only naming. But if that is all that I am doing, then I am not saying anything at all. I can be neither wrong nor right. But directly I go beyond naming and try to describe something, then, it may be argued, I run the risk of being mistaken even about the character of my own immediate experience. For to describe anything is to relate it to something else, not necessarily to anything in the future, or to anything that other people experience, but at least to something that one has oneself experienced in the past. And the attributed relation may not, in fact, obtain.

Now this is a very common view, but I am persuaded that it is mistaken. No doubt, if I have learned to use a senseory predicate correctly in the first place, it will in fact be true that any object to which I properly apply it on any occasion other than the first will resemble some object to which I have properly applied it in the past. But it does not follow that in using the predicate I am making any reference to the past. Many philosophers have thought that it did follow, because they have assumed that an ostensive word was defined in terms of the resemblance of the objects which it denoted to some standard object. Thus, allowing, what is undoubtedly true, that I learned the use of the English word 'green' by being shown certain objects which resembled each other in respect of being green, it is suggested that what I now assert when I say, for example, that the blotting paper in front of me is green is that it resembles these objects in the way that they resembled one another. But this suggestion is false; and to see that it is false we have only to reflect that from the statement that this piece of blotting paper is green it cannot be deduced that anything else exists at all. No doubt, what justifies me in calling it green, as opposed, say, to blue, is the fact that it resembles one set of objects rather than another; but this does not mean that in calling it green I am saying that it resembles any other objects. There are two propositions here which we must be careful not to confuse. One is that if *a* and *b* are both green they resemble one another in colour more than either of them resembles in colour anything outside the class of green things; and the other is that if *a* is green there is at least one other thing *b* which it resembles in colour more than it resembles in colour anything outside the class of green things. The first of these two propositions is analytic, it exemplifies the grammar of colour classification; but the second is empirical. That there is such another thing *b* is at best a matter of fact which has to be established independently. It does not follow from the fact that *a* is green.

This shows, incidentally, how little is accomplished by talking about classes in preference to talking about predicates. For suppose that for '*a* is green' we substitute '*a* belongs to the class of green things'. Then how is the expression 'belongs to the class of green things' to be interpreted? If it is merely a way of saying 'is a green thing' there is no point in the substitution. If it is taken as equivalent to 'is one of the things that are green', it is a mistranslation, since from the fact that *a* is green it does not follow that there are any other green things. If it is taken as equivalent to 'resembles other things in being green', it is again a mistranslation for the same reason as before. There remains the possibility that the class is to be defined by enumeration. But then we have the strange consequence that all ascriptions of class membership become either analytic or self-contradictory: analytic, in our example, if *a,* in fact, is green, since '*a* is green' will then mean '*a* is either *a* or *b* or *c* or *d* . . .', where the alternatives comprise the list of green things; and self-contradictory if it is not, since '*a* is green' will then mean '*a* is either *b* or *c* or *d* . . .', where it is understood that *b, c, d* . . . are other than *a*. Another strange consequence will be that '*a* is green' does not formally contradict '*a* is not green'; for if, in fact, *a* is not green, then '*a* is not green' will mean '*a* is not either *b* or *c* or *d* . . .', and if in fact *a* is green, then '*a* is green' will mean '*a* is either *a* or *b* or *c* or *d* . . .'; and these two propositions, so far from being incompatible, are both necessarily true. The explanation of this is that when it is interpreted in this way the meaning of the word 'green' varies according to its denotation. So that the result of turning predicates into classes and treating these classes extensionally is that one cannot tell what a sentence means until one knows whether it is true. Now I agree that to know what a sentence means is to know what would make it true. But it would ordinarily be held, and I think with reason, that one could not tell whether it was in fact true unless one already knew what it meant. For otherwise what would it be that one was verifying?

However this may be, the fact remains that the ascription to one member of a class of the predicate by which the class is defined does not imply that the class has any other members. And from this it follows that if I use a sensory predicate to describe what I am now experiencing I need not be making any claim about a situation other than the one one before me. Accordingly, no appeal to such other situations can show that I am mistaken. They are not relevant, since my statement makes no reference to them. But then am I saying anything even about this situation? We seem here to have fallen into a dilemma. Either I just name the situation, in which case I am not making any statement about it, and no question of truth or falsehood, knowledge or ignorance, certainty or uncertainty, arises; or I describe it. And how can I describe it except by relating it to something else?

The answer is, I suggest, that I do describe it, not by relating it to anything else, but by indicating that a certain word applies to it in virtue of a meaning rule of the language. I may be in doubt as to its description in the sense that I may hesitate over what word to apply to it, and I may be mistaken about it in the sense that I may describe it incorrectly, the standard of correctness being furnished by my own verbal habits, or by the verbal habits of others who use the same language. Let me try to explain this further.

It would now be generally conceded that a descriptive language, as opposed to a merely formal language, is not sufficiently characterized by its formation and transformation rules. The formation rules prescribe what combinations of signs are to constitute proper sentences of the language; and the transformation rules prescribe what sentences are validly derivable from one another. But if we are to use and understand a language descriptively, we require also rules which correlate certain signs in the language with actual situations; and it is these that I am calling meaning rules. Thus it is a meaning rule of English that anyone who observes something green will be describing it correctly if he says that it is green; or that anyone who feels pain will be describing what he feels correctly if he says that he feels pain. These examples sound trivial, because the statement of these rules is not informative, except where it is a question of translation from one language into another.

The rules are learned ostensively. The verbal statement of them is normally superfluous. For that reason it may even be misleading to call them 'rules' at all. But, whatever they may be called, unless one knows how to employ them, one does not understand the language. Thus, I understand the use of a word if I know in what situations to apply it. For this it is essential that I should be able to recognize the situations when I come upon them; but in order to effect this recognition it is not necessary that I should consciously compare these situations with memories of their predecessors. Neither is it necessary, as some philosophers have mistakenly supposed, that I should have a previous image with which the situation is found to agree. For if I can recognize the image, then I can recognize the situation without the image; and if I cannot recognize the image, then it does not help me to identify the situation. In either case its presence is superfluous. Whether I recognize the situation or not is to be decided by my behaviour; and one of the criteria is my being disposed to use the appropriate words.

Thus, the sense in which statements like 'This is green', 'I feel a headache', 'I seem to remember . . .' can be said to be indubitable is that, when they are understood to refer only to some immediate experience, their truth or falsehood is conclusively determined by a meaning rule of the language in which they are expressed. To deny them in the situations to which they refer is to misapply the language. And it is in this sense also that one can know for certain that they are true. But it is to be remarked that this is rather a case of knowing how than of knowing that. If I have an expereince, say an experience of pain, it does not follow that I know what experience I am having. It is perfectly possible for me to have the experience without knowing anything at all. My knowing what experience it is is my being able to identify it as falling under a particular meaning rule. It is therefore not a matter of my knowing or ignoring some empirical fact but of my knowing or not knowing how to use my language. I have certain knowledge in the sense that the truth of what I say is not open to question, on the assumption that I am using my words correctly; but this is an assumption which remains open to doubt. And here the doubt is not like the ordinary empirical doubt, which turns upon the accuracy of some extrapolation, but like the logical doubt which we considered at the outset. It is to be settled by looking up the rules. But this again lets in the empirical doubt as to whether one has actually carried out the correct procedure. I am told that 'magenta' is the correct name for this colour, and I find this confirmed by the colour atlas. But perhaps my informant is deceiving me, or perhaps I misheard him, or perhaps this colour atlas is untrustworthy, or perhaps my eyes are playing me false. There are ways in which these suppositions can be tested, but the results of such tests can be questioned in their turn. So that here again the doubt may become neurotic and interminable. In this sense, therefore, nothing need be certain. Only, if nothing is allowed to be certain, the word 'certain' ceases to have any use.

It is sometimes made an objection to the choice of sensory predicates as basic that sense-experience is private. For it is argued that the fact that I have the sensations that I do is not of any great significance, since I cannot communicate them to anybody else. But the answer to this is that I can and do communicate them, inasmuch as my coming out with such and such a statement on such and such an occasion will count for another person as evidence in favour of the proposition that I am having such and such a sensation, and of any other proposition for which this proposition counts as evidence. His assumption is that I am using the language correctly; and this he can test by his own observations of my behaviour and of my environment. The meaning rules are impersonal in the sense that they do no more than prescribe what words are to be used in what situations. That some other person is in such and such a situation is an empirical hypothesis which I test by making observations, the proper description of which will in its turn depend upon a further meaning rule. The making of an observation is, of course, a private experience. But this is not to say that my description of it cannot be understood by anybody else.

It is, however, to be noted that while it is necessary that a descriptive language should contain meaning rules, it is not necessary that it should contain any sentences which express basic propositions, if a basic proposition is defined as one whose truth or falsehood is conclusively established, in a given situation, by a meaning rule of the language. It might be that the rules were such that every correct description of an empirical situation involved some reference beyond it; and in that case, while the use of the sentence which was dictated by the relevant meaning rule would be justified in the given situation, its truth would not be conclusively established. Suppose, for example, that our language contained no purely sensory predicates, so that the lowest level sentence that one could express in it was a sentence which ascribed some property to a physical object. Such a language could perfectly well be understood and consistently applied. Words like 'table' would be introduced, as indeed they normally are introduced, by meaning rules; and understanding these words would again be a matter of knowing in what situations to apply them. The difference would be that from the fact that it was correct to use a given sentence in a given situation it would not follow that what the sentence expressed was true. That the use of the sentence was prescribed in these circumstances by a meaning rule would establish that what the sentence stated was probable but not that it was certain.

Thus, if my reasoning is sound, it is at least misleading to say that unless something is certain nothing can be even probable. What is true is that no proposition can ever be discovered to be even probable unless someone has some experience. But to say that someone has some experience is not, in any ordinary sense, to say that anything is certain. Whether anything is certain or not, in the sense which is here in question, will depend upon the meaning rules of the language; whether they are such as guarantee the truth or falsehood of a given statement in the appropriate situation, or merely justify its use. In neither case, as we have seen, is doubt excluded; but at the point where such doubt becomes perpetual, it ceases to be of any theoretical importance.

Hans Reichenbach

Are Phenomenal Reports Absolutely Certain?

There is no doubt that all our knowledge begins with experience, says Kant. He goes on to say that we should not conclude that all our knowledge is derived from experience. He argues that, in addition to the experimental source, there exists a rational source of knowledge, which supplies us with synthetic a priori principles. All his philosophy can be regarded as a commentary on this basic proposition.

Modern empiricism has shown Kant's thesis to be fallacious. There is no synthetic a priori; what reason contributes to knowledge are analytic principles only. I will not elaborate on this counterthesis within this discussion group, within which the rejection of the synthetic a priori can be regarded as accepted. In particular, Professor Lewis has repeatedly made it clear that he shares this empiricist criticism of Kant's views, and has made many valuable contributions to the purification of phi-

Hans Reichenbach, "Are Phenomenal Reports Absolutely Certain?," *The Philosophical Review,* 61 (1952), 147–59. Reprinted by permission.

Paper read at the forty-eighth annual meeting of the Eastern Division of the American Philosophical Association at Bryn Mawr College, Bryn Mawr, Pennsylvania, December 29, 1951.

losophy from the remnants of a philosophic rationalism. It is true that certain contemporary philosophers have attempted to reintroduce a synthetic a priori, reviving arguments that some forty years ago were quite fashionable; but their attempts are too obviously fallacious, and I cannot but regard their attacks on empiricism as a *Putschversuch* which need not be taken seriously. I will therefore proceed on the assumption that our discussion is to be grounded on a common empiricist basis; and the names of my partners in this discussion encourage me to take this common presupposition for granted.

If all knowledge not only begins with experience, but is also validated through experience, there arises the problem of whether there is a certain experiential basis of the elaborate structure of knowledge, a substratum which is composed of the experiential data alone and which carries the total edifice that includes so many results of highest abstraction. Speaking in terms of sentences, we speak here of report propositions. It is well known, and has often been discussed, that the derivational processes, leading from report propositions to laws of nature and predictions of future occurrences, include inductive inferences and therefore can only lead to probable conclusions; certainty is excluded when induction is at work. There remains the question whether such uncertainty also creeps into the experiential basis itself, or whether the basis, at least, is exempt from doubt. Can report propositions be absolutely certain? That is the question I should like to examine as my contribution to the present discussion.

This is the point at which the paths of empiricists diverge. Professor Lewis thinks that there are absolutely certain report propositions; and this view is shared by some other outstanding empiricists, such as Bertrand Russell and C. D. Broad. However, I do not think that this conception is tenable. Within an historical inquiry, I would argue that it is but another remnant of rationalism, taken over even by those who are willing to renounce the synthetic a priori, but who cannot dispense with a synthetic a posteriori which is as apodictic as the corresponding a priori. But historical classification is no logical argument; my thesis requires an analysis on logical grounds, and this is the subject to which I now shall turn.

For this purpose, I should like first to make the thesis of my opponents as clear as possible to me. The absolutely certain report propositions, of which Lewis thinks, are of course not conceived as referring to physical objects. In this respect, Lewis' view differs fortunately from G. E. Moore's opinions, according to which the simple statements concerning our daily environment are absolutely certain. Lewis shows convincingly that this cannot be maintained because later observations can always invalidate such statements. He speaks here of *nonterminating* judgments; they include in their meanings an infinite number of implications for the future and can therefore never be completely verified. In contrast, Lewis calls report propositions of the kind considered *terminating* judgments; their meaning is completely given in the observation to which they refer. They therefore do not include any implications for the future and can be completely verified in the act of observation.

The language of these statements, Lewis insists, is not physical language. When I say, "There is a flight of stairs," later observation can disprove my statement; this would be the case, for instance, if I find out that I cannot walk up these stairs because they are merely a perspective drawing by a clever architect. However, there is another statement, says Lewis, which remains true even if this further consequence is observed. It seems difficult to formulate this statement. Some of us would give it the wording: "I see a flight of stairs"; others would say that there is a flight of stairs, "optically speaking," or "subjectively speaking"; others again would speak of a perceptual existence of the stairs. It seems we all know what we mean, and differ only as to the formulation.

The language of these statements Lewis calls *expressive* language. Using a more familiar name, I would prefer to call it *phenomenal* language. Its terms strangely duplicate those of physical language; but they do not have the same meanings. They do not, because they do not have the same implications; for instance, the phenomenal term "flight of stairs" does not include any implications concerning my later walking up stairs, whereas the physical term does. If we are aware of the peculiar nature of this language, Lewis maintains, we can understand why report propositions are absolutely certain; they merely express a momentary observation and are not subject to later revision.

Yet these statements are synthetic. They inform us about something that is there, and do not merely give labels to the individual observation. They tell us, for instance, that what there is now resembles something I saw yesterday. They draw lines of comparison into the picture offered by experience.

Here we have to be careful. We cannot directly compare what we see now with what we saw yesterday. We have a recollection image of what we saw yesterday, which we compare with what we see now. We cannot observationally compare the recollection image with what we saw yesterday. This comparison can only be made after certain coordinative definitions have been laid down, comparable to those known from space-time measurement, which make it a rule of language (an extension rule) to call the original object of sight similar to its recollection image. Yet there are, in addition, certain empirical statements involved. For instance, when we look at the same blue paper twice, we find that the visual aspect of the second observation is similar to the recollection image of the first. This constancy of the perceptual function [1] does not always hold; we know that the subjective color of an object may change when the color of its surroundings changes, while the object retains its color in the physical sense (contrast colors). But, I think, Lewis would not include an hypothesis about the constancy of the perceptual function in his expressive, or phenomenal, language. He would regard it as already belonging in physical language.

Let us assume that this phenomenal language as proposed by Lewis can be carried through. Can we then maintain that there are absolutely certain report propositions, formulated in phenomenal language? I will try to collect the arguments for and against Lewis' thesis of the existence of such propositions and, examining the pros and cons, attempt to arrive at a conclusion.

The first argument in favor of Lewis' thesis stems from a consideration of the procedure by means of which we construct phenomenal propositions. When we discover that a report formulated in physical language is incompatible with later observations, we change its interpretation by reducing it to its phenomenal content; we say, for instance, "Though it was false to believe that there was a flight of stairs, it remains true that there was the phenomenon of a flight of stairs." In other words, the method by means of which we introduce the phenomenal reports seems to guarantee their absolute certainty: we eliminate that component of the original sentence which is falsified by later observation, and which may be called its physical component; thus we construct its phenomenal component as a residue exempt from doubt. Phenomenal language is constructed by elimination of all physical implications; it therefore appears plausible that the sentences of this language cannot be disproved.

Second, if we reduce the sentence to its phenomenal content, it seems quite impossible that we are mistaken if only certain precautions are taken. Observation cannot lie, we would like to argue; a mistake can only spring from our interpretation of the observation. It is true that observers can lie; so we must make sure that lying is excluded. Although this condition may involve some difficulties if reports by other persons are concerned, it offers no difficulties regarding our own reports: we know whether or not we lie. Now it is also true that there are certain sources of error even for our personal language: we sometimes make mistakes in speaking, say "red" when we mean "green," or "John" when we mean "Peter," and therefore have to be sure that no mistakes

[1] As to this term and the use of co-ordinative definitions for the comparison of perceptions, see my book, *Experience and Prediction* (Chicago, 1938), pp. 183, 251.

of this kind occur. But we may argue that while we use the words incorrectly they have, at the moment we use them, the correct meaning for us; the word "John," at this moment, has the meaning of "Peter" for us, and, though a slip of the tongue may misinform other persons, it cannot deceive us who know what we mean. In other words, errors can only spring from the linguistic formulation, but cannot concern its meaning as it is intended by the speaking person. So, if we take care that no error creeps into the linguistic formulation, report sentences are absolutely reliable.

The third argument is of a logical nature. It refers to the empiricist conception that statements about physical objects are merely probable, and proceeds by a sort of deductive reasoning. If something is claimed to be probable, so goes the argument, something else must be certain; for how can we arrive at probabilities unless we have some firm basis from which we can derive those probabilities?

Sometimes this argument is given a more mathematical form. We say, for instance, that the probability of the event is p. Assume that this statement about a probability is not absolutely certain, but is itself merely probable to the degree q. This weakens the probability of the event, which can now be asserted merely with the probability p·q. What if even the sentence concerning the probability q is not certain, but merely probable to the degree r? This would once more weaken the probability of the event, which is now =p·q·r. And so on: If there is no certainty on any level, the ultimate probability of the event is a product of infinitely many factors each of which is smaller than 1 and which do not converge to 1, and thus the product is equal to 0. So, if the empiricist claims that he can maintain empirical knowledge with some probability, he must have certainty on some level of language. This argument was advanced by Bertrand Russell.[2]

These are the most important arguments in favor of the thesis that there are absolutely certain report sentences. I will now turn to analyzing these arguments and thereby develop the arguments which I raise against the thesis. Let me begin with an analysis of the third argument. I will then proceed to advance arguments against the thesis and shall thereby be led to a criticism of the second and first argument set forth above.

The argument that probability presupposes certainty on some other level appears very persuasive, in particular if it is given the mathematical form in which a product of infinitely many factors smaller than 1 goes to 0. Unfortunately—or should I say, fortunately?—there is a flaw in it. If q is the probability of the sentence s, "The probability of

2 Bertrand Russell, *Human Knowledge* (New York, 1948), p. 416.

the event is p," then the probability of the event is not given by the product p·q, but by a more complicated formula, the rule of elimination. Its application requires a knowledge about the probability of the event in case the sentence s is false. Let this probability be $=p'$; then the probability of the event is equal to $q \cdot p + (1 - q) \cdot p'$.[3] This expression need not be smaller than p, and can even be larger. So the convergence to 0 for infinitely many levels of language cannot be derived. In fact, the infinite product p·q·r . . . does not give the probability of the event, but supplies the probability that all these infinitely many sentences are true simultaneously; and such a probability is, of course, equal to 0. Thus the argument is invalid for mathematical reasons.

But why is it so persuasive? It seems so clear that something must be certain in order that some other thing can be probable. I think this is just one of those fallacies in which probability theory is so rich. We are accustomed to thinking in terms of truth and falsehood and wish to extend this habit to probability statements. We argue: if events are merely probable, the statement about their probability must be certain, because . . . Because of what? I think there is tacitly a conception involved according to which knowledge is to be identified with certainty, and probable knowledge appears tolerable only if it is embedded in a framework of certainty. This is a remnant of rationalism. An empiricist theory of probability can be constructed only if we are willing to regard knowledge as a system of posits. And posits do not require certainty on any level. But I will not go into these problems here, as I have treated them in other publications.

I will rather turn to another argument against the thesis of absolutely certain report sentences, an argument also referring to probabilities, but which uses the theory of probability in the opposite direction, so to speak, namely, for the proof that such sentences cannot be certain. The logic of this argument is very simple. Since report sentences, even when formulated in phenomenal language, are the only basis of knowledge, they must enable us to make predictions of further report sentences. Now it is true that, according to Lewis' definition of phenomenal language, report sentences cannot *strictly imply* predictions; i.e., any implications to the future cannot be analytic implications, or, what is perhaps the same thing, strict implications in the sense of Lewis' famous term, or even synthetic nomological implications, when I use this term to denote the form of implication represented by the laws of nature.[4] So the implications from report sentences to predictions of further report

[3] For an exact treatment of this probability see my *Theory of Probability* (Berkeley, 1949), p. 321 (German edition [Leiden, 1935], p. 315).
[4] See my *Elements of Symbolic Logic* (New York, 1947), ch. viii.

sentences must be probability implications. This seems to me to be the only solution for Lewis' problem of terminating judgments which still allow for predictions: if these predictions are not strictly implied, in any of the above senses, they do not belong to the meaning of the terminating judgment, and thus Lewis' condition is satisfied; whereas it still makes sense to use terminating judgments for predictions if such predictions are implied with probability.

Now if there exist probability implications between phenomenal sentences, they establish a concatenation between such sentences; and this concatenation works in both directions, from the past to the future as well as from the future to the past. If the phenomenal sentence *a,* in a certain context, makes the phenomenal sentence *b* highly probable, whereas non-*a* would make non-*b* highly probable, then conversely, the verification of *b* will make *a* highly probable, whereas the verification of non-*b* would make *a* highly improbable. I refer here to the theorem of inverse probability, known as Bayes' rule. It is true that the use of this rule requires a knowledge of quite a few probabilities, among which the antecedent probabilities play an important part; but the system of knowledge is elaborate enough to supply all these probabilities, though perhaps sometimes only in the form of rough estimates.[5] It follows, then, that any phenomenal sentence is capable of being tested in terms of other such sentences; and though the other sentences cannot completely verify, or falsify, the given sentence, they can verify it, or falsify it, to a high degree.

I will call this the *argument from concatenation.* It shows that phenomenal sentences are not exempt from probability tests. Let us examine in what sense it can be used for a proof that phenomenal sentences are not absolutely certain.

In defense of Lewis' thesis, the objection might be raised that, although the probability of the phenomenal sentence *a* may be very low if it is based on the totality of other phenomenal sentences, we need not abandon sentence *a*. Once this sentence has been verified by direct observation, we shall prefer this kind of evidence to all the evidence collected in the other sentences, for the reason that direct observation confers the probability 1 upon the sentence *a,* whereas the probability of non-*a* derived from the totality of other sentences is smaller than 1. In fact, similar situations do admittedly occur. It is very improbable that

[5] From the existence of a probability P (a,b) alone we cannot infer that a probability P (b,a) exists; see my *Theory of Probability* (Berkeley, 1949), pp. 109–110. But this inference can be made if, in addition, the probabilities P (a) and P (ā,b) exist; this follows from formula (9) *(ibid.,* p. 92), when the general reference class A is omitted. I may add the remark that all these considerations, of course, belong in what I have called advanced knowledge.

when I step on the brake my car starts speeding up. But assume such experience did actually occur; would I be willing to doubt my observation? Would I argue that I was mistaken in believing that my car speeded up, because the probability against the production of such an effect by a stepped-on brake pedal is very high? We would usually refuse to make such an inference; the direct observational evidence for the individual occurrence is stronger than the indirect evidence against it derived from other observations. Would we not be willing to defend in a similar way any individual phenomenal sentence against the totality of other sentences?

The logic of this defense must be carefully analyzed. When we are willing to retain the individual sentence in spite of indirect evidence against it, we do so because we believe that further observational evidence will support it. In the example of the car, we might ask other people whether they, too, saw our car speed up; and we might ask them to check, in a repeated performance of the unusual event, whether our foot is actually on the brake pedal. If both observations are endorsed by other observers, we might proceed to further investigation and may perhaps eventually discover that the sole of our shoe, while pressing down the brake pedal, touched the gas pedal slightly and moved it downward. We then have found an explanation of the unusual occurrence. We have found further observation sentences of such a kind that the totality of observation sentences now confers a high probability on the individual sentence considered. This is, in fact, the maxim of any defense of individual observation sentences: retaining an observation sentence against indirect evidence is equivalent to predicting that the class of observation sentences, on suitable experimentation, will be so extended as to turn the negative indirect evidence into positive evidence.

In the example considered I used not phenomenal sentences but physical sentences, since I referred to such physical occurrences as the motion of a brake pedal and the speeding of a car. But I do not see any reason why the procedure should be different in principle for phenomenal sentences. Retaining a phenomenal sentence against the indirect evidence derived from the total system of phenomenal sentences in which it is embedded is equivalent to assuming that the class of phenomenal sentences, on suitable experimentation, will be so extended as to supply positive evidence for the sentence. I will call this maxim the principle of *inductive consistency*. It goes beyond deductive consistency. A sentence system relative to which, on further extension, the probability of some individual sentence *a* goes to zero, is deductively consistent if the sentence *a* is retained in it; but it is not inductively consistent. It appears obvious that for our system of knowledge we require inductive consistency, because this system cannot be constructed by deductive inferences alone but is based on inductive inferences.

I arrive at the result that phenomenal sentences cannot be absolutely certain, because retaining an individual sentence against any possible indirect evidence may lead to the abandonment of inductive consistency. This argument I regard as a conclusive proof against the thesis.

It may perhaps be objected that we would rather sacrifice inductive consistency than give up a phenomenal sentence. However, it can be shown that such a practice contradicts our actual procedure. This consideration leads back to the second argument advanced above in favor of Lewis' thesis.

It was said there that the only sources of error for phenomenal sentences are lying and mistakes in the verbal formulation. Now assume that such errors actually have occurred; for instance, that I said "John" when I meant "Peter." How would I find it out later? Obviously, by inferences from the totality of other report sentences. Now, in these inferences I do not use the fact that the error stemmed from a slip of the tongue; I merely refer to the high probability derived from other phenomenal sentences against the correctness of the word "John," i.e., I use inductive consistency. When I then proceed to maintain that there must have been a mistake in speaking, I merely advance a psychological explanation of the error, and thus attempt to make my inductive system even more consistent. This is, in fact, the meaning of such qualifications as that the observer must not use the wrong words, or must not lie: they represent possible explanations for false phenomenal sentences.

But it is by no means understood that they are the only possible explanations for such sentences. It is true that there are situations in which we say "John" and mean "Peter," in which, therefore, at least subjectively the correct meaning can be said to exist. There are other situations, however, in which our attention is not fully focused on our words, and for which we cannot maintain that any distinct meaning was attached to our words. These transitional situations play a greater part than is usually recognized. That is true, likewise, for the case of lying. Although we intend to make a truthful statement, wishful thinking may bias our report; this fact is known to astronomers and physicists, who are afraid that their pointer readings may be slightly falsified in the direction of the result which they wish to find for theoretical reasons, and prefer to have their readings checked by an observer who does not know the theoretical background. The psychological sources of error in phenomenal sentences cannot be simply classified into lying and verbal mistake.

It may perhaps be argued that error presupposes truth, that speaking of possible errors in phenomenal sentences indicates our willingness to assume that there exist true phenomenal sentences. But this objection misses its point. What matters is the sentences we possesss, or are willing to accept; it does not help us to know that there are other sentences which we *should* accept. That there are true sentences describing phenomenal occurrences is no greater miracle than that there is a truly descriptive sentence for any physical occurrence. Our knowledge is built up, not from facts, but from what we know about facts; and knowing refers to language. Phenomenal knowledge must somehow be given in linguistic form, even if it is not the articulate form of conversational language; and for this very reason it can be false. The gap between facts and language cannot be abridged by the belief that the phenomenal sentences known to us cannot be false—this belief is incompatible with the principle of inductive consistency.

Although I think that the argument from concatenation settles the problem of absolutely certain phenomenal sentences in a negative way, I should like to add some remarks concerning the use of a phenomenal language. This consideration will lead us back to the first argument which I advanced in favor of Lewis' thesis.

It was said there that our actual procedure of checking and correcting physical report sentences exhibits a method of denying physical truth to those sentences and reducing them to mere phenomenal reports. In the example used, the physical object "flight of stairs" was replaced by a phenomenal object carrying the same name. Although at first glance this method seems to support the view that there exists a specific phenomenal language, I wish to show now that the contrary is true, that this method speaks against the psychological priority of a so-called phenomenal language.

I wish to argue that, in a psychological sense, the primary meaning of all terms is given by their reference to physical objects. The term "flight of stairs" means the physical objects so called; and when I speak of a tree I saw in a dream, the term "tree" refers to the kind of physical object usually denoted by it. It is very well possible to base all empirical knowledge on a list of observation sentences having physical reference, in this sense. This list would include reports of dreams and hallucinations. Subjecting the list to inductive concatenation, i.e., constructing physical knowledge in the usual way, we then find that, if all report sentences are assumed to be true, some must be false, i.e., we eliminate dream reports, etc., by an inductive form of *reductio ad absurdum*. We then can ask: How must the eliminated sentences be modified in order to make them compatible with the total system? It is at this point that their phenomenal interpretation is introduced. We say, for instance, that there was no tree, but that we had a dream in which we believed we saw a tree. This sentence can be completely translated into physical language.[6] It is merely a convenient abbreviation if we speak of a subjective tree, or the phenomenon of a tree, and thus construct a phenomenal language.

The phenomenal language appears, therefore, as the product of a logical construction starting with terms of the physical language. This is the reason that the phenomenal language cannot be freed from terms of the physical language, that we cannot help but use such terms as "something that looks like a tree," "something that resembles a flight of stairs." If we wish to define the meaning of phenomenal terms, we have to refer to physical objects.

The usual objection to this view is that there are direct ostensive definitions of phenomenal terms. But I doubt whether such definitions can be completely separated from physical terms. When we define shades of color by means of a color scale, we refer to a physical object, the scale, and say, for instance, "sand beige is the color of this object." If we try also to replace the scale by a phenomenal object, we come into difficulties when we wish to reproduce the standards of color, and arrive at sentences like "this here equals that here." This sentence contains terms like "equals," "this," the meaning of which must already be known. If it was introduced in a previous ostensive definition, we must somehow be able to reproduce the defining standards, which procedure involves physical objects and physical language. It seems that phenomenal language is not an actual language, but merely a program which some of us hope to be able to carry through.

This leads me to another interpretation of phenomenal language. When a sentence like "There is a tree" is given, in the ordinary meaning of physical language, and we discover that it is false, we ask: How can we reinterpret the sentence in order to make it true? We then come to such interpretations as, "I dreamed that there was a tree." This sentence contains the term "I," which belongs to physical language, since the ego is by no means phenomenally given; and the same holds for the term "dreamed." The program of a phenomenal language seems therefore to be the directive: replace every observation sentence that is false, physically speaking, by a true sentence which explains why we uttered the original sentence. In other words, we look for a psychological explanation of false observation sentences. When we have found a true explanation, i.e., a true reinterpretation of the sentence, the resulting sentence is true—this is, of course, trivially analytic. If we regard the property of being a true explanation as the criterion of phenomenal

[6] See my *Elements of Symbolic Logic* (New York, 1947), p. 275, and a note in *Philosophical Studies*, II (1951), 92.

language, it thus follows trivially that all sentences of this language are true. But we cannot say beforehand what these sentences will be; whether they refer to a dream, or a slip of the tongue, or a falsification of observation by an unconscious motive. The construction of phenomenal language then merely appears as a procedure supplying psychological knowledge; we can achieve it step by step, but will never be able to say that we have found the truly phenomenal language, because we can never say when we have found the ultimate truth.

These are a few sketchy ideas to show how we may incorporate a phenomenal language in an empiricist philosophy. My main argument is that such a philosophy does not need a basis of absolutely certain sentences. The system of knowledge can be based on observation sentences of the physical language of everyday life. Those among these sentences which are tenable are found by inductive concatenation; and those which are not tenable are given a reinterpretation, by the same method, which makes them tenable as psychological reports. Empiricism does not need absolute certainty, either for so-called principles of knowledge, or for observation sentences. There is no synthetic a priori; and there is no synthetic a posteriori that is absolutely certain.

Nelson Goodman

Sense and Certainty

The argument for empirical certainties has two phases. The first is the effort to point out actual statements or kinds of statements that are plainly immune to doubt. The second is the effort to show, quite aside from the question just *what* statements are certain, that on theoretical grounds there must be *some* empirical certainties.

The popular hunting ground for empirical certainty is among statements confined to immediate phenomena. Statements concerning physical objects involve prediction in one way or another, and so may always turn out to be wrong. But, the argument runs, between the presentation of an element in experience and my simultaneous judgment that it is presented, there is no room for error or doubt. We may have trouble formulating these judgments correctly in language, but misuses of language or slips of tongue must not be confused with errors in judgment. If the judgment is immediate and confined to what is fully before me, it cannot be wrong. For how can I be mistaken at a given moment about the sheer content of my experience at that moment?

Despite the forthright appeal of this argument, the fact seems to

Nelson Goodman, "Sense and Certainty," *Problems and Projects* (Indianapolis, Indiana: Bobbs-Merrill Company, Inc., 1972). Reprinted by permission of the publisher.

be that my judgments at a moment about what I immediately apprehend at that moment are often wrong. That is to say, they are often withdrawn for good reason. This is sometimes denied on the ground that, since the momentary experience is instantly gone, the judgment is forever safe from further test. But the judgment I made a few moments ago that a reddish patch occupied the center of my visual field at that moment will be dropped if it conflicts with other judgments having a combined stronger claim to preservation. For example, if I also judged that the patch occupying the same region an instant later was blue, and also that the apparent color was constant over the brief period covering the two instants, I am going to have to drop one of the three judgments; and circumstances may point to the first as well as to either of the others. Indeed judgments concerning immediate phenomena may be rejected in favor of judgments concerning physical objects, as happens when I conclude that it could not have been a reddish patch after all since I was looking at a bluebird in sunlight with my eyes functioning normally. In either sort of case, I cannot reasonably plead a mere slip of the tongue; I am deciding that a judgment was wrong. If a statement may be withdrawn in the interest of compatibility and other statements, it is not certain in any ordinary sense; for certainty consists of immunity to such withdrawal.

Now someone may object that all I have shown is that a judgment concerning phenomena at a given moment may be doubted at some later moment, while what is being claimed is merely that such a judgment is certain *at* the moment in question. This seems to me a confusion. When we talk of certainty we are not—I take it—talking about a feeling of utter conviction; nor are we asking whether a judgment made at a given moment can be withdrawn at that same moment. We are talking of knowledge without possibility of error—or, in practice, of judgment immune to subsequent withdrawal for cause. I cannot be said to be certain about what occurs at a given moment, even at that moment, if I may justifiably change my mind about it at a later moment.

The advocate of empirical certainty, however, is not put off by a failure to find instances or by the problems encountered in arriving at an unexceptionable statement of his thesis. The difficulty of formulating the given must not, Mr. Lewis warns, lead us to suppose that there is no given; for if there were no given there would be no experience as we know it at all. No argument can erase the fact that experience and knowledge are not purely arbitary, willful inventions. The sheer stubborness of experience recognized by even the most thorough-going idealists is proof enough that there is *something there* in experience, some element not manufactured but given. This cannot be denied whatever may be the difficulties of articulating it.

But this all seems to me to point, to, or at least to be compatible with, the conclusion that while something is given, nothing given is true; that while some things may be indubitable, nothing is certain. What we have been urged to grant amounts at most to this: materials for or particles of experiences are given, sensory qualities or events or other elements are not created at will but presented, experience has some content even though our description of it may be artificial or wrong and even though the precise differentiation between what is given and what is not given may be virtually impossible. But to such content or materials or particles or elements, the terms "true," "false," and "certain" are quite inapplicable. These elements are simply there or not there. To grant that some are there is not to grant that anything is certain. Such elements may be indubitable in the vacuous sense that doubt is irrelevant to them, as it is to a desk; but they, like the desk, are equally devoid of certainty. They may be before use, but they are neither true nor false. For truth and falsity and certainty pertain to statements or judgments and not to mere particles or materials or elements. Thus, to deny that there are empirical certainties does not imply that experience is a pure fiction, that it is without content, or even that there is no given element.

Some of Mr. Lewis' arguments, however, are aimed directly at showing that there must be some indubitable judgments or statements, not merely that there is something presented. Unless some statements are certain, he argues, none is even probable. Mr. Reichenbach has disputed this argument on mathematical grounds, but perhaps Mr. Lewis intends only to make a somewhat less technical point. It plainly does us no good to know that a statement is probable with respect to certain premises unless we have some confidence in these premises. And we cannot just say that the premises themselves need merely be probable; for this means only that they in turn are probable with respect to other premises, and so on without end. Probability will be genuinely useful in judging the truth of sentences—the argument runs—only if the chain of probability relationships is somewhere moored to certainty. This is closely akin to the argument against a pure coherence theory of truth. Internal coherence is obviously a necessary but not a sufficient condition for the truth of a system; for we need also some means of choosing between equally tight systems that are incompatible with each other. There must be a tie to fact through, it is contended, some immediately certain statements. Otherwise compatibility with a system is not even a probable indication of the truth of any statement.

Now clearly we cannot suppose that statements derive their credibility from other statements without ever bringing this string of statements to earth. Credibility may be transmitted from one statement to another through deductive or probability connections; but credibility does not spring from these connections by spontaneous generation. Somewhere along the line some statements, whether atomic sense reports or the entire system or something in between, must have initial credibility. So far the argument is sound. To use the term "probability" for this initial credibility is to risk misunderstanding since probability, strictly speaking, is not initial at all but always relative to specified premises. Yet all that is indicated is credibility to some degree, not certainty. To say that some statements must be initially credible if any statement is ever to be credible at all is not to say that any statement is immune to withdrawal. For indeed, as remarked earlier, no matter how strong its initial claim to preservation may be, a statement will be dropped if its retention—along with consequent adjustments in the interest of coherence—results in a system that does not satisfy as well as possible the totality of claims presented by all relevant statements. In the "search for truth" we deal with the clamoring demands of conflicting statements by trying, so to speak, to realize the greatest happiness of the greatest number of them. These demands constitute a different factor from coherence, the wanted means of choosing between different systems, the missing link with fact; yet none is so strong that it may be denied. That we have probable knowledge, then, implies no certainty but only initial credibility.

Still, I am not satisfied that we have as yet gone to the heart of the matter. Just why is it so important to decide whether or not there is some empirical certainty? Mr. Reichenbach says that Mr. Lewis' view is a vestige of rationalism; but unlike the rationalists, Mr. Lewis obviously is not seeking certainties in order to use them as axioms for a philosophical system. If he could once prove that there are some empirical certainties, I doubt if he would be much disposed to go catch one. Rather he is convinced that such certainties are somehow essential to knowledge as we possess it. And I suspect that both his specific arguments and my counterarguments may leave him, as they leave me, with a feeling that the real issue has not yet been brought into relief. The underlying motivation for Mr. Lewis's whole argument is to be found, I think, in the problem of relating language to what it describes.

Consider the familiar problem faced by a common version of pragmatism. The meaning and truth of a statement are said to lie in its predictive consequences. These consequences are themselves statements; for from statements we can deduce, or even infer with probability, nothing but other statements. But, if the truth of these predictions depends in turn upon the truth of others derived from them, we are lost in an endless regress. The theory rests upon our being able, when a particular moment arrives, to decide with some degree of confidence whether a prediction made concerning that moment is or is not fulfilled. Accordingly, statements describing immediate experience are specifically exempted from the predictive criterion. But what, then, is to be said concerning them? What sort of relationship to experience makes such a statement true or credible? The connection between a statement and the very dissimilar experience it describes is not easy to grasp. Testimony to the rather mysterious character of the relation is found in the oblique way it is referred to in the literature. Mr. Quine wrote recently that a system of statements "impinges at its edges" upon experience; and he has been twitted for waxing so metaphorical. I suspect that the metaphorical term was chosen purposely to intimate that we have here an inadequately understood relationship. Again, Mr. Lewis, choosing simile rather than metaphor, merely likens the relationship to that between an outcry and the fearful apparition that evokes it.

What I am suggesting is that Mr. Lewis is actually more vitally concerned with the directness and immediacy and irreducibility of this relation between sensory experience and sentences describing it than with the certainty of these sentences. For, if this crucial relation seems inexplicable, perhaps—the thought runs—that is just because it is so fundamental and simple as to require no explanation. Learning a language may involve becoming acquainted with this elementary and irreducible relation, of which subsequent cases are instantly recognized. The claim that statements describing bare sense experience are certain then becomes an accidental by-product of the view that their truth is immediately and directly apprehended. And the real challenge that emerges is not to muster arguments showing that there are no empirical certainties, but to point a way of explaining the root relation between language and the nonlinguistic experience it describes.

Plainly we cannot look to resemblance for any help. The English statement "There is a blue patch" and its Chinese equivalent are very unlike, and both are even more unlike the blue patch itself. In no literal sense does language mirror experience. Yet this false start has something in its favor. The explanation in terms of resemblance is very good except for being so wrong. By that I mean that to explain the relation in question is to subsume it under or analyze it into more general relations. Such terms as "describes," "is true," "denotes," and "designates," require explanation because they are idiosyncratic to cases where the first element in question is linguistic. Only words and strings of words denote or are true. Our problem is to reduce these purely semantic predicates to predicates that have familiar instances in nonlinguistic experience.[1]

A clue to a better starting point than resemblance lies in the fact that a toot may warn of an oncoming train or that a ray of dawn foretells the approach of daylight. Here are nonverbal events standing as *signals* for others. In like fashion two sensory experiences or phenomena are often such that the earlier is a promise or warning or signal of the later. A feeling of warmth may signal the imminent appearance of a fiery red patch in the visual field; an evenly shaded patch may signal a certain tactual experience to come. Of course, the situation is seldom quite so simple. More often, an isolated presentation signals another only conditionally upon certain behavior; that is, the tactual experience ensues only if I reach out my hand in a certain way. But this can be accommodated without difficulty merely by recognizing that a presentation is itself usually a partial, incomplete signal that combines with other presentations (such as those of bodily movements) to constitute a signal for a subsequent experience. In other words, a signal is often comprised of more than one presentation; but this does not affect the important point that some nonlinguistic experiences function as signals.

If asked for a psychological account of signaling, we might say that the earlier experience arouses an expectation that is fulfilled, or a tension that is released, by the later one. But this and the various questions it inspires are not quite apposite to the present task. Our primary objective is not to explain this relation but to explain certain semantic predicates in terms of it. So long as we are satisfied that the relation clearly obtains in nonlinguistic experience, we can postpone consideration of its anatomy and genealogy.

If experiences comprised of such presentations as shaded patches can signal, there is no mystery about how an irregular black patch or a brief stretch of sound may function in the same way. And a statement-event,[2] or other string of word-events, is simply some such patch or stretch. Just as a blue patch and some kinaesthetic presentations may signal the coming appearance of a red patch, so also does a statement-event—let us name it *"F"*—saying in advance that there will be a red patch in the visual field at the time in question, *t*. Statements are merely

[1] Thus our problem differs from that considered by Tarski in *Der Wahrheitsbegriff in den formalisierten Sprachen,* in which he defines truth in terms of the purely semantic notion of *satisfaction.*

[2] I use the term "statement-event" at times to emphasize that I think of a statement as an actual utterance or inscription-at-a-moment.

more complicated, and hence often more specific, than some other signals. It is clear enough how a signaling system can be elaborated and refined, once even a few signaling relationships are available. Under some circumstances or other, almost anything can be made to serve as a signal for almost any subsequent experience. Differentiation between conditioned and unconditioned signaling is irrelevant to our present purpose.

It may be contended that statements signal by virtue of their meaning, and that their signaling is thus essentially different from that of nonlinguistic elements. On the contrary, I should say rather that statements mean by virtue of their signaling; for "means," like "denotes," is one of the puzzling semantic predicates that constitute our problem. Yet this is not to say that a statement either means or denotes what it signals; the explanation of meaning or denoting in terms of signaling would have to be much more complex than that.

So far, however, only statements like *F* that are in the future tense have been provided for. What are we to do about statements in the present tense? Suppose the statement *P* "There is now a red patch in the visual field" occurs at the time *t* above in question. *P* does not *signal* the simultaneous occurrence of the red patch; for signaling is always forecasting. Nevertheless, we know that *P* is true if and only if *F* is true. Hence *P* is true just in case *F* is a genuine signal. Although *P* does not itself signal the occurrence of the red patch, the truth of *P* is explained in terms of the truth of the earlier statement *F*, which does signal this occurrence. Statements in the past tense can be handled in the same way as those in the present tense; and tenseless statements, depending on whether they occur before, during, or after the time they pertain to, in the same way as statements in, respectively, the future, present, and past tense. A key point of the present proposal lies in its radical departure from the usual attack, which rests the truth of all statements upon that of statements in the present tense and leaves us at a loss to deal with these. After all, a thoroughly predictive theory can be carried through only by basing all truth upon the truth of statement-events concerning later events.

What I have been saying is meant to apply just to rather simple statements, like those illustrated, about phenomena. The relation of other statements to these is not part of my present problem. But even with respect to the simple statements in question, a number of problems must be left untouched. For example, I cannot here discuss the means available for dealing with a statement, in the present tense, such that no correlative statement in the future tense ever happened to occur.

I expect to be told that what I offer is a fragment of a time-worn theory in a somewhat topsy-turvy version. But I make no claim to a complete or unprecedented or pretty theory. Nor am I at all complacent about pragmatic-predictive epistemology in general. What I have tried to do here is to suggest how, in terms of a pragmatism not entirely alien to Mr. Lewis' point of view, the connection between language and what it describes may be given a reasonable explanation. In that case, this relation need no longer be regarded as immediate, mystic, and inexplicable. And this, if I am correct, will remove the last and deepest motivation for the defense of empirical certainty.

C. I. Lewis

The Given Element in Empirical Knowledge

Since I have already said in print how I would propose to deal with our present topic, and my colleagues on this program have made references to that view, let me here omit any attempted summary and try instead to emphasize those basic considerations which, as I see it, dictate this conception of an incorrigible datum-element underlying empirical beliefs which are justified.

Empirical knowledge—if there be any such thing—is distinguished by having as an essential factor or essential premise something disclosed in experience. That is a tautology. To express this tautological fact circumstantially and circumspectly can be a matter of some difficulty; but, if anyone should deny what we so attempt to state, he must impress us as philosophizing by the Russian method of the big lie, and argument with him might well be useless. It is this essential factor in knowledge which comes from experience which I would speak of as 'the given.'

C. I. Lewis, "The Given Element in Empirical Knowledge," *The Philosophical Review*, 61 (1952), pp. 168–75. Reprinted by permission.
Paper read at the forty-eighth annual meeting of the Eastern Division of the American Philosophical Association at Bryn Mawr College, Bryn Mawr, Pennsylvania, December 29, 1951.

But since experience and the functioning of it as the basis of empirical knowledge is something open to the inspection of all of us, each in his own case, how comes it that we tell such different tales about it? The account which I have offered has frequently met with dissent; and this dissent with respect to something which, if correctly stated, should be obvious gives me pause. If those who so find fault held a rationalistic theory, I might offer myself the excuse that they philosophize in the interest of an unsound major premise. But the greater number of my critics have been as firmly empiricistic in their professed convictions as myself. That is just what puzzles me most, because I seem to find only two alternatives for a plausible account of knowledge: either there must be some ground in experience, some factuality it directly affords, which plays an indispensable part in the validation of empirical beliefs, or what determines empirical truth is merely some logical relationship of a candidate-belief with other beliefs which have been accepted. And in the latter case any reason, apart from factualities afforded by experience, why these *antecedent* beliefs have been accepted, remains obscure. Even passing that difficulty, this second alternative would seem to be merely a revival of the coherence theory of truth, whose defects have long been patent.

There undoubtedly is some logical relation of facts—or more than one—to which the name 'coherence' might aptly be given. And there is equally little doubt that such logical and systemic relationships are important for assuring credibility—once a sufficient number of antecedent and relevant facts have been otherwise determined. But no logical relationship, by itself, can ever be sufficient to establish the truth, or the credibility even, of any synthetic judgment. That is one point which logical studies of the last half century have made abundantly clear. Unless the beliefs so related, or some of them, have a warrant which no logical principle can assure, no logical relation of them to one another constitutes a scintilla of evidence that they are even probable.

Let us assume that the whole of the truth has even that strongest type of coherence illustrated by a system of geometry. The statements of the system (postulates and theorems together) are so related that, if we should be doubtful of any one of them, the other statements of the system would be sufficient to assure it with deductive certainty. But that relationship, as we know, is insufficient to determine any truth about the geometric properties of actual things. If Euclid is thus coherent, then so too are Riemann and Lobachevsky; though given any denotation of the geometric vocabulary, these three geometries are mutually incompatible systems. If the truth about our space is ever to be ascertained, something disclosed in experience must be the final arbiter. Since this is the case for geometric truths, which cohere by the strong relations of deductive logic, *a fortiori* it must be the case for empirical truth at large, for the determination of which we must so often rely upon induction, which affords a probability only, on the supposition that our premises are certain or that they have some antecedent probability on other grounds.

In brief, we have nothing but experience and logic to determine truth or credibility of any synthetic judgment. Rule out datum-facts afforded by experience, and you have nothing left but the logically certifiable. And logic will not do it.

Such argument by elimination is admittedly not final, and I would not rest upon that but would appeal additionally to the facts of life. However, I would ask my critics where they stand on this point. Have they repudiated a fundamental requirement of any empiristic theory? Are they rationalists who think to extract from logical considerations alone some sufficient ground for empirical beliefs? Or are they really skeptics who dislike to acknowledge that fact in so many words? Or do they find some third alternative which I have overlooked?

One class of those who disagree have made their point of objection clear; it concerns my supposition that what is given in experience is incorrigible and indubitable. Empiricists generally are agreed that non-perceptual synthetic knowledge rests finally on knowledge which is perceptual, and so find the root problem in the nature of perception. Practically all empiricists recognize that some items of perceptual cognition are less than indubitable; perception is subject to illusion and mistake. They differ among themselves as to whether all perceptions, or some only, are subject to doubt. Mr. Moore, for example, regards such convictions as "This is my hand" (under appropriate circumstances) as subject to no doubt. But many, perhaps most of us, can find differences of degree only in the valid assurance of perceptual judgments: we recognize that most of them have what may be called 'practical certainty' but think that none of them is theoretically and validly certain. Those of us who come to this conclusion are then confronted with the following question: Is there, either antecedent to and supporting the perceptual belief in objective fact, or in the perceptual experience itself, an element or factor which is the basis of the perceptual judgment but is not, like this judgment of objective fact, subject to theoretical doubt?

My own answer to this question is affirmative. When I perceive a door, I may be deceived by a cleverly painted pattern on the wall, but the presentation which greets my eye is an indubitable fact of my experience. My perceptual belief in a real door, having another side, is not an explicit inference but a belief suggested by association; nevertheless the *validity* of this interpretation is that and that only which could attach to it as an inductive inference from the given visual presentation. The given element is this incorrigible presentational element; the criticizable and dubitable element is the element of interpretation.

The arguments which have been offered in criticism of this view are literally too numerous to be mentioned here. Some of them have been of the causal variety which may be advanced without reference to any attempted full account of empirical knowledge. The objections of Goodman and Reichenbach, however, are not of that sort but are made in the interest of alternative views which are complex and worked out. Neither of them has had time to do more than suggest his alternative conceptions; and I shall have time only to suggest where, as it seems to me, some of the critical issues lie.

I hope I shall not give offense if I say that Reichenbach's view impresses me as being an unabridged probabilism; a modernized coherence theory with two immense advantages over the older one so named. First, he makes provision for observation-statements, though he insists that these should be in objective ('physical') language, and that they are both dubitable and corrigible. And second, he substitues for the vague relation, historically called 'coherence,' meticulously described relations of probability-inference.

First, as to observation-statements: Let us suppose that I look over yonder and report that I see a horse. You (being epistemologists) may reply that you find my report ambiguous; that statements of the form "I see an X" are assertions of objective fact if and only if the constants substitutable for 'X' are understood to be confined to expressions denoting physical entities, but that statements of this form are in the protocol or expressive idiom if and only if the expressions substitutable for 'X' are understood to be designations of *appearances*. In the one case—you observe—I have made a dubitable assertion of an existent horse; in the other case, I have merely reported a specific given presentation which, whether dubitable or not, at least asserts no real horse as being present. This protocol statement, in its intended meaning—so I would claim—will be true just in case I am not lying or making some verbal mistake in the words I use. I am unable to see that Reichenbach's denial of this second and expressive idiom, is other than a dogmatism. (Even his 'phenomenal language' seems not to coincide with what I deem essential for any formulation of the given in experience.) I would, moreover, emphasize that the near absence of any restricted vocabulary or syntax for expressive statements is an unimportant matter for empirical knowledge itself: no one needs verbal formulation of his own present experience in order to be aware of it; and obviously, nobody else's protocols are indubitable to us. Protocol expression is as inessential to what it expresses as a cry of fear is to the fearful apparition which may cause it. It is for purposes of epistemological discussion that the notion of protocol statements is principally needed; though there are, of course, statements so intended, and the requisite idiom is one which finds exemplification in natural language.

Let us pass these points, however, and take it that the observer of the horse has formulated his observation in objective ('physical') language, and that what he reports is dubitable and only probable. Reichenbach himself refers to the difficulty which then arises (attributing the objection to Russell): a statement justified as probable must have a ground; if the ground is only probable, then there must be a ground of it; and so on. And to assess the probability of the original statement, its probability relative to its ground must be multiplied by the probability of this ground, which in turn must be multiplied by the probability of its own ground, and so on. Reichenbach denies that the regressive series of probability-values so arising must approach zero, and the probability of the original statement be thus finally whittled down to nothing. That matter could be discussed for the rest of the afternoon or longer; it makes a difference whether one is talking about determined probabilities on known grounds, or merely what are called 'a priori probabilities.' However, even if we accept the correction which Reichenbach urges here, I disbelieve that it will save his point. For that, I think he must prove that, where any such regress of probability-values is involved, the progressively qualified fraction measuring the probability of the quaesitum will converge to some determinable value other than zero; and I question whether such proof can be given. Nor do I think that the difficulty can be removed by his 'argument from concatenation.' It is true that, by the rule of inverse probabilities, we may proceed in either direction, determining the probability of a 'consequence' from the probability of a 'ground,' or of a 'ground' from a 'consequence.' But what I would emphasize is that, as Reichenbach mentions, you cannot take even the first step in either direction until you are prepared to assign numerical values to the 'antecedent probabilities' called for by the rule. These must literally be determined *before* use of the rule will determine the probability of anything. And, if the answer be given that these can be determined by another use of the rule, the rebuttal is obvious: in that case you must make that *other* use of it *before* you can make *this* one. An interminable progressus or regressus need not defeat theoretical purposes provided you are on the right end of it—the end from which its members are successively determinable. But in the kind of case here in point, one is always on the wrong end of any segment of the series, always required to determine something else first before one can determine what one wants to determine. The supposition that the probability of anything whatever always depends on something else which is only probable itself, is flatly incompatible with the justifiable assignment of any probability at all. Reichenbach suggests that the craving for some certainty here is a retained trace of rationalism; my countersuggestion would be that it is the attempt to retain a trace of empiricism.

Even more crudely put: the probabilistic conception strikes me as supposing that if enough probabilities can be got to lean against one another they can all be made to stand up. I suggest that, on the contrary, unless some of them can stand alone, they will all fall flat. If no non-analytic statement is categorically assertable, without probability qualification, then I think the whole system of such could provide no better assurance of anything in it than that which attaches to the contents of a well-written novel. I see no hope for such a coherence theory which repudiates data of experience which are simply given—or no hope unless a postulate be added to the effect that *some* synthetic statements are probable a priori; the postulate, for example, that every perceptual belief has *some* probability just on account of being a perceptual belief.[1]

There is time only for very brief comment on one other point. Both Goodman and Reichenbach would impose a requirement of consistency—or 'inductive consistency'—on protocols. This goes along with their supposition that what protocols report is dubitable and corrigible. Briefly and inadequately, there is no requirement of consistency which is relevant to protocols. A protocol is a report of given appearances, of experience as such. Looking out over this audience, I see in one place two heads on one neck. When I lift my own head a bit, I see only one head there. But that is no reason to alter my first protocol and deny this apparition of two heads. I do not, of course, believe the two apparent heads to be actual. It is at *that* point that the requirement of inductive consistency comes in. But the critique by which I avoid that conclusion as to objective fact is criticism of a suggested interpretation—of a perceptual *belief*—and not a criticism of what the protocol reports. What it further indicates is only the desirability of some objective explanation of this apparition. The careless observer's protocols, the insane man's direct experience, and the content of the dreamer's dream must not be corrected or eliminated in the interest of consistency; to do that would be simple falsification of facts of experience. The problem of empirical knowledge at large is the problem of an account of objective facts which will accord with the occurrence of the experiences reported in all truthful and verbally accurate protocols. That is one test of adequate empirical knowledge. And the capacity of the objective account to explain any puzzling and apparent incongruities of experience is a further such test. To call a given experience an illusion, or a dream, or a careless observa-

[1] This was suggested to me by Professor Paul Henle—though not as a supposition which he would adopt.

tion, is to indicate the kind of objective fact which will explain it—just as the laws of optics and the fact of my looking through the edge of my glasses explains my apparition of two heads. We must not forget that experience is all that is given to us for the purposes of empirical knowing, and that such knowledge of objective facts as we achieve is simply that body of beliefs which represents our over-all interpretation of experience. If we could not be sure of our experience when we have it, we should be in poor position to determine any objective fact, or confirm the supposition of one, or assign any probability to one.

I regret not to make the further and detailed comments which Goodman's paper merits. Disbelieving that my conception of an indubitable given element in experience can be maintained, he suppresses further criticisms he might have, in the interest of a possible pragmatic reformulation of statements describing experience.

Putting it oversimply one may say that what he proposes is the interpretation of observation-statements in terms of the forward looking import of what they lead us to expect. But that proposal is, I fear, a little more pragmatic than I dare to be. However plausibly such reformulation could be carried out, it would fail to satisfy me because of a conviction I have concerning the task of epistemological study; the conviction, namely, that a principal business of epistemology is with the *validity* of knowledge. And validity concerns the character of cognition as warranted or justified.

In order to be knowledge, empirical judgment must not only have predictive import of what will verify or confirm it; it must also be distinguished from a merely lucky or unlucky guess or hazard of belief by having some justifying ground. And in the nature of the case, what so justifies an empirical judgment cannot be something future to it and presently uninspectable but must lie in something antecedent to or compresent with it. Where it is perceptual cognition which is in question, the point is that the interpretation of experience—the perceptual belief—*is* significant of the future and verifiable, but, in order that this belief have *validity,* that which functions as the ground of it must be present and given.

That is precisely the point with which I am here principally concerned. It is on account of that point that I have felt it necessary to depart from or to supplement other pragmatic theories. And it is on account of that point that I could not accept Goodman's pragmatic proposal: by interpreting empirical findings in terms of what is future to them, it would invite confusion of the ground of knowledge which is there and given with what is not there but anticipated. It is also on the same account that I must disagree with various other current theories, put forward as empirical, which fail to recognize the datum-element of experience. In terms of such conceptions—so I think—no explanation of the validity of knowledge is forthcoming or even possible, and the holders of them can escape the skeptical conclusion only by failing to look where they are going.

I consider skepticism something worse than unsatisfactory; I consider it nonsense to hold or to imply that just any empirical judgment is as good as any other—because none is warranted. A theory which implies or allows that consequence is not an explanation of anything but merely an intellectual disaster.

William Alston

Varieties of Privileged Access

It is a very common, though by no means uncontested, view that the kind of knowledge a person has of his own mental (psychological) states, such as thoughts and feelings, is in principle not only fundamentally different from but also superior to the knowledge of his thoughts and feelings that is available to anyone else. Following an established usage, we may express this view by saying that a person has "privileged access" to his own mental states. It is obvious that this thesis will vary in content with variations in the specific mode of superiority imputed. Nevertheless, discussions of privileged access, both pro and con, have never been sufficiently alive to these variations or to their significance.

The central task of this paper is the exhibition and interrelation of the most important of the ways in which one's access to one's own mental states has been, or might be, thought to be privileged. In addition I shall show, though only sketchily, how failure to be alive to the full range of possibilities has vitiated some prominent discussions of the topic.

William Alston, "Varieties of Privileged Access," *American Philosophical Quarterly,* 8 (1971), 223–41. Reprinted by permission.

I

First, a couple of preliminary points. Privileged access claims vary not only with variations in the mode of epistemic superiority imputed, but also with variations in the category of "mental states" with respect to which the claim is made. Many philosophers have advanced privileged access as a *criterion* for the mental or the psychological; they have held that a state of a person is mental (psychological) if and only if that person's knowledge that he has the state is in principle superior, in some specified way, to the knowledge of that fact that is available to anyone else.[1] Others have made distinctions within this class of states and have asserted their favored form of privileged access of some sub-class thereof. Thus it is not uncommon to hold that one cannot be mistaken with respect to what may be called "phenomenal states," i.e., present contents of consciousness, such as sensations, images, feelings, and thoughts, but not to assert infallibility with respect to what may be called "dispositional states," such as beliefs, desires, and attitudes.[2] However the most common procedure is simply to work with particular examples, e.g., sensations or, more specifically, pains, and not even attempt to make clear the several classes of states of which privileged access is being asserted.[3] In this paper I mention this dimension of variation only to set it aside. My sole concern will be to distinguish and compare various types of epistemic superiority; I shall not also be concerned to distinguish and compare various classes of entities with respect to which one or another of these has been asserted. Hence for our purposes we can just work with the rather loose rubric, "mental state," remembering that if anyone is to

[1] See, e.g., G. E. Moore, "The Subject Matter of Psychology," *Proceedings of the Aristotelian Society,* vol. 10 (1909–1910), pp. 36–62, reprinted in G. N. A. Vesey (ed), *Body and Mind* (London 1964); and F. Bretano, selection from *Psychology from an Empirical Standpoint,* in *ibid.*

[2] See, e.g., J. Shaffer, "Persons and Their Bodies," *The Philosophical Review,* vol. 75 (1966), pp. 59–77.

[3] Thus Norman Malcolm, in "Direct Perception" (in *Knowledge and Certainty,* Englewood Cliffs, N.J., 1963) restricts his discussion to after-images; while in "The Privacy of Experience" (in A. Stroll, ed., *Epistemology, New Essays in the Theory of Knowledge,* New York, 1967), he specifically discusses pain, and sometimes more generally "sensations." Presumably Malcolm supposes that the things he says about after-images (pains) have a wider scope of application, but he does not make explicit just what he takes this to be. Again, most of A. J. Ayer's discussion in his essay "Privacy" (in *The Concept of a Person and Other Essays,* New York, 1963) is in terms of "thoughts and feelings," but he makes no attempt to say exactly how far he means his remarks to extend.

put forward a privileged access thesis, he should be more specific as to the range of states involved.

We can hardly avoid taking note, however briefly, of those philosophers who would make short shrift of our entire problem by dismissing it, on the grounds that it makes no sense to speak of a person *knowing* that he has, e.g., a certain sensation. (See L. Wittgenstein, *Philosophical Investigations,* Pt. I, para. 246.) If that is the case, there is no problem as to whether one's own knowledge of his own sensations is in some way necessarily superior to that available to any other person. I cannot really go into the issue in this paper, but it may not be out of place to explain briefly why it seems to me that any argument for this conclusion must be defective in *some* way. Clearly someone else can be in doubt as to whether I am in a given mental state, e.g., whether I am thinking about tomorrow's lecture, whether I am worrying about my job prospects, whether I feel elated. That is, he may not know how to answer a certain question, "Does he (Alston) feel elated?" But it seems that normally I *would* be in a position to answer that question, the *same* question to which he does not know the answer. But how can we understand my being in that position without supposing that I know something he doesn't, e.g., that I do feel elated? Thus it seems to be as undeniable as anything could be that persons normally do know what mental states they are in at a given moment, and that no argument designed to show that this is false or meaningless can be sound.

II

I shall begin by extracting a number of possible modes of privileged access from a rather wide sampling of the literature. We may begin with the following.

> Am I not that being who now doubts nearly everything, who nevertheless understands certain things, who affirms that one only is true, who denies all the others, who desires to know more, is averse from being deceived, who imagines many things, sometimes indeed despite his will, and who perceives many likewise, as by the intervention of the bodily organs? Is there nothing in all this which is as true as it is certain that I exist, even though I should always sleep and though he who has given me being employed all his ingenuity in deceiving me? . . . Finally, I am the same who feels, that is to say, who perceives certain things, as by the organs of sense since in truth I see light. I hear noise, I feel heat. But it will be said that these phenomena are false and that I am dreaming. Let it be so; still

it is at least quite certain that it seems to me that I see light, that I hear noise, and that I feel heat. That cannot be false; . . .

R. Descartes, *Meditations,* II

. . . for a man cannot conceive himself capable of a greater certainty than to know that any idea in his mind is such as he perceives it to be; and that two ideas, wherein he perceives a difference, are different and are not precisely the same.

J. Locke, *Essay Concerning Human Understanding,* IV, 2

For since all actions and sensations of the mind are known to us by consciousness, they must necessarily appear in every particular what they are, and be what they appear. Everything that enters the mind, being in *reality* as the perception, tis impossible anything should to *feeling* appear different. This were to suppose that even where we are most intimately conscious, we might be mistaken.

D. Hume, *Treatise of Human Nature,* I, iv, 2

The facts of consciousness are to be considered in two points of view; either as evidencing their own ideal or phaenomenal existence, or as evidencing the objective existence of something else beyond them. A belief in the former is not identical with a belief in the latter. The one cannot, the other may possibly be refused. . . . Now the reality of this, as a subjective datum—as an ideal phaenomenon, it is absolutely impossible to doubt without doubting the existence of consciousness, for consciousness is itself this fact; and to doubt the existence of consciousness is absolutely impossible; for as such a doubt could not exist, except in and through consciousness, it would, consequently, annihilate itself.

Sir W. Hamilton, *Lectures on Metaphysics,* XV, p. 188

It is a further general characteristic of all mental phenomena that they are perceived only in inner consciousness. . . . One could believe that such a definition says little, since it would seem more natural to take the opposite course, defining the act by reference to its object, and so defining inner perception of mental phenomena. But inner perception has still another characteristic, apart from the special nature of its object, which distinguishes it: namely, that immediate, infallible self-evidence, which pertains to it alone among all the cases in which we know objects of experience. Thus, if we say that mental phenomena are those which are grasped by means of inner perception, we have accordingly said that their perception is immediately evident.

F. Brentano, *Psychology from an Empirical Standpoint,*
selection in G. N. A. Vesey, ed., *op. cit.,* p. 151.

Subtract in what we say that we see, or hear, or otherwise learn from direct experience, *all that conceivably could be mistaken;* the remainder is the given content of the experience inducing this belief. . . . Apprehensions of the given which such expressive statements formulate, are not judgments, and they are not here classed as knowledge, because they are not subject to any possible error. Statement of such apprehension is, however, true or false; there could be no doubt about the presented content of experience as such at the time when it is given, but it would be possible to tell a lie about it.

C. I. Lewis, *An Analysis of Knowledge and Valuation*,
La Salle, Ill.: Open Court, 1946, pp. 182–183
[pp. 138, this volume, Eds.]

Some Philosophers . . . have thought it possible to find a class of statements which would be both genuinely informative and at the same time logically immune from doubt. . . . The statements usually chosen for this role . . . characterize some present state of the speaker, or some present content of his experience. I cannot, so it is maintained, be in any doubt or in any way mistaken about the fact. I cannot be unsure whether I feel a headache, nor can I think that I feel a headache when I do not.[4]

A. J. Ayer, *The Problem of Knowledge*,
London: Macmillan & Co., 1956, p. 55

Besides what is logically certain there are a number of immediately known propositions which we can regard as absolutely certain although there would be no self-contradiction in denying them. In this class I put more specific propositions based on introspection. I cannot see any self-contradiction in supposing that I might make mistakes in introspection; and there is therefore no *logical* absurdity in supposing that I might be mistaken now when I judge that I feel warm or that I have a visual presentation of a table. But I still cannot help being absolutely certain of the truth of these propositions and I do not think that I ought to be otherwise. . . . As we have seen, it is however hardly possible to claim this absolute certainty for judgments about physical objects, and, as we shall see, there are similar difficulties in claiming it for judgments about minds other than one's own.

A. C. Ewing, *The Fundamental Questions of Philosophy,* ch. V

I think the facts that give rise to the illusion of privacy would be the following: (a) you can be *in doubt* as to whether I am in pain, but I can-

[4] It should be noted that this passage sets forth a view that Ayer is examining rather than propounding.

not; (b) you can *find out* whether I am in pain, but I cannot; and (c) you can be *mistaken* as to whether I am in pain, but I cannot.

N. Malcolm, "The Privacy of Experience," in A. Stroll, ed., *op. cit.,* p. 146

But there is also a sense in which a person's report that he sees an after-image *cannot* be mistaken; and it is this sense that I intend when I say that his report is "incorrigible."

N. Malcolm, "Direct Perception," in *Knowledge and Certainty,* p. 85

Among the incorrigible statements are statements about "private" experiences and mental events, e.g., pain statements, statements about mental images, reports of thought, and so on. These are incorrigible in the sense that if a person sincerely asserts such a statement it does not make sense to suppose, and nothing could be accepted as showing, that he is mistaken, i.e., that what he says is false.

S. Shoemaker, *Self-Knowledge and Self-Identity,* Ithaca, N.Y.: Cornell U. Press, 1963, pp. 215–216

All of these quotations represent one's epistemic position *vis-à-vis* one's own mental states (or some subclass thereof) as highly favorable in some way or other. In most of the passages quoted there is no contrast explicitly drawn with the epistemic position of other persons, but such a contrast is implicit in what is said. None of these philosophers would suppose that other persons have the kind of cognitive access to my mental states which they impute to me; hence by being in this kind of position one enjoys a kind of special epistemic privilege.

How many distinguishable types of favorable epistemic position are involved in these passages? One type that is clearly imputed in several of the quotations is the impossibility of mistake. Thus one's judgments or beliefs about his own mental states "cannot be false" (Descartes), "are not subject to any possible error" (Lewis), "cannot . . .be . . .in any way mistaken" (Ayer), "it does not make sense to suppose that he is mistaken" (Shoemaker). A great many terms have been used for this kind of epistemic privilege. I prefer "infallibility."

There is also much talk in these passages about immunity from doubt (Descartes, Hamilton, Lewis, Ayer, Ewing, Malcolm). But we can distinguish several different indubitability claims, each of which can be attributed to one or more of our authors. First there is the claim that it is impossible to *entertain a doubt* as to the truth of a proposition attributing a current mental state to oneself. I am *incapable of being in doubt* as to whether I am now thinking about my lecture for tomorrow, or whether there is now an image of my boyhood home before my mind's eye. This impossibility might be logical, or it might be nomological (based, e.g., on psychological laws). Malcolm in the first quotation is clearly asserting the former, for he asserts the three points as facts about the "grammar" of the word "pain"; because of the way we use the word, no sense can be attached to speaking of a person having a doubt as to whether he is in pain. On the other hand Lewis might be plausibly interpreted as claiming that it is a psychological impossibility for one to doubt whether he is currently in some conscious state.

However, we can also discern a quite different concept of indubitability at work in these authors. This is a normative rather than a factual concept—not the impossibility of being, in fact, in a psychological state of doubt, but rather the impossibility of having any grounds for doubt, the impossibility of a rational doubt. In our quoted material this comes out most clearly in the passage from Hamilton. What he is arguing there, in the spirit of Descartes, is not so much that there are psychological bars to the formation of a doubt, but rather that such a doubt would necessarily lack any foundation, since it presupposes that which is called into question, viz., the fact of consciousness.[5] Again, if, as we shall argue later, we can take Ewing to be using "certainty" as equivalent to "indubitability," he clearly distinguishes our two main senses of indubitability and asserts both. "But I still cannot help being absolutely certain of the truth of these propositions and I do not think that I ought to be otherwise." That is, I find it psychologically impossible to have any doubt of their truth, and I am justified in this incapacity, since there could be no grounds for any doubt.

Thus we have distinguished three forms of indubitability: logical impossibility of entertaining a doubt, psychological impossibility of entertaining a doubt, impossibility of there being any grounds for doubt. Although for any of them it is worth considering whether propositions about one's own current mental states are indubitable in that sense, still it is only the third that constitutes a distinctively *epistemic* privilege. If I am so related to a certain group of propositions that whenever I believe one of those propositions to be true, there can be no grounds for doubt that it is true, then I am in a very favorable position to obtain knowledge in this sphere; for, unlike the usual situation, whatever I believe, no one can have any justification for refusing to accept my belief as true. But that means that I have every right to accept the proposition; so that in this sphere, each and every one of my beliefs will automatically count as knowledge. This is certainly to be in a highly favorable epistemic posi-

[5] The merits of Hamilton's argument, and any other *substantive* question concerning privileged access, are not within the jurisdiction of this article.

tion. On the other hand, the mere fact that I find it psychologically impossible to doubt the truth of any such proposition does not in itself confer any cognitive superiority. We can think of many cases where people are unable to entertain doubts about certain matters, and where we regard this as a liability rather than an asset. Very small children are often unable to imagine that what their parents say is mistaken, and religious fanatics are sometimes psychologically unable to doubt the tenets of their sect. We do not take such people to be thereby in a better position for acquiring knowledge; quite the contrary, we suppose this critical incapacity to be hampering them in the cognitive enterprise. To be sure, when the second sort of indubitability is imputed to propositions about one's own mental states, it is supposed that this holds for all men as such, and it may be thought that this renders inappropriate an epithet such as "lack of critical faculty" which one might suppose to be applicable only when the disability in question is peculiar to certain stages of development, types of personality, or kinds of social groups. Nevertheless, if we suppose that a universally shared psychological inability to doubt confers some advantage in the acquisition of knowledge, it is only because we think that this *psychological* inability is conjoined with, and perhaps is a reflection of, indubitability in the normative sense, the impossibility of any *grounds* for doubt. If it *should* be the case that the psychological impossibility of doubting the truth of one's beliefs about one's own current mental states is due to an ingrained weakness in the human critical apparatus, or to an irresistible partiality to one's own case, then this inability would *not* indicate any first person epistemic advantage in these matters.

We shall have to make the same judgment concerning Malcolm's thesis of the logical impossibility of entertaining a doubt. Suppose we grant that the meanings we attach to our conscious state terms are such that it makes no sense to suppose that a given person is in doubt as to whether he is currently in a certain kind of conscious state. That would be a noteworthy feature of our conceptual scheme, but we still have to ask whether or not it is well founded. Unless we accept normative indubitability, or some other principle according to which a person is in a particularly favorable position to discriminate true from false propositions concerning his present conscious states, then we will have to conclude that the features of our "logical grammar" to which Malcolm alludes are ill-advised; and that the fact that this "logical grammar" is as it is does nothing to show that persons are in a specially favorable epistemic position *vis-à-vis* their own current conscious states.

Thus I conclude that normative indubitability is the only variety that clearly constitutes a cognitive advantage. We shall henceforth restrict the term "indubitability" to that variety.

We might think of indubitability as a weaker version of infallibility. To be infallible *vis-à-vis* one's present conscious states is to be in such a position that no belief one has to the effect that one is in such a state *can* be mistaken. Whereas an indubitability thesis does not commit one to the impossibility of mistakes, but to the weaker claim that no one could have grounds for questioning the accuracy of one's belief. There is a still weaker derivative of infallibility that can be found in the literature, though more rarely. It is set out clearly in the following passage from A. J. Ayer's British Academy lecture on "Privacy."

> If this is correct, it provides us with a satisfactory model for the logic of the statements that a person may make about his present thoughts and feelings. He may not be infallible, but still his word is sovereign. The logic of these statements that a person makes about himself is such that if others were to contradict him we should not be entitled to say that they were right so long as he honestly maintained his stand against them.[6]

What Ayer is saying here is that it is impossible that anyone else should show that I am mistaken in what I say (believe) about my present thoughts and feelings. This is an inherent impossibility, for the "logic of these statements" requires us to give the person in question the last word. We may term this kind of epistemic position "incorrigibility."[7] Incorrigibility is weaker than indubitability, for whereas the latter rules out the possibility of any grounds for doubt, however weak, the former only rules out someone else's having grounds for the contradictory that are so strong as to be sufficient to *show* that I was mistaken.[8]

"Certainty" is another term that figures prominently in our quotations. A person's judgments concerning his own mental states are said to exhibit the highest degree of certainty; one can be *absolutely* certain about such matters (Descartes, Locke, Ewing). How are we to interpret these claims *vis-a-vis* the others we have been considering? Here too we may distinguish factual and normative senses. Being certain of something may be construed as a matter of feeling assurance, feeling confident that one is correct; this is presumably the reverse side of the (*de facto*) absence

[6] A. J. Ayer, "Privacy," in *op. cit.*, p. 73.

[7] The use of this term presents the usual chaotic picture. We have seen Malcolm and Shoemaker using it to mean infallibility. Thomas Nagel in his essay, "Physicalism," (*The Philosophical Review*, vol. 74 [1965], p. 344) uses it to mean what I shall next be distinguishing as "omniscience." I believe that the present usage is a more apt one.

[8] It may be contended, e.g., by partisans of the "private language argument," that there is no significant difference between an impossibility of anyone else's showing that I am mistaken and an impossibility of my being mistaken. I am unable to go into those issues in this paper.

of doubt. To feel complete confidence that one is correct is to entertain no doubt about the matter. And a psychological (logical) impossibility of the entertaining of any doubt would be the same thing as a psychological (logical) necessity of feeling completely assured that one is correct. Thus this kind of certainty comes under the scope of the arguments just given to dismiss the corresponding forms of indubitability from further consideration.

However there is also a normative concept of certainty, a concept employed by Ewing when after saying "I still cannot help being absolutely certain of the truth of these propositions" he adds, ". . . and I do not think that I ought to be otherwise." To be certain in this sense is to be justified in feeling complete assurance. How is this normative concept related to the modes of epistemic superiority already distinguished? It seems impossible to make a general identification of normative certainty with any of the other modes. To be justified in feeling complete assurance that *S* is to have a very strong warrant for one's belief that *S*. But views may differ as to just how strong a warrant is required: the strongest conceivable, the strongest one could reasonably ask for in the subject matter under consideration, and so on. Thus the general concept of normative certainty is really a sort of family or continuum of concepts, differing as to the chosen locus along the dimension of strength of warrants for belief. Whereas our other modes of epistemic superiority are not subject to variations in degree; they are absolute concepts. If one's belief is indubitable, *no* doubt can have any basis: if one is infallible, one's belief must be *wholly* correct; and so on.[9]

But although we cannot make any general identification of the concept of normative certainty with the other modes of epistemic superiority we have distinguished, still I think that the degree of certainty typically ascribed to one's beliefs about one's own mental states amounts either to infallibility or to indubitability. Sometimes it is claimed (Descartes, Locke) that such beliefs enjoy the highest conceivable certainty; in that case one is in effect ascribing infallibility, for the highest warrant one could conceive for a belief is one which would render the falsity of the belief *impossible*. In other cases something weaker is being claimed; thus Ewing conjoins his assertion of certainty with the admission that "there is no self-contradiction in supposing that I might make mistakes in introspection." However, in such cases it is plausible to suppose that a

[9] One could, of course, construct degree-concept derivatives of these absolute concepts. Thus one could distinguish various degrees of immunity to rational doubt, depending on what kinds of doubts are excluded, how strong or weak the grounds would have to be, and so on. However, so far as I know, such degree concepts are not in fact employed in connection with the present topic.

warrant strong enough to exclude all grounds for doubt is being imputed, and hence that what is being ascribed is indubitability. Thus I do not feel that we need "certainty" as a separate item in our list.

We have still not exhausted the conceptual riches of our initial list of quotations. Going back to the passage from Hume, we note that he not only says of "actions and sensations of the mind" that they "must necessarily . . . be what they appear," which is infallibility, but that they "must necessarily appear in every particular what they are." In other words, it is not only that every belief or judgment which I form about my present mental states must be correct; it is also necessary that every feature of those states must find representation in those (necessarily correct) beliefs. *Ignorance* as well as *error* is excluded. Let us use the term "omniscience" for the logical impossibility of ignorance concerning a certain subject-matter. Although the Hume quotation contains the only omniscience claim in our original list, we can find other passages in which it is asserted that one is omniscient *vis-à-vis* his own mental states.

> It requires only to be stated to be admitted, that when I know, I must know that I know,—when I feel, I must know that I feel,—when I desire, I must know that I desire. The knowledge, the feelings, the desire, are possible only under the condition of being known, and being known by me.[10]
>
> Thinking and perceiving are essentially conscious processes, which means that they cannot be said to occur unless the person to whom they are ascribed knows that they occur.[11]

We can better represent and interrelate the modes of epistemic privilege we have distinguished, and will be distinguishing, if we have a standard formula for favorable epistemic positions, a formula containing blanks such that when these blanks are filled in differently we get specifications of different modes. One might at first suppose that our formula could simply be: *X*'s knowledge of ———— is ————, where the first blank is filled with a specification of the subject-matter, and the second blank with a specification of a particular mode of cognitive superiority—infallibility, omniscience, or whatever. However this will not work, since it is not in general true that the modes we are distinguishing are features of pieces of knowledge, features which a given piece of knowledge might or might not have. This is particularly clear with respect to infallibility and omniscience. We cannot first ascertain that *P* knows that *S*, and then go on to ask whether that bit of *P*'s knowledge is or is

[10] Sir William Hamilton, *op. cit.*, Lect. XI, p. 133.

[11] D. Locke, *Myself and Others*, ch. II, p. 17.

not infallible or omniscient. The reason is somewhat different in the two cases. Infallibility in the sense of *cannot be mistaken* is a feature necessarily possessed by every piece of *knowledge* in a strong sense of "knowledge." That is, it would not be correct to attribute knowledge that *S* to *P* unless *P*'s supposition that *S* were correct. That is part of what we mean by "know." If I do not feel elated now, then that is enough to (logically) rule out the possibility that I, or anyone else, know that I am elated now. Thus infallibility does not constitute a feature that distinguishes one kind of *knowledge* from another. With omniscience (in a certain area) on the other hand, the point is that this is a feature of one's position with respect to the possession or non-possession of knowledge (of certain matters), rather than a feature of any particular instance of such knowledge; it is a matter of what kinds of knowledge one (necessarily) has, rather than a matter of the character of that knowledge once obtained.

But although infallibility and omniscience are not characteristics that (may) attach to some pieces of knowledge and not to others, they clearly have something to do with knowledge. They are, in some way, features of one's epistemic position, powers, or status, *vis-à-vis* some domain of knowledge. Perhaps we can find an illuminating way of representing these modes of privileged access if we dig into the structure of the concept of knowledge, rather than just using it in an unanalyzed form. For our purposes we can work with the following familiar tripartite analysis of "*P* knows that *S*." The analysans consists of a conjunction of the following:

A. *P* believes that *S*.
B. *P* is justified in believing that *S*.
C. It is the case that *S*.[12]

As for infallibility, although a piece of knowledge is not the sort of thing that may or may not be capable of error, there is, according to the above analysis, a constituent of *P*'s knowledge that *S* which may or may not be capable of error, viz., *P*'s belief that *S*.[13] Thus one can be said

[12] Recent criticism has shown that this analysis is not generally adequate without some modification. See, e.g., E. L. Gettier, "Is Justified True Belief Knowledge?" *Analysis*, vol. 23 (1962–63), pp. 121–123. However these difficulties do not attach to the sorts of cases with which we are concerned in this paper, and so we may take the above as a sufficient approximation for present purposes.

[13] It will be noted that in the previous discussion we were already presenting infallibility as an impossibility of error for one's *beliefs* or *judgments*.

to be infallible *vis-à-vis* a certain subject matter provided one cannot be mistaken in any beliefs he forms concerning that subject matter.

> A person enjoys infallibility[14] *vis-à-vis* his own mental states $=_{\text{df}}$. It is logically impossible that a belief of his about his own mental states should be mistaken.

Now if one is so situated relative to a given belief, he is amply, indeed maximally, *justified* in holding that belief. For one could hardly have a stronger (epistemic) justification for holding a certain belief than the logical impossibility of the belief's being mistaken. Hence where the mere possession of the belief logically guarantees truth, it equally guarantees the belief's being justified, i.e., it guarantees the satisfaction of both the other two conditions for knowledge. Hence we can just as well state our definition as follows (generalizing now over subject-matters, so as not to restrict the general concept of infallibility to the topic of one's own mental states):

> (D1) *P* (a person) enjoys infallibility with respect to a type of proposition, $R =_{\text{df}}$. For any proposition, *S*, of type *R*, it is logically impossible that *P* should believe that *S*, without knowing that *S*. (Condition A. for *P*'s knowing that *S* logically implies conditions B. and C.)

The philosophers who shy away from speaking of a person's *knowing* that he has certain thoughts and sensations will probably be even more leary of speaking of a person's *believing* that he has a certain thought or sensation. And it must be admitted that one does not ordinarily speak in this vein. But, so far as I can see, this is simply because we ordinarily use the word "belief" in such a way that it contrasts with knowledge, as in the following dialogue:

> What was that noise in the kitchen?
> I believe that the tap was leaking.
> You *believe* it was leaking! Couldn't you see whether it was or not?

In this paper, as quite frequently in philosophy, we are using the word in a wider sense. This sense can be indicated by making it explicit that a sufficient condition for *P*'s believing that *S* is that *P* would have a tendency to assert that *S* if he were asked whether it were the case that *S*,

14 We use this cumbersome locution rather than the more natural "is infallible," so that our standard form will be usable for concepts such as indubitability that are not predicated of persons.

if he understood the question, and if he were disposed to be sincere. In this wider sense one often believes that he has certain thoughts and feelings. At this point the Wittgensteinian will, no doubt, cavil at the idea that one can correctly be said to *assert* that he has a certain feeling, but I cannot pursue the controversy further in this paper.

Omniscience can be given a parallel formulation as follows:

(D2) *P* enjoys omniscience *vis-à-vis* a type of proposition $R =_{df.}$ For any true proposition, *S*, of type *R*, it is logically impossible that *P* should not know that *S*. (Condition C. for *P*'s knowing that *S* logically implies conditions A. and B.)[15]

Thus this familiar analysis of knowledge permits us to give a neat presentation of the infallibility-omniscience distinction. They differ just as to which of the three conditions for knowledge entails the other two.[16] Indubitability does not fit into the model in quite so neat a fashion, but of course it can be represented there. To say that one's beliefs in a certain area are immune from doubt is just to say that given any such belief, it is impossible for anyone to have any grounds for doubting that the other two conditions for knowledge hold. Again, in the first instance, indubitability entails that there can be no grounds for doubting that one belief is true (condition C.); but if that is the case, then surely no one can have any grounds for doubting that one is justified in holding one's belief.

(D3) *P* enjoys indubitability *vis-à-vis* a type of proposition, $R =_{df.}$ For any proposition, *S*, of type *R*, it is logically impossible that *P* should believe that *S* and that anyone should have any grounds for doubting that *P* knows that *S*. (Condition A. for *P*'s knowing that *S* logically implies that there can be no grounds for doubting that conditions B. and C. hold.)

Incorrigibility can be given a similar formulation as follows:

(D4) *P* enjoys incorrigibility *vis-à-vis* a type of proposition, $R =_{df.}$ For any proposition, *S*, of type *R*, it is logically impossible that *P* should believe that *S* and that someone should show that *P* is mistaken in this

[15] Here too we might build up this formulation by first thinking of the fact that *S* (condition C.) entailing belief that *S* (condition A.), and then deriving the entailment of condition B. from that. For if a certain range of facts is such that it is impossible for such a fact to obtain without my believing that it does, it would seem clear that any such belief would be amply warranted. It would be amply warranted since it inevitably stems from the fact believed in.

[16] For a similar presentation, see D. M. Armstrong, *A Materialist Theory of the Mind* (London, 1968), p. 101.

belief. (Condition A. for *P*'s knowing that *S* logically implies that no one else can show that condition C. does not hold.)[17, 18]

Having now defined four different favorable epistemic positions in which a person may be *vis-à-vis* a given range of propositions, we can use these concepts to specify four ways in which a person may be said to have privileged access to his current mental states. To say that a person has *privileged* access to his current mental states is to say that his epistemic position *vis-à-vis* propositions ascribing current mental states to himself is favorable in a way no one else's position is. The simplest standard formula for a privileged access claim would be:

> Each person enjoys ——— *vis-à-vis* propositions ascribing current mental states to himself, while no one else enjoys ——— *vis-à-vis* such propositions.

By successively filling in the blank with the four terms we have defined, we get four different privileged access theses.

However, it will be useful in our further discussions to have the different versions of a privileged access thesis spelled out more explicitly, with the content of the chosen mode of favorable epistemic position explicitly represented. We can give these more explicit formulations as follows:

(T1) (Infallibility) Each person is so related to propositions ascribing current mental states to himself that it is logically impossible for him to believe that such a proposition is true without knowing it to be true; while no one else is so related to such propositions.

(T2) (Omniscience) Each person is so related to propositions ascribing current mental states to himself that it is logically impossible for such a proposition to be true without his knowing that it is true; while no one else is so related to such propositions.

[17] It will be noted that all these definitions have been stated in terms of logical modalities. Later we shall explore the possibility of employing other modalities.

[18] We could, of course, make incorrigibility more parallel with the other modes by construing it to involve also the impossibility of anyone else's showing that *P* is not justified in believing that *S*. However, since this goes beyond what is either stated by our sources, or implied by what they say, I have avoided strengthening it in this way. It is clear that an impossibility of anyone else's showing that I am mistaken does not necessarily carry with it an impossibility of showing that my belief is unjustified. And this general possibility of dissociation might conceivably apply to beliefs about one's own mental states. It is conceivable, e.g., that one might show, through psychoanalysis, that I have a general tendency to deceive myself about my attitudes toward my daughter. This might well be taken to show that I am not justified in what I believe about those attitudes, even though no one is able to show (conclusively) that any particular belief I have about those attitudes is mistaken.

(T3) (Indubitability) Each person is so related to propositions ascribing current mental states to himself that it is logically impossible both for him to believe that such a proposition is true and for anyone to have any grounds for doubting that he knows that proposition to be true; while no one else is so related to such propositions.

(T4) (Incorrigibility) Each person is so related to propositions ascribing current mental states to himself that it is logically impossible both for him to believe that such a proposition is true and for someone else to show that that proposition is false; while no one else is so related to such propositions.

III

As I pointed out earlier, it is not my aim in this work to determine in just what way, if any, one does have privileged access to just what kinds of mental states. However it may help to motivate our consideration of other modes of privileged access if we briefly allude to some of the considerations that have led many thinkers to reject the modes so far considered. If we think of the range of mental states as including dispositional (belief, desire) as well as phenomenal (sensations, thoughts, feelings) states, there would seem to be strong reasons for denying that one enjoys infallibility, omniscience, indubitability, or incorrigibility *vis-à-vis* all the items within this range. The most dramatic reasons come from the sorts of cases highlighted by psycho-analysis, in which one hides certain of one's desires or beliefs from oneself, and in the process attributes to oneself desires or beliefs that one does not have. Thus consider the classic overprotective mother, who is preventing her daughter from going out in society in order to prevent her from developing into a feared rival. This mother stoutly and sincerely denies wanting to prevent her daughter's development and believing that her policy is likely to lead to any such result. Instead, she says, she is motivated solely by a desire to protect her daughter from harm. It certainly does seem at least possible that there are such cases in which the person both has desires and beliefs without knowing that he has them and attributes to himself desires and beliefs he does not have (at least not to the extent he supposes). Moreover, in such cases other people will have substantial grounds for doubting what the woman says about the desires and beliefs in question, and it even seems possible that others may sometimes be in a position to *show* (using realistic standards for this) that she is mistaken; so that not even indubitability or incorrigibility hold for beliefs and desires.

There is no doubt that proponents of these modes of privileged access are in a stronger position with respect to phenomenal states. I do not feel that this issue is definitely settled by a long way, but there are substantial negative arguments here.[19] For example, a general argument against infallibility is that knowledge of particular facts essentially involves the application of general concepts to those facts and hence is inherently liable to error. At the very least these negative arguments provide a stimulus to consider whether there is not some weaker sense in which a person might be said to be in a necessarily superior epistemic position *vis-à-vis* his own mental states.

Another candidate that is well represented in the literature is "immediacy" or "directness." The notion that a person is privileged in having *immediate* knowledge of his own mental states is expressed incidentally in several of our original quotations. Thus Brentano says that the perception of mental phenomena is "immediately evident"; Ewing speaks of propositions based on introspection as "immediately known"; Hume speaks of our consciousness of the "actions and sensations of the mind" as that domain of experience where we are "most intimately conscious." Immediacy is closer to the center of the stage in the following quotations.

> It has been suggested, namely, that any entity, which *can be directly known by one mind only* is a mental entity, and is "in the mind" of the person in question, and also, conversely, that all mental entities can be directly known only by a single mind.[20]
>
> It is one such essential feature of what the word "mind" means that minds are private; that one's own mind is something with which one is directly acquainted—nothing more so—but that the mind of another is something which one is unable directly to inspect.[21]

The terms "immediate" and "direct" are susceptible of a variety of interpretations. Malcolm, in his essay, "Direct Perception,"[22] maintains that "impossibility of error" is the main feature of the standard philosophical conception of direct perception (p. 89). He cites several eminent philosophers in support of this claim, including Berkeley, Moore, and Lewis. He then goes on to construct the following definition: "*A directly* perceives *x* if and only if *A*'s assertion that he perceives *x* could not be mistaken; . . ." (*loc. cit.*). Of course if this is what we mean by directness, we have already discussed it under the heading of infallibility. We are therefore led to look for some other interpretation.

19 For some recent presentation of such arguments, see D. M. Armstrong, *op. cit.*, ch. 6, sect. 10; and B. Aune, *Knowledge, Mind, and Nature* (New York, 1967), ch. II, sect. 1.

20 G. E. Moore, "The Subject Matter of Psychology," in Vesey, *op. cit.*, p. 241.

21 C. I. Lewis, "Some Logical Considerations Concerning the Mental," in Vesey, *op. cit.*, p. 332.

22 In *Knowledge and Certainty*, *op. cit.*

Moore, in typical fashion, tries to explain "direct knowledge" by pointing to a certain not further analyzable feature of our conscious experience. Immediately following the passage quoted above he writes:

> By "direct knowledge" is here meant the kind of relation we have to a colour, when we actually see it, or to a sound when we actually hear it.

But if we simply leave the matter there it is not very satisfactory. Presumably *something* can be said about the relation one has to a color when one actually sees it. And if it is not made explicit what the relation(s) in question is, we shall have no basis for resolving controversies over whether something or other is (or can be) directly known, whether, e.g., one directly knows that one has a certain belief, or whether it is conceivable that another person could directly know one's own thoughts. Let us try to find something more explicit.

Talk about immediate knowledge has traditionally been powerfully influenced by a spatial-causal model of mediacy. When people deny that perceptual knowledge of physical objects is immediate, it is often on the grounds that there is a spatial and causal gap between my knowledge (or rather the beliefs and/or sense-impressions involved) and the object of knowledge—the tree or whatever. There are spatial and causal intermediaries involved, and if these are not aligned properly, things can be thrown off. Similarly there are causal and spatial intermediaries between my desire or feeling and your belief that I have that desire or feeling. Your belief (in the most favorable case) is evoked by some perceptions of yours, which are in turn evoked by some behavior of mine, which is in turn evoked by my desire or feeling. But when it comes to my knowledge of my desires or feelings, no such intermediaries are involved, and here we do not have the same possibilities of distortion. I am "right up next to" my own mental states; I am "directly aware" of them; they give rise to my knowledge without going through a causal chain of any sort. Let us call immediacy so construed "causal immediacy."

The main reason for not using this sense of "immediacy" here is that we do not know how to determine either spatial or causal directness for knowledge of one's own mental states. We are not able to assign precise spatial locations to mental states.[23] Insofar as such location is possible, it is something rough, like "in the body," or "in the head," or maybe "in the brain." For the other cases that is enough for a judgment

[23] I am not maintaining, like some opponents of the identity theory, that such determinations are logically impossible. I am merely pointing out that at present we lack the resources for doing so.

of mediacy; as long as my belief that there is a tree out there is somewhere in my head, it is clearly not spatially contiguous to the tree; and as long as your desire is in your head and my belief that you have that desire is in my head, then they are not spatially contiguous (even if our heads are touching). But when both the belief and the object of the belief are mental states of the same person, we would need a more precise method of location to determine whether or not they are spatially contiguous. They are both "in the head", but just where in the head? Similar comments can be made concerning judgments of causal immediacy. With no more precise assumption than that the immediate causal antecedents of a belief of mine consist of processes in the brain, I can be sure that no belief of mine has its immediate causal antecedents in a tree. But if I am to determine whether my desire to go to Europe is an immediate causal antecedent of my belief that I have a desire to go to Europe, I need to have a more fine-grained view of the causal processes involved, and unfortunately we do not have any such view. We are in almost total ignorance of the causal processes, if any, involved in the origin of beliefs about our own mental states, and so we simply do not know what intermediaries there may be.

The upshot of this discussion is that although we can have sufficient reasons for terming many cases of knowledge "mediate" in the causal sense, we can have no assurance that any particular kind of knowledge is causally *immediate,* for when we come to the only plausible candidates for such immediacy, we do not know enough about the spatial and causal relations involved (if any) to have any basis for the denial of intermediaries. Thus our criterion is quite unworkable if we interpret it in terms of causal immediacy. It will be noted that we have argued for this without casting doubt on the intelligibility of the term "causal immediacy." Such a doubt could be raised, but that is another story.

There is a more distinctively epistemic sense of the mediate-immediate contrast, a sense that is suggested by such talk as the following. "You can know what I am thinking and feeling only *through* something (some signs, indications, criteria, or whatever); your knowledge of my thoughts and feelings is *based on* something else you know." But I, by contrast, know directly what I am thinking and feeling. I don't have to "derive" this knowledge from anything else. Let's say that in the sense of the contrast suggested by these remarks, mediate knowledge is, while immediate knowledge is not, *based on* other knowledge.

However the term "based on" does not wear a unique interpretation on its face. It is often used in such a way that to say that my knowledge that *S* is based on my knowledge that *T* is to say that I arrived at the knowledge that *S* by inferring *S* from *T*. Thus philosophers have often used the presence or absence of inference as the crucial consideration in deciding whether a given piece of knowledge is to be called "direct" or "indirect."

> I affirm, for example, that I hear a man's voice. This would pass, in common language, for a direct perception. All, however, which is really perception, is that I hear a sound. That the sound is a voice, and that voice the voice of a man, are not perceptions but inferences.[24]

However, it is clear that this contrast in terms of inference is not going to make the desired discriminations if we confine ourselves to conscious inference. The perception of speech does not ordinarily involve a conscious inference from the existence of a sound (under some acoustical description) to the existence of a human voice as its source. And more to the present point, it is clear that one's knowledge of the mental states of others is not always mediate if conscious inference is a necessary condition of mediacy. Quite often when I see that my companion feels dejected I am not aware of performing any inference from specifiable features of his speech, demeanor, and bearing to his dejection. And we certainly want to develop a concept of mediacy which is such that our ordinary knowledge of the mental states of others counts as mediate. Hence if we are going to make the desired discriminations in terms of the presence or absence of inference, we are going to have to rely heavily on the postulation of unconscious inference. I would not wish to subscribe to any general ban on such postulation, and it may be that we are justified in postulating unconscious inferences in just those cases where they are needed to discriminate between mediate and immediate knowledge along the present lines. However, in view of the obscurities surrounding the concept of unconscious inferential processes, and in view of present uncertainties concerning the conditions under which the postulations of such processes is justified, it would seem desirable to search for some other interpretation of "based on."

I would suggest that the tripartite analysis of knowledge introduced earlier provides us with the materials for such an interpretation. Using that schema we can distinguish between mediate and immediate knowledge in terms of what satisfies the second condition. If what justifies *P* in believing that *S* is some other knowledge that *P* possesses, then his knowledge is mediated by (based on) that other knowledge in a strictly epistemological sense. If, on the other hand, what satisfies condition (B.)

[24] J. S. Mill, *A System of Logic,* Bk. IV, ch. 1, sect. 2. Quoted by N. Malcolm, "Direct Perception," p. 88.

is something other than *P*'s having some knowledge or other, we can say that his knowledge that *S* is *im*mediate, not based on other knowledge. Let us call this kind of immediacy "epistemic immediacy." If I know that there was a fire last night at the corner of Huron and 5th because I read it in the *Ann Arbor News*, my knowledge is mediate; since what warrants me in believing that there is such a fire is my knowledge that such a fire was reported in the *Ann Arbor News*, plus my knowledge that it is a reliable source for local news. (The fact that the *Ann Arbor News did* carry this story and the fact that it *is* reliable in such matters will not justify *me* in believing that the fire took place, unless *I* know them to be the case.) Again if I know that my brother is dissatisfied with his job because he has complained to me about it, what warrants me in believing that he is dissatisfied is my knowledge that he has been complaining about it (and means what he says). On the other hand, it seems overwhelmingly plausible to suppose that what warrants me in believing that I feel disturbed, or am thinking about the mind-body problem, is not some other knowledge that I have. There is no bit of knowledge, or disjunction of bits of knowledge, such that if I do not have it (or some of them) my belief is not warranted. What would such bits of knowledge be? This is reflected in the oft-cited, but almost as often misunderstood,[25] fact that it "sounds odd,"or even "nonsensical" to respond to a person who has just told us how he feels or what he is thinking, with "What reason do you have for saying that?" or "What is your evidence for that?" One does not know how to answer such a question; there is no answer to give.

This characterization of "immediate" is purely negative. It specifies what sort of thing does *not* satisfy condition B. where the knowledge is immediate, but it does not further limit the field of alternative possibilities. Clearly we can have different sorts of immediate knowledge claims depending on what is taken to satisfy condition B. If we consider the most explicit claims to immediate knowledge of one's own mental states in the literature, those of Ayer and Shoemaker, we shall see that in both cases condition C. is taken to imply condition B.

> This gives us the clue also to what may be meant by saying that knowledge of this kind is direct. In other cases where knowledge is claimed, it is not sufficient that one be able to give a true report of what one claims to know: it is necessary also that the claim be authorized, and this is done

[25] It is misunderstood when it is taken to show that it makes no sense to speak of a person knowing that he feels disturbed, rather than taken to show what kind of knowledge this is.

> by adducing some other statement which in some way supports the statement for which the claim is made. But in this case no such authority is needed; . . . Our knowledge of our thoughts and feelings accrues to us automatically in the sense that having them puts us in a position and gives us the authority to report them.[26]
>
> . . . it is characteristic of a certain kind of statements, what I there called "first-person experience statements," that being entitled to assert such a statement does not consist in having established that the statement is true, i.e., in having good evidence that it is true or having observed that it is true, but consists simply in the statement's *being* true.[27]

Let us use the term "truth-sufficiency" for the sort of epistemic position described by these authors. We can put this notion into our standard format as follows:

(D5) *P* enjoys truth-sufficiency *vis-à-vis* a type of proposition, $R =_{df}$. For any true proposition, *S*, of type *R*, it is logically impossible that *P* should not be justified in believing that *S*. (Condition C. for *P*'s knowing that *S* logically implies condition B.)[28]

The privileged access thesis that makes use of this concept can be formulated as follows.

(T5) (Truth-sufficiency) Each person is so related to propositions ascribing current mental states to himself that it is logically impossible both for such a proposition to be true and for him not to be justified in believing it to be true; while no one else is so related to such propositions.

Knowledge involving truth-sufficiency is a sort of limiting case of direct knowledge; for here what is taken to justify the belief is something that is independently required for knowledge, viz., the truth of the belief. Thus nothing over and above the other two conditions for knowledge is required for the satisfaction of condition B., and so B. becomes, in a way, vacuous. We may call cases of knowledge in which nothing is

26 "Privacy," in *The Concept of a Person*, p. 64.

27 S. Shoemaker, *op. cit.*, p. 216.

28 This is the first time we have envisaged an implication of condition B. while the question of the satisfaction of condition A. is left undecided. It may seem that this is impossible, on the grounds that B. presupposes that A. is satisfied. How can I be justified in having a belief that I do not have? To make the three conditions logically independent, we shall have to interpret B. as: "P is in such a position that he will thereby be justified in believing that *S* if he has such a belief."

required to satisfy B. over and above the other conditions for knowledge, "autonomous" knowledge.[29]

However, one can hold that a certain kind of knowledge is direct without considering it to be autonomous. Whenever condition B. is satisfied by something other than the possession of one or more pieces of other *knowledge* by the person in question, *and* this something goes beyond the other conditions for knowledge, we have knowledge that is direct but not autonomous. Thus a "direct realist," who denies that one's perceptual knowledge of physical objects is based on an epistemically prior knowledge of sense data, will think of perceptual knowledge as direct in the present sense of that term. However, he will certainly not think that nothing but the truth of *S* (a proposition describing a perceivable state of affairs) is required to justify a perceptual belief in *S*. The mere fact that it is true that there is now a fire in my living room fireplace does not justify me in believing this, and more specifically does not justify me in accepting it as a perceptual belief. I shall not be so justified if I am out of sensory range of the fire, if, e.g., there is a thick wall between me and the living room, or if my sense organs are not functioning properly. Thus justifiability will at least require the belief that *S* to have resulted from the normal operation of one's sense organs and central nervous system, as set into operation by stimuli from *S*. Perceptual knowledge so construed is direct but not autonomous.

In the light of these distinctions we can see that Ayer and Shoemaker have an inadequate conception of the alternatives to their version of direct knowledge. Let us recall that Ayer says:

> In other cases where knowledge is claimed, it is not sufficient that one be able to give a true report of what one claims to know: it is necessary also that the claim be authorized, and this is done by adducing some other statement which in some way supports the statement for which the claim is made.

Ayer is constrasting (his version of) *autonomous* knowledge with mediate knowledge, ignoring the intermediate category of knowledge that is

[29] Actually the concepts of infallibility and omniscience, as we have introduced them, satisfy our criteria for both directness and autonomy. If one is infallible or omniscient relative to a type of proposition, *R*, then when one knows that *S*, where *S* is an instance of that type, one's knowledge is both direct and autonomous. For what satisfied condition B. is, in the case of infallibility, condition A., and, in the case of omniscience, condition C. In considering autonomy as an alternative to infallibility and omniscience, we are restricting ourselves to cases in which one of the other conditions is sufficient for B., but not also sufficient for the third condition. We could, of course, build that further restriction into a definition of autonomy, but there will be no need to do so, since our list of modes of privileged access will not contain autonomy as such.

direct but not autonomous. As our reference to the direct realist view of perception shows, there may be additional "authorizations" required where these "authorizations" do not consist in the putative knower's having some other knowledge that can count as evidence for *S*. Shoemaker is a bit more inclusive; he gives as alternative modes of "entitlement," "having established that the statement is true, i.e., in having good evidence that it is true or having observed that it is true." The latter disjunct could presumably be construed so as to cover perceptual knowledge as viewed by the direct realist, though as stated the condition is uninformatively circular; to say that one has observed that it is true that *S* is just to say that one has perceptual knowledge that *S*. However, there are still many other possibilities for direct knowledge. For example, one might hold (with what justice I shall not inquire) that a belief about what makes for successful teaching is justified merely by the fact that one has engaged in a lot of teaching for a long time. More generally one may hold that long experience in an activity puts one in a position to make justified statements (of certain sorts) about that activity, regardless of whether one has any knowledge that could count as sufficient evidence for those statements.

Ayer and Shoemaker have not only overlooked the possibility of direct but non-autonomous knowledge; they have also failed to notice another possibility for autonomous knowledge, viz., taking A. instead of C. as a sufficient condition for B. To say that this is true of one's epistemic position *vis-à-vis* a certain range of propositions is to say that *any* belief in such a proposition is necessarily a justified one. We may use the term "self-warrant" for such a position.

> (D6) *P* enjoys self-warrant *vis-à-vis* a type of proposition, $R =_{\text{df}}$. For any proposition, *S*, of type *R*, it is logically impossible that that *P* should believe that *S* and not be justified in believing that *S*. (Condition A. for *P*'s knowing that *S* logically implies condition B.)

The corresponding privileged access thesis may be formulated as follows:

> (T6) (Self-warrant) Each person is so related to propositions ascribing current mental states to himself that it is logically impossible both for him to believe that such a proposition is true and not be justified in holding this belief; while no one else is so related to such propositions.

It is clear that self-warrant and truth-sufficiency are weaker analogues of infallibility and omniscience, respectively. In the stronger modes, a given condition for knowledge is held to entail the other two, while in the weaker analogue that condition is held to entail *only* condition B. If one enjoys infallibility, then A. entails both B. and C., while with self-warrant, A. entails only B., leaving open the logical possibility of error. If one enjoys omniscience, C. entails both A. and B., while with truth-sufficiency C. entails only B., leaving open the logical possibility of ignorance.

Let us look more closely at the relations of self-warrant and truth-sufficiency. In a way they are equivalent. Both insure that conditions A. and C., which are required for knowledge in any event, are sufficient for any given piece of knowledge in the appropriate range. Whether I enjoy self-warrant or truth-sufficiency (or both) *vis-à-vis* my current thoughts and feelings, it will follow in either case that whenever I have a true belief to the effect that I am thinking or feeling x at the moment, I can correctly be said to *know* that I am thinking or feeling x. And neither privilege carries any guarantee that anything less will suffice for knowledge. However, they carry different implications as to what can be said short of a full knowledge claim. Enjoying self-warrant in this area guarantees that *any* belief of this sort is justified; it protects one against the possibility of unjustified belief formation. Whereas truth-sufficiency makes no such guarantee; it is compatible with the existence of some unjustified beliefs in the appropriate range. Does truth-sufficiency confer a contrasting partial advantage? Does it put the agent into some favorable position (short of knowledge) that he is not put into by self-warrant? It may seem to. For it guarantees that for any thought or feeling possessed by P at t_1, P is justified in believing that he currently has that thought or feeling. That is, with respect to whatever thought or feeling I have at a given time, the fact that I enjoy truth-sufficiency means that I possess the conditional guarantee that my belief that I currently have that thought or feeling will be justified *if* I have such a belief. But in fact this adds nothing to the guarantee given by self-warrant. For the latter involves the claim that *any* of P's belief in the appropriate range, whether true or not, will (necessarily) be justified. Whereas truth-sufficiency guarantees this only for such beliefs as are true. The latter guarantee is a proper part of the former.[30]

[30] In fact, if we should interpret truth-sufficiency as involving the claim that C. is a necessary as well as a sufficient condition for the justification of the belief (for B.), then not only does truth-sufficiency not confer any additional cognitive advantage over self-warrant; it puts one in a less advantageous position. For, contrary to self-warrant, it entails that one cannot be justified in a belief about one's own mental state unless that belief is true. That is, it entails a reduction in the range of cases (intensionally even if not extensionally) in which one's beliefs are justified.

My formulation of truth-sufficiency did not represent C. as a necessary condition for B., though Shoemaker could be interpreted in this way. Of course for Shoemaker it is hardly a live issue, since he also commits himself to infallibility without explicitly

Thus we may conclude that within the range of varieties of privileged access weaker than omniscience, infallibility, indubitability, and incorrigibility, self-warrant is the more interesting and important, since it provides everything in the way of cognitive superiority that is provided by truth-sufficiency, but not vice-versa. I would suggest that Ayer and Shoemaker missed the boat when they singled out truth-sufficiency for consideration.

The greater interest of self-warrant is also shown by its greater utility as a principle of cognitive evaluation. We are now taking the standpoint of another person evaluating *P*'s knowledge claims, rather than the standpoint of *P* and his cognitive capacities. The basic point is that the criteria of justification provided by self-warrant are more accessible than those in terms of which the truth-sufficiency principle is stated. It is generally much easier to determine whether *P* believes that he has a certain thought, than it is to determine whether in fact he does have that thought. At least that is the case, insofar as a determination of the latter is a task that goes beyond the determination of the former. And of course where we are employing truth-sufficiency *instead of* self-warrant as a principle for the evaluation of knowledge claims, we must be taking the verification of condition C. to be distinguishable from the verification of condition A.; otherwise the use of the truth-sufficiency principle could not be distinguished from the use of the self-warrant principle.

IV

I believe that (T6) is the most defensible of the privileged access principles we have considered. It escapes the objections urged against claims of infallibility, omniscience, indubitability, and incorrigibility. It allows for cases in which a person is mistaken about his current mental states (and of course it puts no limit at all on the extent to which a person may be ignorant of his current mental states), and it even allows for cases in which someone else can show that one is mistaken. And at the same time it specifies a very definite respect in which a person is in a superior

---

distinguishing it from truth-sufficiency. If one accepts the infallibility principle, then the question whether C. is necessarily as well as sufficient for B. becomes otiose. For since A. entails C. there is not even a logical possibility of a case in which one would justifiably believe that *S* (A. and B.) without *S*'s being true (C.). However in the case of someone like Ayer, who rejects infallibility, it would seem unjustifiable to make C. a necessary condition for B. For this would be to put a person in a worse cognitive position, in a way, with respect to his own mental states than he is in other fields of knowledge. For when it comes to knowledge of the physical world and historical events it is possible to be justified in believing that *S*, even though it is not true that *S*.

epistemic position *vis-à-vis* his own mental states. To be sure, it is not immune from criticism. A thorough examination of such criticism is outside the scope of this paper, but there is one plausible criticism a consideration of which will afford a convenient entrée to still further varieties of privileged access.

The criticism in question is an attack on the logical entailment (and logical impossibility) claim that is imbedded in (T6). It maintains that what the principle holds to be logically impossible, viz., that a first-person-current-mental-state-belief (FPCMSB) should be unwarranted, is in fact consistently conceivable.[31] More specifically, it claims that it is just a matter of fact that people are highly reliable in the reports they give us about their feelings, thoughts, and beliefs, i.e., that things generally turn out as they could be expected to on the hypothesis that those reports are correct. As things are, if a person tells us that he is feeling depressed or that he is thinking about his income tax, then subsequent events tend to bear this out, insofar as we can form any definite rational expectations, given the complexity of the connections, the underdeveloped state of our knowledge of general connections in this area, and the varied possibilities for dissimulation. However, it is quite conceivable that the world should be such that a person's reports of his feelings, thoughts, and beliefs would be no better guide to the future than, say, his reports of his immediate physical environment, which are still highly reliable, but by no means so overbearingly so as to be rightly accepted as self-warranted. If the world were like this, it would depend on further factors whether a given FPCMSB were warranted, just as is now the case with perceptual beliefs. Such factors might include how alert the person is at the moment, how good a judge he has proved himself to be in such matters, and so on. Thus in this logically possible world FPCMSB's would be sometimes unwarranted, viz., in those cases in which the requisite additional factors were not present. But then even in our world it cannot be *logically* impossible for a FPCMSB to be unwarranted.[32]

There are various ways in which a defender of self-warrant may try to meet this criticism. First he may roundly deny that what the criticism maintains to be logically impossible is indeed so. This denial may take varying forms, but I would suppose that the most plausible is one based

31 There are also arguments to the effect that it is logically possible for other persons to enjoy self-warrant (and/or other modes of favorable epistemic position) *vis-à-vis* one's own mental states; but I will not have time to go into that side of the criticism.

32 Such a criticism could, of course, also be brought against the other varieties of privileged access we have distinguished since they all were stated in terms of logical entailment and logical impossibility. However, I have chosen to state the criticism in opposition to self-warrant, since I take this to be the strongest form of privileged access that does not fall victim to other objections.

on the claim that as we now use mental state terms like "feel ———," "think about ———," etc., it is "part of their meaning" that FPCMSB's are self-warranted. It is impossible, in *our language,* to make sense of the supposition that such a belief should not be warranted. What the critic is doing, in effect, is envisaging a situation in which the meanings of mental state terms would have changed in this respect. But the fact that such a change in meaning is possible leaves untouched the point that, given the present meaning of mental-state terms, having a FPCMSB logically guarantees a warrant for the belief.[33]

At the other end of the spectrum would be a capitulation; one might concede, in the face of the criticism, that the epistemic superiority enjoyed by FPCMSB's is only an "empirical" one; it is just a matter of fact that one's own reports of one's current mental states are more reliable in general than the estimates of those states formed by other people.

For present purposes we are interested in replies that lie between these extremes, replies that develop conceptions of self-warrant that lie between a *logical* impossibility of unwarranted belief and a mere *de facto* superior reliability. For this purpose let us imagine that the self-warrant theorist agrees with the critic that the situations adduced by the latter can be consistently described, using terms with their current meanings. Thus he has to give up the claim that FPCMSB's logically entail their own warrant. Nevertheless he still feels inclined to assert a stronger kind of superiority of such beliefs over their third-person counterparts than merely a greater frequency of accuracy.

An obvious move at this point is to consider the possibility of defining self-warrant in terms of modalities other than logical. Two kinds that are familiar from other contexts are nomological modalities and normative modalities. The former is illustrated by such sentences as:

Water can't run uphill.
If the cream's been around that long it has to be sour.
An airplane *could* go 1200 miles an hour.

Here the modalities are based on laws of nature rather than on logical principles. There is nothing logically impossible about water running uphill, but to do so would be contrary to physical laws. The sourness of the cream in question follows from biochemical laws plus antecedent conditions. And so on.

33 Just as the criticism in question may be made of stronger forms of a privileged access principle, so this sort of reply may be made in defense of those stronger forms. Malcolm and Shoemaker seem to think that infallibility is guaranteed by the meaning we now attach to mental state terms.

Normative modalities are employed in sentences like the following:

Bringing happiness to another person can't be a sin.
To get a Ph.D. you have to write a thesis.
You can't win without scoring runs.

Here the necessities and impossibilities are based on normative principles of one sort or another; in these examples they are moral standards, institutional regulations, and rules of games, respectively.

Can we conceive the impossibility of a FPCMSB's being unwarranted in one of these other ways, rather than as logical? It would seem that nomological impossibility is inapplicable here. If it were applicable, the laws involved would presumably be psychological laws, more specifically laws governing the formation of beliefs about one's own mental states. If these laws either asserted or implied a universal connection between a belief's being about one's own mental states and that belief's being warranted, then it would be nomologically impossible for such a belief to be unwarranted. The trouble with this is that warrantedness, being a normative concept, is not of the right sort of figure in a scientific law. To say that a belief is warranted is to say that it comes up to the proper epistemic standards, and to determine what the proper standards are for one or another kind of belief is not within the province of an empirical science, anymore than is any other normative question.[34] Hence it could not be nomologically impossible for a belief to be unwarranted.

But for just the same reasons normative modalities are quite appropriate here. If there is a justifiable epistemic norm to the effect that any FPCMSB is *ipso facto* warranted just by virtue of its being the belief it is, then it would thereby be normatively impossible for such a belief to be unwarranted. Thus an alternative formulation of the self-warrant principle would be:

(T6A) Each person is so related to propositions ascribing current mental states to himself that it is normatively impossible both for him to believe that such a proposition is true and not be justified in holding this belief; while no one else is so related to such propositions.

[34] This conclusion is of course controversial, and it may be contested on the grounds that it presupposes an unwarranted distinction between the scientific (factual) and normative. However, it is not essential to this paper to take a definite stand on this issue. If normative matters are deemed to be within the province of science, it just means that nomological modalities are more widely applicable than I am supposing here, and the varieties of privileged access are even more numerous than I am representing them to be.

(T6A) presupposes that a defensible epistemic standard would effect a direct connection between being a FPCMSB and being warranted; hence it can be stated in terms of normative modalities alone. A more complicated case can also be envisaged, one in which both nomological and normative modalities are involved. Suppose that there is no such defensible epistemic standard as the one just mentioned; suppose instead that there is a standard to the effect that any belief possessing a certain property, *F*, is warranted, *and* that it is nomologically necessary that all FPCMSB's have the property *F*. In that case it would be nomologically-normatively impossible for FPCMSB's to be unwarranted; the impossibility would derive from a combination of epistemic norms and psychological laws. This gives rise to another version of the self-warrant principle:

> (T6B) Each person is so related to propositions ascribing current mental states to himself that it is nomologically impossible for him to believe such a proposition without his belief having property *F*, and it is normatively impossible for any belief having the property *F* to be unjustified; while no one else is so related to such propositions.

Both of these alternative versions of a self-warrant principle are immune to the criticisms that launched us on the search for alternative modalities. Since neither version asserts any logical necessity for the warrant of FPCMSB's, they allow for the possibility of consistently describing, in our present language, a situation in which (some) FPCMSB's would not be warranted. According to (T6A) such a situation would involve some difference in epistemic standards, and according to (T6B) it would involve either that or a difference in psychological laws. But there is nothing in these principles to suggest that such differences cannot be described by the use of current mentalistic language.

This discussion suggests the possibility of a considerable proliferation of privileged access theses, through varying the modalities in terms of which each of our six modes of favorable epistemic position is stated. However we should not suppose that every such mode can be construed in terms of every modality. We have already seen that self-warrant is not amenable to statement in terms of a purely nomological modality. The question of just which modalities are combinable with each mode of favorable epistemic position is a complicated one, and we shall have time only for a few sketchy and dogmatic remarks. It would seem that indubitability, incorrigibility, and truth-sufficiency cannot be stated in terms of nomological modalities alone, for the same reasons we gave in the case of self-warrant. With truth-sufficiency, which has the same structure, exactly the same argument applies. Our concept of indubitability being a normative one, it seems clear that an appeal to epistemic standards is essentially involved in the claim that there can be no *grounds* for any doubt. And since incorrigibility involves the impossibility of someone else's showing the person to be mistaken (not just the impossibility of someone else's being correct while one is mistaken), again it would seem that standards defining what counts as a demonstration in this area would be involved. By similar arguments I think it could be shown that these three modes are all construable, like self-warrant, in terms of both pure normative modalities and a combination of nomological and normative modalities.

The situation is quite different with respect to infallibility and omniscience. Here what is implied most basically is the correctness of a belief, and the possession of a belief, respectively. Whether or not a certain (factual) belief is correct, and whether or not a given person has a given belief, is sheerly a matter of fact and not within the jurisdiction of norms or standards. It would not make sense to adopt a standard to the effect that all beliefs of a certain category are correct; that would be as if a city council were to adopt an ordinance according to which all public housing in the city is free of rats. If a certain belief is in fact mistaken, we cannot alter that fact by legislating it away. On the other hand, it might conceivably be *nomologically* necessary that beliefs of a certain category all be correct. The mechanisms of belief formation might be such as to guarantee this. However, since both infallibility and omniscience, as we have formulated them, involve the implication of the warrant condition, B., as well, it would seem, for the reasons given in connection with self-warrant, that they cannot involve nomological modalities alone.[35] Thus a mixed nomological-normative modality would seem to be the only alternative to the logical modalities (at least among the alternatives we are considering). An infallibility principle could be stated in those terms as follows:

(T1A) Each person is so related to propositions ascribing current mental states to himself that it is nomologically impossible for him to believe such a proposition without that proposition's being true, and it is normatively impossible for a belief that satisfies this condition

[35] Of course we could excise this implication from our construal of infallibility and omniscience, in which case infallibility would be defined simply as the impossibility of mistake and omniscience simply as the inevitability of belief-formation. (It would still be the case that the beliefs that satisfy these conditions would be warranted and so count as knowledge; it is just that this would not be made explicit in the definition.) As so conceived these modes would be amenable to a formulation in terms of nomological modalities alone.

to be unjustified; while no one else is so related to such propositions.

In addition, there is the possibility of non-modal, *de facto* universal, versions of each of our six basic types. The following is a rough indication of how privileged access principles will look as so construed.

Infallibility—FPCMSB's are, in fact, never mistaken.
Omniscience—A person is, in fact, never ignorant of one of his mental states.
Indubitability—No one, in fact, ever has grounds for doubting a FPCMSB.
Incorrigibility—No one else ever, in fact, succeeds in showing that a FPCMSB is mistaken.
Self-warrant—FPCMSB's are, as a matter of fact, always warranted.
Truth-sufficiency—True FPCMSB's are, as a matter of fact, always warranted.

It is dubious that these formulations in terms of *de facto* universals are of much use. For it is doubtful that anyone could have solid grounds for supposing that, e.g., FPCMSB's are *always* correct, unless his claim were based on some sort of modal consideration to the effect that something in the nature of the case makes it impossible for FPCMSB's to be mistaken; and in that case he would be in a position to formulate the infallibility thesis in modal terms. We can derive a more usable non-modal formulation by weakening the universals to a "for the most part" status, thus replacing "never" with "rarely," and "always" with "usually." So construed, infallibility and self-warrant, e.g., would become:

Infallibility—FPCMSB's are, in fact, rarely mistaken.[36]
Self-warrant—FPCMSB's are, as a matter of fact, usually warranted.

It does seem *conceivable* that one should acquire solid grounds for, e.g., a "for the most part" version of an infallibility principle without thereby putting himself in a position to assert a corresponding modal principle. One might argue, e.g., that we are rarely, if ever, in a position to show that a FPCMSB is incorrect, and to the extent that we have an independent check on their accuracy, they almost always turn out to be correct. Therefore we have every reason to suppose that they are, in fact, usually correct. This line of argument is not based on any fundamental considerations concerning the concepts, natural laws, or epistemic norms

36 Absolutistic terms like "infallibility" and "omniscience" are not aptly used for formulations that are weakened to this extent, but that is a merely verbal point.

involved, and therefore it does not support any claim as to what is necessary or impossible.

Another way of deviating from unrestricted universality involves a restriction to "normal" conditions. Thus we might construe self-warrant, e.g., as follows:

> Self-warrant—FPCMSB's are normally warranted (are always warranted in normal conditions).

Certain lines of argument support a "normal conditions" version instead of, or in addition to, a "by and large" version. For example, one may think that he can give an (open-ended) list of "abnormal" factors that are usually absent but which when present would prevent a FPCMSB from having the warrant it usually has. These might include such things as extreme preoccupation with other matters, extreme emotional upset, and derangement of the critical faculties.

Our list of varieties of privileged access has now swollen to a staggering 34: 16 modal principles, 6 *de facto* unrestrictedly universal principles, 6 "by and large" principles, and 6 "normal conditions" principles. No doubt with sufficient ingenuity the list could be further expanded, but perhaps the results already attained will suffice to bring out the main dimensions of variation.

V

Attacks on privileged access invariably fail to take account of the full range of possibilities. Their arguments are directed against only some of the possible versions of the position they are attacking; hence at best they fall short of showing that no privileged access principle is acceptable. To illustrate this point I shall take two of the best and most prominent recent attacks on privileged access, those of Bruce Aune in his book *Knowledge, Mind, and Nature,*[37] and those of D. M. Armstrong in his book *A Materialist Theory of the Mind.*[38]

Aune's arguments occur in chap. II, "Does Knowledge Have An Indubitable Foundation?" and they form part of his attack on the general idea that our knowledge rests on a foundation that is made up of beliefs, each of which is wholly noninferential and completely infallible. Although at the beginning of the discussion (pp. 32–33) he wobbles a bit between talking of the "reliability of our beliefs concerning immediate

[37] New York, 1967.
[38] London, 1968.

experience" (p. 32) and talking about "the alleged infallible character of immediate awareness," (p. 33) it is clear that his actual arguments are directed against an infallibility thesis, and indeed a logical infallibility thesis. The arguments are designed to show that "identifications of even feelings and mental images are not logically incapable of error" (p. 33), and to demonstrate "the possibility of being mistaken about the character of one's momentary experience" (p. 34). But having presented what he claims to be possible cases of mistake about such matters, he then supposes himself to have shown that statements about one's immediate experience are not "intrinsically acceptable," in the sense that their "truth is acceptable independently of any inference" (p. 41). And he seems to suppose that the only alternative to an infallibility claim is the view that there are strong empirical reasons for accepting one's statements about his immediate experience.

> The point seems to be securely established that judgments of phenomenal identification are not, in fact, infallible. We may come to have enormous confidence that, after a protracted period of training, a man's opinions about the character of his own experiences are never really wrong. But our confidence here is based on empirical considerations. There is no longer any reason to think that such opinions *cannot* be erroneous; rather we have fairly good, though not infallible, reasons to think that they are normally reliable (P. 37).

In supposing that having disposed of logical infallibility, he has thereby disposed of "intrinsic acceptability" and left a clear field for an acceptability based on empirical evidence, it is clear that Aune has overlooked most of the modes of epistemic superiority we have distinguished, in particular self-warrant and truth-sufficiency. For to say that one enjoys self-warrant *vis-à-vis* his own immediate experience is to say that any of the person's beliefs about that experience is justified (acceptable) just by virtue of the fact that it is held, whether or not one possesses anything that has the status of evidence for that belief; and to say that one enjoys truth-sufficiency *vis-à-vis* one's immediate experience is to say the same thing for one's true beliefs about that experience. These are two forms of "intrinsic acceptability" without infallibility, and Aune will have to mount arguments against these before he can lay claim to having disposed of "intrinsic acceptability." At the most basic level what is overlooked here is the distinction between a belief's guaranteeing its own truth, and a belief's guaranteeing its own justification (acceptability), i.e., the difference between the justification (B.) and the truth (C.) conditions for knowledge.

Moreover Aune has overlooked the possibility of working, within any of those modes of epistemic superiority, with modalities other than the logical modalities. In the quotation just cited, he presents a "normal conditions" variety of infallibility as the only alternative to a logical infallibility thesis. But even within the bounds of infallibility there is also the view that it is *nomologically* impossible that FPCMSB's should be mistaken. And as for self-warrant, even if we should reject the claim that it is logically impossible for FPCMSB's to be unwarranted, there is still the view that their being unwarranted is a normative impossibility, a view that is also distinct from the position that FPCMSB's are "normally reliable."

Armstrong's discussion (in chap. 6, sect. x of the above mentioned book, entitled, "The alleged indubitability of consciousness") draws more distinctions than Aune. He distinguishes logical infallibility, logical omniscience, and logical incorrigibility (pp. 101–102), in much the same way as I, though he uses for these concepts the terms "indubitability" (alternatively "incorrigibility"), "self-intimation," and "logically privileged access," respectively. He then presents arguments against the claims that FPCMSB's enjoy any of these kinds of privilege. Furthermore he explicitly recognizes nomological infallibility.[39] In chap. 9, sect. ii, entitled "The nature of non-inferential knowledge" he defines non-inferential knowledge as follows: "*A* knows *p* non-inferentially, if, and only if, *A* has no good reasons for *p* but:

(1) *A* believes *p;*
(2) *p* is true;
(3) *A*'s belief-that-*p* is empirically sufficient for the truth of *p*." (P. 189.)

He goes on to make it explicit that the "empirical sufficiency" involved here is based on some law of nature (p. 190); hence whenever one has non-inferential knowledge of *p* it is nomologically impossible that his belief should be mistaken. Thus he does not, like Aune, regard some kind of *de facto* reliability as the only alternative to a logically necessary epistemic privilege. However, like Aune, he fails to note both the possibility of self-warrant (and truth-sufficiency) as distinct modes of epistemic privilege, and the possibility of formulating at least some of the modes in terms of normative modalities. Thus even if he has effectively disposed of logical infallibility, omniscience, and incorrigibility, he cannot yet conclude that nomological infallibility is the only plausible version of a modal privileged access thesis.

[39] Where this is construed simply as matter of condition *A*'s nomologically implying *C* without the further stipulation of an implication of *B*.

V

DOES EMPIRICAL KNOWLEDGE HAVE A FOUNDATION?

Moritz Schlick

The Foundation of Knowledge

All important attempts at establishing a theory of knowledge grow out of the problem concerning the certainty of human knowledge. And this problem in turn originates in the wish for absolute certainty.

The insight that the statements of daily life and science can at best be only probable, that even the most general results of science, which all experiences confirm, can have only the character of hypotheses, has again and again stimulated philosophers since Descartes, and indeed, though less obviously, since ancient times, to search for an unshakeable, indubitable, foundation, a firm basis on which the uncertain structure of our knowledge could rest. The uncertainty of the structure was generally attributed to the fact that it was impossible, perhaps in principle, to construct a firmer one by the power of human thought. But this did not inhibit the search for the bedrock, which exists prior to all construction and does not itself vacillate.

This article, originally entitled "Über das Fundament der Erkenntnis," first appeared in *Erkenntnis,* Vol. IV (1934). Translated by David Rynin.
Moritz Schlick, "The Foundation of Knowledge," trans. David Rynin, in *Logical Positivism,* ed. A. J. Ayer (New York: The Macmillan Company, 1959), 209–27.

This search is a praiseworthy, healthy effort, and it is prevalent even among "relativists" and "sceptics, who would rather not acknowledge it." It appears in different forms and leads to odd differences of opinion. The problem of "protocol statements," their structure and function, is the latest form in which the philosophy or rather the decisive empiricism of our day clothes the problem of the ultimate ground of knowledge.

What was originally meant by "protocol statements," as the name indicates, are those statements which express the *facts* with absolute simplicity, without any moulding, alteration or addition, in whose elaboration every science consists, and which precede all knowing, every judgment regarding the world. It makes no sense to speak of uncertain facts. Only assertions, only our knowledge can be uncertain. If we succeed therefore in expressing the raw facts in "protocol statements," without any contamination, these appear to be the absolutely indubitable starting points of all knowledge. They are, to be sure, again abandoned the moment one goes over to statements which are actually of use in life or science (such a transition appears to be that from "singular" to "universal" statements), but they constitute nevertheless the firm basis to which all our cognitions owe whatever validity they may possess.

Moreover, it makes no difference whether or not these so-called protocol statements have ever actually been made, that is, actually uttered, written down or even only explicitly "thought"; it is required only that one know what statements form the basis for the notations which are actually made, and that these statements be at all times reconstructible. If for example an investigator makes a note, "Under such and such conditions the pointer stands at 10.5," he knows that this means "two black lines coincide," and that the words "under such and such conditions" (which we here imagine to be specified) are likewise to be resolved into definite protocol statements which, if he wished, he could in principle formulate exactly, although perhaps with difficulty.

It is clear, and is so far as I know disputed by no one, that knowledge in life and science in *some* sense *begins* with confirmation of facts, and that the "protocol statements" in which this occurs stand in the same sense at the *beginning* of science. What is this sense? Is "beginning" to be understood in the temporal or logical sense?

Here we already find much confusion and oscillation. If I said above that it is not important whether the decisive statements have been actually made or uttered, this means evidently that they need not stand at the beginning *temporally,* but can be arrived at later just as well if need be. The necessity for formulating them would arise when one wished to make clear to oneself the meaning of the statement that one had actually written down. Is the reference to protocol statements then to be understood in the *logical* sense? In that event they would be distinguished by definite logical properties, by their structure, their position in the system of science, and one would be confronted with the task of actually specifying these properties. In fact, this is the form in which, for example, Carnap used explicitly to put the question of protocol statements, while later [1] declaring it to be a question which is to be settled by an arbitrary decision.

On the other hand, we find many expositions which seem to presuppose that by "protocol statements" only those assertions are to be understood that also temporally precede the other assertions of science. And is this not correct? One must bear in mind that it is a matter of the ultimate basis of knowledge of *reality,* and that it is not sufficient for this to treat statements as, so to speak, "ideal constructions" (as one used to say in Platonic fashion), but rather that one must concern oneself with real occurrences, with events that take place in time, in which the making of judgments consists, hence with psychic acts of "thought," or physical acts of "speaking" or "writing." Since psychic acts of judgment seem suitable for establishing inter-subjectively valid knowledge only when translated into verbal or written expressions (that is, into a physical system of symbols) "protocol statements" come to be regarded as certain spoken, written or printed sentences, i.e., certain symbol-complexes of sounds or printer's ink, which when translated from the common abbreviations into full-fledged speech, would mean something like: "Mr. N. N. at such and such a time observed so and so at such and such a place." (This view was adopted particularly by O. Neurath.) [2] As a matter of fact, when we retrace the path by which we actually arrive at all our knowledge, we doubtless always come up against this same source: printed sentences in books, words out of the mouth of a teacher, our own observations (in the latter case we are ourselves N. N.).

On this view protocol statements would be real happenings in the world and would temporally precede the other real processes in which the "construction of science," or indeed the production of an individual's knowledge consists.

I do not know to what extent the distinction made here between the logical and temporal priority of protocol statements corresponds to differences in the views actually held by certain authors—but that is not important. For we are not concerned to determine who expressed the correct view, but what the correct view *is.* And for this our distinction between the two points of view will serve well enough.

As a matter of fact, these two views are compatible. For the statements that register simple data of observation and stand temporally at

[1] See Carnap, "Über Protokollsätze," *Erkenntnis,* Vol. III, pp. 216 ff.

[2] Neurath, "Protokollsätze," *Erkenntnis,* Vol. III, pp. 104 ff.

the beginning could at the same time be those that by virtue of their structure would have to constitute the logical starting-point of science.

II

The question which will first interest us is this: What progress is achieved by formulating the problem of the ultimate basis of knowledge in terms of protocol statements? The answer to this question will itself pave the way to a solution of the problem.

I think it a great improvement in method to try to aim at the basis of knowledge by looking not for the primary *facts* but for the primary *sentences*. But I also think that this advantage was not made the most of, perhaps because of a failure to realize that what was at issue, fundamentally, was just the old problem of the basis. I believe, in fact, that the position to which the consideration of protocol statements has led is not tenable. It results in a peculiar relativism, which appears to be a necessary consequence of the view that protocol statements are empirical facts upon which the edifice of science is subsequently built.

That is to say: when protocol statements are conceived in this manner, then directly one raises the question of the certainty with which one may assert their truth, one must grant that they are exposed to all possible doubts.

There appears in a book a sentence which says, for example, that N. N. used such and such an instrument to make such and such an observation. One may under certain circumstances have the greatest confidence in this sentence. Nevertheless, it and the observation it records, can never be considered *absolutely* certain. For the possibilities of error are innumerable. N. N. can inadvertently or intentionally have described something that does not accurately represent the observed fact; in writing it down or printing it, an error may have crept in. Indeed the assumption that the symbols of a book retain their form even for an instant and do not "of themselves" change into new sentences is an empirical hypothesis, which as such can never be strictly verified. For every verification would rest on assumptions of the same sort and on the presupposition that our memory does not deceive us at least during a brief interval, and so on.

This means, of course—and some of our authors have pointed this out almost with a note of triumph—that protocol statements, so conceived, have in principle exactly the same character as all the other statements of science: they are hypotheses, nothing but hypotheses. They are anything but incontrovertible, and one can use them in the construction of the system of science only so long as they are supported by, or at least not contradicted by, other hypotheses. We therefore always reserve the right to make protocol statements subject to correction, and such corrections, quite often indeed, do occur when we eliminate certain protocol statements and declare that they must have been the result of some error.

Even in the case of statements which we ourselves have put forward we do not in principle exclude the possibility of error. We grant that our mind at the moment the judgment was made may have been wholly confused, and that an experience which we now say we had two minutes ago may upon later examination be found to have been an hallucination, or even one that never took place at all.

Thus it is clear that on this view of protocol statements they do not provide one who is in search of a firm basis of knowledge with anything of the sort. On the contrary, the actual result is that one ends by abandoning the original distinction between protocol and other statements as meaningless. Thus we come to understand how people come to think [3] that any statements of science can be selected at will and called "protocol statements," and that it is simply a question of convenience which are chosen.

But can we admit this? Are there really only reasons of convenience? It is not rather a matter of where the particular statements come from, what is their origin, their history? In general, what is meant here by convenience? What is the end that one pursues in making and selecting statements?

The end can be no other than that of science itself, namely, that of affording a *true* description of the facts. For us it is self-evident that the problem of the basis of knowledge is nothing other than the question of the criterion of truth. Surely the reason for bringing in the term "protocol statement" in the first place was that it should serve to mark out certain statements by the truth of which the truth of all other statements comes to be measured, as by a measuring rod. But according to the viewpoint just described this measuring rod would have shown itself to be as relative as, say, all the measuring rods of physics. And it is this view with its consequences that has been commended as the banishing of the last remnant of "absolutism" from philosophy.[4]

But what then remains at all as a criterion of truth? Since the proposal is not that all scientific assertions must accord with certain definite protocol statements, but rather that all statements shall accord with one another, with the result that every single one is considered as, in principle, corrigible, truth can consist only in a *mutual agreement of statements.*

[3] K. Popper as quoted by Carnap, *op. cit., Erkenntnis,* Vol. III, p. 223.
[4] Carnap, *op. cit.,* p. 228.

III

This view, which has been expressly formulated and represented in this context, for example, by Neurath, is well known from the history of recent philosophy. In England it is usually called the "coherence theory of truth," and contrasted with the older "correspondence theory." It is to be observed that the expression "theory" is quite inappropriate. For observations on the nature of truth have a quite different character from scientific theories, which always consist of a system of hypotheses.

The contrast between the two views is generally expressed as follows: according to the traditional one, the truth of a statement consists in its agreement with the facts, while according to the other, the coherence theory, it consists in its agreement with the system of other statements.

I shall not in general pursue the question here whether the latter view can not also be interpreted in a way that draws attention to something quite correct (namely, to the fact that in a quite definite sense we cannot "go beyond language" as Wittgenstein puts it). I have here rather to show that, on the interpretation required in the present context, it is quite untenable.

If the truth of a statement is to consist in its coherence or agreement with the other statements, one must be clear as to what one understands by "agreement," and *which* statements are meant by "other."

The first point can be settled easily. Since it cannot be meant that the statement to be tested asserts the same thing as the others, it remains only that they must be *compatible* with it, that is, that no contradictions exist between them. Truth would consist simply in absence of contradiction. But on the question whether truth can be identified simply with the absence of contradiction, there ought to be no further discussion. It should long since have been generally acknowledged that only in the case of statements of a tautological nature are truth (if one will apply this term at all) and absence of contradiction to be equated, as for instance with the statements of pure geometry. But with such statements every connection with reality is purposely dissolved; they are only formulas within a determinate calculus; it makes no sense in the case of the statements of *pure* geometry to ask whether they agree with the facts of the world: they need only be compatible with the axioms arbitrarily laid down at the beginning (in addition, it is usually also required that they follow from them) in order to be called true or correct. We have before us precisely what was earlier called *formal* truth and distinguished from *material* truth.

The latter is the truth of synthetic statements, assertions of matters of fact, and if one wishes to describe them by help of the concept of absence of contradiction, of agreement with other statements, one can do so only if one says that they may not contradict *very special* statements, namely just those that express "facts of immediate observation." The criterion of truth cannot be compatibility with any statements whatever, but agreement is required with certain exceptional statements which are not chosen arbitrarily at all. In other words, the criterion of absence of contradiction does not by itself suffice for material truth. It is, rather, entirely a matter of compatibility with very special peculiar statements. And for this compatibility there is no reason not to use—indeed I consider there is every justification for using—the good old expression "agreement with reality."

The astounding error of the "coherence theory" can be explained only by the fact that its defenders and expositors were thinking only of such statements as actually occur in science, and took them as their only examples. Under these conditions the relation of non-contradiction was in fact sufficient, but only because these statements are of a very special character. They have, that is, in a certain sense (to be explained presently) their "origin" in observation statements, they derive, as one may confidently say in the traditional way of speaking, "from experience."

If one is to take coherence seriously as a general criterion of truth, then one must consider arbitrary fairy stories to be as true as a historical report, or as statements in a textbook of chemistry, provided the story is constructed in such a way that no contradiction ever arises. I can depict by help of fantasy a grotesque world full of bizarre adventures: the coherence philosopher must believe in the truth of my account provided only I take care of the mutual compatibility of my statements, and also take the precaution of avoiding any collision with the usual description of the world, by placing the scene of my story on a distant star, where no observation is possible. Indeed, strickly speaking, I don't even require this precaution; I can just as well demand that the others have to adapt themselves to my description; and not the other way round. They cannot then object that, say, this happening runs counter to the observations, for according to the coherence theory there is no question of observations, but only of the compatibility of statements.

Since no one dreams of holding the statements of a story book true and those of a text of physics false, the coherence view fails utterly. Something more, that is, must be added to coherence, namely, a principle in terms of which the compatibility is to be established, and this would alone then be the actual criterion.

If I am given a set of statements, among which are found some that contradict each other, I can establish consistency in a number of ways, by, for example, on one occasion selecting certain statements and abandoning or altering them and on another occasion doing the same with the other statements that contradict the first.

Thus the coherence theory is shown to be logically impossible; it fails altogether to give an unambiguous criterion of truth, for by means of it I can arrive at any number of consistent systems of statements which are incompatible with one another.

The only way to avoid this absurdity is not to allow any statements whatever to be abandoned or altered, but rather to specify those that are to be maintained, to which the remainder have to be accommodated.

IV

The coherence theory is thus disposed of, and we have in the meantime arrived at the second point of our critical considerations, namely, at the question whether *all* statements are corrigible, or whether there are also those that cannot be shaken. These latter would of course constitute the "basis" of all knowledge which we have been seeking, without so far being able to take any step towards it.

By what mark, then, are we to distinguish these statements which themselves remain unaltered, while all others must be brought into agreement with them? We shall in what follows call them not "protocol statements," but "basic statements" for it is quite dubious whether they occur at all among the protocols of science.

The most obvious recourse would doubtless be to find the rule for which we are searching in some kind of economy principle, namely, to say: we are to choose those as basic statements whose retention requires a *minimum* of alteration in the whole system of statements in order to rid it of all contradictions.

It is worth noticing that such an economy principle would not enable us to pick out certain statements as being basic once and for all, for it might happen that with the progress of science the basic statements that served as such up to a given moment would be again degraded, if it appeared more economical to abandon them in favor of newly found statements which from that time on—until further notice—would play the basic role. This would, of course, no longer be the pure coherence viewpoint, but one based on economy; "relativity," however, would characterize it also.

There seems to me no question but that the representatives of the view we have been criticizing did in fact take the economy principle as their guiding light, whether explicitly or implicitly; I have therefore already assumed above that on the relativity view there are purposive grounds which determine the selection of protocol statements, and I asked: Can we admit this?

I now answer this question in the negative. It is in fact not economic purposiveness but quite other characteristics which distinguish the genuine basic statements.

The procedure for choosing these statements would be called economic if it consisted say in conforming to the opinions (or "protocol statements") of the majority of investigators. Now it is of course the case that we do not doubt the existence of a fact, for example a fact of geography or history, or even of a natural law, when we find that in the relevant contexts its existence is very frequently reported. It does not occur to us in those cases to wish to investigate the matter ourselves. We acquiesce in what is universally acknowledged. But this is explained by the fact that we have precise knowledge of the manner in which such factual statements tend to be made, and that this manner wins our confidence; it is not that it agrees with the view of the majority. Quite the contrary, it could only arrive at universal acceptance because everyone feels the same confidence. Whether and to what extent we hold a statement to be corrigible or annulable depends solely on its *origin,* and (apart from very special cases) not at all upon whether maintaining it requires the correction of very many other statements and perhaps a reorganization of the whole system of knowledge.

Before one can apply the principle of economy one must know to *which* statements it is to be applied. And if the principle were the *only* decisive rule the answer could only be: to *all* that are asserted with any claim to validity or have ever been so asserted. Indeed, the phrase "with any claim to validity" should be omitted, for how should we distinguish such statements from those which were asserted quite arbitrarily, as jokes or with intent to deceive? This distinction cannot even be formulated without taking into consideration *the derivation* of the statements. So we find ourselves once more referred to the question of their origin. Without having classified statements according to their origin, any application of the economy principle of agreement would be quite absurd. But once one has examined the statements with respect to their origin it becomes immediately obvious that one has thereby already ordered them in terms of their validity, and that there is no place left for the application of the principle of economy (apart from certain very special cases in still unfinished areas of science). We can see also that the establishment of this order points the way to the basis of which we are in search.

V

Here of course the greatest care is necessary. For we are treading on the path which has been followed from ancient times by all those who have ever embarked upon the journey towards the ultimate grounds of truth. And always they have failed to reach the goal. In the ordering of statements according to their origin which I undertake for the purpose of judging their certainty, I start by assigning a special place to those that I make *myself*. And here a secondary position is occupied by those that lie in the past, for we believe that their certainty can be impaired by "errors of memory"—and indeed in general the more so the farther back in time they lie. On the other hand, the statements which stand at the top, free from all doubt, are those that express facts of one's own "perception," or whatever you like to call it. But in spite of the fact that statements of this sort seem so simple and clear, philosophers have found themselves in a hopeless labyrinth the moment they actually attempted to use them as the foundation of all knowledge. Some puzzling sections of this labyrinth are for example those formulations and deductions that have occupied the center of so many philosophical disputes under the heading "evidence of inner perception," "solipsism," "solipsism of the present moment," "self-conscious certainty," etc. The Cartesian *cogito ergo sum* is the best-known of the destinations to which this path has led —a terminating point to which indeed Augustine had already pushed through. And concerning *cogito ergo sum* our eyes have today been sufficiently opened: we know that it is a mere pseudo-statement, which does not become genuine by being expressed in the form *"cogitatio est"*— "the contents of consciousness exist." [5] Such a statement, which does not express anything itself, cannot in any sense serve as the basis of anything. It is not itself a cognition, and none rests upon it. It cannot lend certainty to any cognition.

There exists therefore the greatest danger that in following the path recommended one will arrive at empty verbiage instead of the basis one seeks. The critical theory of protocol statements originated indeed in the wish to avoid this danger. But the way out proposed by it is unsatisfactory. Its *essential* deficiency lies in ignoring the different rank of statements, which expresses itself most clearly in the fact that for the system of science which one takes to be the "right" one, one's *own* statements in the end play the only decisive role.

[5] Cf. "Positivismus und Realismus," *Erkenntnis,* Vol. III, p. 20.

It would be theoretically conceivable that my own observations in no way substantiate the assertions made about the world by other men. It might be that all the books that I read, all the teachers that I hear are in perfect agreement among themselves, that they never contradict one another, but that they are simply incompatible with a large part of my own observation statements. (Certain difficulties would in this case accompany the problem of learning the language and its use in communication, but they can be removed by means of certain assumptions concerning the place in which the contradictions are to appear.) According to the view we have been criticizing I would in such a case simply have to sacrifice my own "protocol statements," for they would be opposed by the overwhelming mass of other statements which would be in mutual agreement themselves, and it would be impossible to expect that these should be corrected in accordance with my own limited fragmentary experience.

But what would actually happen in such a case? Well, under no circumstances would I abandon my own observation statements. On the contrary, I find that I can accept only a system of knowledge into which they fit unmutilated. And I can always construct such a system. I need only view the others as dreaming fools, in whose madness lies a remarkable method, or—to express it more objectively—I would say that the others live in a different world from mine, which has just so much in common with mine as to make it possible to achieve understanding by means of the same language. In any case no matter what world picture I construct, I would test its truth always in terms of my own experience. I would never permit anyone to take this support from me: my own observation statements would always be the ultimate criterion. I should, so to speak, exclaim "What I see, I see!"

VI

In the light of these preliminary critical remarks, it is clear where we have to look for the solution of these confusing difficulties: we must use the Cartesian road in so far as it is good and passable, but then be careful to avoid falling into the *cogito ergo sum* and related nonsense. We effect this by making clear to ourselves the role which really belongs to the statements expressing "the immediately observed."

What actually lies behind one's saying that they are "absolutely certain"? And in what sense may one describe them as the ultimate ground of all knowledge?

Let us consider the second question first. If we imagine that I at once recorded every observation—and it is in principle indifferent whether this is done on paper or in memory—and then began from that point the construction of science, I should have before me genuine "protocol statements" which stood temporally at the beginning of knowledge. From them would gradually arise the rest of the statements of science, by means of the process called "induction," which consists in nothing else than that I am stimulated or induced by the protocol statements to establish tentative generalizations (hypotheses), from which those first statements, but also an endless number of others, follow logically. If now these others express *the same* as is expressed by later observation statements that are obtained under quite definite conditions which are exactly specifiable beforehand, then the hypotheses are considered to be confirmed so long as no observation statements appear that stand in contradiction to the statements derived from the hypotheses and thus to the hypotheses themselves. So long as this does not occur we believe ourselves to have hit correctly upon a law of nature. Induction is thus nothing but methodically conducted guessing, a psychological, biological process whose conduct has certainly nothing to do with "logic."

In this way the actual procedure of science is described schematically. It is evident what role is played in it by the statements concerning what is "immediately perceived." They are not identical with those written down or memorized, with what can correctly be called "protocol statements," but they are the *occasions* of their formation. The protocol statements observed in a book or memory are, as we acknowledged long ago, so far as their validity goes, doubtless to be compared to hypotheses. For, when we have such a statement before us, it is a mere assumption that it is true, that it agrees with the observation statements that give rise to it. (Indeed it may have been occasioned by no observation statements, but derived from some game or other.) What I call an observation statement cannot be identical with a genuine protocol statement, if only because in a certain sense it cannot be written down at all—a point which we shall presently discuss.

Thus in the schema of the building up of knowledge that I have described, the part played by observation statements is first that of standing temporally at the beginning of the whole process, stimulating it and setting it going. How much of their content enters into knowledge remains in principle at first undetermined. One can thus with some justice see in the observation statements the ultimate origin of all knowledge. But should they be described as the basis, as the ultimate certain ground? This can hardly be maintained, for this "origin" stands in a too questionable relation to the edifice of knowledge. But in addition we have conceived of the true process as schematically simplified. In reality what is actually expressed in protocols stands in a less close connection with the observed, and in general one ought not to assume that any pure observation statements ever slip in between the observation and the "protocol."

But now a second function appears to belong to these statements about the immediately perceived, these "confirmations" * as we may also call them, namely, the corroboration of hypotheses, their *verification.*

Science makes prophecies that are tested by "experience." Its essential function consists in making predictions. It says, for example: "If at such and such a time you look through a telescope adjusted in such and such a manner you will see a point of light (a star) in coincidence with a black mark (cross wires)." Let us assume that in following out these instructions the predicted experience actually occurs. This means that we make an anticipated confirmation, we pronounce an expected judgment of observation, we obtain thereby a feeling of *fulfilment,* a quite characteristic satisfaction: we are *satisfied.* One is fully justified in saying that the confirmation or observation statements have fulfilled their true mission as soon as we obtain this peculiar satisfaction.

And it is obtained in the very moment in which the confirmation takes place, in which the observation statement is made. This is of the utmost importance. For thus the function of the statements about the immediately experienced itself lies in the immediate present. Indeed we saw that they have so to speak no duration, that the moment they are gone one has at one's disposal in their place inscriptions, or memory traces, that can play only the role of hypotheses and thereby lack ultimate certainty. One cannot build any logically tenable structure upon the confirmations, for they are gone the moment one begins to construct. If they stand at the beginning of the process of cognition they are logically

* The term used by the author is "Konstatierung" which he sometimes equates with "observation statement" i.e., "Beobachtungssatz," and generally tends to quote, in a manner indicating his awareness that it is a somewhat unusual usage and perhaps a not altogether adequate technical term. Wilfred Sellars in a recently published essay ("Empiricism and the Philosophy of Mind," *Minnesota Studies in the Philosophy of Science,* Volume I, University of Minnesota Press, 1956) [pp. 471–541, this volume. Eds.] uses the term "report" in referring to what seems to be the kind of statement Schlick is discussing. I do not adopt this term, despite some undoubted advantages it has over "confirmation," because of the close connection that "Konstatierung" has with confirmation or verification, a connection so close that Schlick uses the same term unquoted to refer to confirmation. Furthermore, as the text shows, confirmations are never false, as Schlick understands them; but this is certainly not a characteristic of reports, as the term "report" is used in everyday or even scientific language. (Translator's note.)

of no use. Quite otherwise however if they stand at the end; they bring verification (or also falsification) to completion, and in the moment of their occurrence they have already fulfilled their duty. Logically nothing more depends on them, no conclusions are drawn from them. They constitute an absolute end.

Of course, psychologically and biologically a new process of cognition begins with the satisfaction they create: the hypotheses whose verification ends in them are considered to be upheld, and the formulation of more general hypotheses is sought, the guessing and search for universal laws goes on. The observation statements constitute the origin and stimuli for these events that follow in time, in the sense described earlier.

It seems to me that by means of these considerations a new and clear light is cast upon the problem of the ultimate basis of knowledge, and we see clearly how the construction of the system of knowledge takes place and what role the "confirmations" play in it.

Cognition is originally a means in the service of life. In order to find his way about in his environment and to adjust his actions to events, man must be able to foresee these events to a certain extent. For this he makes use of universal statements, cognitions, and he can make use of them only in so far as what has been predicted actually occurs. Now in science this character of cognition remains wholly unaltered; the only difference is that it no longer serves the purposes of life, is not sought because of its utility. With the confirmation of prediction the scientific goal is achieved: the joy in cognition is the joy of verification, the triumphant feeling of having guessed correctly. And it is this that the observation statements bring about. In them science as it were achieves its goal: it is for their sake that it exists. The question hidden behind the problem of the absolutely certain basis of knowledge is, as it were, that of the legitimacy of this satisfaction with which verification fills us. Have our predictions actually come true? In every single case of verification or falsification a "confirmation" answers unambiguously with a yes or a no, with joy of fulfilment or disappointment. The confirmations are final.

Finality is a very fitting word to characterize the function of observation statements. They are an absolute end. In them the task of cognition at this point is fulfilled. That a new task begins with the pleasure in which they culminate, and with the hypotheses that they leave behind does not concern them. Science does not rest upon them but leads to them, and they indicate that it has led correctly. They are really the absolute fixed points; it gives us joy to reach them, even if we cannot stand upon them.

VII

In what does this fixity consist? This brings us to the question we postponed earlier: in what sense can one speak of observation statements as being "absolutely certain"?

I should like to throw light on this by first saying something about a quite different kind of statement, namely about *analytic* statements. I will then compare these to the "confirmations." In the case of analytic statements it is well known that the question of their validity constitutes no problem. They hold *a priori;* one cannot and should not try to look to experience for proof of their correctness for they say nothing whatever about objects of experience. For this reason only "formal truth" pertains to them, i.e., they are not "true" because they correctly express some fact. What makes them true is just their being correctly constructed, i.e. their standing in agreement with our arbitrarily established definitions.

However, certain philosophical writers have thought themselves obliged to ask: Yes, but how do I know in an individual case whether a statement really stands in agreement with the definition, whether it is really analytic and therefore holds without question? Must I not carry in my head these definitions, the meaning of all the words that are used when I speak or hear or read the statement even if it endures only for a second? But can I be sure that my psychological capacities suffice for this? Is it not possible, for example, that at the end of the statement I should have forgotten or incorrectly remembered the beginning? Must I not thus agree that for psychological reasons I can never be sure of the validity of an analytic judgment also?

To this there is the following answer: the possibility of a failure of the psychic mechanism must of course always be granted, but the consequences that follow from it are not correctly described in the sceptical questions just raised.

It can be that owing to a weakness of memory, and a thousand other causes, we do not understand a statement, or understand it erroneously (i.e. differently from the way it was intended)—but what does this signify? Well, so long as I have not understood a sentence it is not a statement at all for me, but a mere series of words, of sounds or written signs. In this case there is no problem, for only of a statement, not of an uncomprehended series of words, can one ask whether it is analytic or synthetic. But if I have misinterpreted a series of words, but nevertheless interpreted it as a statement, then I know of just *this* statement whether it is analytic or synthetic and therefore valid *a priori* or not.

One may not suppose that I could comprehend a statement as such and still be in doubt concerning its analytic character. For if it is analytic I have understood it only when I have understood it as analytic. To understand means nothing else, that is, than to be clear about the rules governing the use of the words in question; but it is precisely these rules of usage that make statements analytic. If I do not know whether a complex of words constitutes an analytic statement or not, this simply means that at that moment I lack the rules of usage: that therefore I have simply not understood the statement. Thus the case is that either I have understood nothing at all, and then nothing more is to be said, or I know whether the statement *which* I understand is synthetic or analytic (which of course does not presuppose that these words hover before me, that I am even acquainted with them). In the case of an analytic statement I know at one and the same time that it is valid, that formal truth belongs to it.

The above doubt concerning the validity of analytic statements was therefore out of order. I may indeed doubt whether I have correctly grasped the meaning of some complex of signs, in fact whether I shall ever understand the meaning of any sequence of words. But I cannot raise the question whether I can ascertain the correctness of an analytic statement. For to understand its meaning and to note its *a priori* validity are in an analytic statement *one and the same* process. In contrast, a synthetic assertion is characterized by the fact that I do not in the least know whether it is true or false if I have only ascertained its meaning. Its truth is determined only by comparison with experience. The process of grasping the meaning is here quite distinct from the process of verification.

There is but one exception to this. And we thus return to our "confirmations." These, that is, are always of the form "Here now so and so," for example "Here two black points coincide," or "Here yellow borders on blue," or also "Here now pain," etc. What is common to all these assertions is that *demonstrative* terms occur in them which have the sense of a present gesture, i.e. their rules of usage provide that in making the statements in which they occur some experience is had, the attention is directed upon something observed. What is referred to by such words as "here," "now," "this here," cannot be communicated by means of general definitions in words, but only by means of them together with pointing or gestures. "This here" has meaning only in connection with a gesture. In order therefore to understand the meaning of such an observation statement one must simultaneously execute the gesture, one must somehow point to reality.

In other words: I can understand the meaning of a "confirmation" only by, and when, comparing it with the facts, thus carrying out that process which is necessary for the verification of all synthetic statements. While in the case of all other synthetic statements determining the meaning is separate from, distinguishable from, determining the truth, in the case of observation statements they coincide, just as in the case of analytic statements. However different therefore "confirmations" are from analytic statements, they have in common that the occasion of understanding them is at the same time that of verifying them: I grasp their meaning at the same time as I grasp their truth. In the case of a confirmation it makes as little sense to ask whether I might be deceived regarding its truth as in the case of a tautology. Both are absolutely valid. However, while the analytic, tautological, statement is empty of content, the observation statement supplies us with the satisfaction of genuine knowledge of reality.

It has become clear, we may hope, that here everything depends on the characteristic of immediacy which is peculiar to observation statements and to which they owe their value and disvalue; the value of absolute validity, and the disvalue of uselessness as an abiding foundation.

A misunderstanding of this nature is responsible for most of the unhappy problems of protocol statements with which our enquiry began. If I make the confirmation "Here now blue," this is *not* the same as the protocol statement "M. S. perceived blue on the nth of April 1934 at such and such a time and such and such a place." The latter statement is a hypothesis and as such always characterized by uncertainty. The latter statement is equivalent to "M. S. made . . . (here time and place are to be given) the confirmation 'here now blue.' " And that this assertion is not identical with the confirmation occurring in it is clear. In protocol statements there is *always* mention of perceptions (or they are to be added in thought—the identity of the perceiving observer is important for a scientific protocol), while they are never mentioned in confirmations. A genuine confirmation cannot be written down, for as soon as I inscribe the demonstratives "here," "now," they lose their meaning. Neither can they be replaced by an indication of time and place, for as soon as one attempts to do this, the result, as we saw, is that one unavoidably substitutes for the observation statement a protocol statement which as such has a wholly different nature.

VIII

I believe that the problem of the basis of knowledge is now clarified.

If science is taken to be a system of statements in which one's interest as a logician is confined to their logical connections, the question of its basis, which would then be a "logical" question, can be answered quite arbitrarily. For one is free to define the basis as one wishes. In an abstract system of statements there is no priority and no posteriority. For instance, the most general statements of science, thus those that are normally selected as axioms, could be regarded as its ultimate foundation; but this name could just as well be reserved for the most particular statements, which would then more or less actually correspond to the protocols written down. Or any other choice would be possible. But all the statements of science are collectively and individually *hypotheses* the moment one considers them from the point of view of their truth value, their validity.

If attention is directed upon the relation of science to reality the system of its statements is seen to be that which it really is, namely, a means of finding one's way among the facts; of arriving at the joy of confirmation, the feeling of finality. The problem of the "basis" changes then automatically into that of the unshakeable point of contact between knowledge and reality. We have come to know these absolutely fixed points of contact, the confirmations, in their individuality: they are the only synthetic statements that are not *hypotheses*. They do not in any way lie at the base of science; but like a flame, cognition, as it were, licks out to them, reaching each but for a moment and then at once consuming it. And newly fed and strengthened, it flames onward to the next.

These moments of fulfilment and combustion are what is essential. All the light of knowledge comes from them. And it is for the source of this light the philosopher is really inquiring when he seeks the ultimate basis of all knowledge.

Bertrand Russell

Epistemological Premisses

Theory of knowledge is rendered difficult by the fact that it involves psychology, logic, and the physical sciences, with the result that confusions between different points of view are a constant danger. This danger is particularly acute in connexion with the problem of our present chapter, which is that of determining the premisses of our knowledge from an epistemological point of view. And there is a further source of confusion in the fact that, as already noted, theory of knowledge itself may be conceived in two different ways. On the one hand, accepting as knowledge whatever science recognizes as such, we may ask: how have we acquired this knowledge, and how best can we analyse it into premisses and inferences? On the other hand, we may adopt the Cartesian standpoint, and seek to divide what passes for knowledge into more certain and less certain portions. These two inquiries are not so distinct as they might seem, for, since the forms of inference involved are not demonstrative, our premisses will have more certainty than our conclusions.

Bertrand Russell, "Epistemological Premisses," "Basic Propositions," and "Factual Premisses," in *An Inquiry into Meaning and Truth* (London: George Allen & Unwin Ltd., 1940), pp. 124–57. Reprinted by permission.

But this fact only makes it the more difficult to avoid confusion between the two inquiries.

An epistemological premiss, which we shall now seek to define, must have three characteristics. It must be (*a*) a logical premiss, (*b*) a psychological premiss, and (*c*) true so far as we can ascertain. Concerning each of these something must be said.

(*a*) Given any systematic body of propositions, such as is contained in some science in which there are general laws, it is possible, usually in an indefinite number of ways, to pick out certain of the propositions as premisses, and deduce the remainder. In the Newtonian theory of the solar system, for example, we can take as premisses the law of gravitation together with the positions and velocities of the planets at a given moment. Any moment will do, and for the law of gravitation we can substitute Kepler's three laws. In conducting such analyses, the logician, as such, is indifferent to the truth or falsehood of the body of propositions concerned, provided they are mutually consistent (if they are not, he will have nothing to do with them). He will, for example, just as willingly consider an imaginary planetary system and a gravitational law other than that of the inverse square. Nor does he pretend that his premisses give the grounds for believing in their consequences, even when both are true. When we are considering grounds of belief, the law of gravitation is an inference, not a premiss.

The logician, in his search for premisses, has one purpose which is emphatically not shared by the epistemologist, namely, that he seeks a *minimum* set of premisses. A set of premisses is a minimum set, in relation to a given body of propositions, if from the whole set, but not from any part of the set, all the given body of propositions can be deduced. Usually many minimum sets exist; the logician prefers those that are shortest, and, among two equally short, the one that is simplest. But these preferences are merely aesthetic.

(*b*) A psychological premiss may be defined as a belief which is not caused by any other belief or beliefs. Psychologically, any belief may be considered to be inferred when it is caused by other beliefs, however invalid the inference may be for logic. The most obvious class of beliefs not caused by other beliefs are those that result directly from perception. These, however, are not the only beliefs that are psychological premisses. Others are required to produce our faith in deductive arguments. Perhaps induction also is based, psychologically, upon primitive beliefs. What others there may be I shall not at the moment inquire.

(*c*) Since we are concerned with theory of *knowledge,* not merely of *belief,* we cannot accept all psychological premisses as epistemological premisses, for two psychological premisses may contradict each other, and therefore not all are true. For example I may think 'there is a man coming downstairs', and the next moment I may realize that it is a reflection of myself in a mirror. For such reasons, psychological premisses must be subjected to analysis before being accepted as premisses for theory of knowledge. In this analysis we are as little sceptical as possible. We assume that perception *can* cause knowledge, although it *may* cause error if we are logically careless. Without this fundamental assumption, we should be reduced to complete scepticism as regards the empirical world. No arguments are logically possible either for or against complete scepticism, which must be admitted to be one among possible philosophies. It is, however, too short and simple to be interesting. I shall, therefore, without more ado, develop the opposite hypothesis, according to which beliefs caused by perception are to be accepted unless there are positive grounds for rejecting them.

Since we can never be completely certain that any given proposition is true, we can never be completely certain that it is an epistemological premiss, even when it possesses the other two defining properties and seems to us to be true. We shall attach different 'weights' (to use a term employed by Professor Reichenbach) to different propositions which we believe and which, if true, are epistemological premisses: the greatest weight will be given to those of which we are most certain, and the least to those of which we are least certain. Where there is a logical conflict we shall sacrifice the less certain, unless a large number of these are opposed to a very small number of the more certain.

Owing to the absence of certainty, we shall not seek, like the logician, to reduce our premisses to a minimum. On the contrary, we shall be glad when a number of propositions which support one another can all be accepted as epistemological premisses, since this increases the probability of all of them. (I am not thinking of logical deducibility, but of inductive compatibility.)

Epistemological premisses are different according as they are momentary, individual, or social. Let us illustrate. I believe that $16^2 = 256$; at the moment, I believe this on grounds of memory, but probably at some time I did the sum, and I have convinced myself that the received rules of multiplication follow from the premisses of logic. Therefore taking my life as a whole, $16^2 = 256$ is inferred, not from memory, but from logic. In this case, if my logic is correct, there is no difference between the individual and the social premisses.

But now let us take the existence of the Straits of Magellan. Again, my momentary epistemological premiss is memory. But I have had, at various times, better reasons: maps, books of travel, etc. *My* reasons have been the assertions of others, whom I believed to be well-informed and honest. *Their* reasons, traced back, lead to percepts: Magellan, and others who have been in the region concerned when it was not foggy, saw what they took to be land and sea, and by dint of systematized inferences made maps. Treating the knowledge of mankind as one whole, it is the percepts of Magellan and other travellers that provide the epistemological premisses for belief in the Straits of Magellan. Writers who are interested in knowledge as a social phenomenon are apt to concentrate upon social epistemological premisses. For certain purposes this is legitimate, for others not. Social epistemological premisses are relevant in deciding whether to spend public money on a new telescope or an investigation of the Trobriand Islanders. Laboratory experiments aim at establishing new factual premisses which can be incorporated in the accepted system of human knowledge. But for the philosopher there are two prior questions: what reason (if any) have I for believing in the existence of other people? And what reason (if any) have I now for believing that I existed at certain past times, or, more generally, that my present beliefs concerning past times are more or less correct? For me now, only my momentary epistemological premisses are really premisses; the rest must be in some sense inferred. For me as opposed to others, my individual premisses are premisses, but the percepts of others are not. Only those who regard mankind as in some mystical sense a single entity possessed of a single persistent mind have a right to confine their epistemology to the consideration of *social* epistemological premisses.

In the light of these distinctions, let us consider possible definitions of empiricism. I think that the great majority of empiricists are *social* empiricists, a few are *individual* empiricists, and hardly any are *momentary* empiricists. What all empiricists have in common is emphasis upon *perceptive premisses.* We shall seek a definition of this term presently; for the moment I shall say only a few preliminary words.

Speaking psychologically, a 'perceptive premiss' may be defined as a belief caused, as immediately as possible, by a percept. If I believe there *will be* an eclipse because the astronomers say so, my belief is not a perceptive premiss; if I believe there *is* an eclipse because I see it, that is a perceptive premiss. But immediately difficulties arise. What astronomers call an eclipse is a public event, whereas what I am seeing may be due to a defect in my eye or my telescope. While, therefore, the belief 'there is an eclipse' may arise in me without conscious inference, this belief goes beyond the mere expression of what I see. Thus we are driven, in epistemology, to define 'perceptive premiss' more narrowly than would be necessary in psychology. We are driven to this because we want a 'perceptive premiss' to be something which there is never good reason to think false, or, what comes to the same thing, something so defined that two perceptive premisses cannot contradict each other.

Assuming 'perceptive premisses' to have been adequately defined, let us return to the definition of 'empiricism'. My momentary knowledge consists largely of memory, and my individual knowledge consists largely of testimony. But memory, when it is veridical, is related to a previous perceptive premiss, and testimony, when it is veridical, is related to some one else's perceptive premiss. Social empiricism takes these perceptive premisses of other times or other persons as *the* empirical premisses for what is now accepted, and thus evades the problems connected with memory and testimony. This is plainly illegitimate, since there is reason to believe that both memory and testimony sometimes deceive. I, now, can only arrive at the perceptive premisses of other times and other persons by an inference from memory and testimony. If I, now, am to have any reason to believe what I read yesterday in the Encyclopaedia, I must, now, find reason to trust my memory, and to believe, in suitable circumstances, what comes to me in the form of testimony. I must, that is to say, start from *momentary* epistemological premisses. To do anything else is to evade problems which it is part of the business of epistemology to consider.

It follows from the above considerations that epistemology cannot say: 'knowledge is wholly derivable from perceptive premisses together with the principles of demonstrative and probable inference'. Memory premisses, at least, must be added to perceptive premisses. What premisses, if any, must be added in order to make testimony admissible (with common sense limitations), is a difficult question, which must be borne in mind, but need not be discussed at the moment. The paramount importance of perception, in any tenable form of empiricism, is causal. Memory, when veridical, is causally dependent upon a previous perception; testimony, when veridical, is causally dependent upon some one else's perception. We may say, therefore: 'all human knowledge of matters of fact is in part *caused* by perception'. But a principle of this sort is clearly one which can only be known by inference, if at all; it cannot be a premiss in epistemology. It is fairly clear that part of the *cause* of my believing in the Straits of Magellan is that certain people have seen them, but this is not the *ground* of my belief, since it has to be proved to me (or rather made probable) that such people have had such percepts. To me, their percepts are inferences, not premisses.

BASIC PROPOSITIONS

'Basic Propositions', as I wish to use the term, are a subclass of epistemological premisses, namely those which are caused, as immediately as possible, by perceptive experiences. This excludes the premisses required for inference, whether demonstrative or probable. It excludes also any extra-logical premisses used for inference, if there be such—e.g., 'what is red is not blue', 'if A is earlier than B, B is not earlier than A'. Such propositions demand careful discussion, but whether premisses or not, they are in any case not 'basic' in the above sense.

I have borrowed the term 'basic proposition' from Mr. A. J. Ayer, who uses it as the equivalent of the German *Protokollsatz* employed by the logical positivists. I shall use it, perhaps, not in exactly the same sense in which it is used by Mr. Ayer, but I shall use it in connexion with the same problems as those which have led him and the logical positivists to require such a term.

Many writers on theory of knowledge hold that from a single occurrence nothing is to be learnt. They think of all empirical knowledge as consisting of inductions from a number of more or less similar experiences. For my part, I think that such a view makes history impossible and memory unintelligible. I hold that, from any occurrence that a man notices, he can obtain knowledge, which, if his linguistic habits are adequate, he can express in sentences. His linguistic habits, of course, have been generated by past experiences, but these only determine the words he uses. The truth of what he says, given the meanings of his words, can, given adequate care, be wholly dependent upon the character of one occurrence that he is noticing. When this is the case, what he is asserting is what I call a 'basic proposition'.

The discussion of basic propositions has two parts. First, it is necessary to argue, as against opposing opinions, that there are basic propositions. Secondly, it is necessary to determine just what sort of thing they can affirm, and to show that this is usually much less than common sense asserts on the occasions on which the basic propositions in question are epistemologically justifiable.

A basic proposition is intended to have several characteristics. It must be known independently of inference from other propositions, but not independently of evidence, since there must be a perceptive occurrence which gives the cause and is considered to give the reason for believing the basic proposition. Then again, from a logical point of view, it should be possible so to analyse our empirical knowledge that its primitive propositions (apart from logic and generalities) should all have been, at the moment when they were first believed, basic propositions. This requires that basic propositions should not contradict each other, and makes it desirable, if possible, to give them a logical form which makes mutual contradiction impossible. These conditions demand, therefore, that a basic proposition should have two properties:

(1) It must be caused by some sensible occurrence;
(2) It must be of such a form that no other basic proposition can contradict it.

As to (1): I do not wish to insist upon the word 'caused', but the belief must arise on the occasion of some sensible occurrence, and must be such that, if questioned, it will be defended by the argument 'why, I see it' or something similar. The belief refers to a certain time, and the reasons for believing it did not exist before that time. If the event in question had been previously inferred or expected, the evidence beforehand was different from that afforded by perception, and would generally be considered less decisive. Perception affords for the belief evidence which is considered the strongest possible, but which is not verbal.

As to (2): the judgements that common sense bases upon perception, such as 'there is a dog', usually go beyond the present datum, and may therefore be refuted by subsequent evidence. We cannot know, from perception alone, anything about other times or about the perceptions of others or about bodies understood in an impersonal sense. That is why, in the search for data, we are driven to analysis: we are seeking a core which is logically independent of other occurrences. When you think you see a dog, what is really given in perception may be expressed in the words 'there is a canoid patch of colour'. No previous or subsequent occurrence, and no experience of others, can prove the falsehood of this proposition. It is true that, in the sense in which we infer eclipses, there can be evidence against a present judgement of perception, but this evidence is inductive and merely probable, and cannot stand against 'the evidence of the senses'. When we have analysed a judgement of perception in this way, we are left with something which cannot be *proved* to be false.

We may then define a 'basic proposition' as follows: it is a proposition which arises on occasion of a perception, which is the evidence for its truth, and it has a form such that no two propositions having this form can be mutually inconsistent if derived from different percepts.

Examples would be: 'I am hot', 'that is red', 'what a foul smell'. All basic propositions in the above sense are personal, since no one else can share my percepts, and transitory, for after a moment they are replaced by memories.

In place of the above definition, we *can* adopt a logical definition. We can consider the whole body of empirical knowledge, and define 'basic propositions' as those of its logically indemonstrable propositions which are themselves empirical, i.e., assert some temporal occurrence. This definition, I think, is extensionally equivalent to the above epistemological definition.

Some among logical positivists, notably Neurath and Hempel, deny that any set of propositions can be singled out as 'basic', or as in any important epistemological sense premisses for the remainder. Their view is that 'truth' is a *syntactical,* not a *semantic* concept: a proposition is 'true' within a given system if it is consistent with the rest of the system, but there may be other systems, inconsistent with the first, in which the proposition in question will be 'false'. There is no such process, according to them, as deriving the truth of a proposition from some non-verbal occurrence: the world of words is a closed self-contained world, and the philosopher need not concern himself with anything outside it.

In logic and mathematics, the view that 'truth' is a syntactical concept is correct, since it is syntax that guarantees the truth of tautologies. Truth, in this sphere, is discoverable by studying the *form* of the proposition concerned; there is no need to go outside to something that the proposition 'means' or 'asserts'. The authors in question assimilate empirical to logical truth, thus reverting unconsciously to the tradition of Spinoza, Leibniz, and Hegel. In rejecting their view, as I shall contend that we must, we are committing ourselves to the opinion that 'truth' in empirical material has a meaning different from that which it bears in logic and mathematics.

The coherence theory of truth, as I have just said, is that of Hegel. It is worked out, from a Hegelian point of view, in Joachim's book *The Nature of Truth,* which I criticized, from the standpoint of the correspondence theory, in *Philosophical Essays* (1910). The Hegelian theory, however, differs from that of Neurath, since it holds that only one body of mutually coherent propositions is possible, so that every proposition remains definitely true or false. Neurath, on the contrary, takes the view of Pirandello: 'so it is, if you think so'.

The theory of Neurath and Hempel is set forth in articles in *Erkenntnis* and *Analysis.* The following are quotations or paraphrases of their words.

An assertion is called right when we can fit it in (*eingliedern*).

Assertions are compared with assertions, not with 'experiences' (*Erlebnissen*).

There are no primary *Protokollsätze* or propositions needing no confirmation.

All *Protokollsätze* should be put into the following form: 'Otto's protocol at 3.17: {Otto's word-thought at 3.16 (In the room at 3.15 was a table perceived by Otto)}.'

Here the repeated use of the word 'Otto' instead of 'I' is essential.

Although, according to the above, it would seem as if we were debarred from knowing anything about the physical world except that physicists make certain assertions about it, Neurath nevertheless commits himself to the statement that sentences are mounds of ink or systems of air-waves (*Erkenntnis* IV, 209). He does not tell us how he discovered this fact; presumably he only means that physicists assert it.

Neurath in 'Radikaler Physikalismus and Wirkliche Welt' (*Erkenntnis* IV, 5, 1934), maintains the following theses:

1. All *Realsätze* of science including *Protokollsätze,* are chosen as the result of *Entschlüsse* (decisions), and can be altered.
2. We call a *Realsatz false* when it cannot fit into the edifice of science.
3. The control of certain *Realsätze* is compatibility with certain *Protokollsätze:* instead of *die Wirklichkeit* we have a number of mutually incompatible but internally coherent bodies of propositions, choice between which is *'nicht logisch ausgezeichnet'*.

The practice of life, Neurath says, quickly reduces ambiguity; moreover the opinions of neighbours influence us.

Carl G. Hempel 'On the logical positivist's theory of truth' (*Analysis* II, 4 January 1935) sets forth the history of the views of logical positivists as to *Protokollsätze.* He says the theory developed step by step from a correspondence theory into a restrained coherence theory. He says that Neurath denies that we can ever compare reality with propositions, and that Carnap agrees.

We started, he says, from Wittgenstein's atomic propositions; these were replaced by *Protokollsätze,* at first thought to express the results of observation. But then *Protokollsätze* were no longer the result of observation, and then no class of statements was admitted as basic.

Carnap (Hempel continues) says there are *no* absolutely first statements for science; even for *Protokollsätze* further justification may be demanded. Nevertheless:

'Carnap and Neurath do by no means intend to say: "There are no facts, there are only propositions"; on the contrary, the occurrence of certain statements in the protocol of an observer or in a scientific book is regarded as an empirical fact, and the propositions occurring as empirical objects. What the authors do intend to say, may be expressed more precisely thanks to Carnap's distinction between the material and the formal mode of speech. . . .

'The concept of truth may be characterized in this formal mode of speech, namely, in a crude formulation, as a sufficient agreement between the system of acknowledged *Protokollsätze* and the logical consequences which may be deduced from the statement and other statements which are already adopted. . . .

'Saying that empirical statements "express facts" and consequently that truth consists in a certain correspondence between statements and the "facts" expressed by them, is a typical form of the material mode of speech.' (p. 54) [i.e., 'truth' is syntactic, not semantic.]

'In order to have a relatively high degree of certainty, one will go back to the *Protokollsätze* of reliable observers.' [Two questions arise: A. How do we know who are reliable? B. How do we know what they say?]

'The system of *Protokollsätze* we call true . . . may only be characterized by the historical fact, that it is the system which is actually adopted by mankind, and especially by the scientists of our culture circle.

'A *Protokollsatz,* like every other statement, is at the end adopted or rejected by a decision.'

Protokollsätze are now superfluous. It is implied that there is no definite world with definite properties.

I think Neurath and Hempel may be more or less right as regards *their* problem, which is the construction of an encyclopaedia. They want public impersonal propositions, incorporated in public science. But *public* knowledge is a construction, containing less than the sum of *private* knowledges.

The man who is constructing an encyclopaedia is not expected himself to conduct experiments; he is expected to compare the opinions of the best authorities, and arrive, so far as he can, at the standard scientific opinion of his time. Thus in dealing with a scientific question his data are opinions, not direct observations of the subject-matter. The individual men of science, however, whose opinions are the encyclopaedist's premisses, have not themselves merely compared other investigators' opinions; they have made observations and conducted experiments, on the basis of which they have been prepared, if necessary, to reject previously unanimous opinions. The purpose of an observation or experiment is to give rise to a perceptive experience, as a result of which the percipient has new knowledge, at first purely personal and private. Others may repeat the experiment, and in the end the result becomes part of *public* knowledge; but this public knowledge is merely an abstract or epitome of private knowledges.

All theory of knowledge must start from 'what do *I* know?' not from 'what does mankind know?' For how can I tell what mankind knows? Only by (*a*) personal observation of what it says in the books it has written, and (*b*) weighing the evidence in favour of the view that what is said in the books is true. If I am Copernicus, I shall decide against the books; if I am a student of cuneiform, I may decide that Darius did not say what he is supposed to have said about his campaigns.

There is a tendency—not confined to Neurath and Hempel, but prevalent in much modern philosophy—to forget the arguments of Descartes and Berkeley. It may be that these arguments can be refuted, though, as regards our present question, I do not believe that they can be. But in any case they are too weighty to be merely ignored. In the present connexion, the point is that *my* knowledge as to matters of fact must be based upon *my* perceptive experiences, through which alone I can ascertain what is received as public knowledge.

This applies, in particular, to what is to be found in books. That Carnap's books say whatever they do say is the sort of thing that would be generally accepted as public knowledge.

But what do I know?

(1) What I see when I look at them
(2) What I hear when others read them aloud
(3) What I see when others quote them in print
(4) What I see when I compare two copies of the same book.

Hence, I pass, by elaborate and doubtful inferences, to *public* knowledge.

On Neurath's view, language has no relation to non-linguistic occurrences, but this makes many every-day experiences inexplicable. For instance: I arrived in Messina from a sea voyage in 1901 and found flags at half-mast; on inquiry I learnt that McKinley had been murdered. If language has no relation to the non-linguistic, this whole procedure was frivolous.

As we saw, Neurath says the proper form of a protocol sentence is: 'Otto's protocol at 3.17: {Otto's word-thought at 3.16 was: (In the room at 3.15 there was a table perceived by Otto)}.'

It seems to me that, in giving this form to protocol sentences, Neurath shows himself far more credulous than the man who says 'there's a dog'. In the inside bracket he perceived a table, which is just as bad as perceiving a dog. In the outside bracket he finds words for what he has perceived, viz.: 'in the room at 3.15 there was a table perceived by Otto'. And a minute later he writes down the words at which he has arrived. This last stage involves memory and the continuity of the ego. The second stage involves memory also, and in addition involves introspection.

Let us take the matter in detail.

To begin with the inner bracket: 'in the room at 3.15 there was a table perceived by Otto'. We may take the words 'in the room' as merely meaning that the table had a perceptual background, and in that sense they may be allowed to pass. The words 'at 3.15' imply that Otto was looking at his watch as well as at the table, and that his watch was right. These are grave matters, if taken seriously. Let us suppose that, instead of 'at 3.15' we say 'once upon a time', and instead of '3.16' we say 'a little later', and instead of '3.17' we say 'a little later still'. This eliminates the difficulties of time-measurement, which surely Neurath cannot have intended to introduce. We come now to the words 'there was a table'. These are objectionable on the same grounds as 'there's a dog'. It may not have been a table, but a reflection in a mirror. Or perhaps it was like Macbeth's dagger, a phantasm called up by the intention of committing a murder on a table. Or perhaps a very unusual collocation of quantum phenomena caused a momentary appearance of a table, which was going to disappear in another moment. It may be conceded that this last hypothesis is improbable, that Dr. Neurath is not the sort of person who would think of murdering anybody, and that his room probably contains no mirror large enough for the reflection of a table that is elsewhere. But such considerations ought not to be necessary where protocol-sentences are concerned.

I come now to a still more serious matter. We are told, not only that there was a table, but that there was a table 'perceived by Otto'. This last is a social statement, derived from experience of social life, and by no means primitive; in so far as there is reason to believe it, it is based upon argument. Otto perceives the table, or rather a tabular appearance —well and good—but he does not perceive that Otto perceives it. What is 'Otto'? So far as he can be known, either to himself or others, he is a series of occurrences. One of them is the visual appearance which he rashly calls a table. By the help of conversation, he is led to the conclusion that the occurrences people mention form bundles, each of which is one person, and that the appearance of the table belongs to the same bundle as the subsequent word-thought and the still more subsequent act of writing. But all this elaboration is no part of the visual datum. If he always lived alone, he would never be led to distinguish between 'there's a table' and 'I see a table'; in fact, he would always use the former phrase, if one could suppose him using phrases at all. The word 'I' is a word of limitation, meaning 'I, not you'; it is by no means part of any primitive datum. And this is still more evident when, instead of 'I', Neurath says 'Otto'.

So far we have only been concerned with what happened at 3.15. It is now time to consider what happened at 3.16.

At 3.16, Otto put into words what had happened at 3.15. Now I am willing to admit that the words he used are such as well might be employed by a man who was not on the lookout for pitfalls. There is, therefore, less to criticize at this stage. What he thought may well not have been true, but I am quite willing to concede that he thought it, if he says so.

At 3.17, Otto carried out an act of introspection, and decided that, a minute ago, a certain phrase had been in his thoughts, not just as a phrase, but as an assertion concerning an earlier perception which, at 3.16, he still remembered. It is only what happens at 3.17 that is actually asserted. Thus according to Neurath the data of empirical science are all of the following form:

'A certain person (who happens to be myself, but this, we are told, is irrelevant) is aware at a certain time that a little while ago he believed a phrase which asserted that a little while before that he had seen a table.'

That is to say, all empirical knowledge is based upon recollections of words used on former occasions. Why recollections should be preferred to perceptions, and why no recollections should be admitted except of thought-words, is not explained. Neurath is making an attempt to secure publicity in data, but by mistake has arrived at one of the most subjective forms of knowledge, namely recollection of past thoughts. This result is not encouraging to those who believe that data can be public.

The particular form given to protocol-sentences by Neurath is, perhaps, not an essential part of his doctrine. Let us therefore examine it more generally.

Let us repeat some quotations.[1] 'Statements are compared with statements, not with experiences' (N). 'A protocol-statement, like every other statement, is at the end adopted or rejected by a decision' (N). 'The system of *Protokollsätze* we call true . . . may only be characterized by the historical fact, that it is the system which is actually adopted by mankind, and especially by the scientists of our culture circle' (H). 'Instead of *reality* we have a number of mutually incompatible but internally coherent bodies of propositions, choice between which is not logically determined (*logisch ausgezeichnet*)' (N).

This attempt to make the linguistic world self-sufficient is open to many objections. Take first the necessity of empirical statements about words, e.g., 'Neurath says so-and-so'. How do I know this? By seeing certain black marks on a white ground. But this experience must not, according to Neurath and Hempel, be made a ground for my assertion that Neurath says so-and-so. Before I can assert this, I must ascertain the opinion of mankind, and especially of my culture circle, as to what Neurath says. But how am I to ascertain it? I go round to all the scientists of my culture circle, and say: 'what does Neurath say on p. 364?' In reply I hear certain sounds, but this is an experience, and therefore does not give any ground for an opinion as to what they said. When A answers, I must go round to B, C, D, and the rest of my culture circle, to ascertain what they think A said. And so on throughout an endless regress. If eyes and ears do not enable me to know what Neurath said, no assemblage of scientists, however distinguished, can enable me to know. If Neurath is right, his opinions are not known to me through his writings, but through my decisions and those of my culture circle. If we choose to attribute to him opinions completely different from those which he in fact holds, it will be useless for him to contradict, or to point to pages in his writings; for by such behaviour he will only cause us to have experiences, which are never a ground for statements.

Hempel, it is true, denies such consequences of his doctrine. He says: 'Carnap and Neurath do by no means intend to say: "there are no facts, there are only propositions"; on the contrary, the occurrence of certain statements in the protocol of an observer or in a scientific book is regarded as an empirical fact, and the propositions occurring as empirical objects.' But this makes nonsense of the whole theory. For what is an 'empirical fact'? To say: 'A is an empirical fact' is, according to Neurath and Hempel, to say: 'the proposition "A occurs" is consistent with a certain body of already accepted propositions'. In a different culture circle another body of propositions may be accepted; owing to this fact, Neurath is an exile. He remarks himself that practical life soon

[1] In what follows, 'N' stands for 'Neurath' and 'H' for 'Hempel'.

reduces the ambiguity, and that we are influenced by the opinions of neighbours. In other words, empirical truth can be determined by the police. This doctrine, it is evident, is a complete abandonment of empiricism, of which the very essence is that only experiences can determine the truth of falsehood of non-tautologous propositions.

Neurath's doctrine, if taken seriously, deprives empirical propositions of all meaning. When I say 'the sun is shining', I do not mean that this is one of a number of sentences among which there is no contradiction; I mean something which is not verbal, and for the sake of which such words as 'sun' and 'shining' were invented. The purpose of words, though philosophers seem to forget this simple fact, is to deal with matters other than words. If I go into a restaurant and order my dinner, I do not want my words to fit into a system with other words, but to bring about the presence of food. I could have managed without words, by taking what I want, but this would have been less convenient. The verbalist theories of some modern philosophers forget the homely practical purposes of every-day words, and lose themselves in a neo-neo-Platonic mysticism. I seem to hear them saying 'in the beginning was the Word', not 'in the beginning was what the word means'. It is remarkable that this reversion to ancient metaphysics should have occurred in the attempt to be ultra-empirical.

FACTUAL PREMISSES

Assuming, as I shall do henceforth, that there are basic propositions, it seems to me that, for theory of knowledge, 'basic propositions' may be alternatively defined as 'those propositions about particular occurrences which, after a critical scrutiny, we still believe independently of any extraneous evidence in their favour'.

Let us consider the clauses of this definition, and let us begin at the end. There may be evidence in favour of a basic proposition, but it is not this evidence *alone* that causes our belief. You may wake up in the morning and see that it is daylight, and you may see from your watch that it must be daylight. But even if your watch pointed to midnight, you would not doubt that it is daylight. In any scientific system, a number of propositions based on observations support each other, but each is capable of commanding belief on its own account. Moreover mutual support among basic propositions is only possible on the basis of some theory.

There are cases, however—chiefly where memory is concerned—in which our belief, though not inferential, is more or less uncertain. In such cases, a system composed of such beliefs wins more acceptance than any one of them singly. I think Mr Z. invited me to dinner on Thursday; I look in my diary, and find an entry to that effect. Both my memory and my diary are fallible, but when they agree I think it unlikely that they are both wrong. I will return to this kind of case later; for the present, I wish to exclude it. It is to be observed, meantime, that a non-inferential belief need not be either certain or indubitable.

Now comes the question of critical scrutiny, and a very awkward question it is. You say 'there's a dog', and feel quite satisfied of the truth of your statement. I shall not suppose your faith attacked by Bishop Berkeley, but by one of his allies in modern business. The producer comes to you and says: 'ah, I hoped you would think it was a dog, but in fact it was recorded by the new system of Technicolor, which is revolutionizing the cinema'. Perhaps the physiologist in future will be able to stimulate the optic nerve in the way necessary for seeing a dog; I have gathered from the works of Bulldog Drummond that contact of a fist with the eye enables people to see the starry heavens as well as the moral law. And we all know what hypnotists can do; we know also how emotional excitement can produce phenomena like Macbeth's dagger. On these grounds, which are all derived from common sense, not from philosophy, a man possessed of intellectual prudence will avoid such rash credulity as is involved in saying 'there's a dog'.

But what, then, will such a man say on such an occasion? Having been badly brought up, he will have an *impulse* to say 'dog', which he will have to restrain. He will say: 'there is a canoid patch of colour'. Suppose, now, having been impressed by the method of Cartesian doubt, he tries to make himself disbelieve even this. What reason can he find for disbelieving it? It cannot be disproved by anything else that he may see or hear; and he can have no better reason for believing in other sights or sounds than in this one; if he carries doubt to this length, he cannot even know that he said 'dog', if he did say so.

We should note that basic propositions must be just as true when applied to dreams as when applied to waking life; for, after all, dreams do really occur. This is a criterion for discriminating between what is basic and what is interpretative.

We thus arrive at the momentary object of perception as the least questionable thing in our experience, and as therefore the criterion and touchstone of all other certainties and pseudo-certainties.

But for theory of knowledge it is not sufficient that we should perceive something; it is necessary that we should express what we perceive in words. Now most object-words are condensed inductions; this is true of the word 'dog', as we have already had occasion to notice. We must avoid such words, if we wish to be merely recording what we perceive. To do this is very difficult, and requires a special vocabulary. We have seen that this vocabulary includes predicate-words such as 'red', and relation-words such as 'precedes', but not names of persons or physical objects or classes of such terms.

We have considered the subject of 'basic propositions' or *Protokollsätze,* and tried to show that empirical knowledge is impossible without them. It will be remembered that we defined a 'basic proposition' by two characteristics:

(1) It arises on occasion of a perception, which is the evidence for its truth;
(2) It has a form such that no two propositions having this form can be mutually inconsistent if derived from different percepts.

A proposition having these two characteristics cannot be disproved, but it would be rash to say that it *must be* true.

Perhaps no actual proposition quite rigidly fulfils the definition. But pure perceptive propositions remain a limit to which we can approach asymptotically, and the nearer we approach the smaller is the risk of error.

Empirical knowledge requires, however, other premisses asserting matters of fact, in addition to pure perceptive propositions. I shall give the name 'factual premiss' to any uninferred proposition which asserts something having a date, and which I believe after a critical scrutiny. I do not mean that the date is part of the assertion, but merely that some kind of temporal occurrence is what is involved in the truth of the assertion.

Factual premisses are not alone sufficient for empirical knowledge, since most of it is inferred. We require, in addition, the premisses necessary for deduction, and those other premisses, whatever they may be, that are necessary for the non-demonstrative inferences upon which science depends. Perhaps there are also some general propositions such as 'if A precedes B, and B precedes C, then A precedes C' and 'yellow is more like green than like blue'. Such propositions, however, as already mentioned, call for a lengthy discussion. For the present, I am only concerned with those premisses of our empirical knowledge which have to do with particular occurrences, i.e., with those that I am calling 'factual premisses'. These, it seems to me, are of four kinds:

I. Perceptual propositions.
II. Memory propositions.
III. Negative basic propositions.
IV. Basic propositions concerning present propositional attitudes, i.e. concerning what I am believing, doubting, desiring, etc.

I. Perceptual Propositions. Suppose, as in an earlier chapter, that we see a red square inscribed in a blue circle. We may say 'there is a square in a circle', 'there is a red figure in a blue one', 'there is a red square in a blue circle'. All these are judgements of perception. The perceptual datum always allows many propositions, all expressing some aspect of it. The propositions are more abstract than the datum, of necessity, since words classify. But there is no theoretical limit to the accuracy of specification that is possible, and there is nothing in the perceptual datum that is essentially incapable of being expressed in words.

The correspondence theory of truth, as applied to judgements of perception, may be interpreted in a way which would be false. It would be a mistake to think that, corresponding to every true judgement of perception, there is a separate fact. Thus in the above case of the circle and the square, there is a circle of a certain colour and of certain angular dimensions, and inside it there is a square of a certain other colour and of certain other angular dimensions. All this is only one datum, from which a variety of judgements of perception can be derived. There is not, outside language, a fact 'that there is a square in a circle', and another fact 'that there is a red figure in a blue figure'. There are no facts 'that so-and-so'. There are percepts, from which, by analysis, we derive propositions 'that so-and-so'. But so long as this is realized, it will do no harm if percepts are called 'facts'.

II. Memory Propositions. There are considerable difficulties about basic propositions of this class. For, first, memory is fallible, so that in any given case it is difficult to feel the same degree of certainty as in a judgement of perception; secondly, no memory proposition is, strictly speaking, verifiable, since nothing in the present or the future makes any proposition about the past necessary; but thirdly, it is impossible to doubt that there have been events in the past, or to believe that the world has only just begun. This third consideration shows that there must be factual premisses about the past, while the first and second make it difficult to say what they are.

I think, to begin with, that we must exclude from the category of memories what we know about the *immediate* past. For instance, when we see a quick movement, we know that the object concerned was in one place and is in another; but this is all to be included in perception, and cannot be counted as a case of memory. This is shown by the fact that seeing a movement is different from seeing a thing first in one place and then in another.[1]

[1] Ah, yet doth beauty, like a dial-hand,
Steal from his figure, and no pace perceived.
[Shakespeare, Sonnet CIV]

It is by no means easy to distinguish between memory and habit; in ordinary speech, the distinction is ignored where verbal habits are concerned. A child is said to 'remember' the multiplication table if he has the correct verbal habits, although the multiplication table never happened and he may not remember any of the occasions on which he learnt it. Our memory of past events is sometimes of the same sort: we have a verbal habit of narrative, but nothing more. This happens especially with incidents that one relates frequently. But how about past incidents that one has never recalled till now, or at any rate not for a long time? Even then, the memory may be recalled by association, which is a form of habit. Turgenev's *Smoke* opens with the smell of heliotrope recalling a long-past love affair. Here the memory is involuntary; there is, however, also deliberate recollection, for example in writing an autobiography. I think that association is still the main agent here. We start from some prominent incident that we remember easily, and gradually associations lead us on to things that we had not thought of for a long time. The prominent incident itself has remained prominent, usually, because it has many associative links with the present. It is obvious that we are not always remembering everything that we can remember, and that what causes us to remember a given occurrence at a given moment is some association with something in the present. Thus association is certainly a vital factor in the occurrence of a recollection. But this leaves us still in doubt as to the epistemological status of memory.

Take, first, the fact that we know what is meant by the past. Would this be possible without memory? It may be said that we know what is meant by the future, although we have no memory of it. But I think the future is defined by relation to the past: it is 'a time when what is now the present is past'. Lapse of time, up to a point, can be understood from the specious present: when a person utters a short sentence, say 'dinner is served', we know there is a lapse of time between the first word and the last, though the whole sentence comes within the specious present. But in true memory there is a pastness of an altogether different kind, and this is something with which association has nothing to do. Say you meet a man whom you have not seen for twenty years: association will account for any words or images connected with the previous meeting that may come into your mind, but will not account for the reference of these words or images to the past. You may find it impossible to refer them to the present, but why not treat them as mere imaginative fantasies? You do not do this, but treat them as referring to something that really happened. It would seem, therefore, that the mere fact that we can understand the word 'past' implies knowledge that *something* happened in the past. Since it is hardly possible that our most primitive knowledge of the past should refer to a vague 'something', there must be more definite memories which are to be accepted as basic propositions.

Let us take some recollection that it is very difficult to doubt. Suppose you receive a telegram to say that your uncle in Australia has left you a million pounds, and you go upstairs to tell your wife. By the time you reach her, your first reading of the telegram has become a memory, but you can hardly doubt that it occurred. Or take more ordinary events: at the end of the day, you can recall many things that you have done since you got up, and concerning some, at least, you feel a high degree of certainty. Suppose you set to work to remember as many as you can. There are things that you know because they always happen: that you dressed, breakfasted, and so on. But in regard even to them, there is a very clear difference between knowing that they must have occurred and remembering them. It seems to me that, in true memory, we have images to which we say 'yes' or 'no'. In some cases, we say 'yes' emphatically and without hesitation; in others, we depend partly upon context. For our purpose, the emphatic cases are the important ones. Images come, it seems to me, in three ways: as merely imaginary, or with a yes-feeling, or with a no-feeling. When they come with a yes-feeling, but do not fit into the present, they are referred to the past. (I do not mean that this is a complete account of what happens in memory.) Thus all memory involves propositional attitudes, meaning, and external references; in this it differs from judgements of perception.

No memory is indubitable. I have had memories in dreams, just as definite as the best memories of waking life, but wholly untrue. I once, in a dream, remembered that Whitehead and I had murdered Lloyd George a month ago. Judgements of perception are just as true when applied to dreams as when applied to waking life; this, indeed, is a criterion for the correct interpretation of judgements of perception. But memory judgements in dreams, except when they consist in remembering an earlier part of the dream or a real event of waking life, are erroneous.

Since memories are not indubitable, we seek various ways of reinforcing them. We make contemporary records, or we seek confirmation from other witnesses, or we look for reasons tending to show that what we recollect was what was to be expected. In such ways we can increase the likelihood of any given recollection being correct, but we cannot free ourselves from dependence on memory in general. This is obvious as regards the testimony of other witnesses. As regards contemporary records, they are seldom *strictly* contemporary, and if they are, it cannot be subsequently known except through the memory of the person making the record. Suppose you remember on November 8th that last night you saw a very bright meteor, and you find on your desk a note in your handwriting saying: 'at 20h. 32m. G.M.T. on November 7th, I saw a bright meteor in the constellation Hercules. Note made at 20h. 33m. G.M.T.' You may remember making the note; if so, the memory of the meteor and the note confirm each other. But if you are discarding memory as a source of knowledge, you will not know how the note got there. It may have been made by a forger, or by yourself as a practical joke. As a matter of logic, it is quite clear that there can be no demonstrative inference from a set of shapes now seen on paper to a bright light seen in the sky last night. It would seem, therefore, that, where the past is concerned, we rely partly on coherence, and partly on the strength of our conviction as regards the particular memory which is in question; but that our confidence as regards memory in general is such that we cannot entertain the hypothesis of the past being wholly an illusion.

It will be remembered that, in an earlier chapter, we decided that memory propositions often require the word 'some'. We say 'I know I saw that book somewhere', or 'I know he said something very witty'. Perhaps we can remember even more vaguely, for instance 'I know something happened yesterday'. We *might* even remember 'there have been past events', which we rejected as a factual premiss a little while ago. I think that to accept this as a factual premiss would be going too far, but there certainly are uninferred memory propositions (at any given moment) which involve 'some'. These are logically deducible from propositions not involving 'some' which were, at some previous time, expressions of present perception. You say to yourself one day 'oh there is that letter I had lost', and next day ' I know I saw that letter *somewhere* yesterday'. This is an important logical difference between memory and perception, for perception is never general or vague. When we say it is vague, that only means that it does not allow so many inferences as some other perception would allow. But images, in their representative capacity, may be vague, and the knowledge based upon them may involve the word 'some'. It is worthy of note that this word may occur in a factual premiss.

In admitting memory propositions among factual premisses, we are conceding that our premisses may be doubtful and sometimes false. We are all willing, on occasion, to admit evidence against what we think we remember. Memories come to us with different grades of subjective certainty; in some, there is hardly more doubt than as regards a present percept, whereas in others the hesitation may be very great. Memories, in practice, are reinforced by inferences as casual as is possible, but such inferences are never demonstrative. It would be a great simplification if we could dispense with memory premisses, or if, failing that, we could distinguish two kinds of memory, of which one is infallible. Let us examine these possibilities.

In an attempt to dispense with memory, we shall still allow knowledge of whatever falls within the specious present; thus we shall be still aware of temporal sequence. We shall know what is meant by 'A is earlier than B'. We can therefore define 'the past' as 'what is earlier than the specious present'. We shall construct our knowledge of the past by means of causal laws, as we do in geology, where memory does not come in. We shall observe that we have a habit of making a record of an event that for any reason is important to us, either in writing or by creating in ourselves a verbal habit. We do the latter, for example, if, when we are introduced to a man, we repeat his name over and over to ourselves. We may do this so often that, when we next see him, we think of his name at once. We are then said, in popular language, to 'remember' his name, but we do not necessarily recall any past event. Is it possible to build up our knowledge of the past in this way, by means of records and verbal habits alone? In this view, if I see a man and know that his name is Jones, I shall infer that I must have met him on some former occasion, just as I do if his face is vaguely familiar. When I see a record, I can know that it is in my handwriting without having to invoke recollection, because I can copy the record now and make comparisons; I can then go on to infer that the record tells of something that once happened to me. In theory, the small but finite stretch of time comprised within the specious present should suffice for the discovery of causal laws, by means of which we could infer the past without having to appeal to memory.

I am not prepared to maintain that the above theory is logically untenable. There is no doubt that we could, without the help of memory, know *something* of the past. But I think it is clear that, in fact, we know more of the past than can be accounted for in this way. And while we must admit that we are sometimes mistaken as to what we think we remember, some recollections are so nearly indubitable that they would still command credence, even if much contrary evidence were produced. I do not see, therefore, on what ground we could reject memory as one of the sources of our knowledge concerning the course of events.

It remains to inquire whether there are two kinds of memory, one fallible and one infallible. We might maintain this without maintaining that we could know infallibly to which kind a given recollection belonged; we should then still have reason for some degree of uncertainty in every particular case. But we should at least have reason to think that *some* memories are correct. The theory, therefore, is worth examining.

I should not have considered seriously the possibility of there being two kinds of memory of which one is infallible, but for the fact that I heard this theory advocated in discussion by G. E. Moore. He did not then elaborate it, and I do not know how tenaciously he held it. I shall, therefore, independently attempt to give it as much plausibility as I can.

It must be held, on logical grounds, that no occurrence gives *demonstrative* grounds in favour of belief in any other occurrence. But the grounds are often such as we cannot fail to accept as giving *practical* certainty. We saw that there can be no reason for disbelieving the proposition 'that is red' when made in the presence of a red percept; it must, however, be admitted that belief in this proposition is logically possible in the absence of a red percept. Such grounds as exist for supposing that this does not occur are derived from causal laws as to the occurrence of language. We can, however, in theory, distinguish two cases in relation to a judgement such as 'that is red': one, when it is caused by what it asserts, and the other when words or images enter into its causation. In the former case it must be true, in the latter not.

This, however, is a statement which needs elaborating. What can be meant when we say that a percept 'causes' a word or a sentence? On the face of it, we have to suppose a considerable process in the brain, connecting visual centres with motor centres; the causation, therefore, is by no means direct. Perhaps we may state the matter as follows: in the course of learning to speak, certain causal routes (language-habits) are established in the brain, which lead from percepts to utterances. These are the shortest possible routes from percepts to utterances; all others involve some further association or habit. When an utterance is associated with a percept by a minimal causal route, the percept is said to be the 'meaning' of the utterance, and the utterance is 'true' because what it means occurs. Thus wherever this state of affairs exists, the truth of a judgement of perception is logically guaranteed.

We have to inquire whether anything similar is possible in the case of memory.

The stimulus to a judgement of recollection is obviously never the event recollected, since that is in the not immediate past. The stimulus may be a percept, or may be a 'thought'. Let us take the former case as the simpler. You find yourself, let us suppose, in some place where an interesting conversation occurred, and you remember the conversation. The cerebral mechanism involved is as yet hypothetical, but we may suppose it very similar to that involved in the passage from a percept to a word which 'means' it. When two percepts A and B occur together, the occurrence of a percept closely similar to A on a future occasion may cause an image closely similar to B. It may be argued that a certain type of association between a percept like A and an image like B can only occur if, on a previous occasion, A and B, as percepts, have occurred together, and that, therefore, the recollection resulting from the percept resembling A must be correct. Where fallacious memories occur, it may be said, the associative causal chains involved must be longer than in the case of correct memories. Perhaps, in this way, the case of memory can be assimilated to that of perception.

The above type of argument, however, while it may be correct at its own level, can have no direct relevance to the question of factual premisses, since it presupposes elaborate knowledge concerning the brain, which, obviously, can only be built up by means of factual premisses some of which are recollections.

It must be admitted that a factual premiss need not be indubitable, even subjectively; it need only command a certain degree of credence. It can therefore always be reinforced if it is found to harmonize with other factual premisses. What characterizes a factual premiss is not indubitability, but the fact that it commands a greater or less degree of belief on its own account, independently of its relations to other propositions. We are thus led to a combination of self-evidence with coherence: sometimes one factor is very much more important than the other, but in theory coherence always plays some part. The coherence required, however, is not strict logical coherence, for factual premisses can and should be so stated as to be deductively independent of each other. The kind of coherence involved is a matter which I shall consider at a later stage.

III. Negative Basic Propositions. We have already had occasion to consider negative empirical propositions, but I want now to consider afresh whether they are ever themselves factual premisses, or are always derived from incompatibility propositions.

The question to be considered is: how do we know negative empirical propositions, such as 'there is no cheese in the larder' or 'there are no snakes in Ireland'? We entertained the hypothesis, when we considered this question in an earlier chapter, that such propositions are inferred from premisses among which there are propositions such as 'where there is red there is not yellow', or 'what feels hard does not feel soft'. I want now to examine afresh the whole question of negative empirical knowledge.

It is plain, to begin with, that sensible qualities fall into genera. There are colours, there are sounds, there are smells and tastes, there are various sorts of sensations of touch, there are sensations of temperature. As to these, certain things are to be noted. We can see two colours at once, but not in the same place. We can hear two sounds at once, and there need be no discoverable difference in their direction of origin. Smells have no location except in the nose, and two smells are not essentially incompatible. A sensation of touch has qualities of which we may note two kinds: a local quality, according to the part of the body touched, and a quality of greater or less pressure; in each kind, different qualities have the sort of incompatibility that colours have, i.e. they can be experienced simultaneously, but not in the same place on the surface of the body. The same applies to temperature.

It thus appears that, as regards incompatibility, there are differences between qualities belonging to different senses. But as regards negative judgements there are no such differences. If someone brings you, in the dark, into the neighbourhood of a ripe Gorgonzola, and says 'can't you smell roses?' you will say no. When you hear a foghorn, you know it is not the song of the lark. And when you smell nothing or hear nothing, you can be aware of the fact. It seems that we must conclude that pure negative propositions can be empirically known without being inferred. 'Listen. Do you hear anything?' 'No.' There is nothing recondite about this conversation. When you say 'no' in such a case, are you giving the result of an inference, or are you uttering a basic proposition? I do not think this kind of knowledge has received the attention that it deserves. If your 'no' gives utterance to a basic proposition (which must obviously be empirical), such propositions may not only be negative, but apparently general, for your 'no' may, if logic is to be believed, be expressed in the form: 'all sounds are unheard by me now'.[2] Thus the logical difficulties of general empirical knowledge will be greatly lessened. If, on the other hand, your 'no' expresses an inference, it must use some general premiss, for otherwise no general conclusion could be inferred; and thus we shall still have to admit that some basic propositions not belonging to logic are general.

When a person says 'listen', and then you hear no sound, you are in a condition to notice a noise if there were one. But this does not always apply. 'Didn't you hear the dinner-bell?' 'No, I was working.' Here you have a negative memory judgement, and a cause (not a ground) assigned for its truth; and in this case you are sure of the negative although you were *not* listening at the time.

The conclusion seems irresistible that a percept or a memory may give rise to a negative factual premiss as well as to a positive one. There is an important difference: in the case of a positive basic proposition, the percept may cause the words, whereas in the case of a negation the words, or corresponding images, must exist independently of the percept. A negative basic proposition thus requires a propositional attitude, in which the proposition concerned is the one which, on the basis of perception, is denied. We may therefore say that, while a positive basic proposition is caused only by a percept (given our verbal habits), a negative one is caused by the percept plus a previous propositional

[2] I shall argue later that theory of knowledge need not accept this logical interpretation.

attitude. There is still an incompatibility, but it is between imagination and perception. The simplest way of expressing this state of affairs is to say that, in consequence of perception, you know that a certain proposition is false. In a word: it is possible, in a certain sense, to notice what is not there as well as what is there. This conclusion, if true, is important.

IV. Factual Premisses concerning present propositional attitudes. These propositions, just as much as 'this is red', report a present occurrence, but they differ from basic propositions of Class I by their logical form, which involves mention of a proposition. They are propositions asserting that something is believed, doubted, desired, and so on, in so far as such propositions are known independently of inference. The something believed or doubted or desired can only be expressed by means of a subordinate proposition. It is clear that we can be aware of believing or desiring something, in just as immediate a way as we can be aware of a red patch that we see. Someone says, let us suppose, 'is today Wednesday?' and you reply 'I think so'. Your statement 'I think so' expresses, in part at least, a factual premiss as to your opinion. The analysis of the proposition offers difficulties, but I do not see how to deny that it contains at least a kernel which expresses a datum.

It will be observed that propositions of this class are usually, if not always, psychological. I am not sure that we could not use this fact to define 'psychology'. It might be said that dreams belong to psychology, and that basic propositions concerning percepts in dreams are exactly on a level with other basic propositions concerning percepts. But to this it may be replied that the scientific study of dreams is only possible when we are awake, and that, therefore, all the data for any possible science of dreams are memories. Similar answers could be made as regards the psychology of perception.

However that may be, there is certainly an important department of knowledge which is characterized by the fact that, among its basic propositions, some contain subordinate propositions.

The factual premisses considered in the above discussions all have in common a certain characteristic, namely that they each refer to a short period of time, which is that at which they (or other propositions from which they are deducible) first became premisses. In the case of recollections, if they are veridical, they are either identical with or logically inferrable from judgements of perception made at the times to which the recollections refer. Our knowledge of the present and the past consists partly of basic propositions, whereas our knowledge of the future consists wholly of inferences—apart, possibly, from certain immediate expectations.

An 'empirical datum' might be defined as a proposition referring to a particular time, and beginning to be known at the time to which it refers; this definition, however, would be inadequate, since we may infer what is now happening before we perceive it. It is essential to the conception of an empirical datum that the knowledge should be (in some sense) caused by what is known. I do not wish, however, to introduce the conception of cause by a back door, and I shall therefore, at present, ignore this aspect of empirical knowledge.

Among the premisses of our knowledge there must be propositions not referring to particular events. Logical premisses, both deductive and inductive, are generally admitted, but it seems possible that there are others. The impossibility of two different colours in the same part of the visual field is perhaps one. The question of propositions of this sort is difficult, and I will say nothing dogmatic about them.

I will observe, however, that empiricism, as a theory of knowledge, is self-refuting. For, however it may be formulated, it must involve *some* general proposition about the dependence of knowledge upon experience; and any such proposition, if true, must have as a consequence that itself cannot be known. While, therefore, empiricism may be true, it cannot, if true, be known to be so. This, however, is a large problem.

Roderick Firth

Coherence, Certainty, and Epistemic Priority

Near the end of his annual lectures on epistemology at Harvard, Lewis used to tell his students that they must ultimately choose between the theory of justification that he had been defending—or something very similar to it—and a coherence theory like that of Bosanquet. These two alternatives may not seem to confront each other quite so directly in Lewis's books on epistemology, but in his paper entitled "The Given Element in Empirical Knowledge" [1] he again offers us this same choice. He explicitly defends his own theory of the given as one of "two alternatives for a plausible account of knowledge" (168) [p. 369, this volume. Eds.], the other alternative being an "unabridged probabilism" like that of Reichenbach—"a modernized coherence theory" (171) [p. 371, this

Presented in a Commemorative Symposium on C. I. Lewis, at the sixty-first annual meeting of the American Philosophical Association, Eastern Division, December 28, 1964. A revised and extended version of a paper presented in the Lewis Memorial Symposium, Harvard University, April 23, 1964.
Roderick Firth, "Coherence, Certainty, and Epistemic Priority," *The Journal of Philosophy,* LXI, No. 19 (October 15, 1964), 545–57. Reprinted by permission.

[1] In a symposium with Hans Reichenbach and Nelson Goodman, in *The Philosophical Review,* 61, 2 (April, 1952): 168–175. [pp. 368–375, this volume. Eds.]

volume. Eds.]. Although "logical and systemic relationships are important for assuring credibility," such a "probabilistic conception" of knowledge is incompatible with the fact that "no logical relationship, by itself, can ever be sufficient to establish the truth, or the credibility even, of any synthetic judgment" (169) [p. 369, this volume. Eds.]. "Crudely put," Lewis asserts, it . . . strikes me as supposing that if enough probabilities can be got to lean against one another they can all be made to stand up. . . . I think the whole system of such could provide no better assurance of anything in it than that which attaches to the contents of a well-written novel. (173) [p. 373, this volume. Eds.].

The issue outlined here is apparently one which Lewis continued to take very seriously, for in a letter written to me as recently as three years ago he expressed the fear that contemporary philosophers are, in his words, "headed back toward Bosanquet." It seems especially appropriate, therefore, in this memorial symposium, to consider some of the problems that arise when we attempt to formulate a precise definition of the issue Lewis had in mind. What kind of coherence theory did Lewis want to avoid, and what are the alternatives to it? I am convinced that we can ask no questions more important than these if we wish to understand Lewis's philosophical motivation and the full implications of his theory of knowledge.

It is possible to distinguish at least three theories (or perhaps I should say three types of theory) which can appropriately be labeled "coherence theories," and which can be defined, I believe, in such a way that none of them logically entails either of the others. These are (1) the coherence theory of truth, (2) the coherence theory of concepts, and (3) the coherence theory of justification. I shall say nothing about the coherence theory of truth except that the arguments offered in its support all seem to me to presuppose the coherence theory of justification. And I shall comment on the coherence theory of concepts only to suggest that it might be quite acceptable to Lewis even though he rejects the coherence theory of justification. It is clearly this last theory, the coherence theory of justification, which Lewis is primarily concerned to refute in his epistemological writings.

I

The coherence theory of concepts is the doctrine that all our concepts are related to one another in such a way that we cannot be said fully to have grasped any one of them unless we have grasped all the others: they form an organic conceptual scheme, it is said, a system of meanings which cohere in such a way that introducing a new concept at any one point in the system has repercussions which are felt throughout the system. It is easy to illustrate this doctrine by restricting it to the technical concepts of some particular science and tracing the changes produced by the introduction of a new concept of space, matter, or energy. But the broader implications of the doctrine can better be suggested by appealing to some commonplace concept like that of "mirror image." It can plausibly be argued that the young child who has not yet acquired the concept of "mirror image" cannot yet use the words 'see', 'touch', 'same', 'real', 'thing', 'space', 'colored', 'myself', 'left' and 'right'—or perhaps *any* words in his vocabulary—to mean quite what they mean to his older brother. And once the pattern of this argument has been accepted, it can easily be extended to any other concept we may select.

Now it might seem at first thought that this coherence theory of concepts is incompatible with Lewis's analysis of the "sense meaning" of statements about physical objects—and incompatible, indeed, even with the more moderate view of Locke and many other philosophers that some material-object *predicates* (e.g., "red") can be analyzed by means of supposedly simpler predicates (e.g., "looks red") which we use to describe sense experience. For if a philosopher maintains that 'The apple is red' can be analyzed as meaning "The apple would look red under such and such physical conditions," he is assuming that "looks red" is logically prior to "is red," i.e., that it is at least *logically* possible to have the concept "looks red" *before* we acquire the concept "is red." But if the coherence theory of concepts is correct, and we cannot fully understand "looks red" unless we possess the contrasting concept "is red," then it would seem that it is *not* logically possible to have the concept "looks red" before we have the concept "is red." This paradox might even lead us to wonder, indeed, whether the conceptual interdependence of "looks" and "is" is enough to undermine Lewis's basic assumption that we can make "expressive judgments" (e.g., "I seem to see a doorknob," "It looks as if I am seeing something red") without at the same time asserting something about the nature of "objective reality." It is these expressive judgments, according to Lewis, that enable us to escape the coherence theory of justification; and if it should turn out that these judgments all make some covert reference to physical objects, then—depending, of course, on the *kind* of "covert reference"—it might no longer be possible to make the epistemological distinction that Lewis requires.

There are many subtle facets of this question which cannot be explored here, but for our present purpose it is sufficient to point out that the underlying paradox is easily dissolved if we do not confuse concepts with the words used to express them. It is a genetic fact, but a fact with philosophical implications, that when a child first begins to use the word 'red' with any consistency he applies it to things that *look* red to him whether these things are, as we should say, "really red," or whether they are merely made to appear red by abnormal conditions of observation. Thus the child calls white things "red" when he sees them through red glass. In fact at this stage the child says 'red' just in those circumstances in which we, as adults, could truthfully say "looks red to me now," so that it would not be unreasonable to assert that the child is using 'red' to express a primitive form of the concept "looks red." To call this a "primitive form" of the concept "looks red" is to acknowledge that in some sense the child cannot *fully* understand adult usage until he is able to distinguish things that merely look red from things that really are red; but we must not suppose that the child somehow *loses* his primitive concept when he acquires a more sophisticated one. As Lewis points out in Chapter III of *Mind and the World Order*,[2] the scientist and the nonscientist are able to share what Lewis calls "our common world" precisely because the scientist does not necessarily forget how to use words in their nontechnical senses; and for the same reason there is no inconsistency in maintaining that even as adults we continue to have *a* concept "looks red" which is logically prior to our concept "is red."

To grant Lewis this crucial point is not to deny that the *vocabulary* of "looks" and "seems" expressions that we use to describe sense experience is in some respect derivative from the *vocabulary* that we use to describe the physical world. Thus when Lewis describes his sense experience by saying "I seem to see a doorknob" his choice of words appears to reflect a linguistic rule to the effect that a sense experience should be "named after" its normal condition (in this case the condition of actually seeing a real doorknob). But such a rule, like the rule in some societies that sons should be named after their fathers, is merely a *baptismal* rule. The fact that Young Rufus is named after Old Rufus does not prevent us from learning to recognize Young Rufus before we have met Old Rufus. Analogously, the fact that key words in our "looks" and "seems" expressions are inherited from our "is" expressions does not prevent the child from consistently identifying things that look red to him (or situations in which he seems to see a doorknob) before he can consistently identify things that *are* red (or situations in which he really sees an "objective" doorknob). If we do not confuse baptismal rules with semantical rules (e.g., the semantical rule followed by the child who says "red" when something looks red to him) the coherence theory of concepts does not seem to be incompatible with Lewis's theories of meaning and knowledge. Let us turn, therefore, to the coherence theory of justification.

[2] New York: Scribner's, 1929; hereafter referred to as MWO.

II

Philosophers have sometimes construed the problems of justification as though they were problems concerning the knowledge possessed by a social group; and it does of course make perfectly good sense to ask what statements *we* (e.g., you and I, our "culture circle," etc.) are justified in believing, and why we are justified in believing them. But Lewis seems clearly to be right in maintaining that such a question cannot be answered without first answering a more fundamental, egocentric, question: Why am *I*, at the present moment, justified in believing some statements and not justified in believing other statements? This is to be interpreted as an epistemological question—not as an ethical question to which someone might in principle reply: "Because you will be happier (or more loyal to your friends) if you believe these statements rather than those"; and the ambiguous expression 'justified in believing' is to be interpreted so that we may assert without self-contradiction that someone is justified in believing a statement he does not in fact believe. It is helpful, therefore, to reformulate the question as a question about the "epistemic warrant" (or, for short, "warrant") that statements have "for me" at a particular time; and in these terms I think that the heart of the coherence theory of justification, as Lewis probably construes it, is the thesis that *ultimately* every statement that has some degree of warrant for me has that particular degree of warrant because, and only because, it is related by valid principles of inference to (that is to say "coheres with") certain other statements.

To explain why I have used an italicized the word 'ultimately' in formulating this central thesis of the coherence theory, and to facilitate comparison with alternative theories of justification, it is helpful to refine the issue still further and construe the coherence theory as an answer to the question: What properties or characteristics of a statement may serve to increase its warrant? This question may in turn be formulated in a slightly different way by employing the term 'warrant-increasing property', interpreted so that, in saying that a statement *S* has a warrant-increasing property *P* for a particular person at a particular time, we imply that *S* would be *less* warranted, and that *not-S* would be *more* warranted, for that person at that time if, other things remaining the same, *S* did not have property *P*. In this terminology the question becomes: What properties of statements are warrant-increasing properties?

It is clear that advocates of the coherence theory would want to reply that, if *P* is a warrant-increasing property of statement *S*, *P* might consist simply in *S*'s being validly inferable from certain other statements of a specified kind. In such a case, since the warrant of *S* is increased, so to speak, by the *fact that* *S* is validly inferable from certain other statements, *P* might appropriately be called an "inferential" property. Advocates of the coherence theory would surely be willing to grant, however, that there are noninferential properties (e.g., the property of being believed by scholars with such and such characteristics) which might also increase the warrant of a statement; but to preserve coherence as the ultimate court of appeal they would insist that such a noninferential property (*P'*) can be a warrant-increasing property of a statement *S* only if a particular statement *about* *S*—the statement, namely, "If *S* has property *P* then *S* is true"—is validly inferable from (coheres with) certain other specified statements.[3] (This requirement might be met, for example, if *P'* were the property of being believed by certain scholars and if there were evidence that these scholars have usually had correct beliefs about statements similar to *S* in certain respects.) Thus we may say that the coherence theory of justification maintains that, if *P* is a warrant-increasing property of *S*, then either (1) *P* is an inferential property, or (2) *P* is a warrant-increasing property only because the statement "If *S* has the property *P* then *S* is true" has an inferential warrant-increasing property. It is convenient to summarize this by saying that all warrant-increasing properties, according to the central thesis of the coherence theory, must be "ultimately inferential."

To convert this central thesis into a fully determinate coherence theory, it would have to be elaborated in two ways. (1) We should have to specify the "valid" principles of inference, deductive and inductive, that determine whether one statement coheres with, and thus confers warrant on, another. And (2) we should have to specify the nature of the "certain other statements" with which a warranted statement must cohere —the class of statements that are, we might say, "warrant-conferring." Although the problems involved in (1) are very important—especially those which arise when we ask whether there is a set of principles of inference, and only one set, that can be selected and justified by reapplying the same standard of coherence—these problems are neutral with respect to the central issues at stake between Lewis and the coherence theory. The problems involved in (2), however, are more directly relevant to these central issues, and we shall return to them after considering Lewis's position.

[3] For simplicity I assume that the noninferential warrant-increasing property *P'* is only one step removed from the ultimate appeal to coherence; but in principle there might be a long intervening chain of noninferential warrant-increasing properties.

III

In clear opposition to the coherence theory of justification, Lewis flatly denies that all warrant-increasing properties are ultimately inferential. It is a matter of some importance, which we shall consider later, that Lewis often discusses the problems of epistemic justification as problems concerning *judgments,* and may thus be restricting his attention to the epistemic status of statements that are actually *believed* (judged to be true) by a particular person at a particular time. But in any case he maintains that those statements which do reflect my present judgments about my own present experience—including statements about sense experience, memory experience, occurrent feelings, etc.—are *certain* (and hence warranted) for me at the present time, and that their certainty is not derived directly or indirectly from their coherence with other statements. There is room for debate, however, about the meaning of the word 'certain' in this context, and I think that Lewis's writings actually suggest several different alternatives to the coherence theory of justification.

There are a number of passages in *Mind and the World Order,* in *An Analysis of Knowledge and Valuation,*[4] and elsewhere in which Lewis says that "expressive judgments" (e.g., "I seem to see a doorknob") *cannot be mistaken.* "One cannot be mistaken," he asserts, "about the content of an immediate awareness" (MWO, 131). This is perhaps the most extreme alternative to a coherence theory of justification, and is often taken to be the only alternative that Lewis offers us. In another place in *Mind and the World Order,* however, Lewis says, interestingly enough: "All those difficulties which the psychologist encounters in dealing with reports of introspection may be sources of error in any report of the given. It may require careful self-questioning, or questioning by another, to elicit the full and correct account of the given" (62). This of course seems to imply that, in some important sense of 'can', our expressive judgments *can* be mistaken, and it suggests the need to distinguish what we might call "truth-evaluative" senses of 'certain' from "warrant-evaluative" senses of 'certain'. To say that a judgment is certain in a truth-evaluative sense of the word entails that the judgment is true, but to say that a judgment is certain in a warrant-evaluative sense is merely to say that the judgment (whether it be in fact true or false) is completely warranted in some specifiable sense of 'completely'. Although Lewis does sometimes assert that expressive judgments cannot be false, I believe that

[4] La Salle, Ill.: Open Court, 1964; hereafter referred to as AKV.

all the *arguments* he gives for the certainty of expressive judgments are are arguments to show that these judgments are certain in a warrant-evaluative sense. Indeed Lewis sometimes uses the words 'indubitable' and 'incorrigible' as synonyms of 'certain', and these two words are more naturally interpreted as warrant-evaluative than as truth-evaluative. There is no logical inconsistency in asserting that someone has a false belief which he cannot rationally *doubt* and which he is not in a position to *correct;* consequently there is no inconsistency in asserting that expressive judgments are indubitable and incorrigible, while at the same time granting that some of them may be false.

In defending the doctrine that expressive judgments are certain in a warrant-evaluative sense, Lewis sometimes tries to prove much more than is necessary to refute the coherence theory of justification. Some of his arguments are apparently intended to show that, if I now judge, for example, that it looks as if I am seeing something red, I shall never, at any time in the future, be justified in revoking this judgment. But problems concerning the future revocation of an expressive judgment, at a time when my decision must depend in part on my memory of my present experience, are not directly relevant to the question: Are my *present* expressive judgments certain (and hence warranted) for me *now?* And, if they are, is their warrant derived entirely from coherence? I believe that Lewis's answers to these two questions are (1) that my present expressive judgments, being certain, are not only warranted for me but warranted to so high a degree that no other judgments are *more* warranted for me, and (2) that their warrant is not derived to the slightest degree from coherence nor defeasible through failure to cohere with other judgments. "There is no requirement of consistency," Lewis asserts, "which is *relevant* to protocols." [5]

Again, however, it is important to observe that there are at least three weaker, and therefore perhaps more plausible, positions that are also incompatible with the coherence theory of justification as we have been construing it. It might be maintained (1) that the warrant of an expressive judgment may be increased by its coherence with other judgments, and to some extent decreased by failure to cohere, but that failure to cohere can never decrease its warrant to a point at which a contradictory judgment would be more (or even equally) warranted. This would allow us to say that my present expressive judgments, although they may be false, are not now *falsifiable* for me. Or it might be maintained (2) that present expressive judgments, although falsifiable by failure to cohere, always have *some* degree of warrant which is not derived from coherence and which is not defeasible through failure to

[5] "The Given Element in Empirical Knowledge," p. 173 [p. 373, this volume. Eds.] Italics mine.

cohere. Or, even more moderately, it might be maintained (3) that expressive judgments have some degree of "initial" noninferential warrant which *is* defeasible through failure to cohere—perhaps even allowing, in principle, for the possibility that the contradictory of an expressive judgment may be as fully warranted as any other empirical judgment.[6] Although Lewis's strong position and each of these weaker positions differ markedly from one another, each of them entails a proposition which we may call "the central thesis of epistemic priority"—the thesis that some statements have some degree of warrant which is independent of (and in this sense "prior to") the warrant (if any) that they derive from their coherence with other statements. If we decide that there are statements of this kind, our next task is to determine what warrant-increasing property these statements have in addition to properties that are ultimately inferential.

In considering this problem there is a strong temptation for those who accept the thesis of epistemic priority to say that the statement (for example) "It looks as if I am seeing something red" is warranted (or given some warrant) for me simply by the fact that it *does* look as if I am seeing something red; but to say this seems to imply that the statement is warranted because it is *true*—because it asserts what is in fact the case. To preserve the important distinction between truth and warrant, so that in principle *any* empirical statement may be true but unwarranted, or false but warranted, it would be preferable to maintain that the statement has a certain degree of warrant for me because it is a statement (whether true or false) that *purports* to characterize (and only to characterize) the content of my present experience. (This could of course be made more precise by the use of examples and other devices.) But this condition is clearly insufficient, for we should not want to hold that *all* statements, including all possible pairs of contradictory statements, have some degree of warrant if they satisfy this requirement.

The obvious way to meet this difficulty is to add the further condition that a statement about my present experience can have some degree of ultimate noninferential warrant for me only if I believe it to be true. This condition is suggested, as we have already observed, by Lewis's use of the word 'judgment', and I am inclined to think that Lewis would consider these two conditions, taken together, to constitute a *sufficient* con-

[6] Lewis himself defends a position analogous to (3) with respect to present memory judgments about the *past*—as opposed to present judgments about experiences (including memory judgments) occurring in the *present* (AKV, 354 ff.). H. H. Price's "Principle of Confirmability" represents an analogous position with respect to judgments about presently perceived material things; see *Perception* (New York: McBride, 1933), p. 185. But "initial" warrant is derived by Lewis and Price from an "assumption" or "principle," and can thus be construed as "inferential."

dition of epistemic priority. If he were also to maintain that these two conditions are *necessary,* it would not be inappropriate to say that for Lewis expressive judgments are "self-warranted" (perhaps even "self-evident"), implying by this, so to speak, that, for a statement about my present sense experience, its being now judged by me to be true is an ultimate warrant-increasing property. Because of the ambiguity of the word 'judgment', however, it is unclear to me whether Lewis would actually consider this second condition (viz., that statements with non-inferential warrant must be believed) to be necessary. There are of course many statements which are warranted for me, which I am justified in believing, but which I do not in fact believe; and a philosopher who accepts the thesis of epistemic priority might maintain that among these statements are some that are ultimately warranted, at least in part, non-inferentially. Presumably, however, these noninferentially warranted statements would all be statements that I would now believe if I had just *decided* whether they were true or false; and thus it would probably be close to the spirit of Lewis's position to maintain that in the last analysis a statement can now have for me only one warrant-increasing property that is not ultimately inferential—that compound property which consists in (1) purporting to characterize (and only to characterize) the content of my present experience, and (2) being a statement that I either now believe to be true or should now believe to be true if I had just decided whether it were true or false.

This formulation of a possible theory of epistemic priority raises a number of important and puzzling questions. We might wonder, for example, whether (2) should include some restriction on the method by which I arrive at my belief, and whether it is possible to formulate such a restriction without circularity. And we might wonder whether the *strength* of my belief (the *confidence* with which I hold it) does not have some role in determining at least the *degree* to which a statement has a warrant that is ultimately noninferential. Within the limits of this paper, however, I can make only a few concluding remarks about Lewis's criticism of the coherence theory, in particular about his statement, already quoted, that "no logical relationship, by itself, can ever be sufficient to establish the truth, or the credibility even, of any synthetic judgment."

IV

This statement, which I think represents the crux of many familiar arguments against the coherence theory, seems to me to reflect a conception of the coherence theory which is unnecessarily narrow and much too narrow to make the theory at all plausible. It is sometimes said (cf. AKV, 340) that the coherence theory provides us with no way of distinguishing the actual world from other "possible worlds," since statements describing any of these worlds will form equally coherent systems; and this seems also to be Lewis's point when he says that a system of statements that stand only because they "lean against one another" gives us "no better assurance of anything in it than that which attaches to the contents of a well-written novel." As we have observed, however, a philosopher who accepts what we have called the "central thesis" of the coherence theory is not thereby committed to any particular way of identifying the class of "warrant-conferring" statements with which any warranted statement must ultimately cohere. If he insists that the power to confer warrant resides only in warranted statements, and that warranted statements constitute a perfectly democratic society in which each member receives its warrant from coherence with all the others, then indeed he will not be able to explain why one system of coherent statements is warranted and another is not. But this difficulty can be avoided if he adopts a less democratic position and recognizes an elite class of "basic" warrant-conferring statements which, although it may include some statements that are not warranted, excludes a great many statements that *are* warranted. If he can identify this class by reference to something other than mere coherence, he may be able, so to speak, to tie the entire set of warranted statements to the possible world in which we actually live. In fact he would then be in a position to agree with Lewis, without giving up the coherence theory, that no logical (inferential) relationship, *by itself,* "can ever be sufficient to establish the truth, or even the credibility, of any synthetic judgment."

There are many interesting ways in which we might delimit such a class of basic warrant-conferring statements for a particular person at a particular time, but perhaps the traditional and most plausible way is to restrict this class to statements, whatever their logical form or subject matter, that are actually believed by that person at that time.[7] If 'believed' is interpreted liberally enough so that this class includes a large number of very general theoretical statements, there is some ground for holding that the inferential relationships among them—and at some points the lack of any inferential relationship—are sufficient to determine which statements are warranted, which statements are not, and the rela-

[7] Cf. Brand Blanshard, *The Nature of Thought* (New York: Macmillan, 1940), vol. II, p. 272: "What the ultimate standard means *in practice* is the system of present knowledge as apprehended by a particular mind."

tive degrees of warrant among them.[8] Within this elite class, so to speak, each statement, whether itself warranted or not, would have a voice in determining the epistemic status of every other statement in the class. And statements outside the class—statements which have not yet been thought about, or which, for some other reason are neither believed nor disbelieved—could be said to be "derivatively" warranted if in fact—whether anybody knows it or not—they cohere with the warranted statements in this warrant-conferring class. This would mean, in effect, that these derivatively warranted statements are second-class citizens: they receive warrant from members of the class of basic warrant-conferring statements (and are thus tied down to the actual world), but they have no independent authority in determining whether any other statement is warranted.

A position of this kind seems to me to avoid Lewis's logical objection to the coherence theory of justification and thus to demonstrate that the issue between this theory and the thesis of epistemic priority must ultimately be decided on purely empirical grounds. It is of course difficult to formulate precise criteria for settling such an issue, but advocates of the coherence theory have commonly tried to defend their position by appealing to the actual practices of scientists and other rational men, and presumably these practices are relevant to the issue even if not absolutely decisive. On this basis I think it would be very difficult to defend Lewis's strong position that some statements are certain in a sense that makes coherence *completely* irrelevant to their warrant. But I think, on the other hand, that rational men often believe statements about their own sense experience with much greater confidence than they could justify by inference from other beliefs; and this suggests that we may accept the thesis of epistemic priority and try to choose among the three weaker positions that entail this thesis. It has been my intention in this paper to formulate an issue and not to defend this particular conclusion. But if the thesis of epistemic priority is, as I think, correct, the methodological consequences are momentous whether or not we accept Lewis's doctrine of certainty. For at least we can say in that case that Lewis has always been right in maintaining that the major task of a theory of empirical knowledge is to show how it is possible—by means of a theory of meaning and suitable principles of inference—for statements that have independent, noninferential, warrant to serve as the ground of all the rest of our empirical knowledge.

[8] The rules that would determine these things might be similar to those proposed by R. B. Brandt for the selection of warranted memory beliefs (recollections) in his "Memory Beliefs," *The Philosophical Review*, 64, 1 (January, 1955), 88 [pp. 279–280, this volume. Eds.]. Brandt's rule, however, "advises accepting recollections when there is no positive support from the system" and is thus compatible with the thesis of epistemic priority.

Wilfrid Sellars

Empiricism and the Philosophy of Mind

I. AN AMBIGUITY IN SENSE-DATUM THEORIES

I presume that no philosopher who has attacked the philosophical idea of givenness or, to use the Hegelian term, immediacy, has intended to deny that there is a difference between *inferring* that something is the case and, for example, *seeing* it to be the case. If the term "given" referred merely to what is observed as being observed, or, perhaps, to a proper subset of the things we are said to determine by observation, the existence of "data" would be as noncontroversial as the existence of philosophical perplexities. But, of course, this just isn't so. The phrase "the given" as a piece of professional—epistemological—shoptalk carries a substantial theoretical commitment, and one can deny that there are

This paper was first presented as the University of London Special Lectures on Philosophy for 1955–56, delivered on March 1, 8, and 15, 1956, under the title "The Myth of the Given: Three Lectures on Empiricism and the Philosophy of Mind."

Wilfrid Sellars, "Empiricism and the Philosophy of Mind," in *Minnesota Studies in the Philosophy of Science,* Vol. I, ed. H. Feigl and M. Scriven (Minneapolis: University of Minnesota Press, 1956), pp. 253–329.

"data" or that anything is, in this sense, "given" without flying in the face of reason.

Many things have been said to be "given": sense contents, material objects, universals, propositions, real connections, first principles, even givenness itself. And there is, indeed, a certain way of construing the situations which philosophers analyze in these terms which can be said to be the framework of givenness. This framework has been a common feature of most of the major systems of philosophy, including, to use a Kantian turn of phrase, both "dogmatic rationalism" and "skeptical empiricism." It has, indeed, been so pervasive that few, if any, philosophers have been altogether free of it; certainly not Kant, and, I would argue, not even Hegel, that great foe of "immediacy." Often what is attacked under its name are only specific varieties of "given." Intuited first principles and synthetic necessary connections were the first to come under attack. And many who today attack "the whole idea of givenness"—and they are an increasing number—are really only attacking sense data. For they transfer to other items, say physical objects or relations of appearing, the characteristic features of the "given." If, however, I begin my argument with an attack on sense datum theories, it is only as a first step in a general critique of the entire framework of givenness.

2. Sense-datum theories characteristically distinguish between an *act* of awareness and, for example, the color patch which is its *object.* The act is usually called *sensing.* Classical exponents of the theory have often characterized these acts as "phenomenologically simple" and "not further analyzable." But other sense-datum theorists—some of them with an equal claim to be considered "classical exponents"—have held that sensing is analyzable. And if some philosophers seem to have thought that if sensing is analyzable, then it can't be an *act,* this has by no means been the general opinion. There are, indeed, deeper roots for the doubt that sensing (if there is such a thing) is an act, roots which can be traced to one of two lines of thought tangled together in classical sense-datum theory. For the moment, however, I shall simply assume that however complex (or simple) the fact that x is sensed may be, it has the form, whatever exactly it may be, by virtue of which for x to be sensed is for it to be the object of an act.

Being a sense datum, or sensum, is a relational property of the item that is sensed. To refer to an item which is sensed in a way which does not entail that it *is* sensed, it is necessary to use some other locution. *Sensible* has the disadvantage that it implies that sensed items could exist without being sensed, and this is a matter of controversy among sense-datum theorists. *Sense content* is, perhaps, as neutral a term as any.

There appear to be varieties of sensing, referred to by some as *visual sensing, tactual sensing,* etc., and by others as *directly seeing, directly hearing,* etc. But it is not clear whether these are species of sensing in any full-blooded sense, or whether "x is visually sensed" amounts to no more than "x is a color patch which is sensed," "x is directly heard" than "x is a sound which is sensed" and so on. In the latter case, being a *visual sensing* or a *direct hearing* would be a relational property of an act of sensing, just as being a sense datum is a relational property of a sense content.

3. Now if we bear in mind that the point of the epistemological category of the given is, presumably, to explicate the idea that empirical knowledge rests on a 'foundation' of non-inferential knowledge of matter of fact, we may well experience a feeling of surprise on noting that according to sense-datum theorists, it is *particulars* that are sensed. For what is *known,* even in non-inferential knowledge, is *facts* rather than particulars, items of the form *something's being thus-and-so* or *something's standing in a certain relation to something else.* It would seem, then, that the sensing of sense contents *cannot* constitute knowledge, inferential or non-inferential; and if so, we may well ask, what light does the concept of a sense datum throw on the 'foundations of empirical knowledge?' The sense-datum theorist, it would seem, must choose between saying:

(a) It is *particulars* which are sensed. Sensing is not knowing. The existence of sense-data does not *logically* imply the existence of knowledge.

or

(b) Sensing *is* a form of knowing. It is *facts* rather than *particulars* which are sensed.

On alternative (a) the fact that a sense content was sensed would be a *non-epistemic* fact about the sense content. Yet it would be hasty to conclude that this alternative precludes *any* logical connection between the sensing of sense contents and the possession of non-inferential knowledge. For even if the sensing of sense contents did not logically imply the existence of non-inferential knowledge, the converse might well be true. Thus, the non-inferential knowledge of a particular matter of fact might logically imply the existence of sense data (for example, *seeing that a certain physical object is red* might logically imply *sensing a red sense content*) even though the sensing of a red sense content were not itself a cognitive fact and did not imply the possession of non-inferential knowledge.

On the second alternative, (b), the sensing of sense contents would logically imply the existence of non-inferential knowledge for the simple reason that it would *be* this knowledge. But, once again, it would be facts rather than particulars which are sensed.

4. Now it might seem that when confronted by this choice, the sense-datum theorist seeks to have his cake and eat it. For he characteristically insists *both* that sensing is a knowing *and* that it is particulars which are sensed. Yet his position is by no means as hopeless as this formulation suggests. For the 'having' and the 'eating' *can* be combined without logical nonsense provided that he uses the word *know* and, correspondingly, the word *given* in two senses. He must say something like the following:

> The non-inferential knowing on which our world pitcure rests is the knowing that certain items, e.g. red sense contents, are of a certain character, e.g. red. When such a fact is non-inferentially known about a sense content, I will say that the sense content is sensed *as being,* e.g., *red.* It will then say that a sense content is *sensed* (full stop) if it is *sensed as being* of a certain character, e.g. red. Finally, I will say of a sense content that it is *known* if it is sensed (full stop), to emphasize that sensing is a *cognitive* or *epistemic* fact.

Notice that, given these stipulations, it is logically necessary that if a sense content be *sensed,* it be *sensed as being of a certain character,* and that if it be *sensed of a certain character,* the *fact that it is of this character* be *non-inferentially known.* Notice also that the being sensed of a sense content would be *knowledge* only in a stipulated sense of *know.* To say of a *sense content*—a color patch, for example—that it was 'known' would be to say that *some fact about it* was non-inferentially known, e.g. that it was red. This *stipulated* use of *know* would, however, receive aid and comfort from the fact that there is, in ordinary usage, a sense of *know* in which it is followed by a noun or descriptive phrase which refers to a particular, thus

> Do you know John?
> Do you know the President?

Because these questions are equivalent to "Are you acquainted with John?" and "Are you acquainted with the President?" the phrase "knowledge by acquaintance" recommends itself as a useful metaphor for this stipulated sense of *know* and, like other useful metaphors, has congealed into a technical term.

5. We have seen that the fact that a sense content is a *datum* (if, indeed, there are such facts) will logically imply that someone has non-inferential knowledge *only* if to say that a sense content is given is contextually defined in terms of non-inferential knowledge of a fact

about this sense content. If this is not clearly realized or held in mind, sense-datum theorists may come to think of the givenness of sense contents as the *basic* or *primitive* concept of the sense-datum framework, and thus sever the logical connection between sense data and non-inferential knowledge to which the classical form of the theory is committed. This brings us face to face with the fact that in spite of the above considerations, many if not most sense-datum theorists *have* thought of the givenness of sense contents as the basic notion of the sense-datum framework. What, then, of the logical connection in the direction *sensing sense contents* → *having non-inferential knowledge?* Clearly it is severed by those who think of sensing as a unique and unanalyzable act. Those, on the other hand, who conceive of sensing as an *analyzable* fact, while they have prima facie severed this connection (by taking the sensing of sense contents to be the basic concept of the sense-datum framework) will nevertheless, in a sense, have maintained it, if the result they get by analying *x is a red sense datum* turns out to be the same as the result they get when they analyze *x is non-inferentially known to be red.* The entailment which was thrown out the front door would have sneaked in by the back.

It is interesting to note, in this connection, that those who, in the classical period of sense-datum theories, say from Moore's "Refutation of Idealism" until about 1938, analyzed or sketched an analysis of sensing, did so in *non-epistemic* terms. Typically it was held that for a sense content to be sensed is for it to be an element in a certain kind of relational array of sense contents, where the relations which constitute the array are such relations as spatiotemporal juxtaposition (or overlapping), constant conjunction, mnemic causation—even real connection and belonging to a self. There is, however, one class of terms which is conspicuous by its absence, namely *cognitive* terms. For these, like the 'sensing' which was under analysis, were taken to belong to a higher level of complexity.

Now the idea that epistemic facts can be analyzed without remainder—even "in principle"—into non-epistemic facts, whether phenomenal or behavioral, public or private, with no matter how lavish a sprinkling of subjunctives and hypotheticals is, I believe, a radical mistake—a mistake of a piece with the so-called "naturalistic fallacy" in ethics. I shall not, however, press this point for the moment, though it will be a central theme in a later stage of my argument. What I do want to stress is that whether classical sense-datum philosophers have conceived of the givenness of sense contents as analyzable in non-epistemic terms, or as constituted by acts which are somehow both irreducible *and* knowings, they have without exception taken them to be fundamental in another sense.

6. For they have taken givenness to be a fact which presupposes no learning, no forming of associations, no setting up of stimulus-response connections. In short, they have tended to equate *sensing sense contents* with *being conscious,* as a person who has been hit on the head is *not* conscious whereas a new born babe, alive and kicking, *is* conscious. They would admit, of course, that the ability to know that a *person,* namely oneself, is *now,* at a certain time, feeling a pain, *is* acquired and does presuppose a (complicated) process of concept formation. But, they would insist, to suppose that the simple ability to *feel a pain* or *see a color,* in short, to sense sense contents, is *acquired* and involves a process of concept formation, would be very odd indeed.

But if a sense-datum philosopher takes the ability to sense sense contents to be unacquired, he is clearly precluded from offering an analysis of *x senses a sense content* which presupposes acquired abilities. It follows that he could analyze *x senses red sense content s* as *x non-inferentially knows that s is red* only if he is prepared to admit that the ability to have such non-inferential knowledge as that, for example, a red sense content is red, is itself unacquired. And this brings us face to face with the fact that most empirically minded philosophers are strongly inclined to think that all classificatory consciousness, all knowledge *that something is thus-and-so,* or, in logicians' jargon, all subsumption of particulars under universals, involves learning, concept formation, even the use of symbols. It is clear from the above analysis, therefore, that *classical* sense-datum theories—I emphasize the adjective, for there are other, 'heterodox,' sense-datum theories to be taken into account—are confronted by an inconsistent triad made up of the following three propositions:

A. *X senses red sense contents* entails *x non-inferentially knows that s is red.*
B. The ability to sense sense contents is unacquired.
C. The ability to know facts of the form *x is* ϕ is acquired.
A and B together entail not-C; B and C entail not-A; A and C entail not-B.

Once the classical sense-datum theorist faces up to the fact that A, B, and C do form an inconsistent triad, which of them will he choose to abandon?

1) He can abandon A, in which case the sensing of sense contents becomes a noncognitive fact—a noncognitive fact, to be sure which may be a necessary condition, even a *logically* necessary condition, of non-inferential knowledge, but a fact, nevertheless, which cannot *constitute* this knowledge.

2) He can abandon B, in which case he must pay the price of cutting off the concept of a sense datum from its connection with our ordinary talk about sensations, feelings, afterimages, tickles and itches, etc., which are usually thought by sense-datum theorists to be its common sense counterparts.
3) But to abandon C is to do violence to the predominantly nominalistic proclivities of the empiricist tradition.

7. It certainly begins to look as though the classical concept of a sense datum were a mongrel resulting from a crossbreeding of two ideas:

(1) The idea that there are certain inner episodes—e.g. sensations of red or of C♯ which can occur to human beings (and brutes) without any prior process of learning or concept formation; and without which it would *in some sense* be impossible to *see,* for example, that the facing surface of a physical object is red and triangular, or *hear* that a certain physical sound is C♯.
(2) The idea that there are certain inner episodes which are the non-inferential knowings that certain items are, for example, red or C♯; and that these episodes are the necessary conditions of empirical knowledge as providing the evidence for all other empirical propositions.

And I think that once we are on the lookout for them, it is quite easy to see how these two ideas came to be blended together in traditional epistemology. The *first* idea clearly arises in the attempt to explain the facts of sense perception in scientific style. How does it happen that people can have the experience which they describe by saying "It is as though I were seeing a red and triangular physical object" when either there is no physical object there at all, or, if there is, it is neither red nor triangular? The explanation, roughly, posits that in every case in which a person has an experience of this kind, whether veridical or not, he has what is called a 'sensation' or 'impression' 'of a red triangle.' The core idea is that the proximate cause of such a sensation is *only for the most part* brought about by the presence in the neighborhood of the perceiver of a red and triangular physical object; and that while a baby, say, can have the 'sensation of a red triangle' without either *seeing* or *seeming to see that the facing side of a physical object is red and triangular,* there usually *looks,* to adults, *to be* a physical object with a red and triangular facing surface, when they are caused to have a 'sensation of a red triangle'; while *without* such a sensation, no such experience can be had.

I shall have a great deal more to say about this kind of 'explanation' of perceptual situations in the course of my argument. What I want to emphasize for the moment, however, is that, as far as the above formulation goes, there is no reason to suppose that having the sensation of a red triangle is a *cognitive* or *epistemic* fact. There is, of course, a temptation to assimilate "having a sensation of a red triangle" to "thinking of a celestial city" and to attribute to the former the epistemic character, the 'intentionality' of the latter. But this temptation *could* be resisted, and it *could* be held that having a sensation of a red triangle is a fact *sui generis,* neither epistemic nor physical, having its own logical grammar. Unfortunately, the idea that there are such things as sensations of red triangles—in itself, as we shall see, quite legitimate, though not without its puzzles—seems to fit the requirements of another, and less fortunate, line of thought so well that it has almost invariably been distorted to give the latter a reinforcement without which it would long ago have collapsed. This unfortunate, but familiar, line of thought runs as follows:

> The seeing that the facing surface of a physical object is red and triangular is a *veridical* member of a class of experiences—let us call them 'ostensible seeings'—some of the members of which are non-veridical; and there is no inspectible hallmark which guarantees that *any* such experience is veridical. To suppose that the non-inferential knowledge on which our world picture rests consists of such ostensible seeings, hearings, etc., as *happen* to be veridical is to place empirical knowledge on too precarious a footing—indeed, to open the door to skepticism by making a mockery of the word *knowledge* in the phrase "empirical knowledge."
>
> Now it is, of course, possible to delimit subclasses of ostensible seeings, hearings, etc., which are progressively less precarious, i.e. more reliable, by specifying the circumstances in which they occur, and the vigilance of the perceiver. But the possibility that any given ostensible seeing, hearing, etc., is non-veridical can never be entirely eliminated. Therefore, given that the foundation of empirical *knowledge* cannot consist of the veridical members of a class not all the members of which are veridical, and from which the non-veridical members cannot be weeded out by 'inspection,' this foundation cannot consist of such items as *seeing that the facing surface of a physical object is red and triangular.*

Thus baldly put, scarcely anyone would accept this conclusion. Rather they would take the contrapositive of the argument, and reason that *since* the foundation of empirical knowledge *is* the non-inferential knowledge of such facts, it *does* consist of members of a class which contains non-veridical members. But before it is thus baldly put, it gets tangled up with the first line of thought. The idea springs to mind that *sensations of red triangles* have exactly the virtues which *ostensible seeings of red triangular physical surfaces* lack. To begin with, the grammatical similarity of 'sensation of a red triangle' to "thought of a celestial city" is interpreted to mean, or, better, gives rise to the presupposition, that *sensations* belong in the same general pigeonhole as *thoughts*—in short, are cognitive facts. *Then,* it is noticed that sensations are *ex hypothesi* far more intimately related to mental processes than external physical objects. It would seem easier to "get at" a red triangle of which we are having a sensation, than to "get at" a red and triangular physical surface. But, above all, it is the fact that it *doesn't make sense* to speak of unveridical sensations which strikes these philosophers, though for it to strike them as it does, they must overlook the fact that if it makes sense to speak of an experience as *veridical* it must correspondingly make sense to speak of it as *unveridical.* Let me emphasize that not *all* sense-datum theorists—even of the classical type—have been guilty of *all* these confusions; nor are these *all* the confusions of which sense-datum theorists have been guilty. I shall have more to say on this topic later. But the confusions I have mentioned are central to the tradition, and will serve my present purpose. For the upshot of blending all these ingredients together is the idea that a sensation of a red triangle is the very paradigm of empirical knowledge. And I think that it can readily be seen that this idea leads straight to the orthodox type of sense-datum theory and accounts for the perplexities which arise when one tries to think it through.

II. ANOTHER LANGUAGE?

8. I shall now examine briefly a heterodox suggestion by, for example, Ayer (1) (2) to the effect that discourse about sense data is, so to speak, another language, a language contrived by the epistemologist, for situations which the plain man describes by means of such locutions as "Now the book looks green to me" and "There seems to be a red and triangular object over there." The core of this suggestion is the idea that the vocabulary of sense data embodies no increase in the content of descriptive discourse, as over and against the plain man's language of physical objects in Space and Time, and the properties they have and appear to have. For it holds that sentences of the form

X presents S with a ϕ sense datum

are simply *stipulated* to have the same force as sentences of the form

X looks ϕ to S.

Thus "The tomato presents S with a bulgy red sense-datum" would be the contrived counterpart of "The tomato looks red and bulgy to S" and would mean exactly what the latter means for the simple reason that it was stipulated to do so.

As an aid to explicating this suggestion, I am going to make use of a certain picture. I am going to start with the idea of a *code,* and I am going to enrich this notion until the codes I am talking about are no longer *mere* codes. Whether one wants to call these "enriched codes" codes at all is a matter which I shall not attempt to decide.

Now a code, in the sense in which I shall use the term, is a system of symbols each of which represents a complete sentence. Thus, as we initially view the situation, there are two characteristic features of a code: (1) Each code symbol is a unit; the parts of a code symbol are not themselves code symbols. (2) Such logical relations as obtain among code symbols are completely parasitical; they derive entirely from logical relations among the sentences they represent. Indeed, to speak about logical relations among code symbols is a way of talking which is introduced in terms of the logical relations among the sentences they represent. Thus, if "○" stands for "Everybody on board is sick" and "△" for "Somebody on board is sick," then "△" would follow from "○" in the sense that the sentence represented by "△" follows from the sentence represented by "○".

Let me begin to modify this austere conception of a code. There is no reason why a code symbol might not have parts which, without becoming full-fledged symbols on their own, do play a role in the system. Thus they might play the role of *mnemonic devices* serving to put us in mind of features of the sentences represented by the symbols of which they are parts. For example, the code symbol for "Someone on board is sick" might contain the letter S to remind us of the word "sick," and, perhaps, the reversed letter E to remind those of us who have a background in logic of the word "someone." Thus, the flag for "Someone on board is sick" might be '∃*S*'. Now the suggestion at which I am obviously driving is that someone might introduce so-called sense-datum sentences as code symbols or "flags," and introduce the vocables and printables they contain to serve the role of reminding us of certain features of the sentences in ordinary perceptual discourse which the flags as wholes represent. In particular, the role of the vocable or printable "sense datum" would be that of indicating that the symbolized sentence contains the context ". . . looks . . . ," the vocable or printable "red" that the correlated sentence contains the context ". . . looks red . . ." and so on.

9. Now to take this conception of sense datum 'sentences' seriously is, of course, to take seriously the idea that there are no independent logical relations between sense-datum 'sentences.' It *looks* as though there were such independent logical relations, for these 'sentences' look like

sentences, and they have as proper parts vocables or printables which function *in ordinary usage* as *logical words.* Certainly if sense-datum talk is a code, it is a code which is easily mistaken for a language proper. Let me illustrate. At first sight it certainly seems that

A. The tomato presents S with a red sense datum
   entails both
B. There are red sense data
   and
C. The tomato presents S with a sense datum which has some specific shade of red.

This, however, on the kind of view I am considering, would be a mistake. (B) would follow—even in the inverted commas sense of 'follows' appropriate to code symbols—from (A) only because (B) is the flag for (β), "Something looks red to somebody," which *does* follow from (α), "The tomato looks red to Jones" which is represented in the code by (A). And (C) would 'follow' from (A), in spite of appearances, only if (C) were the flag for a *sentence* which *follows* from (α).

I shall have more to say about this example in a moment. The point to be stressed now is that to carry out this view consistently one must deny to such vocables and printables as "quality," "is," "red," "color," "crimson," "determinable," "determinate," "all," "some," "exists," etc., etc., *as they occur in sense-datum talk,* the full-blooded status of their counterparts in ordinary usage. They are rather *clues* which serve to remind us which sense-datum 'flag' it would be proper to fly along with which other sense-datum 'flags.' Thus, the vocables which make up the two 'flags'

(D) All sense-data are red

and

(E) Some sense data are not red

remind us of the genuine logical incompatibility between, for example,

(F) All elephants are grey

and

(G) Some elephants are not grey,

and serve, therefore, as a clue to the impropriety of flying these two 'flags' together. For the sentences they symbolize are, presumably,

(δ) Everything looks red to everybody

and

(ε) There is a color other than red which something looks to somebody to have,

and these *are* incompatible.

But one would have to be cautious in using these clues. Thus, from the fact that it is proper to infer

(H) Some elephants have a determinate shade of pink

from

(I) Some elephants are pink

it would clearly be a mistake to infer that the right to fly

(K) Some sense data are pink

carries with it the right to fly

(L) Some sense data have a determinate shade of pink.

9. But if sense-datum sentences are really sense-datum 'sentences'—i.e. code flags—it follows, of course, that sense-datum talk neither *clarifies* nor *explains* facts of the form *x looks* ϕ *to S* or *x is* ϕ. That it would appear to do so would be because it would take an almost superhuman effort to keep from taking the vocables and printables which occur in the code (and let me now add to our earlier list the vocable "directly known") to be *words* which, if homonyms of words in ordinary usage, have their ordinary sense, and which, if invented, have a meaning specified by their relation to the others. One would be constantly tempted, that is, to treat sense-datum flags as though they were sentences in a *theory*, and sense-datum talk as a *language* which gets its use by coordinating sense-datum sentences with sentences in ordinary perception talk, *as molecule talk gets its use by coordinating sentences about populations of molecules with talk about the pressure of gases on the walls of their containers*. After all,

x looks red to S · ≡ · there is a class of red sense data which belong to x, and are sensed by S

has at least a superficial resemblance to

g exerts pressure on w · ≡ · there is a class of molecules which make up g, and which are bouncing off w,

a resemblance which becomes even more striking once it is granted that the former is not an *analysis* of *x looks red to S* in terms of sense data.

There is, therefore, reason to believe that it is the fact that both codes and theories are contrived systems which are under the control of the language with which they are coordinated, which has given aid and comfort to the idea that sense-datum talk is "another language" for ordinary discourse about perception. Yet although the logical relations between sentences in a theoretical language are, in an important sense, under the control of logical relations between sentences in the observation language, nevertheless, within the framework of this control, the theoretical language has an *autonomy* which contradicts the very idea of a code. If this essential difference between theories and codes is overlooked, one may be tempted to try to eat his cake and have it. By thinking of sense-datum talk as *merely another language,* one draws on the fact that codes have no surplus value. By thinking of sense-datum talk as *illuminating* the "language of appearing," one draws on the fact that theoretical languages, though *contrived,* and depending for their meaningfulness on a coordination with the language of observation, have an explanatory function. Unfortunately, these two characteristics are incompatible; for it is just because theories have "surplus value" that they can provide explanations.

No one, of course, who thinks—as, for example, does Ayer—of the existence of sense data as entailing the existence of "direct knowledge," would wish to say that sense *data* are theoretical entities. It could scarcely be a theoretical fact that I am directly knowing that a certain sense content is red. On the other hand, the idea that sense *contents* are theoretical entities is not *obviously* absurd—so absurd as to preclude the above interpretation of the plausibility of the "another-language" approach. For even those who introduce the expression "sense content" by means of the context ". . . is directly known to be . . ." may fail to keep this fact in mind when putting this expression to use—for example, by developing the idea that physical objects and persons alike are patterns of sense contents. In such a specific context, it is possible to forget that sense *contents,* thus introduced, are essentially sense *data* and not merely items which exemplify sense qualities. Indeed, one may even lapse into thinking of the *sensing* of sense contents, the givenness of sense *data,* as *non-epistemic* facts.

I think it fair to say that those who offer the "another-language" interpretation of sense data find the illumination it provides to consist primarily in the fact that in the language of sense data, physical objects are patterns of sense contents, so that, viewed in this framework, there is no "iron curtain" between the knowing mind and the physical world. It is to elaborating plausible (if schematic) translations of physical-object statements into statements about sense contents, rather than to spelling out the force of such sentences as "Sense content *s* is directly known to be red," that the greater part of their philosophical ingenuity has been directed.

However this may be, one thing can be said with confidence. If the language of sense data *were* merely a code, a notational device, then the cash value of any philosophical clarification it might provide must lie in its ability to illuminate logical relations *within* ordinary discourse about physical objects and our perception of them. Thus, the fact (if it were a fact) that a code can be constructed for ordinary perception talk which 'speaks' of a "relation of identity" between the components ("sense data") of "minds" and of "things," would presumably have as its cash value the insight that ordinary discourse about physical objects and perceivers could (in principle) be constructed from sentences of the form "There looks to be a physical object with a red and triangular facing surface over there" (the counterpart in ordinary language of the basic expressions of the code). In more traditional terms, the clarification would consist in making manifest the fact that persons and things are alike logical constructions out of *lookings* or *appearings* (*not* appearances!). But any claim to this effect soon runs into insuperable difficulties which become apparent once the role of "looks" or "appears" is understood. And it is to an examination of this role that I now turn.

III. THE LOGIC OF 'LOOKS'

10. Before turning aside to examine the suggestion that the language of sense data is "another language" for the situations described by the so-called "language of appearing," I had concluded that classical sense-datum theories, when pressed, reveal themselves to be the result of a mismating of two ideas: (1) The idea that there are certain "inner episodes," e.g. the sensation of a red triangle or of a C♯ sound, which occur to human beings and brutes without any prior process of learning or concept formation, and without which it would—in *some* sense—be impossible to *see,* for example, that the facing surface of a physical

object is red and triangular, or *hear* that a certain physical sound is C♯; (2) The idea that there are certain "inner episodes" which are the non-inferential knowings that, for example, a certain item is red and triangular, or, in the case of sounds, C♯, which inner episodes are the necessary conditions of empirical knowledge as providing the evidence for all other empirical propositions. If this diagnosis is correct, a reasonable next step would be to examine these two ideas and determine how that which survives criticism in each is properly to be combined with the other. Clearly we would have to come to grips with the idea of *inner episodes,* for this is common to both.

Many who attack the idea of the given seem to have thought that the central mistake embedded in this idea is exactly the idea that there are inner episodes, whether thoughts or so-called "immediate experiences," to which each of us has privileged access. I shall argue that this is just not so, and that the Myth of the Given can be dispelled without resorting to the crude verificationisms or operationalisms characteristic of the more dogmatic forms of recent empiricism. Then there are those who, while they do not reject the idea of inner episodes, find the Myth of the Given to consist in the idea that knowledge of these episodes furnishes *premises* on which empirical knowledge rests as on a foundation. But while this idea has, indeed, been the most widespread form of the Myth, it is far from constituting its essence. Everything hinges on *why* these philosophers reject it. If, for example, it is on the ground that the learning of a language is a *public* process which proceeds in a domain of *public* objects and is governed by *public* sanctions, so that *private* episodes—with the exception of a mysterious nod in their direction—must needs escape the net of rational discourse, then, while these philosophers are immune to the form of the myth which has flowered in sense-datum theories, they have no defense against the myth in the form of the givenness of such facts as that *physical object x looks red to person S at time t,* or that *there looks to person S at time t to be a red physical object over there.* It will be useful to pursue the Myth in this direction for a while before more general issues are raised.

11. Philosophers have found it easy to suppose that such a sentence as "The tomato looks red to Jones" says that a certain triadic relation, *looking* or *appearing,* obtains among a physical object, a person, and a quality.[1] "A looks ϕ to S" is assimilated to "x gives y to z"—or, better, since giving is, strictly speaking, an action rather than a relation—to "x is between y and z," and taken to be a case of the general form "R(x,y,z)." Having supposed this, they turn without further ado to the question, "Is this relation analyzable?" Sense-datum theorists have, on

[1] A useful discussion of views of this type is to be found in (9) and (13).

the whole, answered "Yes," and claimed that facts of the form *x looks red to X* are to be analyzed in terms of sense data. Some of them, without necessarily rejecting this claim, have argued that facts of this kind are, at the very least, to be *explained* in terms of sense data. Thus, when Broad (4) writes "If, in fact, nothing elliptical is before my mind, it is very hard to understand why the penny should seem *elliptical* rather than of any other shape (p. 240)," he is appealing to sense-data as a means of *explaining* facts of this form. The difference, of course, is that whereas if *x looks* ϕ *to S* is correctly *analyzed* in terms of sense data, then no one could believe that x looks ϕ to S without believing that S has sense data, the same need not be true if *x looks* ϕ *to S* is explained in terms of sense data, for, in the case of some types of explanation, at least, one can believe a fact without believing its explanation.

On the other hand, those philosophers who reject sense-datum theories in favor of so-called theories of appearing have characteristically held that facts of the form *x looks* ϕ *to S* are ultimate and irreducible, and that sense data are needed neither for their analysis nor for their explanation. If asked, "Doesn't the statement 'x looks red to S' have as part of its meaning the idea that s stands in some relation to something that *is* red?" their answer is in the negative, and, I believe, rightly so.

12. I shall begin my examination of "X looks red to S at t" with the simple but fundamental point that the sense of "red" in which things *look* red is, on the face of it, the same as that in which things *are* red. When one glimpses an object and decides that it looks red (to *me, now,* from here) and wonders whether it really *is* red, one is surely wondering whether the color—red—which it looks to have is the one it really does have. This point can be obscured by such verbal manipulations as hyphenating the words "looks" and "red" and claiming that it is the insoluble unity "looks-red" and not just "looks" which is the relation. Insofar as this dodge is based on insight, it is insight into the fact that *looks* is not a relation between a person, a thing, and a quality. Unfortunately, as we shall see, the reason for this fact is one which gives no comfort at all to the idea that it is *looks-red* rather than *looks* which is the relation.

I have, in effect, been claiming that *being red* is logically prior, is a logically simpler notion, than *looking red;* the function "x is red" to "x looks red to y." In short, that it just won't do to say that *x is red* is analyzable in terms of *x looks red to y*. But what, then, are we to make of the necessary truth—and it is, of course, a necessary truth—that

x *is* red $\cdot \equiv \cdot$ x would *look* red to standard observers in standard conditions?

There is certainly some sense to the idea that this is at least the schema for a definition of *physical redness* in terms of *looking red.* One begins to see the plausibility of the gambit that *looking-red* is an insoluble unity, for the minute one gives "red" (on the right-hand side) an independent status, it becomes what it obviously is, namely "red" as a predicate of physical objects, and the supposed definition becomes an obvious circle.

13. The way out of this troubling situation has two parts. The *second* is to show how "x *is* red" can be necessarily equivalent to "x would *look* red to standard observers in standard situations" without this being a definition of "x is red" in terms of "x looks red." But the *first,* and logically prior, step is to show that "x looks red to S" does not assert either an unanalyzable triadic relation to obtain between x, red, and S, or an unanalyzable dyadic relation to obtain between x and S. Not, however, because it asserts an *analyzable* relation to obtain, but because *looks* is not a relation at all. Or, to put the matter in a familiar way, one can say that *looks* is a relation if he likes, for the sentences in which this word appears show some grammatical analogies to sentences built around words which we should not hesitate to classify as relation words; but once one has become aware of certain other features which make them very unlike ordinary relation sentences, he will be less inclined to view his task as that of *finding the answer* to the question "Is looks a relation?"

14. To bring out the essential features of the use of "looks," I shall engage in a little historical fiction. A young man, whom I shall call John, works in a necktie shop. He has learned the use of color words in the usual way, with this exception. I shall suppose that he has never looked at an object in other than standard conditions. As he examines his stock every evening before closing up shop, he says "This is red," "That is green," "This is purple," etc., and such of his linguistic peers as happen to be present nod their heads approvingly.

Let us suppose, now, that at this point in the story, electric lighting is invented. His friends and neighbors rapidly adopt this new means of illumination, and wrestle with the problems it presents. John, however, is the last to succumb. Just after it has been installed in his shop, one of his neighbors, Jim, comes in to buy a necktie.

"Here is a handsome green one," says John.

"But it *isn't* green," says Jim, and takes John outside.

"Well," says John, "it was green in there, but now it is blue."

"No," says Jim, "you know that neckties don't change their color merely as a result of being taken from place to place."

"But perhaps electricity changes their color and they change back again in daylight?"

"That would be a queer kind of change, wouldn't it?" says Jim.

"I suppose so," says bewildered John. "But we *saw* that it was green *in there.*"

"No, we didn't see that it was green in there, because it wasn't green, and you can't see what isn't so!"

"Well, this is a pretty pickle," says John. *"I just don't know what to say."*

The next time John picks up this tie in his shop and someone asks what color it is, his first impulse is to say "It is green." He suppresses this impulse, and, remembering what happened before, comes out with "It is blue." He doesn't *see* that it is blue, nor would he say that he sees it to be blue. What does he see? Let us ask him.

"I don't know *what* to say. If I didn't know that the tie is blue—and the alternative to granting this is odd indeed—I would swear that I was seeing a green tie and seeing that it is green. It is *as though* I were seeing the necktie to be green."

If we bear in mind that such sentences as "This is green" have both a *fact-stating* and a *reporting* use, we can put the point I have just been making by saying that once John learns to stifle the *report* "This necktie is green" when looking at it in the shop, there is no other *report* about color and the necktie which he knows how to make. To be sure, he now says "This necktie is blue." But he is not making a *reporting* use of this sentence. He uses it as the conclusion of an inference.

15. We return to the shop after an interval, and we find that when John is asked "What is the color of this necktie?" he makes such statements as "It looks green, but take it outside and see." It occurs to us that perhaps in learning to say "This tie *looks* green" when in the shop, he has learned to make a new kind of report. Thus, it might seem as though his linguistic peers have helped him to notice a new kind of *objective* fact, one which though a relational fact involving a perceiver, is as logically independent of the beliefs, the conceptual framework of the perceiver, as the fact that the necktie is blue; but a *minimal* fact, one which it is safer to report because one is less likely to be mistaken. Such a minimal fact would be the fact that the necktie looks green to John on a certain occasion, and it would be properly reported by using the sentence "This necktie *looks* green." It is this type of account, of course, which I have already rejected.

But what is the alternative? If, that is, we are not going to adopt the sense-datum analysis. Let me begin by noting that there certainly seems to be something to the idea that the sentence "This looks green to me now" has a reporting role. Indeed, it would seem to be essentially a report. But if so, *what* does it report, if not a minimal objective fact, and if what it reports is not to be analyzed in terms of sense data?

16. Let me next call attention to the fact that the experience of having something look green to one at a certain time is, insofar as it is an experience, obviously very much like that of seeing something to be green, insofar as the latter is an experience. But the latter, of course,

is not *just* an experience. And this is the heart of the matter. For to say that a certain experience is a *seeing that* something is the case, is to do more than describe the experience. It is to characterize it as, so to speak, making an assertion or claim, and—which is the point I wish to stress—to *endorse* that claim. As a matter of fact, as we shall see, it is much more easy to see that the statement "Jones sees that the tree is green" ascribes a propositional claim to Jones' experience and endorses it, than to specify how the statement *describes* Jones' experience.

I realize that by speaking of experiences as containing propositional claims, I may seem to be knocking at closed doors. I ask the reader to bear with me, however, as the justification of this way of talking is one of my major aims. If I am permitted to issue this verbal currency now, I hope to put it on the gold standard before concluding the argument.

16. It is clear that the experience of seeing that something is green is not *merely* the occurrence of the propositional claim 'this is green'—not even if we add, as we must, that this claim is, so to speak, evoked or wrung from the perceiver by the object perceived. Here Nature— to turn Kant's simile (which he uses in another context) on its head—puts us to the question. The something more is clearly what philosophers have in mind when they speak of "visual impressions" or "immediate visual experiences." What exactly is the logical status of these "impressions" or "immediate experiences" is a problem which will be with us for the remainder of this argument. For the moment it is the propositional claim which concerns us.

I pointed out above that when we use the word "see" as in "S sees that the tree is green" we are not only ascribing a claim to the experience, but endorsing it. It is this endorsement which Ryle has in mind when he refers to *seeing that something is thus and so* as an *achievement,* and to *"sees"* as an *achievement word.* I prefer to call it a "so it is" or "just so" word, for the root idea is that of *truth.* To characterize S's experience as a *seeing* is, in a suitably broad sense—which I shall be concerned to explicate—to apply the semantical concept of truth to that experience.

Now the suggestion I wish to make is, in its simplest terms, that the statement "X looks green to Jones" differs from "Jones sees that x is green" in that whereas the latter both ascribes a propositional claim to Jones' experience *and endorses it,* the former ascribes the claim but does not endorse it. This is the essential difference between the two, for it is clear that two experiences may be identical as *experiences,* and yet one be properly referred to as a *seeing that* something is green, and the other *merely* as a case of something's *looking* green. Of course, if I say "X *merely looks* green to S" I am not only failing to endorse the claim, I am rejecting it.

Thus, when I say "X looks green to me now" I am *reporting* the fact that my experience is, so to speak, intrinsically, *as an experience,* indistinguishable from a veridical one of seeing that x is green. Involved in the report is the ascription to my experience of the claim 'x is green'; and the fact that I make this report rather than the simple report "X is green" indicates that certain considerations have operated to raise, so to speak in a higher court, the question 'to endorse or not to endorse.' I may have reason to think that x may not after all be green.

If I make at one time the report "X looks to be green"—which is not only a report, but the withholding of an endorsement—I may later, when the original reasons for withholding endorsement have been rebutted, endorse the original claim by saying "I saw that it was green, though at the time I was only sure that it looked green." Notice that I will only say "I see that x is green" (as opposed to "X is green") when the question "to endorse or not to endorse" has come up. "I see that x is green" belongs, so to speak, on the same level as "X looks green" and "X merely *looks* green."

17. There are many interesting and subtle questions about the dialectics of "looks talk," into which I do not have the space to enter. Fortunately, the above distinctions suffice for our present purposes. Let us suppose, then, that to say that "X looks green to S at t" is, in effect, to say that S has that kind of experience which, if one were prepared to endorse the propositional claim it involves, one would characterize as *seeing x to be green at t.* Thus, when our friend John learns to use the sentence "This necktie looks green to me" he learns a way of reporting an experience of the kind which, as far as any categories I have yet permitted him to have are concerned, he can only characterize by saying that as an experience it does not differ from seeing something to be green, and that evidence for the proposition. 'This necktie is green' is *ipso facto* evidence for the proposition that the experience in question is *seeing that the necktie is green.*

Now one of the chief merits of this account is that it permits a parallel treatment of 'qualitative' and 'existential' seeming or looking. Thus, when I say "The tree looks bent" I am endorsing that part of the claim involved in my experience which concerns the existence of the tree, but withholding endorsement from the rest. On the other hand, when I say "There looks to be a bent tree over there" I am refusing to endorse any but the most general aspect of the claim, namely, that there is an 'over there' as opposed to a 'here.' Another merit of the account is that it explains how a necktie, for example, can look red to S at t, without looking scarlet or crimnson or any other determinate shade of red. In short it explains how things can have a *merely generic* look, a fact which would be puzzling indeed if looking red were a *natural* as opposed to *epistemic* fact about objects. The core of the explanation, of course, is that the propositional claim involved in such an experience may be, for example, either the more determinable claim 'This is red' or the more determinate claim 'This is crimson.' The complete story is more complicated, and requires some account of the role in these experiences of the 'impressions' or 'immediate experiences' the logical status of which remains to be determined. But even in the absence of these additional details, we can note the resemblance between the fact that x can look red to S, without it being true of some specific shade of red that x looks to S to be of that shade, and the fact that S can believe that Cleopatra's Needle is tall, without its being true of some determinate number of feet that S believes it to be that number of feet tall.

18. The point I wish to stress at this time, however, is that the concept of *looking green,* the ability to recognize that something *looks green,* presupposes the concept of *being green,* and that the latter concept involves the ability to tell what colors objects have by looking at them—which, in turn, involves knowing in what circumstances to place an object if one wishes to ascertain its color by looking at it. Let me develop this latter point. As our friend John becomes more and more sophisticated about his own and other people's visual experiences, he learns under what conditions it is as though one were seeing a necktie to be of one color when in fact it is of another. Suppose someone asks him "Why does this tie look green to me?" John may very well reply "Because it is blue, and blue objects look green in this kind of light." And if someone asks this question when looking at the neckties in plain daylight, John may very well reply "Because the tie *is* green"—to which he may add "We are in plain daylight, *and in daylight things look what they are.*" We thus see that

x is red · ≡ · x looks red to standard observers in standard conditions

is a necessary truth *not* because the right-hand side is the definition of "x is red," but because "standard conditions" means conditions in which things look what they are. And, of course, *which* conditions are standard for a given mode of perception is, at the common-sense level, specified by a list of conditions which exhibit the vagueness and open texture characteristic of ordinary discourse.

19. I have arrived at a stage in my argument which is, at least prima facie, out of step with the basic presuppositions of logical atomism. Thus, as long as *looking green* is taken to be the notion to which *being green* is reducible, it could be claimed with considerable plausibility that fundamental concepts pertaining to observable fact have that logical independence of one another which is characteristic of the empiricist tradition. Indeed, at first sight the situation is *quite* disquieting, for if

the ability to recognize that x looks green presupposes the concept of *being green,* and if this in turn involves knowing in what circumstances to view an object to ascertain its color, then, since one can scarcely determine what the circumstances are without noticing that certain objects have certain perceptible characteristics—including colors—it would seem that one couldn't form the concept of *being green,* and, by parity of reasoning, of the other colors, unless he already had them.

Now, it just won't do to reply that to have the concept of green, to know what it is for something to be green, it is sufficient to respond, when one is *in point of fact* in standard conditions, to green objects with the vocable "This is green." Not only must the conditions be of a sort that is appropriate for determining the color of an object by looking, the subject must *know* that conditions of this sort *are* appropriate. And while this does not imply that one must have concepts before one has them, it does imply that one can have the concept of green only by having a whole battery of concepts of which it is one element. It implies that while the process of acquiring the concept of green may —indeed does—involve a long history of acquiring *piecemeal* habits of response to various objects in various circumstances, there is an important sense in which one has *no* concept pertaining to the observable properties of physical objects in Space and Time unless one has them all—and, indeed, as we shall see, a great deal more besides.

20. Now, I think it is clear what a logical atomist, supposing that he found any merit at all in the above argument, would say. He would say that I am overlooking the fact that the logical space of physical objects in Space and Time rests on the logical space of sense contents, and he would argue that it is concepts pertaining to sense contents which have the logical independence of one another which is characteristic of traditional empiricism. "After all," he would point out, "concepts pertaining to theoretical entities—molecules, for example—have the mutual dependence you have, perhaps rightly, ascribed to concepts pertaining to *physical* fact. But," he would continue, "theoretical concepts have empirical content because they rest on—are coordinated with—a more fundamental logical space. Until you have disposed, therefore, of the idea that there is a more fundamental logical space than that of physical objects in Space and Time, or shown that it too is fraught with coherence, your incipient *Meditations Hegeliènnes* are premature."

And we can imagine a sense-datum theorist to interject the following complaint: "You have begun to write as though you had shown not only that *physical redness* is not to be analyzed in terms of *looking red* —which I will grant—but also that physical redness is not to be analyzed at all, and, in particular, not to be analyzed in terms of the redness of red sense contents. Again, you have begun to write as though you had shown not only that observing that x *looks* red is not more basic than observing that x *is* red, but also that there is *no* form of visual noticing more basic than seeing that x is red, such as the sensing of a red sense content. I grant," he continues, "that the tendency of sense-datum theorists has been to claim that the *redness* of physical objects is to be analyzed in terms of *looking red,* and *then* to claim that *looking red* is itself to be analyzed in terms of *red sense contents,* and that you may have undercut this line of analysis. But what is to prevent the sense-datum theorist from taking the line that the properties of physical objects are *directly* analyzable into the qualities and phenomenal relations of sense contents?"

Very well. But once again we must ask, How does the sense-datum theorist come by the framework of sense contents? and How is he going to convince us that there are such things? For even if *looking red* doesn't enter into the analysis of physical redness, it is by asking us to reflect on the experience of having something look red to us that he hopes to make this framework convincing. And it therefore becomes relevant to note that my analysis of *x looks red to S at t* has not, at least as far as I have pushed it to date, revealed any such items as sense-contents. And it may be relevant to suggest that once we see clearly that physical redness is not to be given a dispositional analysis in terms of *looking red,* the idea that it is to be given *any* kind of dispositional analysis loses a large measure of its plausibility. In any event, the next move must be to press further the above account of qualitative and existential looking.

IV. EXPLAINING LOOKS

21. I have already noted that sense-datum theorists are impressed by the question "How can a physical object look red to S, unless something in that situation *is* red and S is taking account of it? If S isn't experiencing something red, how does it happen that the physical object looks *red,* rather than green or streaky?" There is, I propose to show, *something* to this line of thought, though the story turns out to be a complicated one. And if, in the course of telling the story, I shall be led to make statements which resemble *some* of the things sense-datum theorists have said, this story will amount to a sense-datum theory only in a sense which robs this phrase of an entire dimension of its traditional epistemological force, a dimension which is characteristic of even such heterodox forms of sense-datum theory as the "another language" approach.

Let me begin by formulating the question: "Is the fact that an object looks to S to be red and triangular, or that there looks to S to be a red and triangular object over there, to be explained in terms of the idea that Jones has a sensation—or impression, or immediate experience—of a red triangle? One point can be made right away, namely that if these expressions are so understood that, say, the immediate experience of a red triangle implies the existence of something—not a physical object—which *is* red and triangular, and if the redness which this item has is the same as the redness which the physical object *looks* to have, then the suggestion runs up against the objection that the redness physical objects *look* to have is the same as the redness physical objects actually *do* have, so that items which *ex hypothesi* are not physical objects, and which radically, even categorially, differ from physical objects, would have the same redness as physical objects. And while this is, perhaps, not entirely out of the question, it certainly provides food for thought. Yet when it is claimed that "obviously" physical objects can't *look* red to one unless one is experiencing something that *is* red, is it not presumed that the redness which the *something* has is the redness which the physical object *looks to have*?

Now there are those who would say that the question "Is the fact that an object looks red and triangular to S to be explained—as opposed to notationally reformulated—in terms of the idea that S has an impression of a red triangle?" simply doesn't arise, on the ground that there are perfectly sound explanations of qualitative and existential lookings which make no reference to 'immediate experience' or other dubious entities. Thus, it is pointed out, it is perfectly proper to answer the question "Why does this object look red?" by saying "Because it is an orange object looked at in such and such circumstances." The explanation is, in principle, a good one, and is typical of the answers we make to such questions in everyday life. But because these explanations are good, it by no means follows that explanations of other kinds might not be equally good, and, perhaps, more searching.

22. On the face of it there are at least two ways in which additional, but equally legitimate explanations *might* be forthcoming for such a fact as that *x looks red*. The first of these is suggested by a simple analogy. Might it not be the case that just as there are two kinds of good explanation of the fact that this balloon has expanded, (a) in terms of the Boyle-Charles laws which relate the empirical concepts of volume, pressure, and temperature pertaining to gases, and (b) in terms of the kinetic theory of gases; so there are two ways of explaining the fact that this object looks red to S: (a) in terms of empirical generalizations relating the colors of objects, the circumstances in which they are seen, and the colors they look to have, and (b) in terms of a theory of perception in which 'immediate experiences' play a role analogous to that of the molecules of the kinetic theory.

Now there is such an air of paradox to the idea that 'immediate experiences' are *mere* theoretical entities—entities, that is, which are postulated, along with certain fundamental principles concerning them, to explain uniformities pertaining to sense perception, as molecules, along with the principles of molecular motion, are postulated to explain the experimentally determined regularities pertaining to gases—that I am going to lay it aside until a more propitious context of thought may make it seem relevant. Certainly, those who have thought that qualitative and existential lookings are to be explained in terms of 'immediate experiences' thought of the latter as the most untheoretical of entities, indeed, as *the* observables *par excellence.*

Let us therefore turn to a second way in which, at least prima facie, there might be an additional, but equally legitimate explanation of existential and qualitative lookings. According to this second account, when we consider items of this kind, we *find* that they contain as components items which are properly referred to as, for example, 'the immediate experience of a red triangle.' Let us begin our exploration of this suggestion by taking another look at our account of existential and qualitative lookings. It will be remembered that our account of qualitative looking ran, in rough and ready terms, as follows:

> 'x looks red to S' has the sense of 'S has an experience which involves in a unique way the idea *that x is red* and involves it in such a way that if this idea were true, the experience would correctly be characterized as a seeing that x is red.'

Thus, our account implies that the three situations

(a) Seeing that x, over there, is red
(b) Its looking to one that x, over there, is red
(c) Its looking to one as though there were a red object over there

differ primarily in that (a) is so formulated as to involve an endorsement of the idea that x, over there, is red, whereas in (b) this idea is only partially endorsed, and in (c) not at all. Let us refer to the idea *that x, over there, is red* as the *common propositional content* of these three situations. (This is, of course, not strictly correct, since the propositional content of (c) is *existential,* rather than about a presupposedly designated object x, but it will serve my purpose. Furthermore, the common propositional content of these three experiences is much more complex and determinate than is indicated by the sentence we use to describe our experience to others, and which I am using to represent it. Nevertheless it is clear that, subject to the first of these qualifications, the propositional content of these three experiences *could* be identical.)

The propositional content of these three experiences is, of course, but a part of that to which we are logically committed by characterizing them as situations of these three kinds. Of the remainder, as we have seen, part is a matter of the extent to which this propositional content is endorsed. It is the residue with which we are now concerned. Let us call this residue the *descriptive content*. I can then point out that it is implied by my account that not only the *propositional content*, but also the *descriptive content* of these three experiences may be identical. I shall suppose this to be the case, though that there must be some factual difference in the *total* situations is obvious.

Now, and this is the decisive point, in characterizing these three experiences as, respectively a *seeing that x, over there, is red, its looking to one as though x, over there, were red,* and *its looking to one as though there were a red object over there,* we do not specify this common *descriptive* content save *indirectly,* by implying that *if the common propositional content were true,* then all these three situations would be cases of *seeing* that *x,* over there is red. Both existential and qualitative lookings are experiences that would be *seeings* if their propositional contents were true.

Thus, the very nature of "looks talk" is such as to raise questions to which it gives no answer: What is the *intrinsic* character of the common descriptive content of these three experiences? and How are they able to have it in spite of the fact that whereas in the case of (a) the perceiver must be in the presence of a red object over there, in (b) the object over there need not be red, while in (c) there need be no object over there at all?

23. Now it is clear that if we were required to give a more direct characterization of the common descriptive content of these experiences, we would begin by trying to do so in terms of the quality *red.* Yet, as I have already pointed out, we can scarcely say that this descriptive content is itself something red unless we can pry the term "red" loose from its prima-facie tie with the category of physical objects. And there is a line of thought which has been one of the standard gambits of perceptual epistemology and which seems to promise exactly this. If successful, it would convince us that *redness*—in the most basic sense of this term—is a characteristic of items of the sort we have been calling sense contents. It runs as follows:

> While it would, indeed, be a howler to say that we don't see chairs, tables, etc., but only their facing surfaces, nevertheless, although we see a table, say, and although the table has a back as well as a front, we do not see the back of the table as we see its front. Again, although we see the table, and although the table has an 'inside,' we do not see the inside of

> the table as we see its facing outside. Seeing an object entails seeing its facing surface. If we are seeing that an object is red, this entails seeing that its facing surface is red. A red surface is a two-dimensional red expanse—two dimensional in that though it may be *bulgy*, and in *this* sense three-dimensional, it has no *thickness*. As far as the analysis of perceptual consciousness is concerned, a red physical object is one that has a red expanse as its surface.
>
> Now a red expanse is not a physical object, nor does the existence of a red expanse entail the existence of a physical object to which it belongs. (Indeed, there are "wild" expanses which do not belong to any physical object.) The "descriptive content"—as you put it—which is common to the three experiences (a), (b) and (c) above, is exactly this sort of thing, a bulgy red expanse.

Spelled out thus baldly, the fallacy is, or should be, obvious; it is a simple equivocation on the phrase "having a red surface." We start out by thinking of the familiar fact that a physical object may be of one color "on the surface" and of another color "inside." We may express this by saying that, for example, the 'surface' of the object is red, but its 'inside' green. But in saying this we are *not* saying that there is a 'surface' in the sense of a bulgy two-dimensional particular, a red 'expanse' which is a component particular in a complex particular which also includes green particulars. The notion of two-dimensional bulgy (or flat) particulars is a product of philosophical (and mathematical) sophistication which can be *related* to our ordinary conceptual framework, but does not belong in an *analysis* of it. I think that in its place it has an important contribution to make. (See below, Section 61, (5), pp. 325–26.) [pp. 537–38, this volume. Eds.] But this place is in the logical space of an ideal *scientific* picture of the world and not in the logical space of ordinary discourse. It has nothing to do with the logical grammar of our ordinary color words. It is just a mistake to suppose that as the word "red" is actually used, it is ever surfaces in the sense of two-dimensional particulars which are red. The only particular involved when a physical object is "red on the outside, but green inside" is the physical object itself, located in a certain region of Space and enduring over a stretch of Time. The fundamental grammar of the attribute *red* is *physical object x is red at place p and at time t*. Certainly, when we say of an object that it is red, we commit ourselves to no more than that it is red "at the surface." And sometimes it is red at the surface by having what we would not hesitate to call a "part" which is red through and through—thus, a red table which is red by virtue of a layer of red paint. But the red paint is not itself by virtue of a component—a 'surface' or 'expanse'; a particular with no thickness—which is red. There may, let me repeat, turn out to be some place in the total philosophical picture for the statement that there "really are" such particulars, and that they are elements in perceptual experience. But this place is not to be found by an analysis of ordinary perceptual discourse, any more than Minkowski four-dimensional Space-Time worms are an *analysis* of what we mean when we speak of physical objects in Space and Time.

V. IMPRESSIONS AND IDEAS: A LOGICAL POINT

24. Let me return to beating the neighboring bushes. Notice that the common descriptive component of the three experiences I am considering is itself often referred to (by philosophers, at least) as an *experience*—as, for example, an *immediate experience.* Here caution is necessary. The notorious "ing-ed" ambiguity of "experience" must be kept in mind. For although *seeing that x, over there, is red is* an *experiencing*—indeed, a paradigm case of experiencing—it does not follow that the descriptive content of this experiencing is itself an experiencing. Furthermore, because the fact that *x, over there, looks to Jones to be red* would be a *seeing,* on Jones' part, *that x, over there, is red,* if its propositional content were true, and because if it *were* a seeing, it *would be* an experiencing, we must beware of concluding that the fact that *x, over there, looks red to Jones* is itself an *experiencing.* Certainly, the fact that something looks red to me can itself be *experienced.* But it is not itself an experiencing.

All this is not to say that the common descriptive core may not turn out to be an experiencing, though the chances that this is so appear less with each step in my argument. On the other hand, I can say that it is a component in states of affairs which are experienced, and it does not seem unreasonable to say that it is itself experienced. But what kind of experience (in the sense of experienced) *is* it? If my argument to date is sound, I cannot say that it is a *red* experience, that is, a red experienced item. I could, of course introduce a new use of "red" according to which to say of an 'immediate experience' that it was red, would be the stipulated equivalent of characterizing it as that which could be the common descriptive component of a *seeing* that something is red, and the corresponding qualitative and existential *lookings.* This would give us a *predicate* by which to describe and report the experience, but we should, of course, be only verbally better off than if we could only refer to this kind of experience as *the kind which* could be the common descriptive component of a *seeing* and a qualitative or existential *looking.* And this makes it clear that one way of putting what we are after is by saying that we want to have a *name* for this kind of experience which is truly a *name,* and not just shorthand for a definite description. Does ordinary usage have a *name* for this kind of experience?

I shall return to this quest in a moment. In the meantime it is important to clear the way of a traditional obstacle to understanding the status of such things as *sensations of red triangles.* Thus, suppose I were to say that while the experience I am examining is not a red experience, it is an experience *of red.* I could expect the immediate challenge: "Is 'sensation of a red triangle' any better off than 'red and triangular experience'? Does not the existence of a sensation of a red triangle entail the existence of a red and triangular item, and hence, *always on the assumption that red is a property of physical objects,* of a red and triangular physical object? Must you not, therefore abandon this assumption, and return to the framework of sense contents which you have so far refused to do?"

One way out of the dilemma would be to assimilate "Jones has a sensation of a red triangle" to "Jones believes in a divine Huntress." For the truth of the latter does not, of course, entail the existence of a divine Huntress. Now, I think that most contemporary philosophers are clear that it is possible to attribute to the context

. . . sensation of . . .

the *logical* property of being such that "There is a sensation of a red triangle" does not entail "There is a red triangle" without assimilating the context ". . . sensation of . . ." to the context ". . . believes in . . ." in any closer way. For while mentalistic verbs characteristically provide nonextensional contexts (when they are not "achievement" or "endorsing" words), not all nonextensional contexts are mentalistic. Thus, as far as the purely *logical* point is concerned, there is no reason why "Jones has a sensation of a red triangle" should be assimilated to "Jones believes in a divine Huntress" rather than to "It is possible that the moon is made of green cheese" or to any of the other nonextensional contexts familiar to logicians. Indeed there is no reason why it should be assimilated to any of these. ". . . sensation of . . ." or ". . . impression of . . ." could be a context which, though sharing with these others the logical property of nonextensionality, was otherwise in a class by itself.

25. Yet there is no doubt but that *historically* the contexts " . . . sensation of . . ." and ". . . impression of . . ." *were* assimilated to such mentalistic contexts as ". . . believes . . .," ". . . desires . . .," ". . . chooses . . .," in short to contexts which are either themselves 'propositional attitudes' or involve propositional attitudes in their analysis. This assimilation took the form of classifying sensations with *ideas* or *thoughts.* Thus Descartes uses the word "thought" to cover not only *judgments, inferences, desires, volitions,* and (occurrent) *ideas* of

abstract qualities, but also *sensations, feelings,* and *images.* Locke, in the same spirit, uses the term "idea" with similar scope. The apparatus of Conceptualism, which had its genesis in the controversy over universals, was given a correspondingly wide application. Just as objects and situations were said to have 'objective being' in our *thoughts,* when we think of them, or judge them to obtain—as contrasted with the 'subjective' or 'formal being' which they have in the world—so, when we have a sensation of a red triangle, the red triangle was supposed to have 'objective being' in our sensation.

In elaborating, for a moment, this conceptualistic interpretation of sensation, let me refer to that which has 'objective being' in a *thought* or *idea* as its *content* or *immanent object.* Then I can say that the fundamental difference between occurrent *abstract ideas* and *sensations,* for both Locke and Descartes, lay in the *specificity* and, above all, the *complexity* of the content of the latter. (Indeed, both Descartes and Locke assimilated the contrast between the simple and the complex in ideas to that between the generic and the specific.) Descartes thinks of sensations as confused thoughts of their external cause, Spinoza of sensations and images as confused thoughts of bodily states, and still more confused thoughts of the external causes of these bodily states. And it is interesting to note that the conceptualistic thesis that abstract entities have only *esse intentionale* (their *esse* is *concipi*) is extended by Descartes and, with less awareness of what he is doing, Locke, to include the thesis that colors, sounds, etc., exist "only in the mind" (their *esse* is *percipi*) and by Berkeley to cover all perceptible qualities.

Now, I think we would all agree, today, that this assimilation of sensations to thoughts is a mistake. It is sufficient to note that if "sensation of a red triangle" had the sense of "episode of the kind which is the common descriptive component of those experiences which *would be* cases of seeing that the facing surface of a physical object is red and triangular if an object *were* presenting a red and triangular facing surface" then it would have the nonextensionality the noticing of which led to this mistaken assimilation. But while we have indeed escaped from this blind alley, it is small consolation. For we are no further along in the search for a 'direct' or 'intrinsic' characterization of 'immediate experience.'

VI. IMPRESSIONS AND IDEAS: AN HISTORICAL POINT

26. There are those who will say that although I have spoken of exploring blind alleys, it is really I who am blind. For, they will say, if that

which we wish to characterize intrinsically is an *experience,* then there *can* be no puzzle about knowing *what kind of* experience it is, though there may be a problem about how this knowledge is to be communicated to others. And, indeed, it is tempting to suppose that if we *should* happen, at a certain stage of our intellectual development, to be able to classify an experience *only* as *of the kind which* could be common to a *seeing* and corresponding qualitative and existential *lookings,* all we would have to do to acquire a 'direct designation' for this kind of experience would be to pitch in, 'examine' it, locate the kind which it exemplifies and which satisfies the above description, name it—say "ϕ"—and, in full possession of the concept of ϕ, classify such experiences, from now on, as ϕ experiences.

At this point, it is clear, the concept—or, as I have put it, the myth—of the given is being invoked to explain the possibility of a direct account of immediate experience. The myth insists that what I have been treating as one problem really subdivides into two, one of which is really no problem at all, while the other may have no solution. These problems are, respectively

(1) How do we become aware of an immediate experience as of one sort, and of a simultaneous immediate experience as of another sort?
(2) How can I know that the labels I attach to the sorts to which my immediate experiences belong, are attached by you to the same sorts? May not the sort I call "'red" be the sort you call "green"—and so on systematically throughout the spectrum?

We shall find that the second question, to be a philosophical perplexity, presupposes a certain answer to the first question—indeed the answer given by the myth. And it is to this first question that I now turn. Actually there are various forms taken by the myth of the given in this connection, depending on other philosophical commitments. But they all have in common the idea that the awareness of certain *sorts*—and by "sorts" I have in mind, in the first instance, determinate sense repeatables—is a primordial, non-problematic feature of 'immediate experience.' In the context of conceptualism, as we have seen, this idea took the form of treating sensations as though they were absolutely specific, and infinitely complicated, *thoughts.* And it is essential to an understanding of the empiricist tradition to realize that whereas the contemporary problem of universals primarily concerns the status of repeatable *determinate* features of particular situations, and the contemporary problem of abstract ideas is at least as much the problem of what it is to be aware of determinate repeatables as of what it is to be aware of determinable repeatables, Locke, Berkeley and, for that matter, Hume saw the problem of abstract ideas as the problem of what it is to be aware of *determinable* repeatables.[2] Thus, an examination of Locke's *Essay* makes it clear that he is thinking of a sensation of white as the sort of thing that can become an abstract idea (occurrent) of White—a thought of White "in the Understanding"—merely by virtue of being separated from the context of other sensations (and images) which accompany it on a particular occasion. In other words, for Locke an abstract (occurrent) idea of the determinate repeatable Whiteness is nothing more than an isolated *image of white,* which, in turn, differs from a *sensation of white* only (to use a modern turn of phrase) by being "centrally aroused."

In short, for Locke, the problem of how we come to be aware of *determinate* sense repeatables is no problem at all. Merely by virtue *of having sensations* and *images* we have this awareness. *His* problem of abstract ideas is the problem of how we come to be able to think of generic properties. And, as is clear from the *Essay,* he approaches *this* problem in terms of what might be called an "adjunctive theory of specification," that is, the view that (if we represent the idea of a determinable as *the idea of being A*) the idea of a determinate form of *A* can be represented as *the idea of being A and B.* It is, of course, notorious that this won't account for the relation of *the idea of being red* to *the idea of being crimson.* By thinking of *conjunction* as the fundamental logical relation involved in building up complex ideas from simple ones, and as the principle of the difference between determinable and determinate ideas, Locke precluded himself from giving even a plausible account of the relation between ideas of determinables and ideas of determinates. It is interesting to speculate what turn his thought might have taken had he admitted *disjunctive* as well as *conjunctive* complex ideas, *the idea of being A or B* alongside *the idea of being A and B.*

27. But my purpose here is not to develop a commentary on the shortcomings of Locke's treatment of abstract ideas, but to emphasize that something which is a problem for us was not a problem for him. And it is therefore important to note that the same is true of Berkeley. His problem was not, as it is often construed, "How do we go from the awareness of *particulars* to ideas of *repeatables?*" but rather "Granted that in immediate experience we are aware of absolutely *specific* sense qualities, how do we come to be conscious of genera pertaining to them, and in what does this consciousness consist?" (This is not the only dimension of "abstraction" that concerned him, but it is the one that is

[2] For a systematic elaboration and defence of the following interpretation of Locke, Berkeley, and Hume, the reader should consult (11).

central to our purpose.) And, contrary to the usual interpretation, the essential difference between his account and Locke's consists in the fact that whereas Locke was on the whole [3] committed to the view that there can be an idea which is *of* the genus without being *of* any of its species, Berkeley insists that we can have an idea *of* a genus only by having an idea *of* the genus *as,* to borrow a useful Scotist term, *'contracted' into one of its species.*

Roughly, Berkeley's contention is that if *being A* entails *being B,* then there can be no such thing as an idea which is *of A* without being *of B.* He infers that since *being triangular* entails *having some determinately triangular shape,* there cannot be an idea which is *of triangle* without being *of some determinately triangular shape.* We can be aware of generic triangularity only by having an idea which is of triangularity as 'contracted' into one of the specific forms of triangularity. Any of the latter will do; they are all "of the same sort."

28. Now, a careful study of the *Treatise* makes it clear that Hume is in the same boat as Berkeley and Locke, sharing with them the presupposition that we have an unacquired ability to be aware of determinate repeatables. It is often said that whereas he begins the *Treatise* by characterizing 'ideas' in terms which do not distinguish between *images* and *thoughts,* he corrects this deficiency in Book I, Part I, Section vii. What these students of Hume tend to overlook is that what Hume does in this later section is given an account *not* of what it is to think of *repeatables* whether determinable or determinate, but of what it is to think of *determinables,* thus of color as contrasted with particular shades of color. And his account of the consciousness of determinables takes for

[3] I say that Locke was "on the whole" committed to the view that there can be an idea which is *of* the genus without being *of* any of its species, because while he saw that it couldn't be *of* any one of the species to the exclusion of the others, and saw no way of avoiding this except by making it *of none* of the species, he was greatly puzzled by this, for he saw that in some sense the idea *of the genus* must be *of all the species.* We have already noted that if he had admitted disjunction as a principle of compounding ideas, he could have said that the idea *of the genus* is the idea *of the disjunction of all its species,* that the idea of *being triangular* is the idea of *being scalene or isosceles.* As it was, he thought that to be of all the species it would have to be the idea of *being scalene and isosceles,* which is, of course, the idea of an impossibility.

It is interesting to note that if Berkeley had faced up to the implications of the criterion we shall find him to have adopted, this disjunctive conception of the generic idea is the one he would have been led to adopt. For since *being* G—where 'G' stands for a generic character—entails being S_1 or S_2 or S_3 . . . . . or S_n,—where 'S_1' stands for a specific character falling under G—Berkeley should have taken as the unit of ideas concerning triangles, the idea of the genus Triangle as differentiated into the set of specific forms of triangularity. But, needless to say, if Berkeley *had* taken this step, he could not have thought of a sensation of crimson as a determinate *thought.*

granted that we have a primordial ability to take account of *determinate* repeatables. Thus, his later account is simply built on, and in no sense a revision of, the account of ideas with which he opens the *Treatise.*

How, then, does he differ from Berkeley and Locke? The latter two had supposed that there must be such a thing as an *occurrent* thought of a determinable, however much they differed in their account of such thoughts. Hume, on the other hand, assuming that there are occurrent thoughts of *determinate* repeatables, *denies* that there are occurrent thoughts of *determinables.* I shall spare the reader the familiar details of Hume's attempt to give a constructive account of our consciousness of determinables, nor shall I criticize it. For my point is that however much Locke, Berkeley, and Hume differ on the problem of abstract ideas, they all take for granted that the human mind has an innate ability to be aware of certain determinate sorts—*indeed, that we are aware of them simply by virtue of having sensations and images.*

29. Now, it takes but a small twist of Hume's position to get a radically different view. For suppose that instead of characterizing the initial elements of experience as impressions *of, e.g. red,* Hume had characterized them as *red particulars* (and I would be the last to deny that not only Hume, but perhaps Berkeley and Locke as well, often treat impressions or ideas *of red* as though they were *red particulars*) then Hume's view, expanded to take into account determinates as well as determinables, would become the view that all consciousness of sorts or repeatables rests on an association of *words* (e.g. "red") with classes of resembling particulars.

It clearly makes all the difference in the world how this association is conceived. For if the formation of the association involves not only the occurrence of resembling particulars, but also the occurrence of the awareness *that they are resembling particulars,* then the givenness of determinate kinds of repeatables, say crimson, is merely being replaced by the givenness of *facts* of the form *x resembles y,* and we are back with an unacquired ability to be aware of repeatables, in this case the repeatable *resemblance.* Even more obviously, if the formation of the association involves not only the occurrence of red particulars, but the awareness *that they are red,* then the conceptualistic form of the myth has merely been replaced by a realistic version, as in the classical sense-datum theory.

If, however, the association is not mediated by the awareness of facts either of the form *x resembles y,* or of the form *x is* ϕ, then we have a view of the general type which I will call *psychological nominalism,* according to which *all* awareness of *sorts, resemblances, facts,* etc., in short, all awareness of abstract entities—indeed, all awareness even of particulars—is a linguistic affair. According to it, not even the awareness of such sorts, resemblances, and facts as pertain to so-called immediate experiences is presupposed by the process of acquiring the use of a language.

Two remarks are immediately relevant: (1) Although the form of psychological nominalism which one gets by modifying Hume's view along the above lines has the essential merit that it avoids the mistake of supposing that there are pure episodes of being aware of sensory repeatables or sensory facts, and is committed to the view that any event which can be referred to in these terms must be, to use Ryle's expression, a mongrel categorical-hypothetical, in particular, a verbal episode as *being the manifestation of associative connections of the word-object and word-word types,* it nevertheless is impossibly crude and inadequate as an account of the simplest concept. (2) Once sensations and images have been purged of epistemic aboutness, the primary reason for supposing that the fundamental associative tie between language and the world must be between words and 'immediate experiences' has disappeared, and the way is clear to recognizing that basic word-world associations hold, for example, between "red" and red *physical objects,* rather than between "red" and a supposed class of private red particulars.

The second remark, it should be emphasized, does not imply that private sensations or impressions may not be essential to the formation of these associative connections. For one can certainly admit that the tie between "red" and red physical objects—which tie makes it possible for "red" to mean the quality red—is *causally* mediated by sensations of red without being committed to the mistaken idea that it is "really" sensations of red, rather than red physical objects, which are the primary denotation of the word "red."

VII. THE LOGIC OF 'MEANS'

30. There is a source of the Myth of the Given to which even philosophers who are suspicious of the whole idea of *inner episodes* can fall prey. This is the fact that when we picture a child—or a carrier of slabs—learning his *first* language, *we,* of course, locate the language learner in a structured logical space in which *we* are at home. Thus, we conceive of him as a person (or, at least, a potential person) in a world of physical objects, colored, producing sounds, existing in Space and Time. But though it is *we* who are familiar with this logical space, we run the danger, if we are not careful, of picturing the language learner as having *ab initio* some degree of awareness—"pre-analytic," limited and fragmentary though it may be—of this same logical space. We picture his state as though it were rather like our own when placed in a strange

forest on a dark night. In other words, unless we are careful, we can easily take for granted that the process of teaching a child to use a language is that of teaching it to discriminate elements within a logical space of particulars, universals, facts, etc., of which it is already undiscriminatingly aware, and to associate these discriminated elements with verbal symbols. And this mistake is in principle the same whether the logical space of which the child is supposed to have this undiscriminating awareness is conceived by *us* to be that of physical objects or of private sense contents.

The real test of a theory of language lies not in its account of what has been called (by H. H. Price) "thinking in absence," but in its account of "thinking in presence"—that is to say, its account of those occasions on which the fundamental connection of language with nonlinguistic fact is exhibited. And many theories which look like psychological nominalism when one views their account of thinking in absence, turn out to be quite "Augustinian" when the scalpel is turned to their account of thinking in presence.

31. Now, the friendly use I have been making of the phrase "psychological nominalism" may suggest that I am about to *equate* concepts with words, and thinking, in so far as it is episodic, with verbal episodes. I must now hasten to say that I shall do nothing of the sort, or, at least, that if I *do* do *something* of the sort, the view I shall shortly be developing is only in a relatively Pickwickian sense an equation of thinking with the use of language. I wish to emphasize, therefore, that as I am using the term, the primary connotation of "psychological nominalism" is the denial that there is any awareness of logical space prior to, or independent of, the acquisition of a language.

However, although I shall later be distinguishing between *thoughts* and their verbal *expression*, there is a point of fundamental importance which is best made before more subtle distinctions are drawn. To begin with, it is perfectly clear that the word "red" would not be a *predicate* if it didn't have the logical syntax characteristic of predicates. Nor would it be the predicate it is, unless, in certain frames of mind, at least, we tended to respond to red objects in standard circumstances with something having the force of "This is red." And once we have abandoned the idea that learning to use the word "red" involves antecedent episodes of the *awareness of redness*—not to be confused, of course, with *sensations of red*—there is a temptation to suppose that the word "red" means the quality *red* by virtue of these two facts: briefly, the fact that it has the *syntax* of a predicate, and the fact that it is a *response* (in certain circumstances) to red objects.

But this account of the meaningfulness of "red," which Price has correctly stigmatized as the "thermometer view," would have little plausibility if it were not reinforced by another line of thought which takes its point of departure from the superficial resemblance of

(In German) *"rot"* means *red*

to such relational statements as

Cowley adjoins Oxford.

For once one assimilates the form

". . ." means - - -

to the form

x R y

and thus takes it for granted that meaning is a relation between a word and a nonverbal entity, it is tempting to suppose that the relation in question is that of association.

The truth of the matter, of course, is that statements of the form "'. . .' means - - -" are *not* relational statements, and that while it is indeed the case that the word *"rot"* could not mean the quality *red* unless it were associated with red things, it would be misleading to say that the semantical statement "*'Rot'* means *red*" says of *"rot"* that it associated with red things. For this would suggest that the semantical statement is, so to speak, definitional shorthand for a longer statement about the associative connections of *"rot,"* which is not the case. The rubric "'. . .' means - - -" is a linguistic device for conveying the information that a *mentioned* word, in this case *"rot,"* plays the same role in a certain linguistic economy, in this case the linguistic economy of German-speaking peoples, as does the word "red," which is not *mentioned* but *used*—used in a unique way; *exhibited,* so to speak—and which occurs "on the right-hand side" of the semantical statement.

We see, therefore, how the two statements

"Und" means *and*

and

"Rot" means *red*

can tell us quite different things about *"und"* and *"rot,"* for the first conveys the information that *"und"* plays the purely formal role of a certain logical connective, the second that *"rot"* plays in German the role of the observation word "red"—in spite of the fact that *means* has the same sense in each statement, and without having to say that the first says of *"und"* that it stands in "the meaning relation" to Conjunction, or the second that *"rot"* stands in "the meaning relation" to Redness.[4]

These considerations make it clear that nothing whatever can be inferred about the complexity of the role played by the word "red" or about the exact way in which the word "red" is related to red things, from the truth of the semantical statement " 'red' means the quality *red*." And no consideration arising from the 'Fido'-Fido aspect of the grammar of "means" precludes one from claiming that the role of the word "red" by virtue of which it can correctly be said to have the meaning it does is a complicated one indeed, and that one cannot understand the meaning of the word "red"—"know what redness is"—unless one has a great deal of knowledge which classical empiricism would have held to have a purely contingent relationship with the possession of fundamental empirical concepts.

VIII. DOES EMPIRICAL KNOWLEDGE HAVE A FOUNDATION?

32. One of the forms taken by the Myth of the Given is the idea that there is, indeed *must be,* a structure of particular matter of fact such that (a) each fact can not only be noninferentially known to be the case, but presupposes no other knowledge either of particular matter of fact, or of general truths; and (b) such that the noninferential knowledge of facts belonging to this structure constitutes the ultimate court of appeals for all factual claims—particular and general—about the world. It is important to note that I characterized the knowledge of fact belonging to this stratum as not only noninferential, but as presupposing no knowledge of other matter of fact, whether particular or general. It might be thought that this is a redundancy, that knowledge (not belief or conviction, but knowledge) which logically presupposes knowledge of other facts *must* be inferential. This, however, as I hope to show, is itself an episode in the Myth.

Now, the idea of such a privileged stratum of fact is a familiar one, though not without its difficulties. Knowledge pertaining to this level is *noninferential,* yet it is, after all, *knowledge.* It is *ultimate,* yet it has

4 For an analysis of the problem of abstract entities built on this interpretation of semantical statements, see (20).

authority. The attempt to make a consistent picture of these two requirements has traditionally taken the following form:

> Statements pertaining to this level, in order to 'express knowledge' must not only be made, but, so to speak, must be worthy of being made, *credible,* that is, in the sense of worthy of credence. Furthermore, and this is a crucial point, they must be made in a way which *involves* this credibility. For where there is no connection between the making of a statement and its authority, the assertion may express *conviction,* but it can scarcely be said to express knowledge.
>
> The authority—the credibility—of statements pertaining to this level cannot exhaustively consist in the fact that they are supported by *other* statements, for in that case all *knowledge* pertaining to this level would have to be inferential, which not only contradicts the hypothesis, but flies in the face of good sense. The conclusion seems inevitable that if some statements pertaining to this level are to express *noninferential* knowledge, they must have a credibility which is not a matter of being supported by other statements. Now there does seem to be a class of statements which fill at least part of this bill, namely such statements as would be said to *report observations,* thus, "This is red." These statements, candidly made, have authority. Yet they are not expressions of inference. How, then, is this authority to be understood?
>
> Clearly, the argument continues, it springs from the fact that they are made in just the circumstances in which they are made, as is indicated by the fact that they characteristically, though not necessarily or without exception, involve those so-called token-reflexive expressions which, in addition to the tenses of verbs, serve to connect the circumstances in which a statement is made with its sense. (At this point it will be helpful to begin putting the line of thought I am developing in terms of the *fact-stating* and *observation-reporting* roles of certain sentences.) Roughly, two verbal performances which are tokens of a non-token-reflexive sentence can occur in widely different circumstances and yet make the same statement; whereas two tokens of a token-reflexive sentence can make the same statement only if they are uttered in the same circumstances (according to a relevant criterion of sameness). And two tokens of a sentence, whether it contains a token-reflexive expression—over and above a tensed verb—or not, can make the same *report* only if, made in all candor, they express the *presence*—in *some* sense of "presence"—of the state of affairs that is being reported; if, that is, they stand in that relation to the state of affairs, whatever the relation may be, by virtue of which they can be said to formulate observations of it.
>
> It would appear, then, that there are two ways in which a sentence token can have credibility: (1) The authority may accrue to it, so to speak, from above, that is, as being a token of a sentence type *all* the tokens of which, in a certain use, have credibility, e.g. "$2 + 2 = 4$." In this case, let us say that token credibility is inherited from type authority. (2) The

credibility may accrue to it from the fact that it came to exist in a certain way in a certain set of circumstances, e.g. "This is red." Here token credibility is not derived from type credibility.

Now, the credibility of *some* sentence types appears to be *intrinsic*—at least in the limited sense that it is *not* derived from other sentences, type or token. This is, or seems to be, the case with certain sentences used to make analytic statements. The credibility of *some* sentence types accrues to them by virtue of their logical relations to other sentence types, thus by virtue of the fact that they are logical consequences of more basic sentences. It would seem obvious, however, that the credibility of empirical sentence types cannot be traced without remainder to the credibility of other sentence types. And since no empirical sentence type appears to have *intrinsic* credibility, this means that credibility must accrue to *some* empirical sentence types by virtue of their logical relations to certain sentence tokens, and, in deed, to sentence tokens the authority of which is not derived, in its turn, from the authority of sentence types.

The picture we get is that of their being two *ultimate* modes of credibility: (1) The intrinsic credibility of analytic sentences, which accrues to tokens as being tokens of such a type; (2) the credibility of such tokens as "express observations," a credibility which flows from tokens to types.

33. Let us explore this picture, which is common to all traditional empiricisms, a bit further. How is the authority of such sentence tokens as "express observational knowledge" to be understood? It has been tempting to suppose that in spite of the obvious differences which exist between "observation reports" and "analytic statements," there is an essential similarity between the ways in which they come by their authority. Thus, it has been claimed, not without plausibility, that whereas *ordinary* empirical statements can be *correctly* made without being *true,* observation reports resemble analytic statements in that being correctly made is a sufficient as well as necessary condition of their truth. And it has been inferred from this—somewhat hastily, I believe—that "correctly making" the report "This is green" is a matter of "following the rules for the use of 'this,' 'is' and 'green.' "

Three comments are immediately necessary:

(1) First a brief remark about the term "report." In ordinary usage a report is a report made *by* someone *to* someone. To make a report is to *do* something. In the literature of epistemology, however, the word "report" or *"Konstatierung"* has acquired a technical use in which a sentence token can play a reporting role (a) without being an *overt* verbal performance, and (b) without having the character of being "by someone to someone"—even oneself. There is, of course, such a thing as "talking to oneself"—*in foro interno*—but, as I shall be emphasizing in the closing stages of my argument, it is important not to suppose that all "covert" verbal episodes are of this kind.

(2) My second comment is that while *we* shall not assume that because 'reports' in the *ordinary sense* are *actions*, 'reports' in the sense of *Konstatierungen* are also actions, the line of thought we are considering treats them as such. In other words, it interprets the correctness of *Konstatierungen* as analogous to the rightness of actions. Let me emphasize, however, that not all *ought* is *ought to do*, nor all correctness the correctness of *actions*.

(3) My third comment is that if the expression "following a rule" is taken seriously, and is not weakened beyond all recognition into the bare notion of exhibiting a uniformity—in which case the lightning, thunder sequence would "follow a rule"—then it is the knowledge or belief that the circumstances are of a certain kind, and not the mere fact that they *are* of this kind, which contributes to bringing about the action.

34. In the light of these remarks it is clear that *if* observation reports are construed as *actions*, *if* their correctness is interpreted as the correctness of an *action*, and *if* the authority of an observation report is construed as the fact that making it is "following a rule" in the proper sense of this phrase, *then* we are face to face with givenness in its most straightforward form. For these stipulations commit one to the idea that the authority of *Konstatierungen* rests on nonverbal episodes of awareness—awareness *that* something is the case, e.g. *that this is green*—which nonverbal episodes have an intrinsic authority (they are, so to speak 'self-authenticating') which the *verbal* performances (the *Konstatierungen*) properly performed "express." One is committed to a stratum of authoritative nonverbal episodes ("awareness") the authority of which accrues to a superstructure of *verbal actions*, provided that the expressions occurring in these actions are properly *used*. These self-authenticating episodes would constitute the tortoise on which stands the elephant on which rests the edifice of empirical knowledge. The essence of the view is the same whether these intrinsically authoritative episodes are such items as the awareness that a certain sense content is green or such items as the awareness that a certain physical object looks to someone to be green.

35. But what is the alternative? We might begin by trying something like the following: An overt or covert token of "This is green" in the presence of a green item is a *Konstatierung* and expresses observational knowledge if and only if it is a manifestation of a tendency to produce overt or covert tokens of "This is green"—given a certain set—if and only if a green object is being looked at in standard conditions. Clearly on this interpretation the occurrence of such tokens of "This is green" would be "following a rule" only in the sense that they are instances of a uniformity, a uniformity differing from the lightning-thunder case in that it is an acquired causal characteristic of the lan-

guage user. Clearly the above suggestion, which corresponds to the "thermometer view" criticized by Professor Price, and which we have already rejected, won't do as it stands. Let us see, however, if it can't be revised to fit the criteria I have been using for "expressing observational knowledge."

The first hurdle to be jumped concerns the *authority* which, as I have emphasized, a sentence token must have in order that it may be said to express knowledge. Clearly, on this account the only thing that can remotely be supposed to constitute such authority is the fact that one can infer the presence of a green object from the fact that someone makes this report. As we have already noticed, the correctness of a report does not have to be construed as the rightness of an *action*. A report can be correct as being an instance of a general mode of behavior which, in a given linguistic community, it is reasonable to sanction and support.

The second hurdle is, however, the decisive one. For we have seen that to be the expression of knowledge, a report must not only *have* authority, this authority must *in some sense* be recognized by the person whose report it is. And this is a steep hurdle indeed. For if the authority of the report "This is green" lies in the fact that the existence of green items appropriately related to the perceiver can be inferred from the occurrence of such reports, it follows that only a person who is able to draw this inference, and therefore who has not only the concept *green*, but also the concept of uttering "This is green"—indeed, the concept of certain conditions of perception, those which would correctly be called 'standard conditions'—could be in a position to token "This is green" in recognition of its authority. In other words, for a *Konstatierung* "This is green" to "express observational knowledge," not only must it be a *symptom* or *sign* of the presence of a green object in standard conditions, but the perceiver must know that tokens of "This is green" are symptoms of the presence of green objects in conditions which are standard for visual perception.

36. Now it might be thought that there is something obviously absurd in the idea that before a token uttered by, say, Jones could be the expression of observational knowledge, Jones would have to know that overt verbal episodes of this kind are reliable indicators of the existence, suitably related to the speaker, of green objects. I do not think that it is. Indeed, I think that something very like it is true. The point I wish to make now, however, is that if it *is* true, then it follows, as a matter of simple logic, that one couldn't have observational knowledge of *any* fact unless one knew many *other* things as well. And let me emphasize that the point is not taken care of by distinguishing between *knowing how* and *knowing that,* and admitting that observational knowledge requires a lot of "know how." For the point is specifically that observational

knowledge of any particular fact, e.g. that this is green, presupposes that one knows general facts of the form *X is a reliable symptom of Y*. And to admit this requires an abandonment of the traditional empiricist idea that observational knowledge "stands on its own feet." Indeed, the suggestion would be anathema to traditional empiricists for the obvious reason that by making observational knowledge *presuppose* knowledge of general facts of the form *X is a reliable symptom of Y,* it runs counter to the idea that we come to know general facts of this form only *after* we have come to know by observation a number of particular facts which support the hypothesis that X is a symptom of Y.

And it might be thought that there is an obvious regress in the view we are examining. Does it not tell us that observational knowledge at time t presupposes knowledge of the form *X is a reliable symptom of Y,* which presupposes *prior* observational knowledge, which presupposes *other* knowledge of the form *X is a reliable symptom of Y,* which presupposes still other, and *prior,* observational knowledge, and so on? This charge, however, rests on too simple, indeed a radically mistaken, conception of what one is saying of Jones when one says that he *knows* that p. It is not just that the objection supposes that knowing is an *episode;* for clearly these are episodes which we can correctly characterize as knowings, in particular, *observings.* The essential point is that in characterizing an episode or a state as that of *knowing,* we are not giving an empirical description of that episode or state; we are placing it in the logical space of reasons, of justifying and being able to justify what one says.

37. Thus, all that the view I am defending requires is that no tokening by *S now* of "This is green" is to count as "expressing observational knowledge" unless it is also correct to say of *S* that he *now* knows the appropriate fact of the form *X is a reliable symptom of Y,* namely that (and again I oversimplify) utterances of "This is green" are reliable indicators of the presence of green objects in standard conditions of perception. And while the correctness of this statement about Jones requires that Jones could *now* cite prior particular facts as evidence for the idea that these utterances *are* reliable indicators, it requires only that it is correct to say that Jones *now* knows, thus remembers, that these particular facts *did* obtain. It does not require that it be correct to say that at the time these facts did obtain he *then knew* them to obtain. And the regress disappears.

Thus, while Jones' ability to give inductive reasons *today* is built on a long history of acquiring and manifesting verbal habits in perceptual situations, and, in particular, the occurrence of verbal episodes, e.g. "This is green," which is superficially like those which are later properly said to express observational knowledge, it does not require that any episode in this prior time be characterizeable as expressing knowledge. (At this point, the reader should reread Section 19 above.)

38. The idea that observation "strictly and properly so-called" is constituted by certain self-authenticating nonverbal episodes, the authority of which is transmitted to verbal and quasi-verbal performances when these performances are made "in conformity with the semantical rules of the language," is, of course, the heart of the Myth of the Given. For the *given*, in epistemological tradition, is what is *taken* by these self-authenticating episodes. These 'takings' are, so to speak, the unmoved movers of empirical knowledge, the 'knowings in presence' which are presupposed by all other knowledge, both the knowledge of general truths and the knowledge 'in absence' of other particular matters of fact. Such is the framework in which traditional empiricism makes its characteristic claim that the perceptually given is the foundation of empirical knowledge.

Let me make it clear, however, that if I reject this framework, it is not because I should deny that observings are *inner* episodes, nor that *strictly speaking* they are *nonverbal* episodes. It will be my contention, however, that the sense in which they are nonverbal—which is also the sense in which thought episodes are nonverbal—is one which gives no aid or comfort to epistemological givenness. In the concluding sections of this paper, I shall attempt to explicate the logic of inner episodes, and show that we can distinguish between observations and thoughts, on the one hand, and their verbal expression on the other, without making the mistakes of traditional dualism. I shall also attempt to explicate the logical status of *impressions* or *immediate experiences*, and thus bring to a successful conclusion the quest with which my argument began.

One final remark before I begin this task. If I reject the framework of traditional empiricism, it is not because I want to say that empirical knowledge has *no* foundation. For to put it this way is to suggest that it is really "empirical knowledge so-called," and to put it in a box with rumors and hoaxes. There is clearly *some* point to the picture of human knowledge as resting on a level of propositions—observation reports—which do not rest on other propositions in the same way as other propositions rest on them. On the other hand, I do wish to insist that the metaphor of "foundation" is misleading in that it keeps us from seeing that if there is a logical dimension in which other empirical propositions rest on observation reports, there is another logical dimension in which the later rest on the former.

Above all, the picture is misleading because of its static character. One seems forced to choose between the picture of an elephant which rests on a tortoise (What supports the tortoise?) and the picture of a great

Hegelian serpent of knowledge with its tail in its mouth. (Where does it begin?). Neither will do. For empirical knowledge, like its sophisticated extension, science, is rational, not because it has a *foundation* but because it is a self-correcting enterprise which can put *any* claim in jeopardy, thogh not *all* at once.

IX. SCIENCE AND ORDINARY USAGE

39. There are many strange and exotic specimens in the gardens of philosophy: Epistemology, Ontology, Cosmology, to name but a few. And clearly there is much good sense—not only rhyme but reason—to these labels. It is not my purpose, however, to animadvert on the botanizing of philosophies and things philosophical, other than to call attention to a recent addition to the list of philosophical flora and fauna, the Philosophy of Science. Nor shall I attempt to locate this new speciality in a classificatory system. The point I wish to make, however, can be introduced by calling to mind the fact that classificatory schemes, however theoretical their purpose, have practical consequences: nominal causes, so to speak, have real effects. As long as there was no such subject as 'philosophy of science,' all students of philosophy felt obligated to keep at least one eye part of the time on both the methodological and the substantive aspects of the scientific enterprise. And if the result was often a confusion of the task of philosophy with the task of science, and almost equally often a projection of the framework of the latest scientific speculations into the common-sense picture of the world (witness the almost unquestioned assumption, today, that the common-sense world of physical objects in Space and Time must be *analyzable* into spatially and temporally, or even spatiotemporally, related *events*), at least it had the merit of ensuring that reflection on the nature and implications of scientific discourse was an integral and vital part of philosophical thinking generally. But now that philosophy of science has nominal as well as real existence, there has arisen the temptation to leave it to the specialists, and to confuse the sound idea that philosophy is not science with the mistaken idea that philosophy is independent of science.

40. As long as discourse was viewed as a map, subdivided into a side-by-side of sub-maps, each representing a sub-region in a side-by-side of regions making up the total subject matter of discourse, and as long as the task of the philosopher was conceived to be the piecemeal one of analysis in the sense of *definition*—the task, so to speak, of "making little ones out of big ones"—one could view with equanimity the existence of philosophical specialists—specialists in formal and mathematical logic, in perception, in moral philosophy, etc. For if discourse were as

represented above, where would be the harm of each man fencing himself off in his own garden? In spite, however, of the persistence of the slogan "philosophy is analysis," we now realize that the atomistic conception of philosophy is a snare and a delusion. For "analysis" no longer connotes the definition of terms, but rather the clarification of the logical structure—in the broadest sense—of discourse, and discourse no longer appears as one plane parallel to another, but as a tangle of intersecting dimensions whose relations with one another and with extra-linguistic fact conform to no single or simple pattern. No longer can the philosopher interested in perception say "let him who is interested in prescriptive discourse analyze its concepts and leave me in peace." Most if not all philosophically interesting concepts are caught up in more than one dimension of discourse, and while the atomism of early analysis has a healthy successor in the contemporary stress on journeyman tactics, the grand strategy of the philosophical enterprise is once again directed toward that articulated and integrated vision of man-in-the-universe—or, shall I say discourse-about-man-in-all-discourse—which has traditionally been its goal.

But the moral I wish specifically to draw is that no longer can one smugly say "Let the person who is interested in scientific discourse analyze scientific discourse and let the person who is interested in ordinary discourse analyze ordinary discourse." Let me not be misunderstood. I am not saying that in order to discern the logic—the polydimensional logic—of ordinary discourse, it is necessary to make use of the results or the methods of the sciences. Nor even that, within limits, such a division of labor is not a sound corollary of the journeyman's approach. My point is rather that what we call the scientific enterprise is the flowering of a dimension of discourse which already exists in what historians call the "prescientific stage," and that failure to understand this type of discourse "writ large"—in science—may lead, indeed, has often led to a failure to appreciate its role in "ordinary usage," and, as a result, to a failure to understand the full logic of even the most fundamental, the "simplest" empirical terms.

41. Another point of equal importance. The procedures of philosophical analysis as such may make no use of the methods or results of the sciences. But familiarity with the trend of scientific thought is essential to the *appraisal* of the framework categories of the common-sense picture of the world. For if the line of thought embodied in the preceding paragraphs is sound, if, that is to say, scientific discourse is but a continuation of a dimension of discourse which has been present in human discourse from the very beginning, then one would expect there to be a sense in which the scientific picture of the world *replaces* the common-

sense picture; a sense in which the scientific account of "what there is" *supersedes* the descriptive ontology of everyday life.

Here one must be cautious. For there is a right way and a wrong way to make this point. Many years ago it used to be confidently said that science has shown, for example, that physical objects aren't really colored. Later it was pointed out that if this is interpreted as the claim that the sentence "Physical objects have colors" expresses an empirical proposition which, though widely believed by common sense, has been shown by science to be false, then, of course, this claim is absurd. The idea that physical objects aren't colored can make sense only as the (misleading) expression of one aspect of a philosophical critique of the very framework of physical objects located in Space and enduring through Time. In short, "Physical objects aren't really colored" makes sense only as a clumsy expression of the idea that there are no such things as the colored physical objects of the common-sense world, where this is interpreted, not as an empirical proposition—like "There are no nonhuman featherless bipeds"—*within* the common-sense frame, but as the expression of a rejection (in *some* sense) of this very framework itself, in favor of another built around different, if not unrelated, categories. This rejection need not, of course, be a *practical* rejection. It need not, that is, carry with it a proposal to brain-wash existing populations and train them to speak differently. And, of course, as long as the existing framework is used, it will be *incorrect* to say—otherwise than to make a philosophical point *about the framework*—that no object is really colored, or is located in Space, or endures through Time. But, *speaking as a philosopher,* I am quite prepared to say that the common-sense world of physical objects in Space and Time is unreal—that is, that there are no such things. Or, to put it less paradoxically, that in the dimension of describing and explaining the world, science is the measure of all things, of what is that it is, and of what is not that it is not.

43. There is a widespread impression that reflection on how we learn the language in which, in everyday life, we describe the world, leads to the conclusion that the categories of the common-sense picture of the world have, so to speak, an unchallengeable authenticity. There are, of course, different conceptions of just what this fundamental categorical framework is. For some it is sense contents and phenomenal relations between them; for others physical objects, persons, and processes in Space and Time. But whatever their points of difference, the philosophers I have in mind are united in the conviction that what is called the "ostensive tie" between our fundamental descriptive vocabulary and the world rules out of court as utterly absurd any notion that there are no such things as this framework talks about.

An integral part of this conviction is what I shall call (in an extended sense) the *positivistic conception of science,* the idea that the framework of theoretical objects (molecules, electromagnetic fields, etc.) and their relationships is, so to speak, an *auxiliary* framework. In its most explicit form, it is the idea that theoretical objects and propositions concerning them are "calculational devices," the value and status of which consist in their systematizing and heuristic role with respect to confirmable generalizations formulated in the framework of terms which enjoy a direct ostensive link with the world. One is tempted to put this by saying that according to these philosophers, the objects of ostensively linked discourse behave *as if* and *only as if* they were bound up with or consisted of scientific entities. But, of course, these philosophers would hasten to point out (and rightly so) that

> X behaves as if it consisted of Y's

makes sense only by contrast with

> X behaves as it does because it *does* consist of Y's

whereas their contention is exactly that where the Y's are *scientific* objects, no such contrast makes sense.

The point I am making is that as long as one thinks that there is a framework, whether of physical objects or of sense contents, the absolute authenticity of which is guaranteed by the fact that the learning of this framework involves an "ostensive step," so long one will be tempted to think of the authority of theoretical discourse as entirely derivative, that of a calculational auxiliary, an effective heuristic device. It is one of my prime purposes, in the following sections, to convince the reader that this interpretation of the status of the scientific picture of the world rests on two mistakes: (1) a misunderstanding (which I have already exposed) of the ostensive element in the learning and use of a language—the Myth of the Given; (2) a reification of the *methodological* distinction between theoretical and non-theoretical discourse into a *substantive* distinction between theoretical and non-theoretical existence.

44. One way of summing up what I have been saying above is by saying that there is a widespread impression abroad, aided and abetted by a naive interpretation of concept formation, that philosophers of science deal with a mode of discourse which is, so to speak, a peninsular offshoot from the mainland of ordinary discourse. The study of scientific discourse is conceived to be a worthy employment for those who have the background and motivation to keep track of it, but an em-

ployment which is fundamentally a hobby divorced from the perplexities of the mainland. But, of course, this summing up won't quite do. For all philosophers would agree that no philosophy would be complete unless it resolved the perplexities which arise when one attempts to think through the relationship of the framework of modern science to ordinary discourse. My point, however, is not that any one would reject the idea that this is a proper task for philosophy, but that, by approaching the language in which the plain man describes and explains empirical fact with the presuppositions of *givenness,* they are led to a "resolution" of these perplexities along the lines of what I have called the positivistic or peninsular conception of scientific discourse—a "resolution" which, I believe, is not only superficial, but positively mistaken.

X. *PRIVATE EPISODES: THE PROBLEM*

45. Let us now return, after a long absence, to the problem of how the similarity among the experiences of *seeing that an object over there is red, its looking to one that an object over there is red* (when in point of fact it is *not* red) and *its looking to one as though there were a red object over there* (when in fact there is *nothing* over there at all) is to be understood. Part of this similarity, we saw, consists in the fact that they all involve the idea—the proposition, if you please—that the object over there is red. But over and above this there is, of course, the aspect which many philosophers have attempted to clarify by the notion of *impressions* or *immediate experience.*

It was pointed out in Sections 21 ff. above that there are prima facie two ways in which facts of the form *x merely looks red* might be explained, in addition to the kind of explanation which is based on empirical generalizations relating the color of objects, the circumstances in which they are seen, and the colors they look to have. These two ways are (a) the introduction of impressions or immediate experiences as theoretical entities; and (b) the *discovery,* on scrutinizing these situations, that they contain impressions or immediate experiences as components. I called attention to the paradoxical character of the first of these alternatives, and refused, at that time, to take it seriously. But in the meantime the second alternative, involving as it does the Myth of the Given, has turned out to be no more satisfactory.

For, in the first place, how are these impressions to be described, if not by using such words as "red" and "triangular." Yet, if my argument, to date, is sound, physical objects alone can be literally red and triangular. Thus, in the cases I am considering, there is nothing to be red and triangular. It would seem to follow that "impression of a red triangle" could mean nothing more than "impression of *the sort which* is common to those experiences in which we either see that something is red and triangular, or something merely looks red and triangular or there merely looks to be a red and triangular object over there." And if we can never characterize "impressions" intrinsically, but only by what is logically a definite description, i.e., as *the kind of entity which* is common to such situations, then we would scarcely seem to be any better off than if we maintained that talk about "impressions" is a notational convenience, a code, for the language in which we speak of how things look and what there looks to be.

And this line of thought is reinforced by the consideration that once we give up the idea that we begin our sojourn in this world with any—even a vague, fragmentary, and undiscriminating—awareness of the logical space of particulars, kinds, facts, and resemblances, and recognize that even such "simple" concepts as those of colors are the fruit of a long process of publicly reinforced responses to public objects (including verbal performances) in public situations, we may well be puzzled as to how, even if there are such things as impressions or sensations, we could come to know that there are, and to know what sort of thing they are. *For we now recognize that instead of coming to have a concept of something because we have noticed that sort of thing, to have the ability to notice a sort of thing is already to have the concept of that sort of thing, and cannot account for it.*

Indeed, once we think this line of reasoning through, we are struck by the fact that if it is sound, we are faced not only with the question "How could we come to have the idea of an 'impression' or 'sensation?' " but by the question "How could we come to have the idea of something's looking red to us, or," to get to the crux of the matter, "of seeing that something is red?" In short, we are brought face to face with the general problem of understanding how there can be *inner episodes*—episodes, that is, which somehow combine *privacy,* in that each of us has privileged access to his own, with *intersubjectivity,* in that each of us can, in principle, know about the other's. We might try to put this more linguistically as the problem of how there can be a sentence (e.g. "S has a toothache") of which it is *logically* true that whereas *anybody* can use it to state a fact, only *one* person, namely S himself, can use it to make a report. But while this is a useful formulation, it does not do justice to the supposedly *episodic* character of the items in question. And that this is the heart of the puzzle is shown by the fact that many philosophers who would not deny that there are short-term hypothetical and mongrel hypothetical-categorical facts about behavior which others can ascribe to us on behavioral evidence, but which only *we* can *report,* have found it to be logical nonsense to speak of non-behavioral *episodes* of which this is true. Thus, it has been claimed by Ryle (17) that the very idea that there are such episodes is a category mistake, while others have argued that though there are such episodes, they cannot be characterized in intersubjective discourse, learned as it is in a context of public objects and in the 'academy' of one's linguistic peers. It is my purpose to argue that both these contentions are quite mistaken, and that not only are inner episodes *not* category mistakes, they are quite "effable" in intersubjective discourse. And it is my purpose to show, positively, *how* this can be the case. I am particularly concerned to make this point in connection with such inner episodes as sensations and feelings, in short, with what has—unfortunately, I think—been called "immediate experience." For such an account is necessary to round off this examination of the Myth of the Given. But before I can come to grips with these topics, the way must be prepared by a discussion of inner episodes of quite another kind, namely *thoughts.*

XI. THOUGHTS: THE CLASSICAL VIEW

46. Recent empiricism has been of two minds about the status of *thoughts.* On the one hand, it has resonated to the idea that insofar as there are *episodes* which are thoughts, they are *verbal* or *linguistic* episodes. Clearly, however, even if candid overt verbal behaviors by people who had learned a language *were* thoughts, there are not nearly enough of them to account for all the cases in which it would be argued that a person was thinking. Nor can we plausibly suppose that the remainder is accounted for by those inner episodes which are often very clumsily lumped together under the heading "verbal imagery."

On the other hand, they have been tempted to suppose that the *episodes* which are referred to by verbs pertaining to thinking include all forms of "intelligent behavior," verbal as well as nonverbal, and that the "thought episodes" which are supposed to be manifested by these behaviors are not really episodes at all, but rather hypothetical and mongrel hypothetical-categorical facts about these and still other behaviors. This, however, runs into the difficulty that whenever we try to explain what we mean by calling a piece of *nonhabitual* behavior intelligent, we seem to find it necessary to do so in terms of *thinking.* The uncomfortable feeling will not be downed that the dispositional account of thoughts in terms of intelligent behavior is covertly circular.

47. Now the classical tradition claimed that there is a family of episodes, neither overt verbal behavior nor verbal imagery, which are *thoughts,* and that both overt verbal behavior and verbal imagery owe their meaningfulness to the fact that they stand to these *thoughts* in

the unique relation of "expressing" them. These episodes are introspectable. Indeed, it was usually believed that they could not occur without being known to occur. But this can be traced to a number of confusions, perhaps the most important of which was the idea that *thoughts* belong in the same general category as sensations, images, tickles, itches, etc. This mis-assimilation of thoughts to sensations and feelings was equally, as we saw in Sections 26 ff. above, a mis-assimilation of sensations and feelings to thoughts, and a falsification of both. The assumption that if there are thought episodes, they must be immediate experiences is common both to those who propounded the classical view and to those who reject it, saying that they "find no such experiences." If we purge the classical tradition of these confusions, it becomes the idea that to each of us belongs a stream of episodes, not themselves immediate experiences, to which we have privileged, but by no means either invariable or infallible, access. These episodes can occur without being "expressed" by overt verbal behavior, though verbal behavior is—in an important sense—their natural fruition. Again, we can "hear ourselves think," but the verbal imagery which enables us to do this is no more the thinking itself than is the overt verbal behavior by which it is expressed and communicated to others. It is a mistake to suppose that we must be having verbal imagery—indeed, any imagery—when we "know what we are thinking"—in short, to suppose that "privileged access" must be construed on a perceptual or quasi-perceptual model.

Now, it is my purpose to defend such a revised classical analysis of our common-sense conception of thoughts, and in the course of doing so I shall develop distinctions which will later contribute to a resolution, in principle, of the puzzle of *immediate experience.* But before I continue, let me hasten to add that it will turn out that the view I am about to expound could, with equal appropriateness, be represented as a modified form of the view that thoughts are *linguistic* episodes.

XII. OUR RYLEAN ANCESTORS

48. But, the reader may well ask, in what sense can these episodes be "inner" if they are not immediate experiences? and in what sense can they be "linguistic" if they are neither overt linguistic performances, nor verbal imagery *"in foro interno"*? I am going to answer these and the other questions I have been raising by making a myth of my own, or, to give it an air of up-to-date respectability, by writing a piece of science fiction—anthropological science fiction. Imagine a stage in prehistory in which humans are limited to what I shall call a Rylean language, a language of which the fundamental descriptive vocabulary

speaks of public properties of public objects located in Space and enduring through Time. Let me hasten to add that it is also Rylean in that although its basic resources are limited (how limited I shall be discussing in a moment), its total expressive power is very great. For it makes subtle use not only of the elementary logical operations of conjunction, disjunction, negation, and quantification, but especially of the subjunctive conditional. Furthermore, I shall suppose it to be characterized by the presence of the looser logical relations typical of ordinary discourse which are referred to by philosophers under the headings "vagueness" and "open texture."

I am beginning my myth *in medias res* with humans who have already mastered a Rylean language, because the philosophical situation it is designed to clarify is one in which we are not puzzled by how people acquire a language for referring to public properties of public objects, but are very puzzled indeed about how we learn to speak of inner episodes and immediate experiences.

There are, I suppose, still some philosophers who are inclined to think that by allowing these mythical ancestors of ours the use *ad libitum* of subjunctive conditionals, we have, in effect, enabled them to say anything that *we* can say when we speak of *thoughts, experiences* (seeing, hearing, etc.), and *immediate experiences.* I doubt that there are many. In any case, the story I am telling is designed to show exactly *how* the idea that an intersubjective language *must* be Rylean rests on too simple a picture of the relation of intersubjective discourse to public objects.

49. The questions I am, in effect, raisng are "What resources would have to be added to the Rylean language of these talking animals in order that they might come to recognize each other and themselves as animals that *think, observe,* and have *feelings* and *sensations,* as we use these terms?" and "How could the addition of these resources be construed as reasonable?" In the first place, the language would have to be enriched with the fundamental resources of semantical discourse—that is to say, the resources necessary for making such characteristically semantical statements as "*'Rot'* means red," and "*'Der Mond ist rund'* is true if and only if the moon is round." It is sometimes said, e.g., by Carnap (6), that these resources can be constructed out of the vocabulary of formal logic, and that they would therefore already be contained, in principle, in our Rylean language. I have criticized this idea in another place (20) and shall not discuss it here. In any event, a decision on this point is not essential to the argument.

Let it be granted, then, that these mythical ancestors of ours are able to characterize each other's verbal behavior in semantical terms; that, in other words, they not only can talk about each other's predictions as causes and effects, and as indicators (with greater or less reliability) of other verbal and nonverbal states of affairs, but can also say of these verbal productions that they *mean* thus and so, that they say *that* such and such, that they are true, false, etc. And let me emphasize, as was pointed out in Section 31 above, that to make a semantical statement about a verbal event is not a shorthand way of talking about its causes and effects, although there is a sense of "imply" in which semantical statements about verbal productions do *imply* information about the causes and effects of these productions. Thus, when I say "*'Es regnet'* means it is raining," my statement "implies" that the causes and effects of utterances of *"Es regnet"* beyond the Rhine parallel the causes and effects of utterances of "It is raining" by myself and other members of the English-speaking community. And if it didn't imply this, it couldn't perform its role. But this is not to say that semantical statements are definitional shorthand for statements about the causes and effects of verbal performances.

50. With the resources of semantical discourse, the language of our fictional ancestors has acquired a dimension which gives considerably more plausibility to the claim that they are in a position to talk about *thoughts* just as we are. For characteristic of thoughts is their *intentionality, reference,* or *aboutness,* and it is clear that semantical talk about the meaning or reference of verbal expressions has the same structure as mentalistic discourse concerning what thoughts are about. It is therefore all the more tempting to suppose that the intentionality of *thoughts* can be traced to the application of semantical categories to overt verbal performances, and to suggest a modified Rylean account according to which talk about so-called "thoughts" is shorthand for hypothetical and mongrel categorical-hypothetical statements about overt verbal and nonverbal behavior, *and* that talk about the *intentionality* of these "episodes" is correspondingly reducible to semantical talk about the verbal components.

What is the alternative? Classically it has been the idea that not only are there overt verbal episodes which can be characterized in semantical terms, but, *over and above these,* there are certain inner episodes which are properly characterized by the traditional vocabulary of *intentionality.* And, of course, the classical scheme includes the idea that semantical discourse about overt verbal performances is to be analyzed in terms of talk about the intentionality of the mental episodes which are "expressed" by these overt performances. My immediate problem is to see if I can reconcile the classical idea of thoughts as inner episodes which are neither overt behavior nor verbal imagery and which are properly referred to in terms of the vocabulary of intentionality, with the idea that the categories of intentionality are, at bottom, semantical categories pertaining to overt verbal performances.[5]

XIII. THEORIES AND MODELS

51. But what might these episodes be? And, in terms of our science fiction, how might our ancestors have come to recognize their existence? The answer to these questions is surprisingly straightforward, once the logical space of our discussion is enlarged to include a distinction, central to the philosophy of science, between the language of *theory* and the language of *observation*. Although this distinction is a familiar one, I shall take a few paragraphs to highlight those aspects of the distinction which are of greatest relevance to our problem.

Informally, to construct a theory is, in its most developed or sophisticated form, to postulate a domain of entities which behave in certain ways set down by the fundamental principles of the theory, and to correlate—perhaps, in a certain sense to identify—complexes of these theoretical entities with certain non-theoretical objects or situations; that is to say, with objects or situations which are either matters of observable fact or, in principle at least, describable in observational terms. This "correlation" or "identification" of theoretical with observational states of affairs is a tentative one "until further notice," and amounts, so to speak, to erecting temporary bridges which permit the passage from sentences in observational discourse to sentences in the theory, and vice versa. Thus, for example, in the kinetic theory of gases, empirical statements of the form "Gas g at such and such a place and time has such and such a volume, pressure, and temperature" are correlated with theoretical statements specifying certain statistical measures of populations of molecules. These temporary bridges are so set up that inductively established laws pertaining to gases, formulated in the language of observable fact, are correlated with derived propositions or theorems in the language of the theory, and that no proposition in the theory is correlated with a falsified empirical generalization. Thus, a good theory (at least of the type we are considering) "explains" established empirical laws by deriving theoretical counterparts of these laws from a small set of postulates relating to unobserved entities.

These remarks, of course, barely scratch the surface of the problem of the status of theories in scientific discourse. And no sooner have I made them, than I must hasten to qualify them—almost beyond rec-

[5] An earlier attempt along these lines is to be found in (18) and (19).

ognition. For while this by now classical account of the nature of theories (one of the earlier formulations of which is due to Norman Campbell (5), and which is to be bound more recently in the writings of Carnap (8), Reichenbach (15, 16), Hempel (10), and Braithwaite (3)) does throw light on the logical status of theories, it emphasizes certain features at the expense of others. By speaking of the construction of a theory as the elaboration of a postulate system which is tentatively correlated with observational discourse, it gives a highly artificial and unrealistic picture of what scientists have actually done in the process of constructing theories. I don't wish to deny that logically sophisticated scientists today *might* and perhaps, on occasion, *do* proceed in true logistical style. I do, however, wish to emphasize two points:

(1) The first is that the fundamental assumptions of a theory are usually developed not by constructing uninterpreted calculi which might correlate in the desired manner with observational discourse, but rather by attempting to find a *model,* i.e. to describe a domain of familiar objects behaving in familiar ways such that we can see how the phenomena to be explained would arise if they consisted of this sort of thing. The essential thing about a model is that it is accompanied, so to speak, by a commentary which *qualifies* or *limits*—but not precisely nor in all respects—the analogy between the familiar objects and the entities which are being introduced by the theory. It is the descriptions of the fundamental ways in which the objects in the model domain, thus qualified, behave, which, transferred to the theoretical entities, correspond to the postulates of the logistical picture of theory construction.

(2) But even more important for our purposes is the fact that the logistical picture of theory construction obscures the most important thing of all, namely that the process of devising "theoretical" explanations of observable phenomena did not spring full-blown from the head of modern science. In particular, it obscures the fact that not all commonsense inductive inferences are of the form

All observed A's have been B, *therefore (probably)* all A's are B.

or its statistical counterparts, and leads one mistakenly to suppose that so-called "hypothetic-deductive" explanation is limited to the sophisticated stages of science. The truth of the matter, as I shall shortly be illustrating, is that science is continuous with common sense, and the ways in which the scientist seeks to explain empirical phenomena are refinements of the ways in which plain men, however crudely and schematically, have attempted to understand their environment and their fellow men since the dawn of intelligence. It is this point which I wish to stress at the present time, for I am going to argue that the distinction between theoretical and observational discourse is involved in the logic of concepts pertaining to inner episodes. I say "involved in" for it would be paradoxical and, indeed, incorrect, to say that these concepts *are* theoretical concepts.

52. Now I think it fair to say that some light has already been thrown on the expression "inner episodes"; for while it would indeed be a category mistake to suppose that the inflammability of a piece of wood is, so to speak, a hidden burning which becomes overt or manifest when the wood is placed on the fire, not all the unobservable episodes we suppose to go on in the world are the offspring of category mistakes. Clearly it is by no means an illegitimate use of "in"—though it is a use which has its own logical grammar—to say, for example, that "in" the air around us there are innumerable molecules which, in spite of the observable stodginess of the air, are participating in a veritable turmoil of episodes. Clearly, the sense in which these episodes are "in" the air is to be explicated in terms of the sense in which the air "is" a population of molecules, and this, in turn, in terms of the logic of the relation between theoretical and observational discourse.

I shall have more to say on this topic in a moment. In the meantime, let us return to our mythical ancestors. It will not surprise my readers to learn that the second stage in the enrichment of their Rylean language is the addition of theoretical discourse. Thus we may suppose these language-using animals to elaborate, without methodological sophistication, crude, sketchy, and vague theories to explain why things which are similar in their observable properties differ in their causal properties, and things which are similar in their causal properties differ in their observable properties.

XIV. METHODOLOGICAL VERSUS PHILOSOPHICAL BEHAVIORISM

53. But we are approaching the time for the central episode in our myth. I want you to suppose that in this Neo-Rylean culture there now appears a genius—let us call him Jones—who is an unsung forerunner of the movement in psychology, once revolutionary, now commonplace, known as Behaviorism. Let me emphasize that what I have in mind is Behaviorism as a methodological thesis, which I shall be concerned to formulate. For the central and guiding theme in the historical complex known by this term has been a certain conception, or family of conceptions, of how to go about building a science of psychology.

Philosophers have sometimes supposed that Behaviorists are, as such, committed to the idea that our ordinary mentalistic concepts are *analyzable* in terms of overt behavior. But although Behaviorism has often been characterized by a certain metaphysical bias, it is not a thesis about the *analysis* of *existing* psychological concepts, but one which concerns the construction of new concepts. As a methodological thesis, it involves no commitment whatever concerning the logical analysis of common-sense mentalistic discourse, nor does it involve a denial that each of us has a privileged access to our state of mind, nor that these states of mind can properly be described in terms of such common-sense concepts as believing, wondering, doubting, intending, wishing, inferring, etc. If we permit ourselves to speak of this privileged access to our states of mind as "introspection," avoiding the implication that there is a "means" whereby we "see" what is going on "inside," as we see external circumstances by the eye, then we can say that Behaviorism, as I shall use the term, does not deny that there is such a thing as introspection, nor that it is, on some topics, at least, quite reliable. The essential point about 'introspection' from the standpoint of Behaviorism is that *we introspect in terms of common sense mentalistic concepts*. And while the Behavorist admits, as anyone must, that much knowledge is embodied in common-sense mentalistic discourse, and that still more can be gained in the future by formulating and testing hypotheses in terms of them, and while he admits that it is perfectly legitimate to call such a psychology "scientific," he proposes, for his own part, to make no more than a heuristic use of mentalistic discourse, and to construct his concepts "from scratch" in the course of developing his own scientific account of the observable behavior of human organisms.

54. But while it is quite clear that scientific Behaviorism is not the thesis that common-sense psychological concepts are *analyzable* into concepts pertaining to overt behavior—a thesis which has been maintained by some philosophers and which may be called 'analytical' or 'philosophical' Behaviorism—it is often thought that Behaviorism is committed to the idea that the concepts of a behavioristic psychology must be so analyzable, or, to put things right side up, that properly introduced behavioristic concepts must be built by explicit definition—in the broadest sense—from a basic vocabulary pertaining to overt behavior. The Behaviorist would thus be saying "Whether or not the mentalistic concepts of everyday life are definable in terms of overt behavior, I shall ensure that this is true of the concepts that I shall employ." And it must be confessed that many behavioristically oriented psychologists have believed themselves committed to this austere program of concept formation.

Now I think it reasonable to say that, *thus conceived*, the behavioristic program would be unduly restrictive. Certainly, nothing in the nature of sound scientific procedure requires this self-denial. Physics, the methodological sophistication of which has so impressed—indeed, overly impressed—the other sciences, does not lay down a corresponding restriction on its concepts, nor has chemistry been built in terms of concepts explicitly definable in terms of the observable properties and behavior of chemical substances. The point I am making should now be clear. The behavioristic requirement that all concepts should be *introduced* in terms of a basic vocabulary pertaining to overt behavior is compatible with the idea that some behavioristic concepts are to be introduced as *theoretical* concepts.

55. It is essential to note that the theoretical terms of a behavioristic psychology are not only *not* defined in terms of overt behavior, they are also *not* defined in terms of nerves, synapses, neural impulses, etc., etc. A behavioristic theory of behavior is not, as such, a physiological explanation of behavior. The ability of a framework of theoretical concepts and propositions successfully to explain behavioral phenomena is logically independent of the identification of these theoretical concepts with concepts of neurophysiology. What *is* true—and this is a logical point—is that each special science dealing with some aspect of the human organism operates within the frame of a certain regulative ideal, the ideal of a coherent system in which the achievements of each have an intelligible place. Thus, it is part of the Behaviorist's business to keep an eye on the total picture of the human organism which is beginning to emerge. And if the tendency to premature identification is held in check, there may be considerable heuristic value in speculative attempts at integration; though, until recently, at least, neurophysiological speculations in behavior theory have not been particularly fruitful. And while it is, I suppose, noncontroversial that when the total scientific picture of man and his behavior is in, it will involve *some* identification of concepts in behavior theory with concepts pertaining to the functioning of anatomical structures, it should not be assumed that behavior theory is committed *ab initio* to a physiological identification of *all* its concepts,—that its concepts are, so to speak, physiological from the start.

We have, in effect, been distinguishing between two dimensions of the logic (or 'methodologic') of theoretical terms: (a) their role in explaining the selected phenomena of which the theory is the theory; (b) their role as candidates for integration in what we have called the "total picture." These roles are equally part of the logic, and hence the "meaning," of theoretical terms. Thus, at any one time the terms in a theory will carry with them as part of their logical force that which it is reasonable to envisage—whether schematically or determinately—

as the manner of their integration. However, for the purposes of my argument, it will be useful to refer to these two roles as though it were a matter of a distinction between what I shall call *pure theoretical concepts,* and hypotheses concerning the relation of these concepts to concepts in other specialties. What we *can* say is that the less a scientist is in a position to conjecture about the way in which a certain theory can be expected to integrate with other specialties, the more the concepts of his theory approximate to the status of pure theoretical concepts. To illustrate: We can imagine that Chemistry developed a sophisticated and successful theory to explain chemical phenomena before either electrical or magnetic phenomena were noticed; and that chemists developed as pure theoretical concepts, certain concepts which it later became reasonable to identify with concepts belonging to the framework of electromagnetic theory.

XV. THE LOGIC OF PRIVATE EPISODES: THOUGHTS

56. With these all too sketchy remarks on Methodological Behaviorism under our belts, let us return once again to our fictional ancestors. We are now in a position to characterize the original Rylean language in which they described themselves and their fellows as not only a *behavioristic* language, but a behavioristic language which is restricted to the *non-theoretical* vocabulary of a behavioristic psychology. Suppose, now, that in the attempt to account for the fact that his fellow men behave intelligently not only when their conduct is threaded on a string of overt verbal episodes—that is to say, as we would put it, when they "think out loud"—but also when no detectable verbal output is present, Jones develops a *theory* according to which overt utterances are but the culmination of a process which begins with certain inner episodes. *And let us supposes that his model for these episodes* which initiate the events which culminate in overt verbal behavior *is that of overt verbal behavior itself. In other words, using the language of the model, the theory is to the effect that overt verbal behavior is the culmination of a process which begins with "inner speech."*

It is essential to bear in mind that what Jones means by "inner speech" is not to be confused with *verbal imagery*. As a matter of fact, Jones, like his fellows, does not as yet even have the concept of an image.

It is easy to see the general lines a Jonesean theory will take. According to it the true cause of intelligent nonhabitual behavior is "inner speech." Thus, even when a hungry person overtly says "Here is an edible object" and proceeds to eat it, the true—theoretical—cause of his eating, given his hunger, is not the overt utterance, but the "inner utterance of this sentence."

57. The first thing to note about the Jonesean theory is that, as built on the model of speech episodes, *it carries over to these inner episodes the applicability of semantical categories.* Thus, just as Jones has, like his fellows, been speaking of overt utterances as *meaning* this or that, or being *about* this or that, so he now speaks of these inner episodes as *meaning* this or that, or being *about* this or that.

The second point to remember is that although Jones' theory involves a *model,* it is not identical with it. Like all theories formulated in terms of a model, it also includes a *commentary* on the model; a commentary which places more or less sharply drawn restrictions on the analogy between the theoretical entities and the entities of the model. Thus, while his theory talks of "inner speech," the commentary hastens to add that, of course, the episodes in question are not the wagging of a hidden tongue, nor are any sounds produced by this "inner speech."

58. The general drift of my story should now be clear. I shall therefore proceed to make the essential points quite briefly:

(1) What we must suppose Jones to have developed is the germ of a theory which permits many different developments. We must not pin it down to any of the more sophisticated forms it takes in the hands of classical philosophers. Thus, the theory need not be given a Socratic or Cartesian form, according to which this "inner speech" is a function of a separate substance; though primitive peoples may have had good reason to suppose that humans consist of two separate things.

(2) Let us suppose Jones to have called these discursive entities *thoughts.* We can admit at once that the framework of thoughts he has introduced is a framework of "unobserved," "nonempirical" "inner" episodes. For we can point out immediately that in these respects they are no worse off than the particles and episodes of physical theory. For these episodes are "in" language-using animals as molecular impacts are "in" gases, not as "ghosts" are in "machines." They are "nonempirical" in the simple sense that they are *theoretical*—not definable in observational terms. Nor does the fact that they are, *as introduced,* unobserved entities imply that Jones could not have good reason for supposing them to exist. Their "purity" is not a *metaphysical* purity, but, so to speak, a *methodological* purity. As we have seen, the fact that they are not introduced as physiological entities does not preclude the possibility that at a later methodological stage, they may, so to speak, "turn out" to be such. Thus, there are many who would say that it

is already reasonable to suppose that these *thoughts* are to be "identified" with complex events in the cerebral cortex functioning along the lines of a caluculating machine. Jones, of course, has no such idea.

(3) Although the theory postulates that overt discourse is the culmination of a process which begins with "inner discourse," this should not be taken to mean that overt discourse stands to "inner discourse" *as voluntary movements stand to intentions and motives.* True, overt linguistic events *can* be produced as means to ends. But serious errors creep into the interpretation of both language and thought if one interprets the idea that overt linguistic episodes *express* thoughts, on the model of the use of an instrument. Thus, it should be noted that Jones' theory, as I have sketched it, is perfectly compatible with the idea that the ability to have thoughts is acquired in the process of acquiring overt speech and that only after overt speech is well established, can "inner speech" occur without its overt culmination.

(4) Although the occurrence of overt speech episodes which are characterizable in semantical terms is explained by the theory in terms of *thoughts* which are *also* characterized in semantical terms, this does not mean that the idea that overt speech "has meaning" is being *analyzed* in terms of the intentionality of thoughts. It must not be forgotten that *the semantical characterization of overt verbal episodes is the primary use of semantical terms, and that overt linguistic events as semantically characterized are the model for the inner episodes introduced by the theory.*

(5) One final point before we come to the *dénouement* of the first episode in the saga of Jones. It cannot be emphasized too much that although these theoretical discursive episodes or *thoughts* are introduced as *inner* episodes—which is merely to repeat that they are introduced as *theoretical* episodes—they are *not* introduced as *immediate experiences.* Let me remind the reader that Jones, like his Neo-Rylean contemporaries, does not as yet have this concept. And even when he, and they, acquire it, by a process which will be the second episode in my myth, it will only be the philosophers among them who will suppose that the inner episodes introduced for one theoretical purpose—thoughts—must be a subset of immediate experiences, inner episodes introduced for another theoretical purpose.

59. Here, then, is the *dénouement.* I have suggested a number of times that although it would be most misleading to say that concepts pertaining to thinking are theoretical concepts, yet their status might be illuminated by means of the contrast between theoretical and non-theoretical discourse. We are now in a position to see exactly why this is so. For once our fictitious ancestor, Jones, has developed the theory that overt verbal behavior is the expression of thoughts, and taught his

compatriots to make use of the theory in interpreting each other's behavior, it is but a short step to the use of this language in self-description. Thus, when Tom, watching Dick, has behavioral evidence which warrants the use of the sentence (in the language of the theory) "Dick is thinking 'p' " (or "Dick is thinking that p"), Dick, using the same behavioral evidence, can say, in the language of the theory, "I am thinking 'p' " (or "I am thinking that p.") And it now turns out—need it have?—that Dick can be trained to give reasonably reliable self-descriptions, using the language of the theory, without having to observe his overt behavior. Jones brings this about, roughly, by applauding utterances by Dick of "I am thinking that p" when the behavioral evidence strongly supports the theoretical statement "Dick is thinking that p"; and by frowning on utterances of "I am thinking that p," when the evidence does not support this theoretical statement. Our ancestors begin to speak of the privileged access each of us has to his own thoughts. *What began as a language with a purely theoretical use has gained a reporting role.*

As I see it, this story helps us understand that concepts pertaining to such inner episodes as thoughts are primarily and essentially *intersubjective,* as intersubjective as the concept of a positron, and that the reporting role of these concepts—that fact that each of us has a privileged access to his thoughts—constitutes a dimension of the use of these concepts which is *built on* and *presupposes* this intersubjective status. My myth has shown that the fact that language is essentially an *intersubjective* achievement, and is learned in intersubjective contexts—a fact rightly stressed in modern psychologies of language, thus by B. F. Skinner (21), and by certain philosophers, e.g. Carnap (7), Wittgenstein (22)—is compatible with the "privacy" of "inner episodes." It also makes clear that this privacy is not an "absolute privacy." For if it recognizes that these concepts have a reporting use in which one is not drawing inferences from behavioral evidence, it nevertheless insists that the fact that overt behavior *is* evidence for these episodes *is built into the very logic of these concepts,* just as the fact that the observable behavior of gases is evidence for molecular episodes is built into the very logic of molecule talk.

XVI. THE LOGIC OF PRIVATE EPISODES: IMPRESSIONS

60. We are now ready for the problem of the status of concepts pertaining to immediate experience. The first step is to remind ourselves that among the inner episodes which belong to the framework of *thoughts* will be perceptions, that is to say, *seeing that the table is brown,*

hearing that the piano is out of tune, etc. Until Jones introduced this framework, the only concepts our fictitious ancestors had of perceptual *episodes* were those of overt verbal *reports,* made, for example, in the context of looking at an object in standard conditions. *Seeing that something is the case* is an inner episode in the Jonesean theory which has as its model *reporting on looking that something is the case.* It will be remembered from an earlier section that just as when I say that Dick *reported* that the table is green, I commit myself to the truth of what he reported, so to say of Dick that he *saw* that the table is green is, in part, to ascribe to Dick the idea '*this* table is green' and to endorse this idea. The reader might refer back to Sections 16 ff. for an elaboration of this point.

With the enrichment of the originally Rylean framework to include inner perceptual episodes, I have established contact with my original formulation of the problem of inner experience (Sections 22 ff.). For I can readily reconstruct in this framework my earlier account of the *language of appearing,* both *qualitative* and *existential.* Let us turn, therefore to the final chapter of our historical novel. By now our ancestors speak a quite un-Rylean language. But it still contains no reference to such things as impressions, sensations, or feelings—in short, to the items which philosophers lump together under the heading "immediate experiences." It will be remembered that we had reached a point at which, as far as we could see, the phrase "impression of a red triangle" could only mean something like "that state of a perceiver—over and above the idea that there is a red and triangular physical object over there—which is common to those situations in which

(a) he sees that the object over there is red and triangular;
(b) the object over there looks to him to be red and triangular;
(c) there looks to him to be a red and triangular physical object over there."

Our problem was that, on the one hand, it seemed absurd to say that impressions, for example, are theoretical entities, while, on the other, the interpretation of impressions as theoretical entities seemed to provide the only hope of accounting for the positive content and explanatory power that the idea that there are such entities appears to have, and of enabling us to understand how we could have arrived at this idea. The account I have just been giving of *thoughts* suggests how this apparent dilemma can be resolved.

For we continue the myth by supposing that Jones develops, in crude and sketchy form, of course, a theory of sense perception. Jones' theory does not have to be either well-articulated or precise in order to be the first effective step in the development of a mode of discourse which today, in the case of some sense-modalities at least, is extraordinarily subtle and complex. We need, therefore, attribute to this mythical theory only those minimal features which enable it to throw light on the logic of our ordinary language about immediate experiences. From this standpoint it is sufficient to suppose that the hero of my myth postulates a class of inner—theoretical—episodes which he calls, say, *impressions,* and which are the end results of the impingement of physical objects and processes on various parts of the body, and, in particular, to follow up the specific form in which I have posed our problem, the eye.

61. A number of points can be made right away:

(1) The entities introduced by the theory are *states* of the perceiving subject, *not a class of particulars.* It cannot be emphasized too strongly that the particulars of the common-sense world are such things as books, pages, turnips, dogs, persons, noises, flashes, etc., and the Space and Time—Kant's *Undinge*—in which they come to be. What is likely to make us suppose that *impressions* are introduced as particulars is that, as in the case of thoughts, this ur-theory is formulated in terms of a *model.* This time the model is the idea of a domain of "inner replicas" which, when brought about in standard conditions, share the perceptible characteristics of their physical source. It is important to see that the model is the occurrence "in" perceivers of *replicas,* not of *perceivings of replicas.* Thus, the model for an impression of a red triangle is a *red and triangular replica,* not a *seeing of a red and triangular replica.* The latter alternative would have the merit of recognizing that impressions are not particulars. But, by misunderstanding the role of models in the formulation of a theory, it mistakenly assumes that if the entities of the model are particulars, the theoretical entities which are introduced by means of the model must themselves be particulars—thus overlooking the role of the commentary. And by taking the model to be *seeing a red and triangular replica,* it smuggles into the language of impressions the logic of the language of thoughts. For seeing is a *cognitive* episode which involves the framework of thoughts, and to take it as the model is to give aid and comfort to the assimilation of impressions to thoughts, and thoughts to impressions which, as I have already pointed out, is responsible for many of the confusions of the classical account of both thoughts and impressions.

(2) The fact that *impressions* are theoretical entities enables us to understand how they can be *intrinsically* characterized—that is to say, characterized by something more than a *definite description,* such as "entity of *the kind which* has as its standard cause looking at a red and triangular physical object in such and such circumstances" or "entity of *the kind which* is common to the situations in which there looks

to be a red and triangular physical object." For although the predicates of a theory owe their meaningfulness to the fact that they are logically related to predicates which apply to the observable phenomena which the theory explains, the predicates of a theory are not shorthand for definite descriptions of properties in terms of these observation predicates. When the kinetic theory of gases speaks of molecules as having *mass,* the term "mass" is not the abbreviation of a definite description of the form "the property which . . ." Thus, "impression of a red triangle" does not simply mean "impression such as is caused by red and triangular physical objects in standard conditions," though it is true—*logically* true—of impressions of red triangles that they are of that sort which *is* caused by red and triangular objects in standard conditions.

(3) If the theory of impressions were developed in true logistical style, we could say that the intrinsic properties of impressions are "implicitly defined" by the postulates of the theory, as we can say that the intrinsic properties of subatomic particles are "implicitly defined" by the fundamental principles of subatomic theory. For this would be just another way of saying that one knows the meaning of a theoretical term when one knows (a) how it is related to other theoretical terms, and (b) how the theoretical system as a whole is tied to the observation language. But, as I have pointed out, our ur-behaviorist does not formulate his theory in textbook style. He formulates it in terms of a model.

Now the model entities are entities which *do* have intrinsic properties. They are, for example, red and triangular wafers. It might therefore seem that the theory specifies the intrinsic characteristics of impressions to be the familiar perceptible qualities of physical objects and processes. If this were so, of course, the theory would be ultimately incoherent, for it would attribute to impressions—which are clearly not physical objects—characteristics which, if our argument to date is sound, only physical objects can have. Fortunately, this line of thought overlooks what we have called the commentary on the model, which qualifies, restricts and interprets the analogy between the familiar entities of the model and the theoretical entities which are being introduced. Thus, it would be a mistake to suppose that since the *model* for the impression of a red triangle is a red and triangular wafer, the impression itself is a red and triangular wafer. What can be said is that the impression of a red triangle is *analogous,* to an extent which is by no means neatly and tidily specified, to a red and triangular wafer. The *essential* feature of the analogy is that visual impressions stand to one another in a system of ways of resembling and differing which is structurally similar to the ways in which the colors and shapes of visible objects resemble and differ.

(4) It might be concluded from this last point that the concept of the impression of a red triangle is a "purely formal" concept, the concept of a "logical form" which can acquire a "content" only by means of "ostensive definition." One can see why a philosopher might want to say this, and why he might conclude that in so far as concepts pertaining to immediate experiences are *intersubjective,* they are "purely structural," the "content" of immediate experience being incommunicable. Yet this line of thought is but another expression of the Myth of the Given. For the theoretical concept of the impression of a red triangle would be no more and no less "without content" than *any* theoretical concept. And while, like these, it must belong to a framework which is logically connected with the language of observable fact, the logical relation between a theoretical language and the language of observable fact has nothing to do with the epistemological fiction of an "ostensive definition."

(5) The impressions of Jones' theory are, as was pointed out above, states of the perceiver, rather than particulars. If we remind ourselves that these states are not introduced as physiological states (see Section 55), a number of interesting questions arise which tie in with the reflections on the status of the scientific picture of the world (Sections 39–44 above) but which, unfortunately, there is space only to adumbrate. Thus, some philosophers have thought it obvious that we can expect that in the development of science it will become reasonable to identify *all* the concepts of behavior theory with definable terms in neurophysiological theory, and these, in turn, with definable terms in theoretical physics. It is important to realize that the second step of this prediction, at least, is either a *truism* or a *mistake.* It is a truism if it involves a tacit redefinition of "physical theory" to mean "theory adequate to account for the observable behavior of any object (including animals and persons) which has physical properties." While if "physical theory" is taken in its ordinary sense of "theory adequate to explain the observable behavior of physical objects," it is, I believe, mistaken.

To ask how *impressions* fit together with *electromagnetic fields,* for example, is to ask a mistaken question. It is to mix the framework of *molar* behavior theory with the framework of the *micro*-theory of physical objects. The proper question is, rather, "What would correspond in a *micro*-theory of sentient organisms to *molar* concepts pertaining to impressions?" And it is, I believe, in answer to this question that one would come upon the *particulars* which sense-datum theorists profess to find (by analysis) in the common-sense universe of discourse (cf. Section 23). Furthermore, I believe that in characterizing these particulars, the micro-behaviorist would be led to say something like the following: "It is such particulars which (from the standpoint of the theory) are being responded to by the organism when it looks to a *person* as though there were a red and triangular physical object over there." It would, of course, be incorrect to say that, in the ordinary sense, such a particular is red or triangular. What *could* be said,[6] however, is that whereas in the common-sense picture physical objects are red and triangular but the impression "of" a red triangle is neither red nor triangular, in the framework of this micro-theory, the theoretical counterparts of sentient organisms are Space-Time worms characterized by two kinds of variables: (a) variables which also characterize the theoretical counterparts of *merely* material objects; (b) variables peculiar to sentient things; and that these latter variables are the counterparts in this new framework of the perceptible qualities of the physical objects of the common-sense framework. It is statements such as these which would be the cash value of the idea that "physical objects aren't really colored; colors exist only in the perceiver," and that "to see that the facing surface of a physical object is red and triangular is to *mistake* a red and triangular sense content for a physical object with a red and triangular facing side." Both these ideas clearly treat what is really a speculative philosophical critique (see Section 41) of the common-sense framework of physical objects and the perception of physical objects in the light of an envisaged ideal scientific framework, as though it were a matter of distinctions which can be drawn *within* the common-sense framework itself.

62. This brings me to the final chapter of my story. Let us suppose that as his final service to mankind before he vanishes without a trace, Jones teaches his theory of perception to his fellows. As before in the case of *thoughts,* they begin by using the language of impressions to draw theoretical conclusions from appropriate premises. (Notice that the evidence for theoretical statements in the language of impressions will include such introspectible inner episodes as *its looking to one as though there were a red and triangular physical object over there,* as well as overt behavior.) Finally he succeeds in training them to make a *reporting* use of this language. He trains them, that is, to say "I have the impression of a red triangle" when, and only when, according to the theory, they are indeed having the impression of a red triangle.

Once again the myth helps us to understand that concepts pertain-

[6] For a discussion of some logical points pertaining to this framework, the reader should consult the essay, "The Concept of Emergence," by Paul E. Meehl and Wilfrid Sellars, on pp. 239–52 of this volume. [H. Feigl and M. Scriven (eds.), *Minnesota Studies in the Philosophy of Science,* vol. I. Eds.]

ing to certain inner episodes—in this case *impressions*—can be primarily and essentially *intersubjective,* without being resolvable into overt behavioral symptoms, and that the reporting role of these concepts, their role in introspection, the fact that each of us has a privileged access to his impressions, constitutes a dimension of these concepts which is *built on* and *presupposes* their role in intersubjective discourse. It also makes clear why the "privacy" of these episodes is not the "absolute privacy" of the traditional puzzles. For, as in the case of thoughts, the fact that overt behavior is evidence for these episodes is built into the very logic of these concepts as the fact that the observable behavior of gases is evidence for molecular episodes is built into the very logic of molecule talk.

Notice that what our "ancestors" have acquired under the guidance of Jones is not "just another language"—a "notational convenience" or "code"—which merely enables them to say what they can already say in the language of qualitative and existential looking. They have acquired another language, indeed, but it is one which, though it rests on a framework of discourse about public objects in Space and Time, has an autonomous logical structure, and contains an *explanation of,* not just a *code for,* such facts as that *there looks to me to be a red and triangular physical object over there.* And notice that while our "ancestors" came to notice impressions, and the language of impressions embodies a "discovery" that there are such things, the language of impressions was no more tailored to fit *antecedent* noticings of these entities than the language of molecules was tailored to fit antecedent noticings of molecules.

And the spirit of Jones is not yet dead. For it is the particulars of the micro-theory discussed in Section 61 (5) which are the solid core of the sense contents and sense fields of the sense-datum theorist. Envisaging the general lines of that framework, even sketching some of its regions, he has taught himself to play with it (in his study) as a report language. Unfortunately, he mislocates the truth of these conceptions, and, with a modesty forgivable in any but a philosopher, confuses his own creative enrichment of the framework of empirical knowledge, with an analysis of knowledge as it was. He construes as *data* the particulars and arrays of particulars which he has come to be able to observe, and believes them to be antecedent objects of knowledge which have somehow been in the framework from the beginning. It is in the very act of *taking* that he speaks of the *given.*

63. I have used a myth to kill a myth—the Myth of the Given. But is my myth really a myth? Or does the reader not recognize Jones as Man himself in the middle of his journey from the grunts and groans of the cave to the subtle and polydimensional discourse of the drawing room, the laboratory, and the study, the language of Henry and William

James, of Einstein and of the philosophers who, in their efforts to break out of discourse to an *arché* beyond discourse, have provided the most curious dimension of all.

References

1. Ayer, A. J. *Foundations of Empirical Knowledge*. London: Macmillan, 1940.
2. Ayer, A. J. "The Terminology of Sense Data," in *Philosophical Essays*, pp. 66–104. London: Macmillan, 1954. Also in *Mind*, 54, 1945, pp. 289–312.
3. Braithwaite, R. B. *Scientific Explanation*. Cambridge: Cambridge Univ. Pr., 1953.
4. Broad, C. D. *Scientific Thought*. London: Kegan Paul, 1923.
5. Campbell, Norman. *Physics: The Elements*. Cambridge: Cambridge Univ. Pr., 1920.
6. Carnap, Rudolf. *Introduction to Semantics*. Chicago: Univ. of Chicago Pr., 1942.
7. Carnap, Rudolf. *"Psychologie in Physikalischer Sprache," Erketnntnis*, 3:107–42 (1933).
8. Carnap, Rudolf. "The Interpretation of Physics," in H. Feigl and M. Brodbeck (eds.), *Readings in the Philosophy of Science*, pp. 309–18. New York: Appleton-Century-Crofts, 1953. This selection consists of pp. 59–69 of his *Foundations of Logic and Mathematics*. Chicago: Univ. of Chicago Pr., 1939.
9. Chisholm, Roderick. "The Theory of Appearing," in Max Black (ed.), *Philosophical Analysis*, pp. 102–18. Ithaca: Cornell Univ. Pr., 1950.
10. Hempel, C. G. *Fundamentals of Concept Formation in Empirical Science*. Chicago: Univ. of Chicago Pr., 1952.
11. Linnell, John. "Berkeley's Critique of Abstract Ideas." A Ph.D. thesis submitted to the Graduate Faculty of the University of Minnesota, June 1954.
12. Paul, G. A. "Is there a Problem about Sense Data?" in Supplementary Volume XV of the *Aristotelian Society Proceedings*. Also in A. G. N. Flew (ed.), *Logic and Language*. New York: Philosophical Lib., 1951.
13. Price, H. H. *Perception*. London: Methuen, 1932.
14. Price, H. H. *Thinking and Experience*. London: Hutchinson's Univ. Lib., 1953.
15. Reichenbach, H. *Philosophie der Raum-Zeit-Lehre*. Berlin: de Gruyter, 1928.
16. Reichenbach, H. *Experience and Prediction*. Chicago: Univ. of Chicago Pr., 1938.
17. Ryle, Gilbert. *The Concept of Mind*. London: Hutchinson's Univ. Lib., 1949.

18. Sellars, Wilfrid. "Mind, Meaning and Behavior," *Philosophical Studies,* 3:83–94 (1952).
19. Sellars, Wilfrid. "A Semantical Solution of the Mind-Body Problem," *Methodos,* 5:45–84 (1953).
20. Sellars, Wilfrid. "Empiricism and Abstract Entities," in *Paul A. Schilpp* (ed.), *The Philosophy of Rudolf Carnap*. Evanston (Ill.): Library of Living Philosophers (forthcoming). (Available in mimeograph form from the author.)
21. Skinner, B. F. "The Operational Analysis of Psychological Terms," *Psychological Review,* 52:270–77 (1945). Reprinted in H. Feigl and M. Brodbeck (eds.), *Readings in the Philosophy of Science,* pp. 585–94. New York: Appleton-Century-Crofts, 1953.
22. Wittgenstein, Ludwig. *Philosophical Investigations.* London: Macmillan, 1953.

Anthony Quinton

The Foundations of Knowledge

I

The idea that knowledge forms an ordered, hierarchical system is not a new one, but it has been particularly prominent in British philosophy in the last fifty years. It was anticipated by the theory of self-evidence put forward by Aristotle in the *Posterior Analytics* and assumed by Descartes in his pursuit of an indubitable starting-point for the reconstruction of his beliefs. But where Aristotle and Descartes took the ultimate truths on which the edifice of knowledge was reared to be *a priori* principles, the more recent adherents of this general position have understood them to be particular statements of empirical fact.

The inspiration behind the recurrences of this theory has in each case been mathematical and logical. Aristotle's version was in accord with his own discovery of deductive logic, and with the beginnings of Greek geometry in Pythagoras and perhaps Thales, eventually to be

Anthony Quinton, "The Foundations of Knowledge," in *British Analytical Philosophy*, ed. Bernard Williams and Alan Montefiore (London: Routledge & Kegan Paul Ltd., and New York: Humanities Press, Inc., 1966). Reprinted by permission of the publishers.

systematized by Euclid. Descartes was explicit about his debt to the pure mathematics of his own time, to which he extensively contributed, and was concerned also to found a systematic science of mechanics. In the case of Russell, the central figure of the contemporary revival of the doctrine, there is an equally close connection between theory of knowledge on the one hand, and mathematics and logic on the other. The essential aim of *Principia Mathematica* [RUSSELL–WHITEHEAD] [1] was to demonstrate the identity of logic and mathematics by showing that the whole of mathematics could be derived from an improved deductive logic. The unitary discipline they composed was set out by him in a Euclidean manner as a vast body of theorems derived with the aid of three intuitively acceptable rules of inference from five equally self-evident logical axioms. By organizing a particular body of knowledge in a fully logically articulate way *Principia Mathematica* provided a model for the systematic presentation of knowledge in general. The idea of a comparable systematic presentation of our knowledge of empirical fact, in which the justification of every kind of thing we empirically know or have reason to believe is made clear by displaying its logical derivation from its ultimate empirical evidence, lies behind a long sequence of important and influential treatises: RUSSELL'S *Our Knowledge of the External World, Inquiry into Meaning and Truth,* and *Human Knowledge,* SCHLICK'S *Allgemeine Erkenntnislehre,* WITTGENSTEIN'S *Tractatus Logico-Philosophicus,* CARNAP'S *Der Logische Aufbau der Welt,* C. I. LEWIS'S *Mind and the World Order* and *Analysis of Knowledge and Valuation,* PRICE'S *Perception,* REICHENBACH'S *Experience and Prediction* and AYER'S *Foundations of Empirical Knowledge.*[2]

In each of these works it is said that knowledge has foundations and that the task of a philosophical theory of knowledge is to identify and describe these foundations and to reveal the logical dependence, whether deductive or inductive, of every other sort of justified belief

[1] Russell, B.A.W., and Whitehead, A.N. *Principia Mathematica,* 2nd ed. Cambridge University Press, 1925–7.

[2] Russell, B.A.W. *Our Knowledge of the External World.* London: Open Court, 1914.
Russell, B.A.W. *Inquiry into Meaning and Truth.* London: Allen and Unwin, 1940.
Russell, B.A.W. *Human Knowledge: Its Scope and Limits.* London: Allen and Unwin, 1948.
Schlick, M. *Allgemeine Erkenntnislehre.* Berlin: Springer, 1918.
Wittgenstein, L. *Tractatus Logico-Philosophicus.* London: Kegan Paul, 1922.
Carnap, R. *Der Logische Aufbau der Welt.* Berlin: Weltkreis-Verlag, 1928.
Lewis, C.I. *Mind and the World Order.* New York: Scribner, 1929.
Lewis, C.I. *An Analysis of Knowledge and Valuation.* La Salle: Open Court, 1946.
Price, H.H. *Perception.* London: Methuen, 1932.
Reichenbach, H. *Experience and Prediction.* University of Chicago Press, 1947.
Ayer, A.J. *The Foundations of Empirical Knowledge.* London: Macmillan, 1940.

upon them. As distinct from such earlier empiricists as Locke, Hume and Mill, the members of this tradition, which has been the standard or classical form of epistemology, in Britain at any rate, in this century, have been quite definite that their purpose is to give a logical analysis of knowledge as it actually exists and not a genetic or historical or psychological account of its growth. In Reichenbach's useful phrase, they are offering a rational reconstruction of our knowledge which sets out the reasons that logically justify our beliefs and not a narrative of the causes that in fact led us to adopt them.

This standard theory of the foundations of knowledge has been exposed to two kinds of criticism. In the first place it has had to contend with the objections of those who, while not denying that knowledge has foundations, disagree with the actual specification of them that Russell and his followers have given. Secondly, there have been more radical critics who reject the general presumption that knowledge has foundations at all. The traditional alternative to the doctrine of foundations is the coherence theory which argues that the elements of our knowledge do not stand in any sort of linear dependence on a set of self-evident basic truths about the given but hang together, rather, in systematic mutual corroboration. A version of the coherence theory was revived by some radical positivists in the 1930s, and another by Quine, under the influence of Duhem, more recently. In a series of publications stretching over the past thirty years Popper has argued for a fallibilism with interesting affinities to the critique of Cartesian intuitionism put forward by Peirce at the end of the nineteenth century. He does not deny that there are basic statements, but contends that their basicness is not absolute but relative. There are no statements for which further evidence cannot be acquired; but no further evidence need be sought for those which are not disputed by anyone. Goodman has also maintained that the basicness of a statement is relative, but in a very different sense. Bodies of assertions can be systematized in many alternative ways between which the analyst has a free choice. A statement is basic only in relation to a particular, freely chosen, way of systematizing the set to which it belongs. Finally, Austin has argued that the doctrine of foundations is altogether misconceived.

In what follows I shall first consider the arguments that have been advanced for the general thesis that knowledge has foundations. In particular I shall examine the infinite regress arguments that have been brought in support of the view that there must be some intuitive statements which have not been inferred from anything else and for the view that there must be some ostensive statements whose meaning is not introduced by correlating them with other statements whose meaning is already understood. Secondly, I shall consider the specification given by the standard theory of the detailed characteristics of these intuitive and ostensive statements as (*a*) certain or incorrigible, and (*b*) sensory or phenomenal. Thirdly, I shall look at the alternatives to these two specifications: the theories that basic statements may be probable or corrigible, on the one hand, and that they may report public, physical states of affairs, on the other. Finally, I shall turn to the more radical view that knowledge has no foundations of the kind the doctrine supposes, and thus that there are no absolutely or logically basic statements. A discussion of these topics will cover the main elements of epistemological controversy among analytic philosophers in the English-speaking world during the past fifty years.

II

The traditional form of the doctrine of foundations holds that there must be some intuitive beliefs if any beliefs are to be justified at all. By an intuitive belief is meant one which does not owe its truth or credibility to some other belief or beliefs from which it can be inferred. For a belief to be justified it is not enough for it to be accepted, let alone merely entertained. There must also be good reason for accepting it. Certainly some beliefs are justifiable by reference to others, but only if these other beliefs are themselves established or well confirmed. If every belief was dependent on others for its justification, no belief would be justified at all, for in this case to justify any belief would require the justification of an infinite series of beliefs. So if any belief is to be justified, there must be a class of basic, non-inferential beliefs to bring the regress of justification to a halt. These terminal, intuitive beliefs need not be strictly self-evident in the sense that the belief is its own justification. All that is required is that what justifies them should not be another belief.

The point can be made by reference to a widely accepted definition of knowledge. I know that *p*, it is often said, if I believe that *p*, if *p* is true and if I have sufficient reason for my belief in it. This sufficient reason cannot always be another belief since it will only be a sufficient reason if, besides being something from which the original belief can be validly inferred, deductively or inductively, it is also something which I know to be true. That today is the 30th is a logically sufficient reason for the conclusion that this month is not February. But only if the statement that today is the 30th is true, or some other statement is true which is a sufficient reason for the conclusion, will it be true that this month is not February; and only if I know that this or some comparable statement is true do I know that the conclusion is true. In other words not all beliefs can have other beliefs as their sufficient reasons but some must be justified by, for example, the occurrence of an experience or sense-impression. Valid inference only establishes the truth of a conclusion if the premises from which it is made are true. Inference cannot justify unless its ultimate premises are given. The argument for intuitive statements is simply a generalization of this argument in which the concept of justification has been widened to include making statements rationally credible or worthy of acceptance as well as their establishment as certainly true.

Empiricist philosophers are usually uncomfortable at the mention of intuition, which they identify with some perhaps mystical, and at any rate uncheckable, alternative to observation. But it is being used here in an approximately Kantian sense which would count our ultimate observational beliefs as themselves intuitive. To say that a belief is intuitive is to say that it does not owe its justification to other justified beliefs from which it can be validly derived. It is desirable at this stage to distinguish three possible senses of the word 'intuition'. There is, first, the common-or-garden, vernacular sense of the word in which it refers to the capacity to form correct beliefs in the absence of the sort of evidence ordinarily required to justify them. Unless the beliefs formed are, at least predominantly, correct, this is just guessing. They can be shown to be correct only if there is an authoritative, laborious and inferential way of justifying the beliefs in question. Secondly, there is a psychological sense of the word in which the formation of a particular belief by a particular person may be said to be intuitive if he has not got or cannot provide any reason for accepting it. Thirdly, there are what may be called logically intuitive beliefs where the belief is of such a kind that no reason in the form of another supporting belief is required for it to be worthy of acceptance. Beliefs that are logically intuitive will ordinarily be psychologically intuitive as well. But they do not have to be. From the fact that statable reasons are not *required* it does not follow that they are not *available*. Equally psychologically intuitive beliefs need not be logically intuitive. First we find ourselves inclined to accept a belief, then we look round for reasons in support of it. Finally, no common-or-garden intuition can be logically intuitive though all will be psychologically intuitive.

There do not have to be common-or-garden intuitions but there are, and it is a good thing that there are for otherwise the accumulation of knowledge would be a very plodding, laborious and uneconomical business. There must be psychologically intuitive beliefs if there are logically intuitive beliefs, and also, it would seem, if the number of beliefs held by a person at any given moment is finite. At any rate, if there was a time before which he had no beliefs at all, this must be so since he could have had no reason for his first belief or beliefs. These first beliefs may cease to be intuitive in this sense if he acquires reasons for them, but then some of these reasons will have to be intuitive since they cannot be based on the beliefs that they are used to support.

The traditional form of the doctrine of foundations is clearly concerned with logically intuitive beliefs. What it maintains is that there must be a set of statements which do not require for their justification the establishment of any other beliefs.

III

This familiar line of argument has been supplemented and fortified in recent times by an analogous train of reasoning which derives the necessity of foundations for knowledge not from the conditions which must be satisfied if any belief is to be justified but from the conditions which must be satisfied if any statement is to be understood. It seeks to show that there must be ostensive statements, in other words, statements whose meaning is not explained in terms of other statements already understood. Its starting-point is the fact that we often explain the meaning of a form of words by asserting it to be the same as that of some other statement or statements, and it argues that to avoid an infinite regress of explanation there must be a class of statements whose meaning is explained in some other way, not by correlation with other statements but by correlation with the world outside language. The parallels between this theory of ostensive statements and the theory of intuitive statements are obvious. Both rest on infinite regress arguments; in one case applied to the idea that all statements are explained by definition in terms of others, in the other applied to the idea that all statements are justified by inference from others.

The classic presentation of what might be called the pure theory of ostensive statements is to be found in the account of elementary propositions in Wittgenstein's *Tractatus* [WITTGENSTEIN].[3] He contends that if any statement is to have a definite sense it must be, or be equivalent and so reducible to, a statement or set of statements which correspond directly to the facts of which the world is composed. The underlying principle of this theory is less original than the way in which it is expressed. For what it really does is to present in a new way a generalized version of the principle of traditional empiricism that all ideas or concepts must be, or be definable in terms of, ideas or concepts that are directly derived from and correlated with experience. But in Wittgenstein

[3] Wittgenstein, L. *Tractatus Logico-Philosophicus*. London: Kegan Paul, 1922.

there is no commitment to the empirical nature of terms of the analysis. The novelty of Wittgenstein's version of the theory is that it takes the ultimate units or elements of meaning to be not words but sentences. Underlying this assumption is a theory of the logical priority of sentences to words, first propounded by Frege in his precept of philosophical method: 'Never to ask for the meaning of a word in isolation, but only in the context of a proposition.' In closely similar words Wittgenstein remarks: 'Only propositions have sense; only in the nexus of a proposition does a name have meaning.' This fact is concealed by the occurrence of intelligible one-word utterances, such as 'fire' or 'stop'. But to make anything of such one-word utterances we have to take them as sentences by supplying the missing elements, for example, 'there is a fire here', 'this place is on fire', 'fire that gun', 'light the fire', etc. To understand the meaning of a word is necessarily to understand the kinds of sentence in which it can occur. As our mastery of language increases we realize that many groups of words play similar syntactical parts, and this makes the definition of single words in terms of other words possible. When told that 'spinster' means the same as 'unmarried woman' I understand that the defined word can occur in all the sentences in which I already understand the defining phrase to be capable of occurring significantly.

IV

The arguments for intuitive and ostensive statements are connected as well as similar in form. The ostensive statement is given its meaning by correlation with some kind of observable situation. It has a meaning to the extent that observable situations are divided into those of which it is true and those of which it is not. To know what it means or to understand it is to be able to pick out the situations in which it is true, or at least to have been trained to respond to such situations with an inclination to utter it. Now the occurrence of a situation of the appropriate, verifying kind will be the sufficient reason for the assertion of an intuitive statement, the non-inferential kind of justification required to bring an end to the infinite regress. Intuitive statements must be ostensively learnt, for if they were explained in terms of other statements these latter could serve as premises for an inference to them; and ostensive statements must be intuitive, for the occurrence of a situation of the kind by correlation with which they were explained would be a sufficient reason of a non-inferential kind for their acceptance. As will emerge more fully later, it would be going too far to say that all ostensive statements are intuitive in the sense that the sufficient reason for their acceptance must always be non-inferential. For if we have found that when and only when an ostensive statement *o* is true, another statement *p* is true, we can reasonably infer from a new case of the truth of *p* that *o* is true even though we are unaware of the non-inferential sufficient reason for asserting it in this case.

From now on I shall refer to statements that are both ostensive and intuitive as basic. Basic statements are the axioms of the system of factual or empirical knowledge. Non-basic or derived statements are explained in terms of them and are established or confirmed by inference from them. Derived statements can be divided into two classes at this stage. First, there are those which are equivalent to some closed or finite set of basic statements, the conjunctions, disjunctions and conditionals called molecular propositions by Russell and Wittgenstein. Secondly, there are general propositions, equivalent to an open set of basic statements. The former can be established conclusively by deductive inference from the closed set of basic statements that makes up the ultimate evidence for them. But the latter can be confirmed only inductively by establishing some finite subset of the open set of basic statements that follow from them. It is worth noticing that this way of classifying the main elements of discourse does something to support the traditional view of induction, to be found in the writings of Mill, as primarily a matter of confirming general statements by establishing their singular, basic, consequences and thus as the inverse of deduction. A less restricted idea of induction is now widely accepted which defines any inference as inductive in which the conclusion is supported but not entailed by the premises (cf., for example, STRAWSON).[4] But unless the relevance of the premises of a non-deductive inference to its conclusion is established by the fact that they follow from it, and thus are part of its logical content, this relevance can be established only by reference to a general statement which has been confirmed in the primary, traditional way.

Basic statements, defined as intuitive and ostensive, have been given a variety of names in recent works on the theory of knowledge. They are the atomic propositions of Russell's logical atomism, the elementary propositions of Wittgenstein's *Tractatus,* the protocol propositions of the Vienna Circle. Schlick called them constatations, Lewis expressive judgements. But however they have been described they have been taken to be the ultimate statable evidence of all the factual assertions we have any good reason to assert, and to constitute the ultimate analysis of everything we can significantly assert. They are held to be the indispensable support of whatever we know or have reason to believe and to be entailed by everything significant that we say.

[4] Strawson, P.F. *Introduction to Logical Theory*. London: Methuen, 1952.

So far I have treated them in a purely formal and generalized way. But most theorists of basic statements, with the exception of Wittgenstein, have gone farther. In the first place they have maintained that all basic statements are certain, usually stating or implying the corollary that no derived statement can be more than probable. Secondly, they have identified them with phenomenal reports of immediate experience, expressed in the first person singular and in the present tense. But both of these consequential theories have been firmly rejected by some of those who accept the general principle that there must be some basic statements if any statement is to be understood or rationally accepted. Russell has always been doubtful of the certainty or incorrigibility of any contingent statement whatever, and has been content to claim that phenomenal basic statements are less uncertain and corrigible than anything else, a position endorsed by Ayer in his first book [AYER],[5] but later abandoned by him. Price, in his lecture *Truth and Corrigibility* [PRICE],[6] and Ayer, in his essay 'Basic Propositions' [AYER],[7] [pp. 335–347, this volume. Eds.] have both considered the possibility of basic statements that are no more than probable; but their consideration has been only in a conjectural, exploratory spirit. As to the phenomenal or experiential interpretation of the concrete character of basic statements, this was ruled out by the theory of physicalism which occurred as a kind of left-wing deviation within logical positivism; and, with a certain licence, a theory similar to physicalism can be attributed to Ryle, whose *Concept of Mind* [RYLE][8] does seem to imply a general theory of knowledge of the kind that sees knowledge as a structure with foundations.

V

It has been widely assumed that basic statements must be certain and incorrigible. The most general argument for this assertion is not often stated, but it is similar in character to the arguments used to establish that intuitive and ostensive statements are indispensable if any beliefs are to be justified or understood. It is clearly presented by Lewis in his *Analysis of Knowledge and Valuation* [C. I. LEWIS],[9] where he writes: 'If anything is to be probable, then something must be certain. The data

5 Ayer, A.J. *Language, Truth and Logic.* London: Gollancz, 1936; 2nd edition, 1946.

6 Price, H.H. *Truth and Corrigibility.* Oxford: Clarendon Press, 1936.

7 Ayer, A.J. 'Basic Propositions.' In Black, M. (ed.). *Philosophical Analysis.* Ithaca: Cornell University Press, 1950.

8 Ryle, G. *The Concept of Mind.* London: Hutchinson, 1949.

9 Lewis, C.I. *An Analysis of Knowledge and Valuation.* La Salle: Open Court, 1946.

which support a genuine probability must themselves be certainties.' One merely probable statement may be supported by another, but 'such confirmation is only provisional and hypothetical, and it must have reference eventually to confirmation by direct experience, which alone is capable of being decisive and providing any sure foundation' [C. I. LEWIS, Ch. II].[10] What lies behind this conviction is the view that probability is essentially relative in character, that no statement is probable by itself but only in relation to its evidence, the presumed truth of some other statement. Clearly, if this were correct it would follow that not all statements could be no more than probable. The chain of probabilifying evidence could never be completed. Price, in his *Truth and Corrigibility* [PRICE],[11] has drawn a useful distinction between hypothetical and categorical probability. A statement of hypothetical probability is non-committal with regard to the acceptability of its evidence. 'If he has caught the train he will probably be there by six', leaves the question of his having caught the train open and says only that he will probably arrive by six *if* he has caught it. A statement of categorical probability, set out in full, is of the form 'since he has caught the train he will probably be there by six', and any such statement as 'he will probably be there by six' presupposes the acceptance of some such since-clause.

What makes Lewis's argument suspect is that certainty would appear to be just as much relative to evidence as probability. For just the same reasons exist for denying that certainty is an intrinsic property of statements as for denying that probability is. Both properties of statements vary with time. What was not, in the light of the evidence available a month ago, either probable or certain may be probable or certain now. So the more or less Cartesian identification of the certain with the necessarily true is a mistake. A statement is necessarily true, if it is, whether anybody has any good reason for thinking so or not. It has always been necessarily true that there is no largest prime number, but before Euclid discovered his proof of the fact it was not certain that this was so.

We are faced here by another version of the difficulty we discovered in accepting as a general account of the conditions under which it was correct to say 'A knows that p' the requirements that X believes that p, p is true and X has sufficient reason for believing p. And the difficulty can be circumvented by the same manoeuvre of distinguishing between the type of evidence or sufficient reason that can be expressed as a statement and the type that cannot. We can allow that both certainty and

10 See footnote 9.

11 Price, H.H. *Truth and Corrigibility*. Oxford: Clarendon Press, 1936.

probability are relative to evidence provided that we admit that the evidence may be propositional, in other words, a belief, certain or probable, from which the initial statement can be inferred with certainty or probability, or experiential, the occurrence of an experience or awareness of the existence of some observable situation. The infinite regress argument rules out the idea that there must be propositional evidence for every certain or probable statement but, if evidence is allowed to be experiential as well, the argument cannot be brought to bear against the view that all statements that we have any reason to believe must rest on evidence.

In PRICE [12] Price opposes to the view that probability presupposes certainty a conception of the intrinsic probability of statements. He suggests that it is possessed by statements of perception, introspection and memory. Such statements, he continues, will be as corrigible as any other empirical assertions, but they will differ from these others in being also, as he puts it, 'corrigent', that is to say, 'capable of correcting other judgements, as well as receiving correction from them'. But he confesses to some doubts about the concept of intrinsic probability, wondering if it is not as nonsensical an idea as that of being intrinsically longer. Recognition that if probability is relative so is certainty, together with the distinction between propositional and experiential evidence, should go some way towards removing these doubts. Instead of 'intrinsic' we can speak of 'experiential' probability, contrasting it with the propositional probability of a statement relative to the statable evidence for it. But these doubts cannot be wholly seat at rest until a positive account is forthcoming of the manner in which experience confers intrinsic probability on statements.

Another general argument for the view that probability presupposes certainty, outlined in an essay of Hampshire's on 'Self-Knowledge and Will' [HAMPSHIRE],[13] will help to show what sort of thing this positive account of experiential probability must be. Hampshire says that to understand a statement is to be aware of the conditions in which it can be known to be true. There is, he says, 'a necessary connection between learning the meaning of an expression and learning what are the standard conditions of its use'. So for every statement whose meaning is understood there must be some conditions in which it can be known for certain to be true, namely, conditions of the sort that are standard for introducing someone to the meaning of the statement in question. Hampshire's point is a seemingly inevitable development of the idea that the meaning of a statement is given by its truth-conditions. One weak-

[12] See footnote 11.

[13] Hampshire, S.N. 'Self-Knowledge and the Will.' *RIP,* VII (1953), pp. 230–45.

ness of the argument as Hampshire puts it is that it can only apply to ostensive statements. The statement that this stone is infinitely divisible has an intelligible meaning (perhaps several), but, except on an interpretation that renders it analytic, it is hard to see that we can envisage circumstances in which we should conclude that it was certainly true. But is it even correct to say that ostensive statements must be incorrigible?

In his first discussion of the subject in AYER[14] Ayer held that there were no incorrigible empirical statements on the ground that a sentence could refer to nothing outside the current experience of the speaker only if it consisted entirely of demonstrative expressions. But if so, it would not be a genuine statement which must contain, as well as a demonstrative to indicate what it referred to, a general predicative term, whose application to the object of reference involves a comparison of that object with other objects satisfying the same predicate and serving as the standard for its application. In his later essay, AYER[15] [pp. 335–347, this volume. Eds.], however, he says that, in applying purely sensory predicates to our current immediate experience, we describe it, not by relating it to anything else, 'but by indicating that a certain word applies to it in virtue of a meaning rule of the language'. Meaning rules of this ostensive kind are necessary for any language that can be used for purposes of empirical description.

> Unless one knows how to employ (these rules), one does not understand the language. Thus, I understand the use of a word if I know in what situations to apply it. For this it is essential that I should be able to recognize the situations when I come upon them; but in order to effect this recognition it is not necessary that I should consciously compare these situations with memories of their predecessors. [p. 345, this volume. Eds.]

But, he continues, although a language must have ostensive meaning rules, these do not have to be of the kind which conclusively establish the truth of falsehood of the statements they are used to introduce. Meaning rules can be of this certifying kind, and Ayer believes that the rules governing the use of such statements as 'this looks green' and 'I am in pain' actually are. But they do not have to be, they could be merely probabilifying, so to speak. 'It might be that the rules were such that every correct description of an empirical situation involved some reference beyond it; and in that case, while the use of the sentence which was dictated by the given meaning rule would be justified in the given situation, its truth would not be conclusively established.' In other words

[14] Ayer, A.J. *Language, Truth and Logic*. London: Gollancz, 1936.

[15] Ayer, A.J. 'Basic Propositions.' In Black, M. (ed.). *Philosophical Analysis*. Ithaca: Cornell University Press, 1950.

ostensive rules determine the conditions in which it is correct to make a statement or in which one is justified in doing so, but to do this is not necessarily to lay down the conditions in which the statement is conclusively established and thus known for certain to be true. Ayer's distinction between the correct use as that in which the making of a statement is justified and as that in which it is conclusively established as certainly true, and so, as it were, absolutely justified, removes the obstacle to Price's hypothesis of intrinsically probable statements presented by Hampshire's argument. To understand the meaning of an ostensive statement is to know in what circumstances it is correct to make it and these need not, *a priori,* be those in which it is certainly true.

VI

While it has been widely, though not universally, assumed that basic statements are incorrigible, it has not usually been deduced in Lewis's way that this is so from the concept of a basic statement. A common procedure has been to say that the basic statements of our language are, in fact, phenomenal or sensory statements about our immediate, current experience, whether perceptual or introspective, and that these phenomenal statements are, as it happens, incorrigible. On the other hand, however, the identification of phenomenal statements as basic is not ordinarily presented simply as a matter of straightforwardly discoverable fact about our use of language. It is supported by the principle that the ultimate source of our knowledge about matters of fact is experience, observation or perception. At the level of common sense it might seem that a statement reporting what we experience, observe or perceive would refer to medium-sized material things currently in our fairly close environment. But the usual view of observation statements is that they report the current sense-impressions of the speaker. And the main reason for this is that statements about material things are susceptible to doubt and correction, that, by carrying implications about what may be observed at other times, or with other senses, or by other people, they go beyond what we directly apprehend or are aware of and so embody an element of inference. Thus Price, in his *Perception,* says 'When I see a tomato there is much that I can doubt . . . One thing, however, I cannot doubt: that there exists a red patch of a round and somewhat bulgy shape (which) is directly present to my consciousness' [PRICE, Ch. 1].[16] This patch of colour, private to my consciousness, is what is given in perception, it is the type of empirical datum from which all the rest

[16] Price, H.H. *Perception.* London: Methuen, 1932.

of my factual beliefs are inferred. And Ayer, in *Foundations of Empirical Knowledge,* takes basic statements to be those which we discover by direct awareness and he defines 'direct awareness' as entailing that 'if someone is directly aware of an object *x,* it follows that *x* exists and that it really has whatever properties it is appearing to have' and again 'that whenever we are directly aware of a sense-datum, it follows that we know some proposition which describes the sense-datum to be true' [AYER, Ch. 2].[17] The upshot of these accounts of the matter is that in every perceptual situation, in every situation in which we perceive or think we perceive something, it is at least certain that we seem to perceive something and this is held to be equivalent to the statement that we know for certain that a seeming object, or sense-impression, in other words, exists.

The standard view, then, is that the basic statements which are the foundations of our knowledge of matters of fact are phenomenal reports of our immediate experience. These are incorrigible in the sense that since they do not go beyond what we are directly aware of and have nothing predictive about them, they cannot be falsified by any subsequent experience. Statements about material things, on the other hand, are subsequently corrigible. The implications they carry may turn out to be false. But the only ways in which statements about impressions can be false are by the deliberate intent of the person who has the impression being reported (for since they are contingent there is no contradiction in denying them), and by merely verbal error. Statements about material things are or seem intuitive in the psychological sense. We do not ordinarily, if ever, infer them consciously from statements about impressions. But, it is argued, since they are corrigible conjectures about what is going on outside the field of our direct awareness they cannot be logically intuitive, but must be implicitly inferred from statements about impressions if their assertion is to be justified.

Initially, two main lines of objection were developed to this theory of the phenomenal character of basic statements. The first of these started from the difficulty of giving an acceptable account of the way in which beliefs about material things were supported and justified by reports of immediate experience. Statements about objects could only be confirmed by statements about impressions that followed logically from them, and they could only have a definite meaning if they were capable in principle of translation into ostensive impression statements. But the only acceptable-looking translations failed to eliminate the reference to material things from the translation. 'There is a table in the next room' did not entail 'if I were having the impression of being in the next room,

[17] Ayer, A.J. *The Foundations of Empirical Knowledge.* London: Macmillan, 1940.

I should be having the impression of a table', but only 'if I actually were in the next room, I should be having the impression of a table'. Another difficulty arose from widely felt insufficiency of any set of hypothetical statements, however extensive, to add up to a categorical statement about material things.

More important than this negative objection, which led to no clear alternative account of the problem and no serious scrutiny of its underlying assumptions, was the criticism of Carnap and Neurath which was directed against the private and uncommunicable character of the facts reported by phenomenal statements. They argued that science, and therefore ordinary common knowledge, was a public, intersubjective affair and could not be based on private experiences that individuals had no way of communicating to one another. Neurath further objected to the momentary and unfalsifiable nature of phenomenal basic statements like Schlick's constatations. As momentary they could only be used to confirm or refute other beliefs at the instant of utterance and as unfalsifiable expressions of subjective conviction they were foreign to science. Schlick defended the phenomenal theory, in his essay 'On the Foundation of Knowledge' [SCHLICK][18] [pp. 413–430, this volume. Eds.], partly by admitting the momentary character of constatations but declaring it to be harmless, arguing that they were used antecedently to suggest and consequently, at any time the question arose, to confirm derived, theoretical statements, and partly by criticizing the conventionalism of the alternative theory proposed by Neurath, which, by regarding the acceptance of basic statements as a matter of social convention, was open to the objections traditionally raised against the coherence theory. But there are other difficulties connected with the privacy of phenomenal basic statements which undermine them more effectively: first, that our private languages seem to be based on public language rather than the other way round and, secondly, that a strictly private language is, according to Wittgenstein, an impossibility.

VII

It is phenomenal statements that are basic, not merely must we say that all public statements, to the extent that they are justified at all, are inferred from or supported by them, we must also admit something much harder to accommodate: that all public statements acquire their meaning from correlation with statements in an *antecedently understood* private

[18] Schlick, 'The Foundation of Knowledge.' In Ayer, A.J. (ed.). *Logical Positivism.* Glencoe, Illinois: The Free Press, 1959.

language. It is plain that the private language we actually have, that in which we report our own sensations and emotions, is taught to us by other people on the basis of our publicly observable behaviour. Furthermore, we draw on the public language in developing it. We describe our sensations in terms of the material things that cause them and our emotions in terms of the behaviour to which they incline us. The theory that phenomenal statements are logically intuitive could be saved only by claiming that the inference from them to other statements was implicit. Similarly, the theory that phenomenal statements are ostensive can be saved only by the claim that basic statements are originally private in a double sense, being expressed in some internal symbolism or imagery as well as referring to private entities, and that we must have acquired the capacity to use this inner language not from teaching by others but by having made it up for ourselves. The teaching of language as a social activity clearly begins with statements about material things. If phenomenal statements alone are basic, we must come to understand the statements about material things that we are taught by correlating them with the already understood phenomenal statements of our inner language which are present to our minds in the circumstances in which the teaching is taking place.

In his *Philosophical Investigations* Wittgenstein argued that this exceedingly unplausible conjecture was in fact a senseless one. A language is a practice of utterance governed by rules which distinguish correct utterances from incorrect ones. It might seem that a man could construct a private, inner language by naming a particular experience, and adopting the rule that every subsequent experience of the same kind should have the same name. But how, he asks, are we to tell whether any subsequent experience is of the same kind? It will not do to say that I call this experience '*x*' because I remember the experience used to introduce the term '*x*' and see that they are the same. For it is always possible that my memory is mistaken in any particular case and this is a doubt that I can never set at rest since memory is my sole mode of access to the standard experiences by means of which the terms in my private language were introduced. In these circumstances the private introduction of names for experiences is an 'empty ceremony'.

VIII

The phenomenal basic statements that report sense-impressions are expressed in ordinary language by means of the verbs 'looks', 'appears' and 'seems'. To say that one is having a sense-impression of a brown box is to say that there looks or appears or seems to be a brown box where one is, or that it seems or appears that one can see a brown box. It is clear that in every perceptual situation, which has been defined as one in which we perceive something or think that we do, there appears to be something present to us. The supporters of the theory of a phenomenal basis for knowledge go on from this to conclude that in every perceptual situation there is a private object, an appearance or sense-datum, which is directly present to my mind in the sense that I know for certain that this private object exists. These appearances are never identical with material things or with any parts of them for they are private to a single observer, depend for their existence, like the ideas of Berkeley's philosophy, on the fact that they are being perceived and have all and only the properties that they appear to have.

For some time doubts have been felt as to the validity of this transition from the unquestionable statement that in a perceptual situation I appear to be aware of a material thing to the conclusion that in a perceptual situation I am aware of a non-material appearance. It has been held that this 'reification of appearances' is mistaken and that it commits the 'sense-datum fallacy'. As it stands the move is not obviously legitimate; but it is not obviously illegitimate either. In general, this kind of grammatical transformation of verb into noun is not puzzling or disputable. There is no objection to saying 'he gave the door a kick' instead of 'he kicked the door' or 'she took up a position at the end of the line' instead of 'she placed herself at the end of the line'. But this absence of trouble might be ascribed to the fact that we do not exploit these permitted transformations to ask questions about the nature of kicks and positions and do not assume that they are some sort of objects in the way that doors and lines are. Again there are transformations of this general variety which we should be less willing to endorse. We should not be pleased with the replacement of 'it is probably dark down there' by 'there is a darkness-probability down there'.

In an article on 'The Problem of Perception' [QUINTON] [19] I have tried to show that statements about what appears to be the case are used in two broadly distinguishable ways, in the primary and more usual of which the reification of appearances is unacceptable. In this primary, epistemic sense of 'appears' to say that there appears to be, or that it appears that there is, such-and-such a thing here is not to describe the current state of one's visual field but rather to express an inclination to believe that there actually is such-and-such a thing here, in other words, to make a tentative, qualified statement about the material world. 'It appears that *p*', I suggested, is the way in which we make a qualified claim about observable facts when the evidence is experiential, 'it is

[19] Quinton, A.M. 'The Problem of Perception.' *Mind,* LXIV (1955), pp. 28–51.

probable that *p*' being more appropriate to the case when the evidence is propositional. An epistemic statement about what appears is not, then, a description of appearances, it is a hesitant statement about public, material objects.

There is, however, a secondary, derivative, use of the verb 'appears' in which it is employed for some rather specialized purposes to describe the current character of our sensory fields. At the instance of oculists and art teachers we can, by an effort of attention, suppose that, for example, what we see is all situated on a flat surface a few feet in front of us in conditions of normal illumination. We then describe our visual field by saying what we should be inclined to believe was in front of us if we in fact knew that these special and peculiar conditions of observation prevailed. The result is a genuinely phenomenological statement about patches of colour of various shapes and sizes arranged in a certain way. The conditions mentioned are chosen for the purpose of phenomenological description because they are visually ideal, are those in which, when they actually do obtain, the danger of visual error is minimized. The phenomenological use of the verb 'appears', it should be noticed, is not merely a rather sophisticated one, it is also a development of the more usual, epistemic, one. We say 'there appears to be an *x* here' when we are not sure that the conditions of observation are ideal or that they are unideal in a way that we can allow for. We could say instead, 'I should say that there definitely is an *x* here if I were sure that the conditions of observation are what I am taking them to be; but I am not sure of it.' More important is the effort of attention that we have to make in order to give a phenomenological description. We have to see things as we know, or have very good reason to believe, they are not. Now the ability to adopt this phenomenological frame of mind is one that has to be learnt after that for the perception of the material world has already been mastered. The language in which its findings are expressed is derived from that with which we describe material things and the rules defining the attitude involved are stated in public, material terms. So unless we first make up a private phenomenological language for ourselves ordinary statements about material things cannot acquire their sense from correlation with basic phenomenal statements. Furthermore, the phenomenological attitude or frame of mind, in which by an effort of attention all our background knowledge of where we are and what is around us is suppressed and replaced by a feigned assumption of ideal conditions, is inevitably exclusive of the ordinary frame of mind in which we confront the observable world. We cannot look at the world ordinarily and phenomenologically at the same moment. It follows from this, and is fairly obvious on its own account, that we are very rarely in a phenomenological frame of mind. It cannot, therefore, be the case that our beliefs about material objects are generally inferred from phenomenological statements about appearances or sense-data. For the very much greater part of our conscious life the phenomenological evidence is simply not there for statements about material things to be inferred from. Unless we can be subconsciously in a phenomenological attitude at the same time as we are consciously looking at things in the ordinary way, and unless we subconsciously register the deliverances of this attitude, the only alternative to the view that statements about material things do not have a phenomenological foundation is that the very great majority of our beliefs about the material world never have any justification at all.

Some empirical confirmation for the view that we are only very exceptionally aware of the phenomenologically describable state of our sense-fields is provided by the fact that if asked for a phenomenological report of a past experience, we normally have to reconstruct it from our recollection of the material scene we actually perceived, together with our background knowledge of where we were situated within the scene. What we can reasonably do is to infer that in every perceptual situation our sense-fields are in some appropriate condition, and we can work out what this was in any particular case by working out what phenomenological report we should have given at the time if we had been in the appropriate frame of mind. These conjectured states of our sense-fields may be interpreted as the phenomenological causes of our perceptual beliefs. We can refer to them, for instance, when we want to explain errors of perception. But this is not to admit them as reasons for our perceptual beliefs. Though they can be used as reasons for such beliefs in exceptional cases, and then only in the light of antecedently established correlations between the phenomenological condition and the observable state of affairs in question, they cannot serve as reasons in all cases in which we have some reason for the perceptual beliefs we form.

In its ordinary use an epistemic appearance statement of the form 'there appears to be an *x* here' does not, then, describe a substantive appearance. Its function is to make the assertion that there is an *x* here in a guarded, qualified way. It makes clear that the speaker regards the statement as no more than probable. We can raise these statements to higher probabilities and even certainty, in Moore's sense of absence of reasonable doubt rather than incorrigibility,[20] by assembling other consilient statements of the same sort. 'There appears to be an orange here, but perhaps not, since wax fruit is to be found in places like this. But

20 Cf., e.g., the article 'Certainty' in Moore, G.E. *Philosophical Papers*. London: Allen and Unwin, 1959.

it also appears to be cold and hard and this room does not appear to be refrigerated.' This artificially circumspect soliloquy shows how epistemic appearance statements mutually corroborate each other. More usually the requisite corroborative material is already to hand embedded in our background knowledge, (in the example given, perhaps, that this room is a prison larder).

What I suggest is that these epistemic appearance statements are ways of affirming, in an explicitly qualified fashion, the experientially probable basic statements whose possibility was argued for earlier. To say 'there is an orange here' may be no more than probably true. In saying 'there appears to be an orange here' the fact that it is no more than probable is made explicit. By putting in the explicit qualification the statement is protected from the kind of falsification wrought by the discovery that the object involved is in fact made of wax. These appearance statements have, then, a kind of certainty. But it is rather the unqualified statements which we have an inclination to believe, and not the qualified appearance statements associated with them, that are basic on the theory that I am advancing. Ordinary statements about material things, I claim, are, as they appear to be, both the ostensive basis in terms of which all other statements are introduced and the intuitive basis by reference to which they are confirmed. In themselves, they are never more than probable. But associated, as they commonly are, with a large background of other statements, probable and certain, they can attain certainty, at least in the straightforward, Moorean sense.

It remains to be shown how, in the process of ostensive teaching of ordinary statements about material things, they are endowed with the experiential probability that the theory ascribes to them. This can be shown by a consideration of the way in which their meaning is learnt. I learn when to say 'this is an orange', or its infantile equivalent 'orange', by being exposed to oranges in carefully selected situations, that is, where my teachers have assured themselves that the object involved really is an orange, and not a piece of wax fruit or a piece of soap or a rubber ball, and where the conditions of observation are favourable. Equipped by this training I start to make use on my own of the statement I have learnt and, still unaware, in my ostensive innocence, of the existence of orange-like non-oranges, and again of the effect of fog on the look of traffic lights or of distance on the look of large orange globes, I make mistakes. These mistakes are corrected and my understanding of the statement 'this is an orange' undergoes a change. It becomes loaded with theory, as it were, for I find out about the insides of oranges, their characteristic taste and their causal dependence on orange trees. I learn that vision is not enough to certify the belief that there is an orange here. But unless my utterances of 'this is an orange' are more often mistaken than not, this saddening achievement of conceptual maturity will not deprive the statement of its intrinsic probability.

An important consequence of this discussion is the undermining of an assumption which has not been questioned hitherto. It has been assumed that a statement is either ostensive or verbally introduced, that it must be wholly the one or wholly the other. According to this theory of basic statements ordinary assertions about material things are first taught ostensively, but this correlation with observable states of affairs does not complete the teaching process. It has to be supplemented by knowledge of the circumstances in which our inclination to believe something about our material surroundings must be controlled by collateral information about those surroundings. On this theory there are no purely ostensive statements. Partly ostensive basic statements acquire an intrinsic probability from experiential evidence alone, but this is never complete, never sufficient to render them certain. It may well be that Hampshire is correct in saying that the ostensive conditions under which the use of a statement is taught constitute the criteria of its certainty in so far as *purely ostensive* statements are concerned. But in the language we actually have the basic statements in which our observations are reported are not purely ostensive. So the conjecture of Price and Ayer that there could be a language whose basic statements were no more than probable is confirmed in the best possible way, by the fact that what they envisage as a possibility is true of the language we actually have. The initial infinite regress arguments proved that some statements must be ostensively learnt, and that some statements must derive their justification from experience rather than other statements. But these two requirements are satisfied by an account of basic statements which represents them as initially, but not wholly, taught by ostension and as justified to some extent, but not beyond reasonable doubt, by experience.

IX

A complete rejection of the doctrine that knowledge has foundations implies the acceptance of a coherence theory of truth and knowledge. This theory had a central place in the absolute idealism of Bradley, who worked out its consequences with great elaboration. Bradley's idealism was the dominant academic philosophy against which Russell and Moore rebelled, and Russell's earliest strictly philosophical writings, in the first decade of the century, were directly concerned to refute the coherence theory. Some of his criticisms do not apply to it if, as in this discussion, it is restricted to the domain of empirical fact. Certainly we must accept the truth of the laws of logic if the concept of coherence is to be applied; but there is no circularity in this if it is only the truth of non-logical statements that coherence is used to define. Again there is nothing self-refuting, or rather self-enfeebling, about the consequential thesis that no statement is wholly true if the reference of this thesis is not supposed to include itself. Indeed, if Russell's theory of types, by which all self-reference is ruled out, is accepted, the thesis cannot be formulated in this self-destructive way. There remains the crucial difficulty that coherence, while it may be the necessary condition of the truth of a body of statements, cannot be the sufficient condition, since more than one system of statements, all of which are coherent with the other members of the system, can be constructed where there will be members of one system that are incompatible with members of another. The same point is less formally made by the argument that the business of justification can never begin unless some of the statements up for consideration have some ground for acceptance other than their relation to the others.

In the light of these criticisms recent philosophers have seldom openly endorsed a full-blooded coherence theory. Nevertheless, several have taken up positions which commit them to it by implication. The left-wing positivists of the 1930s, abandoning Schlick's view that basic statements were the direct and incorrigible reports of experience, concluded that their nature and their acceptance was a matter of convention. Unwilling to admit that any sense could be attached to the idea that some statements rested on experiential evidence, because of its purportedly metaphysical assertion of a relation between language and fact, they seemed to have no other recourse than conventionalism. Their attempt to show that the actual convention they proposed was not an arbitrary one by pointing to its coincidence with that adopted by scientists, was unsuccessful. In the first place the expedient was viciously regressive in presuming the antecedent truth of some statement about the basic statements actually adopted by scientists. Secondly, it inverted the logical relation between the concepts of a scientist and a basic statement. It is not that a basic statement is one that a scientist accepts without question or further inquiry, but rather that a scientist is one who systematically exposes his beliefs to the judgement of basic statements.

X

Two negative views of the doctrine of foundations of more recent origin, which avoid difficulties by the simple expedient of failing to present an alternative to it, deserve some consideration. In his *Structure of Appearance* [Goodman][21] Goodman rejects the concept of an asymmetrical relation of epistemological priority between basic and derived statements. In his view logical priority is always relative to a particular system and it is well known that the same body of assertions can be equally well derived from different, alternative sets of axioms or primitive propositions. Applying this to systems setting out the definitional relations of empirical concepts, he argues that it is a manner of free choice for the builder of the system as to which concepts he selects as primitive and undefined. He should be guided in his choice by such strictly formal considerations as that of the simplicity and elegance of one choice as compared with another. Certainly there is a formal sense of priority or basicness which is relative to a given way of setting up a system of statements. But philosophical analysts are not concerned simply with the construction of formally consistent systems: their aim, in the first instance, is to set out, as systematically as possible, the order of logical dependence of the apparatus of concepts and statements that we actually possess. But more than this, a formally consistent system may be epistemologically inconsistent. If Wittgenstein's argument against the possibility of private languages is valid, a system in which physical concepts are defined in terms of strictly phenomenal ones, though it might be perfectly consistent as a formal system, would nevertheless be epistemologically impossible and incapable of being used as a language.

In his *Sense and Sensibilia* [Austin][22] Austin delivers a lively but somewhat superficial onslaught on the doctrine of foundations, which he mistakenly identifies with the theory that our knowledge of matters of fact must rest on an incorrigible basis. He agrees that such philosophers as Ayer are right to hold that the truth of some statements must be determined by non-verbal reality, and he asserts that most words are learnt ostensively. To accept these points is to concede the truth of the greater part of the doctrine of foundations, and so a more precise account of the actual object of Austin's criticism must be sought. At one stage of the argument he singles out for criticism the view that it is the particular business of some sub-class of sentences to be evidence for or to verify the rest. Against it he says that no kind of *sentence,* understood as a form of words in a given meaning, could do this job. A given sentence will sometimes be used to express a conclusion from evidence, at others to make a direct report of observation. A given sentence can be used to make many different statements, depending on who is making

[21] Goodman, N. *The Structure of Appearance.* Cambridge, Mass.: Harvard University Press, 1951.

[22] Austin, *Sense and Sensibilia.* Ed. G.J. Warnock. Oxford: Clarendon Press, 1962.

them and on where and when they are made. This is true but doubly irrelevant. The doctrine of foundations can perfectly well be formulated in terms of statements and to the extent that it has not been it is because of the peculiarities of the German word 'Satz'. But, in fact, this is not to go far enough, since two people can make the same statement but only one of them be making a basic statement. Suppose *A*, looking down a well, says, 'There is water at the bottom.' *B*, who is standing beside him and not looking down, may affirm that there is water at the bottom at very much the same time and in exactly the same words because he has heard what *A* said and believes *A* to be a reliable person. In strictness we should perhaps say that a given statement can be made as basic or as derived. But provided we realize that to say that *A*'s statement is basic is not to say that the same statement made by *B* is also basic and is *a fortiori* not to say that every statement made by the use of the sentences *A* utters is basic, no confusion need be caused by the less pedantic way of speaking.

Austin argues penetratingly against the view that there are any strictly incorrigible statements. Every statement can, he maintains, be retracted, and any that are so understood that their seeming to their speaker to be true is a guarantee of their truth, are not really descriptive at all. This, as we have seen, does not invalidate the doctrine of foundations. He goes on to say that in general we do not have to produce or even have evidence for our assertions about material objects. As far as this refers to propositional evidence I have argued that it is correct. But it is not a criticism of the theory of basic statements, only of the identification of them with phenomenal reports. If it refers to experiential evidence as well, it is false, for it suggests that we can assert any material object statement with justification by mere whim. What he perhaps intended to say was that we do not ordinarily call the experience that justifies a statement about material things evidence for it. This would not be very interesting even if it were true. But if a man who, looking into a room, says, 'There's a fire in here', is asked if he has any evidence for saying so, when he has in fact seen the fire, it would be ridiculous for him to answer, 'No.' The proper answer would be, 'Yes, I can see it.'

The real point of Austin's criticism is his claim that 'in general . . . *any* kind of statement, could state evidence for *any* other kind'. 'It is not true, in general,' he goes on, 'that general statements are "based on" singular statements and not vice versa; my belief that *this* animal will eat turnips may be used on the belief that most pigs eat turnips; though certainly, in different circumstances, I might have supported the claim that most pigs eat turnips by saying that this pig eats them at any rate.' It is true that the belief of any particular man that a given pig, not before him, eats turnips may be based on and owe what justification it has to his antecedent conviction that most pigs eat turnips. But there is an obvious asymmetry in the logical relation between the two beliefs. For the general belief, although formally evidence for the singular one by itself and independently of whether there is any reason to accept it, will actually confirm or justify it only if it is itself already supported. This support will normally be provided by the establishment of a number of statements of the form 'this pig eats turnips', and of not more than a very few of the form 'this pig does not eat turnips'. This recourse to the empirical basis may be postponed. That most pigs eat turnips may be inferred from the further generalizations that most curly-tailed animals eat turnips and that all pigs are curly-tailed. And these, if they are really to support it, must themselves rest either on singular statements about particular curly-tailed animals eating turnips and particular pigs being curly-tailed, or else on further generalizations which possess, at some finite remove, singular evidence of the same kind. In other words, general statements can only be contingently or derivatively evidence for singular ones, whereas singular statements are the primary and indispensable evidence for generalizations. We can have sufficient reason for thinking that this pig eats turnips without having any justified belief about what pigs in general do; but we cannot have reason for thinking that most pigs eat turnips unless we have some justified beliefs about the eating habits of particular pigs. That most pigs eat turnips, then, while it does not presuppose for its justification the establishment of any particular statement to the effect that this pig does so, does presuppose that some statements of this kind have been confirmed or established. But the statement that this pig does so, while it may owe its justification to the antecedent establishment of some general statement about pigs in a particular case, does not in general require the establishment or confirmation of any such generalization.

Most specific issues in the theory of knowledge can be conceived as problems about the epistemological priority of one class of statements to another. It has been questioned whether statements about impressions, present memories, behaviour, observables, natural events and feelings of pleasure and pain are epistemologically prior, respectively, to statements about objects, past happenings, mental states, theoretical entities, supernatural beings and values or whether, on the other hand, the types of statement coupled in this list are logically independent of one another. One does not have to accept the reducibility of any of the items in the second part of the list to their partners in the first part to attach sense to the concept of epistemological priority which is involved in the theories that they are so reducible. And whatever may be said about these contentious cases the priority of singular statements to general ones is really too obvious to need labouring.

XI

The most substantial criticism of the doctrine of foundations that has been put forward in recent times is that made by Popper, in his *Logic of Scientific Discovery* [Popper],[23] particularly in the fifth chapter, and in his *Conjectures and Refutations* [Popper],[24] particularly in the introductory chapter. Popper's theory of knowledge is a sustained attack on a traditional body of ideas which he divides into empiricism, the theory that the foundation of knowledge is observation, and inductivism, the theory that knowledge is developed by the generalization of theories from this observational basis. He rejects these theories both as psychological or genetic accounts of the way in which knowledge actually grows, and as logical reconstructions of the order of dependence in which the elements of knowledge stand as regards their justification. On the matter of growth he maintains that theories precede observation and are not, and cannot be, mechanically excogitated from it. There is no such thing as pure observation; we must always observe under the guidance of some hypothesis which directs our attention by telling us what to look for. Theories or hypotheses are not derived from observable facts by applying the rules of a non-existent inductive logic to those facts. They may be suggested by facts to some extent, but an indispensable part is played in the business of theoretical conjecture by the background of knowledge already achieved, as well as an understanding of the unsolved problems that it presents, and by the constructive or imaginative power of the individual theorist. This seems truer of the more strictly theoretical parts of science than of the instantial laws of, say, natural history, and, again, truer of scientific theorizing than of the broad and continuous tide of subconscious, or at any rate not consciously directed, generalization that augments our ordinary knowledge of the world. On the matter of justification he points to the logical asymmetry between general theories and singular descriptions because of which theories can be falsified by observations but not established or verified by them. Science, then, as the most developed method of acquiring knowledge, is defined by him as a method of resolutely seeking for observations that will falsify

23 Popper, K.R. *Logik der Forschung*. Vienna: Springer, 1935; English tr. (*The Logic of Scientific Discovery*), with additions. London: Hutchinson, 1959.

24 Popper, K.R. *Conjectures and Refutations*. London: Routledge, 1963.

our theoretical conjectures. It requires us to formulate our theories in as falsifiable a way as possible and to expose them as vigorously as possible to the test of observation and experiment and to the criticism of others. Our theories can never be certain, but to the extent that they have escaped falsification, without being so formulated as to avoid it, they are corroborated and worthy of provisional acceptance.

Bringing his accounts of the historical order of discovery and of the logical order of justification together, the following picture of the growth of knowledge results: first of all, theories, in the form of general statements, are put forward as conjectures; from them singular statements about observables are derived by deductive logic; these observations are empirically tested; if they pass the tests, the theory is so far corroborated, if they fail, it is refuted and must be replaced by another. The nature of the empirical test to which the observation statements are subjected is plainly crucial in this progression. Popper is prepared to describe these vital singular statements about observable states of affairs as basic, but he does not admit that they can be regarded as certain or as descriptions of experiences. It would appear, he argues, that three possible views can be taken about the status of basic observation statements. First, a dogmatism which accepts them as true without question; secondly, a psychologism which somehow reduces them to or identifies them with perceptual experiences; finally, the acceptance of an infinite regress. His own view of the matter is presented as a combination of elements from all three theories which he believes is free from the defects of all of them.

His theory is that in genuinely rational and scientific thinking we adopt as basic, statements about observable material things and events situated at a definite time and place. The acceptance of basic statements is a matter of convention and thus far dogmatic, but not viciously so since the convention can be abandoned if the convention of some other investigator comes into conflict with it. There is nothing permanent about the convention, and so the dogmatism involved is of a harmless because temporary and provisional kind. If a basic statement is challenged, it can itself be exposed to test by deriving further basic statements from it, together with already accepted theories. This possibility introduces an infinite regress, but it, too, is not vicious. We do not have to go on deducing basic statements from one another *ad infinitum,* but only from any given basic statement if anybody challenges it. And in fact most statements of the form he takes as basic are not challenged. Finally, a measure of dependence on perceptual experience is introduced to explain why we make the conventions that we do, why we choose to accept so very few of the basic statements from among all those that, being significant, are formally suitable for adoption. Experience does not, he says, verify basic statements but it does motivate us to adopt some rather than others.

This is an original and important attempt to solve the problem of the basis of knowledge, and I believe it to be very nearly successful but I do not think it can be accepted as it stands. The first difficulty concerns the idea that experiences do not justify but simply motivate the acceptance of certain singular statements about observables. We may assume that this motivation is not inexorable and can be resisted, in particular, by those who have reflected on the principles of rational thinking. If it could not be resisted, speculations about how one ought, if rational, to manage one's beliefs would be devoid of point. The vital difficulty is this: either the fact that an observational belief is motivated by experience is a reason for accepting it, in which case experience is not just a motivation, or else no belief whatever is justified at all. Unless experience actually supports the beliefs that it prompts us to hold, why should we choose to adopt them in preference to those which are prompted by wishful thinking or the desire to save ourselves trouble or any other emotional factor? In practice, to the extent that we are rational, we resist the promptings of hope and laziness because of their well-established tendency to conflict with the beliefs we are induced to form by experience. But why should we show this partiality as between the different emotional determinants of belief unless there is some necessary connection between experience and the acceptability of the beliefs that it inspires in us?

No conjecture, whether theory or observation statement, derives any support from the mere fact that someone entertains or conjectures it. Before it deserves acceptance a theory must be corroborated by the discovery that the basic statements which could falsify it are in fact false. But, on Popper's theory, should this not apply to basic statements as well? Either a basic statement derives some support from the experience that underlies its conventional adoption, in which case it is qualified to refute or corroborate antecedently conjectured theories, or the convention is a completely arbitrary one. If basic statements have no intrinsic probability, then the derivation of further basic statements from them cannot, for however long it is continued, add anything to their justification.

Why, furthermore, should conventional adoption be restricted to basic statements and not extended to theories themselves? For, as Popper has argued, theories are just as psychologically intuitive, just as much matters of subjective conviction, as basic statements are. It will not do to say that it is because they can at least be subjected to the negative test of exposure to falsification, for this is true of basic statements also.

Popper might argue that we confine conventional adoption to basic statements motivated by experience because we find that there is very little disagreement about them, whereas there is a great deal of disagreement about theories and about basic statements motivated by wishful thinking or laziness. But, waiving the somewhat rhetorical objection that asks how this comforting fact is discovered, we must inquire whether it is simply a happy accident. Even if it is correct it only shows that the most economical or socially harmonious way to go about controlling our beliefs will be by subjecting them to the test of what experience has motivated. But is this relevant? The corroboration of theories will be accelerated by this convention and it will be a more sociable affair, but will it be any better calculated to approximate to truth than the convention of accepting basic statements on grounds of their euphony? Why should the fact that it satisfies our desires for economy and social harmony be regarded as justifying the second-order convention of adopting only those basic statements that are motivated by experience? Popper, in fact, has not really escaped his trilemma. If no statement is worthy of acceptance until it has been corroborated by way of the consequences deducible from it, then a vicious infinite regress ensues and no statement can be justified at all. If some or all statements are justified to some extent by the mere fact of being entertained or conjectured, then his position is arbitrarily dogmatic. The only alternative is to allow himself to be impaled, at least a little, on the remaining horn of psychologism by allowing that basic statements can derive some support from the experiences that motivate them and are not entirely dependent for justification on the consequences that can be derived from them.

This modification of Popper's theory of basic statements, which holds that they acquire some, perhaps small, initial probability from the perceptual experiences that prompt them, is in effect the corrigibilist theory considered by Price. It is wholly consistent with Popper's fallibilist conviction that no statement of fact is ever finally and unalterably established, and that every statement, basic or theoretical, can be corroborated by its consequences. It maintains that the structure of our knowledge has foundations, but does not hold that these are absolutely solid and incorrigible, and while it asserts that it is through their connection with experience that basic statements derive that initial support without which no statement whatever would have any justification, it does not require them to be mere descriptions of experience. If the truth of the matter does lie in some such close interweaving of the correspondence and coherence theories, it would at once explain why the conflict between them has continued for so long and bring it to a conclusion which would not require the unconditional surrender of either contestant.